Dedication

If it wasn't for David Chilton, author of *The Wealthy Barber*, there would be no *Looneyspoons* and no *Collection*. There would be no *Crazy Plates* or *Eat, Shrink & Be Merry!*, either.

Back in 1996, after more than a dozen publishers rejected our *Looneyspoons* manuscript and told us not to quit our day jobs (too late), we cried our hearts out to our mother, Alfreda. We told her how we'd risked everything to write our book, that no one wanted to publish it, that we had amassed $80,000 in debt and were now resorting to holding yard sales, bake sales and bottle drives to pay our bills. Mom listened to our sister sob story, paused for a moment, then declared in her adorable Polish accent, "I vill pray to God to send somevun to help you!"

As if delivered by angels, Dave arrived exactly one month later. He graciously took us under his wings, believed in us when no one else did (except our mom!), lent us money (we still haven't paid him back), opened doors, paved the way, booked interviews, struck deals, negotiated contracts, put out fires and tolerated our monthly mood swings. And he never complained when we named our newly formed company Granet Publishing (Greta + Janet = Granet!), even though he was the president and the only partner who knew anything about publishing.

We truly couldn't have done it without him. Dave is brilliant, funny and humble (though he's quick to tell you when he's leading in his hockey pool!). Ultra-generous with his time and wisdom, he's the person to whom so many turn when they need advice…including us! Fitting that he's known as *The Wealthy Barber*—he's enriched the lives of all who are fortunate enough to know him.

Thank you, Dave, and thank you, Mom, for "helping" send Dave our way. He was the answer to your prayers…and ours, too!

THE
LOONEYSPOONS
COLLECTION

THE
LOONEYSPOONS
COLLECTION

Good Food, Good Health, Good Fun!

JANET & GRETA PODLESKI

Cartoons by Ted Martin

HAY HOUSE, INC.
Carlsbad, California • New York City
London • Sydney • Johannesburg
Vancouver • Hong Kong • New Delhi

...ed in the United States by: Hay House, Inc., P.O. Box 5100, Carlsbad, CA 92018-5100
00) 431-7695 or (800) 654-5126 • *Fax:* (760) 431-6948 or (800) 650-5115 • www.hayhouse.com®

Published and distributed in Australia by: Hay House Australia Pty. Ltd., 18/36 Ralph St., Alexandria NSW 2015
Phone: 612-9669-4299 • *Fax:* 612-9669-4144 • www.hayhouse.com.au

Published and distributed in the United Kingdom by: Hay House UK, Ltd., 292B Kensal Rd., London W10 5BE
Phone: 44-20-8962-1230 • *Fax:* 44-20-8962-1239 • www.hayhouse.co.uk

Published and distributed in the Republic of South Africa by: Hay House SA (Pty), Ltd., P.O. Box 990, Witkoppen 2068
Phone/Fax: 27-11-467-8904 • www.hayhouse.co.za

Published in India by: Hay House Publishers India, Muskaan Complex, Plot No. 3, B-2, Vasant Kunj, New Delhi 110 070
Phone: 91-11-4176-1620 • *Fax:* 91-11-4176-1630 • www.hayhouse.co.in

Printed in Canada

Cartoons by Ted Martin

Cartoons colorized by Pierre Loranger

Edited by Fina Scroppo

Designed by Matrix Four Limited

Cover concept by Jason Smith

Food photography:

Greta Podleski pages 3, 7, 10, 17, 19, 20, 26, 28, 31, 32, 36, 38, 42, 44, 46, 52, 55, 58, 61, 63, 67, 68, 73, 74, 78, 85, 87, 89, 94, 96, 101, 102, 105, 106, 108, 111, 112, 115, 117, 118, 123, 125, 127, 131, 133, 135, 137, 138, 141, 142, 145, 147, 148, 151, 152, 156, 161, 163, 166, 169, 171, 173, 175, 179, 181, 183, 184, 186, 188, 191, 192, 194, 196, 199, 201, 205, 206, 210, 212, 215, 216, 220, 224, 227, 229, 231, 232, 235, 237, 242, 249, 251, 255, 257, 258, 261, 262, 266, 271, 274, 277, 279, 280, 283, 285, 287, 288, 290, 291, 292, 295, 297, 298, 300, 303, 305, 307, 309, 311, 314, 319, 321, 322, 327, 329, 331, 332, 335, 337, 338, 341, 342, 345, 347, 349, 350, 351 (food styling by Greta Podleski)

Colin Erricson pages 23, 51, 71, 98, 128, 154, 177, 218, 246, 269, 317, 325, 353 (food styling by Terry Schacht)

Robert Wigington pages 92, 202 (food styling by Ruth Gangbar)

Library of Congress Control Number: 2012947210

Tradepaper ISBN: 978-1-4019-4196-3
Digital ISBN: 978-1-4019-4197-0

15 14 13 12   4 3 2 1
1st Hay House edition, October 2012

Recipe analyses calculated using NutriBase Professional Nutrition Manager software (CyberSoft, Inc.). When a choice of ingredients is listed, analysis is calculated using the first ingredient. Optional ingredients are not included in the analyses.

Introduction

"It was the best of times, it was the worst of times" is the famous opening sentence of the classic Charles Dickens novel, *A Tale of Two Cities*. Darn. That means someone else thought of it first. Too bad, 'cause it's the perfect way to describe our own nonfiction story, *A Tale of Two Sisters: The Looneyspoons Collection*. "It was the best of times, it was the worst of times." Let us explain.

This year marks the 15th anniversary of the publication of our first cookbook, *Looneyspoons: Low-Fat Food Made Fun!* The surprising success of our "little basement project," as we fondly refer to it, has led to experiences beyond our wildest dreams, including appearances on dozens of popular TV shows, features in newspapers and magazines from coast to coast (including a two-page spread in *People* magazine—with the Barbra Streisand-James Brolin wedding picture on the cover!), our own TV show on Food Network Canada and repeat visits to the huge U.S. shopping network, QVC, where we rubbed elbows with Paula Abdul, Paula Deen, Joan Rivers and Suzanne Somers.

But the best, most satisfying experience of all has been reading the thousands of heartfelt emails and letters that have poured in from "fans" across North America. (We put "fans" in quotations because we're just ordinary people, not movie stars or famous athletes, so the concept of having "fans" feels very strange to us!) The letters describe how our cookbooks and recipes have impacted peoples' lives, and their families' lives, for the better. Sometimes we'd laugh and sometimes we'd cry when reading incredible weight-loss success stories, tales of finicky kids who were eating their vegetables for the first time, accounts of cooking-challenged husbands who were suddenly whipping up tasty masterpieces, and an unforgettable, hilarious letter from an 80-year-old gentleman who confessed that he'd never cooked a single meal from any of our cookbooks, but uses them for bathroom reading, "since that's where all the fiber ends up anyway!"

Despite the overwhelmingly positive response to *Looneyspoons* and, later in 1999, to *Crazy Plates*, our second cookbook, we made the tough decision a few years ago to take both cookbooks out of print. Needless to say, the bookstores were NOT happy! "What!? Are ya nuts?" they said. Yes, and we've been called worse. "Why would you stop selling a bestseller?" But the decision had nothing to do with sales potential or money. It bothered us that some of the nutrition information in our cookbooks was outdated and, in some cases, outright wrong (based on newer studies). For example, back then, fats were classified as "evil" and we were encouraged by experts to drastically cut back on fat consumption, yet they didn't make a distinction between what are now known as "good fats" (avocados, nuts, seeds, salmon, etc.) and "bad fats" (hydrogenated and trans fats). We were advised to cut out ALL fats, which, of course, were replaced by carbs, mostly of the white, refined variety. (Sugar and flour—not a good thing!) In our defense, no one was talking about "good carbs" and "bad carbs," either! So out went the fat and in came the carbs, and the '90s low-fat craze was born.

Ironically, the low-fat frenzy seemed to make people fatter! Yup, as a continent, we were puffing up along with the fat-free puffed rice cakes we were "hoovering" down. Everyone knew the rule: As long as the cookies were labeled "fat-free," they could not (repeat, could not!) make you fat. Calories and sugar simply did not count. Remember those days? Funny thing was, as everyone seemed to be getting fatter from eating fat-free, we were getting loads of letters from readers who were LOSING weight, not gaining it. They were making our recipes, following our books' nutrition advice and shopping for smaller jeans. Say what? How can this be? What revolutionary diet plan or sage words of nutritional wisdom were causing these folks to drop dress sizes and melt their middles like celebrities getting ready for the red carpet? What was it? Enquiring minds want to know!

Well, we're pretty sure we've figured it out: Our cookbooks got people cooking! Yes, cooking! How ingenious! Our mission was (and still is) to make healthy cooking delicious, easy and fun. We gave folks recipes for scrumptious comfort foods that happened to be good for them, too. We made them laugh. That got people more interested in cooking. As they cooked more, they simply ate better. More veggies, more lean meats, more whole grains, more fresh, good stuff. That meant they relied less on packaged, processed, sugar-laden, fat-free concoctions. They lost weight. They felt better. It was sheer, accidental genius (if we do say so ourselves!).

Let's fast-forward to 2011. Today, fewer and fewer people are cooking. It's a sad fact (and not just because we're cookbook authors!). With life's fast pace, we've turned to convenience foods as our daily bread—not the whole-grain variety, either. Take-out, drive-thru, eat-in restaurant, vending machine, microwave...you name it. As long as it doesn't involve cooking, "sign us up!" has been our motto. Heaven forbid we make the effort or take the time to prepare our own meals. Instead,

it seems that everyone's eating out of packages, boxes and bags (oh, my!). That means we're eating more sugar, salt, bad fats, high-fructose corn syrup, MSG and artificial ingredients than ever before. We've forgotten what "real" food is. And that drives us crazy. Absolutely *looney*, in fact. Perhaps the obesity epidemic isn't about people eating too much food. Maybe it's about people eating too much that ISN'T food!

But what if you can't even *identify* food? Then what? On one of Greta's regular visits to her local supermarket, she was shocked and saddened by the food ignorance (and we mean that in the nicest possible way!) of the female cashier, who appeared to be in her late teens or early 20s. As Greta emptied her shopping basket full of produce onto the conveyor belt, the young cashier held up the items, one by one, asking Greta to identify them.

"That's zucchini," Greta answered. "That's a sweet potato. Parsley. Those are beets. Butternut squash." Then the cashier held up a lime. *A lime*! "OK, she's pulling my leg," Greta thought. "Seriously? You don't know what that is?" Greta asked. "Have you ever cooked a meal? I'm just curious."

"No, never," she replied.

"Well, what do you eat?" Greta inquired.

"Subs and pizza, mostly," was her honest answer.

"Oh," Greta replied. "That's a lime, by the way."

"Yeah, I know, I was just testing you."

Greta spices things up in the kitchen.

Janet writes nutrition tips in Greta's home office.

OK, so she could identify a lime. But not a sweet potato? Zucchini? We found this experience seriously alarming. And kinda depressing. What are teenagers eating and how will they ever learn to cook if no one teaches them? Is it any wonder that sales of energy drinks are soaring among the 18- to 25-year-old crowd? They're getting ZERO "real" fuel from their diet!

It was then that we decided on our mission: To boldly go where no cookbook authors have gone before—on a Cross-Country Cooking Crusade! We felt compelled to motivate North Americans to get back into their kitchens, to take platters (and health matters!) into their own hands. We truly believe that the more you cook for yourself (and prepare your own meals), the healthier you and your family will be. We want to encourage everyone to get real! Food, that is! Fresh, natural, whole, unprocessed. Zucchini, sweet potatoes, parsley and, yes, limes!

"I'll take two pain pills, please!"
said Greta post-surgery.

And the idea for *The Looneyspoons Collection* was born. In order to write the best cookbook possible, we sequestered ourselves for a full year at Cookbook Central, otherwise known as Greta's house. Janet moved in, dog and laptop in tow. We had no social lives, we cancelled dental appointments (mostly because we hate going to the dentist) and cut off all contact with the outside world (What's this about a Royal Wedding?). We ate, slept and dreamt "cookbook." We were completely focused on our mission and determined to motivate the world (yes, the world!) to get cookin'. Nothing could stop us. Or could it?

Just a few months into the writing process, Greta's beloved 12-year-old dog, a shepherd-lab mix named Lexi, became ill. Some of you may know Lexi from our *Eat, Shrink & Be Merry!* TV show since she made several cameo appearances on our kitchen set. Greta and Lexi were inseparable best pals. There was nothing the vets could do to save her. Lexi passed away on May 27, 2011. Needless to say, Greta was devastated. She cried for weeks. When the Kleenex ran out, Greta decided that focusing on

recipe development might help take her mind off her loss. She decided to get back in the kitchen and chop to it! After all, we were on a mission.

While slicing an onion, Greta (somehow!) twisted her right knee, forcing her kneecap out of its socket. Yeeeeeeeee-owch! This resulted in unplanned knee surgery less than one week later. On crutches for six weeks and unable to drive for four, Janet was assigned to play both nurse and chauffeur, "Driving Miss Gretty" to doctor's appointments, physiotherapy sessions and the grocery store to buy ingredients for recipes she could no longer develop. (Ever tried cooking with one leg and no hands?)

Enter our saviors and sisters Donna, Theresa and Margie, who took turns acting as Greta's hands and missing leg so that our cookbook project could continue. Greta supervised their work with an ice pack on her swollen knee, dictating recipe instructions from her chaise-lounge-turned-office.

One day, feeling particularly pleased with her revamped, warm spinach salad recipe, Greta decided to snap a picture and post it on Facebook. The responses were immediate. "Yum!" "Wow, I want that NOW!" "Beautiful!" "Great picture!" "You should take photos of ALL your recipes!"

Hmm. Really? Well, OK. Why not? So the one-legged cook became a one-legged food photographer, having absolutely no photography experience whatsoever, taking pictures with a four-year-old, battery-sucking, point-and-shoot camera on her back deck, since she didn't have a studio. Using only natural daylight, props from HomeSense, Janet for a tripod and an ironing board for a table, Greta hopped around on one leg taking 137 photos for this cookbook, just because a Facebook fan said she should. (See the copyright page at the front of the book for a list of Greta's pictures.)

Janet would often find Greta lying facedown on the deck, unable to get up after capturing the "perfect" shot of her whole-grain tortilla pinwheels with chicken and hot red pepper jelly.

It was a summer to remember and a summer to forget. Which isn't quite as catchy as "It was the best of times, it was the worst of times," but it's pretty darn close.

So, besides the Herculean effort that went into the making of TLC, why do we feel this is our best cookbook ever? Please allow us to tell you! First of all, the recipes in *The Looneyspoons Collection* are not simply reprints of reader-favorite recipes from our three cookbooks. No sireee! Though we refer to this book as a "collection," most of our older recipes are really "new," since they've been revised and updated to reflect current nutritional trends and ingredients, getting a much-needed overhaul. That means recipes now have better carbs, better fats, less sodium, less sugar and more fiber—yet with that same great taste that won't go to your waist. White pasta is now whole-grain, white rice is now brown, quinoa (a relatively unknown grain just a few years ago) makes an appearance in several chapters and canned products are now of the "no-salt-added" variety, an option not available in the 1990s. We've taken the "best of our best" recipes and made them even better for you!

Plus (and this is the really exciting part for our biggest fans!), we've included a lot of super-mouthwatering, NEW, never-seen-before, I-can't-believe-these-are-healthy recipes. The book has more than 325 recipes in total, almost one recipe for each day of the year. (See! We really DO want you to cook more!) You'll enjoy brand-new creations like *Stick to Your Ribs* (pork tenderloin "ribs" with a zesty lemon-rosemary sauce), *Honey, I Shrunk My Thighs!* (marinated honey-garlic chicken thighs), *Corn, Black Bean and Mango Fandango* (Greta's favorite salad!) and *Rolls Royce* (ooey, gooey cinnamon rolls with a touch of whole wheat and flax. Yum!). We've also included recipes suitable for diabetics and those following a gluten-free diet. Oh, and lots of goodies for vegetarians, too. You asked for it, you got it! We really believe our new *Moroccan and Rollin' Quinoa Salad* alone is worth the price of the book. And *Greta's Gluten-Free Miracle Brownies*? Grab a napkin, cuz there's some serious drool-factor involved!

We don't mean to sound like groovy TV infomercial hosts, but we can't help it. We're seriously excited. Can you tell? *The Looneyspoons Collection* is a whoppin' 400 pages, so you'll actually burn calories and build muscle just lifting it onto your kitchen counter! Not only that, but you'll also feast your eyes on tons of gorgeous food photos, thanks to Greta's previously mentioned one-legged efforts. Hunger for younger? You'll revel in all of Janet's NEWtrition nuggets—valuable weight-loss and anti-aging tips aimed at keeping all of us looking and feeling great. And of course, our trademark corny jokes and puns are sprinkled generously throughout the chapters to help make healthy eating fun, fun, fun!

Finally, to all of our fans at Weight Watchers, we've heard your pleas and pleases! You'll notice that every recipe in *The Looneyspoons Collection* contains a complete nutritional analysis, including the fiber content, an omission in our first book that drove WW members nuts (½ cup nuts = 12 points).

We feel like this is the cookbook we were meant to write. The first three were just practice! We sincerely hope you enjoy this book as much as we've enjoyed writing it. We literally poured our hearts, souls and every single ounce of love and effort we could muster into writing it. It's not a coincidence that the abbreviation of *The Looneyspoons Collection* is TLC.

Janet & Greta

Contents

In this chapter...

Fairest Wheels, p. 28

Come On, Get Appy!

Crowd-pleasing appetizers for your next gig

Hearty-Choke Dip

Hot roasted artichoke dip with spinach and Asiago cheese

*A hit recipe from our TV show **Eat, Shrink & Be Merry**!*

1 can	(14 oz/398 mL) artichoke hearts (not marinated)
½	large yellow sweet onion, coarsely chopped
3	large cloves garlic, peeled and cut into thirds
1 tbsp	olive oil

Salt and freshly ground black pepper to taste

1 can	(19 oz/540 mL) no-salt-added white kidney beans, drained and rinsed
1 cup	light (5%) sour cream
1 tub	(8 oz/250 g) light garden vegetable cream cheese (such as Philadelphia brand)
½ tsp	grated lemon zest
4 or 5	dashes hot pepper sauce
½ pkg	(10 oz/300 g) frozen spinach, thawed, squeezed dry and chopped (5 oz/150 g total)
1 cup	packed shredded Asiago cheese, divided (4 oz/113 g)

- Preheat oven to 425°F.

- Drain artichokes and pat dry using paper towels. Cut artichokes in half. Place artichokes in a small casserole dish or baking pan. Add chopped onions and garlic. Drizzle with olive oil and sprinkle lightly with salt and pepper. Mix well. Roast uncovered for 30 minutes, stirring once, halfway through roasting time.

- While vegetables are roasting, place kidney beans, sour cream, cream cheese, lemon zest and hot pepper sauce in the bowl of a food processor. Whirl until smooth.

- Remove artichoke mixture from oven. Reduce oven temperature to 375°F. Let vegetables cool for 5 minutes, then add to ingredients in food processor. Pulse on and off until mixture is well blended but still slightly lumpy. Transfer artichoke mixture to a bowl and stir in spinach, a pinch of black pepper and all but 2 tbsp Asiago cheese. Spoon mixture back into casserole dish. Top with remaining 2 tbsp Asiago cheese.

- Bake uncovered on middle oven rack for 30 minutes, until mixture bubbles around edges and top turns a light golden brown. Remove from oven and let cool for 5 minutes before serving. It's hot! Serve with whole-grain pita chips or crackers.

I ♥ this dip!

MAKES ABOUT 4 CUPS

PER SERVING (ABOUT ⅓ CUP)
143 calories, 7.9 g total fat (3.9 g saturated fat), 7 g protein, 12 g carbohydrate, 2.8 g fiber, 22 mg cholesterol, 334 mg sodium

Recipe Tip: Make sure spinach is well drained and patted dry (use paper towels to squeeze out excess moisture) before adding to dip.

Nutrition Nugget
Here's a juicy secret: Add a squirt of fresh lemon juice to your drinking water to spike your metabolism and help your body burn fat!

All Choked Up

An edible thistle that was prized by the Romans as food of nobility, the artichoke is as nutritious as it is delicious. *Choke*-full of fiber, vitamin C, folate and a gold mine of minerals, the healing qualities of the artichoke were well-recognized in ancient times, when it was used as an aphrodisiac, diuretic, breath freshener and even as a deodorant. Today, natural practitioners recommend artichokes for lowering cholesterol and stabilizing blood sugar. Plus, recent research shows that an active compound in artichokes called silymarin is a powerful antioxidant and may help regenerate the liver. After a few too many margaritas, *thistle* really help you! What won't help you, or those around you, is undercooking artichokes, especially Jerusalem artichokes. That can cause flatulence, or as Englishman John Goodyer wrote in 1617, they "...can cause a filthy, loathsome, stinking wind within the body." Oh, those artsy, fartsy culinary writers!

The Skins Game

Crispy potato skins topped with cheddar cheese and bacon crumbles

When you putt these tasty skins in front of the gallery, you'll have their undivotted attention, fore sure!

Keep your eyes on the ball.

MAKES 18 SKINS

PER SKIN
75 calories,
2 g total fat
(0.9 g saturated fat),
3 g protein,
11 g carbohydrate,
1.2 g fiber,
5 mg cholesterol,
100 mg sodium

3	large Russet (baking) potatoes (about 2 lbs/907 g total), unpeeled
2 tsp	olive oil
½ tsp	seasoned salt
¾ cup	packed shredded light old (sharp) cheddar cheese (3 oz/85 g)
3 slices	reduced-sodium bacon, cooked crisp and crumbled or chopped
2 tbsp	minced green onions
1 tbsp	minced fresh cilantro

- Wash potatoes and pat dry. Pierce all over with a fork. Place potatoes on a baking tray and bake at 400°F for about 1 hour, until tender. Allow potatoes to cool completely. (You can bake potatoes one day ahead, cool, wrap in plastic wrap or foil and refrigerate until ready to use.)

- Cut potatoes in half lengthwise. Using a teaspoon, scoop out the flesh (save it for another use), leaving a ¼-inch-thick shell. Cut each half into 3 long wedges. Mix together olive oil and salt in a small dish. Lightly brush both sides of skins with olive oil-salt mixture.

- Preheat broiler. Arrange skins in a single layer on a large baking sheet. Broil skins on top oven rack for about 3 minutes, or until tops begin to get lightly browned and crispy. Remove from oven, sprinkle with cheese, bacon, onions and cilantro. Return to oven and broil for 2 to 3 more minutes, until cheese is completely melted. Serve hot skins with light sour cream and salsa on the side.

> A smile is a facelift that's in everyone's price range.
> *Tom Wilson*

Artificial Unintelligence

It seems that researchers have uncovered an ironic and unfortunate side effect of drinking diet soft drinks...weight *gain*! A 25-year-long study showed that drinking diet soda increases the likelihood of serious weight gain—even more so than regular soda. Wait a minute! How can something with *zero calories* make you fat? Well, there's a lot more to weight gain than simple calories. It also boils down to hormones. Artificial sweeteners like aspartame or sucralose help us pack on the pounds by rapidly boosting the fat-storage hormone insulin, just like real sugar. They also affect leptin, the hormone that tells you when to stop eating. What happens when insulin and leptin levels are out of whack? You're ravenous, you crave sweets, you overeat and you store more fat! Researchers say that fake sugars are making us crave more *real* sugar. Some weight loss aid, huh? To top it all off, diet soda is 100 percent nutrition-free. Plus, the more diet soda you drink, the less healthful beverages, such as filtered water or green tea, you'll consume. For overall good health, your best bet is to develop less of a taste for sweets in general. The less sugar you eat, real or fake, the less you crave. If you think moderation, the occasional diet soda shouldn't pop your pants!

Trivial Tidbit

Did you know that a person who's lost in the woods and starving can obtain nourishment by chewing on his shoes? It's true! Leather has enough nutritional value to sustain life for a short time. And you thought putting your foot in your mouth was a *bad* thing! It's also why people with really small feet should always carry a compass.

Don't Worry, Be Crabby!

I'M REALLY HIP!

This scrumptious hot baked crab dip is a party favorite

If you're feeling down and out,
There's no need to mope and pout,
Don't worry, be crabby.
This recipe is really hip,
Pep up your mood with hot crab dip,
Don't worry, be crabby.

1½ cups	1% cottage cheese
½ pkg	(4 oz/125 g) light cream cheese
¾ cup	packed shredded light old (sharp) cheddar cheese (3 oz/85 g)
2 tbsp	finely minced or grated onions
1 tbsp	freshly squeezed lemon juice
1 tsp	each Worcestershire sauce and dry mustard
1 tsp	minced garlic
3 to 4	dashes hot pepper sauce
1 lb	(454 g) good-quality lump crabmeat

MAKES 10 SERVINGS

PER SERVING (⅓ cup)
115 calories,
5 g total fat
(2.7 g saturated fat),
13 g protein,
3 g carbohydrate,
0 g fiber,
50 mg cholesterol,
357 mg sodium

- Preheat oven to 350°F. Spray a small casserole dish with cooking spray and set aside.

- Whirl together cottage cheese and cream cheese in a food processor until perfectly smooth. Transfer mixture to a large bowl. Stir in all remaining ingredients except crabmeat. Mix well. Chop or break up crabmeat into small pieces and add to cream-cheese mixture. Stir until well blended. Spoon into casserole dish.

- Bake, uncovered, for 25 minutes. Remove from oven and let cool slightly (it's hot). Stir before serving. Serve with whole-grain crackers or pita chips.

Recipe Tip: Imitation crabmeat also works nicely in this recipe.

FOOD BITE

Talk about putting your foot in your mouth! Did you know that if you rub garlic on the heel of your foot, it will be absorbed by the pores and eventually show up on your breath? We've all heard that garlic has *heeling* qualities, though we couldn't help but wonder: If you *eat* garlic, does the smell show up on your feet?

Say it Ain't So, Joe!

Tall, grande, venti, Frappuccino, Cappuccino, Mochaccino. Sure is a whole *latte* lingo goin' down at the gourmet coffee shop—and a whole *latte* sugar-filled calories! Depending on the size of your drink, the type of milk and syrup you choose and whether you say "yes" to whipped cream, you can transform an innocent beverage into an insulin-spiking, belt-busting milkshake. Here's proof: A Starbucks Peppermint White Chocolate Mocha has an unthinkable, drinkable 78 grams of sugar—that's almost 20 teaspoons! Even a less fancy Grande Cinnamon Dolce Latte (2% milk and no whipped cream) packs almost 10 teaspoons! And calories? Chalk up 260 for the latter latte. Imagine, if you drink just one of these syrup-filled concoctions five days a week for one year, you'd not only be broke, but also add almost 70,000 liquid calories to your waistline, the equivalent of 20 pounds of flab! Unless you want your rear to appear venti (large!), make sure sweetened coffees aren't your daily grind.

Chicken Littles

Japanese rumaki: bacon-wrapped, ginger-marinated chicken bites and water chestnuts

Someone run and tell the king, our chicken bites are the greatest thing! Who would believe that bacon-wrapped chicken morsels could be so tasty without tons of fat? They may be little, but their flavor's huge!

¼ cup	reduced-sodium soy sauce		2	large boneless skinless chicken breasts (about 12 oz/340 g)
2 tbsp	brown sugar		12	whole water chestnuts (canned)
1 tbsp	grated gingerroot		12	slices bacon, cut in half crosswise
1 tsp	grated orange zest		24	round wooden toothpicks
¼ tsp	each ground coriander and curry powder			
1 tsp	minced garlic			

- To make marinade, combine soy sauce, brown sugar, gingerroot, orange zest, coriander, curry and garlic in a small bowl. Set aside.

- Cut chicken breasts into 24 bite-sized pieces. Cut water chestnuts in half. Combine chicken, water chestnuts and marinade in a shallow glass baking dish (a pie plate would work) or in a large, heavy-duty, resealable plastic bag. Mix well to coat chicken and water chestnuts with marinade. Marinate in refrigerator for at least 1 hour. (You can marinate overnight for even better flavor.)

- To make rumaki, lay one half-strip of bacon on work surface. Place chicken piece in center of bacon strip and top chicken with water chestnut. Fold over ends of bacon to cover chicken and water chestnut. Secure with toothpick. Make sure toothpick pierces water chestnut or it will fall out (probably when you're eating it!).

- Place rumaki on a wire rack on a baking sheet. (Using a rack prevents the food from soaking in the bacon drippings.) Bake at 400°F for 20 to 25 minutes, until chicken and bacon are cooked through. Serve warm.

MAKES 24 PIECES

PER PIECE
40 calories, 1.8 g total fat
(0.6 saturated fat),
5 g protein,
2 g carbohydrate,
0.3 g fiber,
11 mg cholesterol,
106 mg sodium

Sports energy drinks contain electrolytes, so be sure not to drink them while in the bathtub :)

Recipe Tip: If you're having a large party, you should double this recipe. Everyone goes crazy for this appetizer and there's no such thing as leftover rumaki. Each guest will eat between three and 300 of them, so make lots! When they're almost ready, you'll probably find everyone gathered around the oven, wondering what smells so good. Most traditional rumaki recipes are made with chopped chicken livers, but we prefer chicken breasts.

Yummus

Our lemony version of traditional chickpea hummus gets rave reviews

This is no ho-hum hummus! It's a real humdinger—the yummiest of the yummies—and it only takes a few minutes to prepare. Yummust try it!

1 can	(19 oz/540 mL) no-salt-added chickpeas, drained and rinsed
¼ cup	low-fat Greek yogurt or light (5%) sour cream
2 tbsp	tahini (sesame seed paste)
2 tbsp	freshly squeezed lemon juice
2 tsp	minced garlic
1 tsp	grated lemon zest
1 tsp	liquid honey
½ tsp	sesame oil
½ to 1 tsp	salt
¼ tsp	ground coriander
⅛ tsp	ground cumin

- Place all ingredients in the bowl of a food processor and whirl until smooth. Serve with warmed whole-grain pita wedges or crisp vegetables for dunking (or both!).

Variation: To make roasted red pepper hummus, add 1 large roasted, peeled and chopped red bell pepper plus ¼ tsp paprika and ¼ tsp cayenne pepper to this recipe.

MAKES ABOUT 2 CUPS

PER SERVING (¼ CUP)
104 calories,
3 g total fat (0.4 g saturated fat),
4 g protein,
16 g carbohydrate,
3.1 g fiber,
0.5 mg cholesterol,
229 mg sodium

You're the chick for me!

CHICK PEAS

The Fastest Way 2 Fatville

While we've been busy blaming our ballooning bellies on carbs, fat and white sugar, there's been another nasty villain lurking in the shadows. Who's the dirty rotten scoundrel that's helping to make us fat? It's high-fructose corn syrup (a.k.a. HFCS), the sweetener used to replace sugar in many processed foods. Manufacturers love it because it's cheap and doubly sweet. Problem is, our fat cells love it, too! Research shows that it's more easily turned into fat than any other carbohydrate, and it also shuts off the switches that control appetite. Your liver bears the sole burden for metabolizing HFCS, and it simply hasn't evolved to handle the kind of fructose load we get when we chug 12-ounce cans of Coke daily. So it responds to the fructose flood by shipping much of it directly to our fat cells. In high levels, HFCS also boosts triglycerides (fatty compounds that circulate in the bloodstream and are stored in fat tissue) by as much as 32 percent. That's a heart attack waiting to happen! And you'll find it just about everywhere: soft drinks, juice, energy and sports drinks, candy, barbecue sauce, fruit-flavored yogurt, even some breakfast cereals. The only way to avoid the evil wrath of HFCS is by reading labels carefully. If high-fructose corn syrup, fructose, glucose/fructose or corn syrup appears near the top of the ingredients list, you can bet you're getting a hefty dose of trouble.

Satayday Night Fever

Scrumptious chicken satay with peanut dipping sauce

A low-fat chicken satay that includes a creamy peanut dipping sauce? What Gibbs? And simple to make, too? Discos here and discos there—how easy can it Bee? Gees!

4	large boneless skinless chicken breasts (about 1½ lbs/680 g), cut into 1-inch cubes
2 tbsp	reduced-sodium soy sauce
1 tbsp	each liquid honey and freshly squeezed lemon juice
2 tsp	grated gingerroot
1 tsp	minced garlic

Peanut Dipping Sauce

½ cup	reduced-sodium chicken broth
3 tbsp	each light peanut butter and grape jelly
1 tbsp	reduced-sodium soy sauce
1 tsp	each grated lemon zest and sesame oil
½ tsp	ground coriander
¼ tsp	crushed red pepper flakes

8 small wooden or metal skewers

- Place chicken pieces in a large, heavy-duty, resealable plastic bag. In a small bowl, combine soy sauce, honey, lemon juice, gingerroot and garlic. Pour marinade over chicken pieces in bag. Seal bag and make sure chicken pieces are coated with marinade. Refrigerate for at least 2 hours or overnight, if possible.

- If using wooden skewers, soak them in water for at least 20 minutes before using to prevent burning. Preheat grill to medium-high heat. Thread chicken pieces onto skewers. Discard marinade. Lightly oil grill rack and place skewers on rack. Grill for about 10 minutes, turning often to cook all sides. (If you prefer, cook chicken in oven under broiler, 4 inches from heat, for about 8 minutes total, turning often.)

- While chicken is cooking, prepare dipping sauce. Combine all sauce ingredients in a small saucepan. Heat over medium heat until mixture is bubbly and has thickened. Transfer to a serving dish. Serve hot chicken skewers with dipping sauce.

MAKES 8 SKEWERS

PER SKEWER (NO SAUCE)
113 calories,
2.2 g total fat
(0.6 g saturated fat),
20 g protein,
2 g carbohydrate,
0 g fiber,
53 mg cholesterol,
151 mg sodium

SAUCE (PER 2 TBSP)
67 calories,
2.9 g total fat
(0.6 g saturated fat),
2 g protein,
8 g carbohydrate,
0.5 g fiber,
0 mg cholesterol,
152 mg sodium

Nutrition Nugget

Tea-rrific tummy toner: Drinking strong green tea within two hours after eating a meal increases fat breakdown by one-third!

A good laugh and a long sleep are the best cures in the doctor's book.
Irish proverb

Eat to the Beat

According to researchers at Johns Hopkins University, music affects how fast we eat. The average diner eats five mouthfuls a minute when listening to lively music, four mouthfuls a minute when eating without music, and three mouthfuls a minute when listening to a slow melody. So, listening to slow tunes means it'll take you longer to finish your meal and you'll likely eat less, since it takes about 20 minutes for your stomach to tell your brain that it's had enough. Translation: A Lovin' Spoonful of Meat Loaf with Cranberries and Bread served on The Platters with a glass of April Wine won't make you a Chubby Checker!

Born to be Wild Mushroom Pizza

Herbed wild mushroom appetizer pizza with hummus

*Like a true nature's child, we were born,
born to eat wild…mushrooms, that is!*

1 can	(19 oz/540 mL) tomatoes with Italian herbs
2 tsp	olive oil
1 cup	thinly sliced red onions
1 tsp	minced garlic
4 cups	sliced mixed wild mushrooms (such as cremini, shiitake and portobello)
2 tsp	each minced fresh thyme and fresh rosemary, or ½ tsp each dried
Pinch	salt and freshly ground black pepper
¾ cup	hummus (see tip)
1	12-inch prebaked whole-grain thin-crust pizza shell
¼ cup	freshly grated Parmesan, Romano or Asiago cheese
¾ cup	packed shredded light mozzarella or provolone cheese (3 oz/85 g)

- Preheat oven to 425°F.

- Drain tomatoes in a sieve, pressing down on them to remove as much liquid as possible. Set aside. They won't look pretty at this point, but that's OK.

- Heat olive oil in a large, non-stick skillet over medium heat. Add onions and garlic. Cook and stir until onions have softened, 3 to 4 minutes. Add mushrooms and cook until mushrooms are tender, about 5 more minutes. Stir in thyme, rosemary, salt and pepper. Cook 1 more minute. Remove from heat.

- To assemble pizza, spread hummus over pizza crust, leaving a ½-inch border. Top hummus with drained tomatoes. Sprinkle Parmesan cheese over tomatoes. Spread mushroom mixture evenly over top, followed by mozzarella.

- Place pizza directly on middle oven rack and bake for 10 to 12 minutes, until cheese is completely melted and edges are lightly browned. Remove from oven to cutting board and let cool 1 minute before slicing. Slice into 12 thin wedges and serve immediately.

Recipe Tip: For this recipe, try our hummus on p. 8 or use store-bought hummus. For a variation, substitute crumbled feta cheese with herbs for the Parmesan cheese, and thinly sliced plum (Roma) tomatoes for the canned Italian tomatoes.

MAKES 1 PIZZA, 12 SLICES

PER SLICE
128 calories, 5 g total fat
(1.6 g saturated fat), 6 g protein,
15 g carbohydrate, 2.1 g fiber,
5 mg cholesterol, 254 mg sodium

FOOD BITE

"Dough" and "bread" became slang terms for money because they reflect its historical role in buying life's basic necessities like food (bread!). So, money is appropriately called "dough" because we all *knead* it!

Many a person who goes on a diet finds that he is a poor loser :)

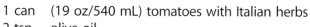

Blame Game

There's no doubt that marketing campaigns for gut-busting, artery-clogging fast foods are everywhere, and they're really persuasive, too. But before you launch a lawsuit alleging that The Hamburglar stole your waistline and left behind an unidentifiable mass of flesh, ask yourself this: Who's really to blame? Sure, the fast-food giants haven't done us too many favors, but remember, we're the ones who keep buying their gargantuan combos and eating them. Every last morsel. Can't we take more personal responsibility for our own health? Do we need lawsuits or even laws to protect us from junk food? A Twinkie tax? Certainly consumers have responsibilities, too. If restaurants are willing to serve food that's better for us, we have to order the healthy stuff, not the Godzilla burger with a side of mammoth fries. Across North America, there's a trend toward innovative menus that dish up plenty of tasty, nutritious, balanced meals. Restaurants will take bigger strides to prepare healthier food choices as long as we keep beating a path to their doors. If we want them to deliver the goods, we've gotta say no to the bads!

Chickadeeahs

Barbecue chicken quesadillas with roasted red pepper hummus

Chick out the ah-some flavor of these ah-mazing chicken quesadillas. Ah-inspiring!

2 tsp	olive oil, divided
1	small red onion, peeled, halved and very thinly sliced
1½ cups	chopped cooked chicken breast (see tip)
¼ cup	smoky barbecue sauce
1 tbsp	minced fresh cilantro
4	large (10-inch) whole-grain flour tortillas
½ cup	roasted red pepper hummus
1 cup	packed shredded light Monterey Jack cheese (4 oz/113 g)

- Heat 1 tsp olive oil in a small non-stick skillet over medium heat. Add onions and cook slowly, stirring often, until onions are very tender. Be careful not to burn them. You may add a bit of water if they start to stick. Remove skillet from heat. Add chicken, barbecue sauce and cilantro to onions and mix well.

- Working one tortilla at a time, brush one side of tortilla with some of the remaining olive oil using a pastry brush. Place oil-side down on a large dinner plate or piece of wax paper. Spread 2 tbsp hummus on one half of tortilla. Top hummus with ¼ chicken-onion mixture. Sprinkle with ¼ cheese. Fold other half of tortilla over filling and press down on tortilla using your hands. This will help hold it together. Repeat process with remaining tortillas and filling. You should now have 4 large half-circles that are ready to be cooked.

- Heat a large (12-inch) skillet over medium-high heat. Place 2 quesadillas in skillet. Do not overlap them. Cook until undersides are lightly browned, about 3 minutes. Carefully turn both quesadillas to brown the other sides, another 3 minutes. Remove quesadillas from skillet and keep warm. Repeat cooking process with remaining 2 tortillas.

- Place hot, cooked quesadillas on a cutting board and slice each half-circle into 4 large wedges. Serve immediately. Tastes great with light sour cream, salsa and guacamole on the side!

Recipe Tip: For convenience, use the breast meat from a store-bought rotisserie chicken for this recipe.

MAKES 16 WEDGES

PER WEDGE
104 calories,
4 g total fat
(1 g saturated fat),
6 g protein,
10 g carbohydrate,
1 g fiber,
13 mg cholesterol,
195 mg sodium

Nutrition Nugget

Seeing red? If not, you should be! Red bell peppers have nine times the wrinkle-fighting, disease-preventing beta carotene of their green cousins, as well as 10 times the vitamin A and more than double the amount of vitamin C. Eat red to feel in the pink!

Jerry Springerolls

Vegetable-filled spring rolls with a spicy Thai dipping sauce

You'll be the host with the most when you serve your friends these light-tasting spring rolls. We've lowered the fat rating by censoring all the heavyweight, controversial ingredients.

MAKES 14 SPRING ROLLS

PER ROLL (NO SAUCE)
48 calories,
0.8 g total fat (0.1 g saturated fat),
1 g protein, 9 g carbohydrate,
0.7 g fiber, 0 mg cholesterol,
30 mg sodium

SAUCE (PER 2 TBSP)
33 calories,
0 g total fat (0 g saturated fat),
0 g protein, 7 g carbohydrate,
0 g fiber, 94 mg sodium

Dipping Sauce

¾ cup	water
⅓ cup	seasoned rice vinegar
¼ cup	brown sugar
1½ tbsp	reduced-sodium soy sauce
1 tbsp	grated gingerroot
2 tsp	cornstarch
1 tsp	minced garlic
¼ tsp	crushed red pepper flakes

2 oz	(57 g) rice vermicelli noodles, uncooked (see tip)
1 cup	each grated carrots and chopped fresh bean sprouts
½ cup	peeled, seeded and finely chopped cucumber
½ cup	chopped green onions
2 tsp	sesame oil
14	6-inch rice paper wraps (see tip)
14	whole fresh mint leaves

- To make dipping sauce, whisk together all sauce ingredients in a small saucepan. Heat over medium-high heat until mixture comes to a boil and thickens slightly. Remove from heat and let cool to room temperature.

- Boil vermicelli in a large pot of water for 4 minutes, or until tender. Drain, rinse with cold water and drain again. Blot dry using paper towels.

- Coarsely chop noodles and place them in a medium bowl. Add carrots, bean sprouts, cucumber and green onions. Mix well. Add sesame oil and mix again.

- Fill a large, shallow dish (such as a pie plate) with very hot water. (Keep some boiling water handy to add to the dish as the water cools.) Working one at a time, soak rice papers in hot water for about 30 seconds, or until soft and pliable (time will vary with brand of rice paper). Transfer to a clean kitchen towel, lay wrapper flat and blot dry.

- Place one mint leaf in center of wrapper and top with ¼ cup filling. Using your fingers, shape filling into a 3-inch-long horizontal cylinder. Fold bottom edge over filling and roll once to enclose. Fold in sides and continue to roll up tightly. Place seam-side down on a plate and cover with a damp towel. Repeat process with remaining wrappers and filling. Wrap tightly and refrigerate until serving time. Serve spring rolls with dipping sauce.

Variation: Add one large cooked shrimp to each spring roll for added protein. Don't forget to remove the tails!

Recipe Tip Rice vermicelli (or rice-flour noodles) are extremely thin, almost thread-like noodles. You'll find them in the Asian food aisle of most supermarkets. Rice papers, made from rice flour and water, look like translucent tortillas. They must be softened by soaking in water before using. Look for rice papers, which are packaged dry and in plastic wrap, at well-stocked grocery stores or Asian markets. Be careful not to confuse rice papers with spring roll wrappers, which are made from wheat flour and are meant to be deep-fried.

Slim Dunk

Super-simple, creamy spinach dip made with Greek yogurt

There's no need to foul-out of your healthy eating plan!
This spinach dip's so light, it won't interfere with your hang time.

2 cups	low-fat Greek yogurt
½ cup	light mayonnaise (not fat-free)
1 pkg	(10 oz/300 g) frozen spinach, thawed, squeezed dry and chopped
1 pkg	(2.7 oz/77 g) Knorr Cream of Leek Soup mix
½ cup	minced water chestnuts
⅓ cup	minced red bell pepper

- Combine all ingredients in a medium bowl. Mix well. Cover and refrigerate for at least 3 hours before serving. (Tastes best when chilled overnight!)

MAKES ABOUT 3½ CUPS

PER SERVING (¼ CUP)
72 calories, 3 g total fat (0.2 g saturated fat), 4 g protein, 7 g carbohydrate, 1 g fiber, 6 mg cholesterol, 324 mg sodium

Nutrition Nugget

Greek is the word! Greek yogurt has three times the protein of regular yogurt. Buy organic varieties if you can and look for brands containing the least amount of sugar.

You Go, 'Gurt!

Ever wonder why your doctor tells you to eat yogurt after you've been taking antibiotics? Well, when antibiotics (which literally means "anti-life") go about gobbling up the "bad" bacteria that make you sick, they also kill off the "good," health-promoting bacteria that live in your gut. Yes, you have beneficial bug buddies inside you! When the good are overtaken by the bad, it can turn ugly and contribute to a variety of ailments, from acne to allergies to arthritis to digestive disorders, largely because 80 percent of your immune system resides in the intestinal tract. That's where yogurt enters the battle. It contains armies of the gut-friendly bugs like acidophilus and bifidus, so by eating yogurt after a course of antibiotics, you're replenishing the troops, so to speak.

Unfortunately, most commercial yogurts are overly pasteurized and the heat kills off plenty of the good bacteria. Plus, the muck at the bottom of fruity yogurts is a sugar-laden buffet for the nasty critters. When possible, choose plain, organic yogurt or Greek yogurt and add your own chopped fruit or nuts. Another option is to simply buy good bacteria (called "probiotics," meaning "for life") in capsule or powder form at the health food store. Nowadays, most of us need probiotics, and not just because we've taken too many antibiotics over the course of our lives. Poor diet (especially sugar and refined foods) and even too much stress can help the bad bacteria knock out the good. Zoinks! Not only that, but factory-farmed animals are routinely given antibiotics, so we're getting a teensy dose every time we eat chicken or beef. Thankfully, beefing up your bifidus helps keep your digestive system in good working order.

Two groups of people are preoccupied with the last supper—clergymen and dieters :)

For Pizza Sake!

An appetizer for the kids:
Hot pizza dip with turkey pepperettes

*It's a funky dunky that won't make them chunky!
Your kids will devour this scrumptious, hot pizza dip—
and it's easy to make, for pizza sake!*

1 tsp	olive oil
1 cup	finely chopped mushrooms
½ cup	minced red onions
½ cup	thinly sliced or chopped turkey pepperettes (see tip)
1 tbsp	minced fresh oregano, or ½ tsp dried
1 tub	(8 oz/250 g) light ranch-flavored cream cheese (such as Philadelphia brand)
½ cup	light (5%) sour cream
1 cup	packed shredded light Monterey Jack or mozzarella cheese (4 oz/113 g)
½ cup	your favorite pizza sauce
2 tbsp	minced green onions

MAKES 12 SERVINGS

PER SERVING (¼ CUP)
96 calories,
5.9 g total fat
(3.3 g saturated fat),
6 g protein,
5 g carbohydrate,
0.4 g fiber,
29 mg cholesterol,
384 mg sodium

- Preheat oven to 350°F. Spray an 8-inch casserole dish with cooking spray and set aside.

- Heat olive oil in a small skillet over medium heat. Add mushrooms, onions, turkey pepperettes and oregano. Cook and stir until vegetables are softened, about 5 minutes. Remove from heat and set aside.

- In a medium bowl, beat together cream cheese and sour cream on medium speed of electric mixer until smooth. Stir in shredded cheese. Spread cheese mixture evenly over bottom of casserole dish. Spread pizza sauce over cheese layer. Spread vegetable-pepperette mixture over sauce.

- Bake, uncovered, for 25 to 30 minutes, until mixture is hot and bubbly. Let cool for 5 minutes before serving (it's hot!). Sprinkle with green onions and serve with whole-grain crackers or toasted pita wedges.

Recipe Tip Look for bags of turkey pepperettes (mini turkey pepperoni sticks) in the deli section at your grocery store where packaged cold cuts are sold.

Portion Distortion

"I'm stuffed! I ate *way* too much!" Sound familiar? One reason we stuff ourselves silly is because we're experiencing "portion distortion." Food has undergone some serious sprawl lately and those ballooning, industrial-sized portions encourage people to eat whether they're hungry or not. Did you know that the correct portion size—the one that's most effectively handled by the body—is the size of your own fist? That corresponds to the size of your stomach. By today's standards, we're double-, triple- and quadruple-fisting, inflating our stomachs like beach balls. Yowch! To prevent your pant size from inflating, too, you've got to get a handle on portion sizes. Always read labels and check both the calories and servings per package. You might think you're eating a 200-calorie snack but, unbeknownst to you, each bag contains two servings. Zoinks! When cooking at home, use measuring cups until you get the hang of what's "normal." One cup of cooked pasta has 200 calories, making the typical three-cup serving worth a whopping 600! For a perfect spaghetti portion, the diameter of a quarter is the exact size of a two-ounce stack (about 200 calories), enough to serve one person. And when it comes to fast food, super size isn't super wise. Is an extra 250 calories, even for a mere 39 cents, really a smart expenditure? Those are the differences, in calories and cost, between a small order of fries and a large one. Remember: Sometimes less is more!

Bewedged

Baked whole wheat pita wedges with Parmesan and rosemary

*Darrin to be different in the appetizer department?
Concocting a spellbinding snack is as easy as wiggling
your nose and sprinkling on some rose (mary, that is).*

1½ tbsp	dried rosemary	
⅔ cup	freshly grated Parmesan cheese	
3	6-inch whole wheat, flax or multigrain pita rounds (with pockets)	
1 tbsp	olive oil	
1 tbsp	butter, melted	
¼ tsp	each garlic powder and onion powder	

MAKES 36 WEDGES

PER WEDGE
29 calories,
1.4 g total fat
(0.6 g saturated fat),
1 g protein,
3 g carbohydrate,
0.5 g fiber,
2 mg cholesterol,
51 mg sodium

- Preheat oven to 350°F.

- Crush the dried rosemary with your fingers and combine it with the Parmesan cheese in a small bowl. Set aside.

- Using a sharp knife or kitchen scissors, cut each pita round into 6 equal wedges. Pull the layers apart and cut each wedge again, so you end up with 12 wedges from each pita (36 wedges total).

- Place the wedges, rough side up, on a large baking sheet. Do not overlap wedges. (You will need to cook 2 separate batches.)

- In another small bowl, combine olive oil, butter, garlic powder and onion powder. Using a pastry brush, lightly brush mixture onto rough side of wedges. Sprinkle with Parmesan-rosemary mixture.

- Bake on middle oven rack for 10 to 14 minutes. Important: Keep an eye on them so they don't burn! One minute they may look pale and the next minute they could be black, so don't wander away from the kitchen for too long. They should be lightly browned. Cool on a wire rack before serving.

Recipe Tip: You can use Asiago or Romano cheese instead of Parmesan.

He Who Laughs, Lasts

Is it possible to laugh your way to better health? Experts believe so! Laughter does your body good, inside and out. In fact, if you're unable to exercise for whatever reason—illness, injury, sports bra's in the wash—laughter's not a bad substitute. Like exercise, it brings more oxygen to your lungs, lowers blood pressure, protects your heart's lining from inflammation and boosts your immune system so viruses, bacteria and tumors won't get the best of you. No wonder George Burns lived to be 100! Plus, when you laugh out loud, your abdomen and diaphragm contract, your liver gets a massage, your facial muscles stretch and your back and shoulders unkink. It's like a half-day spa visit for your upper body and it doesn't cost a cent! And just to prove that laughter really is the best medicine, consider the following: Why do people dip bread into melted cheese? Because it's *fonduing* it! See, don't you feel better already?

The greatest wealth is health.

Virgil

FOOD BITE

Studies show that our taste buds change with age, including a declining sensitivity to bitterness. Fortunately, this makes many health foods more appealing to us as we get older. Eight in 10 older people reported a growing preference for green vegetables, whole-grain foods and bitter fruits like grapefruits and lemons. And you thought Grandma's puckered face came from misplaced dentures!

Skinny Dipping

Dip, dip hooray! These skinny dips won't end up on your hips!

Tzatziki

Serve with warm, fresh, whole-grain pita triangles

1 cup	low-fat Greek yogurt
¾ cup	peeled, seeded and finely chopped English cucumber
1 tbsp	freshly squeezed lemon juice
1 tbsp	minced fresh dill
1 tsp	minced garlic
1 tsp	granulated sugar
½ tsp	salt
¼ tsp	freshly ground black pepper

- Combine all ingredients in a small bowl. Cover and refrigerate for at least 1 hour before serving.

MAKES ABOUT 2 CUPS

PER SERVING (¼ CUP)
24 calories,
0.1 g total fat (0 g saturated fat),
3 g protein, 3 g carbohydrate,
0.4 g fiber, 3 mg cholesterol,
117 mg sodium

Classic Guacamole

Serve with baked, whole-grain tortilla chips, as a burger topper or as an accompaniment to grilled fish

2	large avocados (ripe!), halved, seeded and mashed (see tip)
2 tbsp	freshly squeezed lemon or lime juice
½ cup	finely minced red onions
½ cup	diced tomatoes (grape tomatoes work well)
2 tbsp	minced fresh cilantro
1	jalapeño pepper, seeded and minced, or a couple shakes of hot pepper sauce (optional)
2 tsp	minced garlic
¼ tsp	each salt and ground cumin
Pinch	freshly ground black pepper

Combine all ingredients in a medium bowl. Cover and refrigerate until serving time. Guacamole will keep for about 3 days in the fridge if well covered.

MAKES ABOUT 2½ CUPS

PER SERVING (¼ CUP)
55 calories, 4.7 g total fat (0.7 g saturated fat),
1 g protein, 4 g carbohydrate, 1.8 g fiber,
0 mg cholesterol, 62 mg sodium

Recipe Tip Unlike many other fruits, avocados don't ripen on the tree. They must be picked before the ripening process can start. For guacamole, choose avocados that yield to gentle pressure. Unripe avocados make horrible guacamole! To seed an avocado, cut the avocado in half lengthwise and wiggle both halves to separate them. Tap the big seed with a sharp knife and when the blade catches, rotate the knife and lift out the seed. Scoop out the flesh using a small spoon. Dice or mash as directed in the recipe.

The Tastiest Shrimp Cocktail Sauce

The addition of lemon adds a burst of fresh flavor that pairs perfectly with shrimp

¾ cup tomato-based chili sauce (such as Heinz brand)
¼ cup prepared horseradish
1 tbsp freshly squeezed lemon juice
1 tsp grated lemon zest
1 tsp granulated sugar
½ tsp Worcestershire sauce

• Combine all ingredients in a medium bowl. Mix well. Refrigerate until ready to serve. Sauce may be stored for up to 2 weeks in the fridge. If you like hot cocktail sauce, add a bit more horseradish or a few drops of hot pepper sauce.

Variation: Add 1 tbsp minced fresh dill.

MAKES 1 CUP

PER SERVING (1 TBSP)
15 calories, 0 g total fat (0 g saturated fat),
0 g protein, 4 g carbohydrate, 0.3 g fiber,
0 mg cholesterol, 173 mg sodium

> You can't lose weight by talking about it. You have to keep your mouth shut.
> *The Old Farmer's Almanac*

Chunky Avocado Salsa

Serve with grilled meats, chicken, fish, on scrambled eggs, with whole-grain pita chips or as a burger topper

2 cups quartered grape tomatoes
2 large avocados, peeled, pitted and diced
½ cup finely minced red onions
2 tbsp (or more) minced fresh cilantro
2 tbsp freshly squeezed lime juice
1 tsp granulated sugar
½ tsp each salt and freshly ground black pepper

• Gently mix all ingredients in a medium bowl. Cover and refrigerate until serving time or serve immediately.

MAKES 4½ CUPS

PER SERVING (⅓ CUP)
48 calories, 3.7 g total fat (0.6 g saturated fat), 1 g protein,
4 g carbohydrate, 1.6 g fiber, 0 mg cholesterol, 95 mg sodium

Tangy Orange-Plum Dip

For chicken fingers, chicken skewers, egg rolls or spring rolls

1 cup yellow plum jam
or apricot jam
¼ cup orange juice
2 tbsp white vinegar
1 tsp dry mustard
1 tsp reduced-sodium soy sauce
½ tsp grated orange zest
¼ tsp crushed red pepper flakes
(optional)

• Combine all ingredients in a small pot. Cook over medium heat until jam is melted and dip is bubbly. Serve warm.

MAKES ABOUT 1¼ CUPS

PER SERVING (2 TBSP)
58 calories, 0.1 g total fat (0 g saturated fat),
0 g protein, 15 g carbohydrate,
0.3 g fiber, 0 mg cholesterol,
36 mg sodium

COME ON, GET APPY!

Shrimply Irresistible

Marinated, grilled shrimp skewers with fiery fruit salsa

*Super-lean and super-scrumptious, these shrimp skewers
are shrimple to make, even for a shrimpleton.*

3 tbsp	reduced-sodium soy sauce
2 tbsp	each freshly squeezed lime juice and brown sugar
1 tbsp	each olive oil and ketchup
2 tsp	minced garlic
1 tsp	ground coriander
½ tsp	ground cumin
24	uncooked jumbo shrimp, fresh or frozen (thaw first if using frozen)

Fruit Salsa

¾ cup	orange segments
¾ cup	peeled and diced Granny Smith apples
2 tbsp	freshly squeezed lime juice
2	green onions, white parts plus 1 inch of green parts, minced
1 tbsp	minced fresh cilantro or mint
1 tsp	granulated sugar
½ tsp	crushed red pepper flakes
6	10-inch wooden or metal skewers

- In a small bowl, whisk together soy sauce, lime juice, brown sugar, olive oil, ketchup, garlic, coriander and cumin. Remove shells from shrimp, leaving tails intact. Pour marinade over shrimp in a shallow glass baking dish or in a large, resealable plastic bag. Make sure each piece of shrimp is coated with marinade. Refrigerate for 1 hour. If using wooden skewers, soak them in water until ready to use.

- Meanwhile, prepare salsa. Place all salsa ingredients in a food processor or blender and pulse on and off until mixture is well blended and finely chopped, but not liquified. Pour into a small glass serving bowl, cover and refrigerate until ready to serve.

- Preheat grill to medium-high heat. Lightly oil grill rack. Remove shrimp from marinade and thread 4 pieces onto each skewer. Grill for about 3 to 4 minutes per side or until shrimp turns pink and is cooked through. Be careful not to overcook shrimp. Serve immediately with fruit salsa.

MAKES 6 SERVINGS

PER SKEWER (SHRIMP ONLY)
143 calories, 3.6 g total fat (0.6 g saturated fat),
21 g protein, 6 g carbohydrate, 0.2 g fiber,
152 mg cholesterol, 371 mg sodium

SALSA (PER 2 TBSP)
18 calories, 0 g total fat (0 g saturated fat),
0 g protein, 5 g carbohydrate, 0.6 g fiber,
0 mg cholesterol, 1 mg sodium

Nutrition Nugget

Shrimp doesn't skimp! Once you get through its armor, shrimp offers an ap*peeling* array of nutrients. You'll get muscle-building protein, bone-building vitamin D, energy-producing iron, heart-protecting selenium and sleep-promoting tryptophan. Phew! What a delicious mouthful!

The Early Bird Gets the Burn

If you want to burn fat like there's no tomorrow, then wake up and smell your running shoes! Studies show that exercising first thing in the morning before eating for a mere 20 minutes is more effective in melting fat than a full hour of aerobic exercise performed later in the day after you've eaten. Why? Well, when you first wake up, your blood sugar and carbohydrate reserves are at their lowest levels. So, if you exercise before eating, you force your body to look elsewhere for fuel. That "elsewhere" is stored fat! Exercising in the morning kick-starts your metabolism when it's naturally the slowest, igniting a fat-burning fire that'll blaze all day long. Important: For maximum fat burning and to give your muscles the proper fuel, follow your workout with a high-quality breakfast that includes some protein or a whey protein shake, NOT a carbohydrate- or sugar-loaded breakfast like cereal or a bagel.

Mixed Up Meatballs

Appetizer-size turkey meatballs with cranberry-orange barbecue sauce

Some are sweet, some are sour. But personal differences aside, they do make an unforgettable pair. Delicious!

Meatballs

1½ lbs	(680 g) ground turkey or chicken
½ cup	dry unseasoned bread crumbs
⅓ cup	finely minced or grated onions
¼ cup	minced fresh parsley
1	egg
½ tsp	each garlic powder and dried marjoram
¼ tsp	each salt and freshly ground black pepper

Sauce

1 can	(19 oz/540 mL) jellied cranberry sauce
¼ cup	hickory or chipotle barbecue sauce (smoky)
2 tbsp	freshly squeezed lemon juice
1 tsp	reduced-sodium soy sauce
1 tsp	grated orange zest

MAKES 45 MEATBALLS

PER MEATBALL
44 calories, 1 g total fat (0.3 g saturated fat),
3 g protein, 6 g carbohydrate, 0.3 g fiber,
17 mg cholesterol, 64 mg sodium

- In a large bowl, mix together ground turkey, bread crumbs, onions, parsley, egg, garlic powder, marjoram, salt and pepper (using your hands works best). Form mixture into bite-sized meatballs, about 1 to 1½ inches in diameter. You should end up with about 45 meatballs.

- Place meatballs on a baking sheet that has been lightly coated with cooking spray. Bake at 400°F for 12 to 15 minutes or until cooked through. Stir meatballs once, halfway through cooking time, to brown sides. Remove from oven and transfer to a large pot.

- In a small pot, combine cranberry sauce, barbecue sauce, lemon juice, soy sauce and orange zest. Cook over medium heat until cranberry sauce is melted and mixture is bubbly, about 5 minutes. Pour sauce over meatballs and stir gently until all meatballs are coated with sauce. Cover and simmer over low heat for 5 minutes, stirring occasionally. Serve hot.

Let's Talk Turkey!

When you quit an unhealthy, addictive behavior abruptly—like smoking, drinking or watching reality TV—it's said that you quit "cold turkey." That expression actually originates from the goose bumps and chalky complexion that accompany withdrawal from narcotics like heroin. When an addict stops using drugs, blood is directed toward the internal organs and away from the skin, which then resembles that of a plucked, cold turkey. How fowl!

Dieting: the penalty for exceeding the feed limit :)

COME ON, GET APPY!

Strip T's

Sesame-and-coconut-crusted turkey strips with pineapple-plum sauce

If you add these crispy, baked turkey strips to your cooking repertoire, you'll take it off—you'll take it all off! Your extra weight, that is. That's because we've stripped away most of the fat—and we're not teasing, either.

MAKES 6 SERVINGS
ABOUT 3 STRIPS
PER SERVING

PER SERVING (STRIPS ONLY)
234 calories,
6.8 g total fat (3.3 g saturated fat),
29 g protein, 13 g carbohydrate,
1.5 g fiber, 106 mg cholesterol,
392 mg sodium

SAUCE (PER 2 TBSP)
55 calories,
0.2 g fat (0 g saturated fat),
0 g protein, 13 g carbohydrate,
0.2 g fiber, 0 mg cholesterol,
113 mg sodium

Marinade

1	egg
¼ cup	hoisin sauce
1 tsp	sesame oil
1½ lbs (680 g)	boneless skinless turkey breast, cut into strips (about 1 x 4 inches)

Coating

⅔ cup	sweetened shredded coconut
2 tbsp	sesame seeds
½ cup	dry unseasoned bread crumbs
¼ tsp	each salt, garlic powder and onion powder
⅛ tsp	cayenne pepper

Sauce

½ cup	plum sauce
⅓ cup	unsweetened frozen pineapple juice concentrate, thawed
1½ tsp	each yellow mustard and cornstarch

- In a large bowl, whisk together egg, hoisin sauce and sesame oil. Add turkey strips and (using your hands) toss to coat with marinade. Cover and refrigerate for 30 minutes (or longer if possible).

- Meanwhile, place coconut and sesame seeds in a small dry skillet over medium heat. Cook until golden brown, stirring frequently. Be careful not to burn them! Transfer toasted coconut and sesame seeds to a small pie plate or shallow dish and let cool. Add bread crumbs, salt, garlic powder, onion powder and cayenne pepper. Mix well and set aside.

- Prepare sauce by combining all sauce ingredients in a small pot. Cook over medium heat until sauce is bubbly and has thickened. Keep warm.

- Preheat oven to 450°F. Working one piece at a time, shake excess marinade from turkey strips and roll in crumb mixture. Make sure strips are well coated with crumbs. Place on a cookie sheet that has been sprayed with cooking spray. Repeat with remaining strips and coconut mixture. Spray tops of strips with a light coating of cooking spray. Bake on middle oven rack for 6 minutes. Remove from oven and gently turn pieces over. Spray other side with a light coating of cooking spray. Return to oven and bake about 4 more minutes, until coating is lightly browned and turkey is cooked through.

- Serve strips with warm dipping sauce. Enjoy!

Recipe Tip: You can use boneless, skinless chicken breasts instead of turkey.

Nutrition Nugget

Coconut helps your body burn fat and it's lower in calories than other fats. Plus, it promotes healthy blood-sugar levels and increases satiety, making you feel full longer. That's great news for those with diabetes. No wonder we're loco over coco(nut)!

Bean There, Dunked That

Creamy lemon-dill white bean dip

This simple, creamy dip made of lean, mean beans is sorta like hummus, only better!

1 can	(19 oz/540 mL) no-salt-added white kidney beans (cannellini), drained and rinsed
¼ cup	low-fat Greek yogurt or light (5%) sour cream
2 tbsp	freshly squeezed lemon juice
2 tbsp	tahini (see tip)
2 tsp	minced garlic
1 tsp	liquid honey
1 tsp	olive oil
½ tsp	grated lemon zest
½ tsp	salt
¼ tsp	each ground coriander and freshly ground black pepper
1 tbsp	minced fresh dill (not dried, please!)

MAKES 2 CUPS

PER SERVING (¼ CUP)
98 calories,
2.9 g total fat
(0.3 g saturated fat),
6 g protein,
13 g carbohydrate,
3.5 g fiber,
1 mg cholesterol,
146 mg sodium

- Combine all ingredients except dill in a food processor or blender and process until smooth. Transfer mixture to a bowl and stir in dill. Chill at least 1 hour before serving. Serve with wedges of whole-grain pita bread or sliced cucumber rounds for dunking. Tastes best when eaten within a day or two.

Recipe Tip: Look for tahini in the peanut butter aisle or health food aisle of your grocery store.

You're Darn Tootin'!

When Grandma nagged you to eat your beans, she wasn't just being an old fart. No, she obviously had the inside scoop: Beans are on the Dean's List of superfoods! They're packed with folate, which helps prevent birth defects and cuts your risk of heart disease. Plus, they're also a good source of potassium and magnesium, so they can help stabilize high blood pressure. Some beans, such as black, have levels of disease-fighting antioxidants that are equal to those found in oranges, grapes and cranberries. But it's their mega dose of fiber that gives us real reason to *toot* and holler. The soluble fiber in beans is like an internal Swiffer mop, picking up toxic goop that might otherwise linger in your darkest regions and contribute to cancer, high cholesterol and diabetes. The most exciting news? Beans can be a lethal weight-loss weapon. How's that? Well, beans have both fiber and protein, a dynamic duo that'll keep your blood sugar even Steven, and help you feel full longer, so you're less likely to overeat. Plenty of reasons to jump on the *bean* wagon!

> Exercise is king, nutrition is queen, put them together and you have a kingdom.
>
> *Jack LaLanne*

COME ON, GET APPY!

21

Forever in Blue Cheese

Creamy blue cheese dip for veggies or wings

Yummy talks,
But it don't sing and dance
And it can't walk
As long as I can have some dip
with me
I'd much rather be
Forever in blue cheese…

½ cup	crumbled blue cheese (2 oz/57 g)
⅓ cup	light mayonnaise (not fat-free)
1 tbsp	freshly squeezed lemon juice
1 tsp	granulated sugar
½ tsp	minced garlic
½ tsp	dry mustard
¼ tsp	salt
Dash	freshly ground black pepper

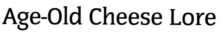

MAKES ABOUT 1 CUP

PER SERVING (2 TBSP)
67 calories,
6 g total fat (2 g saturated fat),
2 g protein, 2 g carbohydrate,
0 g fiber, 13 mg cholesterol,
282 mg sodium

- Combine all ingredients in the bowl of a mini food processor and whirl until almost smooth. The dip shouldn't be perfectly smooth like sour cream; it should have some texture, but no big lumps. You can mash the blue cheese and mix the dip by hand, but it won't be as smooth. Cover and refrigerate until ready to serve. Keeps in the fridge for about 2 days.

Age-Old Cheese Lore

Legend has it that cheese was accidentally discovered by a travelling Arab merchant named Kanana. When he started on a long trip across the Sahara, Kanana put his supply of milk in a pouch made of a sheep's stomach, and slung it over his camel. Apparently, there were still traces of the digestive enzyme, rennet, in the stomach lining. The rennet, heated by the sun and stirred by the camel's trot, caused the curds in the milk to separate from the whey. When he sat down to eat his lunch, Kanana discovered his gouda fortune!

Getting Waisted

If you want to win the No-Belly prize, better banish the bottle. Many people have been fooled into thinking that drinking low-carb beers will help them get six-pack abs. Unfortunately, it's not just the empty-calorie wallop from beer that makes your *Buttwider*, it's the alcohol itself. When you drink, your body's driven to use the calories from alcohol as fuel first, leaving fat as the second choice. Researchers have found that a mere three ounces of alcohol reduced the body's ability to burn fat by one-third! You booze, you don't lose! Even if you're chugging a low-carb beer or using a sugar-free mix with your hard liquor, the alcohol in those drinks still raises blood sugar, which stimulates insulin (the powerful fat-storage hormone), spurring our appetites and compelling us to order a large plate of wings to go with our *Labutt*. Drinking beer and liquor also tends to raise levels of cortisol, a nasty, muscle-eating stress hormone that steers fat toward the waistline, hence the dreaded beer-belly syndrome. Finally, alcohol bogs down your liver, and one of the liver's roles in the body involves fat metabolism. So drinking makes your liverwurst and your beer belly even worster!

On a diet?
Go to the paint store.
You can get
thinner there :)

Lord of the Wings

Boneless, skinless chicken "wings" in a gooey, yummy sauce

They're the wings that everyone's Tolkien about! They sure are hobbit-forming. No bones about it!

12	large boneless skinless chicken thighs (about 2½ lbs/1.1 kg)
⅓ cup	your favorite barbecue sauce
2 tbsp	reduced-sodium soy sauce
2 tbsp	Dijon mustard
2 tbsp	liquid honey (see tip)
2 tbsp	freshly squeezed lemon or lime juice
2 tsp	minced garlic
1 tsp	chili powder
4 to 5	dashes hot pepper sauce (optional)
1 tsp	cornstarch

Recipe Tip: If you're using a barbecue sauce that already has honey in it or a sauce that's quite sweet, you may want to reduce the honey in this recipe from 2 tbsp to 1 tbsp.

MAKES 24 "WINGS"

PER SERVING
(1 WING WITH 1 TSP SAUCE)
56 calories,
1.7 g total fat
(0.4 g saturated fat),
8 g protein,
2 g carbohydrate,
0.1 g fiber,
31 mg cholesterol,
114 mg sodium

(Note: If you skip the extra dipping sauce, the carb count is reduced to about 1.3 g and the sodium drops to about 75 mg.)

- Preheat oven to 400°F. Spray a 9 x 13-inch baking pan with cooking spray and set aside.

- Trim any visible fat from chicken thighs. Cut each thigh in half and place cut pieces in a single layer in prepared baking pan. Fold or roll them up a bit so they resemble the shape of a chicken wing. They should just fit in pan (3 rows of 8 "wings").

- Whisk together barbecue sauce, soy sauce, mustard, honey, lemon juice, garlic, chili powder and hot pepper sauce (if using) in a small bowl. Spoon sauce evenly over chicken pieces.

- Bake, uncovered, for 35 to 40 minutes, until chicken is cooked through and sauce is bubbly. Arrange chicken on a serving platter and keep warm. Pour sauce from pan into a small pot. Combine cornstarch with 2 tsp water and mix until smooth. Stir cornstarch mixture into sauce. Bring to a boil and whisk constantly until mixture has thickened (it won't take long). Serve "wings" with extra sauce for dipping.

Trivial Tidbit

Seems like getting married is *knot* tied to keeping slim. In a 10-year study, men who married gained about 11 pounds. Those who stayed single during the same period gained just 5 pounds. Wedded bliss hit women's waistlines even harder: The single women in the study gained about 6 pounds, while those who married gained a whopping 14. Holy *Fat*rimony!

Tartlett O'Hara

Warm mini crab and cheese tarts

These scrumptious tartlets will play a starring role on your appetizer table. So tasty, they'll be Gone with the Wind!

These will Rhett your appetite.

1 tsp   butter
1 cup   finely chopped mushrooms
⅓ cup   minced shallots or onions
1 tsp   minced garlic
1 can   (4 oz/113 g) lump crabmeat, drained
½ cup   packed shredded light old (sharp)
           cheddar cheese (2 oz/57 g)
¼ cup   freshly grated Parmesan cheese
3 tbsp   light cream cheese
1 tbsp   freshly squeezed lemon juice
1 tbsp   minced fresh parsley
1 tsp   Dijon mustard
¼ tsp   each salt and freshly ground black pepper
1 can   (8 oz/235 g) Pillsbury Crescent rolls

- Preheat oven to 375°F. Spray two 12-cup mini muffin pans with cooking spray and set aside.

- To make filling, heat butter in a small, non-stick skillet over medium heat. Add mushrooms, shallots and garlic. Cook and stir until vegetables are tender, about 4 minutes. Remove from heat and let cool slightly. When cooled, combine mushroom mixture with remaining ingredients, except crescent rolls, in a medium bowl. Mix well.

- Unwrap crescent rolls and lay entire rectangular "sheet" on a lightly floured surface to prevent sticking. Do not separate dough at perforations. Instead, pinch together perforations with your fingers.

- Using a very sharp knife, cut the rectangle into 24 perfect squares by first cutting the dough into 6 equal, short strips, then into 4 equal, long strips. Place dough squares into mini muffin cups. The 4 points of each square will be sticking up—perfect! Fill each cup with crab mixture. Bake for 12 to 14 minutes, until dough is puffed up and golden around the edges. Let tarts cool for a few minutes before serving. They're hot!

MAKES 24 TARTS

PER TART
54 calories, 2.8 g total fat (1.2 g saturated fat),
3 g protein, 4 g carbohydrate, 0.2 g fiber,
10 mg cholesterol, 159 mg sodium

Pretty in Pink

Did you know that baby flamingos are actually born white? They only turn pink once they eat food that's loaded with astaxanthin, a super-powerful carotenoid (antioxidant) found in marine microalgae. Researchers are going gaga over astaxanthin because its list of potential health benefits blows all other antioxidants out of the water. As for its ability as a scavenger of free radicals, this potent compound is 65 times more powerful than vitamin C, 54 times stronger than beta-carotene and 14 times more potent than vitamin E! Can you say "youth serum"? No more wrinkles! Bye-bye brown spots! Hello glowing skin! Bring on the algae! Or wild salmon. Lucky for us, astaxanthin is also responsible for the natural *pink*mentation of wild salmon, so eating this fish means we'll reap the potent disease-fighting and anti-aging benefits of this wonder nutrient. (Farmed salmon uses synthetic astaxanthin as a coloring agent and it's not considered to be healthy.) Supplementing with this miracle carotenoid makes sense, since you'd have to eat a whole lotta salmon to reel in the major health benefits. Look for astaxanthin at well-stocked health food stores and sea for yourself!

I used to have an hourglass figure—then the sands of time shifted :)

Sizzlin' Salsa

Fresh-tasting, flavor-packed, chunky tomato salsa

This salsa really sizzles! Mexican-food fanatics know that homemade salsa beats the store-bought variety any day. It's so good you can eat it with a spoon. (And we have!)

2 tbsp   olive oil
2 cups   diced onions
2 tbsp   minced garlic
5   jalapeño peppers, seeded and finely minced
6 cups   seeded and diced plum tomatoes (fresh, not canned)
1 cup   no-salt-added tomato sauce
2 tbsp   tomato paste
2 tbsp   red wine vinegar
1 tbsp   ground cumin
1 tsp   sea salt
½ tsp   paprika
¼ tsp   cayenne pepper (or to taste)
½ cup   chopped fresh cilantro (important!)
Juice of 1 juicy lime

- Heat olive oil in a large pot over medium heat. Add onions, garlic and jalapeños. Cook and stir until onions begin to soften, about 5 minutes.

- Add tomatoes, tomato sauce, tomato paste, vinegar, cumin, salt, paprika and cayenne pepper. Mix well. Cook, uncovered, for 10 minutes, stirring occasionally.

- Remove pot from heat. Stir in cilantro and lime juice. Serve when cool.

MAKES ABOUT 6 CUPS

PER SERVING (¼ CUP)
31 calories, 1.4 g total fat (0.2 g saturated fat),
1 g protein, 4 g carbohydrate, 1.1 g fiber,
0 mg cholesterol, 98 mg sodium

Recipe Tips Buy the freshest plum tomatoes you can find for this recipe. Cut the plum tomatoes in half and squeeze out (and discard) the seeds before dicing them. Dice the onions and tomatoes into small pieces or the salsa will be too chunky. Store salsa in the fridge in a sealed jar or glass storage container. It will keep for about 1 week (but it will never last that long!). The fresh cilantro is what makes this salsa taste like the kind at Tex-Mex restaurants—don't leave it out.

A Bitter Pill to Swallow

We love finding a good sale, but when it comes to multivitamins and supplements, bargain-basement discount shopping just doesn't make *cents*. Often, the cheaper the price tag, the higher the price your body pays. Inexpensive, poor-quality pills and tablets contain binders, fillers, coatings and other synthetic ingredients that many people can't break down and actually do more harm than good in the body. In particular, older folks, who often lack stomach acid, or those with digestive problems might as well just flush their money down the toilet. In fact, there have been experiments conducted in retirement residences where people were given popular, inexpensive vitamins typically sold at pharmacies. A day or so later, huge, bright-orange pills—whole and intact—were found in bed pans! Talk about a *waste* of money! So, how can you test the digestibility of your multivitamin? Try this simple experiment: Pop your pill into a glass with a half cup of vinegar. A vitamin tablet should dissolve in vinegar within an hour. If it doesn't, your body can't absorb or assimilate it. Remember, health-governing agencies like Health Canada and the FDA certify the *contents* of a supplement, but they don't guarantee that your body can *use* it.

Macho Nacho Dip

Colossal, multilayered Tex-Mex nacho dip, perfect for casual parties

This mucho grande dip is delish!

First Layer (Bottom): Full o' Beans

1 can	(19 oz/540 mL) no-salt-added white kidney beans, drained and rinsed
1 cup	light (5%) sour cream
2 tbsp	reduced-sodium taco seasoning (see tip, p. 234)

- Place beans, sour cream and taco seasoning in the bowl of a mini food processor and purée until smooth. Spread evenly over bottom of 8 x 11 x 2-inch glass baking dish. Cover and refrigerate with plastic wrap while you make second layer.

Second Layer: Easy Peasy Guacamole

1 cup	frozen sweet green peas, thawed
1 can	(4.5 oz/128 mL) diced green chilies
3	large avocados
1½ tbsp	freshly squeezed lime juice
1 tsp	minced garlic
⅓ cup	minced red onions
1 tbsp	minced fresh cilantro
1½ tsp	reduced-sodium taco seasoning
¼ tsp	salt
⅛ tsp	freshly ground black pepper

- Place peas and green chilies (with their liquid) in the bowl of a mini food processor and purée until completely smooth. Set aside.
- Peel and pit avocados and place pieces in a large bowl. Toss with lime juice and garlic. Mash well using a potato masher. Add puréed peas and all remaining guacamole ingredients and mix well. Spread evenly over bean layer. Cover and refrigerate while you make third layer.

Third Layer: Dreamy and Creamy

1 cup	light (5%) sour cream
1 tub	(8 oz/250 g) light garden vegetable cream cheese (such as Philadelphia brand)

- In a medium bowl, stir together sour cream and cream cheese until well blended. Spread cream-cheese mixture evenly over guacamole.

Fourth Layer: Everybody Salsa!

2 cups	medium salsa
2 tsp	minced fresh cilantro

- Mix salsa and cilantro in a small bowl. Spread salsa over cream-cheese layer.

Fifth Layer: Cheesy Decorations

1 cup	packed shredded light old (sharp) cheddar cheese (4 oz/113 g)
1½ cups	chopped iceberg lettuce
⅓ cup	minced red bell pepper
¼ cup	chopped green onions
2 tbsp	minced black olives (optional)

- Sprinkle shredded cheddar evenly over salsa. Top with chopped lettuce, followed by red pepper, green onions and black olives (if using). Cover with plastic wrap and refrigerate for 2 hours before serving. Serve with whole-grain nacho chips.

MAKES ABOUT 15 SERVINGS

PER SERVING (⅔ CUP)
194 calories,
10 g total fat (3.7 g saturated fat),
8 g protein, 19 g carbohydrate,
5.3 g fiber, 23 mg cholesterol,
514 mg sodium

I dropped a tub of margarine in the kitchen and ended up with Parkay floors :)

Deviled in Disguise

Not-so-traditional deviled eggs, flavored with smoked salmon and dill

We took plain ol' deviled eggs and transformed them into a heavenly, sinsational treat. They're a helluva lot better than the boring deviled eggs of the past. Really eggceptional!

8	eggs, hard-boiled and peeled (see tip)
¼ cup	minced smoked salmon (about 1 oz/28 g)
2 tbsp	light mayonnaise
1 tbsp	freshly squeezed lemon juice
1 tbsp	honey mustard
1 tbsp	minced fresh dill, or ½ tsp dried (fresh is best!)
¼ tsp	each salt, freshly ground black pepper and hot pepper sauce
Pinch	paprika for garnish (optional)

- Carefully slice cooked eggs in half lengthwise and remove yolks. Place yolks in a medium bowl and mash well using a fork. Add remaining ingredients and mix well.

- Using a small spoon, fill centers of eggs with egg mixture, mounding slightly. (Note: If you have a pastry bag with a large tip, you can use it to pipe the filling back into the centers of the eggs. The smoked salmon will clog a small tip, so make sure you use a large one.)

- Sprinkle filling with paprika, if desired. Cover loosely with plastic wrap and refrigerate for at least 1 hour before serving.

MAKES 16 DEVILED EGGS

PER SERVING (1 EGG)
46 calories,
3 g total fat
(0.9 g saturated fat),
4 g protein,
1 g carbohydrate,
0 g fiber,
107 mg cholesterol,
103 mg sodium

Recipe Tip

Deviled eggs aren't exactly the fanciest hors d'oeuvres going, but they're always gobbled up before the ritzy appetizers at family gatherings. Because of their added health properties, try using omega-3 eggs when you make this recipe. For perfectly hard-boiled eggs, place the eggs in a single layer in a large saucepan, then add cold water to cover eggs by 1 inch. Bring to a boil over high heat. Remove the saucepan immediately from the heat, cover and let eggs stand for 15 minutes. Using a slotted spoon, transfer eggs to a "bath" of ice cold water. Let them sit in cold water for 5 minutes before peeling.

Nutrition Nugget

Thou shell eat eggs! Your body can effectively use 94 percent of the protein in a whole egg—perfect muscle-building, fat-burning fuel.

Fairest Wheels

Tortilla pinwheels with chicken, cream cheese and hot red pepper jelly

This appetizing chicken pinwheel recipe won first prize in the State Fair's "Fairest of the Fare" recipe contest. And you can say "farewell" when you serve them to your friends!

MAKES 24 PINWHEELS

PER PINWHEEL
44 calories,
1.6 g total fat
(0.9 g saturated fat),
3 g protein,
6 g carbohydrate,
1.1 fiber,
6 mg cholesterol,
120 mg sodium

1 cup	finely chopped cooked chicken breast
½ cup	finely chopped lettuce
½ cup	packed shredded light old (sharp) cheddar cheese (2 oz/57 g)
⅓ cup	chopped green onions
⅓ cup	minced red bell pepper
½ cup	light spreadable cream cheese
2 tbsp	light (5%) sour cream or Greek yogurt
1 tbsp	hot red pepper jelly (see tip)
3	large 10-inch whole-grain flour tortillas (soft and fresh)

- In a medium bowl, combine chicken, lettuce, cheese, onions and red pepper. Set aside.

- In a small bowl, beat together cream cheese, sour cream and red pepper jelly on low speed of electric mixer. Working one at a time, spread ⅓ cream-cheese mixture over one side of tortilla. Sprinkle with ⅓ chicken mixture, leaving a half-inch border at the top just covered with cream-cheese mixture (so you can seal it closed). Roll up tightly, jelly-roll style. Wrap tortilla roll in plastic wrap. Repeat process with remaining tortillas and filling.

- Refrigerate rolls for 2 hours. Trim off ends and cut each roll into 8 equal pinwheels. Serve cold.

Recipe Tip

Hot red pepper jelly is a condiment made from red chili peppers, sugar, vinegar and spices. Look for it in a jar near the ketchup at your grocery store.

Havin' a Ball!

Creamy salmon ball rolled in chopped nuts and parsley

Gillfriends coming over for dinner? Our easy salmon appetizer is always an o-mega hit!

2 cans   (6 oz/170 g each) wild salmon, drained and flaked
1 pkg   (8 oz/250 g) light cream cheese (see tip)
2 tbsp   finely minced onions or shallots
1 tbsp   freshly squeezed lemon juice
1 tsp   prepared horseradish or cocktail sauce
¼ tsp   each salt and freshly ground black pepper
¼ cup   finely chopped walnuts or pecans
¼ cup   finely minced fresh parsley

- Mix together salmon, cream cheese, onions, lemon juice, horseradish, salt and pepper in a medium bowl. You can use an electric mixer if it's easier. Cover salmon mixture and refrigerate for 1 hour so it firms up a little bit.
- Meanwhile, mix together nuts and parsley in a shallow bowl or pie plate. Remove salmon from fridge and form it into a ball (using your hands works best, even though it's a little messy). Roll in nut-parsley mixture so outside of ball is completely coated. Cover with plastic wrap and refrigerate for at least 4 hours before serving.
- To serve, place ball on a small platter and surround with whole-grain crackers or melba rounds, thick red bell pepper strips and thick cucumber slices.

> *Recipe Tip* For this recipe, don't buy spreadable cream cheese (tub) since it's too soft to hold its shape when you roll the mixture into a ball. But, if you want to make a salmon spread instead of a ball, then soft cream cheese is perfect!

MAKES ONE 2-CUP BALL

PER SERVING (2 TBSP)
74 calories, 5 g total fat
(2.3 g saturated fat), 6 g protein,
1 g carbohydrate, 0.2 g fiber,
22 mg cholesterol, 195 mg sodium

I was going to marry a gardener, but he was too rough around the hedges :)

Are You a Craving Lunatic?

If constant cravings for sugary treats are driving you wild, you (and your hips!) will appreciate these tips to help curb the urge to splurge: (1) Most cravings last only about 10 minutes and then subside. Cravings are often your body's cries for water and oxygen, so wait 10 minutes, drink a glass of water with lemon (for an energy boost) and take a few deep breaths. You might try changing activities to clear your mind, too. Go for a walk, take a hot bath or phone a friend. A change of scenery usually works: Researchers in Australia found that visual distractions can help curb cravings. (2) Rate your hunger on a scale of 1 to 10. Unless you're a 9 or 10, fight the urge. Still famished? Give in to your craving, but don't go nuts. Ideally, your "craving cure" should set you back no more than 150 calories. (3) Eat foods containing tryptophan. Say what? Tryptophan is an amino acid that your body uses to make the feel-good brain chemical, serotonin. When serotonin levels are down, we feel down, and the body's way of lifting serotonin, and our spirits, is to load up on sugary or starchy foods. But if you eat foods high in tryptophan (turkey, bananas, pineapple, chicken, whey protein or yogurt), your body can replenish serotonin, preventing you from going on a hip-wrecking carb binge. (4) Brush your teeth! Sometimes the flavor of toothpaste (especially peppermint) can take the edge off a sugar craving. After all, Colgate and Coffee Crisp aren't exactly complementary flavors and, in general, food is less tempting when your mouth feels clean. You'll wonder where the cravings went when you brush your teeth with Pepsodent!

In this chapter...

Easy Peasy Orzo Salad,
p. 52

Become a Beleafer

Lettuce rejoice! These miraculous salads
are the answer to your taste buds' prayers!

Where's Waldorf?

Apples, celery and toasted walnuts tossed with rotini pasta in a light, creamy dressing

If you've been searching high and low for a Waldorf salad that isn't packed with fat and calories, our slimmed-down version is what you're after.

Dressing

¾ cup	vanilla-flavored yogurt
2 tsp	honey mustard
1 tsp	grated lemon zest
½ tsp	salt
⅛ tsp	freshly ground black pepper

Salad

4 cups	cooked rotini pasta (about 2 cups dry)
3 cups	chopped unpeeled Red Delicious apples
1 cup	diced celery
⅓ cup	toasted chopped walnuts (see tip)
¼ cup	minced red onions
2 tbsp	minced fresh parsley

- Combine yogurt, honey mustard, lemon zest, salt and black pepper in a small bowl. Refrigerate until ready to use.

- Toss remaining ingredients in a large bowl. Add dressing and mix well. Chill for 1 hour before serving.

MAKES 4 TO 6 SERVINGS

PER SERVING (BASED ON 6 SERVINGS)
174 calories, 4.5 g total fat (0.3 g saturated fat), 6 g protein, 29 g carbohydrate, 2.3 g fiber, 0.6 mg cholesterol, 254 mg sodium

Recipe Tip Toasting nuts before using them in recipes intensifies their flavor. To toast nuts, place them in a dry skillet over medium heat. Shake the pan often and toast nuts for 4 to 5 minutes, until fragrant. Cool before using. Because nuts have a high fat content, they go rancid quickly. The best way to store shelled nuts is in an airtight container in the refrigerator or freezer.

FOOD BITE

Waldorf salad, originally a mixture of apples, celery and mayonnaise, was invented in 1893 by Oscar Tschirky, a maître d' at the Waldorf Astoria Hotel in New York City.

Good to the Core

You know what they say, "Two apples a day gets the doctor's OK!" Well, that's not exactly what they say, but eating two apples every day is probably a smart idea. Apples are chock-full of nutritional goodies, from pectin, a soluble fiber that helps lower cholesterol, to quercetin, a natural chemical that appears to reduce the risk of heart disease, Alzheimer's, Parkinson's and prostate and lung cancers. And every time you crunch an apple, you may be doing your eyes a favor, too. One of the flavonoids in apples actually protects against cataracts. So what "they're" really saying is that regular daily consumption of apples keeps the cardiologist, the oncologist and the ophthalmologist at bay!

We're Talkin' Small Potatoes

Warm mini-potato salad with bacon and dill

It may be small potatoes we're cookin' for this zesty, filling salad, but we don't want you to think that this is just another mash in the pan. This spud's for you!

Salad

3 lbs	(1.4 kg) mini thin-skinned red or white potatoes
4	slices reduced-sodium bacon, diced
1 cup	diced onions
1 tsp	minced garlic
⅔ cup	finely diced carrots
⅔ cup	finely diced celery
1 tbsp	minced fresh dill
2	green onions, finely chopped (with white parts)
¼ tsp	freshly ground black pepper

Dressing

½ cup	reduced-sodium chicken or vegetable broth
3 tbsp	grainy Dijon mustard
2 tbsp	white balsamic vinegar
1 tbsp	freshly squeezed lemon juice
1 tbsp	granulated sugar
1 tbsp	olive oil
½ tsp	celery seed
½ tsp	salt

Recipe Tip: If you're not a fan of dill, you can substitute minced fresh parsley.

MAKES ABOUT 10 CUPS

PER SERVING (1 CUP)
226 calories, 5 g total fat (1.6 g saturated fat), 6 g protein, 41 g carbohydrate, 3.5 g fiber, 5 mg cholesterol, 414 mg sodium

- Wash potatoes (don't peel) and slice into ¼-inch-thick slices. Arrange in a steamer basket and steam for about 15 minutes or until tender. Let cool to room temperature.

- While potatoes are steaming, whisk together dressing ingredients and set aside until ready to use.

- Cook chopped bacon slowly in a non-stick skillet over medium-high heat until it just begins to crisp. Add onions and garlic and cook until onions are tender. Add carrots and celery. Cook until vegetables are tender, about 3 more minutes. Pour warm bacon and vegetable mixture over cooled potatoes in a large bowl. Pour dressing over potatoes and toss gently to coat. Add dill, green onions and black pepper and mix again. Be careful not to smash the potatoes.

- May be served immediately but tastes best when left to stand for an hour or two for potatoes to absorb dressing.

Trivial Tidbit

It's easy to fall into the habit of matching your dining companion bite for bite, but if your companion is a male and you're a female, it's a sure route to Adipose Alley. The average North American woman needs about one-third fewer calories than her male counterpart. So if you're dining with your beau, aim to eat about two-thirds as much as he does, otherwise, as the country song (kinda) says, you'll "*expand by your man.*"

Nutrition Nugget

According to German researchers, if you drink 16 ounces of cold water first thing in the morning, you'll boost your metabolism by 24 percent for a full 90 minutes! *Water* you waiting for?

Herb gardeners who work on weekends get thyme-and-a-half :)

Thrill of the Grill

Warm grilled vegetable pasta salad with basil and feta

For the grill-seeker in you, here's a flavor-packed, summertime recipe to get fired up about! Our tantalizing blend of colorful grilled veggies, whole wheat pasta, fresh basil, feta cheese and light balsamic vinaigrette will take your breath away!

Salad

1	medium red bell pepper
1	medium orange bell pepper
1	medium yellow zucchini
1	medium green zucchini
1	medium red onion
2	large portobello mushrooms, stems removed
3 cups	uncooked whole wheat rotini pasta

Dressing

2 tbsp	olive oil
2 tbsp	balsamic vinegar
1 tbsp	freshly squeezed lemon juice
1 tsp	Dijon mustard
1 tsp	minced garlic
⅓ cup	chopped fresh basil leaves
Pinch	freshly ground black pepper
½ cup	crumbled light feta cheese (2 oz/57 g)

- Preheat grill to high setting. Remove seeds and stems from bell peppers and chop into 1-inch chunks. Cut zucchini into ½-inch rounds and chop onion and mushrooms into 1-inch chunks. Spray a grill basket with cooking spray or lightly brush with olive oil. Add vegetables and mix well. Place grill basket over hot coals and close lid. Grill vegetables for about 20 minutes, stirring occasionally, until tender with nice grill marks.

- Meanwhile, cook pasta according to package directions. Drain and keep warm.

- In a large serving bowl, whisk together dressing ingredients. Add grilled vegetables and cooked pasta and mix well. Add basil and black pepper and mix again. Serve salad while still warm and top individual servings with crumbled feta cheese and more black pepper, if desired.

Recipe Tips: As a variation, add 1-inch pieces of fresh asparagus to the vegetable mix and substitute small, whole button mushrooms for the portobellos. Add 1 tbsp basil pesto to the dressing in place of the fresh basil leaves. For a more substantial meal, grill chicken breasts, salmon fillets or shrimp skewers alongside the vegetables. Chop the chicken or salmon into bite-sized pieces and add them to the salad. Finally, a non-stick grill basket is a handy, inexpensive piece of cookware that you'll use again and again. Look for grill baskets wherever barbecues and grilling tools are sold.

MAKES 4 SERVINGS

PER SERVING
319 calories, 11 g fat (3.1 g saturated fat),
11 g protein, 46 g carbohydrate,
6.6 g fiber, 13 mg cholesterol,
175 mg sodium

Farewell to Jell-O Arms

Afraid of becoming a hulky, bulky she-man if you start lifting weights? Relax, gals! First of all, if you're over 35, you've been losing muscle for years now, so in most cases, you're just replacing what was there in your younger, slimmer days. Secondly, your hormones won't allow you to become the Incredible Hulk. Women don't produce as much of the growth-enhancing hormone testosterone as men do—some men produce up to 30 times more. Female bodybuilders get their muscle-magazine look only with Olympian-like training programs and possibly performance-enhancing drugs. Mere mortal women who lift weights will lose fat, tone their muscles and still look feminine in a dress! Remember, muscle is more compact than fat, so even if the scale registers weight gain, those extra pounds will appear smaller, shapelier and sexier—not bulkier. You'll look great in your clothes and might even need to shop for new ones. Yee-ha! A reason to shop! (Not that we need one.) Sleek, compact muscle will act like a girdle to shrink and define your waist, thighs, arms and butt. Imagine! No more saddlebags! No more love handles! Goodbye jiggly thighs! Adios adipose!

The Dressing Room

It's time to change the way you dress—your salads, that is!

Maple-Balsamic Vinaigrette

⅓ cup   balsamic vinegar
¼ cup   olive oil
¼ cup   apple juice
3 tbsp   pure maple syrup
2 tbsp   minced shallots
2 tbsp   freshly squeezed lemon juice
1 tbsp   Dijon mustard
1 tbsp   minced fresh dill
1 tsp   minced garlic
¼ tsp   each salt and freshly ground
         black pepper

MAKES ABOUT 1 CUP

PER SERVING (2 TBSP)
95 calories,
6.9 g total fat
(0.9 g saturated fat),
0 g protein,
8 g carbohydrate,
0 g fiber,
0 mg cholesterol,
85 mg sodium

Cheater's Creamy Parmesan Italian

1 cup   bottled fat-free
         Italian dressing
2 tbsp   light mayonnaise
2 tbsp   freshly grated Parmesan cheese
1 tbsp   balsamic vinegar
1 tbsp   liquid honey
¼ tsp   each dried oregano and
         freshly ground black pepper

MAKES ABOUT 1⅓ CUPS

PER SERVING (2 TBSP)
30 calories,
1 g total fat
(0.3 g saturated fat),
1 g protein,
4 g carbohydrate,
0 g fiber,
2 mg cholesterol,
274 mg sodium

Asian Sesame

¾ cup   hoisin sauce
¼ cup   olive oil
3 tbsp   red wine vinegar
2 tbsp   seasoned rice vinegar
1 tbsp   Dijon mustard
1 tbsp   freshly squeezed lime juice
1 tbsp   sesame oil
1 tbsp   grated gingerroot
⅛ tsp   freshly ground black pepper

MAKES ABOUT 1½ CUPS

PER SERVING (2 TBSP)
90 calories,
6.3 g total fat
(0.9 g saturated fat),
1 g protein,
8 g carbohydrate,
0.5 g fiber,
1 mg cholesterol,
266 mg sodium

Directions for all dressings:
Whisk together all ingredients and store in an air-tight container in the refrigerator for up to 1 week. Mix well before using.

Nutrition Nugget

Be the best dressed! Store-bought fat-free or low-fat dressings are often high in sugar. And we know that sugar is stored by the body as fat more readily than...well...fat! So, look for brands with the least amount of sugar or, better yet, make your own dressing.

The Chicken Coup

Chicken salad with pecans and cranberries in a creamy orange dressing

It's the best plan we've ever hatched: Design a chicken salad so extraordinary, it'll cause a revolution! Strategically replace high-fat ingredients with healthier, flavor-packed options in a culinary maneuvre that'll trigger a taste-bud takeover! The plot thickens, and so does our salad dressing! Brilliant!

Dressing

- ¼ cup   light mayonnaise
- ¼ cup   light (5%) sour cream
- 1 tbsp   honey mustard
- 1 tbsp   white vinegar
- 1 tbsp   frozen orange juice concentrate
- ¼ tsp   each salt and freshly ground black pepper

Salad

- 4 cups   chopped cooked chicken (or turkey) breast
- 1 cup   diced celery
- 1   large apple (your favorite kind), unpeeled, cored and chopped
- ⅓ cup   dried cranberries
- ⅓ cup   chopped green onions (with white parts)
- ⅓ cup   chopped pecans
- ¼ cup   chopped fresh parsley

- Combine all dressing ingredients in a small bowl. Cover and refrigerate until ready to use.

- Toss together all salad ingredients in a large bowl. Add dressing and mix well. Cover and refrigerate for 2 hours before serving.

MAKES 6 SERVINGS

PER SERVING
274 calories,
10 g total fat
(1.7 g saturated fat),
28 g protein,
18 g carbohydrate,
2.5 g fiber,
74 mg cholesterol,
284 mg sodium

Not Too Tart, Not Too Sweet

Cranberries, hailed for their antibiotic effect in fighting urinary tract infections, are also a natural probiotic, enhancing good bacteria levels in the gut and even protecting us from foodborne illnesses like E. coli and listeria. And here's some berry good news straight from the science lab: According to the latest studies, it seems that drinking cranberry juice daily can decrease total cholesterol levels and, more importantly, reduce the LDL (lousy) kind. But beware: Cranberries are so tart that most cranberry products, especially juice, are loaded with sugar. And sugar feeds bad bacteria. So that popular brand you've been buying might be a feast for the yeast! Look for concentrated, "100% pure" juices to get the most nutritional bang for your buck. Although more expensive than the sugary variety, you'll dilute an ounce or two with water, so one bottle goes a long way. Some good brands to look for include R.W. Knudson and Lakewood Organics.

Nutrition Nugget

Extend your expiry date! Two ounces of nuts a day can earn you an extra 2.9 years on the planet, according to studies. Buy raw, unsalted nuts for the most health benefits.

Name That Tuna Salad

Tuscan-style tuna and white bean salad

Go ahead. Call our tuna salad whatever you want. Just don't call it bland or boring. Loaded with fiber and easy to make, it's the perfect lunch to take to the office.

Salad

1	large can or two small cans (6 oz/170 g total) solid tuna in olive oil (see tip)
1	can (19 oz/540 mL) no-salt-added white kidney beans (cannellini), drained and rinsed
1½ cups	quartered grape tomatoes
⅔ cup	chopped green onions (with white parts)
¼ cup	coarsely chopped fresh basil leaves

Dressing

2 tbsp	olive oil (from tuna)
2 tbsp	freshly squeezed lemon juice
2 tsp	white wine vinegar
½ tsp	granulated sugar or liquid honey
½ tsp	Dijon mustard
½ tsp	minced garlic
Pinch	salt and freshly ground black pepper

- Drain tuna and reserve olive oil in a small bowl (you should have about 2 tbsp olive oil). Set oil aside.

- In a large bowl, gently toss together drained tuna, beans, tomatoes, onions and basil.

- To make dressing, add lemon juice, vinegar, sugar, mustard and garlic to reserved olive oil. Whisk until ingredients are combined. Pour dressing over bean mixture and stir gently, being careful not to smash the beans. Add salt and pepper to taste and serve immediately or store covered in the refrigerator.

MAKES 4 SERVINGS

PER SERVING

261 calories, 8.3 g total fat (1.2 g saturated fat), 20 g protein, 29 g carbohydrate, 7.6 g fiber, 19 mg cholesterol, 125 mg sodium

Recipe Tip "Borrowing" the olive oil from the tuna to make the dressing means one fewer ingredient and it also adds more flavor to the dressing. Plus, tuna packed in olive oil is moist and not dry like some varieties of water-packed tuna. If you decide to use water-packed tuna, just add 2 tbsp regular olive oil to make the dressing (and don't forget to drain and discard the water from the tuna!).

Heavy Metal Banned

No need to scale back on fish just because you've heard reports that it contains the toxic metal mercury. Just don't swim with the sharks! Fish with higher levels of mercury include shark, swordfish, king mackerel and tilefish. These fish are at the top of the food chain, they're large and live a long time, so they accumulate more mercury. They're the fish that government health regulators suggest limiting to one meal a month for women of childbearing age and young children. The following species are lower in toxic-metal levels, so you can enjoy them more often: sardines, trout, haddock, summer flounder, catfish and wild Pacific salmon. Hooked on tuna sandwiches? The fish used in canned tuna are small, so they don't accumulate as much mercury. But don't overdo it. Once a week is OK. And keep in mind that the fatty acids, vitamin E and selenium contained in fish itself provide protection from mercury. Still smells fishy to you? Then remove the skin and fat, where toxins are likely to lurk, and avoid frying, which can seal in chemical pollutants. Grilling and broiling help drain them away. Another option: Take advantage of fish's health-promoting omega-3 fatty acids with a high-quality fish-oil supplement. They're usually derived from small species like anchovies and sardines and then purified of any pollutants. We'd write more... but we've got bigger fish to fry!

Moroccan and Rollin' Quinoa Salad

Colorful quinoa salad with chickpeas, veggies, lemon and mint

The spices are rockin'...the chickpeas are rollin'...and you'll be droolin'!
(Thanks to Facebook fan Sarah Kisko for contributing this recipe title.)

1 cup	uncooked quinoa (see tip)
2 cups	reduced-sodium vegetable broth
¼ cup	dried currants
1 tsp	curry powder
1 tsp	ground cumin
½ tsp	ground coriander
1 tsp	liquid honey
½ tsp	salt
1 cup	canned no-salt-added chickpeas, drained and rinsed
½ cup	each finely chopped red bell pepper, grated carrots and peeled, diced English cucumber
⅓ cup	chopped green onions
2 tbsp	olive oil
2 tbsp	freshly squeezed lemon juice
2 tbsp	minced fresh mint leaves
¼ tsp	freshly ground black pepper

- Combine quinoa, broth, currants, curry, cumin, coriander, honey and salt in a medium pot. Bring to a boil. Reduce heat to low, cover and simmer for about 20 minutes or until quinoa has absorbed all liquid. Remove from heat. Let stand covered for 10 minutes. Fluff with a fork and leave uncovered to cool completely.

- When quinoa is cool, transfer to large mixing bowl. Stir in all remaining ingredients. Mix well and refrigerate for at least an hour or two before serving. Tastes even better the next day!

Recipe Tip:
Look for quinoa that says "prewashed" or "prerinsed" on the package. Quinoa must be rinsed before using to remove the bitter outer coating. If you buy quinoa that isn't prerinsed, put it in a mesh strainer or sieve and run cold water over it for about 30 seconds.

MAKES 6 SERVINGS
PER SERVING
231 calories, 7.4 g total fat (0.7 g saturated fat), 6 g protein, 36 g carbohydrate, 5.4 g fiber, 0 mg cholesterol, 256 mg sodium

The City of Happiness is found in the State of Mind.

Keen-What?

If we were stranded on a desert island and could choose just one food to live on, it would definitely be quinoa! Pronounced "keen-wah," this recently rediscovered South American ancient grain is truly one of our all-time favorite foods, and we hope it'll soon become one of yours, too. Though commonly referred to as a grain, quinoa is actually a seed of the goosefoot plant, a relative of leafy green vegetables like spinach and Swiss chard. Once considered "the gold of the Incas," Aztec warriors used quinoa to increase their stamina. It's no wonder: quinoa is a nutritional powerhouse! It has twice the protein of brown rice and contains all nine essential amino acids (nutritional building blocks that help form proteins and muscle and other tissue)—rare in the plant kingdom. That's why quinoa is winning the popularity contest among vegetarians and others who don't want to eat meat 'til the cows come home. All that protein plus tons of fiber make it a waist-watcher's dream, a diabetic's dream, a cholesterol-lowering dream and...well...a dream come true for anyone who wants to put the best possible fuel in their body. The tiny seeds can boost energy and also contain lots of magnesium that can help prevent high blood pressure and osteoporosis. As an added bonus, quinoa is gluten-free, ideal for those with Celiac disease or other grain sensitivities. Keen-WOW!

Broccoli Mountain High

Crunchy and creamy broccoli coleslaw with turkey bacon

Shout it from the top: This broccoli coleslaw is full of crunch and full of flavor!
Just be careful not to cause an avalanche. Sure to peak your interest,
it's worth climbing the highest mountain for.

Dressing

½ cup light mayonnaise (not fat-free)
2 tbsp white vinegar
1 tbsp granulated sugar
½ tsp celery seed
¼ tsp each salt and freshly ground black pepper

Salad

1 pkg (12 oz/340 g) broccoli slaw mix (about 5 cups—see tip)
6 slices turkey bacon, cooked and chopped
1 large red apple, unpeeled, cored and diced
½ cup raisins
½ cup packed shredded light old (sharp) cheddar cheese
   (2 oz/57 g)
⅓ cup chopped green onions or minced red onions

MAKES 6 SERVINGS

PER SERVING
196 calories, 9.5 g total fat (2.2 g saturated fat),
7 g protein, 21 g carbohydrate, 2.7 g fiber,
22 mg cholesterol, 406 mg sodium

- In a small bowl, whisk together all dressing ingredients. Refrigerate until ready to use.

- In a large bowl, toss together broccoli slaw mix, bacon, apple, raisins, cheese and onions. Add dressing and mix well. Refrigerate for at least 1 hour before serving.

Recipe Tip: Broccoli slaw mix is made from grated broccoli stems, carrots and red cabbage. Look for it where you find prepackaged salads at the grocery store.

Solid as a Brocc

When it comes to cancer-fighting superfoods, broccoli's definitely at the head of its class. Study after study shows that people who eat their broccoli have fewer cancers of the colon, breast, cervix, lungs, prostate, esophagus, larynx and bladder. Broccoli's power lies in its abundance of powerful disease-fighting compounds called phytochemicals, including beta-carotene, indoles and isothiocyanates. What a crunchy, delicious mouthful! And, if that's not enough, a half cup of cooked broccoli provides more than 100 percent of your daily vitamin C needs, a hefty dose of calcium, plenty of folate to prevent heart disease, more fiber than a slice of whole wheat bread and nearly two-thirds of a banana's potassium—all for just 23 calories! Who needs a multivitamin? Those superpowers seem to run in the family, by the way. All the cruciferous vegetables—cabbage, bok choy, cauliflower, kale, brussels sprouts— are blessed with these impressive cancer-fighting abilities. Eat 'em and watch your health soar to new heights!

FOOD BITE

Mayonnaise originated in the 18th century when a Frenchman, Duc de Richelieu, was taking part in a battle against the British at Mahon, a part of the Mediterranean island of Minorca. It was there that he first tasted the interesting combination of egg yolks, oil and vinegar, so he dubbed it "The Sauce of Mahon." It was later renamed mahonnaise, which means "after the manner of Mahon." Other egg-yolk-based sauces have "aise" endings too, including hollandaise, "after the manner of Holland," and béarnaise, "after the manner of Béarn." As far as fat content goes, these sauces are no yolking matter. Mayo weighs in at close to 100 percent fat! Over *aisey* now!

Corn, Black Bean and Mango Fandango

Colorful corn and black bean salad with mango and avocado

This fresh-tasting, high-fiber salad will make your taste buds dance with joy!

1 can	(19 oz/540 mL) no-salt-added black beans, drained and rinsed
1 can	(14 oz/398 mL) whole-kernel corn, drained
1	large mango, peeled and diced
1 cup	quartered grape tomatoes
1 cup	diced red bell pepper
½ cup	chopped green onions
2 tbsp	minced fresh cilantro
2 tbsp	freshly squeezed lime juice
1 tbsp	olive oil
¼ tsp	each salt and freshly ground black pepper
⅛ tsp	each ground cumin and chili powder (see tip)
1 cup	diced avocado (see tip)

MAKES 4 SERVINGS

PER SERVING
236 calories,
10 g total fat
(1.4 g saturated fat),
7 g protein,
37 g carbohydrate,
10.4 g fiber,
0 mg cholesterol,
385 mg sodium

- Combine all ingredients in a large bowl and mix well. Serve immediately or chill before serving. (We prefer this salad at room temperature.) As with most dishes containing avocado, this dish tastes best when eaten the day it's made.

Recipe Tips: For added kick, try chipotle chili powder—it's sold beside the regular chili powder in the spice aisle. Avocado turns brown quickly, so peel, slice and add it to the salad just before serving.

Nutrition Nugget

You've probably heard that an avocado's monounsaturated fat and 13 grams of fiber help to lower levels of LDL (bad) cholesterol and raise the HDL (good) kind. But, bet you didn't know that avocados also contain boron, a mineral that may help your body absorb calcium. *Bonus!*

Que Se Raw, Se Raw

Let's hear it for the joy of not cooking! Raw! Raw! Raw! Throwing some raw food into your daily menu is crucial to good health. And we're not talking about sushi, egg yolk shakes or steak tartar, either. Raw, uncooked foods like fruits, vegetables, nuts, seeds and sprouts are "live" foods. They're full of living enzymes that act like spark plugs for our cells, providing boundless energy and vitality. In fact, our organs and glands depend on enzymatic activity and can't function properly without it. Problem is, when food is heated above 118°F, enzymes start to break down, just like our bodies would if we had a fever that high. Fortunately, your body can manufacture missing enzymes but, over time, digesting cooked foods overworks the glands, wears out the body and sets the stage for chronic disease. That's why people who live on a diet of cooked protein and starches (the ol' meat and potatoes diet) and very little enzyme-rich fruits and vegetables, are often tired and have little pep in their step. Plus, if we don't get sufficient enzymes, we age faster! That's because our body's own enzyme production slows down as we get older. Now, don't get us wrong—we're not bad-mouthing cooking! How stupid would that be? Why, we'd be out of jobs! Everyone knows that cooking improves the flavor of food, plus it also enhances the digestibility of many foods and, in some cases, makes them safer to eat. But for optimum health and longevity, go ahead and get eatin' alive!

Chop 'Til You Drop

Asian chopped chicken salad with peanut dressing

Attention all choppers! Hack now! Don't delay! Slice and dice your way to an Asian salad masterpiece! Slash the fat! Cut to the chase! Chop to it!

Dressing

⅓ cup	bottled light peanut sauce
¼ cup	hoisin sauce
1 tbsp	red wine vinegar
1 tbsp	sesame oil
1 tsp	grated gingerroot

Salad

3 cups	chopped cooked chicken breast (see tip)
2 cups	packed chopped napa cabbage (see tip)
2 cups	packed chopped romaine hearts
1 cup	grated carrots
1 cup	diced red bell pepper
1 cup	bean sprouts
½ cup	chopped green onions
2 tbsp	minced fresh cilantro
2 tbsp	toasted sesame seeds (optional)

MAKES 6 SERVINGS

PER SERVING

190 calories, 6.2 g total fat (1.2 g saturated fat), 21 g protein, 13 g carbohydrate, 2.4 g fiber, 50 mg cholesterol, 385 mg sodium

- Whisk together all dressing ingredients in a small bowl. Cover and refrigerate until ready to use.

- Toss together all salad ingredients in a large serving bowl. Add half the dressing and toss again. This may be enough dressing for your taste. If not, add more by the tablespoonful until you're happy with the flavor. Serve immediately.

Recipe Tips The ideal chicken for this recipe is grilled teriyaki chicken (see recipe, p. 159), but you can always buy a large rotisserie chicken and use the breast meat to keep things simple. At the grocery store, napa cabbage is often labelled Chinese cabbage.

> If you ignore your health for long enough, it'll go away.

Eat Green Gasoline

Do you treat your car with the utmost care and respect? Tank filled with Ultra-Supreme? Regularly scheduled oil changes? Nothing like a little preventive maintenance to keep ol' Bessie's engine humming, right? But what about your own body's engine? You know, the one that's expected to give you unlimited mileage and last a lifetime? Run it on a steady stream of hamburgers, fries, potato chips and beer, and it's bound to end up in the shop. Many people take their bodies for granted until something goes wrong, and then expect a quick fix, just as they do with their cars. But by the time your doctor tells you there's something seriously wrong "under the hood," it may be too late. Some parts simply can't be replaced. However, with 70 percent of illnesses having a dietary link, preventive maintenance may be as simple as making smarter food choices. So, don't be fuelish! Fill 'er up with whole, natural, nutrient-filled foods and gas up regularly. Green foods give you the most mileage—veggies like broccoli, asparagus, kale, spinach, bok choy, romaine lettuce and other leafy greens, along with any brightly colored vegetables and fruits. Premium-quality gas-o-lean revs up your engine, extends your cellular warranty and keeps your spare tire from inflating!

Rootie Toot Fruit Salad

Simple and simply delicious fruit salad with creamy orange-yogurt dressing

Toss in the fruits that you like best and put your taste buds to the test!

2 cups	low-fat plain Greek yogurt
2 tbsp	liquid honey
1 tbsp	frozen orange juice concentrate
1 tsp	grated orange zest
6 cups	chopped fresh fruit (try a combination of bananas, oranges, kiwi fruit, strawberries, blueberries and apples, or choose your favorites)

- To make dressing, mix first four ingredients together in a small bowl. Cover and refrigerate for 1 hour.

- Stir dressing and fruit together in a large bowl. Serve immediately.

Recipe Tip The creamy, orangey dressing makes this a refreshing, light dessert for that weekend barbecue party. Try topping individual servings with crunchy homemade granola for a fabulous breakfast option. Mix the dressing and fruit together just before serving, otherwise the salad will be runny.

MAKES 6 SERVINGS

PER SERVING
176 calories, 0.6 g total fat (0 g saturated fat), 9 g protein, 36 g carbohydrate, 5 g fiber, 7 mg cholesterol, 119 mg sodium

Trivial Tidbit

A study of smells shows that the scent of grapefruit on women makes them seem about six years younger to men, providing yet another reason to pack up and move to Florida! Interestingly, the perception is not reciprocal and the grapefruit scent on men has no effect on women's estimation of a man's age. Why? No one nose.

Fruity Q & A

Question: Should I cut fruit from my diet to lose weight? *Answer:* Only if you've gone bananas! Not only have we never seen a fat monkey, but we've also never heard anyone complain, "Look at me! I'm a whale! Must be all those blueberries I've been gorging on!" Yes, fruit contains the simple sugar, fructose, and we've been hearing nasty things about fructose lately. But it's the man-made, highly processed corn-syrup concoction that's fattening North Americans, not the fructose Mother Nature manufactured. She wisely made sure that the sugar in fruit comes strategically wrapped in high-fiber packaging, and fiber lessens the blood-sugar peaks, hormonal havoc and weight gain that low-carb dieters fear. In fact, fruit's a fantastic fat fighter! Get a couple of servings under your belt each day and there's less room for fattening junk food. Got a raging sweet tooth? Try some scrumptious raspberries, frozen bananas or juicy pineapple chunks to satisfy cravings. Most fruits are low in calories, high in water content, great-tasting and convenient—what more could you ask for? How about a ton of antioxidants to keep you looking young? Or hundreds of plant chemicals to protect you from disease? Obviously, eating fruit is key to losing weight, feeling great and ensuring you live to a ripe old age!

Rice Capades

Brown rice salad with cantaloupe, cucumber and cilantro in a zesty lime dressing

The gold-medal winner at The World Figure-Slimming Championships, this scrumptious brown rice salad scored a perfect 6 (even from the Russian judge!).

1 cup	uncooked long-grain brown rice (see tip)
1 cup	orange juice
1⅓ cups	reduced-sodium vegetable or chicken broth
1½ cups	diced cantaloupe
1 cup	peeled and diced English cucumber
½ cup	each diced red bell pepper and chopped green onions
2 tbsp	minced fresh cilantro

Dressing

3 tbsp	freshly squeezed lime juice
2 tbsp	liquid honey
1 tbsp	olive oil
1 tsp	Dijon mustard
1 tsp	minced garlic
½ tsp	ground cumin
3 to 4	dashes hot pepper sauce
¼ tsp	salt

MAKES 8 SERVINGS

PER SERVING
152 calories, 2.6 g total fat
(0.4 g saturated fat),
3 g protein, 30 g carbohydrate,
1.6 g fiber, 0 mg cholesterol,
176 mg sodium

- Combine rice, orange juice and broth in a medium pot. Bring to a boil. Reduce heat to medium-low. Cover and simmer until rice is tender and all liquid has been absorbed, about 20 minutes (depending on brand of rice). Let rice cool completely.

- In a large bowl, stir together rice, cantaloupe, cucumber, red pepper, green onions and cilantro. In a small bowl, whisk together all dressing ingredients. Pour dressing over rice mixture and stir well. Cover and refrigerate for 1 hour before serving.

Recipe Tips Make sure your brown rice is the quicker-cooking variety (cooks in 20 minutes), but not instant rice. For an interesting variation, try making this salad with nutrient-packed quinoa (see p. 38 for details).

Don't Avoid THIS Germ!

Every day, about half the world's population gets as many as half its daily calories from rice. In fact, in some Asian languages, the words meaning "to eat" and "to eat rice" are the same. Too bad most of that rice is the white stuff, which is mostly fluff! Sure, white rice does have some protein, but its most precious parts—the bran and the germ—have been polished away in the processing plant. Enter brown rice, white rice's "totally together" cousin. Because its bran and germ are intact—nothing's been stripped away—it's a true whole grain that can help you look and feel great. In fact, just about every nutrition expert will tell you to sub the brown variety for white rice every time. Here's why: Brown rice's germ gives you the antioxidant vitamin E, as well as cholesterol-lowering phytosterols. Its bran is loaded with mood-boosting B vitamins and about five times as much fiber as white rice. All that fabulous fiber makes brown rice gentler on your blood sugar than plain ol' white. Plus, bran acts like a natural detoxifier, swooshing out gunk, such as mercury, that accumulates in the body. Top it off with five grams of protein per cup and you can see why brown wins hands-down!

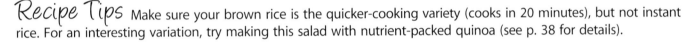

Nutrition Nugget

A variety of muskmelon, the cantaloupe's name is derived from the town of Cantalupo, Italy, where the melon was first grown after being brought into the country from Armenia in the first century AD. Rich in beta-carotene and fiber, half a 5-inch cantaloupe also packs in 100 percent of the recommended daily allowance of vitamins A and C. All that, plus a healthy serving of potassium, means cantaloupe is a heart-health heroine! Your waistline loves it, too—cantaloupe provides slow-digesting carbs that curb your cravings for sweets. Given these health-promoting qualities, maybe we should forget the name cantaloupe and start thinking CANaloupe!

Red, White and Yahoo!

Grape tomatoes, fresh mozzarella and chickpeas tossed with fresh basil and balsamic vinegar

Yippee! This super-easy, flavorsome salad is a real dandy. First you're hit by the color, then you're wowed by the taste. Only a yahoo wouldn't like it!

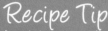

1 can	(19 oz/540 mL) no-salt-added chickpeas, drained and rinsed
2 cups	halved grape tomatoes
1 cup	mini fresh mozzarella balls, halved (4 oz/113 g—see tip)
⅓ cup	minced red onions
⅓ cup	chopped fresh basil leaves
1 tbsp	olive oil
1 tbsp	balsamic vinegar
1 tbsp	freshly squeezed lemon juice
½ tsp	salt
¼ tsp	freshly ground black pepper

- Place all ingredients in a large bowl and mix well. May be served immediately, or salad can stand at room temperature for up to 1 hour before serving. Since tomatoes tend to lose their flavor when refrigerated, we recommend you add them at the last minute if you're preparing this salad in advance.

MAKES 5 SERVINGS

PER SERVING
202 calories, 9 g total fat (3.5 g saturated fat), 10 g protein, 21 g carbohydrate, 4 g fiber, 16 mg cholesterol, 270 mg sodium

Recipe Tip

Look for fresh mini-mozzarella balls, called "mini bocconcini," in small, cottage-cheese-like containers where you buy specialty cheeses at your grocery store or ask for them at the deli-cheese counter. Fresh mozzarella is completely different than regular mozzarella. It's very soft, white and mild, and we know you'll love it!

The further you get from nature, the closer you get to the doctor.

Dr. Bernard Jensen

Grainman

Light-tasting, colorful bulgur salad with dried cranberries, walnuts and fresh mint

Cruisin' for new recipe ideas with whole grains? Well, this nutty, high-fiber, bulgur salad is sheer genius! It's so scrumptious and so healthy, even if you haven't used a pot in years, it's worth Dustin off, man.

1 cup	orange juice
1 cup	bulgur (see tip)
½ cup	chopped dried cranberries
½ cup	each diced celery and peeled, diced English cucumber
¼ cup	minced red onions
¼ cup	chopped walnuts, pecans or natural almonds
⅓ cup	chopped fresh parsley
2 tbsp	chopped fresh mint leaves
1 tbsp	olive oil
1 tbsp	freshly squeezed lemon juice
1 tsp	grated lemon zest
¼ tsp	salt
⅛ tsp	freshly ground black pepper

MAKES 6 SERVINGS

PER SERVING

191 calories, 5.7 g total fat (0.6 g saturated fat), 5 g protein, 33 g carbohydrate, 5.6 g fiber, 0 mg cholesterol, 112 mg sodium

- Combine orange juice and 1 cup water in a medium saucepan. Bring to a boil over high heat. Reduce heat to low and stir in bulgur. Simmer, covered, for 5 minutes. Remove from heat and let stand, covered, until bulgur has absorbed all of the liquid, 15 to 20 minutes.

- Meanwhile, place cranberries, celery, cucumber, red onions and walnuts in a large bowl. Add cooked bulgur, parsley, mint, olive oil, lemon juice, lemon zest, salt and pepper. Mix well. Cover and refrigerate for at least 2 hours before serving.

Recipe Tips What the heck is bulgur? It's a nutritious grain that's created when whole wheat kernels are steamed, dried and crushed. It has a nutty flavor and chewy texture when cooked and is primarily used in pilafs and salads. Look for bulgur in well-stocked supermarkets (check the bulk-food section) and natural/health food stores. For a variation, try this recipe with quinoa instead of bulgur. Delish!

> **Laughter is brightest where food is best.**
> *Irish proverb*

Grain, Grain, Go Away?

Not if you want to lose weight, lower your cholesterol, keep your blood sugar on an even keel, stay regular and prevent disease. Yes, there's a grain of truth to the claim that carbohydrates will make you fat. Today's grocery store shelves are filled with highly refined, overly processed, high-calorie products made from grains: crackers, cakes, cookies, white bread, bagels, pizza and sugary cereals, to name a few. These "bad" carbohydrates are the type we've been overeating and the kind you can blame for your plus-sized pants. But here's the whole truth: Genuine whole grains—the kind that haven't been processed to death, stripped of fiber and depleted of nutrients—are "good" carbs. They're allies, not enemies, in the battle of the bulge because they fill us up, curb our hunger and provide us with a steady supply of energy. And they contain much more than just carbohydrates. Loaded with fiber, vitamins, minerals and phytochemicals, they promote overall health and reduce our risk of disease. Whole grains include brown rice, slow-cooked oatmeal, barley, rye, bulgur, quinoa plus breads, pastas and cereals made with 100 percent whole wheat, millet, flax or spelt. Never *spelt* "quinoa" in your life? Jot it down on your shopping list and give it a try. For optimal health, don't go against the grain!

Unbeleafable Spinach Salad

Spinach salad with crumbled bacon, mushrooms, mandarins and sliced eggs in a warm and tangy maple-Dijon vinaigrette

Beleaf it or not, ho-hum spinach salad can become greens with envy! Tasting is beleafing!

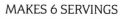

MAKES 6 SERVINGS

PER SERVING
229 calories,
10.7 g total fat
(4 g saturated fat),
13 g protein,
22 g carbohydrate,
2.3 g fiber,
223 mg cholesterol,
395 mg sodium

1 can	(10 oz/284 mL) mandarin orange segments in light syrup, undrained
8 oz	(227 g) fresh baby spinach leaves (a BIG bowlful!)
3 cups	thinly sliced fresh mushrooms
6	slices reduced-sodium bacon
½ cup	diced red onions
1 tsp	minced garlic
3 tbsp	white balsamic vinegar or white wine vinegar
2 tbsp	Dijon mustard
2 tbsp	pure maple syrup or liquid honey
Pinch	salt and freshly ground black pepper
6	hard-boiled eggs, sliced lengthwise into quarters

- Drain orange segments, reserving liquid (you should have about ½ cup syrup). Place drained oranges in a very large salad bowl. Add spinach and mushrooms. Set aside.

- Cook bacon in 10-inch, non-stick skillet over medium-high heat until crisp but not burned. Remove bacon and drain on paper towels. Do not discard bacon drippings. Crumble or chop bacon and add to spinach mixture.

- Add onions, garlic and reserved orange syrup to bacon drippings in skillet. Stir to break up any brown bits on bottom of skillet. Simmer on low heat for 3 minutes, until liquid is slightly reduced. Stir in vinegar, mustard and maple syrup. Mix well. Simmer for 2 more minutes. Add salt and freshly ground black pepper and remove from heat. You should have just under 1 cup dressing.

- Pour hot dressing over salad and mix well using tongs. Spinach will become slightly wilted. Mound salad on individual serving plates and arrange sliced eggs over salad. Serve immediately.

Bone Up on Spinach

If there's one nutritional upgrade you should make when building a salad or a sandwich, it's to swap boring-schmoring iceberg lettuce for spinach. Thanks to Popeye, we know spinach is an energy-boosting iron mine—and a low-calorie, meatless one, to boot. The popular cartoon was credited with increasing spinach sales by 33 percent! Interestingly, it might not have been the iron in spinach that made Popeye so strong. Spinach is a surprisingly good source of bone-building, fat-burning calcium. Just one cup contains 245 mg, about the same as a serving of yogurt, plus the calcium in spinach is much easier for your body to use. This versatile green machine also supplies bone-health superstar vitamin K, muscle-repairing potassium and muscle chillaxin' magnesium, not to mention an impressive lineup of carotenoids like lutein and zeaxanthin that protect against a host of diseases. And it looks like Popeye made another smart choice in the girlfriend department: To get the most out of these fat-soluble nutrients, you need to cook or eat the spinach in combination with a healthy fat. Olive Oyl is an ideal mate!

What did the leftovers say when they were put in the freezer? Foiled again! :)

MAKES 4 SERVINGS

PER SERVING
270 calories, 7 g total fat (2.5 g saturated fat),
35 g protein, 17 g carbohydrate, 3.9 g fiber,
78 mg cholesterol, 387 mg sodium

Nutrition Nugget

Try this anti-bloatation creation: One jug
of pure, filtered water, sliced cucumber,
several mint leaves, squeeze of lemon
juice and some sliced, fresh gingerroot.
Goodbye water retention!

Sugar Shocker

It's official! The average North
American now inhales more than
150 pounds of sugar each year.
That's the equivalent of 30 five-
pound bags going straight to waist!
Studies show that, on average, we're
eating more than 25 teaspoons
of sugar every day. Considering
that experts suggest women
should consume no more than 6.5
teaspoons a day and men no more
than 9.5, we're blowing the lid right
off the sugar bowl with this constant
IV drip of the white stuff. Imagine
piling 8 teaspoons of sugar onto a
plate for breakfast, then 8 teaspoons
at lunch time and another 8 at
dinner. No doubt you'd say, "That's
disgusting! I'm not eating that. It's
so unhealthy!" Yet that's basically
what many people are eating each
day as they scarf back the Standard
American Diet—isn't that S.A.D.?
With sugar now making up the bulk
of our daily calories, no wonder fat's
making up the bulk of our bodies!

Eata Fajita Salad

Warm chicken fajita salad with chili-lime dressing

*Eata fajita and savor the flavor! Traditional fajita fillings—spicy chicken,
peppers and onions—make a filling salad when they're served on
crunchy greens and topped with grated cheese. Giddy up!*

½ cup	light (5%) sour cream
2½ tbsp	freshly squeezed lime juice, divided
1 tsp	granulated sugar
¼ tsp	each chili powder and ground cumin
2 tsp	avocado oil
4	boneless skinless chicken breasts, cut into thin strips (about 1½ lbs/680 g)
1 cup	each sliced green and red bell peppers
1	small red onion, thinly sliced into rings
½ cup	salsa
2 tbsp	minced fresh cilantro
8 cups	shredded romaine lettuce
½ cup	packed shredded light old (sharp) cheddar cheese (2 oz/57 g)

- In a small bowl, combine sour cream, 1½ tbsp of the lime juice, sugar, chili powder and cumin. Refrigerate dressing until ready to use.

- Heat oil in a large, non-stick wok or skillet over medium-high heat. Add chicken. Cook and stir until chicken is no longer pink. Continue to cook until chicken is lightly browned. Add peppers and onions. Cook and stir for 3 more minutes. Add salsa and cook for 2 more minutes.

- Stir in remaining 1 tbsp lime juice and cilantro. Mix well. Remove from heat. To assemble salad, divide lettuce among 4 serving plates. Top with warm chicken mixture. Spoon dressing over salad. Sprinkle with cheese. Serve immediately.

Trivial Tidbit

It is said that the bubbles in
coffee can foretell the day's
weather. Supposedly,
you need to stare at
your coffee before
adding milk. If the
bubbles float toward
the rim of the cup,
the pressure is low,
and you can expect
clouds and stormy weather.
However, if the bubbles float to the
center, the pressure is high, and fair
weather is on its way. Looks like a
meteorologist's job has many perks!

It's All Greek to Me

Traditional Greek salad with fresh oregano, mint and a light vinaigrette dressing

Do you pore over ingredient lists and recipe instructions, scratching your head and muttering, "Graecum est; non potest legi"?*
We sure do. That's why we created this uncomplicated but delicious Greek salad that's so basic, even Janet can make it.

4	large ripe tomatoes (about 2 lbs/907 g), cut into 1-inch chunks
1	English cucumber, peeled, halved lengthwise and cut into 1-inch chunks
1	large green bell pepper, seeded and cut into 1-inch chunks
1	small red onion, halved and very thinly sliced
½ cup	Kalamata olives or other black olives
1 cup	crumbled light feta cheese (4 oz/113 g)
2 tbsp	minced fresh oregano leaves
2 tbsp	minced fresh mint leaves
3 tbsp	red wine vinegar or balsamic vinegar
2 tbsp	olive oil
Pinch	salt and freshly ground black pepper

MAKES 8 SERVINGS

PER SERVING
132 calories,
8.8 g total fat
(2.7 g saturated fat),
4 g protein,
12 g carbohydrate,
2.5 g fiber,
13 mg cholesterol,
271 mg sodium

- Combine tomatoes, cucumber, green pepper, red onion, olives, feta cheese, oregano and mint in a large decorative serving bowl.

- Just before serving, add vinegar, olive oil, salt and pepper and toss gently.

* The phrase, "It's all Greek to me," although attributed to Shakespeare, actually comes from a medieval Latin proverb, Graecum est; non potest legi—meaning "It is Greek; it cannot be read"—and refers to something that is unintelligible.

Recipe Tip
To make this salad in advance, combine all ingredients except the tomatoes and dressing and refrigerate until serving time. Add the tomatoes and dressing just before serving. Never refrigerate tomatoes—they'll lose their flavor! If you can find a beautiful yellow or orange tomato, add it to the mix for extra color.

Don't tell jokes in the kitchen.
The dishes might crack up :)

Beauty Secret for Olive Us

We've all heard that olive oil's good for the heart, but did you know it's also one of the best-kept beauty secrets? By using extra-virgin olive oil topically, you can prevent and treat aging skin. Crow's feet got ya down? Splash a little oil on your salad and on your face! Extra-virgin olive oil is loaded with powerful antioxidants like vitamins A and E that protect your skin from free-radical damage. It also strengthens connective tissue so your skin does a better job of repairing and regenerating itself, and it helps prevent inflammation, one of the leading causes of wrinkles. Olive oil is naturally rich in squalene, an ingredient found in many store-bought skin-care products. Squalene keeps skin moist, giving you that radiant appearance we see on faces that grace magazine covers. Olive oil's antibacterial and antifungal properties can even soothe acne, eczema and psoriasis. An added bonus is that a top-quality bottle of this organic, extra-virgin, skinsational wrinkle cure is easier on the wallet than most other creams and schemes. Oil's well that ends well!

Hail Caesar!

Lightened-up Caesar salad with thick and creamy dressing, crumbled bacon and multigrain croutons

According to the history books, this delicious Caesar salad was one of the most popular recipes in the entire Romaine Empire!

Dressing

½ cup	light mayonnaise or Miracle Whip
2 tbsp	olive oil
¼ cup	freshly grated Parmesan cheese
1	hard-boiled egg
2 tbsp	freshly squeezed lemon juice
1 tbsp	balsamic vinegar
2 tsp	minced garlic
1 tsp	liquid honey or granulated sugar
½ tsp	each Dijon mustard and Worcestershire sauce
½ tsp	anchovy paste (optional)
⅛ tsp	freshly ground black pepper

Salad

1	very large head romaine lettuce, torn (or one large bag prewashed, chopped romaine)
8	slices reduced-sodium bacon, cooked and chopped or crumbled
1 cup	multigrain seasoned croutons
2 tbsp	freshly shaved Parmesan cheese for garnish

MAKES 6 SERVINGS

PER SERVING

217 calories, 16 g total fat (4 g saturated fat), 8 g protein, 13 g carbohydrate, 2 g fiber, 52 mg cholesterol, 471 mg sodium

- Whirl all dressing ingredients in mini food processor until smooth. Refrigerate at least 2 hours or overnight if possible (for flavors to develop).

- To assemble salad, place torn lettuce, crumbled bacon and croutons in a large salad bowl. Add dressing and toss well to distribute dressing evenly. Top with shaved Parmesan. Serve immediately.

Recipe Tip: Add thinly sliced grilled chicken to turn this salad into a meal.

Dress for Success

Think you're a dietary saint because you've been drizzling fat-free dressing on your salad? Well, we hate to put a crimp in your halo, but the latest research shows that "no fat" might be no good—and we're not just talking about flavor! Nope, we're talkin' vitamins, minerals and antioxidants, and how your body absorbs them from the food you eat. Turns out that some of the healthy stuff in vegetables like beta-carotene, lycopene and even calcium can only be absorbed in the presence of fat. Now, that doesn't mean you should soak your salad with vats of full-fat dressing or sauté your veggies in gobs of butter. It's all about balance and moderation. To get the most nutritional bang for your buck, top your naked salad with olive-oil- or flax-oil-based dressings and add a sprinkling of nuts or sliced avocado. Try sautéing veggies in coconut oil or avocado oil. If you wanna dress for success, a little fat'll do ya!

Nutrition Nugget

Mind over platter: Turns out that meditating is as good for your waistline as it is for your psyche. Researchers say just seven minutes of meditation every day could help you control food cravings. Sweet!

Nat's King Coleslaw

Asian coleslaw with a sesame-ginger dressing

It's unforgettable, in every way. But how can coleslaw so unforgettable be so incredible too? We've added sesame oil and gingerroot to make our coleslaw fit for a king.

Dressing

½ cup   seasoned rice vinegar
¼ cup   pure maple syrup (see tip)
2 tbsp   reduced-sodium soy sauce
1 tbsp   sesame oil
1 tsp   grated gingerroot

Salad

1 pkg   (1 lb/454 g) coleslaw mix (see tip)
2 cups   bean sprouts
⅓ cup   chopped green onions
1   large Red Delicious apple, unpeeled, cored and shredded

- To make dressing, whisk together vinegar, maple syrup, soy sauce, sesame oil and gingerroot in a small bowl.

- In a large bowl, combine coleslaw mix, bean sprouts, green onions and apple. Pour dressing over salad and mix well. Refrigerate for 1 hour before serving.

MAKES 6 TO 8 SERVINGS

PER SERVING (BASED ON 8 SERVINGS)
79 calories, 2 g total fat (0.3 g saturated fat),
2 g protein, 15 g carbohydrate, 2.5 g fiber,
0 mg cholesterol, 171 mg sodium

Recipe Tip: If you don't have any maple syrup, use liquid honey. Instead of coleslaw mix, you can use 6 cups shredded green cabbage, 1 cup shredded red cabbage and 1 cup shredded carrots.

When the inventor of the first elastic girdle was asked if it worked, he replied, "Of corset does!" :)

Hailing a Cabbage

Growing up in a Polish household, we certainly ate our fair share of cabbage. Whether she shredded it, rolled it, souped it or tucked it into the sauerkraut pancakes (seriously!) that were part of our traditional Christmas Eve dinner, our Mom must've known that cabbage would give our bodies a head start to healthy! Armed with disease-fighting antioxidants like vitamin C, cabbage is also well-endowed with sulfur compounds that literally kick the butts of suspicious cancer-causing substances in our bodies. In fact, scientists say that women who regularly eat cabbage have a 45 percent lower risk of developing breast cancer! Cabbage can heal an ulcer, too, so if your new boss or daughter's boyfriend has you chewing on Tums like there's no *tum*orrow, you can safely trade the antacids for a glass of cabbage juice. (For more info on juicing, see p. 367.) By the way, red cabbage has 15 times the beta-carotene of its green cousin, so go *ahead* and give the green light to red!

Feast from the East

Asian beef-noodle salad with grilled sirloin and a zesty sesame-orange dressing

Feast your eyes on this! East meats West when oodles of beef and noodles are paired with colorful veggies and a lip-smacking Asian dressing. Lotsa fiber and lean protein make it a waist-watcher's dream.

MAKES 4 TO 6 SERVINGS

PER SERVING
(BASED ON 6 SERVINGS)
340 calories,
7.6 g total fat
(2.1 g saturated fat),
25 g protein,
46 g carbohydrate,
6.3 g fiber,
46 mg cholesterol,
619 mg sodium

Dressing

½ cup	reduced-sodium chicken broth
⅓ cup	hoisin sauce
2 tbsp	reduced-sodium soy sauce
2 tbsp	seasoned rice vinegar (see tip)
1 tbsp	sesame oil
1 tbsp	grated gingerroot
1 tsp	grated orange zest
1 tsp	minced garlic
¼ tsp	each salt, freshly ground black pepper and crushed red pepper flakes

Salad

8 oz	(227 g) uncooked whole wheat spaghetti
1 lb	(454 g) sirloin steak, grilled and cut into strips
2 cups	small broccoli florets
1 cup	thinly sliced red bell pepper
1 cup	peeled, seeded and diced cucumber
1 cup	grated carrots
1 cup	frozen green peas, thawed
½ cup	chopped green onions
⅓ cup	chopped fresh basil leaves

- Whisk together all dressing ingredients in a small bowl and refrigerate until ready to use.

- Cook spaghetti according to package directions. Drain. Rinse well with cold water and drain again. Transfer spaghetti to a large salad bowl and toss with remaining ingredients. Add dressing just before serving and toss again.

Recipe Tip: Rice vinegar is mild, slightly sweet and comes in regular and seasoned varieties. Seasoned rice vinegar has a little salt and sugar added.

FOOD BITE It took scientists until 1970 to figure out what has been folk knowledge for centuries—that cucumbers really are cool. In fact, on a warm day, the inside of a field cucumber registers about 20°F lower than the air around it. How cool is that?

Easy Peasy Orzo Salad

Orzo pasta salad with green peas,
cucumbers, tomatoes, mint
and feta cheese

It's easy, it's peasy, it's feta cheesy!

Dressing

⅓ cup	light bottled Italian dressing
1 tbsp	each balsamic vinegar and freshly squeezed lemon juice
2 tsp	liquid honey
1 tsp	Dijon mustard

Salad

2 cups	uncooked orzo (rice-shaped pasta)
1 cup	quartered grape tomatoes
1 cup	peeled, seeded and diced cucumber
½ cup	diced orange or yellow bell pepper
½ cup	chopped green onions
½ cup	frozen green peas, thawed
½ cup	crumbled light feta cheese (2 oz/57 g)
¼ cup	chopped black olives (optional)
2 to 3 tbsp	minced fresh mint leaves
¼ tsp	freshly ground black pepper

MAKES 6 SERVINGS

PER SERVING
303 calories,
3.2 g total fat
(1.5 g saturated fat),
12 g protein,
59 g carbohydrate,
4 g fiber,
9 mg cholesterol,
295 mg sodium

- To make dressing, whisk together all dressing ingredients in a small bowl. Set aside.

- Cook orzo according to package directions. Drain. Rinse with cold water and drain again. Mix together orzo and all remaining ingredients in a large bowl. Add dressing and toss to coat salad. Cover with plastic wrap and refrigerate overnight for best flavor.

Get In Mint Condition

Ahhh, the cool smell of peppermint. Fights bad breath and fights...fat? It's true! The essential oil of peppermint can help you lose weight because it suppresses appetite and curbs cravings. Simply add one drop to a glass of water and they won't be calling you Peppermint Fatty! Plus, sniffing some peppermint before a workout boosts your mood and reduces fatigue, motivating you to keep moving. Weight-loss benefits aside, peppermint also blocks headache pain, soothes a sore stomach, unclogs stuffy sinuses and even relieves joint pain. And in a recent study, when subjects inhaled peppermint oil before taking a test, their memory retention and recall increased by 28 percent! Sure beats writing answers on your hand! (Not that *we* ever did that.)

Nutrition Nugget

Peas on Earth and goodwill toward men's and women's waistlines! Green peas are a potent weight-loss aid because they're little magic bullets full of fiber and protein. In fact, one cup of peas has more protein than a whole egg! They're also rich in B vitamins that are needed for the proper metabolism of fats, proteins and carbohydrates. To get on the healthy-eating track, take a ride on the peas train!

Do the Chunky Chicken

High-protein, chunky chicken salad with chopped vegetables and a creamy dill dressing

Wanna ruffle some feathers at your next potluck luncheon? Don't show up with the same ol' song and dance—try this little number: A sensational and satisfying chicken salad that'll have everyone flapping their arms with joy.

Dressing

¾ cup	lemon-flavored yogurt (see tip)
¼ cup	light mayonnaise
3 tbsp	white vinegar
2 tbsp	minced fresh dill
1 tbsp	Dijon mustard
½ tsp	salt
¼ tsp	freshly ground black pepper

Salad

4 cups	chopped cooked chicken breast
1½ cups	diced celery
1 cup	chopped red bell pepper
½ cup	chopped green onions (with white parts)
½ cup	sliced almonds, toasted (optional)
½ cup	frozen green peas, thawed
⅓ cup	chopped fresh parsley
4	hard-boiled eggs, sliced

- To make dressing, whisk together all dressing ingredients in a medium bowl. Cover and refrigerate until ready to use.

- Combine all salad ingredients in a large bowl. Mix well. Add dressing and toss gently. Cover and refrigerate for at least 1 hour before serving.

Recipe Tip: If you can't find lemon yogurt, use plain yogurt (not vanilla!) in its place, and add 1 tbsp lemon juice plus 1 tbsp granulated sugar to the dressing.

MAKES 6 SERVINGS

PER SERVING

250 calories, 7.2 g total fat (1.9 g saturated fat), 34 g protein, 11 g carbohydrate, 1.9 g fiber, 214 mg cholesterol, 461 mg sodium

Become a Stalker

Got high blood pressure? Then stalk up on celery! Researchers at the University of Chicago Medical Center showed that a very small amount of a compound in celery called 3-n-butyl phthalide (don't worry, this will not appear on your final exam!) can lower blood pressure in animals by 12 to 14 percent. That's a lot! The study was inspired by the father of one of the researchers, who, after eating about two stalks of celery every day for one week, was pumped to see his blood pressure drop from 158 over 96 to a normal reading of 118 over 82. Want a hot *stalk* tip? Don't leave out the leaves! Celery leaves are actually the most nutritious part of the plant, containing more calcium, iron, potassium and vitamins A and C than the stalks. You can use the leaves in soups, chilies, salads, juices or in other recipes that are enhanced by the flavor of celery.

FOOD BITE

More than just a pickle pal, dill has been recognized for both its culinary and medicinal benefits for centuries. The Greeks and Romans regarded dill as a sign of wealth and held it in high regard for its many healing properties. Dill's name comes from the Norse word *Dilla*, which means "to lull." That makes sense given the herb's traditional uses as a stomach soother and an insomnia reliever. Some of its volatile oils even neutralize the toxins from cigarette and charcoal grill smoke. Why does dill give us such a thrill? Because it's dillicious, of course!

On organic farms they till it like it is :)

Cool Chick Salad

Chicken and black bean salad with lime and cilantro

What's so cool about this chicken salad? Well, it's really hoppin' with black beans, not to mention a zesty, rockin' and rollin' combination of lime and cilantro that'll knock your socks off.

Salad

2 cups	chopped cooked chicken breast
1 cup	canned no-salt-added black beans, drained and rinsed
1½ cups	diced tomatoes
1 cup	whole-kernel corn (canned or frozen)
½ cup	diced red onions
¼ cup	chopped fresh cilantro

Dressing

2 tbsp	freshly squeezed lime juice
1 tbsp	olive oil
½ tsp	each ground cumin and granulated sugar
¼ tsp	each salt and freshly ground black pepper

- Combine salad ingredients in a large bowl and mix well.

- In a small bowl, whisk together dressing ingredients. Pour over bean-chicken mixture and stir until dressing is evenly distributed.

- Cover and refrigerate until ready to serve.

MAKES 4 SERVINGS

PER SERVING
242 calories, 7 g total fat (1.3 g saturated fat), 26 g protein, 18 g carbohydrate, 5.6 g fiber, 60 mg cholesterol, 225 mg sodium

Trivial Tidbit
People who eat beans are 23 percent less likely to have thick waists, and that's not just a bunch of hot air!

The Soaperb Herb

Cilantro, also called Chinese parsley or coriander, is an herb commonly used to add flavor to chili, salsa and other highly spiced Mexican, Asian and Caribbean dishes. It's one of those tastes you either love or hate—some people describe cilantro's distinctive, pungent odor and taste as "soapy." (For the record, we love it!) Regardless, you'll probably want to wash your mouth out with cilantro when you find out how it cleanses your insides. The leaves are rich in calcium, iron, beta-carotene and vitamin C, and studies have shown that cilantro is one of the few substances that can help remove heavy metals, such as mercury and aluminum, from the central nervous system. That's great news for those with Alzheimer's disease, depression and other neurological disorders worsened by toxic overload, but it's also useful for the rest of us who are constantly exposed to harmful heavy metals from environmental pollution, certain foods and even cosmetics and other consumer products. Still feelin' wishy-washy 'bout cilantro?

Sign on church bulletin: Have trouble sleeping? Try counting your blessings.

Let It Bean

Easy, colorful, high-fiber, multi-bean salad

When we found ourselves in times of trouble trying to concoct a great-tasting, nutritious salad, our mother, Alfreda, came to us, speaking words of wisdom, and said, "Let it bean."
Realizing that a high-fiber diet is the cornerstone of good health, she's been eating this salad regularly and recommended that we include her scrumptious recipe in our cookbook so that you can be regular, too.

MAKES 8 SERVINGS

PER SERVING
283 calories, 8.6 g total fat
(0.7 g saturated fat), 11 g protein,
43 g carbohydrate, 11.2 g fiber,
0 mg cholesterol, 239 mg sodium

Salad

2 cups	fresh or frozen cut green beans, cooked (see tip)
1 can	(19 oz/540 mL) no-salt-added chickpeas, drained and rinsed
1 can	(19 oz/540 mL) no-salt-added black beans, drained and rinsed
1 can	(19 oz/540 mL) no-salt-added red kidney beans, drained and rinsed
1 can	(12 oz/340 mL) whole-kernel corn, drained
1 cup	diced red onions
1 cup	diced red or orange bell pepper
½ cup	chopped fresh parsley

Dressing

¼ cup	safflower oil or light olive oil
¼ cup	cider vinegar or white vinegar
2 tbsp	granulated sugar
1 tsp	Dijon mustard
½ tsp	celery seed
¼ tsp	each salt and freshly ground black pepper

- Combine all salad ingredients in a large bowl. Mix well.

- Whisk together oil, vinegar, sugar, mustard, celery seed, salt and pepper in a small pot. Bring to a boil. Remove from heat and pour over bean mixture. Stir gently. Cover and refrigerate overnight for the best flavor. Stir occasionally if possible. (We think this salad tastes great as soon as it's made, but our mom insists you wait 'til tomorrow. Darn.)

Recipe Tip

Steam or boil the green beans just until they're tender. Be careful not to overcook them. Some people use canned green beans in their bean salad, but they're a little on the mushy side and have a faded green color, so we don't recommend them for this salad.

FOOD BITE Ever wonder where the expression "spill the beans" came from? Legend has it that members of Greek societies used to vote on the admission of new members by dropping beans into jars or helmets. White beans signified a "yes" vote and black beans a "no." As tensions mounted and the anticipation became unbearable, anxious voters would accidentally knock over the jar or helmet, revealing the secret vote. In other words, they would spill the beans.

55

Slaw & Order

Classic creamy coleslaw for picnics and potlucks

If great taste is a crime, this coleslaw's headed straight to flavor prison!

Dressing

½ cup	light mayonnaise
⅓ cup	light (5%) sour cream
2 tbsp	seasoned rice vinegar (or cider vinegar)
1 tbsp	freshly squeezed lemon juice
1½ tbsp	liquid honey
1 tsp	grainy Dijon mustard
1 tsp	celery seed
½ tsp	salt
¼ tsp	freshly ground black pepper

Salad

1 bag	(1 lb/454 g) coleslaw mix (green and red cabbage plus carrots)
½ cup	chopped green onions
½ cup	finely minced red bell pepper
½ cup	finely minced celery

- Whisk together all dressing ingredients in a small bowl. Refrigerate until ready to use.

- Empty the bag of coleslaw mix onto a large cutting board and chop it up a bit so the pieces of cabbage and carrots are smaller. Combine coleslaw mix, onions, bell pepper and celery in a large bowl. Pour dressing over salad. Mix well. Cover and refrigerate for at least 4 hours for the best flavor. Stir before serving.

MAKES 5 CUPS

PER SERVING (½ CUP)
77 calories, 4.7 g total fat (0.7 g saturated fat), 1 g protein, 9 g carbohydrate, 1.5 g fiber, 7 mg cholesterol, 255 mg sodium

"Gotta Try It" Diets

Though we aren't crazy about diets in general, we actually love them when we make them up ourselves. Just kidding! Actually, the following week-long "Janet and Greta Mini Diets" truly are beneficial because they can help you improve your overall eating habits. At week's end, take stock of which foods you missed and which you could live without. (1) The Think-Outside-the-Box Diet: Eating out of packages, boxes and bags will not only boost your intake of calories, sodium and sugar, but these highly processed, "edible food-like substances," as author Michael Pollan calls them, can also burden your body with loads of chemical additives and preservatives. Instead, prepare your own meals using "real" foods that are the product of nature, not of industry; (2) The Meatless-in-Seattle Diet: Bypass the meat market and get your protein by eating beans, lentils, quinoa, nuts, seeds and other plant-based protein sources; (3) The BYOF (Bring Your Own Food) Diet: That means no meals of fast food, take-out or convenience food. Eat breakfast at home. Brown-bag it for lunch and snacks, and be sure to pack a balanced blend of protein, fat and fiber, a combo that'll keep you full until dinner. Incidentally, a man from Elmira, Ontario, combined all three diets and lost more than 100 percent of his body weight in seven days. (Just making sure you're still reading!)

Nacho Ordinary Taco Salad

Layered taco salad, without the tacos!

It's buenos without the nachos! Toss the tacos and you can say adios to bad fat and bad carbs. What's left is all good: A mexy, mouthwatering, multilevel salad that's ideal for a hot summer night or a backyard party. Olé!

Beef Mixture

1½ lbs	(680 g) extra-lean ground beef
1 cup	chopped onions
1	large jalapeño pepper, seeded and minced
2 tsp	minced garlic
1 tbsp	chili powder
2 tsp	ground cumin
2 cups	quartered grape tomatoes
⅓ cup	ketchup
½ tsp	salt
¼ tsp	freshly ground black pepper

Salad

12 cups	torn romaine and iceberg lettuce (see tip)
1 cup	canned whole-kernel corn, drained
1 cup	canned no-salt-added black beans, drained and rinsed
½ cup	diced green bell pepper
1 cup	packed shredded light old (sharp) cheddar cheese (4 oz/113 g)
1 cup	quartered grape tomatoes
⅓ cup	chopped green onions
1	small ripe avocado, peeled and sliced (optional)
1 cup	each light (5%) sour cream and medium salsa

MAKES 6 TO 8 SERVINGS

PER SERVING (BASED ON 8 SERVINGS)
284 calories,
11.2 g total fat
(6.1 g saturated fat),
25 g protein,
22 g carbohydrate,
6.4 g fiber,
65 mg cholesterol,
594 mg sodium

Recipe Tips: To save some time, use bagged, prewashed, precut lettuce. This salad tastes best when the beef mixture is warm or at room temperature. Try to assemble it just before serving for the best flavor. If you like salad dressing with your taco salad, try mixing 1 cup Catalina or ranch salad dressing with 2 tbsp hickory-flavored barbecue sauce.

- Heat a large, non-stick skillet over medium-high heat. Add beef, onions, jalapeño pepper and garlic. Cook and stir until beef is no longer pink, breaking up any large pieces. Add chili powder and cumin. Cook 1 more minute. Add grape tomatoes, ketchup, salt and pepper. Cook and stir for 2 more minutes. Remove skillet from heat and set aside.

- To assemble salad, spread lettuce over bottom of a serving platter. (If you want to make individual salads instead of one large salad, spread lettuce over bottom of individual-sized plates or shallow bowls.) Top with beef mixture, followed by corn, beans, green pepper, cheese, tomatoes, green onions and avocado slices (if using), in that order. Top with sour cream and salsa just before serving.

Go Ahead—Havacado!

Avocado, the fruit formerly known as full o' fat, has made a healthy comeback! Turns out the experts now give the "butter pear" triple thumbs-up for its nutritional benefits. Yes, avocados are high in fat—about 30 grams in each—but it's mostly the good, monounsaturated kind that helps our tickers keep on tickin'. Avocados are an excellent source of another heart helper, the B vitamin folate. The good fat and high fiber of avocados also keep us feeling full and satisfied, so we might eat less and lose weight. Plus, avocados are rich in phytosterols, which lower cholesterol, and they offer more potassium per gram than bananas, which is helpful in lowering high blood pressure. No wonder health experts are singing the praises of this saintly, do-gooder. Holy guacamole!

Pessimist's blood type: B negative :)

Crabsolutely Fabulous Pasta Salad

Shell pasta with crabmeat and vegetables in a creamy, mustard-dill dressing

We've got the gift of crab! Our creamy pasta salad with crabmeat and dill will really give you something to talk about. Plus, it's crabnormally easy to make, even for the crabsent-minded!

½ cup	each light (5%) sour cream and light mayonnaise
1 tbsp	each freshly squeezed lemon juice, honey mustard and minced fresh dill
½ tsp	salt
¼ tsp	freshly ground black pepper
12 oz	(340 g) uncooked medium shell pasta (about 5 cups dry)
1 lb	(454 g) lump crabmeat (real or imitation), chopped
½ cup	each diced red and green bell peppers
½ cup	chopped green onions

MAKES 8 SERVINGS

PER SERVING
230 calories,
1.8 g total fat
(0.1 g saturated fat),
15 g protein,
39 g carbohydrate,
0.4 g fiber,
1 mg cholesterol,
531 mg sodium

- In a small bowl, combine sour cream, mayonnaise, lemon juice, honey mustard, dill, salt and pepper. Refrigerate dressing until ready to use.

- Cook shells according to package directions. Drain well. Rinse with cold water and drain again. Transfer pasta to a large bowl. Add crabmeat, bell peppers, onions and dressing. Mix well. Cover and refrigerate until ready to serve.

Recipe Tip: To reduce the sodium content, compare product labels for sour cream, mayonnaise and crabmeat and choose the brands with the lowest amounts of sodium.

Twinkie, Twinkie, Little Star

After dieting for a while, you can get obsessed with the idea of eating. Ever try singing to take your mind off food? Go ahead. Try it. Gumdrops keep fallin' on my head...Ain't nothin' but a hot dog...The farmer in the deli. It just doesn't work. And dieting doesn't work either—in fact, diets stink. They're unrealistic and temporary, putting us in a voluntary state of famine. Funny that we'd starve ourselves to death, hoping we'll live longer. And how about those diet programs with the boot-camp mentality? You know, they say you have to eat their food, they tell you what time of day to eat it and that you have to eat all of it. This isn't a diet, it's living with your parents! No wonder 95 percent of diets fail. It's time to forget about dieting and get on with living! Changing your eating habits doesn't always mean eating less, it means eating better. Now that's something to sing about.

Trivial Tidbit

Contrary to popular belief, the strongest muscle in the body is not the heart— it's the tongue! And it's no wonder. Most people exercise it far too much! And bet you didn't know that tongue prints are as unique as fingerprints. Could this be another way to lick crime?

Melrose Plates

Rotini pasta salad with chicken, celery, almonds and mandarins in a creamy poppy seed dressing

Why not invite everyone in your trendy condo over for a taste of this tangy, zesty, California-style salad? Invite the fashion designer who lives upstairs, invite her nasty sister, invite the advertising executives, call over the owner of the local bar and his photographer friend, invite the doctors…

THIS SALAD IS WICKED!

6 oz	(170 g) uncooked high-fiber rotini or other shaped pasta (about 2 cups dry)
2 cups	chopped cooked chicken breast
1 cup	diced celery
1 cup	mandarin orange segments
½ cup	sliced or slivered almonds
2 tbsp	chopped fresh parsley
¾ cup	low-fat plain yogurt (Greek yogurt works well)
2 tbsp	liquid honey
1 tbsp	frozen orange juice concentrate
1 tsp	poppy seeds
½ tsp	dry mustard
¼ tsp	freshly ground black pepper
Lettuce (any kind you like)	

MAKES 4 SERVINGS

PER SERVING
355 calories, 4.7 g total fat (1.1 g saturated fat), 32 g protein, 50 g carbohydrate, 9 g fiber, 63 mg cholesterol, 124 mg sodium

Recipe Tip: If you don't have any chicken on hand (or on foot or on head or on…), try tuna, turkey, crabmeat or shrimp in its place.

- Cook pasta according to package directions. Drain and rinse with cold water. Transfer pasta to a large bowl. Add chicken, celery, orange segments, almonds and parsley. Mix well.

- In a separate bowl, whisk together yogurt, honey, orange juice concentrate, poppy seeds, mustard and pepper. Pour yogurt mixture over chicken-pasta mixture and mix well. Serve on a bed of lettuce.

No Snooze, No Lose

Ever notice you're a lot hungrier on days when you haven't had enough sleep? That's because your body's crying out for more energy. As your energy plummets, so does your mood, and that's a prime-time trigger for bingeing on sugar-loaded snacks. Most importantly, it's during deep sleep that feel-good brain chemicals like serotonin are replenished. But when you're sleep-deprived, your body tries boosting serotonin by making you crave sugary and starchy carbohydrates. Need another reason to replace the late-night news with more snooze? Chronic sleep deprivation is a major stressor on the body. Your body instinctively perceives lack of sleep as a legitimate threat to its well-being and it reacts by raising levels of stress hormones like cortisol. When lack of quality shut-eye becomes chronic, the extra cortisol can cause our bodies to store fat—and it's usually around the gut. So, if you're losing sight of your belly button, try hitting the snooze button!

Nutrition Nugget

Bite into a "Christmas orange" and you just might receive the gift of good health! Scientists say compounds in the peels of mandarin oranges, called polymethoxylated flavones (PMFs, for short) have the potential to lower cholesterol and blood pressure as effectively as prescription drugs—without the nasty side effects. It seems that PMFs can slow the growth of cancer cells, too, especially in cancers of the breast, lung and colon. Try grating the peel of a well-washed, organic mandarin and use the zest to flavor yogurt, salad dressings, marinades, rice pilafs, quinoa or oatmeal.

Minutes at the table don't make you put on weight—it's the seconds :)

In this chapter...

Rome on the Range,
p. 68

Ladle Gaga

Become a pot star with these sensational
soups that top the flavor charts

Super-Corny Crab Chowder

Creamy, hearty crab and corn chowder with veggies and herbs

YOU HAVE GREAT LEGS!

Our souper-satisfying, scrumptious crab chowder is claws for applause!

1 tbsp	olive oil
1 tbsp	butter
1 cup	diced onions
1 cup	diced celery
²∕₃ cup	diced red bell pepper
2 tsp	minced garlic
1 cup	peeled, cubed Yukon Gold potatoes
1 tsp	dried thyme
1 tsp	dried tarragon
1 tsp	Seafood Magic spice (see tip)
2½ cups	reduced-sodium chicken broth
½ cup	clam juice
½ tsp	each salt and freshly ground black pepper
1 can	(14 oz/398 mL) no-salt-added cream-style corn
1 cup	half-and-half (10%) cream
3 tbsp	all-purpose flour
10 oz	(284 g) lump crabmeat (see tip)

Recipe Tip: Seafood Magic spice blend is similar to Old Bay Seasoning, only much more flavorful, in our humble opinions. It gives this soup some "kick." It is made by Chef Paul Prudhomme and you can usually find it in gourmet or specialty food shops. It's produced by Magic Seasoning Blends, New Orleans, (504) 731-3590. The higher the quality of your crabmeat, the better this chowder will taste! We use Phillips crabmeat which is sold refrigerated near the seafood counter at the grocery store.

- Heat olive oil and butter in a large pot over medium heat until butter is melted. Add onions, celery, red pepper and garlic. Cook and stir until vegetables begin to soften, about 5 minutes.

- Stir in potatoes, thyme, tarragon and seafood spice. Mix well. Cook for 1 more minute. Add broth, clam juice, salt and pepper. Bring to a boil. Reduce heat to low and simmer, covered, for about 12 minutes, or until potatoes are tender.

- Add corn and mix well. Whisk together cream and flour in a measuring cup until smooth. Add to pot. Increase heat to medium-high. Cook and stir until mixture comes to a boil and soup thickens. Reduce heat to low and stir in crabmeat. Cook just until crabmeat is heated through. Serve hot.

MAKES 8 SERVINGS

PER SERVING
161 calories, 7.4 g total fat
(3.4 g saturated fat),
9 g protein, 16 g carbohydrate, 2 g fiber,
45 mg cholesterol, 400 mg sodium

> No disease that can be treated by diet should be treated by any other means.
>
> *Maimonides,*
> *Jewish father of medicine*

Grape Expectations

If media reports about the health benefits of red wine are driving you to drink, you should know that not everything about de*wine* is divine. Yes, there's plenty of research praising the nectar of the gods' antioxidant properties. The perceived health benefits revolve around a plant chemical called resveratrol, found in grape skin and seeds. When scientists saw promise for resveratrol in preventing heart disease and cancer in animal studies, Merlot mania was uncorked. Before having grape expectations, don't forget the damage that alcohol and its empty calories can cause. Booze, whether in beer, vodka or wine, raises blood sugar, spurs appetite and slows fat burning. If you're trying to lose fat, better go on a low-cab(ernet) diet! Because alcohol in any form is tough on the liver, and even moderate amounts have been linked to breast and colon cancers, bone loss, weakening of heart muscle and other health problems, medical experts suggest if you sip on Shiraz, make it one drink a day for women and two drinks a day for men, max. Fortunately, there are plenty of other, less-risky ways to give your heart a boost: Eat garlic, fish and olive oil; curb the junk food; quit smoking; hug your kids; pet your dog; stop and smell the roses; be kind to strangers; give to a charity—none of which will leave you with a hangover!

Thai One On

Exotic sweet potato and coconut soup with shrimp

Loaded with shrimp, half-cut veggies and an intoxicating blend of spices, this savory, Thai-inspired soup will have you seeing double helpings!

Gee Honey, you've really come out of your shell tonight!

1 tbsp	butter or olive oil
1 cup	each chopped onions and chopped red bell pepper
¾ cup	chopped celery
2 tsp	minced garlic
4 cups	peeled, cubed sweet potatoes (about 2 large)
1 tbsp	grated gingerroot
¾ tsp	each ground cumin, ground coriander and curry powder
¼ tsp	ground cinnamon
2 cups	reduced-sodium chicken or vegetable broth
1 can	(14 oz/398 mL) light coconut milk
½ tsp	salt
¼ tsp	freshly ground black pepper
3 tbsp	each minced fresh cilantro and minced fresh basil leaves
2 tbsp	light peanut butter
1 tbsp	brown sugar
1 tbsp	freshly squeezed lime juice
1 lb	(454 g) cooked medium shrimp, tails removed (thaw first if using frozen)

MAKES 6 SERVINGS

PER SERVING
249 calories, 9.4 g total fat (5.2 g saturated fat),
19 g protein, 23 g carbohydrate,
3 g fiber, 122 mg cholesterol,
404 mg sodium

- Heat butter in a large pot over medium heat. Add onions, red pepper, celery and garlic. Cook and stir until vegetables begin to soften, about 4 minutes.

- Stir in sweet potatoes, gingerroot, cumin, coriander, curry powder and cinnamon. Cook and stir for 30 more seconds. Add broth, coconut milk, salt and pepper. Bring soup to a boil. Reduce heat to low, cover and simmer for 10 minutes, just until sweet potatoes are tender.

- Carefully transfer half the soup to a blender and purée until smooth. Return puréed soup to pot with remaining soup. Stir in cilantro, basil, peanut butter, brown sugar and lime juice. Mix well. Add shrimp and heat for about 2 more minutes, just until shrimp is hot.

Nutrition Nugget

Eating the "right" fats, like those found in coconuts or avocados, will make you fat just as much as eating money will make you rich!

Taking Platters into Your Own Hands

Dining out again? If restaurants are where you get your daily bread, you might need to pull up a larger chair for your blossoming buns. Did you know that many restaurant entrées have 1,000 to 1,500 calories? And that's not even counting the bread, appetizer, beverage or dessert? Rich, creamy sauces, gratuitous use of refined cooking oil, gargantuan portions and the triple threat of sugar, fat and salt—your adipose cells are salivating just thinking about them! If you're a frequent diner, try sharing your meal, ordering an appetizer as the main course or asking for a doggie bag and keeping half your meal for lunch the next day. And here's our No. 1 waist-saving tip: Once in a while, stay home and cook! That way, you control what goes on your plate and into your body. You'll likely consume far fewer calories and less trans fat, sodium, sugar and oil. Plus, cooking from scratch is fun, fun, fun! (What do you expect cookbook authors to say?)

The Souper Bowl

Hearty, creamy, turkey and vegetable chowder

We interrupt this cookbook to bring you coverage of Chowderbowl XXIV, live from Bowlivia. The crowd favorites—turkey and vegetables—are sure to score extra points with soup fans.

2 tsp	olive oil
8 oz	(227 g) boneless skinless turkey breast, cut into 1-inch cubes
3 oz	(85 g) Canadian bacon, diced
½ cup	chopped onions
1 tsp	minced garlic
3 cups	reduced-sodium chicken broth
2 cups	diced carrots
1 cup	peeled and cubed potatoes
1 tsp	dried thyme
½ tsp	dried rosemary
½ tsp	salt
¼ tsp	freshly ground black pepper
2 cups	broccoli florets
1 can	(14 oz/398 mL) no-salt-added cream-style corn
1 cup	whole-kernel corn
½ cup	light (5%) sour cream

MAKES 4 SERVINGS

PER SERVING
317 calories, 4 g total fat
(0.7 g saturated fat), 27 g protein,
50 g carbohydrate, 4.2 g fiber,
48 mg cholesterol, 540 mg sodium

- Heat olive oil in a large pot over medium-high heat. Add turkey and cook until lightly browned. Add bacon, onions and garlic and cook for 2 more minutes. Add broth, carrots, potatoes, thyme, rosemary, salt and pepper. Bring to a boil. Reduce heat to medium-low, cover and simmer for 8 minutes.

- Stir in broccoli and simmer for 3 more minutes. Add creamed corn and corn kernels. Cook for 2 more minutes, until corn is heated through. Stir in sour cream and serve hot.

Nutrition Nugget

It's about thyme: A teaspoon of thyme has nearly the same amount of antioxidants as a half cup of chopped tomatoes!

The Intensive Carrot Unit

Carrots need a better PR agent! They've been getting a bad rap for their high score on the Glycemic Index and as a result have been snubbed by low-carb fanatics who fear the starchy vegetable will cause crazy blood-sugar spikes, increased hunger and weight gain. Carrots at the root of weight gain? What's up with that, doc? Unless they're chocolate-covered, the chances that carrots will make you fat are pretty slim. Let's set the record straight: Carrots actually have a minimal effect on blood sugar when eaten in normal amounts. When laboratory researchers compare the Glycemic Index of foods, they do so based on portions that deliver 50 grams of carbohydrates. That's a lot! You'd have to eat about one-and-a-half pounds of carrots (roughly 10 medium carrots) to consume that many carbohydrates—an amount even Bugs Bunny would be hard-pressed to chomp down in one sitting. So, put in perspective, nibbling on a carrot or two only has a mild effect on blood sugar. And don't forget that carrots are loaded with vitamins, minerals and antioxidants like beta-carotene that protect against cancer and that promote healthy skin, hair, bones and teeth—plenty of good reasons to start digging carrots!

The Squash Court

Silky butternut squash soup with pears and ginger

When deciding on what to make your family for dinner, the ball's in your court. Why not serve up this spectacular butternut squash soup and score some big points? So healthy and flavorful, it's sure to create a racquet at the dinner table.

2 tsp	olive oil or butter
1 cup	chopped onions
1 tsp	minced garlic
1 tbsp	grated gingerroot
1 tsp	curry powder
½ tsp	ground cumin
4 cups	reduced-sodium chicken or vegetable broth
3 cups	peeled and cubed butternut squash

2 cups	peeled and chopped pears (see tip)
1 cup	peeled and chopped carrots
½ tsp	salt
¼ tsp	freshly ground black pepper (or to taste)
¾ cup	2% evaporated milk or light (5%) cream

MAKES 6 SERVINGS

PER SERVING
142 calories, 3 g total fat
(0.4 g saturated fat), 7 g protein,
23 g carbohydrate, 4.4 g fiber,
13 mg cholesterol,
378 mg sodium

- Heat olive oil in large pot over medium heat. Add onions and garlic. Cook and stir until onions begin to soften, about 3 minutes. Add gingerroot, curry powder and ground cumin. Mix well and cook for 30 more seconds.

- Add broth, squash, pears, carrots, salt and pepper. Bring mixture to a boil. Reduce heat to low and simmer, covered, for 12 to 15 minutes, or until squash and carrots are tender. Stir occasionally.

- Working in two batches, carefully transfer soup to a blender and purée until smooth. Soup will be very thick. Return puréed soup to pot and stir in evaporated milk or cream. Serve hot.

Recipe Tip: You can substitute peeled, chopped apples for pears.

If you get a gift basket from your psychiatrist, chances are it will be shrink-wrapped :)

Chill Out or Fill Out

The car won't start. Bills are piling up. Your boss is a jerk. Your daughter got a tattoo to complement her navel piercing. "Ahhh! Someone pass the cookies!" Wonder why you crave sweets when you're stressed out? Well, when you're under stress, the hormones cortisol and adrenaline rise. These stress hormones take sugar out of your liver and rush it into your blood, making energy readily available for fight or flight. In prehistoric days, Mr. or Mrs. Neanderthal needed that extra burst of energy to fend off hostile beasts or to migrate across rough terrain. Nowadays, most of us experience mental rather than physical stress, but our bodies don't know the difference. Once the stress is gone, our bodies insist on replacing the sugar stolen from our livers. To do that, stress hormones make us hungry, especially for sweets. No wonder "stressed" spelled backwards is "desserts!" Over long periods of time, too much cortisol wreaks havoc on your system and eats away at the muscle you need to burn fat. It also encourages the body to store abdominal fat for easy burning during stressful times. That's why ongoing stress can lead to a flabby abdomen—a flabdomen! Basically, you gotta chill out or you're gonna fill out. Massage, deep breathing, yoga, a hot bath, listening to music and even laughing are effective ways to turn off the cortisol tap.

Chowdown Chickpea Chowda

Hearty chickpea and vegetable chowder

Howdy, pardner! This here soup is dang good grub that would do Granny Clampett proud!

MAKES 6 SERVINGS

PER SERVING
226 calories,
3.7 g total fat
(0.5 g saturated fat),
8 g protein,
40 g carbohydrate,
6.8 g fiber,
0 mg cholesterol,
236 mg sodium

2 tsp	olive oil
1 cup	chopped onions
½ cup	chopped celery
1 tsp	minced garlic
½ tsp	each dried sage and dried thyme
4 cups	reduced-sodium vegetable or chicken broth
1 can	(28 oz/796 mL) no-salt-added chickpeas, drained and rinsed (see tip)
3 cups	peeled, cubed potatoes
1½ cups	chopped carrots
1 tbsp	freshly squeezed lemon juice
1	bay leaf
¼ tsp	each salt and freshly ground black pepper
⅓ cup	chopped fresh parsley

- Heat olive oil in a large pot over medium heat. Add onions, celery and garlic. Cook and stir until vegetables begin to soften, about 5 minutes. Add sage and thyme and cook 1 more minute.

- Add all remaining ingredients except parsley. Bring to a boil. Reduce heat to medium-low. Cover and simmer for 20 minutes.

- Remove bay leaf. Using a potato masher, mash vegetables until soup resembles a coarsely puréed mixture. Stir in parsley and serve hot.

Recipe Tip: Look for larger cans of chickpeas (28 oz/796 mL) in the ethnic food aisle of your grocery store. The regular canned bean section will likely stock only standard cans (19 oz/540 mL).

Nutrition Nugget

Chickpeas, also known as garbanzos, aren't peas at all. They're beans! Call 'em what you will, but they definitely deserve a prominent place in your kitchen. Like all legumes, chickpeas bring to the table both protein and fiber, the superstars of satiety and Nobelly-Prize nominees. Add to that a healthy dose of antioxidants and you have the makings of a marvelous meatless mealtime staple.

> Worries go down better with soup.
> *Jewish proverb*

Dieting is Only Wishful Shrinking

If you want to shed pounds, don't fall victim to the "last supper" syndrome. You know—tomorrow you're "officially" starting that trendy, new diet that's all the rage in Beverly Hills. So today, your final day of food freedom, you devise your own eating strategy—the Beverly Fillbelly Diet—recklessly hoovering down everything you can get your hands on and then some. "Cut me some slack! For the next month, all the foods I love will be off-limits!" And that's precisely why you're doomed. For lots of folks, just the anticipation of going on a diet can trigger drastic overeating, sending them into the vicious, unhealthy cycle of bingeing and crash dieting. Let's face it: Diets stink! They're unrealistic, ineffective and temporary. Depriving yourself of occasional indulgences in the foods you love is not the way to lose pounds and keep them off forever. In restrictive diets, so many tasty foods are taboo, it's only natural that these will become the foods you desperately crave. We're only human, right? So, forget about dieting and try the balanced approach instead: Choose a variety of natural, nutrient-rich foods most of the time, but slip in the occasional treat so you won't feel deprived. And don't forget that healthy foods can also be great-tasting and satisfying. (You're holding the proof!)

Obi Wonton Kenobi

Simple Chinese soup with chicken-filled wontons

What makes our wonton soup outta this world? Why, it's the light-sabery broth, of course. May the forks be with you! (Or, in this case, a spoon might be better.)

Filling

8 oz	(227 g) ground chicken or turkey
¼ cup	minced green onions
2 tsp	reduced-sodium soy sauce
1 tsp	each grated gingerroot, sesame oil and cornstarch
1	egg white
¼ tsp	salt
30	wonton wrappers (see tip)

Broth

6 cups	reduced-sodium chicken broth
¼ cup	chopped green onions
¼ cup	fresh basil leaves, cut into thin strips
1 tbsp	reduced-sodium soy sauce
2 tsp	sesame oil
1 tsp	grated gingerroot

MAKES 6 SERVINGS

PER SERVING
220 calories, 6.6 g total fat
(1.5 g saturated fat), 13 g protein,
27 g carbohydrate, 1 g fiber,
38 mg cholesterol, 632 mg sodium

- Combine all filling ingredients in a medium bowl. Mix well. Working one at a time, place 1 tsp filling in center of wonton wrapper. Fold one side over to enclose filling, making a triangle. Moisten edges and press down to seal. Bring the two points of the base of the triangle around filling, overlap them, moisten and press together. Place filled wonton on a tray and cover with a damp kitchen towel. Repeat with remaining wontons.

- To cook wontons, bring a large pot of water to a boil over high heat. Add wontons. Stir once or twice to prevent wontons from sticking together. Boil for 5 minutes. Remove wontons using a slotted spoon. Drain well.

- To make soup, bring broth to a boil in a medium pot. Add onions, basil, soy sauce, sesame oil and gingerroot. Simmer, uncovered, for 2 minutes.

- To serve soup, place 5 wontons in the bottom of each soup bowl. Ladle hot broth over wontons and serve immediately.

Recipe Tip: Wontons are a Chinese specialty similar to Italian ravioli. The paper-thin dough used to surround the filling comes packaged as wonton wrappers or wonton skins. Look for them in plastic wrap in the produce department of your grocery store. They dry out very quickly, so keep them covered with a damp towel while using. Make sure you don't confuse wonton wrappers with spring roll wrappers!

A Root Worth Taking

Suffering from motion sickness? Next time you're en route, pack some of the "in" root—ginger, that is! Gingerroot, either fresh, preserved or in capsules, can counteract the nausea and vomiting of motion sickness and is as effective as Gravol or Dramamine, but it doesn't make you drowsy like drugs can. Your mom was onto something when she made you drink flat ginger ale for an upset tummy. Ginger helps relieve indigestion, gas pains and stomach cramping by increasing the production of digestive fluids and saliva. And if you've got a bun in the oven, you'll want to know that, according to studies, ginger relieves morning sickness as effectively as meds, without the side effects. According to folk medicine, ginger is also a cure for fever, diarrhea and coughing. In New Guinea, it's considered a contraceptive and in Africa, an aphrodisiac. On Gilligan's Island, Ginger was a castaway and in pop music, an ex-Spice Girl. A root for all reasons, ginger cures what *ales* ya!

Rome on the Range

Roasted tomato and red pepper soup with mini meatballs

Seldom is heard a discouraging word about our tantalizing roasted tomato and meatball soup. There's a little Italy and a lotta flavor packed into this one.

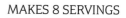

Now that's Italian!

MAKES 8 SERVINGS

PER SERVING
184 calories, 7.8 g total fat
(3.3 g saturated fat), 15 g protein,
16 g carbohydrate, 2.9 g fiber,
64 mg cholesterol,
373 mg sodium

Soup

8	large plum or Roma tomatoes (about 2 lbs/907 g)
2	large red bell peppers, seeded and coarsely chopped
1	large red onion, coarsely chopped
1 tbsp	minced garlic
1 tbsp	olive oil
2 tbsp	each chopped fresh thyme and chopped fresh rosemary, or 2 tsp dried Italian seasoning
2 cups	reduced-sodium beef broth, divided
1 cup	reduced-sodium V8 juice
¼ cup	chopped fresh basil leaves, or 2 tsp dried
1 tbsp	balsamic vinegar
1 tsp	granulated sugar
½ tsp	each salt, freshly ground black pepper and crushed red pepper flakes

Meatballs

12 oz	(340 g) extra-lean ground beef
¼ cup	minced shallots or onions
¼ cup	dry unseasoned bread crumbs
2 tbsp	freshly grated Parmesan cheese
1	egg
½ tsp	dried Italian seasoning
¼ tsp	each salt and freshly ground black pepper

- Preheat oven to 450°F. Coarsely chop tomatoes and combine with red peppers, onion, garlic, olive oil, thyme and rosemary in a very large roasting pan or on a very large rimmed baking sheet. It's best if vegetables are in a single layer.

- Place roasting pan in oven on middle rack and roast vegetables for 15 minutes. Remove vegetables from oven and give them a quick stir. Return pan to oven on middle rack and turn on the broiler. Broil vegetables for 10 minutes.

- Meanwhile, prepare meatballs. Combine all meatball ingredients in a medium bowl and mix well. Using your hands works best! Form 48 mini meatballs using 1 tsp or so of meat mixture per ball. Set aside.

- Remove vegetables from oven. Carefully transfer half the vegetables to a blender or food processor, along with 1 cup beef broth and purée until smooth. Transfer puréed vegetables to a large pot. Chop remaining vegetables into bite-sized pieces (if any tomato or pepper skins come loose, discard them) and add to pot, along with remaining beef broth, V8 juice, basil, balsamic vinegar, sugar, salt, black pepper and crushed red pepper flakes. Bring soup to a boil. Add meatballs. Reduce heat to low, cover and simmer for 5 to 6 minutes, until meatballs are cooked through. Taste soup and add more salt and pepper, if desired.

Recipe Tips Try to use fresh herbs for this recipe if you can—they make a big difference to the flavor of the soup. Also, if you don't feel like making your own meatballs, buy some premade, frozen, lean meatballs, cook them according to package directions, then stir them into the soup before serving. They'll be a bit bigger than our homemade meatballs, so use only about 24 of them. This soup looks nice and tastes great when you sprinkle some freshly grated Parmesan cheese on top of individual servings.

Salmon and Garfunkel

Creamy salmon and corn chowder with dill

Are you going to Scarborough Fair? Don't pick up parsley, sage or rosemary—just thyme (plus tarragon, dill and a bottle of wine!). Then you might want to invite Cecilia and Mrs. Robinson over to taste your dillicious salmon chowder. You'll all be feelin' groovy!

1 tbsp	olive oil or butter
1 cup	sliced leeks (white part only) or chopped onions
¾ cup	each chopped celery and diced red bell pepper
1 tsp	minced garlic
1 tsp	each dried thyme and dried tarragon
3 tbsp	all-purpose flour
3 cups	reduced-sodium chicken broth
1 can	(14 oz/398 mL) no-salt-added cream-style corn
½ cup	light (5%) cream
12 oz	(340 g) boneless skinless salmon fillet, cut into bite-sized pieces
½ tsp	each salt and freshly ground black pepper
2 tbsp	minced fresh dill
1 tbsp	freshly squeezed lemon juice
1 tsp	each grated lemon zest and Dijon mustard

- Heat olive oil in a large pot over medium heat. Add leeks, celery, red pepper and garlic. Cook and stir until vegetables begin to soften, about 3 minutes.

- Add thyme and tarragon. Cook and stir for 30 more seconds. Add flour and mix well, until vegetables are completely coated. Add chicken broth. Bring mixture to a boil, stirring constantly. Soup will thicken slightly. Stir in corn and cream. Reduce heat to medium-low and stir in salmon, salt and pepper. Cover and simmer until salmon is cooked through, about 5 to 6 minutes, depending on size of salmon pieces.

- Remove soup from heat and stir in dill, lemon juice, lemon zest and mustard. Serve immediately.

MAKES 6 SERVINGS

PER SERVING
206 calories, 7.6 g total fat (1.6 g saturated fat), 16 g protein, 20 g carbohydrate, 1.9 g fiber, 40 mg cholesterol, 427 mg sodium

FOOD BITE

A silly *souper*stition? In the court of French King Louis XI, ladies of the upper class dined primarily on soup, believing that excess chewing would cause them to develop premature wrinkles. This practice, of course, led to the creation of the well-known soup opera, *The Bowled and the Beautiful*.

> Fish, to taste right, must swim three times—in water, in butter and in wine.
>
> *Polish proverb*

Keep Them Guessing with Oil of EFA

Did you know that fish oil each day keeps the dermatologist away? Essential Fatty Acids (or EFAs, for short) found in fish promote beautiful, youthful, glowing skin. It's true! You don't need the Ponds, just the fish! EFAs help fight inflammation in the body and, according to the latest research, inflammation is at the root of wrinkles and loss of elasticity in aging skin. One of the worst dietary villains that causes this inflammation? Sugar! So, instead of slathering on the Wrinkle Obliterating Muck Mask or becoming a regular Botox-party crasher, treat your body's cells to nutrients that'll help strengthen them, repair damage and create a more youthful you from the inside out. If you care about your face (and let's face it, who doesn't?), get your wrinkle-fighting, age-defying EFAs from fish or fish oils, krill oil, flaxseed, nuts, seeds and green, leafy vegetables. Why raise eyebrows with a visit to a plastic surgeon when you can get a natural face-lift at home?

The Chicken Soup that Flu the Coop

Comforting, old-fashioned chicken and vegetable soup

When you're suffering from a nasty cold or flu, this tasty hot soup is the best cure in the food doctor's book!

TAKE TWO BOWLFULS AND CALL ME IN THE MORNING.

2 tsp	olive oil
1 cup	each chopped onions, chopped celery and chopped carrots
1 tsp	minced garlic
1½ tsp	dried thyme
1 tsp	dried marjoram
6 cups	reduced-sodium chicken broth
2	plum tomatoes, chopped
¼ cup	chopped celery leaves
2	bay leaves
½ tsp	each salt and freshly ground black pepper
6	bone-in chicken thighs, skin removed (about 1½ lbs/680 g)

MAKES 6 SERVINGS

PER SERVING
153 calories, 6.8 g total fat (1.7 g saturated fat), 14 g protein, 9 g carbohydrate, 2 g fiber, 47 mg cholesterol, 367 mg sodium

- Heat olive oil in a large pot over medium-high heat. Add onions, celery, carrots and garlic. Cook and stir until vegetables begin to soften, about 5 minutes. Stir in thyme and marjoram and cook 30 more seconds. Add broth, tomatoes, celery leaves, bay leaves, salt and pepper. Bring soup to a boil. Add whole chicken thighs. Reduce heat to low and simmer, covered, for 30 minutes.

- Carefully remove chicken thighs from pot. When cool enough to handle, cut meat from bone and chop into bite-sized pieces. Discard bones and return meat to pot. Remove bay leaves. Serve hot.

The Farm Pharm

Good ol' Hippocrates sure knew what he was talking about when he said, "Let food be your medicine and medicine be your food." There are nutrients in certain foods that, when consumed regularly and in proper amounts, allow the body to be its own best pharmacy, protecting and healing itself. In fact, virtually all foods have "drug-like" effects. Just think about the high you get from eating a big slab of chocolate cake! Some foods help improve your health while others destroy it. For instance, when you eat bad fats from a greasy burger and fries, many of your body's cells will falter for hours. Eat too much sugar and you throw your hormones out of whack and weaken your immune system. We can either overdose on the wrong kinds of food like these, or we can buy into a healthy prescription of foods that contain the nutrients our bodies need to flourish. The healthiest products on the market are those packaged and delivered by the world's premier food manufacturer—Mother Nature! Her ideal prescription includes real, natural, whole foods—some cooked, some raw, seasonal, local and organic, if possible. Follow Ma's lead and you'll find the formula for vibrant health at the farm, not the pharmacy.

Did you hear about the farmer who planted bulbs in his garden so it would get more light? :)

FOOD BITE

There's much achoo about black pepper! Because pepper is antifungal, the Egyptians used it for mummification, as evidenced by the discovery of black pepper in the nostrils and abdomen of Ramses the Great. Today, pepper's a hot commodity in weight-loss supplements because it stimulates metabolism and energizes the body. Now that's nothing to sneeze at!

Melancauli Baby

Curried cauliflower soup with Swiss cheese and wild rice

When you're feeling down in the dumps, raise your spirits with this outstanding combination of ingredients that's so tasty, it'll bring tears of joy to your eyes!

You'll cry out for more!

MAKES 8 SERVINGS

PER SERVING
142 calories,
3.9 g total fat
(1.8 g saturated fat),
8 g protein,
20 g carbohydrate,
3 g fiber,
16 mg cholesterol,
308 mg sodium

1 tbsp	butter or olive oil
2 cups	thinly sliced leeks (about 2 large)
2 tsp	minced garlic
4 cups	small cauliflower florets
1½ cups	peeled, cubed sweet potato
1½ tsp	curry powder
1 tsp	ground cumin
4 cups	reduced-sodium chicken or vegetable broth
½ tsp	salt
¼ tsp	freshly ground black pepper
1 cup	cooked brown and wild rice blend (see tip)
1 cup	2% evaporated milk
½ cup	packed shredded light Swiss cheese (2 oz/57 g)

- Heat butter in a large pot over medium heat. Add leeks and garlic. Cook and stir until leeks begin to soften, about 3 minutes.

- Stir in cauliflower, sweet potato, curry and cumin. Cook and stir for 1 more minute. Add broth, salt and pepper. Bring mixture to a boil. Reduce heat to low, cover and simmer for 12 to 15 minutes, until vegetables are tender.

- Carefully transfer half the soup to a blender and purée until smooth. Return puréed soup to pot with remaining soup and mix well. Stir in cooked rice, milk and Swiss cheese. Heat soup for 1 more minute until cheese melts. Serve hot.

Recipe Tips

Rather than using plain ol' (boring!) long-grain white rice in this recipe, you can bump up its nutritional value and flavor by using an interesting variety of brown and wild rices. Look for a blend made up of brown, wild and red rices if you can find it. It looks and tastes great. Or, you can make your own blend by combining brown basmati rice with wild rice in a 2:1 ratio, respectively. Make this soup a complete meal by stirring in some chopped, cooked chicken breast or turkey breast in the final step. Like most soups, this one tastes even better the next day!

Nutrition Nugget
Sweet potatoes may help you look younger! They contain glutathione, a super antioxidant that helps your body manufacture human growth hormone.

Shanks for the Memories

Old-fashioned, smoky ham and split pea soup with lentils

And you thought slicing was a bad thing! Putter around in the kitchen, slicing, dicing and spicing, and you'll end up with a memorable soup that's on par with the best.

Hope you like it!

MAKES 8 SERVINGS

PER SERVING
192 calories,
4 g total fat
(1 g saturated fat),
17 g protein,
22 g carbohydrate,
7.8 g fiber,
30 mg cholesterol,
394 mg sodium

2 tsp	olive oil
1½ cups	chopped onions
1 cup	each chopped celery and chopped carrots
2 tsp	minced garlic
1 tbsp	minced fresh thyme, or 1 tsp dried
½ tsp	dried oregano
7 cups	reduced-sodium chicken broth
1	whole meaty smoked ham shank or ham hock (about 2 lbs/907 g)
1 cup	dry lentils, rinsed
1 cup	dry green split peas, rinsed
2	bay leaves
½ tsp	freshly ground black pepper
¼ cup	minced fresh parsley
1 tbsp	balsamic vinegar

Salt to taste

- Heat olive oil in a large pot over medium heat. Add onions, celery, carrots and garlic. Cook and stir until vegetables begin to soften, about 6 minutes. Add thyme and oregano and cook 1 more minute.

- And remaining ingredients, except parsley, vinegar and salt. Bring soup to a boil. Reduce heat to low. Cover and simmer for 1 hour.

- Remove ham shank from soup. Carefully transfer half the soup to a blender or food processor and purée. Return to pot with remaining soup. Cover to keep hot. Cut meat from ham shank (this part's a little fussy) and return meat to pot. Discard bone. Stir in parsley and vinegar. Taste soup and add more pepper and a bit of salt, if desired.

Trivial Tidbit

Attention all bridegrooms! An ancient Palestinian superstition says that a clove of garlic worn in a groom's buttonhole will ensure a successful wedding night. Why buy cologne when you've got Bold Spice?

Put a Little Love in Your Liver

With more than 500 jobs on its to-do list, the liver is the most overworked and underappreciated organ in the body. Like Rodney Dangerfield, it gets no respect. And that's a shame! While you kick back with a six-pack, your liver is busy processing an astounding 182 pints of blood every hour, filtering toxins, producing bile to break down fats and disposing of excess hormones and cholesterol. But your liver isn't bulletproof. Pummel it each day with processed and fried foods, caffeine, sugar, alcohol, artificial sweeteners and pharmaceutical drugs, and the poor thing becomes congested, fatty and generally dis-organ-ized. A sluggish liver will drop the ball on some of its jobs, one of them being fat metabolism. Translation: A fatty liver means a fatty you! In addition, excess hormones aren't properly flushed from the body, leading to a whole slew of complications, including the protruding, rock-hard, about-to-give-birth-to-twins type of beer gut in men. In women, a bogged-down liver can't clear away excess estrogen. That's called "estrogen dominance," a condition that can trigger PMS symptoms, fibroids and even breast cancer. If you want to be a long liver, better treat yours with respect! Shower it with things it loves: lemons, onion, garlic, turmeric, eggs, beets, leafy greens, artichokes, cruciferous veggies like broccoli and cauliflower, and herbs like milk thistle and dandelion.

Mulligatawnski

Southern Indian soup with curried chicken, apples and quinoa

Get curried away with our scrumptious version of mulligatawny soup.

1 tbsp	butter or olive oil	1 can	(19 oz/540 mL) no-salt-added diced tomatoes, drained
1 cup	each chopped celery, chopped onions and chopped carrots	½ cup	uncooked quinoa or quick-cooking brown rice (not instant)
1 tsp	minced garlic	½ tsp	each salt and freshly ground black pepper
1 lb	(454 g) boneless skinless chicken breast, cubed	1	large apple, peeled and chopped
1 tbsp	grated gingerroot	¾ cup	light coconut milk
2 tsp	curry powder	3 tbsp	minced fresh cilantro or parsley
1 tsp	chili powder		
½ tsp	ground cumin		
3	whole cloves		
4 cups	reduced-sodium chicken broth		

- Melt butter in a large pot over medium heat. Add celery, onions, carrots and garlic. Cook and stir for 3 to 4 minutes, until vegetables begin to soften.

- Add chicken. Cook until chicken is no longer pink. Add gingerroot, curry powder, chili powder, cumin and cloves. Cook and stir for 1 more minute. Add broth, tomatoes, quinoa, salt and pepper. Bring to a boil. Reduce heat to medium-low. Cover and simmer for 15 minutes.

- Add apple. Simmer for 5 more minutes, or until apple is tender but not mushy. Stir in coconut milk and cilantro. Heat for 1 more minute. Serve hot.

MAKES 6 SERVINGS

PER SERVING
229 calories, 6.5 g total fat
(2.2 g saturated fat), 21 g protein,
22 g carbohydrate, 4 g fiber,
47 mg cholesterol, 356 mg sodium

Nutrition Nugget

Make a better butter: By combining butter with olive oil, you can make butter more spreadable (like margarine) and reduce the saturated fat content slightly while adding the heart-healthy benefits of olive oil's monounsaturated fat. In a mixing bowl, combine ½ cup olive oil with 1 cup butter. Beat with a hand mixer until thoroughly blended. Place in an airtight container and refrigerate. Use this better butter for light sautéing and spread it on toast, too.

Butter Be Good To Me

A hundred years ago, when butter (and eggs) were staples in man's diet, heart disease was rare. Between 1930 and 1960, heart disease rose to become North America's No. 1 killer. Coincidentally, during that same period, butter consumption plummeted as people were advised to switch to man-made, fabricated fats like margarine and refined, overly processed polyunsaturated oils. Too bad, because butter's actually a good fat. It contains the antioxidant vitamins A and E, and it also contains lecithin, a substance that helps keep cholesterol moving along in the bloodstream. Butter's fat content and nutrients provide a feeling of satiety when you eat it and it keeps your blood-sugar levels steady. It's still a very concentrated source of calories, though, so don't go slathering it on everything you eat. Moderation is the key to avoiding a large *dairy*erre!

LADLE GAGA

We're Yammin'

Roasted sweet potato soup with orange and ginger

If you make this ever-so-yammy soup recipe, it'll be a huge hit with the entire yamily.

6 cups	peeled, cubed yams or sweet potatoes (about 3 large)
1½ cups	coarsely chopped onions
1 tbsp	olive oil
1 tsp	minced garlic
5 cups	reduced-sodium vegetable or chicken broth
1 tbsp	each grated orange zest and gingerroot
1	whole clove
½ tsp	each ground cumin and salt
¼ tsp	freshly ground black pepper
6 tbsp	light (5%) sour cream

Minced fresh cilantro for garnish (optional)

- Spray a shallow roasting pan with cooking spray. Add yams, onions, olive oil and garlic. Stir well. Roast, uncovered, at 425°F for 25 minutes. Stir once, halfway through cooking time.

- Transfer mixture to a large pot. Add broth, orange zest, gingerroot, clove, cumin, salt and pepper. Bring to a boil. Reduce heat to medium-low and simmer, covered, for 10 minutes.

- Working in batches, carefully transfer soup to a blender or food processor and purée until smooth. Serve hot with a swirl of sour cream in the center. Garnish with fresh cilantro, if desired.

MAKES 6 SERVINGS

PER SERVING
209 calories, 3.7 g total fat
(0.2 g saturated fat), 6 g protein,
39 g carbohydrate, 4.9 g fiber,
1 mg cholesterol, 292 mg sodium

What's the difference between a potato farmer and a baseball fan? One yanks the roots and the other roots for the Yanks :)

Dessert for Breakfast

Looking for a "cool" new way to enjoy your veggies? How about on ice in your morning smoothie? Yes, we're serious, and yes, this is seriously delicious! Our best buddy, Leanne, recently showed us how she uses leftover boiled or roasted squash and sweet potatoes in her morning protein shake for a fiber and antioxidant infusion. At first, we rolled our eyes with skepticism. "That sounds awful!" Well, Leanne sure showed us! Here's her "secret," scrumptious recipe: Add about a ½ cup cooked sweet potatoes or squash (fiber-filled, antioxidant superheroes) to any vanilla protein powder, toss in half a frozen banana, a spoonful of flaxseed or chia seeds, 1 cup cold water or almond milk and some ice. Whirl away, then top it all off with a sprinkle of cinnamon or nutmeg and voilà! Your breakfast will taste like frozen pumpkin pie!

Beef Noodle Doodle

Asian beef-noodle soup with spinach, mint and basil

We doodled over noodles, scribbling while nibbling, to get this souper-duper recipe just right. Finding a better-tasting Asian beef soup would be like searching for a noodle in a haystack!

4 oz	(113 g) uncooked soba noodles, whole wheat spaghetti or rice vermicelli
6 cups	reduced-sodium beef broth
3 tbsp	hoisin sauce (see tip)
1 tbsp	each reduced-sodium soy sauce, grated gingerroot, sesame oil and freshly squeezed lime juice
12 oz	(340 g) beef tenderloin, thinly sliced (see tip)
3 cups	chopped fresh spinach leaves or thinly sliced bok choy
⅓ cup	chopped green onions
¼ cup	each chopped fresh mint leaves and chopped fresh basil leaves

Salt and freshly ground black pepper to taste
1 cup   bean sprouts

MAKES 6 SERVINGS

PER SERVING
225 calories, 6.7 g total fat (1.8 g saturated fat),
18 g protein, 25 g carbohydrate, 2.2 g fiber,
38 mg cholesterol, 506 mg sodium

- Cook noodles according to package directions. Drain well, rinse with cold water and drain again. Set aside until soup is ready to serve.

- In a large pot, combine beef broth, hoisin sauce, soy sauce, gingerroot, sesame oil and lime juice. Bring to a boil. Reduce heat to low and simmer for 3 minutes.

- Add beef, spinach, green onions, mint and basil. Simmer for 5 more minutes, just until beef is cooked through. Taste soup and add salt and pepper, if desired.

- To serve soup, place some cooked noodles in the bottom of a soup bowl. (You can chop the noodles into shorter pieces if you prefer.) Top with a few bean sprouts and ladle hot soup over top. Serve immediately.

Recipe Tips Hoisin sauce, a sweet and spicy Chinese sauce made from soybeans, garlic, chili peppers and various spices, can be found near the soy sauce in the Asian food aisle of your grocery store. That's also where you'll find soba noodles—Japanese buckwheat noodles that resemble spaghetti. For a more economical soup, substitute flank steak for beef tenderloin. (By the way, it's easier to slice beef thinly if it's partially frozen.)

Friend or Foe?

When it comes to maintaining a healthy lifestyle, the gang you hang with may not be helping your cause, especially if all of your social activities revolve around food. Instead of meeting for chicken wings and beer, plan gatherings around enjoyable activities that don't involve food but do involve movement. You can still gab and burn flab while playing tennis, golf or softball, or hiking, biking or Rollerblading. Altering an unhealthy lifestyle begs for encouragement and support, and surrounding yourself with like-minded pals can end up saving you cals!

Nutrition Nugget

It's hard to decide what we like more about herbs—their potent flavor or potent antioxidant properties. Take basil, for example. Eat it at dinnertime and you just might remember where you left the keys to the car you can't find in the airport parking lot! That's because its volatile oils stimulate the area of the brain that controls short-term memory. Basil also contains oils that prevent bacterial growth, and a specific one called eugenol eases inflammation in a similar way to aspirin and ibuprofen. We love basil! In fact, Janet once dated a guy by that name, but he dumped her for Rosemary a long thyme ago.

Chowdy Doody

Smoky roasted chicken and corn chowder

It's Chowdy Doody time! It's Chowdy Doody time! This creamy, dreamy chicken soup is sure to satisfy everyone in your peanut gallery.

4 slices	reduced-sodium bacon, chopped
1 cup	diced onions
½ cup	each diced celery and diced red bell pepper
2 tsp	minced garlic
1½ tbsp	minced fresh thyme, or 1 tsp dried
2 tbsp	all-purpose flour
1½ cups	reduced-sodium chicken broth
1 can	(14 oz/370 mL) 2% evaporated milk
1 can	(19 oz/540 mL) no-salt-added diced tomatoes, well drained (see tip)
1 can	(14 oz/398 mL) no-salt-added cream-style corn
2 cups	chopped roasted chicken breast (see tip)
1 tbsp	hickory-flavored barbecue sauce
½ tsp	freshly ground black pepper
¼ tsp	salt (or to taste)

- Cook chopped bacon in a large, non-stick pot over medium-high heat until lightly browned but not crisp. Stir in onions, celery, red pepper and garlic. Cook and stir until vegetables begin to soften, about 5 minutes.

- Add thyme and flour. Mix well. Stir in broth and evaporated milk. Bring mixture to a gentle boil and stir continuously until soup thickens slightly.

- Reduce heat to medium-low. Stir in remaining ingredients. Cover and let simmer for 10 minutes, stirring occasionally. Serve hot.

MAKES 6 SERVINGS

PER SERVING
272 calories,
7.2 g total fat
(2.6 g saturated fat),
24 g protein,
29 g carbohydrate,
2.6 g fiber,
53 mg cholesterol,
484 mg sodium

Recipe Tips

To drain tomatoes, empty the canned tomatoes into a sieve and press down on them to remove as much liquid as possible. You want the chunks of tomato, but not their juice, which would make this soup a little bitter. To make this soup a snap to prepare, buy a rotisserie chicken at the take-out counter of your grocery store. Remove the skin and use the breast meat for this recipe (it's the perfect amount!). Save the legs for tomorrow's lunch.

The Crying Game

Though onions may bring tears to your eyes, their aromatic flavor and cornucopia of health benefits are well worth the waterworks. The compound that causes eyes to burn is a phytonutrient known as allyl sulfate. It's produced when you slice an onion and rupture its cell, releasing sulfur compounds. Interestingly, this sulfur reaction is not only the culprit behind the pungent aroma and eye irritation, but it's also responsible for increasing an onion's health-promoting properties. That's right—what makes you cry will also make you healthy! In fact, that's why researchers now suggest slicing and dicing an onion and letting it "stand" for 10 minutes before cooking to help you max out on the good stuff. But if dinner guests are at the door and you'd rather not greet them with mascara dripping down your face, try one of the following tear-prevention tricks: (1) Chill the onions for an hour to reduce the effect; (2) Wait as long as possible to trim the root end where the tear-producing fumes are concentrated; (3) Put a slice of bread or a metal spoon in your mouth while cutting to neutralize the compounds; (4) Go to cooking school! Greta insists that the more often you chop onions, the more your eyes adapt to the irritating fumes. Or, follow Janet's lead and wear a scuba mask. Really!

Bean Me Up, Scotty

Spicy, high-fiber black bean soup with a sour cream swirl

Captain's log: It's the most enterprising combination of ingredients on the planet.
Soup that boldly goes where no soup has gone before.

2 tsp	olive oil
1 cup	each chopped onions, chopped red bell pepper and chopped carrots
1 tsp	minced garlic
1	jalapeño pepper, seeded and minced
3 cups	reduced-sodium beef or vegetable broth
1 cup	no-salt-added tomato sauce
2 cans	(19 oz/540 mL each) no-salt-added black beans, drained and rinsed
2 tbsp	minced fresh cilantro
1 tbsp	each freshly squeezed lemon juice and brown sugar
2 tsp	dried oregano
1 tsp	each chili powder, ground cumin and Worcestershire sauce
½ tsp	each dried thyme and salt
¼ tsp	freshly ground black pepper
6 tbsp	light (5%) sour cream

Minced fresh cilantro for garnish (optional)

MAKES 6 SERVINGS

PER SERVING
243 calories,
4.7 g total fat
(1 g saturated fat),
11 g protein, 39 g carbohydrate,
11 g fiber, 5 mg cholesterol,
372 mg sodium

- Heat olive oil in a large pot over medium heat. Add onions, red pepper, carrots, garlic and jalapeño. Cook and stir for 5 minutes, until vegetables begin to soften. Add all remaining ingredients, except sour cream. Bring to a boil. Reduce heat to medium-low and simmer, covered, for 10 minutes.

- Working in batches, carefully transfer soup to a blender or food processor and purée until desired consistency is reached. Return soup to pot. To serve, top each bowl of soup with 1 tbsp sour cream. Garnish with minced cilantro, if desired.

> For this is every cook's opinion
> No savoury dish without an onion
> But lest your kissing should be spoiled
> Your onions must be thoroughly boiled.
> *Jonathan Swift*

Gone with the Wind

All the fuss over fiber's role in weight loss is NOT a bunch of hot air! A high-fiber diet not only helps ward off cancer, diabetes and heart disease, but is also a fantastic fat fighter. Studies show that if you give people virtually the same diet—same calories, similar foods—except that one diet is high in fiber (for example, whole-grain bread versus white bread) and the other is low in fiber, those on the high-fiber diet will lose more weight. No wonder so many nutrition experts consider fiber THE ticket to weight control. How does fiber work its magic? Well, it's like a natural appetite suppressant. Besides keeping you feeling fuller longer on fewer calories, fiber slows the entry of sugar into the bloodstream, minimizing the highs and lows that make you crave sweets. Lower blood sugar means you'll also have lower insulin levels, and that means you're likely to burn fat rather than store it. Like a personal scouring pad for internal use only, fiber (or "roughage," as Grandma called it) mops up suspicious, disease-promoting substances so they don't spend time loitering in your system. And while it's quickly transporting wastes out of your body, fiber also takes some unabsorbed fat (and calories) along for the ride. So, if you eat your beans, fat will be gone with the wind!

It's Only Brocc 'n' Bowl

Creamy broccoli and cheddar soup

But I like it. Like it. Yes I do! Hard to believe that a broccoli and cheese soup so creamy and delicious isn't rollin' in fat.

MAKES 6 SERVINGS

PER SERVING
181 calories,
8.9 g total fat
(4.4 g saturated fat),
10 g protein,
16 g carbohydrate,
2.6 g fiber,
27 mg cholesterol,
417 mg sodium

2 tsp	olive oil
1 cup	chopped onions
½ cup	chopped celery
1 tsp	minced garlic
½ tsp	each dried thyme, dried tarragon and celery seed
2½ cups	reduced-sodium chicken or vegetable broth
1 cup	peeled and diced potatoes
3 cups	small broccoli florets
1 cup	light (5%) cream
2 tbsp	all-purpose flour
¾ cup	packed shredded light old (sharp) cheddar cheese (3 oz/85 g)
¼ cup	freshly grated Parmesan cheese
½ tsp	freshly ground black pepper

Hot pepper sauce (optional) and salt to taste

- Heat olive oil in a large pot over medium heat. Add onions, celery and garlic. Cook and stir until vegetables begin to soften, about 5 minutes. Add thyme, tarragon and celery seed. Cook 30 more seconds. Add broth and potatoes. Bring to a boil. Reduce heat to medium-low. Cover and simmer for 5 minutes. Add broccoli and simmer 5 to 7 more minutes, until broccoli and potatoes are tender.

- Carefully transfer soup to a blender or food processor. Pulse on and off until soup is coarsely puréed (still slightly chunky). Return puréed soup to pot over low heat. Whisk together cream and flour until smooth. Add to soup. Increase heat to medium and cook until mixture is bubbly and has thickened, stirring constantly. Add both cheeses and pepper. Heat until cheeses are melted. Add a few shakes of hot pepper sauce (if desired) and a pinch of salt, if necessary.

Nutrition Nugget

If broccoli was sold at the drugstore, you'd probably need a prescription—it's *that* health-changing! Loaded with beneficial plant chemicals that sweep up cancer-causing free radicals, this super veggie may also ease arthritis, prevent strokes, lower blood pressure, fight cataracts, build bone and prevent diabetes. Oh, and don't forget the leaves and stalks! Most people discard them, but they're packed with nutrients. Simply peel the stalks before cooking.

The Contilentil Divide
Spicy curried vegetable soup with lentils

We raided the spice racks of several continents to create this souperbly flavored, high-fiber veggie and lentil soup.

IT'S OUTTA THIS WORLD!

1 tbsp	olive oil
1½ cups	chopped onions
1 cup	chopped celery
2 tsp	minced garlic
2 cups	small cauliflower florets
1 cup	diced carrots
1 tbsp	grated gingerroot
2 tsp	curry powder
1 tsp	each ground cumin, ground coriander and chili powder
¼ tsp	ground cinnamon
3 cups	reduced-sodium vegetable broth
1 can	(19 oz/540 mL) no-salt-added diced tomatoes, undrained
1 tbsp	brown sugar
¼ tsp	salt
1 can	(19 oz/540 mL) no-salt-added lentils, drained and rinsed
½ cup	light coconut milk
2 tbsp	minced fresh cilantro

MAKES 6 SERVINGS

PER SERVING
190 calories, 4 g total fat (1.4 g saturated fat), 9 g protein, 30 g carbohydrate, 11 g fiber, 0 mg cholesterol, 445 mg sodium

- Heat olive oil in a large pot over medium heat. Add onions, celery and garlic. Cook and stir until vegetables begin to soften, about 3 to 4 minutes. Add cauliflower, carrots, gingerroot, curry powder, cumin, coriander, chili powder and cinnamon. Stir until vegetables are coated with spices and cook 1 more minute.

- Add broth, tomatoes with liquid, brown sugar and salt. Bring soup to a boil. Reduce heat to low and simmer, covered, for 15 minutes. Add lentils and simmer for 5 more minutes. Remove from heat.

- Carefully transfer half the soup to a blender and purée until smooth. Return puréed soup to pot with remaining soup. Add coconut milk and cilantro and mix well. Taste soup and season with salt and pepper, if desired. Serve hot.

When a clock is hungry, does it go back four seconds? :)

FOOD BITE
Why would anyone prefer an apple with a worm in it to one without? The presence of a worm ensures the absence of pesticides.

Garlic: Chop to It!

A culinary sidekick with serious health benefits, garlic (also called "the stinking rose") deserves a regular invitation to your dinner table. Garlic contains allicin, a potent sulfur-based compound responsible not only for the funky odor, but also for protecting us from cancer and heart disease. But allicin only works its magic after garlic's been minced, chopped or crushed. It takes some time for this process to occur, so after you've minced your garlic, let it sit for five to 10 minutes to allow the health-promoting allicin to form. If you jump the gun and heat garlic without waiting (shame on you!), you'll deactivate the enzyme that makes the magic happen, thwarting garlic's cancer-protective properties. Since research confirms the validity of this practice (we're not just making this stuff up, you know!), you'd better set a timer while you stop and smell the stinking roses!

Chicken Soup for the Bowl

Asian chicken soup with coconut and coriander

Fill up your bowl and warm up your soul with a chicken soup that's even better than Mom's. Far East ingredients give it a far-out flavor.

2 lbs	(907 g) skinless bone-in chicken thighs (about 8 large pieces)
6 cups	reduced-sodium chicken broth
3 stalks	lemongrass, cut into 1-inch pieces (see tip)
1 tbsp	grated gingerroot
10	whole black peppercorns
½ tsp	each ground coriander and crushed red pepper flakes
2 cups	thinly sliced shiitake mushrooms
1 can	(14 oz/398 mL) light coconut milk
¼ cup	chopped green onions
1 tsp	granulated sugar
2 tbsp	minced fresh cilantro
1 tbsp	freshly squeezed lime juice
2 cups	cooked basmati or jasmine rice

MAKES 6 SERVINGS

PER SERVING

270 calories, 8.9 g total fat (4.6 g saturated fat), 26 g protein, 21 g carbohydrate, 0.7 g fiber, 98 mg cholesterol, 204 mg sodium

- In a large pot, combine chicken pieces, broth, lemongrass, gingerroot, peppercorns, coriander and crushed red pepper flakes. Bring to a boil. Reduce heat and simmer, partially covered, for 30 minutes. Skim off any foam.

- Remove chicken pieces. When cool enough to handle, cut chicken off bones and set aside. Discard bones.

- Using a mesh strainer, strain the broth and discard the solids. Return broth to soup pot and stir in cooked chicken, mushrooms, coconut milk, green onions and sugar. Cook over medium heat until mushrooms are tender, about 10 minutes. Stir in cilantro and lime juice. Place some cooked rice in each serving bowl. Pour hot soup over top. Serve immediately.

Choose your words with taste. You may have to eat them later.

A Fat That Can Make You Thin

Coconut has made a comeback! Once shunned for its high saturated fat content, researchers have cracked coconut's case wide open, discovering it can actually help you lose weight! Coconut is thermogenic, which means it raises your body's temperature and helps you burn more calories. In fact, people who have low thyroid function (a problem commonly found in women) and have trouble losing weight have noticed great improvement when they add coconut to their diets. Compared to vegetable oils, which the body readily stores as fat, coconut oil is mostly burned and used for energy by the liver. Plus, it's the world's only low-calorie fat! It has 6.8 calories per gram compared to 9 calories per gram for other fats. Studies have shown that when people used coconut oil (a medium-chain fat) in place of vegetable, corn, soy or canola oils (long-chain fats) they lost as much as 36 pounds in a year, even when they had changed nothing else in their diets. Lose weight without trying? That's nutty! As if the weight-loss potential wasn't enough, coconut oil appears to be a great wrinkle preventer, too! It's been an anti-aging, beauty secret in the tropics for years, even reducing the appearance of rashes, scars and warts. Coconut is also antifungal, antibacterial and antiviral, protecting us from the common cold, candida and even parasites. Nuttin' but good!

Recipe Tip

Lemongrass is an herb that grows in slender green stalks that look a bit like woody leeks. It's what gives a lemony flavor and aroma to southeast Asian dishes. Only the bottom four to six inches of the stalk are used in cooking. Many supermarkets carry lemongrass in the produce section, or look for it in Asian markets. In a pinch, substitute the grated zest of one lemon for the lemongrass in this recipe.

Give Peas a Chance

Velvety smooth, minted pea soup that's very high in fiber

When two peas in a pot are united with a handful of other luscious goodies, the result is a silky smooth soup that lives in perfect harmony with your taste buds.

2 tsp	olive oil
1 cup	chopped onions
2 tsp	minced garlic
5 cups	reduced-sodium vegetable or chicken broth
1½ cups	chopped carrots
1½ cups	dried green split peas (see tip)
1 cup	peeled, cubed potatoes
½ cup	chopped fresh mint leaves
1 tbsp	grated gingerroot
½ tsp	dried sage
¼ tsp	each salt and freshly ground black pepper
2 cups	shredded romaine lettuce
1 cup	frozen green peas
½ cup	2% evaporated milk or light (5%) cream

- Heat olive oil in large pot over medium heat. Add onions and garlic. Cook and stir for 3 minutes, until onions begin to soften. Add broth, carrots, split peas, potatoes, mint, gingerroot, sage, salt and pepper. Bring to a boil. Reduce heat to medium-low. Cover and simmer for 30 minutes.

- Add lettuce and frozen peas. Simmer for 5 more minutes, until lettuce is wilted and peas are heated through. Yeah, this seems kinda weird, but stick with us!

- Working in batches, carefully transfer mixture to a blender or food processor. Purée until smooth. Return soup to pot. Stir in evaporated milk and serve immediately.

Recipe Tip: Split peas are a variety of yellow or green pea grown specifically for drying. Unlike whole dried peas, they don't require soaking before cooking. You'd be doing your body a favor by incorporating these tiny health nuggets into your diet. Just 1 cup of cooked split peas has a whopping 16 grams of fiber and less than 1 gram of fat!

MAKES 6 SERVINGS

PER SERVING

274 calories, 3 g total fat (0.5 g saturated fat), 19 g protein, 46 g carbohydrate, 16 g fiber, 2 mg cholesterol, 374 mg sodium

Nutrition Nugget

Pain, pain go away! Did you know that ginger is one of the most common ingredients added to natural arthritis-relief supplements? Scientists went bonkers when they discovered super-potent, anti-inflammatory compounds in ginger, which they creatively named "gingerols" (not to be confused with ginger ale!). In two clinical studies involving patients who responded to conventional drugs and those who didn't, physicians found that 75 percent of arthritis patients and 100 percent of patients with muscular discomfort experienced relief of pain and/or swelling after eating ginger. Raw is best, but you can also steep some sliced gingerroot in hot water to refresh your joints *and* your taste buds.

Just Veggin' Out
Colorful tomato-and-vegetable-packed soup

Maximum taste with minimum fuss! That's what this chunky, hearty soup is all about. Easy to prepare and exploding with vegetable goodness. What more could you ask for?

MAKES 8 SERVINGS

PER SERVING
105 calories, 1.9 g total fat
(0.2 g saturated fat),
3 g protein,
19 g carbohydrate,
3.8 g fiber,
0 mg cholesterol,
444 mg sodium

2 tsp	olive oil
1 cup	each chopped celery and chopped onions
1 tsp	minced garlic
1 tsp	each dried thyme and dried marjoram
4 cups	reduced-sodium beef broth (see tip)
1 can	(19 oz/540 mL) no-salt-added diced tomatoes, undrained
1½ cups	reduced-sodium vegetable juice (such as V8)
3 cups	frozen "California-style" mixed vegetables (broccoli, cauliflower and carrots)
2 cups	peeled and cubed potatoes
2 cups	shredded or chopped cabbage
1 tsp	Worcestershire sauce
1	bay leaf
¾ tsp	salt
½ tsp	freshly ground black pepper

- Heat olive oil in a large pot over medium heat. Add celery, onions and garlic. Cook and stir until vegetables begin to soften, about 5 minutes. Add thyme and marjoram and cook 1 more minute.

- Add all remaining ingredients. Stir well. Bring soup to a boil. Reduce heat to medium-low. Cover and simmer for 25 minutes, until potatoes and cabbage are tender. Remove bay leaf and serve hot.

Recipe Tip: Though we prefer the richness and added flavor of beef broth in this recipe, you can certainly substitute vegetable broth if you're looking for a vegetarian soup option.

Any Way You Slice It

Some say "tomato," some say "tomahto." No matter how you say it, tomatoes are good for you! Lycopene, the phytochemical that makes tomatoes red, is a natural cancer fighter, especially helpful in protecting men from prostate cancer. Research shows that men who consume tomato-based foods at least four times a week—pizza included (hold the gut-busting toppings)—have 20 percent less risk of prostate cancer than those who don't eat tomatoes. Ever wonder why Italian-food-loving star Sophia Loren looks so fabulous, even into her late 70s? Perhaps it's because tomatoes are a sensational skin food. Lycopene helps your skin look great by mopping up skin-ravaging free radicals caused by the sun's ultraviolet rays. Though most produce offers more nutrition when raw, tomatoes are an exception to that rule. You get two to eight times more lycopene from a cooked tomato than from a freshly picked one, and adding a small amount of healthy oil intensifies the effect. That's great news for those of you who love salsa, spaghetti sauce, chili, tomato soup and even ketchup (watch the sodium!). Sliced, diced or chopped—no matter how you eat them—tomatoes can't be topped!

FOOD BITE

Did you know that cabbage played a significant role in history? During Captain James Cook's second great voyage to explore the Pacific in 1772, he ordered thousands of pounds of sauerkraut (cabbage fermented and pickled in a salt solution) for its health properties. Over a period of more than 1,000 days, he lost only one of his 118 men to scurvy, thanks to the abundant supply of vitamin C in the virtuous cabbage!

Mother Souperior's Best Barley

Filling and flavorful, this turkey and barley soup is the perfect comfort food on a cold winter's night

Our unconventional chunky, hearty soup is second to nun.

2 tsp	olive oil
1 lb	(454 g) boneless skinless turkey breasts, cut into cubes
1½ cups	each chopped celery and peeled, chopped carrots
1 cup	chopped onions
1 tsp	minced garlic
1 tsp	each dried thyme, dried sage and dried marjoram
4 cups	reduced-sodium chicken broth
1 can	(28 oz/796 mL) no-salt-added diced tomatoes, undrained
⅓ cup	pearl barley
¼ cup	minced fresh parsley
½ tsp	each salt and freshly ground black pepper

MAKES 6 SERVINGS

PER SERVING
202 calories, 3.2 g total fat (0.4 g saturated fat), 21 g protein, 21 g carbohydrate, 5 g fiber, 37 mg cholesterol, 405 mg sodium

Trivial Tidbit

Although tomatoes are the third most popular vegetable in North America after potatoes and lettuce, our love affair with them is fairly recent. Because the tomato is part of the nightshade plant family, some of whose members are deadly, people once assumed it was poisonous, too, and grew it strictly as a decorative plant. Legend has it that one brave American publicly shocked spectators in his hometown of Salem, New Jersey, in 1820 by safely eating a basketful of tomatoes, disproving the poison theory.

- Heat olive oil in a large pot over medium-high heat. Add turkey cubes and cook until lightly browned. Reduce heat to medium. Add celery, carrots, onions and garlic. Cook and stir for 5 more minutes. Stir in thyme, sage and marjoram. Cook for 1 more minute.

- Add all remaining ingredients. Mix well. Bring soup to a boil over high heat. Reduce heat to low.

- Cover and simmer for 30 to 35 minutes, until turkey and barley are tender. Serve hot.

Variation: Try adding ½ cup uncooked quinoa (see p. 38) to this recipe instead of the barley and replace the turkey breasts with chicken breasts.

If you leave alphabet soup on the stove and go out, it could spell disaster :)

Sweat the Blues Away

Pop a pill or walk a hill? It's your choice. But a growing number of studies are showing that exercise has impressive mood-boosting effects and may even help fight clinical depression. A Duke University study asked people with major depression to exercise moderately for 45 minutes, three times a week, while others simply took their antidepressants. The result: Pills worked no better than push-ups and, in fact, exercise improved patients' symptoms faster than antidepressants—and with pleasant instead of nasty side effects! So next time someone tells you to take a hike, say "I'd be happy to!"

In this chapter...

Eats Without Meats

Vegetarian fare with flavor and flair

Much Ado About Mushrooms,
p. 101

It's a Little Pizza Heaven

Colorful vegetable pizza with pesto and feta

You'll experience supreme happiness when you bite into our flavorful veggie pizza. It's like heaven on Earth!

2 tsp	olive oil
2 cups	sliced mixed mushrooms (such as cremini, shiitake, portobello)
1 cup	broccoli florets, cut small
¾ cup	thinly sliced zucchini
½ cup	each thinly sliced red and yellow bell peppers
1	small red onion, thinly sliced into rings
1 tbsp	pesto sauce (see tip)
⅓ cup	pizza sauce
1	12-inch prebaked whole-grain thin-crust pizza shell
2 tbsp	freshly grated Romano or Parmesan cheese
½ cup	packed shredded light mozzarella cheese (2 oz/57 g)
⅓ cup	crumbled light feta cheese (1.3 oz/37 g)

MAKES 1 PIZZA, 8 SLICES

PER SLICE
177 calories, 7.7 g total fat (3.1 g saturated fat),
9 g protein, 18 g carbohydrate, 2.4 g fiber,
13 mg cholesterol, 350 mg sodium

- Heat olive oil in a 10-inch, non-stick skillet over medium heat. Add mushrooms, broccoli, zucchini, red and yellow peppers and onions. Cook and stir until vegetables are tender, about 6 minutes. Remove from heat and stir in pesto sauce. Mix well.

- Spread pizza sauce evenly over pizza crust. Sprinkle with Romano cheese. Top with vegetable mixture. Sprinkle mozzarella and feta cheese over top.

- Bake at 450°F for about 8 minutes, until crust is lightly browned and cheese is completely melted. Serve immediately.

Recipe Tip Pesto sauce, a combination of fresh basil, garlic, pine nuts, Parmesan cheese and olive oil, is a delicious multipurpose ingredient to keep handy in your fridge. It's most commonly tossed with hot, cooked pasta, but it also makes a tasty addition to pizza. Try jazzing up store-bought pizza sauce or pasta sauce with a spoon of basil pesto to make them taste homemade. It's sold both refrigerated and unrefrigerated in small tubs or jars.

Trivial Tidbit

Top o' the pizza to ya! According to purist Italian chefs, ingredients that should never appear on authentic Italian pizza include bell pepper, pepperoni and chicken. In Australia, the No. 1 topping for pizza is eggs. In Chile, the favorite topping is mussels or clams. In Eastern Europe, ketchup is often served with pizza as a condiment. In Iceland, Domino's Pizza has Reindeer Sausage Pie on its menu—ho, ho, hold the antlers!

Did you hear about the bag of popcorn that was arrested down at the theater? He was charged with a salt and buttery :)

Greek is the Word

Greek-style salad with penne pasta, tomatoes, feta cheese and fresh oregano

If you find yourself saying "It's all Greek to me," then you must be talking about this incredible-tasting pasta and vegetable medley. Feta up with ordinary salads? Ours is food for the gods!

1 lb	(454 g) uncooked whole wheat penne pasta (about 5 cups dry)
1½ cups	peeled, seeded and diced English cucumber
3	medium tomatoes, seeded and chopped
1 cup	crumbled light feta cheese (4 oz/113 g)
½ cup	chopped or thinly sliced red onions
¼ cup	each chopped green onions and pitted, sliced black olives
2 tbsp	minced fresh oregano, or 2 tsp dried

Dressing

½ cup	reduced-sodium vegetable or chicken broth
¼ cup	red wine vinegar
2 tbsp	olive oil
1 tbsp	freshly squeezed lemon juice
1 tsp	each Dijon mustard and granulated sugar
1 tsp	minced garlic
¼ tsp	freshly ground black pepper

MAKES 8 SERVINGS

PER SERVING
327 calories, 9.5 g total fat
(2.8 g saturated fat), 11 g protein,
48 g carbohydrate, 6 g fiber,
17 mg cholesterol,
296 mg sodium

- Cook pasta according to package directions. Drain. Rinse with cold water and drain again.

- In a large bowl, toss together pasta, cucumber, tomatoes, feta cheese, onions, olives and oregano. Set aside.

- In a small bowl, whisk together all dressing ingredients. Pour over salad and mix well. Season with more black pepper, if desired. Cover and refrigerate for at least 1 hour before serving. Tastes even better the next day!

FOOD BITE

Worried about catching infectious diseases? Relax! There's natural protection right in your kitchen. Oregano contains super-potent volatile oils that protect against viruses, bacteria, fungus and even parasites. It's like Mother Nature's antibiotic and you don't need a prescription to get it. Use the herb liberally or look for concentrated oil of oregano at a health food store.

EATS WITHOUT MEATS

Aunt Chilada's Stuffed Tortillas

Veggie and black bean enchiladas with zesty tomato sauce and cheddar cheese

Aunt Chilada sure knows her stuff! She holds the family secret, originating in Mexico, for creatively stuffing tortillas with aromatic, flavorful ingredients.

Ai, Ai, Ai'm one hot dish!

Sauce

2 tsp	olive oil
1 cup	chopped onions
1 tsp	minced garlic
1 can	(28 oz/796 mL) no-salt-added diced tomatoes, undrained
1 can	(5.5 oz/156 mL) tomato paste
1	jalapeño pepper, seeded and minced
1 tbsp	red wine vinegar
1 tsp	each ground cumin and chili powder
½ tsp	freshly ground black pepper
2 tbsp	minced fresh cilantro

Enchiladas

2 tsp	olive oil
1¼ cups	chopped onions
1 cup	each diced carrots and diced green bell pepper
1 tbsp	minced garlic
1	jalapeño pepper, seeded and minced
1 tbsp	chili powder
2 tsp	dried oregano
1 tsp	ground cumin
1 can	(19 oz/540 mL) no-salt-added black beans, drained and rinsed
1½ cups	whole-kernel corn
2 tbsp	freshly squeezed lime juice
2 tbsp	minced fresh cilantro
12	7-inch whole-grain flour tortillas
1 cup	packed shredded light old (sharp) cheddar cheese (4 oz/113 g)
¾ cup	light (5%) sour cream

MAKES 12 ENCHILADAS

PER ENCHILADA
272 calories, 8.9 g total fat
(3.2 g saturated fat), 11 g protein,
36 g carbohydrate, 7.2 g fiber,
12 mg cholesterol,
298 mg sodium

Recipe Tips: If you're in a hurry, we're sure Aunt Chilada won't mind if you go ahead and cheat a little: Substitute 3 cups of prepared salsa for her enchilada sauce. These enchiladas use flour tortillas instead of corn tortillas because the corn variety usually needs to be softened by frying in oil before they're rolled (otherwise they'll break).

- Spray two 9 x 13-inch baking pans with cooking spray and set aside.

- To prepare sauce, heat oil in a large pot over medium heat. Add onions and garlic. Cook and stir until onions are softened, about 5 minutes. Add remaining sauce ingredients, except cilantro. Bring to a boil. Reduce heat to low. Cover and simmer for 15 minutes, stirring occasionally. Remove from heat and stir in cilantro. Taste and add a bit of salt, if needed.

- While sauce is simmering, prepare enchilada filling. Heat oil in a large pot over medium heat. Add onions, carrots, green pepper and garlic. Cook and stir until vegetables are softened, about 5 minutes. Add jalapeño pepper, chili powder, oregano and cumin. Cook for 1 more minute. Remove from heat. Stir in beans, corn, lime juice and cilantro. Mix well.

- To assemble enchiladas, spread 3 heaping tbsp filling down center of one tortilla. Sprinkle with 1 heaping tbsp cheddar cheese. Fold tortilla to enclose filling and place seam-side down in baking dish. Repeat with remaining tortillas, leaving yourself with about ½ cup shredded cheddar.

- Pour prepared sauce evenly over enchiladas, making sure each one is coated. Cover with aluminum foil and bake at 350°F for 25 minutes. Uncover, sprinkle with remaining cheese and return to oven (uncovered) for 5 more minutes. Serve enchiladas with a dollop of sour cream on top.

Nutrition Nugget

As far as pesticides go, bell peppers are one of the most sprayed conventionally grown vegetables. So when you pick a pepper, go organic if possible to avoid the chemicals.

Hakuna Frittata

Simple and delicious vegetable and herb frittata with feta cheese

You'll be singing the praises of this king of frittatas! Kenya imagine waking up to an eggstra-nutritious breakfast that's also eggstra quick and easy to make? Of chorus, you could also serve it for lunch or dinner. It's our problem-free recipe… no worries for the rest of your day!

2 tsp   olive oil
½ cup   diced red onions
1 tsp   minced garlic
½ cup   each diced red bell pepper, thinly sliced
             zucchini and chopped mushrooms
1 tbsp   minced fresh oregano leaves,
             or 1 tsp dried (see tip)
1½ tsp   minced fresh thyme, or ½ tsp dried
8   eggs, lightly beaten
Salt and freshly ground black pepper to taste
½ cup   crumbled light feta cheese (2 oz/57 g)

MAKES 4 SERVINGS

PER SERVING
219 calories, 15.4 g total fat
(5.5 g saturated fat), 15 g protein,
5 g carbohydrate, 1.3 g fiber,
432 mg cholesterol, 416 mg sodium

- Heat olive oil over medium heat in a 10-inch, non-stick skillet. Add onions and garlic. Cook and stir until onions begin to soften, about 2 minutes. Add red pepper, zucchini and mushrooms. Cook and stir until vegetables are tender, about 5 more minutes. Stir in oregano and thyme. Cook for 30 more seconds.

- Reduce heat to low. Pour eggs over vegetables, making sure that vegetables are evenly distributed in skillet. Add salt and pepper. Sprinkle feta cheese evenly over egg mixture.

- Cover skillet with a tight-fitting lid and let cook until eggs are completely set, about 12 minutes. Slice into 4 portions and serve hot.

Recipe Tips: You can substitute fresh dill for oregano for a different (and delicious!) flavor. Make sure you use a good-quality, non-stick skillet to make any frittata. An old skillet with scratch marks and chipped non-stick coating makes removing the frittata a pain in the butt.

> Don't dig your grave with a knife and fork.
> *English proverb*

It's Not Hip to Skip!

Did you know that breakfast eaters are thinner, smarter and nicer to be around? Studies show that lifetime breakfast skippers have, on average, an extra 1.8 inches on their waist versus people who always eat breakfast. Research also shows that breakfast eaters fare better on memory and problem-solving tasks. Skipping breakfast can make you a little weak in the bean—and irritable, too! Think that 10 a.m. coffee and cinnamon danish will perk you up? They'll just fuel the fire, sending your blood-sugar and energy levels soaring to the moon, only to violently crash down to Earth a short while later. Now your coworkers really need to take cover! A hearty, healthy, fiber-and-protein breakfast does more than keep your brain cells, blood sugar and relationships operating smoothly. It also jump-starts your metabolism, so you'll start burning fat and calories right out of the gate. Plus, eating breakfast prevents overeating at lunchtime, when you're sure to be famished if you've skipped your morning meal. No wonder experts say "breaking the fast" is crucial if you're serious about losing weight. So, join the breakfast club and hang with the thin crowd!

Lasagna with Mex Appeal

Layered Mexican tortilla casserole

This dish is so "mexy," it's heating up kitchens all over the country. A great way to add a little spice to your life.

Ai Caramba! Eets Revolutionary!

MAKES 8 SERVINGS

PER SERVING
324 calories, 7.9 g total fat
(3.5 g saturated fat),
15 g protein, 49 g carbohydrate,
12.4 g fiber, 15 mg cholesterol,
407 mg sodium

1 tbsp	olive oil
2 cups	chopped onions
1½ cups	chopped green bell pepper
2 tsp	minced garlic
1 can	(28 oz/796 mL) no-salt-added diced tomatoes, undrained
1 cup	salsa (mild, medium or hot)
2 tsp	ground cumin
1 can	(19 oz/540 mL) no-salt-added black beans, drained and rinsed
1 can	(19 oz/540 mL) no-salt-added red kidney beans, drained and rinsed
2 tbsp	minced fresh cilantro (optional)
12	6-inch corn tortillas or 8 7-inch whole-grain flour tortillas
1½ cups	packed shredded light Monterey Jack cheese (6 oz/170 g)
2	small plum tomatoes, thinly sliced
⅓ cup	chopped green onions

Light (5%) sour cream for garnish (optional)

- Heat olive oil in a large pot over medium heat. Add onions, green pepper and garlic. Cook and stir until vegetables begin to soften, about 5 minutes. Add tomatoes, salsa and cumin. Bring to a boil. Reduce heat to low and simmer, uncovered, for 10 minutes. Stir in black beans and kidney beans. Remove from heat. Stir in cilantro, if using.

- Spray a 9 x 13-inch baking pan with cooking spray. Spread ⅓ of the bean mixture over bottom. Cover with half the tortillas (overlapping as needed) and half the cheese. Spoon another ⅓ bean mixture on top of cheese, followed by remaining tortillas, and last of the bean mixture. Sprinkle remaining cheese on top.

- Cover with foil and bake at 350ºF for 35 minutes. Let cool for 10 minutes before serving. Garnish with tomato slices and green onions. Serve with a dollop of sour cream, if desired.

FOOD BITE

It's nacho ordinary appetizer at the Mexican joint and it just may leave a huge paunch under your poncho! Top a mountain of deep-fried tortilla chips with a third of a pound of melted cheese and a quarter pound of ground beef, then add high-fat sour cream. Whaddya get? A fiesta for cardiologists and muchos pesos for folks in the weight-loss industry! A typical order of beef and cheese nachos at a restaurant will turn you into a stuffed piñata with approximately 1,300 calories and 80 grams of fat! Ai caramba! Share with a few amigos, or you can say adios to your waistline.

They say figures don't lie, but girdles sure condense the truth! :)

Scentilentil Journey

Curried lentils and quinoa with spinach and warm Indian spices

Pack your bags! You're taking a trip to India on us! With an unforgettable blend of aromatic spices, this spectacular lentil and quinoa dish makes it possible to venture to a foreign country—even if it's just for dinner!

½ cup	light (5%) sour cream
½ tsp	curry powder
1 tbsp	olive oil
3 cups	sliced mushrooms
1 cup	chopped onions
1½ cups	chopped carrots
2 tsp	minced garlic
1 tbsp	grated gingerroot
1½ tsp	each ground coriander and ground cumin
1 tsp	ground turmeric
4 cups	reduced-sodium vegetable or chicken broth
1 cup	uncooked quinoa
1 cup	dried red lentils, sorted and rinsed
½ tsp	salt
¼ tsp	freshly ground black pepper
½ pkg	(10 oz/300 g) frozen spinach, thawed, squeezed dry and chopped (about 5 oz/150 g total)
½ cup	chopped green onions

MAKES 4 SERVINGS

PER SERVING
321 calories, 6.1 g total fat
(0.8 g saturated fat), 16 g protein,
52 g carbohydrate, 15.8 g fiber,
3 mg cholesterol,
351 mg sodium

- In a small bowl, combine sour cream with curry powder. Cover and refrigerate until ready to use.

- Heat olive oil in a large pot over medium heat. Add mushrooms, onions, carrots and garlic. Cook and stir until vegetables begin to soften, about 5 to 6 minutes. Add gingerroot, coriander, cumin and turmeric. Cook for 30 more seconds.

- Add broth, quinoa, lentils, salt and pepper. Bring mixture to a boil. Reduce heat to low. Cover and simmer 20 minutes, stirring occasionally.

- Stir in spinach and green onions. Cover and simmer for 3 to 4 more minutes, until quinoa and lentils are tender. Remove from heat and serve immediately. Top each serving with a dollop of sour cream-curry mixture.

Nutrition Nugget

The "original" Old Spice? In India, spices like turmeric are routinely added to food in the same way North Americans shake salt and pepper—only with much tastier and healthier results! Curcumin, the plant chemical that gives turmeric its yellow hue, helps prevent the tiny plaque-related blockages that can form in the brain and lead to Alzheimer's. Researchers say turmeric's prevalence in India might help explain why so few of that country's senior citizens have the disease.

Hara Hachi Bu

The Japanese, who are known for their longevity, have a saying "hara hachi bu," which basically means, "stop eating when you're 80 percent full." On the island of Okinawa, Japan, where citizens live longer and healthier lives than any other people on Earth, "hara hachi bu" is often whispered as a prayer or grace before a meal. They deliberately moderate their portion sizes and their hunger with this simple mealtime ritual. A German expression gives similar guidance: "Tie off the sack before it gets completely full." This is wise advice, since researchers suggest that in one sitting we eat no more than the amount fitting in our hands when they're cupped together. But in North America, Land of the Supersize Combo and Home of the All-You-Can-Eat Buffet, we stuff ourselves silly and we do it all the time, not just on holidays or special occasions. Our mealtime prayer? Give thanks for Spanx! Ironically, if you stop eating before getting full, you'll find you're actually more satisfied with your meal, you won't be sleepy afterward, your brain will operate much better and you'll just generally feel better. It's the best "non-diet" diet going. A little "hara hachi bu" is the *weigh* to go!

EATS WITHOUT MEATS

Chili Chili Bang Bang

**Spicy, stew-like, loaded vegetarian chili...
a Looneyspoons classic!**

*A magical blend of vegetables, beans and spices,
this fiery-hot invention is guaranteed to rev up your engine!*

MAKES 8 SERVINGS

PER SERVING
212 calories,
3.7 g total fat
(0.5 g saturated fat),
9 g protein,
36 g carbohydrate,
10.3 g fiber,
0 mg cholesterol,
246 mg sodium

1 tbsp	olive oil
1¼ cups	chopped onions
1 cup	each chopped green and red bell peppers
¾ cup	each chopped celery and chopped carrots
1 tbsp	minced garlic
1½ cups	quartered mushrooms
1 cup	unpeeled, diced zucchini
1 tbsp	each chili powder and ground cumin
1½ tsp	each dried oregano and dried basil
1 can	(28 oz/796 mL) no-salt-added diced tomatoes, undrained
1 can	(19 oz/540 mL) no-salt-added black beans, drained and rinsed
1 can	(19 oz/540 mL) no-salt-added chickpeas, drained and rinsed
1 can	(12 oz/340 mL) no-salt-added whole-kernel corn, undrained
½ tsp	cayenne pepper (or to taste)
½ tsp	salt
2 tbsp	minced fresh cilantro

- Heat oil in a large pot over medium heat. Add onions, green and red peppers, celery, carrots and garlic. Cook and stir until vegetables begin to soften, about 5 or 6 minutes.

- Add mushrooms and zucchini. Cook and stir for 4 more minutes. Add chili powder, cumin, oregano and basil. Cook for 1 more minute. Add tomatoes, beans, chickpeas, corn (with liquid), cayenne pepper and salt. Mix well. Bring to a boil. Reduce heat to medium-low. Cover and simmer for 20 minutes. Remove from heat and stir in cilantro. Serve hot.

Recipe Tip: Tastes great served with corn muffins on p. 296.

> It is better to wear out than to rust out.
> *Frances E. Willard*

FOOD BITE

Beans, beans, the musical fruit. The more you eat, the more you...lower your cholesterol, stabilize blood-sugar levels and protect yourself against cancer. No wonder it's the musical fruit! We should sing the praises of these health wonders more often. Beans are an important part of every known cuisine and, in fact, they've been eaten for thousands of years. The most famous bean eaters were the pilgrims in Boston, or Beantown, as they say. Because their strict religion forbade them to cook on the Sabbath, they designed a bean pot that baked beans overnight so they'd be ready to eat for Sunday supper. The Pilgrims knew, even back then, that beans were a fantastic, fiber-filled, fat-fighting food. Rootie toot toot!

Garden of Eatin'

Warm roasted vegetable salad with rosemary and feta

If you don't know a good salad from Adam, then take our word for it: This mouthwatering vegetable medley is so tasty, it's sure to lead you into temptation. No need to worry, though—it's sin-free.

It's s-s-s-sinfully delicious!

12	mini red potatoes, unpeeled, quartered
3 cups	whole medium-sized mushrooms
2	medium carrots, peeled and coarsely chopped
2	medium zucchini, cut into bite-sized chunks
1	medium red onion, cut into rings
1	large red bell pepper, cut into bite-sized chunks
1	large yellow bell pepper, cut into bite-sized chunks
2 tsp	minced garlic
1 tbsp	olive oil
1 tbsp	minced fresh rosemary, or 1 tsp dried
1 tbsp	minced fresh oregano, or 1 tsp dried
1 tbsp	balsamic vinegar
¼ tsp	each salt and freshly ground black pepper
½ cup	crumbled light feta cheese (2 oz/57 g)

- Spray a large roasting pan with cooking spray. Add vegetables, garlic, oil and herbs. Mix well. Roast uncovered at 425°F for 30 minutes. Stir once or twice during cooking time. Turn on the broiler and broil vegetables for about 5 minutes, until edges start to brown.

- Remove vegetables from oven and transfer to a serving bowl. Toss with vinegar, salt and pepper. Sprinkle crumbled feta over top. Serve warm.

MAKES 4 SERVINGS

PER SERVING
292 calories, 6.7 g total fat (1.7 g saturated fat), 11 g protein, 52 g carbohydrate, 8.5 g fiber, 10 mg cholesterol, 503 mg sodium

Trivial Tidbit

As far as burning calories goes, 100 hearty, good laughs are considered the equivalent of 10 minutes of rowing. Looks like more giggling leads to less jiggling!

When to Go Organic

There's plenty of evidence that pesticides have a negative impact on our environment and our health. Fortunately, organic produce, free of pesticides and herbicides, is now easy to find in most grocery stores and at local farmers markets. It may be a bit pricier, however (but we think you and your family are worth the extra bucks!). If you're on a tight budget, buying exclusively organic foods might not be realistic. Thankfully, there's a solution! According to the Environmental Working Group, you can reduce your pesticide exposure by nearly 80 percent (Wow!) simply by choosing organic for the 12 fruits and veggies that contain the highest levels of pesticides, based on their tests. They call these "The Dirty Dozen": peaches, apples, sweet bell peppers, celery, nectarines, strawberries, cherries, kale, lettuce, imported grapes, carrots and pears. The more we choose organic foods and demand environmentally safe, organic farming practices, the more the food industry will have to listen and respond (and prices should come down, too). Vote for change with your fork!

Certified Organic green Kale $ 3.00

Livin' on the Vedge

Roasted vegetables with lemon couscous

Looking for more excitement when it comes to roasted vegetables? We've gone over the edge and pushed the flavor limit by adding lemon-scented couscous, sweet potatoes and aromatic herbs. The taste will knock your Birkenstocks off!

It's okay, Honey. Just makin' the garden a little bigger.

2 cups	reduced-sodium vegetable broth
1½ cups	uncooked whole wheat couscous
2 tsp	grated lemon zest
1 large	sweet potato, peeled and diced
1 large	red bell pepper, seeded and chopped
1 large	yellow bell pepper, seeded and chopped
1	medium red onion, chopped
1	medium zucchini, chopped
1	large portobello mushroom, chopped
1 cup	canned no-salt-added chickpeas, drained and rinsed
2 tbsp	olive oil
1 tbsp	balsamic vinegar
2 tsp	minced garlic
1 tsp	dried rosemary
¼ tsp	each salt and freshly ground black pepper
½ cup	crumbled light feta cheese (2 oz/57 g) or ⅓ cup freshly grated Parmesan cheese
¼ cup	chopped fresh basil leaves or mint leaves

- Preheat oven to 450°F.

- Bring vegetable broth to a boil in a medium pot. Stir in couscous and lemon zest. Remove from heat. Cover and let stand until ready to use.

- In a large bowl, toss together all vegetables, chickpeas, olive oil, balsamic vinegar, garlic, rosemary, salt and pepper. Spread vegetable mixture in a large roasting pan that has been sprayed with cooking spray. Roast for about 25 minutes, stirring once or twice, until vegetables are tender.

- To serve, combine hot vegetables, cooked couscous, feta cheese and fresh basil in a large serving bowl and toss well. Add a bit more freshly ground black pepper to taste, if desired.

MAKES 8 SERVINGS

PER SERVING
253 calories, 6.2 g total fat (1.7 g saturated fat),
8 g protein, 42 g carbohydrate,
7.6 g fiber, 6 mg cholesterol,
232 mg sodium

Nutrition Nugget
Don't drink and dine! If you drink liquids during a meal—even water—you actually dilute precious gastric juices in the stomach, slowing and impairing proper digestion. That can lead to bloating, cramps and other "unpleasant" side effects. Little sips are OK, but if you want to digest the best, don't drink anything at least 30 minutes before and after eating.

Beany Baby

Spicy vegetarian chili with meatless ground burger and two kinds of beans

If you're keen about beans, you'll want to stuff yourself silly with this high-protein, meatless, fiber-filled meal. The ingredient list might seem lengthy, but it's really easy to make. Tastes toyriffic with a dollop of light sour cream.

Recipe Tips: When selecting canned beans for this recipe, choose from red kidney beans, black beans, chickpeas, navy beans, cannellini beans or even lentils. Meatless ground burger is precooked, simulated ground beef made from soy. It's a good source of protein, it's cholesterol-free and low in fat, and it's pretty darn tasty when used in chili and spaghetti sauce. Look for it where vegetarian products are sold in the refrigerated deli section of your grocery store.

1 tbsp	olive oil
1½ cups	chopped red onions
1 cup	each chopped green bell pepper and chopped celery
2 tsp	minced garlic
1 pkg	(12 oz/340 g) meatless ground burger (see tip)
1½ tbsp	chili powder
2 tsp	each ground cumin and dried oregano
1 tsp	ground coriander
½ tsp	crushed red pepper flakes
¼ tsp	ground cinnamon
1 can	(28 oz/796 mL) no-salt-added diced tomatoes, undrained
2 cans	(19 oz/540 mL each) no-salt-added beans, drained and rinsed (see tip)
1 can	(14 oz/398 mL) no-salt-added tomato sauce
1 cup	reduced-sodium vegetable or chicken broth
1 tbsp	brown sugar
½ tsp	salt
¼ tsp	freshly ground black pepper
2 tbsp	minced fresh cilantro (optional)

- Heat olive oil in a large pot over medium-high heat. Add onions, green pepper, celery and garlic. Cook and stir until vegetables begin to soften, about 5 minutes.

- Add ground burger, chili powder, cumin, oregano, coriander, red pepper flakes and cinnamon. Mix well and cook for 1 more minute. Add undrained tomatoes, beans, tomato sauce, broth, brown sugar, salt and pepper. Bring mixture to a boil. Reduce heat to low and simmer, covered, for 20 minutes. Remove from heat and stir in cilantro, if using. Serve hot.

MAKES 8 SERVINGS

PER SERVING
242 calories, 2.9 g total fat (0.3 g saturated fat), 19 g protein, 39 g carbohydrate, 13.2 g fiber, 1 mg cholesterol, 636 mg sodium

Choosing the Optimal Cellular Plan

Out with the old, in with the new! Your skin, muscles, bones, even your organs, are constantly degenerating and regenerating. As sure as you're reading the words on this page, your body is in a constant cycle of renewal. Guess what the body uses as fuel to recreate itself? Food! You truly are what you eat. That means *you* are the construction foreman who's responsible for choosing the raw materials to build your foundation. Knowing that, would you order fries to build your eyes? Choose Twinkies to become your pinkies? Pick chips to form your hips? Beer to shape your ear? When Elvis sang, "You ain't nothin' but a…hot dog," was he referring to you? Most people don't have a clue what they're doing to their bodies as a result of poor eating habits. Nor are they aware how much better they could look and feel if they stopped eating mindlessly and started rebuilding themselves intentionally. If you constantly eat junk, you create an inferior, weaker version of what you're capable of being. Eat whole, natural, nutrient-filled foods more often and watch how you'll rejuvenate, replenish and renew. What kind of structure are *you* building?

Bye-Bye Burgie

Broiled portobello "burgers" with sweet peppers, red onions and a spicy chickpea spread

You'll put on a happy face when you bite into these succulent mushroom burgers—and say "farewell" to the thought of any leftovers!

Chickpea Spread

1 cup	canned no-salt-added chickpeas, drained and rinsed
2 tbsp	light (5%) sour cream
2 tbsp	finely minced onions
1 tbsp	minced fresh cilantro
2 tsp	minced garlic
2 tsp	freshly squeezed lemon or lime juice
¾ tsp	ground coriander
½ tsp	granulated sugar or liquid honey
½ tsp	ground cumin

Pinch salt and freshly ground black pepper

Burgers

1 tbsp	each olive oil and balsamic or red wine vinegar
½ tsp	dried basil
4	medium portobello mushrooms, wiped clean
1	large red bell pepper, seeded and cut into wide strips
1	medium red onion, peeled and sliced into thick rings (do not separate)
4	whole-grain burger buns
1 cup	whole baby spinach leaves

- To make chickpea spread, combine all ingredients in the bowl of a food processor and whirl until smooth. Refrigerate until ready to use.

- In a small bowl, combine olive oil, vinegar and basil. Brush oil mixture over both sides of mushrooms, pepper strips and onion rings. Arrange vegetables in a baking pan and place under the broiler, about 5 inches from heat source. Broil for 3 minutes. Remove pan from oven, turn vegetables over, baste with any remaining oil mixture and return to oven. Broil for 3 to 4 more minutes, until vegetables are tender.

- To serve, line bottom of bun with spinach leaves. Place one whole mushroom over top. Spread chickpea mixture over mushroom. Top with peppers, onions and top half of bun. Serve immediately.

MAKES 4 BURGERS

PER BURGER
265 calories, 6.8 g total fat (0.1 g saturated fat), 10 g protein, 45 g carbohydrate, 3.9 g fiber, 1 mg cholesterol, 383 mg sodium

Waiter : A man who believes money grows on trays :)

EATS WITHOUT MEATS

Quiche Me, You Fool!

Crustless roasted pepper and potato quiche

Pucker up and get your taste buds ready for this lip-smacking creation!
One bite and you can kiss the quiche goodbye.

1	large red bell pepper, seeded and halved
1	large yellow or orange bell pepper, seeded and halved
1	small red onion, thinly sliced into rings
2 tsp	olive oil
1 tsp	minced garlic
2 tbsp	minced fresh basil leaves
3	medium potatoes
1 cup	packed shredded light old (sharp) cheddar cheese (4 oz/113 g)
4	eggs
½ cup	2% evaporated milk or light (5%) cream
½ tsp	each dried thyme and salt
¼ tsp	freshly ground black pepper

MAKES 6 SERVINGS

PER SERVING
219 calories, 9.4 g total fat (3.9 g saturated fat),
12 g protein, 21 g carbohydrate, 2.4 g fiber,
156 mg cholesterol, 417 mg sodium

- Spray 1 medium and 1 small baking pan with cooking spray. Place peppers, cut side down, in medium pan. Combine onions, olive oil and garlic in small pan. Place both pans under broiler. Broil onions for 5 minutes and peppers until they begin to blister and char.

- Reduce oven temperature to 375°F. Transfer onion mixture to a medium bowl and set aside. Let peppers sit until cool enough to handle. Using a paring knife, peel off and discard skins. Slice peppers into strips. Add peppers to bowl with onions, along with basil. Mix well.

- Peel potatoes and slice into ¼-inch-thick rounds. Steam potatoes for 10 to 12 minutes, until tender.

- To assemble quiche, spray an 8-inch round quiche pan or cake pan with cooking spray. Layer ½ potatoes over bottom. Top with ½ pepper mixture, followed by ½ cheese. Repeat layering.

- In a medium bowl, whisk together eggs, milk, thyme, salt and pepper. Pour over vegetables. Bake, uncovered, for 35 to 40 minutes, until quiche is firm to touch and cheese is golden brown. Let stand for 10 minutes before slicing.

Nutrition Nugget

At the crack of dawn, eat protein! A Louisiana State University study showed that when people had eggs for breakfast, they ate 264 fewer calories throughout the rest of the day compared to when they ate a bagel. That's because protein is more filling than refined carbohydrates and it keeps blood sugar steadier, too.

The Yoke's on Us

Looks like all the hype about eggs and cholesterol isn't all it's cracked up to be. According to a study published in the prestigious *New England Journal of Medicine*, a group of New Guinea natives (whose diets were extremely low in cholesterol) were fed eggs to measure their cholesterol-raising effect. Figuring that the subjects' blood-cholesterol levels would be blown off the charts, the scientists were surprised to find that egg consumption had no significant effect at all. Another study by the American Cancer Society revealed that egg eaters actually had a lower death rate from heart attacks and strokes than non-egg eaters. (And this was a huge study involving more than 800,000 people!) Maybe that's because the cholesterol in eggs is balanced with lecithin, a substance that keeps cholesterol moving in the bloodstream, preventing it from depositing in the arteries—a great example of how Mother Nature creates balance and synergy in whole, natural foods. Since cholesterol is delicate and can be damaged (oxidized) by high heat, it's healthier to eat poached or boiled eggs rather than fried. That's good news, because a boiled egg in the morning is hard to beat!

Pizza for the Upper Crust

Margherita pizza: Tomatoes, basil and fresh mozzarella on a crispy, thin crust

It's the crown jewel of thin-crust pizzas—in an upper class by itself! One taste of our exquisite tomato and mozzarella pizza and you'll be waisting away in Margheritaville!

1 can (19 oz/540 mL) diced tomatoes with Italian herbs
⅓ cup pizza sauce (see recipe, p. 330)
1   12-inch prebaked whole-grain thin-crust pizza shell
¼ cup freshly grated Romano, Parmesan or Asiago cheese
3 oz   (85 g) fresh mozzarella cheese (see tip)
¼ cup chopped fresh basil leaves
Freshly ground black pepper

- Preheat grill to medium setting and leave lid closed to keep hot. (Or, preheat oven to 425°F.)

- Drain tomatoes in a sieve, pressing down on them to remove as much liquid as possible. Break up any large chunks using your fingers.

- Spread pizza sauce over crust, leaving a ¼-inch border. Top with drained tomatoes. Sprinkle tomatoes evenly with Romano cheese.

- Using a small, sharp knife, cut the mozzarella cheese into thin slices. Distribute the mozzarella evenly over pizza. Sprinkle with basil and some freshly ground black pepper.

- Place pizza directly onto grill or middle oven rack. If grilling, close lid and cook for 4 minutes, checking pizza halfway through cooking time to make sure crust isn't burning (every grill is different!). After 4 minutes, turn grill off, but keep lid down. Cook another 3 minutes or so, until toppings are hot and cheese is melted. If using oven, bake pizza for about 8 to 10 minutes, until cheese is melted and edges are lightly browned.

Royally delicious!

MAKES 1 PIZZA, 8 SLICES

PER SLICE
130 calories,
4.5 g total fat
(2.2 g saturated fat),
6 g protein,
16 g carbohydrate,
1 g fiber,
11 mg cholesterol,
300 mg sodium

Upper crust: A number of people stuck together by their dough :)

Recipe Tip

Fresh mozzarella cheese is milder, softer and whiter than regular mozzarella, which tends to be drier and has an elastic texture. Look for fresh mozzarella at the deli-cheese counter of your supermarket or in small containers where the specialty cheeses are sold.

Fromage à Trois

Three-cheese vegetable lasagna with chunky tomato sauce

It's a meat market out there! Why not stay home and experience this luscious, meatless, three-cheese lasagna with a friend or two? No (cheese) strings attached.

I'm having a grate time!

Tomato Sauce

½ cup	sun-dried tomatoes (not oil-packed)
1 tbsp	olive oil
1½ cups	chopped red onions
2 tsp	minced garlic
3 cups	sliced mushrooms
1 cup	each diced zucchini and diced red or yellow bell pepper
1 tbsp	dried Italian seasoning
1 jar	(22 oz/700 mL) your favorite tomato pasta sauce (see tip)
1 can	(19 oz/540 mL) diced tomatoes with Italian herbs, undrained
⅓ cup	chopped fresh basil leaves
1 tbsp	balsamic vinegar
½ tsp	freshly ground black pepper

2 cups	part-skim ricotta cheese (1 lb/454 g)
1 cup	crumbled feta cheese with herbs (4 oz/113 g—see tip)
1 pkg	(10 oz/300 g) frozen spinach, thawed, squeezed dry and chopped
1	egg
12	oven-ready lasagna noodles (see tip)
1½ cups	packed shredded light mozzarella cheese (6 oz/170 g)

- Place sun-dried tomatoes in a small bowl and pour 1 cup boiling water over top. Let stand for 20 minutes while you prepare the sauce. Spray a 9 x 13-inch baking dish with cooking spray and set aside.

- Heat olive oil in a large pot over medium heat. Add onions and garlic. Cook and stir until onions begin to soften, about 5 minutes. Add mushrooms, zucchini and bell pepper. Cook and stir until vegetables are tender, about 7 more minutes. Stir in Italian seasoning. Cook 1 more minute. Add pasta sauce, undrained tomatoes, basil, balsamic vinegar and pepper. Bring mixture to a boil. Reduce heat to low and simmer, covered, for 20 minutes. When sun-dried tomatoes have softened, chop and add, along with their soaking liquid, to the sauce.

- While sauce is simmering, mix together ricotta cheese, feta cheese, spinach and egg in a medium bowl. Refrigerate until ready to use.

- Preheat oven to 375°F. To assemble lasagna, spread 1½ cups vegetable sauce over bottom of baking dish. Top with 4 lasagna noodles. It's OK to have space between the noodles—they'll expand as they cook. Spread ⅓ of the remaining sauce over noodles, followed by ½ the ricotta mixture. (Use a teaspoon to drop the ricotta in small mounds all over the noodles.) Top with ⅓ mozzarella. Repeat layer: 4 noodles, ⅓ sauce, remaining ricotta, ⅓ mozzarella. For top layer: 4 noodles, ⅓ sauce, ⅓ mozzarella. Cover lasagna with foil. If your baking dish is full, place it on a cookie sheet in case the sauce bubbles over.

- Bake lasagna for 35 minutes. Uncover and bake an additional 15 minutes. Remove lasagna from oven and let stand, uncovered, for 15 minutes before serving.

MAKES 10 SERVINGS

PER SERVING
305 calories, 8.6 g total fat
(5.3 g saturated fat), 19 g protein,
38 g carbohydrate, 4.5 g fiber,
52 mg cholesterol, 664 mg sodium

Recipe Tips

Sure, making a great-tasting veggie lasagna is time-consuming, but worth it! Cut down on your preparation time by making the sauce one day in advance. This way, the process won't seem so overwhelming. Try Healthy Choice Traditional pasta sauce in this recipe and feta cheese flavored with basil and tomatoes. Oven-ready lasagna noodles are the type you don't need to boil before using—a brilliant, time-saving culinary invention! During baking, the moisture from the sauce softens, or rehydrates the noodles, especially when the pan is covered as the lasagna bakes. If you prefer to precook your lasagna noodles (try whole wheat noodles!) instead of using oven-ready noodles, you won't need as much sauce. Therefore, don't add the soaking liquid from the sun-dried tomatoes to the sauce, or your lasagna will be too runny.

Itsy-Bitsy Teeny-Weeny Colored Polka-Dot Rotini

Tricolored rotini with currants and green peas cooked in a spicy coconut broth

Heavens to bitsy! This rotini isn't weeny in the flavor department.
You'll be-keeny to make it again and again.

1½ cups	reduced-sodium vegetable broth
1 cup	light coconut milk
1 tsp	each granulated sugar and ground coriander
½ tsp	each ground cumin and chili powder
¼ tsp	each curry powder and ground ginger
8 oz	(227 g) uncooked tricolored rotini (about 3 cups dry)
1 cup	frozen green peas, thawed
½ cup	finely chopped red bell pepper
¼ cup	dried currants (see tip)

- Combine broth, coconut milk, sugar, coriander, cumin, chili powder, curry powder and ginger in a medium pot (non-stick is best for this recipe). Bring to a boil. Add rotini. Reduce heat to medium-low. Cover and simmer for 6 minutes, stirring occasionally.

- Add peas, red pepper and currants. Simmer for 6 to 7 more minutes, until liquid has been absorbed and pasta is tender. Remove from heat and let stand, covered, for 5 minutes before serving.

MAKES 4 SERVINGS

PER SERVING
326 calories, 4.4 g total fat (2 g saturated fat), 11 g protein, 60 g carbohydrate, 5 g fiber, 0 mg cholesterol, 311 mg sodium

Recipe Tip

There are two different types of fruits that we call currants. The first is a tiny berry related to the gooseberry. It's mainly used to make syrups, sauces, liqueurs and preservatives. The second is a dried Zante grape that looks like a tiny raisin. That's the type you want for this recipe. You'll find dried currants in plastic bags right beside the raisins at your supermarket.

Belly Idol

Think superhuman crunch sessions will give you fab abs? Well, you've got another thing comin'—and it's most likely a stiff neck! Sure, sit-ups will strengthen your core and help lighten the load on your back, but they do not—even if you do 300 every day—make stomach fat disappear. You can't spot-reduce fat. If you want the sculpted-stomach look, you need to shed overall body fat so you can actually see the result of those sit-ups, and that means eating fewer refined carbohydrates (especially sweets!) and moving your muscles more. Remember, muscle is your blubber-burning furnace. The more muscle you have, the more powerful your furnace, and the more fat you'll incinerate 24 hours a day—all over your body, including those nasty, trouble spots. Think of it this way: If you upgraded the furnace in your home, it wouldn't be just the kitchen that receives more heat, right? There'd be more heat in the bedroom and bathrooms, too! Believe it or not, building muscle all over your body, even in your arms, actually helps to flatten your belly. By all means keep doing sit-ups—any strengthening exercise is a boon to your physique. Just make sure you're doing push-ups, pull-ups, stand-ups and jump-ups, too!

> A man's health can be judged by which he takes two at a time—pills or stairs.
>
> *Joan Welsh*

Much Ado About Mushrooms

Marinated, grilled portobello mushroom fajitas with red onions and peppers

There's much ado about mushrooms thanks to these flab-u-less fajitas. Why all the fuss? Well, with red meat out, the fat's way down. And spiced-up, grilled portobellos have the taste and texture of a thick, juicy steak, so you better leave shroom for seconds.

½ cup	light balsamic vinaigrette dressing
2 tbsp	steak spice rub (see tip)
½ tsp	each ground cumin, chili powder and dried oregano
4	large portobello mushrooms (about 6-inch diameter)
1 tbsp	olive oil
1	large red onion, sliced
1	large red bell pepper, seeded and cut into strips
1	large green bell pepper, seeded and cut into strips
1 tbsp	each freshly squeezed lime juice and minced fresh cilantro
8	7-inch whole-grain flour tortillas

Fajita fixin's: light (5%) sour cream, salsa, chopped lettuce, shredded light cheddar cheese, guacamole

MAKES 4 SERVINGS

PER SERVING
343 calories, 10.6 g total fat (0.6 g saturated fat),
12 g protein, 56 g carbohydrate, 8.4 g fiber,
0 mg cholesterol, 651 mg sodium

- To make marinade, combine dressing, steak rub, cumin, chili powder and oregano in a small bowl. Using a pastry brush, coat both sides of mushrooms with marinade. Let stand at room temperature for 1 hour.

- Preheat grill to high setting. Brush grill rack lightly with oil. Grill mushrooms for about 3 minutes per side, until tender with nice grill marks. Remove from heat. Cut each mushroom into 6 slices. Cover with foil and keep warm.

- Heat olive oil in a large, non-stick wok or skillet over medium-high heat. Add onion slices and peppers. Cook and stir until vegetables are tender crisp, about 5 minutes. Add lime juice, cilantro and reserved mushrooms. Stir gently and cook just until mushrooms are hot.

- To prepare fajitas, 10 minutes before serving time, wrap tortillas in foil and heat in a 350°F oven to warm (or wrap in a damp tea towel and heat in microwave). To serve, layer your favorite fajita fixin's on warm tortilla, followed by cooked vegetables. Wrap up and enjoy.

Recipe Tip: The steak spice rub helps give the mushrooms a meaty, steak-like flavor. Our favorite is Club House La Grille Montreal Steak Rub Marinade. It's a thick paste sold in a small jar in the spice aisle. It keeps for months in the refrigerator and, needless to say, it's great on steak, too!

Nutrition Nugget

Portobello mushrooms are actually overgrown cremini mushrooms, the brown mushrooms readily available at supermarkets. Their size and flavor make them an excellent meat substitute for sandwiches, fajitas and, of course, burgers. Just like their smaller cousins, the portobello contains powerful phytonutrients, such as recently discovered lentinan, which seems to protect our DNA from damage. In short, they reduce the risk of cancer! Oh, and there's even shroom for improvement: Cooking them in red wine, which contains the antioxidant resveratrol, magnifies their immunity-boosting power!

Rockin' Moroccan Stew

Moroccan vegetable stew with sweet potatoes, chickpeas and ginger

This unique recipe came right out of Africa! Say "yes, please" to chickpeas and you can eat to the beat!

2 tsp	olive oil
1 cup	chopped onions
½ cup	each diced celery and chopped green bell pepper
1 tsp	minced garlic
2 tsp	grated gingerroot
1 tsp	each ground cumin, curry powder, ground coriander and chili powder
3 cups	reduced-sodium vegetable broth
3 cups	peeled, cubed sweet potatoes
1 can	(19 oz/540 mL) no-salt-added diced tomatoes, drained
1 can	(19 oz/540 mL) no-salt-added chickpeas, drained and rinsed
1 tbsp	freshly squeezed lemon juice
½ tsp	salt
¼ tsp	freshly ground black pepper
¼ cup	raisins
2 tbsp	each light peanut butter and minced fresh cilantro

- Heat olive oil in a large pot over medium-high heat. Add onions, celery, green pepper and garlic. Cook and stir until vegetables begin to soften, about 3 minutes. Add gingerroot, cumin, curry powder, coriander and chili powder. Cook for 30 more seconds.

- Add all remaining ingredients, except raisins, peanut butter and cilantro. Bring to a boil. Reduce heat to low and simmer, covered, for 20 minutes.

- Stir in raisins, peanut butter and cilantro. Mix well. Simmer for 5 more minutes. Serve hot.

MAKES 6 SERVINGS

PER SERVING
253 calories, 5.3 g total fat (0.8 g saturated fat), 8 g protein, 44 g carbohydrate, 6.9 g fiber, 0 mg cholesterol, 355 mg sodium

> After lunch, rest a while.
> After supper, walk a mile.
> *Arabian proverb*

Nutrition Nugget

In a pressure cooker? A small handful of raisins supplies extra potassium, a mineral that has been shown to lower high blood pressure. Plus, like other dried fruits, raisins are a good source of dietary fiber, with nearly 2 grams of fiber in a ¼ cup.

The Soy in the Plastic Bubble

Quick and colorful tofu stir-fry with hoisin-peanut sauce

Sick and tired of the same old stir-fry? Don't confine yourself to the standard chicken and beef varieties. Our scrumptious stir-fry with marinated tofu has contagious flavor and may be just what the doctor ordered.

This recipe's a real ~~germ~~ gem!

⅔ cup	bottled light peanut sauce
2 tbsp	hoisin sauce
1 tsp	sesame oil
2 pkgs	(3 oz/85 g each) instant ramen noodles (see tip)
12 oz	(340 g) teriyaki or Szechuan-flavored firm tofu, cubed
1	medium red onion, sliced
2 cups	broccoli florets
1 cup	baby corn cobs, halved crosswise
1 cup	sliced red bell pepper
1 cup	snow peas or sugar snap peas
⅓ cup	chopped green onions
¼ cup	coarsely chopped fresh basil leaves or 2 tbsp minced fresh cilantro (or a bit of both)
¼ cup	chopped peanuts for garnish (optional)

- Before making this recipe, assemble all of the ingredients. The stir-fry comes together very quickly once you start.

- Whisk together peanut sauce, hoisin sauce and sesame oil in a small bowl. Set aside.

- Place noodles in a glass bowl (discard seasoning packets) and pour boiling water over top to cover. Let soak 1 minute, then drain in a colander. Using kitchen scissors, snip the noodles a bit so they aren't in 10-mile-long wavy pieces. Set aside.

- Spray a large, non-stick wok with cooking spray and heat over medium-high heat. Add tofu. Cook and stir until tofu begins to brown, about 2 minutes. Remove tofu from wok and set aside. Add red onion and ¼ cup water. Cook and stir until onion begins to soften, about 2 minutes. Add broccoli, corn cobs, red pepper and snow peas. Cook and stir for 3 to 4 more minutes, until vegetables are tender crisp. If the vegetables begin to stick, add a little more water. Add green onions and cook 1 more minute. Add reserved sauce and tofu. Mix well. Stir in noodles and basil. Cook 1 more minute. Remove from heat. Sprinkle individual servings with chopped peanuts, if desired.

MAKES 4 SERVINGS

PER SERVING
303 calories, 7.5 g total fat (1 g saturated fat), 14 g protein, 49 g carbohydrate, 6.6 g fiber, 0 mg cholesterol, 576 mg sodium

Recipe Tips: You know those cheap little packs of instant soup noodles that you survived on during your university days? That's what you'll need for this recipe. They come in all sorts of flavors, but it doesn't matter which type you buy because you'll be throwing away the little seasoning packs anyway. If you prefer, you can cook some whole wheat spaghetti (about 3 cups) and substitute for the ramen noodles.

The Vedge Edge

In the healthy-eating game, we all know that vegetables win the Most Valuable Player Award hands down, helping us control weight and feel great. Low in calories, fat and simple sugars, and high in fiber, anti-aging nutrients and cancer-fighting phytochemicals—no wonder health experts keep hounding us to eat five servings every day! But those aren't the only reasons why veggies are an indispensable tool in the weight-watcher's arsenal. They have a very high water content, and that means they're also high in oxygen (hence the "O" in the H_2O formula, in case you spent chemistry class catching up on your zzz's). In order for your lean muscle tissue to burn fat, it needs oxygen to help convert fat into energy. When you eat your greens (and yellows and reds and oranges), you flood your body with water, increasing oxygen levels, improving your metabolism and helping you burn fat. Weigh to go, veggies!

Trivial Tidbit

From tool time to teatime! Researchers have discovered that scattering tea bags throughout a newly remodeled room can reduce the toxicity of chemicals in the air by up to 90 percent. The porous, dry tea bags apparently soak up what's around them, including fumes from paint, polyurethane and glue. Maybe it's time to stop and smell the Red Rose!

Piled-High Veggie Potpie

Vegetable potpie with a colossal pumpkin biscuit crust

It's a potpie piled to the sky! And it's so darn tasty, you'll be begging for a second heaping helping.

Peas get off me!

2 tsp	olive oil
1 cup	each chopped onions and chopped red bell pepper
2 tsp	minced garlic
2½ cups	reduced-sodium vegetable broth, divided
2 cups	peeled, cubed potatoes
1 cup	sliced carrots
1½ tsp	dried rosemary
½ tsp	dried thyme
¼ tsp	each salt and freshly ground black pepper
1 cup	sliced asparagus pieces or sliced green beans
½ cup	frozen green peas, thawed
3 tbsp	all-purpose flour
¼ cup	minced fresh parsley

Pumpkin Biscuit Crust

1 cup	all-purpose flour
½ cup	whole wheat flour
2 tsp	baking powder
1 tsp	baking soda
½ tsp	salt
3 tbsp	frozen butter
¾ cup	cooked mashed pure pumpkin
⅔ cup	buttermilk

- Heat olive oil in a large pot over medium heat. Add onions, red pepper and garlic. Cook and stir over medium heat until vegetables begin to soften, about 5 minutes.

- Add 2 cups broth, potatoes, carrots, rosemary, thyme, salt and pepper. Bring to a boil. Reduce heat to low. Cover and simmer for 12 minutes, until potatoes are almost tender. Stir in asparagus and peas. Cook for 3 more minutes.

- In a small bowl, mix flour with remaining ½ cup vegetable broth until smooth. Add to vegetable mixture. Cook until bubbly and thickened. Stir in parsley. Transfer mixture to a 2-quart casserole dish. Set aside.

- Preheat oven to 425°F. In a large bowl, combine both flours, baking powder, baking soda and salt. Grate frozen butter directly into bowl with flour and mix gently using a fork until butter is evenly distributed. In a separate bowl, whisk together pumpkin and buttermilk, then add to flour mixture. Stir until a soft ball forms. Transfer dough to a lightly floured surface and roll or pat to fit top of casserole. Place dough over vegetables. Bake for 20 minutes, until crust is puffed up and golden brown.

MAKES 6 SERVINGS

PER SERVING
335 calories, 8.6 g total fat (4.1 g saturated fat), 9 g protein, 56 g carbohydrate, 5.5 g fiber, 17 mg cholesterol, 568 mg sodium

FOOD BITE

The name "rosemary" is derived from the Latin words for "dew of the sea" (ros + marinus). According to folklore, the rosemary plant originally had white flowers, but they turned red after the Virgin Mary laid her cloak on the bush. Traditionally, rosemary has been burned as incense to ward off infections, and French hospitals used it to disinfect the air. Today, scientists have found that inhaling the essential oil of rosemary can boost mental alertness and clarity, ease anxiety and even prevent cognitive degeneration. The *genus Rosmarinus* is pure genius!

What's the best place to eat along the highway? Wherever there's a fork in the road :)

Eggplanet Hollywood

Layered eggplant casserole with mozzarella and Parmesan cheeses

Roll out the red carpet for dinner guests! At your next soirée, cast this fabulous eggplant dish in the starring casserole and you're sure to draw rave reviews.

1 cup	dry unseasoned bread crumbs
⅓ cup	freshly grated Parmesan cheese
2 tsp	dried basil
2	eggs
2	medium eggplants (about 2 lbs/907 g total weight) unpeeled, each cut crosswise into 8 slices

Olive oil cooking spray

3 cups	low-sodium tomato pasta sauce
1 cup	packed shredded light mozzarella cheese (4 oz/113 g)
2 tbsp	minced fresh parsley

MAKES 8 SERVINGS

PER SERVING
205 calories, 7.6 g total fat (3.3 g saturated fat),
12 g protein, 24 g carbohydrate, 4.8 g fiber,
63 mg cholesterol, 603 mg sodium

- In a shallow bowl, combine bread crumbs, Parmesan cheese and basil. Mix well.

- In another shallow bowl, lightly beat eggs using a fork. Working one at a time, dip eggplant slices into beaten eggs, shake off excess, then press slices into crumb mixture. Turn to coat both sides with crumbs. Place slices on 1 large or 2 small baking sheets that have been sprayed with cooking spray.

- Spray tops of slices lightly with cooking spray. Bake at 400°F for 15 minutes. Remove eggplant from oven, turn slices over and spray again with cooking spray. Return to oven and bake for 15 more minutes. Remove from oven.

- To assemble casserole, spoon 1 cup pasta sauce over bottom of a 9 x 13-inch baking dish. Top with ½ eggplant slices. Spoon another 1 cup sauce over eggplant, followed by ½ mozzarella. Repeat layering with remaining eggplant slices, sauce and mozzarella. Sprinkle parsley over top.

- Return to oven and bake, uncovered, for 20 minutes, until cheese is completely melted and sauce is bubbly. Serve immediately.

Trivial Tidbit

Parmesan cheese is the most shoplifted item in Italy, making up 10 percent of all thefts!

Nothin' Beats Eats Without Meats!

Did you know that it takes 20 times more land to feed a person on a meat-based diet than it does to feed someone who's vegetarian? That vegetarians have lower rates of heart disease, cancer, diabetes, hypertension, gallstones and obesity? Or that vegetarians live longer and stronger than carnivores? If you *carrot* all about your health (and the environment!), it might be time to try livin' on the vedge! So here's a challenge: Abandon the thought that you have to eat meat every day. Instead, aim for two or three meat-free days a week. C'mon, don't have a cow, man! Just bypass the meat market and pick up meatless sources of protein, such as beans, legumes, nuts, seeds and whole grains like quinoa. Add some brightly colored fruits and veggies to the mix, try it for two months and we'll bet dollars to soy nuts that your energy level will surge and your saddlebags will shrink. Need proof it works? Our famous Eats Without Meats diet plan has been endorsed by such greens-loving celebrities as Okra Winfrey, Dill and Celery Clinton, Beet Midler and Dolly Parsley!

FULLafel Patties

Spicy Middle Eastern mashed chickpea patties

Full of fiber, full of protein, full of flavor! The herbs and spice make falafel taste nice, plus you won't feelawful after eating them, since our version isn't deep-fried.

1 can	(19 oz/540 mL) no-salt-added chickpeas, drained and rinsed
½ cup	diced red onion
3 tbsp	each minced fresh cilantro and parsley
2 tbsp	freshly squeezed lemon juice
2 tbsp	all-purpose flour
1 tbsp	tahini
1 tsp	minced garlic
1 tsp	ground cumin
½ tsp	each ground coriander, chili powder and salt
½ tsp	baking soda
⅛ tsp	cayenne pepper
2 tbsp	olive oil, divided

MAKES 15 PATTIES

PER PATTY
62 calories, 2.9 g total fat
(0.4 g saturated fat), 2 g protein,
7 g carbohydrate, 1.5 g fiber, 0 mg cholesterol, 130 mg sodium

- Add all ingredients except olive oil to the bowl of a food processor. Pulse on and off, occasionally scraping down sides of bowl, until mixture is the consistency of very thick cookie dough. Transfer mixture to a bowl, cover with plastic wrap and refrigerate for at least 1 hour (it will firm up).

- Using about 2 tbsp "dough" per patty, form mixture into 15 balls. Using your hands, flatten balls slightly to form 2-inch patties.

- Heat 1 tbsp oil in a 10-inch skillet over medium-high heat. Add half the patties to skillet. Cover and cook for about 3 to 4 minutes per side, until patties are lightly browned and heated through. Be careful not to burn them. Remove patties from skillet and keep warm. Cook remaining patties in remaining 1 tbsp oil. Patties will firm up a bit if left to cool slightly before serving. Serve warm.

Recipe Tips

Falafel patties taste great when served topped with tzatziki sauce, hummus (try roasted red pepper hummus) or tahini-yogurt sauce. You can stuff falafel patties into whole-grain pita bread with chopped veggies and a dollop of sauce for a filling vegetarian lunch or dinner. We like to eat the cold, leftover patties topped with a spoonful of hummus for a healthy snack.

Most of us spend our lives as if we have another one in the bank.
Ben Irwin

Lentili Chili

Zesty vegetarian chili with lentils

If you're longin' for a different kind of chili that's sure to please your palate, our spicy, meatless creation is the best you'll find this side of the contilentil divide.

2 tsp	olive oil	
1 cup	each diced onions, diced celery, diced green bell pepper and diced carrots	
1 tsp	minced garlic	
1 tbsp	chili powder	
2 tsp	ground cumin	
1½ tsp	dried oregano	
¼ tsp	ground cinnamon	
1 can	(19 oz/540 mL) no-salt-added diced tomatoes, undrained	
1 can	(19 oz/540 mL) cooked lentils, drained and rinsed (see tip)	
1 cup	no-salt-added tomato sauce	
½ cup	unsweetened pineapple juice	
¼ cup	chili sauce (see tip)	
¼ cup	minced fresh cilantro	

Light (5%) sour cream for garnish (optional)

MAKES 6 SERVINGS

PER SERVING
178 calories,
2.2 g total fat
(0.3 g saturated fat),
9 g protein,
31 g carbohydrate,
11 g fiber,
0 mg cholesterol,
321 mg sodium

- Heat olive oil in a large pot over medium heat. Add onions, celery, green pepper, carrots and garlic. Cook and stir for 5 minutes, until vegetables begin to soften.

- Add chili powder, cumin, oregano and cinnamon. Cook and stir for 1 more minute. Add all remaining ingredients, except cilantro and sour cream. Bring to a boil. Reduce heat to medium-low. Cover and simmer for 15 minutes, stirring occasionally.

- Stir in cilantro. Remove from heat. Ladle into serving bowls and top with a dollop of sour cream, if desired.

Nutrition Nugget

Can't remember anything you learned in high school? Eat pineapple! Powerful antioxidants in the fruit attack free radicals that wear away at brain cells and impair memory.

Recipe Tips

A staple throughout much of the Middle East and India, lentils are tiny, dried, lens-shaped seeds. They're a valuable source of protein and fiber, and have long been used as a meat substitute. You'll need cooked lentils for this recipe, so look for them beside the canned beans at your grocery store. Drain the lentils well, then rinse them with cold water to remove the added salt. Bottles of chili sauce (such as Heinz) can be found in the ketchup aisle of your grocery store. For a milder taste, use ketchup instead of chili sauce.

Pick a Potent Packed Pepper

Chili peppers have been recognized for centuries as a cure for a number of illnesses, from indigestion to impotence. Capsaicin, the chemical compound that gives chili peppers their heat, is actually used in some topical creams to relieve the agony of shingles, arthritis and other painful conditions. Like the effect it has on our taste buds, capsaicin first stuns, then anesthetizes when used as an ointment. When we eat chili peppers, our palate translates the heat as burningly tasty, causing our endorphins to kick in, giving us what some people describe as a "runner's high." Apparently, eating a tablespoon of red or green chilies doesn't just burn your mouth, it burns calories, too! Researchers say eating chili peppers increases your metabolic rate by 23 percent. Hot damn!

The Right Stuff

Quinoa-stuffed bell peppers with shiitake mushrooms, spinach, green peas, feta and mint

If you're looking for an interesting twist on ordinary rice-stuffed bell peppers, then you've made the right choice! This tasty, colorful, healthy recipe will leave you filling satisfied.

2 cups	reduced-sodium vegetable broth
1 cup	uncooked quinoa
½ tsp	each ground cumin, ground coriander and curry powder
6	medium bell peppers in a variety of colors
1 tbsp	olive oil
1 cup	chopped onions
1 tsp	minced garlic
3 cups	chopped shiitake mushrooms
3 cups	coarsely chopped baby spinach leaves
½ cup	sweet green peas
½ cup	crumbled light feta cheese (2 oz/57 g)
2 tbsp	minced fresh mint leaves
1 tsp	grated lemon zest
½ tsp	freshly ground black pepper

MAKES 6 SERVINGS

PER SERVING
244 calories, 7.1 g total fat (1.8 g saturated fat), 9 g protein, 38 g carbohydrate, 8 g fiber, 8 mg cholesterol, 187 mg sodium

- Combine vegetable broth, quinoa, cumin, coriander and curry powder in a medium pot. Bring to a boil. Reduce heat to low, cover and simmer for 15 minutes. Remove from heat and let stand, covered, until ready to use.

- Trim the tops off bell peppers. Remove seeds and discard stems. Mince tops and set aside.

- Heat olive oil in a deep, 10-inch skillet over medium heat. Add onions, reserved minced bell pepper tops and garlic. Cook and stir until vegetables begin to soften, about 4 minutes. Add mushrooms and continue to cook until mushrooms are tender, about 5 minutes. Add spinach and cook until wilted, about 2 minutes. Remove from heat.

- In a large bowl, combine cooked quinoa with mushroom mixture, peas, feta, mint, lemon zest and black pepper. Mix well. Spoon filling into bell peppers. Place peppers upright in a 9 x 13-inch baking pan. Cover loosely with foil. Bake at 375°F for 25 minutes. Remove foil and continue baking until bell peppers are tender, about 10 to 15 more minutes. Serve hot.

Nutrition Nugget

Rice 'n' easy swap: If you love rice, try replacing it with quinoa in recipes. It has more protein and fiber, and that means more fat-loss potential!

The Breakfast of Champignons

Wild mushroom, spinach and herb frittata

This simple but flavorful, protein-packed frittata is a winning breakfast or brunch idea!

MAKES 4 SERVINGS

PER SERVING
265 calories, 16 g total fat
(5.9 g saturated fat),
20 g protein,
12 g carbohydrate,
2.5 g fiber,
430 mg cholesterol,
365 mg sodium

2 tsp	olive oil
1 cup	chopped red onions
1 tsp	minced garlic
1 lb	(454 g) mixed wild mushrooms, sliced (such as cremini, shiitake, portobello)
½ tsp	dried basil
¼ tsp	dried thyme
2 cups	packed baby spinach leaves
8	eggs
¼ tsp	each salt and freshly ground black pepper
½ cup	freshly grated Parmesan cheese

- Heat olive oil in a 10-inch, non-stick skillet over medium heat. Add onions and garlic. Cook and stir until onions are tender, about 4 minutes. Add mushrooms. Continue cooking until mushrooms are tender, about 6 to 7 minutes. Stir in basil and thyme. Mix well. Add spinach leaves and cook until spinach is wilted.

- Whisk together eggs, salt and pepper. Pour evenly over mushroom mixture. Sprinkle with Parmesan. Reduce heat to low. Cover skillet with a tight-fitting lid and let cook until eggs are completely set, about 12 minutes. Slice into 4 servings and serve hot.

FOOD BITE

How can something that grows in the dark provide us with the sunshine vitamin? Well, we can thank Mother Nature for this fungal food phenomenon: Mushrooms, even the simple button variety, are one of the few foods that contains vitamin D, which helps the body absorb calcium and boosts our immune systems to prevent disease. If you live in the North, where winters are dark, you can either head to Florida or to the nearest produce department to reap some D-lightful benefits!

Busting the Cholesterol Myth

My LDL cholesterol is too high. My HDL cholesterol is too low. What the H_LL is my doctor talking about? Rather than obsess over the ABCs of HDLs, let's get to the heart of the matter where cholesterol's concerned. The majority of cholesterol in your bloodstream is manufactured by your liver and actually doesn't come from cholesterol-containing foods such as cheese, eggs, shrimp and red meat. The theory that cholesterol causes heart disease has been disproven by modern science. Repeat: Disproven! In fact, having low cholesterol seems to be more of a heart-attack risk. If your doctor keeps advising you to avoid eggs, perhaps he or she needs to get with the 21st century!

According to the latest research, the real culprits in the cholesterol caper are cookies, crackers, chips, white bread, French fries and sweets. That's right! A diet high in processed, refined carbohydrates (read: white flour and sugar) and low in fiber seems to send your liver into a cholesterol-manufacturing frenzy. Fried foods and trans fats are also big villains. Now remember, cholesterol's a sticky subject, and there are lots of other complicated factors, such as a sedentary lifestyle, low thyroid function, alcohol, smoking and just plain ol' bad genes, that affect it. On a more positive note, there are plenty of healthy additions you can make to your diet and lifestyle to keep cholesterol in check. Some proven cholesterol-lowering foods include apples, pears, grapefruit, berries, oatmeal and oat bran, whole grains, beans, nuts, flaxseed or chia seeds, green tea, garlic, onions, artichokes, ginger and cold-water fish (like salmon). Exercise and relaxation (managing stress) can lower LDL cholesterol (the lousy kind) and raise HDL cholesterol (the healthy kind). And it appears that how often you eat is just as important as what you eat. Studies show that people who eat five or six small meals a day have lower LDL cholesterol than those who eat two large meals.

In this chapter...

When Ya Hasta Have Pasta

Oodles of noodle recipes to satisfy your pasta cravings

Pasta Point of No Return, p. 135

Yes We Can-nelloni!

Spinach and cheese cannelloni with roasted tomato sauce

Think you can't create a rich-tasting, flavor-packed cannelloni unless it's stuffed with unhealthy ingredients? Yes, you can! The roasted tomato sauce with fennel is lip-smacking delicious.

Oui! Si! Yes!

Sauce

2 lbs	(907 g) small vine-ripened tomatoes
1	small fennel bulb, coarsely chopped
1	medium onion, coarsely chopped
1	red bell pepper, coarsely chopped
4	cloves garlic, halved
2 tbsp	olive oil
2 tbsp	balsamic vinegar
	Salt and freshly ground black pepper
1 can	(19 oz/540 mL) no-salt-added crushed tomatoes
2 cups	reduced-sodium vegetable broth
1½ tsp	Italian seasoning
⅛ tsp	crushed red pepper flakes
8	whole basil leaves, chopped

Filling

2 cups	part-skim ricotta cheese
1 cup	2% cottage cheese (mash with fork)
½ cup	freshly grated Parmesan cheese
½ pkg	(10 oz/300 g) frozen spinach, thawed, squeezed dry and finely chopped (5 oz/150 g total)
1	egg
¼ tsp	each dried basil and oregano
⅛ tsp	freshly ground black pepper
Pinch	nutmeg
5	sheets fresh, whole-grain lasagna noodles (see tip)
¾ cup	freshly grated Parmesan cheese

Recipe Tip: Packages of fresh, whole-grain lasagna sheets are sold in a cooler near the deli section of your grocery store.

MAKES 10 CANNELLONI

PER CANNELLONI
250 calories, 8.7 g total fat (3.3 g saturated fat), 16 g protein, 28 g carbohydrate, 5 g fiber, 68 mg cholesterol, 511 mg sodium

- To make sauce, quarter the tomatoes and place them on a large rimmed baking sheet with fennel, onions, red pepper and garlic. Drizzle vegetables with olive oil and balsamic vinegar, then sprinkle with some salt and freshly ground black pepper. Mix well using your hands. Roast vegetables at 450°F for 45 minutes on middle oven rack.

- While vegetables are roasting, prepare filling. Combine all filling ingredients in a medium bowl. Cover and refrigerate until ready to use.

- Remove vegetables from oven and let cool slightly. If any tomato skins come loose, you can remove and discard them. Transfer vegetables to a large pot. Add crushed tomatoes, vegetable broth, Italian seasoning, and crushed red pepper flakes. Simmer sauce over low heat, covered, for 15 minutes, stirring occasionally.

- Purée sauce using immersion blender (or carefully transfer to a food processor or regular blender to purée). Stir in basil leaves. Taste and add salt and pepper, if needed.

- Reduce oven temperature to 375°F. Spray a large baking pan (at least 9 x 13-inch) with cooking spray. Coat bottom of baking pan with sauce (about 1 cup should do it). Cut uncooked lasagna noodles in half. Working one at a time, place about ⅓ cup to ½ cup filling in the center of noodle. Roll up tightly to enclose filling. Place seam-side down in pan. Repeat with remaining noodles and filling. Cover cannelloni with sauce. (You won't need all of the sauce; freeze the remaining sauce so you have a quick, delicious sauce ready for a busy weeknight supper.) Sprinkle with Parmesan. Cover with foil and bake for 30 minutes. Uncover and bake an additional 5 minutes. Let stand for 5 minutes before serving (they're hot!).

> The trouble with eating Italian food is that five or six days later, you're hungry again.
>
> *George Miller*

Tickle Me Elbows

Our Mom's simple and delicious tuna noodle casserole with elbow macaroni

Revamped tuna noodle casserole that's so easy to make, it'll tickle your fancy. And if you have finicky kids, it's guaranteed to tickle their taste buds, too.

MAKES 6 SERVINGS

PER SERVING
303 calories,
7.1 g total fat
(3.3 g saturated fat),
19 g protein,
41 g carbohydrate,
4.7 g fiber,
29 mg cholesterol,
519 mg sodium

8 oz	(227 g) uncooked whole-grain or high-fiber white elbow macaroni (about 2 cups dry)
1 can	(6 oz/170 g) water-packed tuna, drained
1 cup	sliced celery
⅓ cup	chopped green onions
¼ cup	diced green bell pepper
¼ cup	diced pimento (see tip)
1 can	(10 oz/284 mL) reduced-fat cream of celery soup, undiluted
½ cup	1% milk
1 cup	packed shredded light old (sharp) cheddar cheese (4 oz/113 g)
½ cup	light mayonnaise
¼ tsp	freshly ground black pepper

Recipe Tip: Pimentos are sweet, red, heart-shaped peppers. They're most commonly used as a stuffing for green olives. Look for them in small jars near the pickles and olives at your grocery store. If you can't find pimentos, roasted red peppers make a good substitute.

- Cook macaroni according to package directions. Drain. Rinse with cold water and drain again. In a large bowl, combine cooked macaroni, tuna, celery, onions, green pepper and pimento. Mix well.

- In a small saucepan, combine soup and milk. Heat over medium heat until smooth. Add cheese and continue to cook until cheese is melted. Remove from heat and stir in mayonnaise and pepper.

- Pour sauce over macaroni mixture. Mix well. Pour into a 1½-quart casserole dish that has been sprayed with cooking spray. Bake at 350°F, uncovered, for 30 minutes. Serve hot.

Nutrition Nugget

Cook once, eat twice! When preparing recipes, why not cook extra to freeze or to take for lunch the next day? With healthy leftovers handy, you'll be less inclined to make impulsive, high-calorie, gut-busting choices. Besides, if you're going to mess up the kitchen, you might as well get two meals out of it.

Pasta La Vista, Baby!

Despite finger-pointing and pooh-poohing by high-protein, low-carb fanatics, there's really no need to place pasta on your list of banned substances. Eating pasta won't make you fat if you just use common sense and moderation. First, drill into your noggin the notion that a serving of pasta is one cup—not four! The typical restaurant portion is enough to feed Tony Soprano and his entire family. Second, realize that pasta, especially cooked firm (al dente), is actually low to moderate on the Glycemic Index. That means it won't cause wild blood-sugar fluctuations and stimulate insulin, the fat-storage hormone—unless, of course, you eat too much. Overeating even a low-glycemic food can send blood sugar and insulin into a frenzy. Third, think balance. When you combine fiber (say, from vegetables), protein (how 'bout some chicken?) and a good fat (maybe some olive oil) with pasta (try whole grain, spelt or kamut), this slows the release of sugar into the bloodstream and dampens the insulin response. No harm done. Those who blame pasta for their weight gain probably eat the white stuff—with plain sauce—and they eat too much, too often. So when ya hasta have pasta, remember that naked noodles are naughty. Cover 'em up. Accessorize. And don't forget to downsize.

Tube Beef or Not Tube Beef?

Slow-cooked beef cubes with mushrooms and onions in a zesty tomato sauce, served over rigatoni noodles

...THAT IS THE QUESTION

Tube beef or not tube beef? That is the question. This extraordinary meal of rigatoni tubes with stewed beef is meant to be shared, but it's only human nature to want to keep something so delicious all to yourself.

1½ lbs	(680 g) stewing beef
1 can	(28 oz/796 mL) no-salt-added diced tomatoes, undrained
1 can	(5.5 oz/156 mL) tomato paste
3 cups	sliced mushrooms
1 cup	chopped onions
2 tbsp	each reduced-sodium soy sauce, brown sugar and white vinegar
2 tsp	low-sodium beef bouillon powder
2 tsp	minced garlic
1 tsp	each dry mustard and dried oregano
½ tsp	freshly ground black pepper
¼ tsp	crushed red pepper flakes
12 oz	(340 g) uncooked rigatoni (about 7 cups dry)

MAKES 6 SERVINGS

PER SERVING
482 calories, 7.2 g total fat
(2.4 g saturated fat),
39 g protein, 61 g carbohydrate,
7 g fiber, 68 mg cholesterol,
250 mg sodium

- Trim all visible fat from beef. Cut into 1-inch cubes. Arrange beef in a small roaster or a large casserole dish with a lid.

- Combine remaining ingredients, except rigatoni, in a large bowl. Mix well. Pour over beef. Cover and bake at 350°F for 1 hour and 45 minutes to 2 hours, until beef is very tender. Stir once, halfway through cooking time. Taste and add a pinch of salt if needed.

- During last 15 minutes of cooking time, prepare rigatoni according to package directions. Drain. Serve hot beef and sauce over rigatoni.

Recipe Tip

When buying canned tomato products, it pays to be a grocery-store detective! Tomato sauce, canned tomatoes, pasta sauce and salsa are notoriously high in sodium, so always inspect the nutrition labels and choose the one with the lowest salt content. Thankfully, there are lots of new "no-salt-added" products appearing on store shelves. Oh, and don't assume the "organic" brand has the lowest sodium, either. We've found organic salsa that blows the lid right off the jar with 500 mg sodium for a measly 2 tbsp serving, compared to just 90 mg sodium in the same serving of regular salsa. Gasp! (Grabbing...chest... reaching for...defibrillator!)

Not a Fungi to be Around

Although they're found in the vegetable section of the grocery store, mushrooms aren't truly vegetables. They're fungi, and some are deadly. Now, don't get all worried—mushrooms are perfectly safe when you buy them at the supermarket. But, if you pick and eat mushrooms out in a field without knowing what you're doing, it might be the last thing you ever do! Since there's no feature that distinguishes toxic mushrooms from the edible kind, never gather or eat wild mushrooms unless a mushroom expert has identified them as safe. Be warned: There are no specific antidotes to some of their lethal poisons! The *morel* of the story: Err on the side of caution and buy your mushrooms at the store.

Less-On-Ya Lasagna

Roasted vegetable lasagna with four kinds of cheese

Translation: You'll end up with less fat on ya since there's less fat in your lasagna. But you'll actually have more healthy stuff in ya, given the heaping layers of veggies hidden under the cheese and noodles.

3 cups	sliced portobello mushrooms
2	medium zucchini, unpeeled and sliced
1	large red bell pepper, seeded and chopped
1	large yellow bell pepper, seeded and chopped
1	large red onion, thinly sliced
1 tbsp	olive oil
2 tsp	minced garlic
1 tsp	balsamic or red wine vinegar
1 tsp	each dried rosemary and dried oregano
1 cup	part-skim ricotta cheese
1 cup	1% cottage cheese
⅓ cup	minced fresh parsley, divided
¼ cup	freshly grated Parmesan cheese
1	egg
12	uncooked whole-grain lasagna noodles
3 cups	your favorite low-sodium tomato pasta sauce
1½ cups	packed shredded light mozzarella or Swiss cheese (6 oz/170 g)

- Spray a large roasting pan with cooking spray. Add mushrooms, zucchini, bell peppers, onion, olive oil, garlic, vinegar, rosemary and oregano. Mix well, until vegetables are coated with seasonings. Roast, uncovered, at 400°F for 25 minutes, stirring once halfway through cooking time.

- While vegetables are roasting, prepare cheese filling and cook pasta. In a medium bowl, combine ricotta and cottage cheeses, ¼ cup parsley, Parmesan cheese and egg. Mix well. Refrigerate until ready to use. Prepare lasagna noodles according to package directions. Drain well. Rinse with cold water and drain again.

- To assemble lasagna, spray a 9 x 13-inch baking dish with cooking spray. Spread ¼ pasta sauce over bottom of pan. Arrange 4 lasagna noodles, 3 lengthwise and one crosswise, over sauce. Spread ½ cheese filling over noodles, followed by ⅓ roasted vegetables. Sprinkle vegetables with ⅓ mozzarella. Repeat layering: 4 noodles, ½ cheese filling, ⅓ roasted vegetables and ⅓ mozzarella. Layer final 4 noodles over mozzarella, followed by remaining pasta sauce. Top sauce with remaining roasted vegetables.

- Cover with foil and bake at 375°F for 35 minutes. Remove lasagna from oven, sprinkle with remaining mozzarella and parsley and return to oven, uncovered, for 5 more minutes. Let cool for 10 minutes before serving.

MAKES 8 SERVINGS

PER SERVING
353 calories, 9.1 g total fat (3.1 g saturated fat), 23 g protein, 47 g carbohydrate, 3 g fiber, 19 mg cholesterol, 619 mg sodium

Actual announcement on church bulletin: Potluck dinner Saturday night. Prayer and medication to follow :)

Lawrence of Arrabbiata

Penne pasta topped with a simple, spicy, oven-roasted tomato sauce

It's no mirage. Penne that's simple to make, yet bursting with flavor. Tasting is believing!

2 lbs	(907 g) plum tomatoes, quartered
1½ cups	chopped red onions
4	slices reduced-sodium bacon, chopped
2 tsp	minced garlic
1 tbsp	balsamic or red wine vinegar
1½ tsp	each dried basil and dried oregano
12 oz	(340 g) uncooked whole-grain penne pasta (about 4 cups dry)
2 tbsp	tomato paste
½ tsp	salt
½ tsp	each freshly ground black pepper and crushed red pepper flakes
¼ cup	freshly grated Parmesan cheese

Minced fresh parsley for garnish

- Spray a roasting pan with cooking spray. Add tomatoes, onions, bacon and garlic. Mix well and spread evenly in pan. Roast, uncovered, at 400°F for 15 minutes. Remove pan from oven. Add vinegar, basil and oregano. Mix well and return pan to oven. Roast for 15 more minutes.

- Meanwhile, prepare pasta according to package directions. Drain well and keep warm.

- Transfer roasted vegetable mixture to a blender or food processor. Work in batches if necessary. Purée until smooth. Transfer mixture to a medium saucepan. Add tomato paste, salt, pepper and crushed red pepper flakes. Bring sauce to a boil, then reduce heat and simmer, uncovered, for 5 minutes. Spoon hot sauce over cooked pasta. Sprinkle with Parmesan cheese and parsley. Serve immediately.

MAKES 4 SERVINGS

PER SERVING
471 calories, 9.3 g total fat (3.3 g saturated fat),
25 g protein, 71 g carbohydrate, 13 g fiber,
20 mg cholesterol, 650 mg sodium

Slow Down to Slim Down

Do you inhale your food like it's The Last Supper? Snort it down like a finalist in a pie-eating contest, like Greta does? Then you probably haven't heard the old Indian proverb that says, "Drink your food, chew your drink!" Translation: We should eat slowly and chew our foods enough to liquefy them and, when drinking, swoosh our beverages around in our mouths before swallowing so that enzymes in our saliva can begin working their magic. Following this sage advice not only improves digestion and absorption of food, but also improves metabolism. Yes, as boring as it sounds, eating slowly is a smart weight-loss strategy! According to researchers at the University of Rhode Island, if you consciously stop to take a breath between bites or put your fork down when you chew, you can cut your food (and calorie) intake by 10 percent. Based on a 2,000-calorie-a-day diet, that would amount to 200 fewer calories each day, 1,400 fewer a week and 72,800 fewer a year—enough to lose 20 pounds of flab!

Nutrition Nugget

Just a spoonful of sugar helps the medicine go down? Think again, Sugar! If you're in the habit of merrily poppin' sweet nothings in your mouth, you might find yourself needing medical attention too often. Studies have shown that eating too much white sugar and other sweets can, in effect, "paralyze" the white blood cells of the immune system for half an hour or more, making you more susceptible to disease. Better practice moderation, since *sugarcalafragilisticmakesyourcellsatrocious!*

Eenie Meenie Fettuccine

Lightened-up fettuccine Alfredo with tuna and sweet green peas

Eenie Meenie Minie Mo! Fet-tuc-ci-ne Al-fre-do! We're justifiably proud of our slimmed-down rendition of this popular classic. Its velvety Alfredo sauce is sheer RAPture! Yo!

MAKES 4 SERVINGS

PER SERVING
550 calories,
13 g total fat
(6.7 g saturated fat),
34 g protein,
75 g carbohydrate,
10.3 g fiber,
51 mg cholesterol,
492 mg sodium

12 oz	(340 g) uncooked whole wheat or spinach fettuccine
2 tbsp	butter
2 tsp	minced garlic
1½ cups	2% milk
1½ tbsp	all-purpose flour
⅓ cup	freshly grated Parmesan cheese
½ tsp	dried basil
¼ tsp	each salt and freshly ground black pepper
1 can	(6 oz/170 g) water-packed tuna, drained
¼ cup	light (5%) sour cream
¾ cup	frozen green peas, thawed
2 tbsp	minced fresh parsley

- Cook fettuccine according to package directions. Drain and return to pot. Keep warm.

- While pasta is cooking, prepare sauce. Melt the butter in a medium pot over medium heat. Add garlic and sauté for 1 minute. Whisk together milk and flour until smooth. Add to garlic. Increase heat to medium-high. Cook and stir until mixture is bubbly and has thickened, about 4 to 5 minutes.

- Reduce heat to low. Stir in Parmesan cheese, basil, salt and pepper. Cook for 1 to 2 more minutes, until cheese is melted. Stir in tuna, sour cream and peas. Cook until heated through, about 2 minutes.

- Pour sauce over fettuccine and toss to coat. Sprinkle parsley over top. Serve with extra Parmesan cheese and black pepper, if desired. Best if served immediately.

FOOD BITE

Alfredo di Lellio, a Roman restaurant owner, was the "Alfredo" who created the popular fettuccine dish in 1920. When movie fans discovered that celebrities Douglas Fairbanks and Mary Pickford patronized Alfredo's every day on their honeymoon in the Eternal City, the dish became very popular in the United States.

Penne from Heaven

Shrimp, scallops, black olives, feta and a zesty tomato sauce served over penne noodles

This miraculously delicious Mediterranean-style pasta dish was created with the help of some divine intervention!

It's divine!

MAKES 4 SERVINGS

PER SERVING
555 calories,
9.9 g total fat
(2.7 g saturated fat),
41 g protein,
71 g carbohydrate,
13 fiber,
117 mg cholesterol,
495 mg sodium

2 tsp	olive oil
1 cup	chopped red onions
2 tsp	minced garlic
1½ cups	chopped zucchini, unpeeled
1 can	(28 oz/796 mL) no-salt-added diced tomatoes, undrained
1 cup	no-salt-added tomato sauce
2 tbsp	tomato paste
1 tbsp	each minced fresh oregano and basil, or 1½ tsp each dried
½ tsp	freshly ground black pepper
¼ tsp	crushed red pepper flakes
12 oz	(340 g) uncooked whole-grain or high-fiber white penne pasta (about 4 cups dry)
8 oz	(227 g) raw jumbo shrimp, peeled
8 oz	(227 g) raw bay scallops
¼ cup	sliced black olives
1 cup	crumbled light feta cheese (4 oz/113 g)

Minced fresh parsley for garnish

- Heat olive oil in a large pot over medium heat. Add onions and garlic. Cook and stir for 3 to 4 minutes, until onions are softened. Add zucchini and cook for 3 more minutes. Add diced tomatoes and their liquid, tomato sauce, tomato paste, oregano, basil, pepper and crushed red pepper flakes. Bring to a boil. Reduce heat to medium-low and simmer, uncovered, for 10 minutes.

- While sauce is simmering, prepare pasta according to package directions. Drain well and keep warm.

- Add shrimp, scallops and olives to sauce. Increase heat to medium-high and cook for 3 to 4 minutes, until shrimp and scallops are cooked through.

- To serve, spoon cooked penne onto serving plates. Top with sauce, followed by crumbled feta and chopped parsley. Serve immediately.

FOOD BITE

The world's rarest coffee comes from Indonesia. At about $300 US a pound, *kopi luwak* is the end product (we really mean end product!) of a catlike marsupial called the *Paradoxurus hermaphroditus* that loves eating coffee beans. The enzymes in the animal's stomach add a unique flavor, and the beans are collected only after they are excreted. Oh, come on! Don't pooh-pooh it until you try it!

WHEN YA HASTA HAVE PASTA

Clamborguini

Whole-grain linguini with a tomato and herb clam sauce

Rev up your engine with this high-performance, high-flavor pasta entrée. The taste will drive you wild!

1 tsp	olive oil
1 cup	chopped red onions
2 tsp	minced garlic
1 can	(28 oz/796 mL) no-salt-added diced tomatoes, undrained
3 tbsp	tomato paste
1 tbsp	balsamic or red wine vinegar
1 tbsp	brown sugar
2 tsp	dried basil
1 tsp	dried oregano
½ tsp	salt
¼ tsp	each freshly ground black pepper and crushed red pepper flakes
12 oz	(340 g) uncooked whole-grain linguini
1 can	(5 oz/142 g) whole baby clams, drained
¼ cup	minced fresh parsley
¼ cup	freshly grated Parmesan cheese

MAKES 4 SERVINGS

PER SERVING
484 calories, 5.3 g total fat (1.7 g saturated fat), 26 g protein, 81 g carbohydrate, 11.1 g fiber, 26 mg cholesterol, 526 mg sodium

- Heat olive oil in a large pot over medium heat. Add onions and garlic. Cook and stir for 3 to 4 minutes, until onions are softened.

- Add diced tomatoes and their liquid, tomato paste, vinegar, brown sugar, basil, oregano, salt, black pepper and crushed red pepper flakes. Bring to a boil. Reduce heat to medium-low. Simmer, uncovered, for 20 minutes, until sauce has thickened.

- Meanwhile, prepare linguini according to package directions. Drain well and keep warm.

- Add drained clams and parsley to sauce. Simmer for 5 more minutes. Serve hot sauce over linguini. Sprinkle with Parmesan cheese.

Trivial Tidbit

In Germany, they insist that eating a bowl of oatmeal with fried onions is a surefire cure for a hangover. Nein danke! (No thanks!)

Hello, My Name is Betty and I'm Dehydrated

Do you have a drinking problem? Well, if you're serious about losing fat, you really should get sloshed. What's on tap? Water! If you're not downing 8 to 10 glasses of water a day, you could be dampening your weight-loss efforts. Without water, your body can't metabolize stored fat efficiently. In fact, even mild dehydration can slow down your metabolism by 3 percent. If you weigh 150 pounds, that's 45 fewer calories burned each day, and over the course of a year, that 45 calories can amount to 5 pounds of stubborn fat strapped to your middle. Bartender! Gimme a double shot of H_2O—on the rocks! Water is the ultimate liquid asset, making up more than 70 percent of our bodies. It regulates body temperature, keeps blood volume up, carries nutrients and oxygen to the cells, promotes proper digestion, tones muscles and gets rid of toxins. Imagine! Drink like a fish and detox at the same time! Plus, water is energizing, and that makes you want to move. When you're dehydrated, you feel sluggish and tired, which will likely send you crawling to the cookie jar. A water shortage makes the body cling to every last drop, and that shows up as swollen feet, legs, hands and eyelids, inflating your weight by as much as 5 to 15 pounds! Ironically, you should drink more water, not less, to beat the bloat. So sneak in some extra H_2O whenever you can. Drink socially! Drink alone! Drink heavily! Join a 12-sip program!

Lanky Noodle Dandy

Chicken and mushroom cream sauce served over egg noodles

Lanky Noodle really went to town when he created this mildly flavored, super-satisfying pasta dish.

12 oz	(340 g) uncooked large whole-grain egg noodles (about 5 cups dry)
1 tbsp	butter
1 tsp	minced garlic
3 cups	sliced mixed mushrooms (see tip)
1½ cups	2% milk
2 tbsp	all-purpose flour
½ cup	reduced-sodium chicken broth
½ cup	freshly grated Romano or Parmesan cheese
½ cup	light (5%) sour cream
½ tsp	each dried thyme and dried basil
¼ tsp	freshly ground black pepper
3 cups	chopped cooked chicken breast
1 cup	frozen green peas, thawed
⅓ cup	minced fresh parsley
¼ cup	chopped roasted red peppers or pimentos (see tip)

- Cook noodles according to package directions. Drain well and keep warm.

- Meanwhile, melt butter in a large, non-stick pot over medium-high heat. Add garlic and mushrooms. Cook and stir for about 4 minutes, until mushrooms are tender.

- Whisk together milk and flour until smooth. Add to mushrooms, along with chicken broth. Cook until sauce is bubbly and has thickened, stirring constantly. Add cheese, sour cream, thyme, basil and pepper. Stir until cheese is melted. Add cooked chicken, peas, parsley and red peppers. Cook until chicken and peas are heated through. Serve over hot noodles.

PER SERVING
470 calories,
10.4 g total fat
(5 g saturated fat),
40 g protein,
54 g carbohydrate,
7.2 g fiber,
80 mg cholesterol,
367 mg sodium

Recipe Tips

Instead of using plain ol' white mushrooms in this recipe, try a mixture of shiitake and cremini mushrooms. Almost all grocery stores carry them. While you're there, look for jars of roasted red peppers and pimentos near the pickles.

Nutrition Nugget

Hot date tonight? Chew on some parsley! Like "nature's mouthwash," its odor-absorbing chlorophyll will freshen your breath, plus its diuretic properties will help you beat the bloat so your little black dress will zip up without a hitch.

Take Our Word for It

English is a crazy language. For instance, there are no grapes in grapefruit, no eggs in eggplant, no horse in horseradish, no ham in hamburger. You won't find any pine or apples in pineapple. English muffins weren't invented in England and French fries didn't originate in France. And here's a little food for thought: If a vegetarian eats vegetables, what does a humanitarian eat?

Thou Shell Eat Beans

Shell-shaped pasta and black beans with a heavenly, spicy tomato sauce

Here's a sin-free recipe you'll want to carve in stone! Miraculous taste!

2 tsp	olive oil
1 cup	diced green bell pepper
½ cup	chopped onions
2 tsp	minced garlic
2 cups	no-salt-added tomato sauce
1 can	(19 oz/540 mL) no-salt-added black beans, drained and rinsed
1 tsp	dried oregano
½ tsp	each ground cumin and crushed red pepper flakes
8 oz	(227 g) uncooked medium-sized shell-shaped pasta (about 3 cups dry)
½ cup	packed shredded light Monterey Jack cheese (2 oz/57 g)

- Heat olive oil in a medium pot over medium heat. Add bell pepper, onions and garlic. Cook and stir until vegetables begin to soften, about 4 minutes. Add tomato sauce, beans, oregano, cumin and crushed red pepper flakes. Bring to a boil. Reduce heat to medium-low, cover and simmer for 5 minutes.

- Meanwhile, prepare pasta shells according to package directions. Drain. Add shells to sauce and mix well. Ladle into individual serving bowls and sprinkle with cheese. Serve hot.

MAKES 4 SERVINGS

PER SERVING
409 calories, 7.4 g total fat (2.5 g saturated fat), 19 g protein, 69 g carbohydrate, 12.9 g fiber, 10 mg cholesterol, 192 mg sodium

Trivial Tidbit

According to an old wives' tale, cumin is said to inspire fidelity in men. In Europe, when young men went off to war, their sweethearts would bake bread sprinkled with cumin seeds to send with them. A soldier would return faithful and full-bellied, thanks to his wife's *dough*nation to the war cause.

May the G-Force Be With You

Boing! Boing! Boing! NASA has long recognized the enormous benefits of bouncing, or rebounding, beginning with its own use of mini trampolines to help astronauts recover from prolonged periods of weightlessness. Get bouncing on a mini trampoline and you might experience "weigh-less-ness," too! Making like a kangaroo for as little as 10 minutes a day can help you shed pounds, tone muscles and conquer cellulite. It also helps protect against cancer, heart disease and many degenerative conditions. That's because with each up and down movement, 50 trillion body cells are pitted against the Earth's gravitational force and the demand on your body's cells to adjust makes them grow stronger. Plus, when cells get squished from all that bouncing, that stimulates your lymphatic system (your internal vacuum cleaner) to force waste products out and deliver nutrients within the body. Talk about *spring* cleaning! The result is a stronger immune system, renewed bone mass and improved overall health. Rebounding is easy on the joints and you can do it just about anywhere or anytime: in your office, backyard, bedroom, or while watching TV, talking on the phone or listening to music. Heck! Maybe you should let your kids bounce on their beds after all!

Part of the secret of life is to eat what you like and let the food fight it out inside.
Mark Twain

A Penne for Your Thoughts

Penne pasta with bacon, mushrooms, spinach and sun-dried tomatoes

Too good for words! The zest and zing of this pasta dish will be stored in your memory bank forever.

1 cup	sun-dried tomatoes (see tip)
12 oz	(340 g) uncooked whole wheat or high-fiber white penne pasta (about 4 cups dry)
4	slices reduced-sodium bacon, cut crosswise into ½-inch sections
2 tsp	minced garlic
3 cups	thinly sliced mushrooms (any kind)
2 cups	chopped fresh baby spinach leaves
1 cup	sliced red onion rings
2 tbsp	minced fresh basil
½ tsp	crushed red pepper flakes

Freshly ground black pepper to taste

¼ cup	freshly grated Parmesan cheese
2 tbsp	minced fresh parsley

- Pour 1 cup boiling water over sun-dried tomatoes and let soak for 15 minutes. Drain and chop. Set aside.

- Meanwhile, cook penne according to package directions. Drain and keep warm.

- Cook bacon in a large skillet over medium-high heat until crisp. Do not discard bacon drippings. Add garlic and cook 1 more minute. Add mushrooms, spinach, onions, sun-dried tomatoes, basil and crushed red pepper flakes. Cook and stir for 5 to 6 minutes, until mushrooms and onions are tender.

- Toss bacon-vegetable mixture with hot pasta until evenly distributed. Divide pasta between 4 serving dishes. Top each with freshly ground black pepper and 1 tbsp Parmesan cheese. Sprinkle with parsley. Serve immediately.

MAKES 4 SERVINGS

PER SERVING
462 calories, 10 g total fat (3.7 g saturated fat), 26 g protein, 64 g carbohydrate, 13 g fiber, 24 mg cholesterol, 534 mg sodium

Recipe Tip

Sun-dried tomatoes (which are actually dried in ovens) provide concentrated flavor and a chewy texture to enliven savory dishes. They're available packaged dry or in oil and have the same nutritional value as fresh tomatoes, which means they're good for you! We prefer the dried version since they don't contain additional ingredients and can be stored in your pantry for months. Sun-dried tomatoes are easily softened by pouring boiling water over them and letting them soak for 15 to 30 minutes. Look for them in bags or plastic containers in the produce section of your supermarket.

Nutrition Nugget

Put a new spin on spinach! Start your day with a mega-dose of iron and cell-protecting plant nutrients by whirling up a spinach smoothie. In a blender, combine a large handful of baby spinach leaves, a few ice cubes and either a frozen banana (cut in chunks) or a cup of frozen ripe mango (or some of each). Add one to two cups water and whirl away! Flavor and nutritional punch that would do Popeye proud!

> A bad habit never disappears miraculously. It's an undo-it-yourself project.
>
> *Abigail Van Buren*

Gringo's Starr

Baked cavatappi pasta with spicy, ground-turkey tomato sauce and two cheeses

While travelling aimlessly through Mexico, our friend Gringo discovered this spicy and ultra-hearty Spanish-style pasta dish that was the star attraction at a local eating house called the Obla Di Obla Diner. He loved it so much that he took a job there drumming up business for the owners.

MAKES 6 SERVINGS

PER SERVING
423 calories,
9 g total fat
(3.1 g saturated fat),
30 g protein,
57 g carbohydrate,
6 g fiber,
69 mg cholesterol,
662 mg sodium

12 oz	(340 g) uncooked cavatappi pasta (corkscrew-shaped macaroni) or medium shell pasta (about 4 cups dry; look for whole wheat)
2 tsp	olive oil
1 lb	(454 g) ground turkey or chicken
1 cup	chopped onions
2 tsp	minced garlic
¾ cup	each diced red and green bell peppers
2	jalapeño peppers, seeded and minced
2 cups	low-sodium tomato pasta sauce
¾ cup	salsa (mild, medium or hot)
1 tsp	each dried oregano, ground cumin and chili powder
¼ tsp	freshly ground black pepper
1 cup	1% cottage cheese or part-skim ricotta cheese
½ cup	packed shredded light Monterey Jack or cheddar cheese (2 oz/57 g)
1 tbsp	minced fresh cilantro or parsley

- Prepare pasta according to package directions. Drain. Rinse with cold water and drain again. Set aside.

- Heat olive oil in a large skillet over medium-high heat. Add turkey, onions, garlic, green and red peppers and jalapeños. Cook and stir until turkey is no longer pink, about 5 minutes. Drain off any fat. Add pasta sauce, salsa, oregano, cumin, chili powder and pepper. Bring to a boil. Reduce heat to medium-low. Cover and simmer for 5 minutes, stirring occasionally. Remove from heat.

- Spray a 9 x 13-inch baking dish with cooking spray. Spread a bit of pasta sauce over bottom, followed by ½ the pasta and ½ the remaining sauce. Spread cottage cheese evenly over sauce. Spread remaining pasta over cottage cheese, followed by remaining sauce. Top with shredded cheese.

- Cover and bake at 350°F for 30 minutes, until completely heated through. Let stand 5 minutes before serving. Sprinkle with cilantro and serve hot.

Trivial Tidbit

An old Transylvanian remedy for easing the pain and swelling of inflamed joints calls for applying a cooked onion directly on the sore spot. What? No garlic?

Tubes and Cubes

Rigatoni tubes with chicken cubes and barbecue sauce

It takes two to tango, and rigatoni and chicken do make a fabulous couple. But when smooth-talking barbecue sauce is permitted to cut in, things really get swingin'.

MAKES 4 SERVINGS

PER SERVING
496 calories,
8.2 g total fat
(2.8 g saturated fat),
47 g protein,
54 g carbohydrate,
6 g fiber,
92 mg cholesterol,
584 mg sodium

2 tsp	olive oil
½ cup	chopped red onions
1 tsp	minced garlic
4	boneless skinless chicken breasts, cut into 1-inch cubes (about 1½ lbs/680 g)
2 cups	sliced mushrooms
1 cup	chopped green bell pepper
1 cup	your favorite low-sodium tomato pasta sauce
⅓ cup	barbecue sauce (see tip)
8 oz	(227 g) uncooked rigatoni (about 5 cups dry)
½ cup	packed shredded light Monterey Jack cheese (2 oz/57 g)

Minced fresh cilantro or parsley for garnish

• Heat oil in a large pot over medium-high heat. Add onions and garlic. Cook and stir for 1 to 2 minutes, until onions are softened. Add chicken and cook until no longer pink. Add mushrooms and green pepper. Continue to cook for 3 to 4 minutes, until vegetables are tender. Add pasta sauce and barbecue sauce. Mix well. Reduce heat, cover and simmer for 5 minutes.

• Meanwhile, prepare rigatoni according to package directions. Drain well. Add rigatoni to chicken and vegetables and mix well. Spoon pasta mixture onto serving plates and sprinkle with cheese and cilantro. Serve immediately.

Recipe Tip: Any type of bottled barbecue sauce will do, but we prefer the kind that says "for chicken and ribs." Make sure you compare sodium levels among different brands. If you like your pasta really saucy, increase pasta sauce to 1½ cups and barbecue sauce to ½ cup.

The Kitchen is Closed!

If you're looking for one small tip that can help you drop clothing sizes faster than a Survivor contestant, then listen up: Put a "closed" sign on the refrigerator door at 7:30 p.m. This kitchen curfew gives your liver a much-deserved break from digestion duties, freeing it to concentrate on its lengthy "to do" list while you're sleeping. That's when repair and rejuvenation are scheduled to happen. Plus, if you don't eat until the next morning, say, at 7:30, you've effectively undertaken a "12-hour mini-fast," allowing your organs and cells to clear some of the debris that's been building up over time. But you'll also cut out a ton of unnecessary calories. Your body doesn't need the energy (calories) at night. So what happens? It's the graveyard shift at the fat factory! Eat at night, make fat all night! Let's face it: If you actually wrote down everything you unconsciously nibble on or absentmindedly swig back after dinner while puttering around the house, watching TV, surfing the Net or helping kids with homework, you might be shocked to see how it all adds up—literally and *figure*atively!

Trivial Tidbit

Coming soon to your local grocer: *Ants* Jemima? Betcha didn't know there are more than 1,450 recorded species of edible insects. (Who are the lucky folks on that taste panel?) Ounce for ounce, many species of insects are lower in fat and higher in protein than beef, pork, lamb or chicken. Talk about guilt-free grub!

Mr. Bowjangles

Simple bow-tie pasta with chicken, broccoli and sun-dried tomatoes in a light broth

The zest and zing of this pasta dish will make your heart sing and your taste buds dance for joy!

¼ cup   reduced-sodium soy sauce
2 tbsp   each liquid honey and freshly squeezed lime juice
1 tbsp   each olive oil, Dijon mustard and balsamic vinegar
1 tsp   minced garlic
4   boneless skinless chicken breasts, cut into
             1-inch cubes (about 1½ lbs/680 g)
½ cup   sun-dried tomatoes (not oil-packed)
8 oz   (227 g) uncooked whole-grain bow-tie pasta (about 5 cups dry)
3 cups   broccoli florets
½ cup   chopped green onions

MAKES 4 SERVINGS

PER SERVING
483 calories, 6.7 g total fat
(1.2 g saturated fat), 46 g protein,
60 g carbohydrate, 8.8 g fiber,
82 mg cholesterol, 743 mg sodium

- In a small bowl, whisk together soy sauce, honey, lime juice, olive oil, mustard, vinegar and garlic. Pour marinade over chicken cubes in a shallow, glass baking dish. Stir until all chicken pieces are coated with marinade. Cover and refrigerate for 30 minutes.

- Pour 1 cup boiling water over sun-dried tomatoes and let soak for 15 minutes. Drain tomatoes and chop. Set aside.

- Prepare pasta according to package directions. Add broccoli florets to pasta cooking water for last 3 minutes. Drain pasta and broccoli and return to pot. Keep warm.

- Transfer chicken and marinade to a large, non-stick skillet. Cook and stir over medium-high heat until chicken is cooked through, about 6 to 7 minutes. Add pasta, broccoli, sun-dried tomatoes and green onions. Mix well. Serve immediately.

Nutrition Nugget

Why is muscle-building exercise so important for losing flab, controlling cravings and preventing diabetes? Because muscle tissue is responsible for 80 percent of blood-sugar uptake following a meal. That means the more muscle you have, the more sugar you'll soak up. Now that's worth the weights!

She feeds him like a god.
Every meal is a burnt offering :)

Manicotti Overboard

Crabmeat and spinach manicotti with Swiss cheese and fresh dill

Help! Help! I'm drowning in a magnificent blend of crabmeat, cheese, dill and spinach! All hands on deck…grab a fork and try some of this! Save me! Save me! Save me some leftovers!

10	uncooked manicotti shells (see tip)
2 tbsp	butter
1 tsp	minced garlic
3 tbsp	all-purpose flour
1½ cups	2% milk
1 can	(19 oz/540 mL) no-salt-added diced tomatoes, drained
1 cup	packed shredded light Swiss cheese (4 oz/113 g)
1 tbsp	minced fresh dill
½ tsp	crushed red pepper flakes
¼ tsp	each salt and freshly ground black pepper
10 oz	(284 g) lump crabmeat, chopped (imitation crabmeat is fine)
1 cup	1% cottage cheese or part-skim ricotta cheese
½ pkg	(10 oz/300 g) frozen spinach, thawed, squeezed dry and chopped (5 oz/150 g total)
¼ cup	freshly grated Parmesan cheese
1	egg

MAKES 10 MANICOTTI

PER MANICOTTI
262 calories, 7.5 g total fat
(3.8 g saturated fat), 20 g protein,
28 g carbohydrate, 2 g fiber,
62 mg cholesterol,
376 mg sodium

- Cook manicotti according to package directions. Drain well. Rinse with cold water and drain again. Set aside.

- Melt butter in a medium pot over medium heat. Add garlic and cook for 1 minute. Whisk together flour and milk until smooth. Add to garlic. Continue to cook, stirring often, until sauce is bubbly and has thickened, about 7 minutes. Stir in tomatoes, ½ cup of the Swiss cheese, dill, crushed red pepper flakes, salt and pepper. When cheese has melted, remove from heat.

- To prepare filling, combine crabmeat, cottage cheese, spinach, remaining Swiss cheese, Parmesan cheese and egg in a large bowl. Mix well.

- Spray a 9 x 13-inch baking pan with cooking spray. Using a teaspoon, carefully spoon filling into each manicotti shell, being careful not to tear them. Place manicotti in baking pan in a single layer. Pour sauce evenly over top. Cover with foil and bake at 350°F for 30 minutes. Remove from oven, uncover and let cool for 5 minutes before serving.

Recipe Tip

If you prefer, you can substitute 5 sheets of fresh, whole-grain lasagna noodles for the manicotti shells. Just cut each sheet in half, spoon filling in center and roll up tightly. There's no need to precook them before using. For this reason alone, they're worth the extra money! Look for packages of fresh, whole-grain lasagna sheets in a cooler near the deli section of your grocery store.

FOOD BITE

Holey moly! It seems that gassy bacteria are behind Swiss cheese's famous holes, which are technically called eyes. In order to make Swiss cheese, starter cultures of bacteria are added to milk, where they create lactic acid, essential for producing cheese. Once the special bacteria are added to the cheese mixture and warmed, bubbles of carbon dioxide form, and these bubbles become the holes in the final product. The longer the cheese cures, the larger the eyes.

The Yellow Bows of Texas

Zesty chili with ground turkey and black beans served over bow-tie pasta

Deep in the heart of Texas, the locals ranked this spicy masterpiece the best pasta dish this side of the Alamo.

2 tsp	olive oil
1 lb	(454 g) ground turkey
1 cup	chopped onions
1 tsp	minced garlic
1 cup	each chopped green bell pepper and diced carrots
1½ cups	no-salt-added tomato sauce
1½ cups	salsa
1 can	(19 oz/540 mL) no-salt-added black beans, drained and rinsed
1½ tsp	chili powder
1 tsp	ground cumin
½ tsp	dried oregano
12 oz	(340 g) uncooked whole-grain bow-tie pasta (about 7 cups dry)
½ cup	light (5%) sour cream
½ cup	packed shredded light old (sharp) cheddar cheese (2 oz/57 g)
½ cup	chopped green onions

MAKES 6 SERVINGS

PER SERVING
506 calories,
11.9 g total fat
(3.7 g saturated fat),
31 g protein,
68 g carbohydrate,
15.4 g fiber,
71 mg cholesterol,
399 mg sodium

> Whatsoever was the father of a disease, an ill diet was the mother.
>
> *George Herbert*

- Heat olive oil in a large pot over medium-high heat. Add ground turkey. Cook and stir until turkey is no longer pink. Break up any large chunks with a fork. Add onions, garlic, green pepper and carrots. Cook and stir for 4 to 5 minutes, until vegetables begin to soften. Stir in tomato sauce, salsa, beans, chili powder, cumin and oregano. Bring mixture to a boil, reduce heat to low, cover and simmer for 10 minutes, stirring occasionally.

- Meanwhile, prepare pasta according to package directions. Drain well. Divide pasta among six serving plates. Ladle chili over pasta. Place a dollop of sour cream in the center, then sprinkle with cheese and onions. Serve immediately.

Nutrition Nugget

Eating a small amount of a high-fiber or high-protein food an hour before a meal helps dilute your appetite, reducing the amount you'll scarf back at mealtime. Try a handful of almonds, a hard-boiled egg, half a can of tuna, half a cup of quinoa or half an avocado (it has more fiber than you think!).

Worth Every Penne

Whole wheat penne noodles with chicken, bacon, vegetables and pesto sauce

To coin a phrase, "Pesto is the besto!" OK, so it's a dumb phrase. We usually make perfect cents. Take this spectacular pasta recipe, for instance: It's penne-wise, but not pound foolish, since we use high-fiber, whole wheat pasta and load up on the veggies and lean chicken. Worth the effort!

Sauce

2 tbsp	basil pesto
2 tbsp	balsamic vinegar
1 tbsp	olive oil
1 tsp	liquid honey
¼ tsp	freshly ground black pepper

8 oz	(227 g) uncooked whole wheat penne noodles (about 2 cups dry)
4	slices reduced-sodium bacon, chopped
3 cups	sliced mushrooms
1 cup	chopped red onions
3	big handfuls baby spinach leaves
12	cherry or grape tomatoes, halved
3 cups	chopped cooked chicken breast (see tip)
¼ cup	shaved Parmesan cheese or ½ cup crumbled light feta cheese (2 oz/57 g)

Freshly ground black pepper to taste

MAKES 6 SERVINGS

PER SERVING
331 calories, 10.6 g total fat (2.9 g saturated fat),
27 g protein, 31 g carbohydrate, 5.7 g fiber,
50 mg cholesterol, 270 mg sodium

- To prepare sauce, whisk together all sauce ingredients in a small bowl and set aside.

- Cook penne noodles according to package directions. Drain and keep warm.

- While pasta is boiling, cook bacon in a large, non-stick skillet or wok over medium-high heat for about 2 minutes. Don't drain bacon drippings! Add mushrooms and onions to skillet. Cook and stir until vegetables begin to soften, about 5 minutes. Add spinach leaves and tomatoes. Cook until spinach is wilted. Stir in chicken and cook just until chicken is heated through. Add cooked penne noodles and mix well. Add reserved sauce and mix again. Remove skillet from heat. Sprinkle pasta with Parmesan cheese and freshly ground black pepper. Serve immediately.

Recipe Tips

To save work and time, buy a rotisserie chicken at your grocery store and chop up all of the breast meat for this meal. Save the dark meat for tomorrow's lunch. For a flavor variation, substitute the following super-simple sauce for the basil pesto sauce:
Place ⅓ cup roasted tomato and oregano salad dressing (Kraft makes a tasty one) and 6 large, fresh basil leaves in a small mini-chopper or food processor. Pulse on and off until mixture is smooth. Add to cooked penne mixture and mix well. Sprinkle with Parmesan cheese and freshly ground black pepper before serving.

Touched by an Angel Hair Pasta

Angel hair pasta with roasted bell peppers and basil pesto

Say halo to a divine creation of delicate angel hair pasta tossed with heavenly roasted sweet peppers and saintly, slimmed-down basil pesto. It's so light and fresh tasting, you'll be floating on cloud nine.

2	large red bell peppers
1	large yellow bell pepper
1	large orange bell pepper
1½ cups	packed fresh basil leaves
2 tbsp	olive oil
2 tsp	minced garlic
½ tsp	salt
8 oz	(227 g) uncooked angel hair pasta (capelli d'angelo)
¼ cup	freshly grated Parmesan cheese

Freshly ground black pepper (optional)

- Preheat broiler. Halve red, yellow and orange peppers. Remove stems and seeds. Place peppers cut-side down on non-stick baking sheet. Broil until blistered and charred. Transfer to large bowl, cover with plastic wrap and let stand for 15 minutes. Peel off skins. Set 1 red pepper half aside. Cut remaining peppers into thin strips. Set aside.

- In food processor, purée reserved red pepper half, basil, olive oil, garlic and salt until smooth.

- Meanwhile, cook pasta according to package directions until tender but firm. Drain and return to pot. Add pepper strips and basil purée. Toss to combine. Serve sprinkled with Parmesan cheese and freshly ground black pepper, if desired.

Variation: Add ½ cup frozen sweet green peas to the pasta cooking water during last 2 minutes of cooking time.

MAKES 4 SERVINGS

PER SERVING
346 calories, 10 g total fat (2.2 g saturated fat), 11 g protein, 53 g carbohydrate, 5.4 g fiber, 5 mg cholesterol, 411 mg sodium

The most difficult part of a diet isn't watching what you eat. It's watching what other people eat :)

Waist Not, Want Not

Polishing off your plate is a good idea, but only if you're doing the dishes! According to a recent study, 27 percent of North Americans said they finished their entire meal, no matter what the size. Blame our parents, who told us we had to eat every single morsel on our plates...or no dessert! Let's face it, despite the guilt trip Mom laid on you, those last few lima beans or lump of meatloaf on your plate weren't going to wipe out the world hunger crisis. Remember, just because a restaurant or your mother-in-law plops 4,325 calories in front of you doesn't mean you have to eat all of them. If you learn to listen to your own gut instinct, it'll tell your brain when enough is enough. So while you're eating, instead of asking, "Am I full?" ask yourself, "Is my hunger gone?" There's a huge difference, and it can prevent you from becoming huge! Consult your gut, practice *not* cleaning your plate and you'll eat less. Perhaps Grandma said it best: Better to go to waste than to waist!

FOOD BITE

According to folklore, the herb basil is a symbol of love. At one time, young girls would place some on their windowsill to indicate they were looking for a suitor. And according to Moldavian folklore, if a woman gives a man a sprig of basil, he is destined to fall in love with her.

Smackaroni and Cheese (1)

Creamy stovetop macaroni and cheese with ground beef

Our totally un-gourmet and totally yummy mac and cheese sure is a whiz to make! And you won't believe your kids are gobbling up veggies and whole wheat macaroni, either.

Lip-smacking good!

1 can	(14 oz/370 mL) 2% evaporated milk
2 tbsp	all-purpose flour
½ tsp	dry mustard
1 cup	light Cheez Whiz
¼ cup	freshly grated Parmesan cheese
¼ tsp	freshly ground black pepper
1 lb	(454 g) extra-lean ground beef (see tip)
1 cup	diced onions
½ cup	diced zucchini
1 to 2 tsp	minced garlic
1 can	(19 oz/540 mL) diced tomatoes with Italian herbs, well drained
4 cups	cooked whole wheat elbow macaroni (about 1½ cups dry)
½ cup	packed shredded light old (sharp) cheddar cheese (2 oz/57 g)

MAKES 8 SERVINGS

PER SERVING
329 calories, 9.6 g total fat (5.2 g saturated fat), 26 g protein, 37 g carbohydrate, 3.6 g fiber, 59 mg cholesterol, 641 mg sodium

- In a medium, non-stick pot, whisk together milk, flour and dry mustard until smooth. Heat over medium-high heat, whisking constantly, until mixture bubbles and thickens. Reduce heat to low. Add Cheez Whiz, Parmesan cheese and pepper. Stir until cheeses are melted. Remove from heat and set aside.

- In a deep, 10-inch, non-stick skillet, cook beef, onions, zucchini and garlic over medium-high heat until meat is no longer pink. Break up any large pieces of beef while it's cooking. Drain off any liquid or fat in pan. Stir in tomatoes and cook 1 more minute.

- Add cooked pasta and reserved cheese sauce. Mix well and cook just until heated through. Remove skillet from heat. Sprinkle macaroni mixture with shredded cheddar. Cover and let stand 5 to 10 minutes before serving.

- Serve hot with a sprinkle of freshly ground black pepper and a salad on the side.

Recipe Tip: You can substitute ground chicken or turkey for ground beef if you prefer.

Trivial Tidbit

If you regularly hire the television as your babysitter, you may be paying an awfully dear price. The latest statistics show that the average North American watches 28 hours of television a week. That means that by the end of high school, the average child has wasted three years of his life in a sedentary TV trance. Better turn off the tube or your kids may end up looking like Telechubbies.

Start Kidding Around

Put more spring in your offspring! Even if you don't want to be more active for your own sake, at least do it for your children. When both parents are active, kids are nearly six times more likely to follow in their footsteps. And that would be a good thing, considering that childhood obesity has reached epidemic levels in North America. So turn off the TV, unplug the computer, hide all the cellphones and tuck the Xbox controller under a pile of laundry. Make exercise a priority, make it fun and make it a family affair. By teaching Buffy and Jody proper sweatiquette, you'll stop them from becoming couch potatoes while they're still small fries!

Smackaroni and Cheese (2)

Super-cheesy mac and cheese with turkey bacon, shiitake mushrooms and green peas

*This interesting twist on macaroni and cheese won a taste-test challenge against a Scottish caterer in a fun-filled episode of our **Eat, Shrink & Be Merry!** TV show.*

NOODLE-LICIOUS!

1 tbsp	butter
⅔ cup	minced onions
4 oz	(113 g) turkey bacon, chopped (about 7 slices)
1 cup	finely chopped shiitake mushrooms
½ cup	frozen sweet green peas
1 can	(14 oz/370 mL) 2% evaporated milk
2 tbsp	all-purpose flour
½ tsp	dry mustard
1 cup	packed shredded light old (sharp) cheddar cheese (4 oz/113 g), divided
1 cup	packed shredded 4-cheese blend (4 oz/113 g—see tip)
¼ tsp	freshly ground black pepper
2 cups	uncooked whole wheat macaroni

MAKES 6 SERVINGS

PER SERVING
384 calories, 14 g total fat (7.1 g saturated fat),
23 g protein, 38 g carbohydrate, 4.1 g fiber,
81 mg cholesterol, 644 mg sodium

Recipe Tip: The cheese blend we prefer is a combination of provolone, Asiago, Parmesan and Fontina cheese. It's sold in a plastic tub where the specialty cheeses are found at your grocery store.

- You will need a deep, 10-inch, oven-safe non-stick skillet. Melt butter in skillet over medium-low heat. Add onions and chopped bacon. Cook slowly, stirring often, until bacon is lightly browned and onions are golden. This will take a good 10 minutes. (In the meantime, cook macaroni according to package directions.) Add mushrooms to skillet and cook until tender. Stir in peas until heated through.

- Preheat broiler. In a large measuring cup or medium bowl, whisk together evaporated milk, flour and dry mustard. Add to bacon and veggies in skillet. Cook and stir until sauce is bubbly and has thickened. Remove from heat and stir in ¾ of the cheddar and ¾ of the 4-cheese blend. Stir until cheeses are melted. Add pepper. Add well-drained macaroni and mix until well-coated with sauce. Sprinkle remaining cheeses over top. Place skillet under broiler until cheeses are melted and lightly browned.

Nutrition Nugget

Don't cut the cheese! Just use less of it. Using strongly flavored or "sharp" cheeses like aged cheddar, Parmesan, Asiago or Swiss means you can use less of them and still get that great cheesy taste in recipes without all the fat.

An elegant frankfurter is a haute dog :)

Thai a Yellow Ribbon

Fettuccine with chicken, red peppers, snow peas and carrots in a spicy peanut sauce

The idea for this scrumptious fettuccine dish came to us while sitting under an old oak tree in Orlando. It was dawn. Yup, that was the exact moment we decided to give it a Thai twist, and it's been three long years since that day.

Sauce

½ cup	reduced-sodium chicken broth
¼ cup	light peanut butter
2 tbsp	each minced fresh cilantro and minced fresh basil leaves
1 tbsp	granulated sugar
2 tsp	each grated gingerroot and lemon zest
1 tsp	each sesame oil and cornstarch
1 tsp	minced garlic
½ tsp	each ground cumin and crushed red pepper flakes

12 oz	(340 g) uncooked high-fiber white or whole-grain fettuccine
2 tsp	olive oil
4	boneless skinless chicken breasts, cut into 1-inch cubes (about 1½ lbs/680 g)
1	large red bell pepper, cut into thin strips
2 cups	snow peas, cut in half diagonally
1	large carrot, cut into thin (julienne) strips

- Combine all sauce ingredients in a blender and whirl until smooth. Set aside.

- Cook fettuccine according to package directions. Drain well and keep warm.

- While pasta is cooking, heat olive oil in a large, non-stick wok or skillet over medium-high heat. Add chicken and cook until no longer pink. Add red pepper, snow peas and carrots. Cook and stir for 3 more minutes, until vegetables are tender-crisp. Add sauce. Cook until sauce is bubbly and has thickened. Remove from heat, stir in cooked fettuccine and serve immediately.

MAKES 4 SERVINGS

PER SERVING
653 calories, 12.6 g total fat (2 g saturated fat), 43 g protein, 84 g carbohydrate, 13.6 g fiber, 83 mg cholesterol, 205 mg sodium

Whole Grain vs. Multigrain

What's the difference between multigrain and whole grain? A whole lot! "Whole grain" is the healthiest grain because it's the least processed and refined. Its germ and bran, where all the vitamins, minerals, healthy fats and fiber are concentrated, haven't been stripped away by food manufacturers. Good for them and good for you! The word "multigrain," on the other hand, technically means "many grains," and depending on the manufacturer and its manufacturing process, each of those grains, whether it's wheat, oats, rye, spelt, millet or kamut, might still be overly refined or processed. Strip away that bran and germ and you're mostly left with starch. Of course, multigrain is still an upgrade from plain ol' refined white or whole wheat. But look for "whole grain" to get the most bang from your buckwheat!

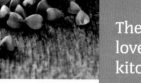

The torch of love is lit in the kitchen.

French proverb

Trivial Tidbit

Dying for a cheeseburger, fries and a chocolate shake? This might make the craving go away: In 2004, an Indiana coffin manufacturer reported selling four or five triple-wide caskets a *month* compared with only one a *year* in the late 1980s. Remember the proverb: Don't dig your grave with a knife and fork.

Orient Express

Linguini, chicken, broccoli and bell peppers in a light, sesame-ginger vinaigrette

Whether you're oriented or disoriented, you're just gonna love this one! Linguini, chicken and vegetables are tossed in a far-out, Far East dressing. Quick and delicious!

12 oz	(340 g) uncooked whole wheat linguini
2 tsp	olive oil
1 cup	chopped onions
2 tsp	minced garlic
1 cup	reduced-sodium chicken broth
¼ cup	each reduced-sodium soy sauce and ketchup
3 tbsp	seasoned rice vinegar
1 tbsp	each freshly squeezed lemon juice, sesame oil and grated gingerroot
2 tsp	liquid honey or brown sugar
1 tsp	hot pepper sauce
½ tsp	freshly ground black pepper
2 tbsp	cornstarch
2 cups	chopped or sliced cooked chicken breast
1½ cups	broccoli florets
1 cup	thinly sliced red bell pepper
1 cup	carrots, cut into thin (julienne) strips

MAKES 4 SERVINGS

PER SERVING
525 calories, 8.8 g total fat
(1.5 g saturated fat), 25 g protein,
87 g carbohydrate, 11.6 g fiber,
25 mg cholesterol, 813 g sodium

- Prepare linguini according to package directions. Drain and keep warm.

- While pasta is cooking, prepare sauce. Heat olive oil in a large pot over medium heat. Add onions and garlic. Cook and stir until vegetables begin to soften, about 4 minutes. Add broth, soy sauce, ketchup, vinegar, lemon juice, sesame oil, gingerroot, honey, hot pepper sauce and black pepper. Mix well and bring to a boil. Blend cornstarch with an equal amount of water until smooth. Add to sauce. Cook and stir until sauce is bubbly and has thickened, about 1 minute.

- Add cooked chicken pieces, broccoli, red pepper and carrots to sauce. Mix well. Cook 3 to 4 minutes, until vegetables are tender-crisp. Pour chicken-vegetable mixture over warm linguini and toss to coat evenly. Serve hot.

Recipe Tip: Give the cooked linguini a quick rinse with very hot water before adding sauce if the linguini has stuck together. Drain linguini well before mixing with sauce. Using low-sodium ketchup will help reduce the sodium content.

Indulging Equals Bulging

Talk about bad food combining! Don'tcha just love it when manufacturers mix together a few of our favorite food vices to launch what was already an indulgence into a whole new caloric stratosphere? As if your thighs really need a cheese-stuffed pizza crust. Or chocolate-chip cookie-dough ice cream. Or gravy-covered, cheese-laden French fries. In most cases, the two-for-one whammy easily doubles your calories, bad fats and pant size. They really should make it a *three-for-one* deal and include a prescription for cholesterol-lowering medication. Use common sense, practice moderation and remember: Those who indulge, bulge!

The Six-Million-Dollar Manicotti

Chicken-and-vegetable-stuffed manicotti with four cheeses

When we set out to revamp plain ol' everyday manicotti, they said it couldn't be done. We replied, "Nonsense. We can rebuild it. We have the technology." The result: creamy, chicken-stuffed manicotti that's so scrumptious, its flavor is bionic!

1 tbsp	olive oil
½ cup	finely chopped onions
1 tsp	minced garlic
1¼ lbs	(568 g) boneless skinless chicken breasts, cut into small pieces (see tip)
1 cup	each grated carrots, grated zucchini and finely chopped mushrooms
3 tbsp	minced fresh basil, or 1½ tsp dried
1 tbsp	minced fresh oregano, or 1 tsp dried
¼ tsp	freshly ground black pepper
½ pkg	(8 oz/250 g) light cream cheese, cut into cubes (4 oz/125 g total)
1 cup	part-skim ricotta cheese
¼ cup	freshly grated Parmesan cheese
12	uncooked manicotti shells
2 cups	your favorite low-sodium, tomato pasta sauce
½ cup	packed shredded light mozzarella cheese (2 oz/57 g)

Minced fresh parsley for garnish (optional)

- To make filling, heat olive oil in a large, non-stick skillet over medium heat. Add onions and garlic. Cook and stir until onions are softened, about 2 minutes. Be careful not to burn them.

- Add chicken, increase heat to medium-high and cook until no longer pink. Add carrots, zucchini, mushrooms, basil, oregano and pepper. Cook for 3 more minutes. Add cream cheese and stir until melted. Remove from heat. Stir in ricotta and Parmesan cheeses. Transfer filling to a large bowl and refrigerate for 20 minutes.

- While filling is chilling, cook manicotti according to package directions. Rinse with cold water and drain well.

- Using a teaspoon, stuff shells equally with filling (see tip). Spread a thin layer of pasta sauce over bottom of one large or two small baking pans Arrange manicotti in a single layer in baking pan(s). Pour remaining sauce over manicotti and sprinkle with mozzarella.

- Cover with foil and bake at 350°F for 40 minutes. Let cool for 5 minutes before serving. Garnish with minced parsley, if desired.

MAKES 12 MANICOTTI

PER MANICOTTI
260 calories, 6.6 g total fat (3.1 g saturated fat), 21 g protein, 28 g carbohydrate, 2.4 g fiber, 43 mg cholesterol, 295 mg sodium

Recipe Tips

Chicken is easier to cut into small pieces if it's partially frozen and manicotti shells are easier to stuff if they're slightly undercooked (it makes them less likely to tear). Drain the cooked shells and rinse them with cold water to stop the cooking process and to keep them from sticking together. Use a teaspoon to stuff them. If you prefer, you can substitute whole-grain lasagna noodles in this recipe and make lasagna roll-ups, or you can use 24 jumbo pasta shells.

Put Up Your Zukes

When people think of foods that help build strong bones, they immediately think of dairy products and maybe nuts and seeds. But here's a juicy secret: Zucchini, even though it's more than 95 percent water, is a bona-fide bone-builder! It's true! This popular summer squash delivers magnesium and phosphorous, two minerals that strengthen the bone matrix, plus manganese and copper that help with bone metabolism. And these minerals are in a form that your body loves, loves, loves to use. Perfect raw materials to build you a stronger foundation! No bones about it!

Pasta Point of No Return

Tricolor pasta primavera with roasted vegetables and Parmesan

There's just no going back to the old way of making the perennial favorite, Pasta Primavera, once you've tried this revamped version from the Try-Light Zone!

I'M SORRY SIR. ONCE YOU'VE TASTED THE PASTA, THERE'S NO GOING BACK.

NO RETURN POLICY

2 cups	whole small button mushrooms
2 cups	cubed zucchini (cut into 1-inch cubes)
2 cups	coarsely chopped tomatoes
1 cup	each sliced red and yellow bell peppers
3 tbsp	minced fresh basil
1 tbsp	olive oil
2 tsp	minced garlic
¼ tsp	freshly ground black pepper
12 oz	(340 g) uncooked tricolor rotini (about 4 cups dry)
1½ cups	broccoli florets
½ cup	frozen green peas, thawed
¼ cup	freshly grated Parmesan cheese
2 tbsp	minced fresh parsley

- Preheat oven to 400°F. Spray a 9 x 13-inch baking pan with cooking spray. Set aside.

- In a large bowl, combine mushrooms, zucchini, tomatoes, bell peppers, basil, olive oil, garlic and pepper. Toss until vegetables are evenly coated with oil and seasonings. Transfer vegetables to prepared baking pan. Bake, uncovered, for 25 minutes. Stir once, halfway through cooking time.

- Meanwhile, prepare pasta according to package directions. About 4 minutes before pasta is done, add broccoli and peas to the boiling water (yup, right along with the rotini). When pasta is cooked, drain pasta and vegetables, then return them to the pot. Stir in roasted vegetables, Parmesan cheese and parsley. Serve with extra freshly ground black pepper, if desired.

MAKES 4 SERVINGS

PER SERVING
449 calories, 8.1 g total fat (2.3 g saturated fat), 21 g protein, 78 g carbohydrate, 9.4 g fiber, 5 mg cholesterol, 199 mg sodium

Nutrition Nugget
Do not exceed the feed limit! According to researchers, exceeding 500 calories at any meal makes it more likely that your body will shift into fat-storage mode. Aim for smaller, more frequent meals, 300 to 500 calories per meal, every 3.5 hours.

New Year's Resolution: Something that goes in one year and out the other.

In this chapter...

Chicken Worth Pickin'

In a fowl mood? These delectable chicken recipes will cheer you up!

Fee Fie Faux Fried Chicken, p. 147

Thigh Master

Braised balsamic chicken with wild mushroom sauce

Make sure you squeeze this simple but succulent chicken-thigh masterpiece into your cooking repertoire. One taste and you'll be weak in the knees!

1 tbsp	olive oil
8	bone-in chicken thighs, skin removed (about 1½ lbs/680 g)
1	small red onion, thinly sliced into rings
2 tsp	minced garlic
3 cups	sliced wild mixed mushrooms (such as cremini and shiitake)
2 tbsp	balsamic vinegar (see tip)
1 tsp	dried tarragon
½ tsp	dried thyme
1 cup	reduced-sodium chicken broth
¼ tsp	freshly ground black pepper
¼ cup	light (5%) sour cream
2 tsp	cornstarch

Minced fresh parsley for garnish

Recipe Tip: Invest in a bottle of good-quality balsamic vinegar (the kind with a cork!). It's a little more expensive but a lot more flavorful.

MAKES 4 SERVINGS

PER SERVING
289 calories, 11.6 g total fat
(3 g saturated fat), 37 g protein,
8 g carbohydrate, 1 g fiber,
146 mg cholesterol, 326 mg sodium

- You'll need a 10-inch, non-stick skillet with a lid for this recipe. Heat olive oil in skillet over medium-high heat. Add chicken thighs and cook for a minute or two on each side, until lightly browned. Remove chicken from skillet and keep warm.

- Add onions and garlic to same skillet. Cook and stir until onions begin to soften, about 3 minutes. Add mushrooms and cook until mushrooms are tender, about 3 more minutes. Stir in balsamic vinegar, tarragon and thyme. Cook for one minute. Add chicken broth and black pepper. Bring mixture to a boil. Reduce heat to medium-low. Return chicken to skillet, cover and simmer for 15 to 20 minutes, or until chicken is cooked through and no longer pink in the center.

- Remove chicken from skillet and keep warm. Return skillet to medium heat. In a small bowl, mix sour cream and cornstarch until smooth. Add sour-cream mixture to sauce in skillet. Cook and stir until sauce bubbles and thickens slightly. Serve hot mushroom sauce over chicken and top with fresh parsley.

Trivial Tidbit
The underside of a mushroom is called the:
(a) meat; (b) gills; (c) fan; or (d) belly.
The answer? (b) gills.
Anything else sounds plain fishy!

One Flew Over the Couscous Nest

Malaysian chicken and sweet potato stew on a bed of couscous

Tired of the same old dinnertime fare? Spice things up with this uniquely flavored chicken stew. It's as good as it gets!

MAKES 4 SERVINGS

PER SERVING
531 calories, 6.4 g total fat
(2.2 g saturated fat),
43 g protein,
74 g carbohydrate,
8.3 g fiber,
82 mg cholesterol,
475 mg sodium

1 tsp	olive oil
4	boneless skinless chicken breasts, cut into 1-inch cubes (about 1½ lbs/680 g)
1 tbsp	grated gingerroot
2 tsp	minced garlic
1 cup	each chopped onions and chopped red bell pepper
1 tsp	each ground coriander and curry powder
½ tsp	ground cumin
¼ tsp	ground cinnamon
1½ cups	reduced-sodium chicken broth
3 cups	peeled and cubed sweet potatoes
1 cup	whole wheat couscous (see tip)
2 tbsp	frozen orange juice concentrate, thawed
¾ cup	light coconut milk
2 tbsp	each cornstarch and minced fresh cilantro

• Heat olive oil in a large pot over medium-high heat. Add chicken, gingerroot and garlic. Cook and stir until chicken is no longer pink. Add onions and red pepper and cook for 3 more minutes. Stir in coriander, curry powder, cumin and cinnamon. Cook for 1 more minute. Add broth and sweet potatoes. Bring to a boil. Reduce heat to medium-low. Cover and simmer for 12 minutes, or until potatoes are tender.

• Meanwhile, prepare couscous. In a medium bowl, combine couscous and orange juice concentrate. Pour 1 cup boiling water over couscous and mix well. Cover and set aside until liquid is absorbed, about 5 minutes.

• Whisk together coconut milk and cornstarch until smooth. Add to chicken and vegetables, along with cilantro. Increase heat to medium-high and cook until stew is bubbly and has thickened.

• Fluff couscous with a fork. Make a "nest" of couscous in individual serving bowls. Ladle stew over top. Serve immediately.

Recipe Tip Couscous is a tiny pasta of North African origin. It doesn't have a lot of flavor on its own, but can be dressed up in a salad, sweetened and mixed with fruits as a dessert or piled high with a savory stew, as in this recipe. It takes less than 10 minutes to cook and comes in white or whole wheat varieties. It's often classified as a grain, not a pasta, so you're likely to find it in the rice section of your grocery store.

It's Soda-Pressing

Look out Sister, look out Jack, you've got pop-o-matic trouble! Back when we were kids, a family-sized bottle of Coke lasted Mom, Dad, Sis and Junior from one week's grocery run to the next. Nowadays, a "single serving" Double Gulp at 7-Eleven convenience stores is packed with an unthinkable, fructose-filled 64 ounces! That's eight cups of soda—the same amount found in that family-sized bottle of days gone by. Gulp! If you don't want to double your pant size, try giving your waistline (and your bladder!) a break and settle for the 12-ounce "kiddie" size. Or better yet, trade that pail o' pop for a bottle o' water. With all those empty calories and enough sugar to sweeten a three-tiered wedding cake, drinking a bucket of pop can make you turn *pail*!

There must be a destiny to shape our ends, but our middles are of our own chewsing :)

Thai Beau

Thai coconut chicken with mango and basil

This colorful, Thai coconut chicken packs a lot of kick and a lot of punch. A real knockout!

1¼ cups	light coconut milk
1 tbsp	grated gingerroot
1 tbsp	reduced-sodium soy sauce
1 tbsp	brown sugar
1 tbsp	Asian fish sauce (see tip, p. 337)
1 tbsp	cornstarch
1 tbsp	freshly squeezed lime juice
1 tsp	minced garlic
Pinch	crushed red pepper flakes (optional)
2 tsp	peanut oil
4	boneless skinless chicken breasts, cut into strips (about 1½ lbs/680 g)
1	large red bell pepper, seeded and cut into strips
4	green onions (with white parts), coarsely chopped
½ cup	frozen green peas
½ cup	coarsely chopped fresh basil leaves
3 tbsp	minced fresh cilantro
1	ripe medium-sized mango, peeled and sliced

MAKES 4 SERVINGS

PER SERVING
341 calories, 9.2 g total fat (4.8 g saturated fat),
43 g protein, 22 g carbohydrate, 2.2 g fiber,
99 mg cholesterol, 634 mg sodium

Recipe Tip: If you like your food spicy, replace the crushed red pepper flakes with 1 tsp Thai green curry paste, available in the Asian food section of your grocery store.

- To make sauce, whisk together coconut milk, gingerroot, soy sauce, brown sugar, fish sauce, cornstarch, lime juice, garlic and crushed red pepper flakes (if using) in a medium bowl. Set aside until ready to use.

- Heat oil in a large, non-stick wok over high heat. Add chicken strips. Cook and stir until chicken is lightly browned, about 4 minutes. Remove chicken from wok and keep warm.

- Reduce heat to medium-high. Add red pepper and onions to same wok. Cook and stir for 3 minutes, until red pepper begins to soften. Return chicken to wok. Add reserved sauce, peas, basil and cilantro. Continue cooking and stirring until sauce is bubbly and has thickened. Reduce heat to medium-low. Simmer for 5 to 6 minutes, or until chicken is cooked through. Stir in mango and cook 1 more minute. Serve over hot basmati or jasmine rice.

> A woman is like a tea bag—only in hot water do you realize how strong she really is.
>
> *Eleanor Roosevelt*

Nutrition Nugget

If you love eating chicken, you might consider buying the organic, pasture-raised variety from a local farmer or butcher once in a while. Though more expensive, organic chicken is the best bet for your health and your family's health in the long run. Why? Well, we are what we eat, but we're also what our food eats! Pasture-raised chickens are healthier (and happier) chickens, allowed to roam free in the yard and feed off insects and grasses, which is more natural to them than eating grains or corn. And that leads to healthier meat. In fact, there are 38 percent more brain-boosting omega-3s in the breast of an organic chicken compared to a caged one. Better for the chickens, better for you! That's chicken worth pickin'.

Slimply Orange Chicken

Quick and delicious skillet-cooked chicken breasts with a simple and tasty orange-mustard sauce

Attention all citrus lovers! This deliciously sweet chicken is the pick of the crop when you're short on time but searching for gourmet flavor.

4	boneless skinless chicken breasts (about 1½ lbs/680 g)
¼ tsp	each salt and freshly ground black pepper
1 tbsp	olive oil
1 can	(10 oz/284 mL) mandarin oranges in light syrup
2 tbsp	honey-Dijon mustard
1 tbsp	cornstarch

MAKES 4 SERVINGS

PER SERVING
283 calories, 5.6 g total fat
(1 g saturated fat),
40 g protein, 16 g carbohydrate,
0.6 g fiber, 98 mg cholesterol,
298 mg sodium

- Sprinkle both sides of chicken breasts with salt and pepper. Heat olive oil in a 10-inch, non-stick skillet over medium-high heat. Add chicken and cook for 3 to 4 minutes on each side, until lightly browned and no longer pink in center. Remove chicken from skillet and keep warm.

- Add mandarin oranges with their syrup to a food processor or blender. Pulse on and off once or twice until oranges are coarsely puréed (still slightly chunky). Add oranges to skillet along with mustard. Cook and stir over medium-high heat for 1 minute. Whisk together cornstarch with an equal amount of water until smooth. Add to orange mixture in skillet. Cook and stir until mixture is bubbly and has thickened.

- Return chicken to skillet. Reduce heat to low. Spoon sauce over chicken. Cover and simmer for 3 to 4 minutes, until chicken is hot and completely cooked through.

Putting the C.A.R.T.S. Before the Hearse

If you want to add years to your life and life to your years, then beware the five deadly dietary sins: **C**affeine, **A**lcohol, **R**efined foods, **T**rans fats and **S**ugar. Known as "anti-nutrients," these nutritional fiends don't contribute anything to your health, but take away from it, draining precious vitamins, minerals and antioxidants from your body. They also make your liver work double overtime to clean up their toxic mess. Abuse them day in and day out, and there's a good chance you'll experience the worm-ridden fruits of their labor: heart disease, stroke, cancer, obesity and diabetes. Even if they don't cut your life short, they can slowly make it miserable by contributing to nasty, nagging conditions like arthritis, allergies, osteoporosis, depression, chronic fatigue, poor sleep and even premature aging. The bottom line is this: It's about self-control and moderation! We're not suggesting you give up your favorite food vices entirely (Greta loves her chicken wings!), but you should limit them. Occasionally savoring special treats is OK. Habitually pigging out on them is not. The good news is, there's a whole lot of healthy food that's also great-tasting (like the recipes in this book!).

Not Humdrumsticks

Baked honey mustard and herb chicken drumsticks

They're not humdrumsticks, they're yumdrumsticks! Bored to tears with your usual weekday fare? Our simple, succulent, finger-lickin' baked chicken will have your family dancing to the beat of a different drumstick!

> Ho hum. He's not humdrum!

12	skinless chicken drumsticks (about 2½ lbs/1.1 kg)
¼ cup	liquid honey
2 tbsp	cider vinegar
2 tbsp	grainy Dijon mustard
1 tsp	minced garlic
1 tsp	dried Herbes de Provence (see tip)
¼ tsp	each salt and freshly ground black pepper

MAKES 6 SERVINGS

PER SERVING
201 calories, 5.4 g total fat (1.3 g saturated fat), 25 g protein, 12 g carbohydrate, 0.2 g fiber, 82 mg cholesterol, 209 mg sodium

- Preheat oven to 400°F. Spray a 9 x 13-inch baking pan with cooking spray. Arrange drumsticks in pan in a single layer.

- Whisk together remaining ingredients in a small bowl. Spoon sauce evenly over chicken pieces. Bake for 20 minutes. Remove pan from oven and baste chicken with sauce. (Tilting the pan to one side helps!) Return chicken to oven and bake an additional 20 to 25 minutes, until chicken is no longer pink in the center.

- Arrange chicken on a serving platter and pour sauce from pan over chicken. Serve hot.

Recipe Tip

What the heck is Herbes de Provence? It's an herb blend that you'll likely find right beside all the other dried herbs you buy at the grocery store. It's simply a combination of herbs commonly used in southern French cooking: basil, marjoram, rosemary, sage, thyme, savory and lavender.

FOOD BITE

Undertakers now report that human bodies are not deteriorating as quickly as they used to. The reason, they believe, is that the modern diet contains so many preservatives, and these chemicals may prevent the body from decomposing rapidly after death. So, eating too much processed food is a self-pickling procedure, of sorts. "Dilly beloved, we are gathered here today...."

Whistle While You Wok

Family-pleasing, orange-ginger chicken stir-fry with vegetables and rotini

Other chicken stir-fries dwarf in comparison. Ours is the fairest of them all! Don't be Grumpy when you can't figure out what to make for dinner. Just whip up this magical recipe and make 'em all Happy.

MAKES 6 SERVINGS

PER SERVING
372 calories,
5.5 g total fat
(0.8 g saturated fat),
35 g protein,
46 g carbohydrate,
5.3 g fiber,
66 mg cholesterol,
510 mg sodium

8 oz	(227 g) uncooked whole wheat rotini (about 3 cups dry—see tip)
½ cup	orange juice
⅓ cup	hoisin sauce
2 tbsp	reduced-sodium soy sauce
1½ tbsp	cornstarch
1 tbsp	each grated gingerroot and sesame oil
1 tsp	minced garlic
¼ tsp	crushed red pepper flakes
1 tbsp	peanut or olive oil
4	boneless skinless chicken breasts, cut into strips or cubes (about 1½ lbs/680 g)
2 cups	broccoli florets
2 cups	halved medium-sized mushrooms
1	large red bell pepper, cut into strips
½ cup	frozen green peas
⅓ cup	coarsely chopped green onions
10	fresh basil leaves, coarsely chopped

- Cook pasta according to package directions. Drain. Rinse with cold water and drain again. Set aside.

- To make sauce, whisk together orange juice, hoisin sauce, soy sauce, cornstarch, gingerroot, sesame oil, garlic and crushed red pepper flakes in a medium bowl. Set aside.

- Heat oil in a large, non-stick wok or skillet over medium-high heat. Add chicken and cook, stirring often, until chicken is lightly browned on the outside but still pink in the center. Add broccoli, mushrooms and red pepper. Cook and stir until vegetables are tender-crisp, about 6 minutes. Add ¼ cup water to prevent sticking, if necessary. Add peas and onions. Cook 1 more minute. Add reserved sauce and basil. Continue cooking until sauce is bubbly and has thickened, about 1 minute. Add rotini and cook 1 more minute, just until rotini is heated through. Serve hot.

Recipe Tip: You can substitute whole wheat spaghetti for the rotini.

> *A commentator is an undistinguished potato :)*

On Shaky Ground

If there's a whole lotta shakin' going on at the dinner table (as in salt shaker), there could be a whole lotta shakin' going on in your body (as in blubber!). When you eat too much refined, processed salt (the typical variety found in most shakers and in packaged and canned foods), your body tries to dilute it with water to get things back in balance. That extra water shows up as swollen feet, legs, hands and eyelids, not to mention bellies. Water retention can inflate your weight by as much as five to 15 pounds. Zoinks! If you're trying to squeeze into a teeny dress for a big event, better not have sushi the night before: One of the worst sodium villains is soy sauce. Always scour the nutrition label and buy the lowest-sodium brand you can find. Some have an astronomical 770 mg sodium in one measly tablespoon! And get this: That's the low-sodium variety! Regular soy sauce has roughly 1,160 mg sodium per one tablespoon—48 percent of your daily recommended limit. Oh, the hypertension is mounting! Luckily, there are natural alternatives in health food stores that use non-GMO soybeans to create the salty taste. Sodium levels are comparable to the regular variety, however, but at least no processed salt or preservatives are used in manufacturing.

Tuskinny Chicken

A hearty, one-pot Italian dinner that is sure to become a family favorite

This delectable chicken dinner is a leaning tower of goodness and contains everything under the Tuscan sun: tender chicken, colorful vegetables, nutritious chickpeas and a hint of white wine. Italeave you satisfied!

MAKES 6 SERVINGS

PER SERVING
371 calories,
10.8 g total fat
(2.9 g saturated fat),
40 g protein,
25 g carbohydrate,
5.7 g fiber,
142 mg cholesterol,
435 mg sodium

1 tbsp	olive oil
12	boneless skinless chicken thighs (about 2¼ lbs/1 kg—see tip)
1½ cups	coarsely chopped red onions
2 tsp	minced garlic
3 cups	sliced mushrooms
1	medium zucchini, sliced
1	large yellow bell pepper, sliced
2 tbsp	each minced fresh basil leaves, oregano leaves and rosemary, or 1½ tsp each dried
1 jar	(22 oz/700 mL) your favorite tomato pasta sauce
½ cup	dry white wine
1 cup	canned no-salt-added chickpeas or white kidney beans, drained and rinsed
¼ tsp	freshly ground black pepper
¼ cup	grated Romano or Parmesan cheese

Recipe Tips: If you prefer, you can substitute 6 boneless, skinless chicken breasts for the thighs. Cut them in half so they're about the same size as thighs. If you're making this meal for a special dinner, it's worth the effort to buy fresh herbs instead of using the dried variety.

- Heat olive oil in a large (14-inch), deep, non-stick skillet over medium-high heat. Add chicken thighs. Cook until chicken is lightly browned, 2 to 3 minutes on each side. Remove chicken from skillet and keep warm.

- Add onions and garlic to the same skillet. Cook and stir until onions begin to soften, about 3 minutes. Be careful not to burn them. Add mushrooms, zucchini and yellow pepper. Cook and stir until vegetables are tender-crisp, about 6 more minutes. Stir in herbs and cook for 1 more minute.

- Add pasta sauce, wine, chickpeas and black pepper. Bring mixture to a boil. Reduce heat to medium-low. Return chicken pieces to skillet. Cover and simmer for 20 minutes. Uncover and cook an additional 10 minutes (this will help thicken sauce). Remove from heat and, if you have the patience, let dish stand, uncovered, for another 5 minutes to cool slightly.

- Serve in shallow bowls, topped with a sprinkling of grated Romano cheese.

Nutrition Nugget

Blue Plate Special: If you're trying to lose weight, consider a blue plate! Since blue is a soothing hue, it can help you slow down at mealtime, and that means you might eat less. Blue as an overall kitchen color works well, too. If you're a waist watcher, avoid red. Because red stimulates, it's the worst color to feast your eyes on since it can lead you to eat more even if you're full. That explains why so many fast-food restaurants are painted red!

Trivial Tidbit

Complete this Spanish proverb: For wine to taste like wine, it should be drunk:
(a) with friends;
(b) in the evening under candlelight;
(c) using only your left hand; or
(d) with fine cheese.
The answer?
(a) with friends! We'd also suggest it must be drunk from a "real" wine glass and not from those cheap, flimsy, plastic ones.

Miss American Thigh

These gooey, saucy, baked chicken thighs are a hit with kids!

Bye-bye Miss American Thigh! Don't waste your time driving your Chevy to the levee. Stay home and savor the delectable taste of these baked chicken thighs—they won't last long!

PER SERVING
343 calories,
7.2 g total fat
(1.8 g saturated fat),
33 g protein,
29 g carbohydrate,
0.2 g fiber,
151 mg cholesterol,
343 mg sodium

⅔ cup	grape jelly
½ cup	ketchup
⅓ cup	minced onions
2 tbsp	white vinegar
1 tsp	dry mustard
12	bone-in chicken thighs, skin removed (about 3 lbs/1.4 kg)

- In a small pot, stir together grape jelly, ketchup, onions, vinegar and dry mustard. Cook over medium-high heat until mixture comes to a boil and jelly is melted. Remove from heat.

- Arrange chicken pieces in a 9 x 13-inch baking dish. Pour sauce evenly over chicken and turn pieces to coat both sides. Bake at 400°F for about 45 minutes, until chicken is very tender. Serve hot.

Does drinking make your liverwurst? :)

The Cause of Youth Decay

Are you unstable and unbalanced? Well, if it makes you feel any better, so are we! Every minute of every day, *everyone's* cells are being ravaged by chemically unstable and unbalanced molecules called free radicals. They may be free, but they're no bargain. They can critically damage cells and contribute to heart disease, cancer, arthritis and other illnesses. Wondering what's causing those new wrinkles and gray hairs? Blame it on the rads. Free radicals cause *youth decay*, accelerating the aging process by making us rust from the inside out. How dare they! And how'd they get inside us in the first place? Well, they're formed naturally when our cells use oxygen to produce energy. Our bodies can handle a certain amount of free radicals, but excessive amounts are created as a result of everyday modern life: poor diet, stress, smoking, alcohol, pollution and electromagnetic fields generated by TVs, computers and power lines. Excess exercise can also pump up the free-radical damage, which explains why some marathoners and triathletes look older than their years. The only way to battle the radicals is with cellular superheroes (no, not Apple iPhones) called antioxidants. Consuming plenty of antioxidant-rich fruits and vegetables is the surest way to remain stable and well-balanced without an expensive visit to the shrink.

I Got Stew, Babe

Chicken stew with balsamic roasted vegetables

Stew that's so irresistibly savory, you'll want to Cher it with everyone!

4 cups	unpeeled, cubed red potatoes
2 cups	whole baby carrots
1 cup	chopped red onions
2 tbsp	balsamic vinegar
1 tbsp	olive oil
1 tsp	minced garlic
1½ tsp	dried thyme, divided
1½ tsp	dried rosemary, divided
1 tsp	dried tarragon
½ tsp	each salt and freshly ground black pepper
1 cup	sliced green beans
½ cup	dry white wine
2 lbs	(907 g) boneless skinless chicken breasts, cut into 1-inch cubes
3 cups	reduced-sodium chicken broth
3 tbsp	all-purpose flour

MAKES 6 SERVINGS

PER SERVING
298 calories,
4.6 g total fat
(0.5 g saturated fat),
31 g protein,
30 g carbohydrate,
3.8 g fiber,
66 mg cholesterol,
368 mg sodium

- Spray a large roasting pan with cooking spray. Add potatoes, carrots, onions, vinegar, oil, garlic, 1 tsp thyme, 1 tsp rosemary, tarragon, salt and pepper. Mix well. Roast, uncovered, at 425°F for 30 minutes. Stir once, halfway through cooking time. Add green beans and roast for 10 more minutes.

- Meanwhile, pour wine into a large pot. Add remaining ½ tsp thyme and ½ tsp rosemary. Bring to a boil. Add chicken pieces and reduce heat to medium-high. Cook, uncovered, until chicken is cooked through, about 12 minutes.

- Add roasted vegetables to chicken and wine. Stir in 2½ cups broth. In a small bowl, whisk together flour with remaining ½ cup broth until lump-free. Add flour mixture to chicken and vegetables. Cook until stew is bubbly and has thickened, about 3 minutes. Serve hot.

Nutrition Nugget

Don't liquefy your asse(t)s! Liquid carbs like soft drinks, syrupy lattes, juice drinks, alcohol coolers and energy and sports drinks will make you fat really fast. The huge amounts of fructose they contain are your BFF: Butt (and Belly) Fat Forever!

In 1950, vegetable farmers from all over the world held an important meeting. It went down in history as the first peas conference :)

Become an Action Figure

Some popular activities just don't burn as many calories as people would like to think. Take running off at the mouth, for example. Sure *sounds* strenuous. So does playing the field, jogging your memory, raking in the bucks, building a reputation, sweeping it under a rug, hiking up your hemline and social climbing. Calories expended during these Olympic-like feats of physical fitness: Zip, zero, zilch! Sorry to burst your bubble (bursting bubbles—zero calories burned). If you're aiming for a leaner, stronger, healthier you, remember that actions speak louder than words. Run, play, jog, rake, build, sweep, hike and climb. Whatever you do, don't rest on your laurels.

Fee Fie Faux Fried Chicken

Oven "fried" chicken pieces with a crispy herb coating

Fee, Fie, Fo Yum! I smell the scent of chicken with crumbs! If you love fried chicken, but hate all the fat, our healthier rendition is a giant step in the right direction.

1 cup	corn flake crumbs
¼ cup	freshly grated Parmesan cheese
1 tsp	paprika
1 tsp	dried marjoram
½ tsp	each dried thyme and seasoned salt
¼ tsp	each garlic powder, onion powder and freshly ground black pepper
⅛ tsp	cayenne pepper
1 cup	buttermilk
½ cup	whole wheat flour
4	large chicken thighs (bone-in; remove skin)
4	large chicken drumsticks (remove skin)
2 tbsp	butter, melted

Safflower oil or cooking spray to coat baking pan

- In a shallow bowl or pie plate, mix corn flake crumbs with Parmesan, paprika, marjoram, thyme, seasoned salt, garlic powder, onion powder, black pepper and cayenne pepper. Set aside.

- Pour buttermilk into a second shallow bowl or pie plate and place flour into a third shallow bowl or pie plate.

- Coat a rimmed baking sheet with safflower oil or spray generously with cooking spray (see tip below). Rinse chicken and pat dry using paper towels. Working one at a time, dip chicken pieces in buttermilk and moisten on all sides. Shake off excess buttermilk. Place chicken in bowl with flour and turn to coat. Dip in buttermilk again, then coat with seasoned corn flake mixture. This process can get a little messy, but hang in there! Double dipping is what makes the chicken extra yummy. Place chicken pieces on prepared baking sheet. Leave some space between chicken pieces (they should not be touching). Using a small spoon, drizzle melted butter evenly over chicken.

- Bake, uncovered, at 400°F for 35 to 40 minutes, until chicken is golden brown and juices run clear. Serve hot.

MAKES 8 PIECES

PER PIECE
258 calories, 8.8 g total fat (4 g saturated fat), 26 g protein, 18 g carbohydrate, 1.4 g fiber, 106 mg cholesterol, 343 mg sodium

Recipe Tip: If you invest in a good-quality oil spray bottle from a gourmet shop or housewares store, you can make your own cooking spray using your favorite oil.

Grill of a Lifetime

Grilled chicken breasts in a mango-curry marinade

These zesty grilled chicken breasts earned top-flavor honors at the annual Spice Grill competition. Ginger Spice failed to make an appearance.

4	boneless skinless chicken breasts (about 1½ lbs/680 g)
⅓ cup	mango chutney (see tip)
3 tbsp	liquid honey
2 tbsp	freshly squeezed lemon juice
1 tbsp	reduced-sodium soy sauce
1 tsp	curry powder
1 tsp	minced garlic
½ tsp	ground cumin

- Arrange chicken breasts in a glass baking dish. Whisk together remaining ingredients in a small bowl. Reserve 3 tbsp marinade (for basting) and pour remaining marinade over chicken. Turn pieces to coat both sides with marinade. Cover and marinate in the refrigerator for at least 1 hour.

- Preheat grill to medium setting. Lightly oil grill rack. Remove chicken from marinade and grill for about 5 minutes per side, until chicken is no longer pink. Baste with reserved marinade. Serve immediately.

Recipe Tip: Mango chutney is a spicy condiment made from mangos, onions, vinegar and spices. The sweetness of the fruit provides a nice contrast to the spicy and sour flavorings. It's commonly used to season grilled meats or to add zing to sauces and salad dressings. You'll find it in a jar near the ketchup at your grocery store.

MAKES 4 SERVINGS

PER SERVING
280 calories, 2.2 g total fat, (0.6 g saturated fat),
40 g protein, 23 g carbohydrate, 0.3 g fiber,
99 mg cholesterol, 500 mg sodium

Nutrition Nugget

Best grill friend: Adding garlic to meat or poultry appears to reduce the production of cancer-causing chemicals that can develop in meat when it's grilled at high temperatures. What's not to clove about that?

Do Re Mi Fa So La-sagna

Layers of roasted chicken with creamy ricotta and spinach filling

Yo! It's here. It's really here. Yay! It's full of chicken, yum! Me. I eat it all myself…OK. You get the drift. Our chicken lasagna is Do Re Mi Fa Sooo delicious!

MAKES 8 SERVINGS

PER SERVING
481 calories,
13 g total fat
(5 g saturated fat),
43 g protein,
44 g carbohydrate,
5.4 g fiber,
88 mg cholesterol,
728 mg sodium

1 cup	part-skim ricotta cheese
¾ cup	1% cottage cheese
½ pkg	(10 oz/300 g) frozen spinach, thawed, squeezed dry and chopped (5 oz/150 g total)
1	egg
½ tsp	dried oregano
12	uncooked whole-grain lasagna noodles
1	small whole rotisserie chicken
4 cups	low-sodium chunky vegetable pasta sauce
1 cup	crumbled light feta cheese (4 oz/113 g)
1½ cups	packed shredded light mozzarella cheese (6 oz/170 g)
¼ cup	chopped black olives
¼ cup	minced fresh parsley

> You don't stop laughing because you grow old. You grow old because you stop laughing.
> *Michael Pritchard*

- In a medium bowl, combine ricotta cheese, cottage cheese, spinach, egg and oregano. Cover and refrigerate until ready to use.

- Prepare lasagna noodles according to package directions. Drain. Rinse with cold water and drain again. While noodles are boiling, remove skin from chicken and chop meat into bite-sized pieces. You should end up with roughly 3½ cups chicken. Set aside.

- Spray a 9 x 13-inch baking pan with cooking spray. To assemble lasagna, spoon 1 cup sauce over bottom of pan. Arrange 4 lasagna noodles, 3 lengthwise and 1 crosswise, over sauce. Top noodles with 1 cup sauce, followed by ⅓ chicken, ⅓ feta, ⅓ mozzarella and ⅓ olives. Arrange 4 more noodles over top, followed by 1 cup sauce, ⅓ chicken, all of the ricotta-spinach mixture, ⅓ feta, ⅓ mozzarella and ⅓ olives. Repeat layering with remaining noodles, sauce, chicken, feta, mozzarella and olives. Sprinkle parsley over top.

- Cover loosely with foil and bake at 375°F for 45 minutes. Remove foil for last 5 minutes of baking time. Let cool for 10 minutes before serving.

FOOD BITE

The only difference between green olives and black olives is their ripeness. Unripe olives are green and fully ripe olives are black. Olives must be cured before eating and aren't typically consumed raw. Fresh olives right from the tree are unbearably bitter. (Just thinking out loud here: What disease did cured olives have in the first place?)

Mom's Famous No-Peek Chicken

Scrumptious yet simple baked chicken and rice casserole

"Look under the foil and the chicken will spoil." Or so our mother told us. Don't ask us why. Ask our mother!

1 can	(10 oz/284 mL) reduced-fat cream of celery soup, undiluted
1 can	(10 oz/284 mL) reduced-fat cream of mushroom soup, undiluted
1½ cups	1% milk
1¼ cups	uncooked brown rice
6	whole chicken legs, skin removed
½ pkg	(1 oz/28 g) dry onion soup mix (0.5 oz/14 g total)

- Spray a 9 x 13-inch baking dish with cooking spray. Set aside.

- In a medium bowl, whisk together celery soup, mushroom soup and milk until smooth. Stir in rice. Pour rice mixture over bottom of baking dish. Arrange chicken legs in a single layer over rice. Sprinkle top of chicken and rice with onion soup mix.

- Cover with foil and bake at 350°F for 1½ hours. DO NOT PEEK! Remove from oven and let stand for 10 minutes before serving. It's hot!

MAKES 6 SERVINGS

PER SERVING
386 calories, 8.2 g total fat (2.2 g saturated fat), 33 g protein, 43 g carbohydrate, 2.1 g fiber, 110 mg cholesterol, 863 mg sodium

Did you hear about the valedictorian of the cooking class? She passed her exams with frying colors :)

Nutrition Nugget

When you lose weight on a very restrictive diet, at least one-quarter of that weight loss comes from water, muscle and bone. Yes, bone! The faster you lose weight, the more bone you lose. And that's not a bunch of boney baloney—it's true! In fact, doctors have found anorexic teens to have bones as porous and brittle as women in their seventies and eighties—all a result of crash dieting. Maybe we should take a lesson from the French, who encourage eating with their famous expression, "Bone appétit!"

Red Meat, White Meat, Dark Meat, Light Meat

Have you ever wondered what makes some meats white and others dark? Well, we thought we'd tell you anyway! It's myoglobin—an oxygen-holding compound—that gives meat its red color. Without getting too complex, myoglobin in muscle cells receives oxygen from the blood and holds it for use in cell metabolism. The amount of myoglobin, and therefore the amount of redness, depends on how often the muscle is used. Since cattle are relatively active, roaming animals, and pigs are raised in pens that confine their activity, beef has more myoglobin than pork. Fish, on the other hand, have very little myoglobin. Their "fast" muscles are designed to burn glycogen, a process that uses less oxygen. That's why most fish meat is white. Chickens have both dark and light meat because their leg muscles are more active than their pectoral (breast) muscles. In contrast, game birds—which do use breast muscles to fly—have mostly dark meat. Looks like the more hustle, the more muscle! What color is *your* leg meat?

Dilly Beloved

Baked chicken breasts with maple, mustard, lemon and dill

It's the wedding of the scentury! One bite of these happily marinated chicken breasts and your dinner guests will be exchanging wows. Easy enough for every day…fancy enough for company.

Marinade

¼ cup	pure maple syrup
3 tbsp	grainy Dijon mustard
2 tbsp	minced fresh dill
2 tbsp	freshly squeezed lemon juice
1 tbsp	olive oil
1 tbsp	balsamic vinegar
2 tsp	grated lemon zest
1 tsp	minced garlic
¼ tsp	each salt and freshly ground black pepper

4	boneless skinless chicken breasts (about 1½ lbs/680 g)

MAKES 4 SERVINGS

PER SERVING
289 calories, 6.4 g total fat
(1.1 g saturated fat), 40 g protein,
16 g carbohydrate, 0.4 g fiber,
99 mg cholesterol, 322 mg sodium

- Whisk together all marinade ingredients in a small bowl. Arrange chicken breasts in a glass or ceramic baking dish that's just large enough to hold the chicken breasts in a single layer. Pour marinade over chicken. Turn pieces to coat both sides with marinade. Cover with plastic wrap and refrigerate for at least 1 hour or up to 1 day.

- Preheat oven to 350ºF. Remove plastic wrap and transfer casserole dish to middle oven rack. Bake, uncovered, for about 35 minutes, or until chicken is no longer pink in the center.

- Place cooked chicken on a serving platter and keep warm. Pour marinade and juices into a small saucepan. Bring to a boil over high heat and cook, stirring constantly, until mixture thickens slightly, about 1 minute. Pour sauce over chicken and serve immediately.

Recipe Tips

Do not use a large casserole dish, such as a lasagna pan, for this recipe. It's too big and will cause the marinade to spread too thinly and likely burn while the chicken is baking. The marinade also makes a great salad dressing when you add an extra tablespoon of balsamic vinegar and olive oil.

CHICKEN WORTH PICKIN'

The Nutcrocker

Slow-cooked peanut-ginger chicken thighs in the Crock-Pot

You'd have to be nuts not to love this one-pot wonderful, peanutty chicken dish.

1 cup	medium salsa
⅓ cup	light peanut butter
2 tbsp	frozen orange juice concentrate
1 tbsp	reduced-sodium soy sauce
1 tbsp	liquid honey
1 tbsp	grated gingerroot
½ tsp	curry powder
12	boneless skinless chicken thighs (about 2¼ lbs/1 kg)

Chopped green onions and chopped peanuts for garnish (optional)

- Whisk together salsa, peanut butter, orange juice concentrate, soy sauce, honey, gingerroot and curry powder in the crock of a slow cooker. Place chicken thighs over sauce. Turn pieces to coat both sides with sauce. Cover and cook on low heat setting for 5 to 6 hours or high heat setting for 2½ to 3 hours, until chicken is tender. Garnish chicken with chopped green onions and chopped peanuts, if desired.

Recipe Tip: This recipe tastes great served on a bed of hot basmati rice or coconut rice with sweet green peas on the side.

MAKES 6 SERVINGS

PER SERVING
283 calories, 11 g total fat
(2.4 g saturated fat),
31 g protein,
13 g carbohydrate,
1 g fiber,
126 mg cholesterol,
479 mg sodium

Calorie Burning 101

Most of us have figured out that protein-rich foods are powerful appetite suppressants. They're filling, satisfying and keep your blood sugar on an even keel so you won't crave junk food. But another interesting way that protein helps fight fat is through something called the "thermic effect of food." The actual process of digesting and absorbing the nutrients in a meal causes us to burn calories as heat. You burn 35 calories when you digest 100 calories of protein—way more heat than what's created by digesting carbs or fat. *Whey* cool! We know what you're thinking: "Cowabunga! Protein seems like a magic potion for weight loss!" Before you go hog wild, realize that eating too much protein can be detrimental to your health. If you'd rather look like Sharon Stone than Fred Flintstone, limit your stops at the Brontosaurus Burger Joint. Aim for small portions (10 to 25 grams) of lean protein with each meal. Some good choices: 3 oz chicken breast (21 g), whey protein shake (25 g), 3 oz salmon (25 g), 1 cup chickpeas (12 g), 2 eggs (12 g), 1 cup quinoa (8 g) and ½ cup cottage cheese (15 g). Eat fish and chicken, get your calorie burner tickin'!

Chicken Pandemonium

Chicken and wild rice skillet meal with grated Parmesan

This wildly delicious, one-pot, stovetop creation is sure to cause an uproar!
Your friends will think you're a gourmet, but it really takes no skillet all.

3	large boneless skinless chicken breasts (about 1¼ lbs/568 g)
2 tsp	olive oil
3 cups	sliced mushrooms (see tip)
¾ cup	chopped onions
1 tsp	minced garlic
1 pkg	(6.3 oz/180 g) Uncle Ben's Long Grain & Wild Rice original recipe
1¼ cups	reduced-sodium chicken broth
½ cup	dry white wine
½ cup	freshly grated Parmesan cheese

MAKES 4 SERVINGS

PER SERVING
404 calories,
6.3 g total fat
(2 g saturated fat),
41 g protein,
37 g carbohydrate,
1.8 g fiber,
89 mg cholesterol,
672 mg sodium

- You will need a 10-inch, non-stick skillet with a tight-fitting lid for this recipe.

- Cut chicken breasts into large chunks (about 6 pieces per breast). Heat oil in skillet over medium-high heat. Add chicken pieces and cook for about 4 minutes, stirring often, until chicken is lightly browned all over. Remove chicken from skillet and set aside.

- Add mushrooms, onions and garlic to the same skillet. Cook and stir until vegetables begin to soften, about 3 minutes. If vegetables start to stick, add a little water or broth.

- Add rice and seasoning pouch. Mix well and cook for 30 seconds. Stir in broth and wine. Return chicken to skillet. Bring mixture to a boil. Reduce heat to medium-low, cover and simmer for about 20 minutes, until rice is tender and liquid is absorbed. Remove from heat. Let stand, covered, for 10 minutes. Stir in Parmesan cheese and serve immediately.

Recipe Tips: To save some time, buy an 8-oz (227 g) package of presliced mushrooms. For a fancier dish, use a blend of sliced wild mushrooms, such as portobello, shiitake and cremini.

Trivial Tidbit

What do wine, coffee, tobacco, blueberries, black tea and soy sauce all have in common? If you guessed "antioxidants," you're wrong (unless tobacco manufacturers have secretly stashed carotenoids in cartons of Camels!). The common bond is that all of the above stain your teeth! However, blueberries are loaded with healthy plant chemicals and are great "skin food," so count on a glowing complexion to offset your blue-tinged smile.

> I cook with wine; sometimes I even add it to the food.
> *W.C. Fields*

FOOD BITE

The first zero-calorie soft drink, introduced in 1952, was called (in a stroke of sheer marketing genius) No-Cal Beverage. The ginger ale drink was invented by Hyman Kirsch, vice-president of the Jewish Sanitarium for Chronic Disease in Brooklyn. Kirsch developed the saccharin-sweetened soda for his patients with diabetes and cardiovascular problems. But when Coke, Pepsi and the other big players in the beverage industry got into the diet-drink business, No-Cal became no more.

Barbecutie Patootie Chicken Pizza

Hungry-man pizza that's perfect for your next party

*Our pizza has pizzazz! Make this tasty pizza-pie for your cutie-pie
when he's in a fowl mood.*

¼ cup	barbecue sauce
¼ cup	pizza sauce
1½ cups	chopped cooked chicken breast
2 tsp	olive oil
2 cups	sliced mixed mushrooms (see tip)
1	medium red onion, sliced thinly into rings
½ tsp	dried oregano
1	12-inch prebaked whole-grain thin-crust pizza shell
1 cup	packed shredded light Monterey Jack cheese (4 oz/113 g)
1 to 2 tbsp	minced fresh cilantro or parsley

• Combine 2 tbsp barbecue sauce with pizza sauce in a small bowl and set aside. Mix remaining barbecue sauce with chopped chicken breast and set aside.

• Heat olive oil in a non-stick skillet over medium-high heat. Add mushrooms and onions. Cook and stir until vegetables are tender, about 5 to 6 minutes. Add oregano and cook for 1 more minute. Remove from heat.

• Spread sauce evenly over pizza crust. Top with mushroom-onion mixture, followed by chicken. Sprinkle with cheese and cilantro. Bake at 425°F for about 8 minutes, until crust is lightly browned and cheese is melted. Serve immediately.

Recipe Tip Common white button mushrooms will work fine in this recipe, but with so many wild varieties to choose from, why not have a little fun(gus) and try something new? Look for fresh Japanese shiitake mushrooms, dark brown cremini mushrooms, meaty portobellos or fan-shaped oyster mushrooms next time you shop. Alone or in combination, these varieties will give your delectable chicken pizza maximum mushroom taste!

MAKES 1 12-INCH PIZZA, 8 SLICES

PER SLICE
184 calories, 6.5 g total fat (2.4 g saturated fat),
13 g protein, 17 g carbohydrate, 1.6 g fiber,
28 mg cholesterol, 341 mg sodium

People who transport salt are movers and shakers :)

The Thigh's the Limit

Marinated, baked chicken thighs in a unique, gingery salsa sauce

Marinated chicken thighs that soar to new flavor heights. Remember: Removing the skin means you won't blimp out. And that's not a bunch of hot air!

12	bone-in chicken thighs, skin removed (about 3 lbs/1.4 kg)
¾ cup	salsa (mild, medium or hot)
⅓ cup	liquid honey
¼ cup	each reduced-sodium soy sauce and orange juice
2 tbsp	Dijon mustard
1½ tbsp	grated gingerroot
2 tsp	olive oil
1 tbsp	cornstarch

- Arrange chicken thighs in a single layer in a 9 x 13-inch baking dish. In a medium bowl, mix together salsa, honey, soy sauce, orange juice, mustard, gingerroot and olive oil. Pour over chicken thighs. Turn thighs to coat both sides with marinade. Cover and refrigerate for at least 4 hours or overnight.

- Bake chicken at 400°F for about 40 minutes, until chicken is tender. Transfer chicken thighs to a serving platter and keep warm. Carefully pour sauce into a small pot. Bring to a boil over medium-high heat. Mix cornstarch with 2 tbsp water until smooth. Add to sauce and stir until mixture thickens, about 1 minute. Pour thickened sauce over chicken and serve immediately.

MAKES 6 SERVINGS

PER SERVING
318 calories, 9 g total fat
(2 g saturated fat), 34 g protein,
20 g carbohydrate, 1 g fiber,
151 mg cholesterol, 628 mg sodium

Bone Appetite

Did you know that North Americans consume more dairy products than anyone else in the world? Sadly, North Americans also have the highest rate of osteoporosis on the planet, no bones about it. What gives? Don't experts say that calcium from dairy products is supposed to prevent thinning of our bones? Though we're milking dairy products for all they're worth, North Americans also consume more "calcium robbers" than anyone else on Earth, and it's definitely our loss. Some of the things that leach calcium from our bones are the same things most common to North American living: caffeine, sugar, soft drinks, alcohol, excessive protein, smoking, stress and inactivity. Amazingly, poor dietary and lifestyle choices have more to do with calcium deficiency and bone loss than not taking in enough calcium. Before boning up on calcium supplements or eating more yogurt, start by repairing the calcium leaks. Beware the calcium bandits, get some exercise and choose real, nutrient-filled food more often.

FOOD BITE

The most famous of the great Dijon mustard firms was founded in 1777 by Monsieur Maurice Grey and his partner, Antoine Poupon, who had developed a secret recipe for a strong mustard made with white wine. But that mustard apparently didn't quite cut the mustard: It was in Dijon, France, in 1856, that Jean Naigeon created what would become known as Dijon mustard. Naigeon substituted a sour liquid made from unripe grapes (called verjuice) in place of vinegar in the traditional mustard recipe, making his mustard smoother and more palatable. Dijon's claim to mustard fame had already been gathering steam, since the Grey Poupon company had created a machine that automated the processing of mustard seeds in 1853. Armed with Naigeon's new-and-improved recipe, the mustard's popularity spread internationally. Today, almost all of the world's mustard is made with seeds from plants grown in Canada!

Chicken Cordon New

Ham-and-cheese-stuffed chicken with Parmesan-herb crumb coating

A prize-worthy chicken cordon bleu that's not oozing with fat? Now, that's something NEW! C'est magnifique!

1   egg
1 tbsp   honey-Dijon mustard
½ cup   whole wheat flour
½ tsp   each salt and freshly ground black pepper
⅓ cup   finely crushed multigrain crackers
2 tbsp   freshly grated Parmesan cheese
2 tsp   minced fresh thyme
¼ tsp   freshly ground black pepper
4   boneless skinless chicken breasts or
          4 large boneless skinless chicken thighs
          (about 1½ lbs/680 g)
4 oz   (113 g) thinly sliced smoked ham
4 oz   (113 g) thinly sliced light Jarlsberg or Swiss cheese
2 tsp   butter
2 tsp   olive oil

MAKES 4 SERVINGS

PER SERVING (WITH CHICKEN BREASTS)
352 calories, 11 g total fat (3.6 g saturated fat), 43 g protein,
17 g carbohydrate, 2.4 g fiber, 154 mg cholesterol, 640 mg sodium

Did you hear about the dog that ate a pound of garlic? His bark was worse than his bite :)

- You will need three shallow bowls (or small pie plates) for this recipe.

- Preheat oven to 350°F. Whisk together egg and honey mustard in first shallow bowl. Combine flour, salt and pepper in second bowl. Mix together cracker crumbs, Parmesan, thyme and pepper in third bowl.

- Place chicken pieces between sheets of plastic wrap and pound with a meat mallet until ¼ inch thick. Be careful not to pound too much or you will tear the meat!

- Place 1 oz ham and 1 oz cheese on each piece of chicken and fold or roll up tightly. (Make sure cheese is in center and not near edge or it will leak out while cooking.) Secure with round wooden toothpicks.

- This process can get a little messy, so hang in there. Working one at a time, place folded chicken in flour mixture and carefully turn to coat both sides. Dip both sides in egg mixture and shake off excess. Dip both sides in crumb mixture. Set aside. Repeat with remaining 3 pieces of chicken.

- Heat butter and olive oil over medium heat in a 10-inch, non-stick skillet. Add chicken pieces and cook for about 2 minutes on each side or until lightly browned. Transfer to a baking pan or rimmed baking sheet and bake for 30 minutes, until chicken is cooked through and juices run clear. Serve hot.

To Stir, With Love

Quick, colorful and delicious chicken and vegetable stir-fry

Eat to your heart's content! One taste of this Asian stir-fry and it's love at first bite!

½ cup	reduced-sodium chicken broth
2 tbsp	each apricot jam and reduced-sodium soy sauce
1 tbsp	each ketchup, grated gingerroot and cornstarch
1 tsp	sesame oil
1 tsp	minced garlic
¼ tsp	crushed red pepper flakes
1 tbsp	olive oil
4	boneless skinless chicken breasts, cut into thin strips (about 1½ lbs/680 g)
1 cup	sliced red bell pepper
1 cup	whole mini corncobs
1 cup	sliced water chestnuts
2 cups	packed whole baby spinach leaves
½ cup	chopped green onions
8	whole basil leaves, coarsely chopped
4 cups	hot cooked brown rice

MAKES 4 SERVINGS

PER SERVING (WITH RICE)
478 calories, 8.2 g total fat
(1 g saturated fat), 35 g protein,
66 g carbohydrate, 7.2 g fiber,
66 mg cholesterol,
557 mg sodium

- To make sauce, whisk together broth, jam, soy sauce, ketchup, gingerroot, cornstarch, sesame oil, garlic and crushed red pepper flakes in a small bowl. Set aside.

- Heat oil in a large, non-stick wok over high heat. Add chicken. Cook and stir until chicken is no longer pink. Continue to cook until chicken is lightly browned. Add red pepper and cook for 2 more minutes. Add corncobs, water chestnuts, spinach leaves and green onions. Cook for 3 more minutes, until spinach is wilted and corncobs are heated through. Add basil leaves and sauce. Cook and stir until sauce is bubbly and has thickened. Serve chicken and vegetables over hot rice.

Trivial Tidbit

Laugh your way to good health! Short, frequent bursts of laughter reduce artery firmness, and that can reduce the risk of heart and other circulatory problems. Looks like a good joke could prevent a stroke. *Hearty* har har!

Believing is Seeing

Losing weight is a lot like driving a car. In order to get results, you need to concentrate on where you want to go. Focusing on what you *don't* want—"I don't want to be fat"—isn't going to work and, in fact, will attract more of what you don't want—fat! It's like staring intently at the curb and saying, "I don't want to drive there." Next thing you know, your fender's wrapped around a light post. To get what you truly want, focus on what you want. Be positive, be specific and speak in terms of "now," not in terms of some vague hope for the future. "I'm too fat. I need to lose weight," isn't nearly as powerful as saying, "I have been transforming my body and now I'm a svelte, sexy, sculpted hottie!" (OK, that's a little over the top, but you get our drift.) Here's the real secret: If you want a slimmer body, picture it vividly, *as if you already have it!* That's right. Act like you're already at your goal weight. Feel it in every cell of your body, and believe it! Go shopping for new, smaller-sized clothes. Try the activities you said you'd try when you lost some weight. Show off those soon-to-be-toned muscles at the gym. BE the change that you want! New science is showing that "living from the outcome," in other words, placing our focus on what our lives would be like if our dreams were *already fulfilled*, can create the conditions within us that transform our beliefs into reality. Like the adage (kinda) says, "We'll see it when we believe it!"

Celine Dijon Chicken

Mildly flavored Dijon chicken with a creamy herb sauce

Even if you have 13 siblings, a grandpa and a Grammy, this Titantilizing dish is sure to make everyone's taste buds sing.

1 cup	unsweetened apple juice
1 tbsp	each Dijon mustard and freshly squeezed lemon juice
1	large shallot, minced (see tip)
½ tsp	dried thyme
¼ tsp	dried rosemary
⅛ tsp	freshly ground black pepper
2 tsp	olive oil
4	boneless skinless chicken breasts (about 1½ lbs/680 g)
¼ cup	light (5%) sour cream
1 tsp	each liquid honey and cornstarch

MAKES 4 SERVINGS

PER SERVING
203 calories, 4.4 g total fat (0.5 g saturated fat), 27 g protein, 12 g carbohydrate, 0.2 g fiber, 67 mg cholesterol, 188 mg sodium

- Whisk together apple juice, Dijon mustard, lemon juice, shallot, thyme, rosemary and black pepper in a small bowl. Set aside.

- Heat olive oil in a large skillet over medium-high heat. Add chicken breasts and cook for 2 to 3 minutes on each side, until lightly browned. Add reserved apple juice mixture. Reduce heat to medium. Simmer, covered, for 5 to 7 minutes, until chicken is cooked through. Remove chicken from skillet and keep warm.

- Gently boil remaining liquid for 3 minutes, until slightly reduced in volume. Mix sour cream, honey and cornstarch in a small bowl. Add to skillet. Cook and stir until sauce is bubbly and has thickened. Pour sauce over warm chicken and serve immediately.

Recipe Tip

Shallots are mild-flavored members of the onion family, though they look like oversized cloves of garlic wrapped in thin, papery brown skins. Because of their delicate, sweet flavor, shallots are a good choice for light sauces. Dry shallots are available year-round in the produce section of your supermarket, sold in mesh bags or in bulk. Look for shallots that are plump and sprout-free. They should be stored like onions in a cool, dry, well-ventilated place, where they'll keep for about a month.

Nutrition Nugget

When light isn't right: Research published in *New Scientist* magazine showed that light destroys many of the antioxidants in olive oil. Oils stored in clear bottles under supermarket lighting lost at least 30 percent of their tocopherols (vitamin E) and carotenoids. Light also oxidizes olive oil, creating free radicals that'll cause, not prevent, premature aging! So always choose oils that come in darkly tinted or opaque containers and reach for a bottle from the back of the supermarket shelf where it's safe from the effects of bright store lighting. Keep the bottle in a dark, cool place in your kitchen (not near a window!).

Chicken Teriwacky

Marinated, grilled orange-teriyaki chicken

What's so wacky about our teriyaki? We added a hint of orange flavor that'll make you cuckoo! Great for salads or grilled chicken sandwiches.

Marinade

2 tbsp	reduced-sodium soy sauce
2 tbsp	freshly squeezed lime juice
2 tbsp	liquid honey
2 tbsp	ketchup
2 tbsp	minced green onions (with white parts)
1 tbsp	grated gingerroot
2 tsp	grated orange zest
1 tsp	minced garlic
4	boneless skinless chicken breasts (about 1½ lbs/680 g)
1 tbsp	toasted sesame seeds

MAKES 4 SERVINGS

PER SERVING
248 calories, 3.3 g total fat
(0.7 g saturated fat), 41 g protein,
7 g carbohydrate, 0.4 g fiber,
99 mg cholesterol,
430 mg sodium

- Whisk together all marinade ingredients in a small bowl. Place chicken breasts in a large, heavy-duty, resealable plastic bag. Add marinade and seal bag. Turn bag several times to coat chicken with marinade. Marinate for at least 4 hours, or overnight if possible.

- Preheat grill to medium setting. Remove chicken from marinade and place on a grill rack that has been lightly brushed with oil. Grill for about 15 minutes, turning occasionally, until chicken is no longer pink in the center. Be careful not to burn the chicken. (You can brush the chicken with extra marinade as long as you boil the marinade first to kill any bacteria.) Sprinkle chicken with toasted sesame seeds before serving.

> **Poultry is for the cook what canvas is for the painter.**
>
> *Jean Anthelme Brillat-Savarin*

FOOD BITE

Did you know that residues from orange juice manufacturing are a hot commodity? The discarded pulp, seeds and peel of oranges are used to make food products, such as cake mixes, candies and soft drinks. The residues also find their way into paints and perfumes. More than 100 million pounds of orange-peel oil are sold annually for cooking purposes, and it's also used by Coca-Cola as a flavoring. We propose a new company slogan: Coke—It's the peel thing!

Starvin Guy Chicken Pie (1)

Chicken and vegetable potpie with a savory herb gravy. A **Looneyspoons** classic!

Our version of the hungry-man dinner is a chicken potpie that's so jammed with hearty goodness, you might have to solicit the help of a few family members to stuff it into the oven!

Filling

2 tsp	olive oil
1 cup	chopped onions
1 tsp	minced garlic
1½ cups	peeled and cubed potatoes
1½ cups	chopped carrots
1 cup	sliced green beans (cut into 1-inch pieces)
½ tsp	each dried basil and dried thyme or 1 tsp dried Herbes de Provence
2½ cups	reduced-sodium chicken broth
½ tsp	freshly ground black pepper
1 can	(10 oz/284 mL) reduced-fat cream of mushroom soup, undiluted
3 cups	chopped cooked chicken breast
2 tbsp	minced fresh parsley
1 to 2 tbsp	cornstarch

Biscuit Crust

1 cup	all-purpose flour
½ cup	whole wheat flour
2 tsp	baking powder
1 tsp	baking soda
½ tsp	dried sage
¼ tsp	salt
3 tbsp	frozen butter
1 cup	plain low-fat yogurt

MAKES 6 SERVINGS

PER SERVING
411 calories, 11.8 g total fat (5.2 g saturated fat), 29 g protein, 47 g carbohydrate, 4.9 g fiber, 80 mg cholesterol, 752 mg sodium

- Heat olive oil in a large pot over medium heat. Add onions and garlic. Cook and stir until onions are tender, about 5 minutes. Add potatoes, carrots, beans, basil and thyme. Cook 1 more minute. Add broth and black pepper. Bring to a boil. Reduce heat to medium-low. Partially cover and simmer for 12 minutes. The potatoes should be slightly undercooked.

- Stir in soup, chicken and parsley. In a small bowl, whisk together cornstarch with an equal amount water until smooth. Add to chicken mixture. Cook and stir until gravy is bubbly and has thickened. Remove from heat. Pour into a medium casserole dish that has been coated with cooking spray.

- To prepare crust, combine both flours, baking powder, baking soda, sage and salt in a large bowl. Grate frozen butter directly into bowl with flour and mix gently using a fork until butter is evenly distributed. Stir in yogurt. Form a ball with the dough. Add a bit more flour if dough is too sticky. Roll out or pat down on a floured surface to fit top of casserole. Place dough over chicken mixture. Prick several times with a fork. (Brush top with a bit of melted butter, if desired.) Bake at 400°F for 20 to 25 minutes, until crust is puffed up and golden brown and filling is bubbling. Let cool 5 minutes before serving. It's hot!

Drinking hard liquor is whiskey business :)

The Pitfalls of Potpie

When you think of comfort food, chicken potpie probably comes to mind. Wanna know what's in store when it comes to store-bought chicken pies (especially the convenient little frozen ones that you can microwave)? Well, we've dissected a few in our day (don't ask!) and this is what we found: Fat and calories. Lots of 'em. Some puny potpies have more than 700 calories and almost 50 grams of fat. There's nothing comforting about that! Hiding under all that pastry and gravy are a few peas, a couple specks of carrot, 1/48th of a potato and, if it's your lucky day, about four mini-cubelets of chicken. If you're craving potpie, forgo convenience and get cooking. The good, old-fashioned kind like Ma used to make (and what you'll find on these pages) will stick to your ribs—not to your arteries!

Starvin Guy Chicken Pie (2)

Individual chicken potpies with roasted chicken, mushrooms, peas, carrots and sweet potato biscuit crusts

*From our recipe makeover show **Eat, Shrink & Be Merry!**, these delicious, individual chicken potpies fooled taste-testers into believing they were eating a high-fat, high-calorie comfort food!*

Filling

1 tsp	olive oil
1 cup	diced onions
½ cup	diced celery
1 tsp	minced garlic
3 cups	thinly sliced mushrooms
¾ cup	frozen mixed peas and carrots, thawed
1 tsp	dried thyme
¼ tsp	poultry seasoning
1¾ cups	reduced-sodium chicken broth
1 cup	cream-style corn
1 cup	2% evaporated milk
3 tbsp	all-purpose flour
1	large rotisserie chicken, meat cut into chunks (light and dark meat; about 3 cups total)
1 tbsp	minced fresh parsley

Biscuit Crusts

1 cup	all-purpose flour
½ cup	whole wheat flour
2 tsp	baking powder
1 tsp	baking soda
¼ tsp	salt
¾ cup	mashed/puréed cooked sweet potato (canned is fine)
½ cup	buttermilk
3 tbsp	butter, melted

MAKES 8 SERVINGS

PER SERVING
321 calories,
8.3 g total fat
(3.7 g saturated fat),
21 g protein,
41 g carbohydrate,
3.5 g fiber,
62 mg cholesterol,
568 mg sodium

- Preheat oven to 400°F. Place eight 7-oz ramekins on a baking sheet lined with foil and set aside.

- To make filling, heat olive oil over medium-high heat in large pot. Add onions, celery and garlic. Cook until onions begin to soften, about 3 minutes. Add mushrooms and cook until mushrooms are tender. Stir in peas and carrots, thyme and poultry seasoning. Cook 1 more minute. Add broth and corn and let mixture simmer, uncovered, for 2 minutes.

- In a small bowl, whisk together evaporated milk and flour until smooth. Add to pot. Cook and stir until mixture thickens. Remove from heat. Add chicken and parsley. Cover and keep warm.

- To make biscuit crusts, combine both flours, baking powder, baking soda and salt in a large bowl. In a medium bowl, whisk together sweet potato, buttermilk and 2 tbsp of the melted butter. Add wet ingredients to dry ingredients and stir gently until a ball is formed. With floured hands, transfer biscuit dough to a lightly floured surface and roll out or pat down to about ⅓-inch thickness. Using 2½-inch-round cookie cutter, cut dough into circles just slightly smaller than the top of your ramekins. Fill ramekins with warm chicken mixture and top with biscuits. Brush tops of biscuits with remaining melted butter. Bake for 13 to 15 minutes, until filling bubbles and biscuits are puffed up and golden brown. Let stand for 5 minutes before serving. They're hot!

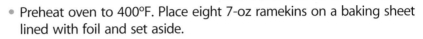

Kickin' Chicken

Spicy baked chicken in a super-simple and extra-flavorful peanut sauce

If you can't take the heat, get outta the chicken! This sizzling, super-spicy creation will leave you hot, but not bothered, since it's so easy to make. It's the perfect choice when you want to kick things up a notch.

12	boneless skinless chicken thighs or 6 boneless skinless chicken breasts (about 2¼ lbs/1 kg)
¾ cup	bottled light peanut sauce (see tip)
½ cup	medium or hot salsa
¼ cup	coarsely chopped fresh basil leaves

- Preheat oven to 400°F. Spray a 9 x 13-inch baking pan with cooking spray. Arrange chicken thighs in pan in a single layer. If you're using chicken breasts, cut them in half, if necessary, to make them fit in pan.

- Combine peanut sauce, salsa and basil in a medium bowl. Pour sauce evenly over chicken and make sure all pieces are well-coated with sauce. Bake, uncovered, for 40 to 45 minutes for thighs and 35 to 40 minutes for breasts, or until chicken is no longer pink in the center and sauce is bubbly.

- To serve, arrange chicken on a serving platter and pour extra sauce from pan over top.

Recipe Tips: Nowadays, it's pretty easy to buy a tasty, low-fat peanut sauce. Bottles of peanut sauce are usually sold near the salad dressings or barbecue sauces at the grocery store. Some are very spicy; others are mild. Make sure you compare brands and labels for sodium and sugar content. Same goes for salsa. You can control the heat factor and the flavor of this recipe by choosing sauces that suit your taste buds and your heat-tolerance level.

MAKES 6 SERVINGS

PER SERVING
(2 THIGHS PLUS SAUCE)
234 calories, 8.8 g total fat
(2 g saturated fat),
32 g protein,
5 g carbohydrate,
0.4 g fiber,
126 mg cholesterol,
546 mg sodium

(1 BREAST PLUS SAUCE)
241 calories, 5 g total fat
(1 g saturated fat),
41 g protein,
5 g carbohydrate,
0.4 g fiber,
99 mg cholesterol,
526 mg sodium

Nutrition Nugget

Skinful is sinful: Removing the skin from chicken reduces the fat content by approximately 50 percent and the calories by 20 percent. That's a lot! Plus, the skin and fat is where toxins can be stored, including Heterocyclic amines (HCAs), compounds created in meats and other foods that have been cooked at high temperatures. Studies show eating large amounts of HCAs can contribute to cancers of the stomach, colon and breast.

SELF-Directed Retirement Plan

As people reach middle age, they usually start to wonder, "Will I have enough money for retirement?" What they really should be taking stock of is the following: "Will I have enough muscle to play with my grandchildren, to pick up grocery bags, to tend the garden or to swing a golf club? Will I have the strength to have any fun at all?" Even if you've never invested in exercise, it's not too late to get in on the action and reap the returns. Like a miracle anti-aging potion, exercise can offset, delay, prevent and even reverse many of the common conditions associated with growing older. One consequence of being active is that you could live longer and stronger than your neighbors. Imagine! You could be climbing Mount Everest when your friends can barely climb the stairs!

Jamaican Me Hungry!

Caribbean jerk-style chicken

What Jamaican for dinner tonight? If you love bold flavors and a little adventure in the kitchen, quit jerkin' around and try our spiced-up grilled chicken recipe.

Marinade

⅓ cup	chopped green onions (with white parts)
¼ cup	freshly squeezed lime juice
2 tbsp	olive oil
2 tbsp	reduced-sodium soy sauce
2 tbsp	liquid honey
1 tbsp	grated gingerroot
2 tsp	minced garlic
2	jalapeño peppers, seeded and minced (wear gloves!)
2 tsp	ground allspice
1 tsp	each dried thyme, salt and freshly ground black pepper
½ tsp	each ground cinnamon and ground nutmeg
12	boneless skinless chicken thighs (about 2¼ lbs/1 kg)

- Whisk together all marinade ingredients in a medium bowl. Place chicken thighs in a large, heavy-duty, resealable plastic bag. Add marinade and seal bag. Turn bag several times to coat chicken with marinade. Marinate in the refrigerator overnight.

- Preheat grill to medium setting. Remove chicken from marinade (discard marinade) and place on a grill rack that has been lightly brushed with oil. Grill for about 15 minutes, turning occasionally, until chicken is no longer pink in the center. Be careful not to burn the chicken.

- Serve hot chicken with mango salsa on p. 273.

MAKES 6 SERVINGS

PER SERVING (WITHOUT SALSA)
242 calories, 9 g total fat (2 g saturated fat), 32 g protein, 5 g carbohydrate, 0.5 g fiber, 141 mg cholesterol, 431 mg sodium

Ya Mon! I hear ya!

GROWL RUMBLE

> If it weren't for Philo T. Farnsworth, inventor of the television, we'd still be eating frozen radio dinners.
>
> *Johnny Carson*

Indian Appleous 500

Indian coconut-curry chicken with chopped apples

Ladies and gentlemen, start your engines! This ultra-healthy Indian curry dish is the perfect vehicle for injecting some high-performance fuel into your system. You'll lap up every last morsel and drive your taste buds around the bend!

1 tbsp	olive oil
12	boneless skinless chicken thighs (about 2¼ lbs/1 kg), each thigh cut in half
1 cup	chopped onions
1 cup	chopped red bell pepper
2 tsp	minced garlic
1½ tbsp	grated gingerroot
1½ tsp	each curry powder and chili powder
½ tsp	each ground turmeric and ground cinnamon
1 can	(14 oz/398 mL) light coconut milk
¼ cup	mango chutney
2 tsp	grated lemon zest
½ tsp	salt
1	large Golden Delicious apple, peeled, cored and chopped (see tip)
½ cup	frozen green peas
2 tbsp	minced fresh cilantro

MAKES 6 SERVINGS

PER SERVING
317 calories, 12.7 g total fat
(5.5 g saturated fat),
33 g protein, 16 g carbohydrate,
2.6 g fiber, 141 mg cholesterol,
378 mg sodium

- You'll need a large, deep, non-stick skillet with a lid for this recipe. Heat olive oil in skillet over medium-high heat. Add chicken pieces and cook until both sides are lightly browned, about 2 minutes per side. Remove chicken and keep warm.

- Add onions, red pepper and garlic to the same skillet. Cook and stir until vegetables begin to soften, about 3 minutes. Add gingerroot, curry powder, chili powder, turmeric and cinnamon. Cook and stir for 1 more minute. Add coconut milk, mango chutney, lemon zest and salt. Mix well. Stir in chicken pieces and apples. Cover and simmer over low heat for 15 minutes. Add peas and cilantro. Simmer, uncovered, for 5 more minutes.

- Serve hot. Tastes great on a bed of basmati rice.

Recipe Tips: Don't cut the apple pieces too small, or they'll turn to mush. Aim for 1-inch pieces. For a different flavor, substitute fresh mango for the apple.

FOOD BITE

During the Renaissance, fashionable ladies used lemon juice as a natural method of reddening their lips. You might have thought they'd use beets, not lemons. As for exactly how lemon works to pinken your pucker? Beets us!

The Battle of the Bulge

Stand at attention, girls! We have the right to bare, flabby arms! When it comes to the war on fat, we're sorely lacking men's arsenal, and that means there's a fat chance we'll beat them in *this* battle of the sexes. Since fat is essential for childbearing, women have more fat cells than men and our fat cells are up to five times larger. Go figure! Stacking the odds against us even further, women have, on average, 40 pounds less muscle than men. And the more muscle you have, the more fat you burn! To add insult to injury, during premenopause, when the ovaries slow down estrogen production, fat cells take up the slack. That's right—fat becomes an estrogen-producing factory! Holy hot flashes, Batman! Because estrogen is so important, women's bodies devise sneaky ways to protect and add to their fat stores so they can keep churning out the hormone. One way is sacrificing fat-burning muscle. It's not unusual for a half pound of muscle to be lost each year during premenopause and to be replaced with one-and-a-half pounds of fat. Over 20 years, that's 30 additional pounds of blubber! With more weapons of body-mass destruction, men will usually beat us in the war against fat. Oh well, we can't have the brains *and* the brawn!

The Roastess with the Mostest

Lemon and herb roasted whole chicken

You'll be the hostess with the mostest when you serve this tantalizing roasted whole chicken to your dinner guests. They're sure to appreciate the carefully plucked, organic, grain-fed chicken that you raised in your backyard coop, infused with freshly snipped, homegrown rosemary and thyme from your greenhouse herb garden, and lovingly presented on the decorative platter that you handcrafted in your very own pottery barn. It's a good thing!

1	whole roasting chicken (about 4 lbs/1.8 kg)
1 tbsp	Dijon mustard
1 tbsp	brown sugar
1 tbsp	minced fresh rosemary
1 tbsp	minced fresh thyme
1 tsp	minced garlic
1 tsp	olive oil
½ tsp	each salt and freshly ground black pepper
1 tsp	grated lemon zest
1 tbsp	freshly squeezed lemon juice

MAKES 4 SERVINGS

PER SERVING (LIGHT & DARK MEAT)
222 calories, 7.3 g total fat
(2 g saturated fat), 33 g protein,
5 g carbohydrate, 0.4 g fiber,
108 mg cholesterol, 417 mg sodium

- Move oven rack to bottom third of oven. Preheat oven to 425°F. Place a small rack inside a roasting pan. Pour 1 cup water in pan. Rinse chicken inside and out, and pat dry with paper towels.

- In a small bowl, mix together mustard, brown sugar, rosemary, thyme, garlic, oil, salt and pepper to make a paste. Add lemon zest and mix again. Set aside.

- Squeeze juice from lemon inside cavity of chicken, then tuck the used lemon half right inside it. Tie legs together with kitchen string. Rub reserved paste over surface of chicken and, using your fingers, carefully rub paste between skin and meat on breast and thighs.

- Place chicken on rack breast-side down. Roast, uncovered, for 30 minutes. Remove chicken from oven and flip over. Add a bit more water if it has evaporated. Return to oven and roast for 35 to 40 more minutes, depending on size of bird. If chicken browns too quickly, cover it loosely with foil. When cooked, legs should move easily in sockets and thigh juices should be clear (not pink) when pierced with a small knife. A meat thermometer inserted in thigh (away from bone) should read 170°F.

- Remove chicken from oven and let rest for 10 minutes before carving.

You know you're overweight when you're living beyond your seams :)

Trivial Tidbit

"Early to bed, early to rise" really is wise, especially if you want to prevent your gut from expanding. A study from Northwestern University showed that night owls, even when they slept seven hours, ate an average of 248 more calories a day than those who hit the sack early. Don't be sleepin' *round*!

The Better Butter Chicken

Fragrant Indian butter chicken

It's the star of India! A real jewel. A gem of a recipe. Our healthier rendition of this popular ethnic dish doesn't use gobs of butter and tons of heavy cream, so you can save those precious calories for dessert.

2 tbsp	butter
1½ cups	chopped onions
2 tsp	minced garlic
1 tbsp	grated gingerroot
1½ tsp	chili powder
¾ tsp	each ground coriander and ground turmeric
½ tsp	each ground cinnamon and ground cumin
1 can	(28 oz/796 mL) no-salt-added diced tomatoes, drained
1½ cups	reduced-sodium chicken broth
1 tbsp	brown sugar
¼ tsp	each salt and freshly ground black pepper
1	whole cooked rotisserie chicken, skin removed and meat cut up (see tip)
⅓ cup	light (5%) sour cream
1 tbsp	minced fresh cilantro
Hot cooked basmati rice (optional)	

MAKES 5 SERVINGS

PER SERVING
297 calories, 10.5 g total fat
(5 g saturated fat), 33 g protein,
18 g carbohydrate, 4 g fiber,
102 mg cholesterol,
395 mg sodium

- Melt butter in a deep, 10-inch skillet over medium heat. Add onions and garlic. Cook slowly, stirring often, until onions are tender, about 5 minutes. Add gingerroot, chili powder, coriander, turmeric, cinnamon and cumin. Cook 1 more minute. Add tomatoes, chicken broth, brown sugar, salt and pepper. Reduce heat to low. Cover and simmer for 10 minutes, stirring occasionally.

- Add cut-up chicken and sour cream. Simmer, uncovered, for 5 more minutes. Remove from heat and stir in cilantro. Serve over hot basmati rice, if desired.

Recipe Tip Using a store-bought rotisserie chicken makes this recipe much tastier than using plain, cooked chicken breast. The combination of dark meat and light meat makes it absolutely scrumptious! Remove all of the skin from the chicken, discard the wings and cut the meat from the thighs and breasts into large chunks. Don't shred or cut the meat too small, or the finished dish won't look very appealing.

Nutrition Nugget

Curry up and get your red-hot super spice! White lab coats across the world are tooting turmeric's horn in a big way these days. Curcumin, the key compound giving turmeric its yellow color and health-promoting superpowers, is now being used to treat arthritis, cancer, diabetes, Crohn's disease, heart disease and Alzheimer's. Who knew the spice rack could get us on the health track?

Sticky Chicky

Baked chicken thighs in a sticky-sweet barbecue sauce

Even if your kids are picky, there's no way they'll call these "icky." Instead of saying "phooey," they'll shout, "Yahooey! These are gooey!"

16	boneless skinless chicken thighs (about 3 lbs/1.4 kg)
½ cup	barbecue sauce (hickory flavor is nice!)
¼ cup	reduced-sodium soy sauce
¼ cup	red wine vinegar
¼ cup	pure maple syrup or liquid honey
1 tbsp	chili powder
1 tbsp	Dijon mustard
1 tbsp	grated gingerroot
2 tsp	minced garlic
1 tsp	ground cumin
1 tbsp	cornstarch

MAKES 8 SERVINGS

PER SERVING
287 calories,
7.1 g total fat
(1.7 g saturated fat),
35 g protein,
19 g carbohydrate,
0.5 g fiber,
141 mg cholesterol,
590 mg sodium

- Preheat oven to 400°F. Spray a 9 x 13-inch baking pan with cooking spray. Arrange chicken thighs in pan in a single layer.

- To make sauce, whisk together remaining ingredients, except cornstarch, in a medium bowl. Pour evenly over chicken. Turn pieces to coat both sides with sauce. Bake, uncovered, for about 40 minutes, or until chicken is no longer pink in the center.

- Remove chicken from pan and keep warm. Carefully pour sauce from pan into a small pot. Bring to a boil over medium-high heat. Combine cornstarch with an equal amount of water and mix until smooth. Add to sauce. Cook until sauce is bubbly and has thickened, about 1 minute. Serve hot chicken with extra sauce on top.

Graze Anatomy

The average person fuels his body the same way he gases up his vehicle—not until it's running on fumes! The red warning light comes on, triggering an emergency pit stop for large fries and a chocolate shake. To avoid crazy blood-sugar spikes and uncontrollable urges to binge, never (ever!) let your tank run dry. Instead, go grazey! Eating smaller meals more often keeps your hunger in check, your energy levels up and your mind sharp all day long. Smaller meals also keep your metabolism stoked—sort of like putting kindling on a fire to keep it burning. Throwing a huge truckload of wood on the fire can dampen and stifle it. Gas up every three hours or so, and make it a high-octane, balanced blend of lean protein (such as turkey or chicken breast), good carbohydrates (such as veggies, fruit or whole grains) and healthy fats (such as olive oil, some nuts or avocado). Warning: Do not overfill the tank! According to researchers, your body can efficiently handle up to 500 calories in one sitting. Any more than that tends to shift your fat-storing engine into overdrive. If you eat small, eat often and eat smart, you won't end up with a wider chassis!

Nutrition Nugget

Nature is the best chemist! Scientists have recently discovered that pure maple syrup contains 54 compounds beneficial to health, and many of those compounds contain antioxidant and anti-inflammatory properties similar to those found in berries, tea and flaxseed. Choose pure, organic maple syrup, not imitations containing high-fructose corn syrup. Aunt Jemima sure seems like a nice lady, plus we've known her since we watched *Sesame Street* from our high chairs, but her syrup just doesn't make the grade, unfortunately.

> Laughter is the shortest distance between two people.
>
> *Victor Borge*

♪ One of these things is not like the others. One of these things is not the same. ♪

Sesame Sweet Chicken

Asian, grilled chicken thighs basted with a sticky-sweet sesame sauce

Can you tell me how you get, how you get your chicken so sweet! These grilled chicken thighs are as easy as 1-2-3. Feeding the whole street? Don't be a grouch—it's a big bird!

12	bone-in chicken thighs, skin removed (about 3 lbs/1.4 kg)
½ cup	hoisin sauce (see tip)
¼ cup	liquid honey
3 tbsp	freshly squeezed lime juice
2 tbsp	reduced-sodium soy sauce
1 tbsp	grated gingerroot
½ tsp	each ground cumin and paprika
1 tbsp	toasted sesame seeds (see tip)

MAKES 6 SERVINGS

PER SERVING
256 calories, 6.8 g total fat (1.6 g saturated fat), 29 g protein, 19 g carbohydrate, 0.8 g fiber, 115 mg cholesterol, 666 mg sodium

- Arrange chicken pieces in a shallow glass dish. Whisk together all remaining ingredients except sesame seeds in a small bowl and pour over chicken. Turn pieces to coat both sides with marinade. Cover with plastic wrap and marinate in the refrigerator for at least 1 hour or overnight.

- Preheat grill to medium setting. Remove chicken from marinade and place on a grill rack that has been lightly brushed with oil. Grill thighs for about 10 minutes per side. Be careful not to burn them. (You can brush the chicken with extra marinade as long as you boil the marinade first to kill any bacteria.) Sprinkle with sesame seeds and serve hot.

Recipe Tips Hoisin sauce is a thick, sweet and spicy sauce used widely in Chinese cooking. It's made from a mixture of soybeans, garlic, chili peppers and various spices. Look for it in a jar in the Asian food aisle of your grocery store. Compare brands and choose the one with the lowest sodium. To toast sesame seeds, place them in a small skillet over medium heat. Cook until seeds turn golden brown, shaking pan frequently. Cool before using.

A balanced meal is one from which the diner has a 50-50 chance of recovering :)

Nutrition Nugget

Just one more reason to remove the skin from cooked chicken: The latest research from leading dermatologists suggests that eating caramelized or browned chicken skin can cause YOUR skin to caramelize! Yikes! That means wrinkled, sagging, aging skin. Cooking meats at high temperatures results in a "browning" effect in which sugars and certain fats react with protein to form something called Advanced Glycation End-Products (appropriately shortened to AGEs). Thing is, this AGEing process can in effect "cook" or brown us—both on the inside and the outside! The skin, arteries, eye lenses, joints and even organs can be affected. That's why constantly eating overly cooked, blackened or charred meats is a big no-no and why ditching the skin is smart. The good news is that we can counter this AGEing effect by eating lots of antioxidant-loaded foods like fruits, veggies and superfoods such as chia seeds, acai berries, spirulina, chlorella and other green foods, plus by getting plenty of omega-3 fats from fish, flaxseed, nuts, seeds and healthy oils.

Grocery Cart Chicken Chili

Zesty, high-fiber chicken chili topped with cheddar cheese

One man's junk is another man's treasure! This super-spicy creation is based on a recipe that was found in an abandoned grocery cart at the side of a dirt road. Yes, we're serious, and no, we're not garbage pickers.

2 tsp	olive oil
3	large boneless skinless chicken breasts, cut into cubes (about 1¼ lbs/568 g)
1½ cups	chopped red onions
1 tbsp	minced garlic
1½ cups	chopped green bell pepper
3	jalapeño peppers, seeded and minced (wear gloves!)
1 can	(19 oz/540 mL) no-salt-added diced tomatoes, undrained
1 cup	tomato-based chili sauce (such as Heinz)
1½ cups	reduced-sodium chicken broth
1½ tbsp	chili powder
2 tsp	ground cumin
1 tsp	dried oregano
¼ tsp	each cayenne pepper and freshly ground black pepper
1 can	(19 oz/540 mL) no-salt-added red kidney beans, drained and rinsed
1 can	(19 oz/540 mL) no-salt-added white kidney beans, drained and rinsed
2 tbsp	minced fresh cilantro (optional)
½ cup	packed shredded light old (sharp) cheddar cheese (2 oz/57 g)

MAKES 6 SERVINGS

PER SERVING
437 calories, 7.4 g total fat
(3.3 g saturated fat), 38 g protein,
51 g carbohydrate, 11.4 g fiber,
69 mg cholesterol, 812 mg sodium

- Heat olive oil in a large pot over medium-high heat. Add chicken and cook until chicken is lightly browned, about 5 to 6 minutes. Add onions, garlic, green peppers and jalapeños. Cook and stir until vegetables begin to soften, about 5 more minutes.

- Add all remaining ingredients, except beans, cilantro and cheese. Bring to a boil. Reduce heat to medium-low. Cover and simmer for 15 minutes, stirring occasionally. Add beans and cook 5 more minutes. Remove from heat. Stir in cilantro, if desired. Ladle chili into individual bowls and top each with a sprinkle of cheddar.

Recipe Tip: Try canned black beans in place of red kidney beans for a nice variation.

Trivial Tidbit

Kiss bad cholesterol goodbye! Literally! Research shows that regular kissing reduces cholesterol in both men and women. Need another reason to plant one on your beloved? Smooching also floods the bloodstream with dopamine, a feel-good neurotransmitter that stimulates the same part of the brain as cocaine for a natural (and legal!) high. To boost your heart and your spirits, make kissing your recreational drug of choice!

Honey, I Shrunk My Thighs!

Marinated, grilled honey-garlic chicken thighs

This slimmed-down, lip-smacking chicken thigh recipe tastes just like honey-garlic chicken wings, only much healthier, since we ditched the skin but kept the meat and bones.

12	bone-in chicken thighs, skin removed (about 3 lbs/1.4 kg)
½ cup	liquid honey
¼ cup	hoisin sauce
3 tbsp	freshly squeezed lemon juice
3 tbsp	reduced-sodium soy sauce
1 tbsp	minced garlic
2 tsp	grated gingerroot
½ tsp	each ground curry and ground coriander
⅛ tsp	cayenne pepper

- Arrange chicken thighs in a shallow glass dish. Whisk together all remaining ingredients in a small bowl and pour over chicken. Turn pieces to coat both sides with marinade. Cover with plastic wrap and marinate in the refrigerator for at least 4 hours or overnight.

- Preheat grill to medium setting. Remove chicken from marinade and place on a grill rack that has been lightly brushed with oil. Grill thighs for about 10 minutes per side. Be careful not to burn them. (You can brush the chicken with extra marinade as long as you boil the marinade first to kill any bacteria.) Serve hot.

MAKES 6 SERVINGS

PER SERVING
294 calories, 7.4 g total fat (1.9 g saturated fat), 34 g protein, 19 g carbohydrate, 0.3 g fiber, 151 mg cholesterol, 445 mg sodium

FOOD BITE

Beelieve it or not, honey is the only food that does not spoil. Honey found in the tombs of Egyptian pharaohs has been tasted by archaeologists and found to be edible. Sweet!

Pump Up the Jam

Here's an important, yet little-publicized reason to exercise: Your lymphatic system depends on it! "My nymphatic what?" That's *lymph* from the Latin word for "water goddess." If the liver is your body's filter, the lymphatic system is its drainage or sewer system. Through a complex series of teensy tubes running throughout your body, the lymph system continually drains excess fluid from cells and carries away waste materials and harmful pollutants, making room for new blood with fresh nutrients. What happens when the sewer gets jammed? Nutrients from the food you eat don't get absorbed properly, your immune system gets bogged down with foreign invaders and you get sick. And if your high-school reunion's approaching, take note: When your drainage pipes are backed up, your tissues can swell, adding 10 to 15 pounds to the scale! Here's where exercise comes into the picture. Unlike blood, which is pumped by the heart, lymphatic fluid has no pump. Instead, what pumps the lymph through its many ducts and tunnels is good ol' movement. That's right—exercise is the liquid Drano that keeps our pipes clear! The fact that our lymph system relies on voluntary movement is proof that Mother Nature intended us to be physically active creatures, constantly in motion, not sedentary couch potatoes or Internet junkies chained to our desks. Baby, we were born to run!

If you wish to grow thinner, diminish your dinner.

H.S. Leigh

Wowie Maui Chicken

One-pot, stovetop chicken, pineapple and rice dinner

This pineapple-chicken dish may not be volcanic, but it's definitely erupting with a luscious, tropical flavor that'll have you dreaming of Hawaii's ocean breezes, white sands and luaus.

1 tbsp	olive oil
4	boneless skinless chicken breasts, cut into 1-inch cubes (about 1½ lbs/680 g)
2½ cups	reduced-sodium chicken broth
1 can	(14 oz/398 mL) pineapple tidbits in juice, undrained
1½ cups	uncooked brown rice (see tip)
¾ cup	finely chopped carrots
½ cup	each chopped red and green bell peppers
⅓ cup	ketchup
2 tbsp	each brown sugar, reduced-sodium soy sauce and white vinegar
2 tsp	minced garlic
¾ cup	chopped green onions

Recipe Tip: Make sure your brown rice is the quicker-cooking variety (cooks in 15 to 20 minutes), but not instant brown rice.

MAKES 6 SERVINGS

PER SERVING
414 calories, 5.3 g total fat
(1 g saturated fat),
32 g protein,
59 g carbohydrate, 3.5 g fiber,
68 mg cholesterol, 442 mg sodium

- Heat olive oil in a large pot over medium-high heat. Add chicken. Cook and stir until chicken is lightly browned, about 5 to 6 minutes.

- Add all remaining ingredients, except green onions. Mix well. Bring to a boil. Reduce heat to low. Cover and simmer for 20 minutes, until rice is tender, stirring occasionally. Add green onions during last 5 minutes of cooking time. Let stand, covered, for 5 minutes before serving. Serve hot.

Nutrition Nugget

Pineapples contain a protein-dissolving enzyme called bromelain. Bromelain breaks down meat fibers, so a pineapple's juice can be used as a natural meat tenderizer. This enzyme also aids digestion and reduces inflammation and swelling, soothing everything from a sore throat to arthritis to a swollen ankle. To get the most out of pineapple's all-body, anti-inflammatory powers, you have to eat it alone between meals, otherwise its bromelain will be used up digesting food. FYI: A piña colada is not a recommended source of bromelain!

The Thigh Who Loved Me

Easy-to-make, extra-tasty, oven-barbecued chicken thighs

As sisters and double agents, we risked our lives and limbs to uncover the secret formula for zesty, gooey, barbecued chicken thighs. You can deliver the goods to your dinner table knowing they're sure to please a crowd. Psst! They make great leftovers, too.

12	boneless skinless chicken thighs (about 2¼ lbs/1 kg)
¾ cup	ketchup
½ cup	salsa
¼ cup	liquid honey
1 tbsp	Dijon mustard
1 tsp	chili powder
½ tsp	ground cumin
1 tbsp	cornstarch

MAKES 6 SERVINGS

PER SERVING
287 calories, 7.3 g total fat
(2 g saturated fat), 33 g protein,
20 g carbohydrate, 0.8 g fiber,
140 mg cholesterol, 586 mg sodium

Recipe Tip: Chicken breasts or drumsticks can be used in place of thighs. If using chicken breasts, bake them for 30 minutes instead of 40.

- Arrange thighs in a single layer in a 9 x 13-inch baking dish. Set aside.

- In a medium bowl, whisk together ketchup, salsa, honey, Dijon mustard, chili powder and cumin until well blended. Pour sauce over chicken. Turn pieces to coat both sides with sauce.

- Bake, uncovered, at 400°F for about 40 minutes. When chicken is done, arrange thighs on a serving platter and keep warm. Pour sauce into a small pot, skimming off as much fat as possible. In a small bowl, mix cornstarch with 1 tbsp water until smooth. Add to sauce. Bring to a boil, and cook until sauce thickens, stirring constantly. Pour extra sauce over chicken or serve it on the side as a dipping sauce.

The first drive-in restaurant was opened for people who wanted to curb their appetites :)

Nutrition Nugget

Don't be afraid of the dark! Yes, the dark meat of chicken contains a bit more fat than white meat, but it's not all bad for you. Dark meat, especially if it's from organic, free-range birds, contains super-healthy omega-3 fats and CLA (conjugated linoleic acid), a type of fat that helps your body burn fat rather than store it. Plus, dark meat has more zinc, B vitamins and iron than white meat. And that's great news for women, in particular, since they're prone to low iron during their monthly cycles.

Trivial Tidbit

Pnigophobia is the intense fear of: (a) ginger ale bubbles going up your nose; (b) finding a fly in your soup; (c) chickens; or (d) choking (such as on a fish bone). And the answer is...(d)! For the record, fear of chickens is called "alektorophobia," and it's nothing to *bock* at, either!

Fake 'n' Bake Chicken

Baked chicken breasts with a lip-smacking barbecue sauce

It's the breast-kept secret! Just slap on some fake grill marks and no one will know this spicy-sweet chicken came out of the oven. Not trying these would be such a sham!

4	boneless skinless chicken breasts (about 1½ lbs/680 g)
⅓ cup	hoisin sauce
⅓ cup	hickory-flavored barbecue sauce
1 tbsp	freshly squeezed lemon juice
2 tsp	grated gingerroot
½ tsp	chili powder

MAKES 4 SERVINGS

PER SERVING
252 calories, 3.3 g total fat (0.7 g saturated fat), 40 g protein, 13 g carbohydrate, 1 g fiber, 99 mg cholesterol, 628 mg sodium

- Preheat oven to 400°F. Spray a medium casserole dish with cooking spray. (The dish should be just large enough to hold the chicken breasts in a single layer.)
- Whisk together all remaining ingredients in a small bowl. Spoon sauce over chicken. Turn pieces to coat both sides with sauce. Bake, uncovered, for about 30 minutes, or until chicken is no longer pink in the center. Spoon sauce from bottom of pan over chicken and serve immediately.

Recipe Tip: You can substitute 12 boneless, skinless chicken thighs for the chicken breasts (add 10 minutes to the cooking time).

It's a Frying Shame

Collecting frequent *fryer* points? If so, you might find yourself on a trip to the heart surgeon! Sure, an order of fries here and there or the occasional fried chicken dinner isn't going to kill you. Every once in a while, it's OK. But if fried foods are your regular, weekly fare, over time that can wreak havoc on your body and trigger chronic disease. That's because eating food that's cooked in oils at the high temperatures involved in deep frying causes inflammation in the body. Researchers now know that inflammation is a culprit behind not only inflamed joints, but also heart disease, cancer, diabetes and even wrinkles and aging! Fry me a river! Even if your fried-food vendor boasts "cooked in trans-fat-free oil," when you crank up the heat, it damages the healthy oil, turning it into an unhealthy oil. The oil's damaged molecules can damage *your* molecules. Not to worry! If you do eat the occasional deep-fried food, just make sure you eat lots of deeply colored vegetables and fruits. Their potent plant chemicals can protect you from the harmful effects of Unidentified Frying Objects.

In this chapter...

A Fine Kettle of Fish

Seaworthy recipes that will
float your boat!

Dilly Whoppers,
p. 192

Rotuni Casserole

The ultimate comfort food: Creamy, cheesy rotini-noodle casserole with tuna and wild salmon

Lemon and dill add zest and zing to this updated classic comfort food!

A PERFECT COUPLE

4 cups	uncooked high-fiber rotini pasta
1 cup	frozen green peas

Sauce

1 tbsp	butter
¾ cup	diced onions
½ cup	diced celery
1 tsp	minced garlic
½ tsp	dried tarragon
1 can	(10 oz/284 mL) reduced-sodium chicken broth, undiluted
1 can	(14 oz/370 mL) 2% evaporated milk
2 tbsp	all-purpose flour
1 tsp	Dijon mustard
1½ tsp	grated lemon zest
¼ tsp	each salt and freshly ground black pepper (or to taste)
¾ cup	packed shredded light Monterey Jack cheese (3 oz/85 g)
½ cup	freshly grated Parmesan cheese
1 can	(6 oz/170 g) tuna, well drained
1 can	(6 oz/170 g) wild salmon, well drained
1 tbsp	minced fresh dill

MAKES 6 SERVINGS

PER SERVING
388 calories, 10.3 g total fat
(4.9 g saturated fat), 28 g protein,
49 g carbohydrate, 6.5 g fiber,
50 mg cholesterol, 613 mg sodium

- It's best to have all ingredients ready to go before starting. Chop the onions and celery, grate the cheeses, drain the canned fish, etc.

- In a large pot, cook pasta according to package directions, adding frozen green peas to pot during last 2 minutes of cooking time. Drain and keep warm.

- Meanwhile, prepare sauce. Melt butter over medium heat in a large, non-stick pot. Add onions, celery and garlic. Cook and stir until vegetables are tender, about 4 minutes. Stir in tarragon and cook 30 more seconds. Add broth. Whisk together evaporated milk and flour until smooth. Add to pot. Cook and stir until sauce is bubbly and has thickened.

- Stir in mustard, lemon zest, salt and pepper. Cook 1 more minute. Remove sauce from heat and stir in both cheeses until melted. Add drained tuna, salmon and dill. Mix well. Add drained noodles and peas and mix well. Serve hot with freshly ground black pepper on top.

Nutrition Nugget

What's the word on the wharf about tuna and the heavy metal mercury? Well, the healthiest canned tuna choice is "light" (skipjack or yellowfin) tuna. It comes from smaller, younger fish, so it doesn't accumulate as much mercury as bigger varieties that live longer. "White" (albacore) tuna is much higher in mercury content. And Atlantic tuna has more mercury than Pacific. If you're on some weird, fad tuna diet or are a bodybuilder who eats three cans a day, then you might have a problem with mercury. Otherwise, Pacific light a couple times a week should be A-OK.

Stay Tuned

In many households, there's a frequent guest at dinnertime: the television! When TV and eating go hand in hand, overconsumption of both is often the result. That's because neither is your real focus. Mindless TV-watching promotes mindless munching, and that makes it easy to forget about the quality and quantity of your food. When you dine in the company of the television, you tend to eat almost anything, including the worst things like chips, crackers, cookies, ice cream, pizza and so on. To avoid the need for a wider-framed La-Z-Boy, switch off the TV and switch your focus to the food you're eating. Mindful eating gives you a better chance of receiving the satellite signal from your brain that shouts, "I'm satisfied! Enough already!" Now *that's* a channel worth tuning into!

Skewer Always On My Mind

Lime-and-cilantro-marinated salmon skewers

"Maybe I didn't feed you…quite as healthy as I should have. Maybe I didn't serve fish…quite as often as I could have." If you constantly fret over your family's poor eating habits, skewer not alone. Make these ultra-nutritious, ultra-delicious salmon kebobs and you'll get one more chance to keep them satisfied…keep them satisfied.

MAKES 4 SERVINGS

PER SERVING
264 calories,
10.9 g total fat
(1.7 g saturated fat),
34 g protein,
5 g carbohydrate,
0.3 g fiber,
94 mg cholesterol,
429 mg sodium

Marinade

¼ cup	freshly squeezed lime juice
2 tbsp	minced fresh cilantro
1 tbsp	reduced-sodium soy sauce
1 tbsp	honey mustard
1 tbsp	barbecue sauce or ketchup
1 tsp	grated lime zest
1 tsp	minced garlic
¼ tsp	each ground cumin, ground coriander, salt and freshly ground black pepper
1½ lbs	(680 g) boneless skinless salmon fillets, cut into chunks
4	12-inch metal skewers

- Combine all marinade ingredients in a small bowl. Mix well.

- Place salmon chunks in a large, heavy-duty, resealable plastic bag. Add marinade and seal bag. Turn bag several times to coat salmon with marinade. Marinate in refrigerator for 30 minutes.

- Meanwhile, preheat grill or broiler to high setting. Remove salmon from marinade (reserve marinade) and thread pieces onto skewers. Brush grill rack lightly with oil. Grill or broil salmon for 3 to 4 minutes per side, brushing often with reserved marinade. Salmon should be just slightly pink in the center. Be careful not to overcook the salmon or it will be dry. Serve hot.

Does eating oysters increase your mussel tone? :)

Trivial Tidbit

Salmonella, the bacteria in contaminated food that causes some intestinal infections, actually has nothing to do with fish. It was named after U.S. veterinary pathologist Daniel E. Salmon, who, in 1885, discovered the first strain in a pig's intestine.

A FINE KETTLE OF FISH

In Cod We Trust

Oven "fried" Cajun cod fillets

Cod almighty! It's a miracle! If you've secretly wished your family would eat more fish, these yummy baked cod fillets with a crumb coating are the answer to your prayers.

6	large cod fillets (about 5 oz/142 g each)
⅔ cup	buttermilk
1½ tsp	grated lemon zest
3 cups	Special K cereal, ground into crumbs (see tip)
¼ cup	freshly grated Parmesan cheese
1 tbsp	minced fresh parsley
1½ tsp	Cajun seasoning
Cooking spray (see tip, p.147)	

MAKES 6 SERVINGS

PER SERVING
206 calories, 2.7 g total fat (1.2 g saturated fat), 31 g protein, 13 g carbohydrate, 0.8 g fiber, 65 mg cholesterol, 314 mg sodium

Recipe Tip: To make fine crumbs, process Special K cereal in your food processor using the pulse feature. Otherwise, you can put the cereal in a heavy-duty, resealable plastic bag and crush it with a rolling pin (your crumbs won't be as fine this way, but they'll be good enough).

- Preheat oven to 450°F. Spray a baking sheet with cooking spray and set aside.

- Pat cod fillets dry with paper towels. Whisk together buttermilk and lemon zest in a shallow bowl or casserole dish. Add cod fillets and turn to coat both sides with buttermilk mixture. Let stand for 10 minutes.

- In another shallow bowl, combine Special K crumbs, Parmesan cheese, parsley and Cajun seasoning.

- Working one piece at a time, remove cod from buttermilk mixture and shake off excess liquid. Press one side of fish into crumb mixture, making sure it's well-coated with crumbs. Place fish, crumb-side up, on prepared pan. Repeat with remaining cod pieces and crumb mixture. Lightly spray tops of fish with cooking spray (or drizzle with a bit of melted butter).

- Bake for 10 to 15 minutes, until fish flakes easily with a fork. Cooking time will depend on thickness of fish. Serve hot. Tastes great with light tartar sauce on top (see recipe, p. 195).

Fight Fat with Fat?

Did you know that you can lose fat by eating fat? We know what you're thinking: Fat chance! Despite what's been drilled into our heads for decades, eating fats is crucial for burning blubber—"good" fats, that is, like the omega-3 fatty acids found in fish, nuts, flaxseed and other seeds. Like other fats, they contain nine calories per gram, but your body prefers not to store them as fat. Instead, they're used for important hormonal, structural and cellular functions. And when these fats make up 12 to 15 percent of your total daily calorie intake, they can send your fat-burning engine off to the races. Omega-3s also help your kidneys flush out excess water held in tissues, acting as a natural bloatation device. That's important, because for many folks, water retention can add serious poundage to the bathroom scale—10, 15, even 20 extra pounds! Plus, having the right fats in your diet helps slow digestion, making you feel fuller longer. Good fat can also be your weight-loss friend because it increases energy levels. And the more energy you have, the more active you'll be, and that's the surest, most direct route to Slim City.

Fish for no compliments. They are generally caught in shallow water. *D. Smith*

Salmon Cowell

Grilled salmon in an orange-ginger marinade

It's absolutely pathetic. Utterly ghastly, if you want our honest opinion. But Paula loves it. You be the judge. We think you'll idolize it.

Marinade

¼ cup   frozen orange juice concentrate
¼ cup   hoisin sauce
1 tbsp   reduced-sodium soy sauce
1 tbsp   grated gingerroot
1 tsp   grated orange zest
Pinch   crushed red pepper flakes (optional)

4   boneless skinless salmon fillets
           (about 5 oz/142 g each)

MAKES 4 SERVINGS

PER SERVING
253 calories, 9.4 g total fat (1.5 g saturated fat), 29 g protein, 11 g carbohydrate, 0.5 g fiber, 78 mg cholesterol, 358 mg sodium

Recipe Tip: If you can't grill the salmon, broil it. Place fish on a baking sheet that has been sprayed with cooking spray. Broil 4 inches from heat source for about 8 minutes, turning salmon once, halfway through cooking time. Salmon should flake easily when tested with a fork.

- Whisk together all marinade ingredients in a small bowl. Place salmon in a large, heavy-duty, resealable plastic bag. Add marinade and seal bag. Turn bag several times to coat salmon with marinade. Marinate in refrigerator for 30 minutes.

- Preheat grill to medium setting. Remove salmon from marinade (reserve marinade) and place on a grill rack that has been lightly brushed with oil. Grill for 3 to 4 minutes per side, until done (salmon should be slightly pink in the center). Do not overcook salmon or it will be dry. Baste salmon with reserved marinade during last minute of cooking time, if desired.

Nutrition Nugget

What's good for the skin is also good for the hair. We know salmon's good fats and proteins help feed our skin and starve our wrinkles, but they can also keep our locks lustrous. Like your skin, oil glands on your scalp need to be well fed in order to stay healthy and hydrated. Yet another reason to get hooked on salmon!

On Golden Prawns

Succulent shrimp simmered in a coconut-curry broth, served over rice

If you're looking for a sensational seafood recipe to serve at a dinner party, here's one the whole gang will be Fonda.

2 tsp	olive oil
½ cup	each minced onions and minced red bell pepper
1 tsp	minced garlic
1 tsp	ground cumin
¾ tsp	ground coriander
½ tsp	curry powder
1 cup	light coconut milk
1 tsp	granulated sugar
¼ tsp	crushed red pepper flakes
1 lb	(454 g) uncooked jumbo shrimp, peeled, deveined and tails removed
1 tbsp	cornstarch
2 tbsp	minced fresh cilantro
4 cups	hot cooked brown rice

- Heat oil in a deep, 10-inch skillet over medium heat. Add onions, red pepper and garlic. Cook and stir until vegetables begin to soften, about 3 minutes.

- Add cumin, coriander and curry powder. Cook for 1 more minute. Add coconut milk, sugar and crushed red pepper flakes. Bring to a boil. Reduce heat and simmer, uncovered, for 2 minutes.

- Stir in shrimp. Increase heat to medium-high. Cook and stir until shrimp turns pink and is cooked through, about 4 minutes.

- In a small bowl, combine cornstarch with 1 tbsp water. Add to shrimp mixture. Cook until sauce is bubbly and has thickened, about 1 minute. Stir in cilantro and remove from heat. Serve shrimp and sauce over hot rice.

MAKES 4 SERVINGS

PER SERVING

426 calories, 9.8 g total fat (4.2 g saturated fat), 29 g protein, 54 g carbohydrate, 4.8 g fiber, 172 mg cholesterol, 192 mg sodium

Bye-Bye Bacteria!

We've always been huge fans of cilantro and just love it in salsa, in fresh salads and in Mexican or Asian dishes. Janet even puts handfuls of the potent green stuff into her vegetable-juice concoctions that she whips together every day. Turns out she's been adding more than just flavor: A recent study in the *Journal of Agricultural Food Chemistry* showed that cilantro can prevent salmonella and other food-borne illnesses! Apparently there's a compound in cilantro leaves and seeds called dodecenal, and scientists found it was twice as strong and more effective than gentamicin, the typical antibiotic treatment for salmonella. They also discovered dozens of additional antibiotic compounds in the green, leafy herb. Based on these findings, it might be a smart idea to add generous portions of cilantro to your food while vacationing in tropical destinations or other places where the food may be questionable. Say "si" to the salsa!

FOOD BITE

Sardines are named after Sardinia, the Italian island where large schools of these fish were once found. It was the emperor Napoleon Bonaparte who helped increase sardine's popularity by initiating the canning of sardines—the first fish ever to be canned—in order to feed his people. Today, sardines are making a comeback as more people realize they're packed with omega-3 fatty acids, bone-building calcium and vitamin D, along with heart-protecting vitamin B12. And since they're small and at the bottom of the aquatic food chain, feeding solely on plankton, they don't accumulate many heavy metals or contaminants. Looks like big things really do come in small packages!

Tuna Turner

Grilled tuna steaks with a tropical fruit marinade

What's lime got to do, got to do with it? Well, lime is diva-vine—especially when it's grouped with tropical friends. These grilled tuna steaks are sure to top the flavor charts!

Marinade

½ cup	mixed tropical fruit jam (a pineapple-mango-orange combination works well)
¼ cup	hoisin sauce
2 tbsp	freshly squeezed lime juice
1 tbsp	minced fresh cilantro
1 tsp	grated gingerroot
1 tsp	sesame oil

4   tuna steaks (about 6 oz/170 g each), 1 inch thick

MAKES 4 SERVINGS

PER SERVING
336 calories, 3.3 g total fat
(0.7 g saturated fat), 40 g protein,
32 g carbohydrate, 0.5 g fiber,
77 mg cholesterol, 322 mg sodium

- To prepare marinade, combine jam, hoisin sauce, lime juice, cilantro, gingerroot and sesame oil in a small bowl. Mix well.

- Rinse tuna steaks and pat dry with paper towels. Arrange steaks in a glass baking dish. Pour marinade over fish. Turn pieces to coat both sides. Cover with plastic wrap and refrigerate for 1 to 2 hours.

- Brush grill with a little oil to prevent fish from sticking. Heat to medium-high. Grill steaks for 4 to 5 minutes per side. Baste with extra marinade during cooking. Be careful not to overcook. Tuna should be lightly browned on outside, but still slightly pink in middle. Serve hot.

Nutrition Nugget

Tuna-up your brain! The types of essential fatty acids found in fish (called EPA and DHA) are super brain foods—better than other sources of omega-3s, in fact. They can help ease depression, boost memory and concentration and even protect against diseases like Alzheimer's and Parkinson's.

Fish and guests smell after three days.
Ben Franklin

Nouveau Quiche

Crustless crab and mushroom quiche

If you like living on easy street, this rich-tasting crab quiche is as simple as it gets. And when you have the good fortune to sample it, you'll see it's loaded with flavor.

2 tsp	olive oil
3 cups	sliced mushrooms
1 cup	each diced onions and diced red bell pepper
2 tsp	minced garlic
6	eggs
¾ cup	2% evaporated milk
¼ cup	freshly grated Parmesan cheese
½ tsp	dry mustard
¼ tsp	each salt and freshly ground black pepper
8 oz	(227 g) canned, fresh or frozen lump crabmeat (see tip)
¾ cup	packed shredded light old (sharp) cheddar cheese (3 oz/85 g)
¼ cup	chopped green onions

Recipe Tip: If using canned crabmeat, drain well before adding to other ingredients. Thaw frozen crabmeat before using.

MAKES 6 SERVINGS

PER SERVING
228 calories, 11.9 g total fat (4.5 g saturated fat), 22 g protein, 9 g carbohydrate, 1.6 g fiber, 258 mg cholesterol, 508 mg sodium

- Heat olive oil in a 10-inch, non-stick skillet over medium heat. Add mushrooms, onions, red pepper and garlic. Cook and stir until vegetables are tender, about 6 to 7 minutes. Remove from heat and let cool slightly.

- In a large bowl, whisk together eggs, milk, Parmesan cheese, dry mustard, salt and pepper. Stir in crabmeat, mushroom mixture, cheddar cheese and green onions. Pour into a 9-inch, deep-dish quiche pan or pie plate that has been sprayed with cooking spray.

- Bake quiche at 350°F for 40 to 45 minutes, until firm to touch. Let stand 10 minutes before slicing.

The Fidget Fitness Plan

Tap your fingers, twirl your hair, bounce your leg, shift here and there. No, we're not callin' a square dance. We're callin' on you to take up fidgeting! Researchers at the Mayo Clinic in Rochester, Minnesota, found that small, habitual movements like tapping your feet, adjusting your posture and pacing back and forth can burn hundreds of calories a day. Golleeee! You'd have to do an awful lot of doe-see-doeing to burn off that many calories! In the study, a group of volunteers aged 20 to 35 were asked to eat 1,000 extra calories a day for eight weeks. As a result, some subjects gained as much as 16 pounds, whereas others gained as little as two pounds. The people who gained the least amount were "the young and the restless." The toe-tappin', knee-bobbin', chair-shiftin', ear-scratchin' crowd may have not made any new friends in the study group, but they didn't make much new fat, either. Looks like any little movement is better than no movement at all.

Why is it that lemonade and lemon pie filling are made with artificial lemon flavoring, but dish soap and furniture polish are made with real lemon juice? :)

FOOD BITE

You'd think that saltwater fish would have a higher sodium content than freshwater fish, but that isn't the case. Saltwater fish aren't any saltier than freshwater fish because their physiology prevents them from becoming as salty as the water they inhabit.

Just for the Halibut

Baked halibut steaks topped with tomatoes, zucchini and feta

Put some fish on your dish! When you pop these simple but sensational halibut steaks into the oven, you'll be waiting with baited breath for them to cook.

Why did the fisherman cross the ocean?

1 tsp	olive oil	¼ tsp	each salt and freshly ground black pepper
1 cup	diced zucchini		
½ cup	minced onions	4	halibut steaks
1 tsp	minced garlic		(about 6 oz/170 g each)
2 cups	diced tomatoes	⅓ cup	crumbled light feta cheese
2 tbsp	minced fresh basil leaves		(1.3 oz/37 g)

- Heat olive oil in a small skillet over medium heat. Add zucchini, onions and garlic. Cook and stir until zucchini is tender, about 5 to 6 minutes. Remove from heat and stir in tomatoes, basil, salt and pepper.

- Rinse fish steaks and pat dry with paper towels. Spray a medium baking pan with cooking spray and place fish in pan. Spoon ¼ tomato-zucchini mixture over each fish steak. Top with feta cheese. Bake at 450°F for 12 to 15 minutes, depending on thickness of fish. Serve immediately.

MAKES 4 SERVINGS

PER SERVING
276 calories, 8.4 g total fat (2.5 g saturated fat), 41 g protein, 8 g carbohydrate, 2 g fiber, 69 mg cholesterol, 392 mg sodium

Recipe Tip To minimize moisture loss when grilling, baking or sautéing fish, use a relatively high heat and cook the fish for a short time. When you cook fish longer than necessary, the juices and flavors are lost, leaving the fish dry and chewy. Plus, overcooked fish is prone to falling apart.

Trivial Tidbit

Take a stroll down memory lane! Scientists say that walking 40 minutes a day, three days a week, can significantly improve memory.

Hook, Line & Simple

Easy broiled salmon with creamy dill sauce

Looking for a reel tasty, reel simple salmon recipe? Well, this dish is the reel McCoy! You'll fall for it hook, line and sinker.

MAKES 6 SERVINGS

PER SERVING
273 calories,
11.2 g total fat
(1.8 g saturated fat),
35 g protein,
6 g carbohydrate,
0.1 g fiber,
94 mg cholesterol,
193 mg sodium

6	boneless skinless salmon fillets (about 6 oz/170 g each)
⅓ cup	light (5%) sour cream
2 tbsp	pure maple syrup
1 tbsp	Dijon mustard
1 tbsp	freshly squeezed lemon juice
1 tbsp	minced fresh dill
1 tsp	grated lemon zest
¼ tsp	each salt and freshly ground black pepper

- Preheat broiler. Sprinkle salmon fillets lightly on both sides with salt and pepper.

- Place salmon on a baking sheet that has been sprayed with cooking spray. Broil 4 to 6 inches from heat source for about 4 minutes per side, or until fish flakes easily but is still just slightly pink in the center.

- While fish is cooking, prepare sauce. In a small bowl, whisk together sour cream, maple syrup, mustard, lemon juice, dill, lemon zest, salt and pepper.

- Remove salmon from oven and drizzle with sauce. Serve immediately.

Wild About Salmon

Low in fat, high in protein and one of the best sources of heart-healthy, brain-boosting, omega-3 fatty acids, salmon is a total catch. Wild-caught sockeye salmon has the highest amount of omega-3s of any fish (about 2.7 grams per 100-gram serving), and it's also higher in vitamin D and much lower in PCBs and other contaminants than farmed salmon. Plus, wild salmon has 20 percent more protein and 20 percent less fat than farm-raised salmon. And when you buy it canned, you also get extra calcium because the canning process makes the bones soft enough to eat. The wild variety is worth fishing for if you want to look younger than your years, too. Besides the skin-friendly essential fats, wild salmon contains the wrinkle fighter CoQ10 and the carotenoid astaxanthin. This member of the carotene family gives wild salmon its pink hue, and it's been shown to provide powerful protection against photoaging of our skin, helping prevent damage from the sun's rays. It also improves skin tone and boosts elasticity, giving you a more youthful, radiant complexion. For glowing health, wild salmon is the *reel* deal!

Low-Fatty Patties

These tender, Thai tuna patties make tasty, unique burgers

Patty-cake, patty-cake, here's the plan: Grill me a burger as fast as you can!
Pull your patty-o-chair up to the patty-o-table and dig in.

1½ lbs	(680 g) fresh tuna steaks (see tip)
½ cup	dry unseasoned bread crumbs
¼ cup	each minced green onions and grated carrots
1 tbsp	each reduced-sodium soy sauce, ketchup, grated gingerroot and minced fresh cilantro
1	egg
1 tsp	sesame oil
½ tsp	ground cumin
¼ tsp	each salt and freshly ground black pepper
6	whole-grain hamburger buns

Lettuce, sliced tomatoes and your favorite burger toppings (optional)

- Cut tuna steaks into chunks and place in food processor. Pulse on and off until tuna is chopped into very small pieces. (If you don't have a food processor, use a very sharp knife and mince the tuna by hand.) Transfer to a large bowl. Add all remaining ingredients. Mix well. Cover with plastic wrap and refrigerate for 30 minutes.

- Form mixture into 6 patties, about ½ inch thick. Brush grill with a little oil to prevent fish from sticking. Heat to medium-high. Grill patties for about 4 minutes per side, until cooked through. Be careful not to overcook. Serve on hamburger buns with burger toppings such as lettuce, sliced tomatoes, honey mustard and ketchup.

MAKES 6 BURGERS

PER BURGER
338 calories,
9.5 g total fat
(1.7 g saturated fat),
32 g protein,
29 g carbohydrate,
3 g fiber, 76 mg cholesterol,
580 mg sodium

Recipe Tips You'll have to can the canned tuna for this recipe and pick up some fresh tuna steaks at the fish counter instead. Fresh tuna has a firm-textured, rich-flavored flesh—perfect for making burgers! Refrigerating the fish before forming it into patties helps it hold together. Try these patties topped with mango salsa (see recipe on p. 273).

Nutrition Nugget

If it's white, don't bite! In your body, one slice of white bread is converted to the same amount of glucose as four tablespoons of sugar! Yowch! When blood-sugar levels go up fast, the hormone insulin swoops in to shuttle that sugar from your bloodstream into your cells for energy. Yes, your body needs some sugar to function, but excess sugar is stored as stubborn fat! There's another hormone called glucagon that takes the fat out of storage and releases it so your body can burn it off. We LOVE this hormone! Thing is, when your body is producing insulin to bring you down from your sugar high, it can't produce glucagon. The result? Not only are you storing extra fat, but your body also isn't able to burn the fat that's already there. Double-fat whammy!

Trivial Tidbit

What does the number 57 on a Heinz Ketchup bottle represent? (a) the number of ripe tomatoes required to manufacture one bottle; (b) the year 1957, when the ketchup formula was invented; (c) the number of products the company sells; (d) the numbers "5" and "7" held a special significance for Henry J. Heinz and his wife. And the answer is…(c) and (d)! Henry John Heinz wanted to advertise the great number of products his company offered. Although the couple actually had more than 60 at the time, they chose the number 57 because "5" was Henry's lucky number and "7" was his wife's.

Did you hear about the restaurant that served submarine sandwiches?
It went under :)

Kinda Nutty Pistachio-Crusted Fish

Scrumptious, restaurant-quality fish with a unique pistachio and Parmesan crumb topping

If you're nuts about pistachios, this flavorful, gourmet baked fish entrée will drive your taste buds looney!

1 tbsp	olive oil	½ tsp	grated lemon zest
1 tbsp	grainy Dijon mustard	¼ tsp	each salt and freshly
2 tsp	hot horseradish		ground black pepper
¾ cup	fresh whole-grain	4	fresh skinless fish fillets
	bread crumbs (see tip, p. 192)		(about 6 oz/170 g each),
⅓ cup	shelled pistachios (see tip)		1 inch thick (see tip)
¼ cup	freshly grated Parmesan cheese	2 tsp	butter, melted
1 tbsp	minced fresh parsley		

MAKES 4 SERVINGS

PER SERVING (USING MONKFISH FILLET)
286 calories, 14.6 g total fat (3.8 g saturated fat), 30 g protein, 8 g carbohydrate, 1.8 g fiber, 53 mg cholesterol, 415 mg sodium

- Preheat oven to 375°F. Spray a shallow baking pan with cooking spray and set aside.

- In a small bowl, mix together olive oil, mustard and horseradish. Set aside.

- Using a food processor or mini chopper, grind pistachios until finely ground, but not powdery. Transfer to a medium bowl and add fresh bread crumbs, Parmesan, parsley, lemon zest, salt and pepper. Stir gently using a fork. Add olive oil mixture and stir again, just until crumb mixture is moistened (like you're making a crust for a cheesecake).

- Rinse fish and pat dry with paper towels. Sprinkle fish lightly with salt and pepper. Place in baking pan. Press ¼ crumb mixture on top of each fish fillet. Drizzle tops with melted butter.

- Bake on middle oven rack for about 12 to 15 minutes, depending on thickness of fish. Be careful not to overcook the fish. Turn on the broiler and broil fish for 1 minute. Crumbs should be golden brown and fish should flake easily with a fork. Serve immediately. May be served with light tartar sauce, if desired (see recipe on p. 195).

Recipe Tips Try fresh monkfish, halibut, salmon or tilapia fillets for this recipe. Fold thin, large pieces of fish (such as tilapia) in half or stack fillets to reach 1-inch thickness. Thin pieces will cook too quickly and the crumb coating won't have enough time to get crusty. You can substitute walnuts or pecans for the pistachios, but the color and flavor of the pistachios in this recipe are hard to beat.

Steak it Up, Baby!

Grilled tuna steaks with a delicious chili-lime marinade

Twist and trout! Oops! These are tuna steaks, not trout steaks. Darn! Trout fit in so nicely with the song. Oh well.

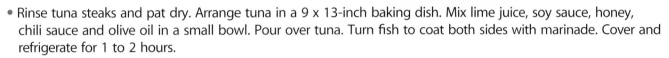

YA KNOW YA GOT ME GOIN' BABY ♪

PER SERVING
241 calories,
2.9 g total fat
(0.6 g saturated fat),
43 g protein,
12 g carbohydrate,
0 g fiber,
68 mg cholesterol,
519 mg sodium

4	tuna steaks (about 6 oz/170 g each), 1 inch thick
2 tbsp	each freshly squeezed lime juice, reduced-sodium soy sauce, liquid honey and tomato-based chili sauce (such as Heinz)
2 tsp	olive oil

- Rinse tuna steaks and pat dry. Arrange tuna in a 9 x 13-inch baking dish. Mix lime juice, soy sauce, honey, chili sauce and olive oil in a small bowl. Pour over tuna. Turn fish to coat both sides with marinade. Cover and refrigerate for 1 to 2 hours.

- Brush grill with a little oil to prevent fish from sticking. Heat to medium-high. Grill steaks for 4 to 5 minutes per side. Baste with extra marinade during cooking. Be careful not to overcook. Tuna should be lightly browned on outside, but still slightly pink in middle. Serve hot.

Recipe Tips

As long as it isn't overcooked, tuna is a tender and moist fish that's great for broiling, baking and grilling. You could substitute other types of fish steaks, such as halibut or shark, for the tuna in this recipe. Too cold for barbecuing in the winter? No problem. Bake the tuna for 10 to 12 minutes in a preheated 425°F oven.

Nutrition Nugget

Add some zest to your life and some zing to your cells! The vibrant, green peel of a lime contains a plant chemical called d-Limonene, a powerful antioxidant that can help prevent damage to your body's cells and DNA. Even the white, pithy portion underneath contains beneficial flavonoids that help lower LDL (bad) cholesterol. When grating limes for zest, be sure to use organically grown limes to avoid wax and pesticide residues.

> You can't plow a field by turning it over in your mind.

Familiarity Breeds Contempt

Have you packed the same lunch for the last 18 years? Do you eat the same brand of cereal every single day? Do you define the five basic food groups as McDonald's, Burger King, Wendy's, KFC and Pizza Hut? Eating the same foods day in and day out supplies you with the exact same vitamins, minerals and nutrients (or lack thereof!) over and over again. Varying the foods you eat provides you with a much broader range of nutrients, and that breeds contentment as far as your body's concerned. Your attitude toward food should be the same as your attitude toward life. To get the most out of both, you have to be willing to try new things. So from now on, every time you visit the grocery store, embark on a shopping safari! Wallet in hand, set out to explore the unknown depths of your supermarket shelves. Bravely venture into uncharted territory and search for one new fruit, vegetable, grain or legume to add to your cart. Your local supermarket probably carries a vast array of foods you've never heard of, let alone eaten. Buy one of them, then take it home and figure out what to do with it! C'mon! Where's your sense of adventure? Every once in a while, go out on a limb. Besides, isn't that where the fruit is?

Stick 'em Up!

Lemon-and-basil-marinated grilled shrimp skewers

Freeze! Caught ya pink-handed! You're guilty of robbing the taste bank and shellfishly hoarding the grilled goods for yourself! Though you'll be tempted to eat these lip-smacking shrimp skewers in solitary confinement, not sharing their arresting flavor with friends would be a crime.

Marinade

⅓ cup	minced fresh basil leaves
2 tbsp	freshly squeezed lemon juice
1 tbsp	each olive oil, melted butter, Dijon mustard and liquid honey
2 tsp	each minced garlic, grated gingerroot and grated lemon zest
1 tsp	balsamic vinegar
½ tsp	salt
¼ tsp	freshly ground black pepper
2 lbs	(907 g) uncooked large or jumbo shrimp, peeled and deveined (leave tails intact)
8	12-inch metal skewers

- Combine all marinade ingredients in a small bowl. Place shrimp in a large, heavy-duty, resealable plastic bag. Pour marinade over shrimp and seal bag. Turn bag several times to coat shrimp with marinade. Marinate in refrigerator for 1 hour.

- Preheat grill to high setting. Thread shrimp onto skewers (5 or 6 shrimp per skewer, depending on size of shrimp). Discard marinade. Brush grill rack lightly with oil. Grill shrimp for about 2 minutes per side, just until shrimp turns pink and no gray remains. Be careful not to overcook shrimp or they will be rubbery. Just stand there and stare at them the entire time they're cooking, OK?

- Serve skewers hot or cold, on a salad or with a hot rice side dish, with grilled vegetables or as an appetizer.

MAKES 8 SERVINGS

PER SERVING
161 calories, 5.3 g total fat (1.5 g saturated fat), 23 g protein, 4 g carbohydrate, 0.2 g fiber, 176 mg cholesterol, 324 mg sodium

Half-Joking Advice

A man goes to the doctor and explains that he hasn't been feeling well. The doctor examines the patient, leaves the room, and returns with three different bottles of pills. The doctor says, "Take the green pill with a big glass of water when you get up. Take the blue pill with a big glass of water at lunch. Then just before going to bed, take the red pill with another big glass of water." Upset at the number of pills he was prescribed, the patient asks, "My goodness, Doc! What's wrong with me?" "You aren't drinking enough water!" replied the doctor.

I'm a Sole Man

Baked sole fillets on a bed of herb-coated vegetables

Or is the proper term "sole person"? For the politically correct and the politically incorrect, too, here's a soleful creation that's lavishly presented on a bed of delicious, herb-coated vegetables.

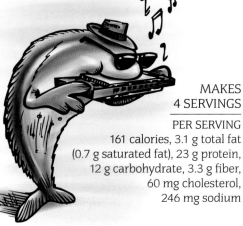

MAKES
4 SERVINGS

PER SERVING
161 calories, 3.1 g total fat
(0.7 g saturated fat), 23 g protein,
12 g carbohydrate, 3.3 g fiber,
60 mg cholesterol,
246 mg sodium

1½ cups	sliced zucchini (cut about ¼ inch thick)
1½ cups	coarsely chopped tomatoes
1 cup	each chopped green and red bell peppers
½ cup	coarsely chopped onions
1 tsp	olive oil
¾ tsp	each dried oregano and dried basil
¼ tsp	freshly ground black pepper
1 lb	(454 g) sole fillets
¼ tsp	each salt and freshly ground black pepper
1 tbsp	freshly squeezed lemon juice

• Preheat oven to 425°F.

• Combine zucchini, tomatoes, bell peppers, onions, olive oil, oregano, basil and black pepper in a large bowl. Stir to evenly distribute seasonings. Transfer to a 9 x 13-inch baking dish that has been sprayed with cooking spray. Bake, uncovered, for 35 minutes.

• Remove baking dish from oven and lay fish fillets over vegetables. Sprinkle fish lightly with salt and pepper. Squeeze lemon juice over fish. Return to oven. Bake an additional 5 to 7 minutes, until fish turns opaque and flakes easily. Remove from oven and serve immediately.

Nutrition Nugget

Can't fit into your bikini? Eat zucchini! A cup of plain, cooked zucchini has only 36 calories and lots of nutrients to help you stay slim and trim. Plus, one cup has more potassium than a medium banana, and that can help flush out water so bloat won't sink your boat!

Thrill of the Krill

Not eating enough fish? Not a fan of fish? Not a problem! You can still get your all-important, wrinkle-fighting, heart-, brain- and immune-boosting essential omega-3 fats from fish oil. One of your best bets is krill oil, which scientists have found to be up to 48 times more potent than regular fish oil. Krill are teensy, shrimp-like creatures that feed the world's largest animal, the whale. Because krill is at the very bottom of the food chain, it's very low in toxins. And krill is so plentiful, it's thought to be one of the most abundant and renewable species on Earth. But what makes krill such a thrill is that it's also swimming in antioxidants, those free-radical scavengers that protect our cells from damage and prevent aging. It's the ultimate two-for-one deal! Other fish oils can't boast that feature. Since fish oil is perishable, especially at higher temperatures, such as the internal temperature of the human body, it can oxidize and go rancid inside your body. Yikes! Antioxidants prevent this from happening. Plus, krill is more absorbable than other fish oils, so you can take one-fifth the amount compared to other oils. It's the krill of a lifetime!

He used to work at a seafood restaurant, but then he pulled a mussel :)

The Soprawnos

Scrumptious Italian shrimp dish with tomatoes, zucchini and feta cheese

When you make this delectable shrimp recipe for the family, it'll be a hit, man! And you won't get whacked with a ton of fat and calories, either.

They mobbed me for the recipe.

2 tsp	olive oil
1 cup	chopped red onions
1	medium zucchini, chopped
2 tsp	minced garlic
½ tsp	dried oregano
½ cup	dry white wine
3 cups	chopped plum tomatoes
1 tbsp	balsamic vinegar
¼ tsp	each salt and freshly ground black pepper
¼ cup	coarsely chopped fresh basil leaves
1 lb	(454 g) uncooked large shrimp, peeled, deveined and tails removed
½ cup	crumbled feta cheese with herbs (2 oz/57 g—see tip)
1 tbsp	minced fresh parsley

MAKES 4 SERVINGS

PER SERVING
253 calories,
7.8 g total fat
(2.9 g saturated fat), 27 g protein,
14 g carbohydrate, 2.9 g fiber, 185 mg cholesterol, 488 mg sodium

Recipe Tip: Look for feta cheese flavored with sun-dried tomatoes and basil. If you prefer, you can use plain feta cheese instead.

- Heat olive oil over medium-high heat in a 10-inch, non-stick skillet. Add onions, zucchini and garlic. Cook and stir until vegetables are softened, about 5 minutes. Add oregano and cook 30 more seconds. Add wine, tomatoes, vinegar, salt and pepper. Mix well. Reduce heat to medium and simmer, uncovered, for about 8 minutes, until most of the wine has evaporated and the tomatoes are broken up.

- Stir in basil and shrimp. Cook and stir until shrimp turns pink and no gray remains, about 4 minutes. Be careful not to overcook shrimp or they will be rubbery. Remove from heat and sprinkle with feta cheese and parsley. Serve hot.

FOOD BITE

Feta is a classic and famous Greek curd cheese whose tradition dates back thousands of years. Homer even wrote about it in his epic, *The Odyssey*. The word "feta" is derived from an ancient Greek word meaning "slice." In fact, to use the word "feta," a cheese must be produced in Greece! Bulgaria, Romania, France and Denmark, among other countries, make similar cheeses, but they can't be called feta. When it comes to feta, it's all Greek to me!

> A stomach 8/10 full needs no doctor.
> *Japanese proverb*

Fear Factor, Reality Check

We're scared. We're really scared. We're afraid of pollution in our air, chemicals in our water, germs in our food, mysterious new viruses and dangers that might be lurking in power lines and cellphones. Perhaps some of these fears are justified but, more often than not, our perceptions of risk don't always match reality. We worry ourselves sick over H1N1, yet smoke a pack a day. We scale back on fish because the morning paper talks of toxins in our waters—yet we scarf down two donuts and a large coffee while reading the headlines. The only time we break a sweat is when we swat frantically at mosquitoes. Honestly! What's more likely to kill us: West Nile Virus or being overweight and sedentary? Scientists are still trying to come to grips with the risks presented by the trappings of modern-day life, but this much is already known: Smoking can actually kill you; eating too much and exercising too little is a lethal combination. The bottom line is this: Yes, wash your hands often, swat those mosquitoes and don't talk on your cellphone while lying in a tanning bed, but keep your perspective. Focus on lowering the truly big health risks, put your butts out and get your butt moving!

Hurry Curry

Thai-style coconut and red curry halibut that's ready in 15 minutes

When you're pressed for time, be impressed with Thai! Thai red curry paste and coconut milk make any fish taste delish.

2 tsp	coconut oil or olive oil		1 tbsp	Thai red curry paste (see tip)
½ cup	finely minced shallots or red onions		1 tbsp	brown sugar
			1 tbsp	freshly squeezed lime juice
2 tsp	grated gingerroot		1 tbsp	minced fresh cilantro or basil
1 tsp	curry powder		4	halibut fillets or other firm white
½ tsp	ground coriander			fish (about 6 oz/170 g each)
1 cup	light coconut milk			

- You'll need a 10-inch, non-stick skillet with a lid for this recipe.

- Heat oil in skillet over medium heat. Add shallots. Cook and stir until shallots are tender, about 3 minutes. Be careful not to burn them. Add gingerroot, curry powder and coriander. Cook for 30 more seconds. Add coconut milk, curry paste, brown sugar and lime juice. Simmer, uncovered, for 5 minutes. Mixture will thicken slightly. Stir in cilantro.

- Add halibut fillets to sauce in skillet. Spoon sauce over fish. Reduce heat to medium-low. Cover and cook for about 7 minutes, or until fish is cooked through and flakes easily with a fork. Serve fish with hot curry sauce spooned over top.

MAKES 4 SERVINGS

PER SERVING
285 calories, 10 g total fat (5.1 g saturated fat), 37 g protein, 10 g carbohydrate, 0.3 g fiber, 55 mg cholesterol, 251 mg sodium

Recipe Tip Red curry paste is an important ingredient in Thai cooking. It's a mixture of ground red chili peppers, garlic, lemongrass, coriander, kaffir lime leaves and other aromatic, super-flavorful herbs and spices. Look for red curry paste in a small jar in the Asian food aisle of your grocery store.

Nutrition Nugget

Ohhhh-mega! Omega-3 fats, like the kind in fish and fish oils, have shown promise in helping kids with attention deficit hyperactivity disorder (ADHD) who are often deficient in this important fatty acid. And if you have children with allergies, note that omega-3s are now recommended by natural practitioners to ease those conditions.

Dilly Whoppers

Pan-fried fresh salmon patties with dill and feta cheese

They're dillightful! They're dillicious! They're dillovely! And healthy, too? Yup, according to the Better Burger Bureau, these heart-smart salmon burgers with whopping good flavor won't make you a fatty Patty.

PER SERVING
236 calories,
10.4 g total fat
(2.8 g saturated fat),
26 g protein,
9 g carbohydrate,
1.1 g fiber,
106 mg cholesterol,
333 mg sodium

1½ lbs	(680 g) boneless skinless salmon fillet, cut into chunks
1 cup	fresh whole-grain bread crumbs (see tip)
½ cup	crumbled light feta cheese (2 oz/57 g)
¼ cup	minced shallots
1 tbsp	honey mustard
1 tbsp	freshly squeezed lemon juice
1	egg
1 tbsp	minced fresh dill
1 tsp	grated lemon zest
¼ tsp	each salt and freshly ground black pepper

- Place salmon chunks in a food processor. Pulse on and off until salmon is chopped into very small pieces. (If you don't have a food processor, use a very sharp knife and mince the salmon by hand.) Transfer salmon to a large bowl. Add remaining ingredients. Mix well using your hands.

- Form mixture into 6 patties, about ¾ inch thick. Place patties on a large plate, cover with plastic wrap and refrigerate for 1 hour. (Chilling will help the patties hold their shape while cooking.)

- Spray a large, non-stick skillet with cooking spray and heat over medium-high heat. Add patties and cook for about 4 minutes per side, until salmon is cooked through. Be careful not to overcook the patties, and be gentle when flipping them so they don't fall apart. If you don't have a high-quality (unscratched!) non-stick pan, you might want to cook the patties in 1 to 2 tbsp olive oil.

- Serve patties on small, whole-grain hamburger buns with sliced tomatoes, lettuce and honey mustard, or top them with spoon of low-fat tartar sauce (see recipe on p. 195) and serve with a salad.

Recipe Tip To make fresh bread crumbs, break up a slice of whole-grain bread into several smaller pieces and place in a food processor or mini chopper. Pulse on and off a few times to create fluffy soft crumbs.

Forrest Gumbo

Hearty, stew-like shrimp gumbo served over rice

If you're hankerin' for a hearty helping of gumbo, then run for Forrest Gumbo, run!

Life is like a pot of gumbo.

¼ cup	all-purpose flour
1 tbsp	butter
1 cup	each chopped onions and chopped green bell pepper
½ cup	diced celery
2 tsp	minced garlic
3 cups	reduced-sodium chicken broth
1 can	(19 oz/540 mL) no-salt-added diced tomatoes, drained
1 cup	diced okra or zucchini (see tip)
1 tsp	ground cumin
½ tsp	each paprika, dried thyme and dried oregano
¼ tsp	each salt and black pepper
⅛ tsp	cayenne pepper
1 lb	(454 g) uncooked large shrimp, peeled, deveined and tails removed
4 cups	hot cooked brown rice

- Sprinkle flour over bottom of a small pie plate. Toast at 400°F for 15 to 20 minutes, until golden brown. Stir once or twice during cooking time. Remove from oven, transfer to a small bowl and let cool.

- Melt butter in a large, non-stick pot over medium-high heat. Add onions, green pepper, celery and garlic. Cook and stir until vegetables begin to soften, about 3 minutes. Stir in toasted flour and cook for 1 more minute. Add broth and mix well. Add drained tomatoes, okra, cumin, paprika, thyme, oregano, salt, pepper and cayenne. Bring to a boil. Reduce heat to low. Cover and simmer for 20 minutes, stirring occasionally.

- Add shrimp and simmer for 5 more minutes, until shrimp is cooked through. To serve, spoon rice over bottom of individual serving bowls. Ladle gumbo over top. Serve hot.

Recipe Tips The name gumbo comes from the African word *kingombo*, which means "okra." In gumbo-making, a browned roux (pronounced "roo") is an essential ingredient. It serves to thicken the gumbo and give it a nutty flavor. Traditionally, roux is made by combining flour and oil, then cooking the mixture until brown. This can add a ton of fat and calories to an otherwise healthy meal. In our recipe, we toast the flour to achieve a heart-healthier result. Using okra (versus zucchini) will result in a thicker gumbo.

MAKES 6 SERVINGS

PER SERVING
316 calories,
4.9 g total fat
(1.8 g saturated fat),
22 g protein,
45 g carbohydrate,
5.1 g fiber,
123 mg cholesterol,
315 mg sodium

Join the Okra Fan Club

Never tried okra before? You don't know what you're missing, especially if weight loss and optimal health are on your radar screen. Not to be confused with the popular daytime TV host, okra, the mild-flavored green pod of a tropical plant, is a typical ingredient of Caribbean cookery. Besides being super low in calories and a source of plant-based protein, okra can help us lose weight because its superior fiber acts as a powerful blood-sugar stabilizer, curbing our urge to splurge and helping us feel full longer. Plus, okra's slippery, film-like fiber is like a ShamWow! that binds to unwanted toxins in the body and swooshes them out, much to the relief of your liver. Fewer toxins swirling around could mean a healthier, slimmer you. Okra's special fiber has unique binding capabilities that can help lower cholesterol, plus it absorbs a ton of water, acting as a gentle laxative, soothing the intestinal tract and calmly ushering out suspicious substances. It's excellent roughage, but it acts like "smoothage!" Bonus! Since most alternative health practitioners believe that "disease begins in the colon," you can see why saying OK to okra is a smart move.

Fab Crab Cakes

Succulent pan-fried crab cakes with creamy lemon-dill sauce

These fabulous crabulous crab cakes are crabnormally delicious!

Crab Cakes

1 lb	(454 g) lump crabmeat, well drained
1¼ cups	fine multigrain cracker crumbs, divided
¼ cup	finely minced red bell pepper
2 tbsp	minced green onions
1 tbsp	minced fresh parsley
1	egg
2 tbsp	light mayonnaise (not fat-free)
1 tbsp	freshly squeezed lemon juice
2 tsp	grainy Dijon mustard
1 tsp	Old Bay Seasoning
1 tsp	Worcestershire sauce
½ tsp	grated lemon zest
¼ tsp	freshly ground black pepper
1 tbsp	each butter and olive oil

Creamy Lemon-Dill Seafood Sauce
(good with any type of fish)

½ cup	light (5%) sour cream
1 tbsp	grainy Dijon mustard
1 tbsp	freshly squeezed lemon juice
1 tbsp	minced fresh dill
1 tsp	grated lemon zest
½ tsp	each Old Bay Seasoning and hot horseradish
Pinch	freshly ground black pepper

MAKES 8 CRAB CAKES AND ¾ CUP SAUCE

PER CRAB CAKE (WITH 1½ TBSP SAUCE)
153 calories, 7 g total fat (2.5 g saturated fat),
12 g protein, 11 g carbohydrate,
0.8 g fiber, 81 mg cholesterol,
471 mg sodium

- To make crab cakes, combine crabmeat, ¾ cup cracker crumbs, red pepper, green onions and parsley in a large bowl. In a small bowl, whisk together egg, mayonnaise, lemon juice, Dijon, Old Bay seasoning, Worcestershire sauce, lemon zest and black pepper. Add wet ingredients to crabmeat mixture. Stir gently using a spatula until well mixed.

- Pour remaining ½ cup cracker crumbs into a shallow bowl. Working one at a time, form crab mixture into 8 crab cakes (use ⅓ cup mixture for each crab cake). Gently dip both sides of crab cake into crumbs. Place on a plate. Cover with plastic wrap and refrigerate for at least 1 hour.

- Meanwhile, make sauce. Whisk together all sauce ingredients in a small bowl. Cover and refrigerate until ready to serve.

- To cook crab cakes, preheat oven to 350°F. Add butter and olive oil to a 10-inch, non-stick skillet and heat over medium heat until butter is melted and bubbly. Add crab cakes. Cook for 2 to 3 minutes per side, until golden brown. Carefully transfer crab cakes to a baking sheet and place in oven for 10 to 12 minutes or until heated through. Serve hot with creamy lemon-dill sauce.

If you don't have time to drink eight glasses of water a day, at least leave your mouth open during rainstorms :)

Cod Up in the Moment

Oven-baked, breaded fish sticks with light tartar sauce

Coddle your taste buds with these simple yet tasty breaded fish sticks.

Tartar Sauce

½ cup	light mayonnaise
1 tbsp	minced fresh dill
1 tbsp	sweet green relish
2 tsp	each prepared horseradish and freshly squeezed lemon juice
⅔ cup	dry unseasoned bread crumbs
3 tbsp	finely grated Parmesan cheese
1 tbsp	minced fresh parsley
¾ tsp	dried thyme
½ tsp	paprika
¼ tsp	each salt and freshly ground black pepper
2	eggs
2 lbs	(907 g) cod fillets, at least ½ inch thick
6	lemon wedges (optional)

- To make tartar sauce, combine all sauce ingredients in a small bowl. Refrigerate until ready to use.

- In a shallow bowl, combine bread crumbs, Parmesan cheese, parsley, thyme, paprika, salt and pepper. Lightly beat eggs in another shallow bowl. Spray a baking sheet with cooking spray and set aside.

- Rinse fish and pat dry with paper towels. Cut fish into thick strips. Working one at a time, dip pieces in egg, then in crumb mixture, coating both sides with crumbs. Place on baking sheet. Allow some space between pieces.

- Bake at 450°F for 8 to 10 minutes, depending on thickness of fish. Fish is ready when it flakes easily with a fork. Serve with tartar sauce and lemon wedges, if desired.

MAKES 6 SERVINGS

PER SERVING (WITH SAUCE)
277 calories, 10.7 g total fat (2.1 g saturated fat), 33 g protein, 12 g carbohydrate, 0.6 g fiber, 167 mg cholesterol, 627 mg sodium

Juicy Gossip About Lemons

Like other vitamin C-rich fruits, the lemon was highly prized by miners during the California Gold Rush in the mid-19th century, since it helped protect against scurvy. Almost as good as gold, people rushed to pay up to $1 a lemon, a price that would be considered high today, never mind in 1849! Making lemons your main squeeze will help boost your immune system and protect your body from disease and the effects of aging, since lemon juice is an effective antioxidant. Consumed before or with a meal, it's also a helpful digestive aid, as it gets the stomach's digestive acids flowing. Interestingly, the custom of serving a slice of lemon with fish dates back to the Middle Ages. It was believed that if a person accidentally swallowed a fish bone, the lemon juice would dissolve it. And if you're a follower of the Glycemic Index, you'll be pleased to know that adding a few tablespoons of lemon juice to a meal can lower its glycemic value by about 30 percent, making lemons a powerful aid in controlling blood sugar. By the way, warmer lemons yield more juice. Leave them at room temperature for at least 30 minutes before juicing, or soak them in hot water for 15 minutes. Roll lemons back and forth on the counter a few times for the juiciest results.

Nutrition Nugget

Fish is usually one of the healthiest choices you can make for a dinner entrée at a restaurant, but when you opt for fish and chips you're opening up a whole new can of worms. Two pieces of fish deep-fried in batter along with a side of fries has a cod-awful amount of bad fats! Forty to 50 grams is common at most fish houses. Feeling a little *gillty*?

Heart and Sole

Baked sole fillets drizzled with a lemon-ginger sauce

Let's get to the heart of the matter: This lemony baked-sole recipe will become dear to your heart when you realize how wonderfully delicious it is. Bonus: You can make it in a heartbeat!

Your taste buds are about to fall in love!

1 lb	(454 g) sole fillets
½ tsp	salt
¼ tsp	freshly ground black pepper
⅓ cup	freshly squeezed lemon juice
¼ cup	reduced-sodium chicken or vegetable broth
3 tbsp	granulated sugar
2 tsp	each grated gingerroot and cornstarch
1 tsp	grated lemon zest
1 tsp	minced garlic
1 tbsp	minced fresh parsley

MAKES 4 SERVINGS

PER SERVING

149 calories, 2.1 g total fat (1 g saturated fat), 22 g protein, 13 g carbohydrate, 0.3 g fiber, 35 mg cholesterol, 400 mg sodium

- Spray a medium baking pan with cooking spray and set aside.

- Rinse fish with cold water and pat dry with paper towels. Sprinkle with salt and pepper. Roll up fish and place seam-side down in baking pan. Bake at 425°F for about 15 minutes, until fish is cooked through and flakes easily with a fork.

- While fish is cooking, prepare sauce. Combine lemon juice, broth, sugar, gingerroot, cornstarch, lemon zest and garlic in a small saucepan. Cook over medium-high heat until mixture is bubbly and has thickened.

- Arrange fish on serving plates and drizzle with sauce. Sprinkle with parsley and serve immediately.

Nutrition Nugget

Heavy metal not music to your ears? Lemon and dill are two foods that can help your liver get rid of or neutralize heavy metals like mercury, lead and aluminum.

Anchors A-weigh Seafood Lasagna

Rich-tasting, creamy seafood lasagna with three cheeses

This super-creamy, triple-cheese lasagna is a seafood lover's dream that won't weigh you down. Go on! Sea for yourself!

9	uncooked whole wheat lasagna noodles
1 cup	trimmed and halved snow peas
1 cup	thinly sliced red bell pepper
1½ cups	part-skim ricotta cheese
¼ cup	freshly grated Parmesan cheese
1	egg
1 tbsp	butter
2 tsp	minced garlic
2½ cups	1% milk
5 tbsp	all-purpose flour
2 tsp	reduced-sodium chicken bouillon powder
½ tsp	each dry mustard and freshly ground black pepper
¼ tsp	salt
¾ lb	(340 g) bay scallops
¾ lb	(340 g) lump crabmeat, chopped or broken into bite-sized pieces
¾ cup	packed shredded light old (sharp) cheddar cheese (3 oz/85 g), divided
¼ cup	minced fresh parsley

- Prepare lasagna noodles according to package directions. Drain. Rinse with cold water and drain again. Set aside.

- Place snow peas and red pepper in a microwave-safe dish with ¼ cup water. Cook on high power for 3 minutes. Drain vegetables and set aside.

- In a medium bowl, mix together ricotta cheese, Parmesan cheese and egg. Set aside.

- To prepare sauce, melt butter in a large pot over medium heat. Add garlic. Cook for 1 minute.

- Whisk together milk and flour until smooth. Add to garlic in pot. Increase heat to medium-high. Stir using a whisk. Cook until mixture is bubbly and has thickened, about 6 to 7 minutes.

- Stir in bouillon powder, dry mustard, pepper and salt. Add scallops. Cook until scallops are opaque, about 5 minutes. Stir in crabmeat, ½ cup cheese, parsley, snow peas and red pepper. Cook for 1 more minute, until cheese is completely melted. Remove sauce from heat.

- Spray a 9 x 13-inch baking dish with cooking spray. To assemble lasagna, cover bottom of baking dish with 3 noodles. Pour ⅓ sauce over top. Layer 3 more noodles over sauce. Spread all of the ricotta-Parmesan mixture over noodles, followed by ⅓ sauce. Top with 3 more noodles and remaining sauce. Sprinkle remaining ¼ cup cheese over top.

- Cover with foil and bake at 350°F for 40 minutes. Let stand 5 minutes before serving.

MAKES 8 SERVINGS

PER SERVING
365 calories, 9.8 g total fat (4.9 g saturated fat), 31 g protein, 37 g carbohydrate, 3 g fiber, 102 mg cholesterol, 516 mg sodium

Sign at dairy farm: You can whip our cream but you can't beat our milk :)

FOOD BITE

The terms "big cheese" and "big wheel" originated in medieval times out of envious respect for those who had money to buy whole wheels of cheese at a time—an expense few could afford. Today, both terms are used sarcastically to describe an important, influential person.

A FINE KETTLE OF FISH

In this chapter...

It's a
Meat Market

Beef and pork that's light on the fork

Stick to Your Ribs,
p. 224

For Goodness Steak

Grilled sirloin steak with an Asian marinade

*Goodness gracious—this steak's bodacious! Our tasty marinade is good
to the last drop—and that's the honest-to-goodness truth.*

It's the tastiest steak, bar nun.

1½ lbs   (680 g) boneless top sirloin steak, about 1½ inches thick

Marinade

5 tbsp   reduced-sodium soy sauce
3 tbsp   steak sauce (such as A1)
2 tbsp   each freshly squeezed lime juice and packed brown sugar
1 tbsp   grated gingerroot
2 tsp   minced garlic
1 tsp   sesame oil
¼ tsp   freshly ground black pepper

- Trim any excess fat from steak and pierce meat in several places with a fork. Combine all marinade ingredients in a small bowl and pour over steak in a large, heavy-duty, resealable plastic bag. Refrigerate for at least 2 hours, or overnight if possible.
- Preheat grill to medium-high setting. Brush grill rack lightly with oil. Remove steak from marinade and grill over hot coals for 4 to 5 minutes per side, until meat is cooked to desired degree of doneness.
- Let meat rest for a few minutes before slicing. Cut against the grain into thin slices. Serve immediately.

MAKES 6 SERVINGS

PER SERVING
210 calories,
7.4 g total fat
(2.8 g saturated fat),
28 g protein,
6 g carbohydrate,
0 g fiber,
81 mg cholesterol,
441 mg sodium

*Television is like
a steak—
a medium rarely
well done :)*

Nutrition Nugget Eyes bigger than your stomach? Not for long! Researchers say that the bigger the portion in front of us, the more we'll eat—close to 30 percent more! That's why it's a good idea to eat more meals at home, where YOU control the portion sizes. And studies show that simply switching from a 12-inch to a 10-inch dinner plate causes people to eat 22 percent less, so buying smaller dinnerware is not a *waist* of money!

Lard Have Mercy!

Hankering for a slab of beef? Don't mosey into a steakhouse or a meat market until you know which cuts are the leanest. Luckily, the most popular ones, top sirloin and filet mignon, are also the lowest in saturated fat. (Remember: "loin" means "lean.") In fact, these cuts are A1 choices! It starts to go downhill from there, though. Choose a New York strip, rib eye or T-bone, for instance, and you'll use up about a day's worth of saturated fat (20 grams). Porterhouse and prime rib are the worst bandits, rustling up almost two days' worth. Steer clear! Need another reason to trim all visible fat, choose the leanest cuts and avoid steak pig-outs? Environmental toxins, pesticides and antibiotics taken in by the animal accumulate in the fat. By the way, if you can afford to buy organic, grass-fed beef from a health-conscious butcher or local farmer, not only will you avoid these toxins, but also your beef will contain less saturated fats and more healthy fats like omega-3s.

DisKEBOBulated Beef Skewers

Succulent grilled sirloin skewers for beef lovers!

Don't confuse these mouthwatering steak skewers with ordinary beef kebobs—our lip-smacking, herb-infused marinade makes them a flavor-packed, grill-time favorite.

Marinade

2 tbsp	grainy Dijon mustard
2 tbsp	balsamic vinegar
1 tbsp	olive oil
1 tbsp	brown sugar
2 tsp	minced garlic
1 tbsp	minced fresh rosemary, or 1 tsp dried
1½ tsp	minced fresh thyme, or ½ tsp dried
½ tsp	each salt and freshly ground black pepper
1½ lbs	(680 g) thick-cut sirloin steak, cut into 1½-inch chunks (see tip)
4	12-inch metal skewers

MAKES 4 KEBOBS

PER KEBOB

249 calories, 11.2 g total fat (3.4 g saturated fat), 29 g protein, 6 g carbohydrate, 0.4 g fiber, 85 mg cholesterol, 397 mg sodium

- Whisk together all marinade ingredients in a small bowl. Place steak cubes in a large, heavy-duty, resealable plastic bag. Add marinade and seal bag. Turn bag several times to coat steak evenly with marinade. Marinate in refrigerator for at least 1 hour (longer if possible).

- Preheat grill to high setting. Thread steak cubes onto skewers. Discard marinade. Place kebobs on a grill rack that has been lightly brushed with oil. Close lid. Grill for 8 to 10 minutes, turning occasionally, until meat is cooked to desired degree of doneness.

Recipe Tip: Ask the butcher at the meat counter for a piece of sirloin steak that's at least 1 inch thick. If you feel like splurging, use beef tenderloin!

FOOD BITE
The city of Chicago got its name from "shikaakwa," a Native American word for the wild garlic plant (*Allium tricoccum*) that grew around Lake Michigan.

Love Me Tenderloin

Grilled pork tenderloin in a rosemary-apple marinade

Love me tenderloin, grill me true, never let me burn.
Though it looks like it ain't nothing but a grilled pork, it's really a fabulous
dinner choice when you're having company. And it's so darn tasty, your guests
will say, "Thank you! Thank you very much!"

Marinade

½ cup	frozen apple juice concentrate, thawed
2 tbsp	honey mustard
2 tbsp	minced fresh rosemary
1 tbsp	olive oil
2 tsp	minced garlic
1	large shallot, minced
¼ tsp	freshly ground black pepper

1½ lbs	(680 g) pork tenderloin, trimmed of fat

- Combine all marinade ingredients in a small bowl. Pour marinade over pork in a glass baking dish or a large, heavy-duty, resealable plastic bag. Turn pork to coat evenly with marinade. Marinate for 2 hours in refrigerator.

- Preheat grill to medium-high setting. Brush grill rack lightly with oil. Remove pork from marinade and cook over hot coals for about 15 minutes, turning several times and basting frequently with reserved marinade. The outside should be nicely browned and the inside should still have a trace of pink. Let pork rest for 5 minutes before carving. Slice into ½-inch-thick slices and place on a serving platter. Bring any remaining marinade to a boil and drizzle over pork. Serve immediately.

MAKES 6 SERVINGS

PER SERVING
199 calories, 6.4 g total fat
(1.4 g saturated fat), 24 g protein,
10 g carbohydrate, 0.1 g fiber,
74 mg cholesterol, 135 mg sodium

Serious Side-Effect Warning!

"Take two dumbbells and call me in the morning." That's what doctors should be prescribing for optimum health. And speaking of prescriptions, if exercise were a pill, the following "warnings" just might appear on the label: May experience dramatically increased muscle tone, significant fat loss, surging energy levels, stronger heart, lungs and bones, lower cholesterol levels, increased immune function and improved sleep. Other side effects may include stress relief, increased confidence and self-esteem and dizzying spells of overall well-being. Take daily with plenty of water and do not skip dosages. In rare case of overdose, get plenty of rest and soak in a bath with Epsom salts. Oh! And please keep within reach of children!

Roast Feast

Colossal beef pot roast with potatoes, onions and cabbage in a zesty gravy

Feast your eyes and your taste buds on this! It's the roast with the most—the most delectable flavor, the most tasty roasted veggies ever and the most eye-appealing, mouthwatering platter ever to be served to a hungry crowd. Beauty and a feast!

1	boneless top sirloin roast (4 lbs/1.8 kg)
1 tsp	salt
1 tbsp	all-purpose flour
2 tsp	olive oil
1½ cups	each barbecue sauce and low-sodium beef broth
¼ cup	Worcestershire sauce
2 tbsp	freshly squeezed lime juice
1 tbsp	minced garlic
1 tsp	dry mustard
¼ tsp	freshly ground black pepper
2	small heads cabbage, each cut into 4 to 6 wedges
25	pearl onions, peeled
4	medium white potatoes, peeled and cut in half lengthwise
4	medium sweet potatoes, peeled and cut in half lengthwise

MAKES 8 SERVINGS

PER SERVING
491 calories, 11.5 g total fat (3.2 g saturated fat), 55 g protein, 41 g carbohydrate, 8.9 g fiber, 139 mg cholesterol, 816 mg sodium

> If people take the trouble to cook, you should take the trouble to eat.
>
> *Robert Morley*

- Preheat oven to 350°F.
- Sprinkle roast lightly on all sides with salt and flour. Heat oil in large non-stick skillet over medium-high heat. Add roast and brown on all sides. Remove roast from skillet and place in a large roasting pan.
- In a medium bowl, combine barbecue sauce, broth, Worcestershire sauce, lime juice, garlic, dry mustard and black pepper. Mix well. Pour over roast. Cover and cook for 1 hour. Reduce heat to 325°F and cook 1 more hour. Baste roast with sauce every ½ hour.
- Remove roasting pan from oven. Arrange vegetables around roast, starting with cabbage, followed by onions, white potatoes and sweet potatoes. Baste roast and vegetables with sauce. Cover, return to oven and cook for 1 more hour (total cooking time for roast: 3 hours).
- Remove roast from oven. Allow to stand 15 minutes before carving. Slice roast thinly. Arrange slices on a serving platter and surround roast with vegetables. Pour off as much fat as possible from sauce in pan. Pour ½ cup sauce over meat and serve immediately.

Trivial Tidbit

Some dairy farmers believe that creating a relaxed, tranquil environment helps cows produce more milk, so farmers sometimes play light country tunes or classical music in the barn. Apparently, rock music makes the cows produce less milk. Looks like The Rolling Stones gather no milk, but when it comes to bigger yields, Beethoven is nothing to Bach at.

Nutrition Nugget

Cabbage is a superhero among vegetables! If you live in a big city (where air pollution is more prevalent) or if you're a smoker, you'll want to put cabbage at the head of your dinner table. Often! It's packed with vitamin C and other plant chemicals that make it a potent toxin fighter, even neutralizing some of the damaging compounds found in cigarette smoke.

Stew Good to Be True

Slow cooker beef and vegetable stew

It's stew good to be true and too good to be stew. But it's true—it is stew. And a mighty good one at that! One bowlful and we guarantee your family will rock around the crock (pot)!

It's all it's crocked up to be...

2 lbs	(907 g) stewing beef, trimmed of fat and cut into 1-inch cubes
3 cups	peeled and cubed potatoes
2 cups	chopped carrots
1½ cups	chopped onions
2 cups	no-salt-added tomato sauce
1 can	(10 oz/284 mL) reduced-sodium beef broth, undiluted
1 tbsp	Dijon mustard
2 tsp	minced garlic
1	bay leaf
1¼ tsp	each dried marjoram and dried thyme
1 tsp	granulated sugar
½ tsp	each salt and freshly ground black pepper
1 tbsp	cornstarch
¼ cup	minced fresh parsley

MAKES 6 SERVINGS

PER SERVING
340 calories, 8.2 g total fat
(2.6 g saturated fat),
36 g protein, 29 g carbohydrate,
3.5 g fiber, 89 mg cholesterol,
608 mg sodium

- Combine all ingredients except cornstarch and parsley in a 3-quart or larger slow cooker. Cover and simmer on low setting for 8 hours.

- Combine cornstarch with an equal amount water and stir until lump-free. Add to stew and mix well. Cook for 1 more hour. Stir in parsley just before serving.

Recipe Tip The larger your slow cooker, the faster the stew will cook. You might need to decrease the cooking time if your slow cooker is very large (5- or 6-quart cookers are common these days, but we still prefer the smaller ones!). For added flavor, brown the beef cubes in a skillet with some olive oil before adding to slow cooker.

FOOD BITE

Thyme heals all wounds! The herb thyme is mentioned in one of the oldest known medical records, Ebers Papyrus (dating from 16th century BC), an ancient Egyptian list of 877 prescriptions and recipes. Nowadays, its most active ingredient, thymol, is used in many over-the-counter products like mouthwash and vapor rubs because it's antiviral, antifungal and antiparasitic.

Nutrition Nugget

Did you know that cooking meats in liquid, like you would when making soups and stews or using marinades, is the healthiest way to cook meat? Without getting into too much scientific mumbo jumbo, when you cook meat at really high temperatures, especially if it gets charred or burned, it causes a reaction in your body that can accelerate aging and cause degenerative disease. But cooking meat slowly in liquid prevents this reaction from happening. Marinate, braise, baste or stew. All are better for you!

Marla's Maple Pork
Roasted pork tenderloin drizzled with a flavorful maple and orange sauce

You can't Trump this recipe! Our roasted pork is so delectable, you'll shout, "Ivanna some more!"

1½ lbs	(680 g) pork tenderloin
½ cup	pure maple syrup
2 tbsp	each reduced-sodium soy sauce and ketchup
1 tbsp	Dijon mustard
2 tsp	grated orange zest
1½ tsp	each curry powder and ground coriander
2 tsp	minced garlic
1 tsp	Worcestershire sauce

- Trim pork of all visible fat. Place pork in a large, heavy-duty, resealable plastic bag. Whisk together all remaining ingredients in a medium bowl. Pour marinade over pork and seal bag. Turn bag several times to coat pork evenly. Marinate in refrigerator for 1 hour.

- Transfer pork and marinade to a small roasting pan or baking dish. Roast, uncovered, at 350°F for 40 minutes. Pork should be slightly pink in middle.

- Let pork stand for 5 minutes before slicing. Slice thinly. Drizzle extra sauce over pork and serve immediately.

MAKES 6 SERVINGS

PER SERVING
226 calories,
4.5 g total fat
(1.4 g saturated fat),
25 g protein,
21 g carbohydrate,
0.5 g fiber,
74 mg cholesterol,
310 mg sodium

If a pig loses his voice, is he disgruntled? :)

Chop Soooo-ey!

Chop suey with marinated pork tenderloin and crunchy vegetables

Call your family to the dinner table for our much-tastier-than-takeout chop suey and they're bound to go hog wild! Squeals of approval guaranteed. Don't be disgruntled over the long ingredients list—it's actually soooo easy to make.

Ah, so good!

Marinade

1 tbsp	reduced-sodium soy sauce
1 tbsp	hoisin sauce
2 tsp	grated gingerroot
1 tsp	minced garlic
1 tsp	cornstarch

1¼ lbs (568 g) pork tenderloin, cut into strips

- Whisk together all marinade ingredients in a medium bowl. Add pork tenderloin and stir to coat evenly with marinade. Let stand for 15 minutes while you prepare sauce and vegetables.

Sauce

½ cup	reduced-sodium beef broth
3 tbsp	hoisin sauce
1 tbsp	reduced-sodium soy sauce
2 tsp	grated gingerroot
2 tsp	cornstarch
1 tsp	sesame oil
¼ tsp	crushed red pepper flakes

- Whisk together all sauce ingredients in a medium bowl. Set aside until ready to use.

Chop Suey

1 tbsp	peanut oil
3 cups	sliced mushrooms
2 cups	sliced celery (cut on angle)
1 cup	coarsely chopped onions
2 cups	sliced baby bok choy
3 cups	bean sprouts
1 cup	snow peas
1 cup	sliced water chestnuts
5	green onions, coarsely chopped
5	large fresh basil leaves, coarsely chopped

- Heat oil in a large wok over high heat. Add marinated pork and cook until outside is lightly browned and pork is no longer pink. Remove pork from wok and keep warm.

- Add mushrooms, celery and onions to same wok. Cook and stir until vegetables are almost tender, about 5 minutes. Add bok choy, bean sprouts and snow peas. Cook for 3 to 4 more minutes. Return pork to wok along with water chestnuts and green onions. Give reserved sauce a quick stir and add to wok. Cook until mixture is hot and bubbly and sauce has thickened. Remove from heat and stir in basil leaves. Serve hot. Tastes great with vegetable fried rice (see recipe on p. 266).

> I was 32 when I started cooking; until then I just ate.
> *Julia Child*

MAKES 6 SERVINGS

PER SERVING
252 calories, 7 g total fat (1.8 g saturated fat), 26 g protein, 23 g carbohydrate, 5 g fiber, 62 mg cholesterol, 548 mg sodium

Reggae Gumbo

Spicy pork tenderloin gumbo with tomatoes, mushrooms and sweet potatoes

We're jammin'...pork and veggies in our stew
We're jammin'...Caribbean flavor—good for you!

MAKES 4 SERVINGS

PER SERVING
337 calories,
5.7 g total fat
(1.6 g saturated fat),
32 g protein,
39 g carbohydrate,
7.5 g fiber,
74 mg cholesterol,
325 mg sodium

1 tsp	olive oil
1 lb	(454 g) pork tenderloin, cut into 1-inch cubes
2 cups	sliced mushrooms
1 cup	chopped onions
2 tsp	minced garlic
½ cup	chopped celery
1 can	(28 oz/796 mL) no-salt-added diced tomatoes, undrained
1 can	(5.5 oz/156 mL) tomato paste
1 tsp	each ground cumin and grated gingerroot
¾ tsp	dried oregano
¼ tsp	each salt, freshly ground black pepper and crushed red pepper flakes
2 cups	peeled and cubed sweet potatoes
1 cup	sliced okra or zucchini
¼ cup	minced fresh cilantro

- Heat oil in a large pot over medium-high heat. Add pork cubes and cook until lightly browned, about 8 to 10 minutes. Add mushrooms, onions, garlic and celery. Cook and stir until vegetables are tender, about 5 minutes.

- Stir in tomatoes and their liquid, tomato paste, cumin, gingerroot, oregano, salt, pepper and crushed red pepper flakes. Bring to a boil. Reduce heat to medium-low. Cover and simmer for 45 minutes, stirring occasionally.

- Stir in sweet potatoes and okra. Cover and simmer another 30 to 35 minutes, until pork and potatoes are very tender. Remove from heat and stir in cilantro. Serve hot.

Trivial Tidbit

The expression "high on the hog" originated from the way meat was once portioned out among ranks in the British army. Officers received the tender cuts "high on the hog," while the lower ranks shared the remains.

Nutrition Nugget

This little piggy lost his potbelly! It *is* possible to eat pork as part of a healthful, well-balanced diet. It just depends on what kind you eat, how much you eat and how you prepare it. The best choice is pork tenderloin. It's about as slim as skinless chicken breast, with a three ounce serving containing just four grams of fat. Don't oink out on spareribs, though. Lotsa bone, little meat, tons of fat! Three small ribs serve up a thigh-bulging 26 grams of fat!

The Way We Stir

Beef and vegetable stir-fry with red bell peppers and sugar snap peas

This beef stir-fry becomes a cherished memory pretty quickly. From wok to plate and poof—it's gone in an instant!

2 tsp	peanut oil
1 lb	(454 g) lean sirloin steak, cut into thin strips (about ¼ inch thick)
1 cup	thinly sliced red bell pepper
2 cups	sugar snap peas
1 cup	coarsely chopped green onions
1 cup	reduced-sodium beef broth
2 tbsp	reduced-sodium soy sauce
2 tbsp	light peanut butter
1 tbsp	grated gingerroot
1 tbsp	cornstarch
1 tsp	sesame oil
½ tsp	crushed red pepper flakes
4 cups	cooked brown rice or quinoa

MAKES 4 SERVINGS

PER SERVING
484 calories,
12.7 g total fat (2.8 g saturated fat),
34 g protein, 60 g carbohydrate,
6.4 g fiber, 70 mg cholesterol,
433 mg sodium

- Heat oil in a large wok over medium-high heat. Add beef and cook until no longer pink, about 4 minutes. Remove beef from wok and set aside.

- Add red pepper, peas and green onions to wok. Cook and stir until vegetables are tender-crisp, about 3 to 4 minutes.

- Whisk together broth, soy sauce, peanut butter, gingerroot, cornstarch, sesame oil and red pepper flakes. Add to vegetables, along with beef. Cook and stir until sauce is bubbly and has thickened, about 2 minutes.

- Serve beef and vegetables over hot rice or quinoa.

Recipe Tips: You can replace the sirloin steak with strips of boneless, skinless chicken or turkey breast. The sesame oil adds a distinct flavor to this stir-fry so don't leave it out of the recipe.

Never eat raw meat unless it's a rare occasion :)

Nutrition Nugget

Brown rice contains a compound that works similarly to blood pressure-reducing drugs! Plus, its germ offers the antioxidant vitamin E, as well as cholesterol-lowering phytosterols.

The Grass is Always Greener

If you're willing to crack open your piggy bank, it's worth investing the extra loot in grass-fed beef. Compared to factory-farmed, grain-fed beef, it's almost a different food! Truth is, real cows eat grass, not grains. Unfortunately, farmers today feed their cattle corn and soybeans so they can fatten them up fast. We wouldn't want the same to happen to you! Grass-fed beef is lower in saturated fat than regular beef and, more importantly, contains higher amounts of conjugated linoleic acid (CLA), a type of fat that's making headlines for its health benefits. These include helping boost metabolism so you burn more fat, helping fend off diabetes and cancer, helping you maintain normal cholesterol levels, and enhancing your immune system. Plus, a recent comprehensive study showed that grass-fed beef has a much healthier ratio of omega-3 fats to omega-6 fats, which means better overall health for you, too. Grain-fed beef has far more omega-6 fats, and that can lead to inflammation in the body and medical problems associated with it. The healthy, grass-fed variety is also higher in beta-carotene, vitamin E, calcium, magnesium and potassium. So in the world of cattle farming, being put out to pasture is a *good* thing!

The Loin King

Delicious marinated pork loin roast for company or Sunday dinner

It's the tastiest pork roast this side of the jungle…and we aren't lion, either!

Marinade

¼ cup	each brown sugar and ketchup
3 tbsp	balsamic vinegar
2 tbsp	olive oil
1 tbsp	reduced-sodium soy sauce
2 tsp	minced garlic
1 tsp	each curry powder, ground coriander and ground ginger
½ tsp	each salt and freshly ground black pepper
1	boneless pork loin roast (4 lbs/1.8 kg)

- Whisk together all marinade ingredients in a medium bowl. Place pork in a large, heavy-duty, resealable plastic bag. Add marinade and seal bag. Turn bag several times to coat roast with marinade. Marinate overnight in refrigerator.

- Preheat oven to 325°F. Remove pork from bag and place on a rack set in a shallow roasting pan. Reserve marinade. Roast pork, uncovered, for about 1 hour and 45 minutes to 2 hours. A meat thermometer inserted in center of roast should read 155°F.

- While roast is cooking, pour reserved marinade into a small saucepan. Bring to a boil, then reduce heat to low and simmer for 1 minute. Brush roast generously with marinade during last 20 minutes of cooking time.

- Remove roast from oven. Cover loosely with foil and let rest for 10 minutes before slicing. Slice thinly and serve hot.

MAKES 10 SERVINGS

PER SERVING
254 calories, 9.9 g total fat (3.2 g saturated fat), 34 g protein, 5 g carbohydrate, 0.2 g fiber, 88 mg cholesterol, 220 mg sodium

FOOD BITE

Garlic is called "the king of vegetables" because it has so many amazing health properties. Most people know it's good for the heart, but in Russia they call it "Russian penicillin" because of its antibiotic qualities. That's why it's an effective remedy for the common cold. Garlic is such a powerful health booster that the Egyptians built the pyramids on a diet of bread, water and garlic, and were often paid in garlic since it helped maintain their strength and stamina.

Happily Ever Apple Pork Chops

Succulent pork chops topped with a sweet and spicy apple-mustard sauce

Once upon a time, there lived a loinly pork chop who was saddened because he had to go topless. Then along came a spicy apple and mustard sauce, and it was love at first bite. The end.

2 tsp	olive oil
6	boneless pork loin chops (about 5 oz/142 g each), trimmed of fat
1 cup	apple butter (see tip)
2 tbsp	yellow mustard
1 tsp	ground cumin
¼ tsp	each salt and freshly ground black pepper
3 cups	peeled and sliced Golden Delicious apples (about 3 large)
½ cup	thinly sliced onions
2 tbsp	cider vinegar

- Heat oil in a large, non-stick skillet over medium-high heat. Cook chops until browned on both sides, about 5 minutes.

- In a small bowl, combine apple butter, mustard, cumin, salt and pepper. Spoon evenly over chops. Reduce heat to medium-low, cover and cook until chops are just slightly pink in the center and juices run clear, about 10 minutes. Remove chops from skillet (leave sauce in skillet) and keep warm.

- Add apples, onions and vinegar to sauce in skillet. Stir to coat apples and onions with sauce. Cover and cook over medium heat for 5 to 7 minutes, until apples are softened and onions are tender.

- To serve, spoon hot apple mixture over warm pork chops.

MAKES 6 SERVINGS

PER SERVING
304 calories, 9.7 g total fat (2.9 g saturated fat), 24 g protein, 23 g carbohydrate, 1.9 g fiber, 66 mg cholesterol, 200 mg sodium

Recipe Tip

Apple butter is a thick, dark brown preserve made by slowly cooking apples, spices, sugar and cider. It's most commonly used as a spread for muffins and breads, but it makes a great addition to sauces, too. Though its name sounds fattening, 1 cup apple butter contains less than 4 g fat! Look for it in a jar near the jams and jellies at your grocery store.

> I've been on a constant diet for the last two decades.
> I've lost a total of 789 pounds. By all accounts,
> I should be hanging from a charm bracelet.
>
> *Erma Bombeck*

Wok This Way

Asian beef and basil with red bell peppers

Ever dream of becoming a wok star? Well, now's your chance for fame and fortune cookies! This flavorful beef stir-fry with fresh basil, red bell peppers and onions will get you wokin' and rollin'!

1 lb	(454 g) sirloin steak, trimmed of fat, thinly sliced
3 tbsp	Asian fish sauce (see tip)
2 tbsp	reduced-sodium soy sauce
1 tbsp	brown sugar
1 tbsp	grated gingerroot
1 tsp	minced garlic
½ tsp	crushed red pepper flakes
1 tbsp	peanut oil
1	large red bell pepper, seeded and cut into strips
1	medium red onion, chopped or sliced

Lots of fresh basil leaves (at least 20)

MAKES 4 SERVINGS

PER SERVING
258 calories, 9.5 g total fat (3 g saturated fat),
26 g protein, 17 g carbohydrate, 2.8 g fiber,
68 mg cholesterol, 732 mg sodium

- Place steak slices in a shallow bowl or casserole dish. In a small bowl, whisk together fish sauce, soy sauce, brown sugar, gingerroot, garlic and crushed red pepper flakes. Pour over steak. Turn to coat both sides evenly with marinade and let sit at room temperature for 30 minutes.

- Heat oil in a large wok over medium-high heat. Remove steak from marinade and shake off excess. Reserve marinade. Cook steak in hot oil just until cooked through, stirring constantly. Remove steak from wok and set aside. Add red pepper and onion to wok. Cook and stir for about 5 minutes, until vegetables are tender. Return steak to wok and add basil and reserved marinade. Cook 1 more minute, until basil leaves are wilted, sauce is bubbly and steak is hot.

Recipe Tip: Asian fish sauce is an essential ingredient for authentic Thai flavor. Most grocery stores stock it near the soy sauce. For more information, see tip on p. 337.

Trivial Tidbit

Eating a fortune cookie will set you back about 30 calories. Luckily, the fortune itself, though usually sugar-coated, is calorie-free and high in fiber!

Having a Bad Air Day?

If you're a shallow breather, you may not be getting enough oxygen to your body's cells, and that can leave you feeling foggy, fatigued and stressed. What's more, lack of oxygen could be contributing to your growing gut! Say what? Well, you need oxygen to burn fat, which is why aerobic exercise (the intense kind that boosts your heart rate and gets you breathing heavily) is necessary if you want to unveil those six-pack abs. But exercise aside, you can avoid bad air days by learning deep-breathing techniques. Deep breathing not only helps detoxify your body, but also kicks up the oxygen level in your cells, boosting your metabolism. Plus, it helps tone your midsection by putting the brakes on cortisol. Cortisol is the nasty stress hormone that promotes weight gain around our middles, giving them the dreaded Pillsbury Doughboy look. Deep breathing also triggers an automatic relaxation response in your body, which lowers blood pressure and heart rate, reduces tension and sharpens thinking. Phew! A little breathing sure goes a long way! Whether you buy a book or DVD on deep-breathing techniques or sign up for a class, you'll be collecting valuable air miles.

Jurassic Pork Roast

Spectacular roasted pork loin with apple gravy

On one of our many archaeological expeditions, we unearthed this prehistoric recipe for a spectacular, juicy pork roast. We later discovered that it was voted "best low-fat pork dish" by Cavemopolitan Magazine.

1	boneless pork top loin roast (3 lbs/1.4 kg)
2	cloves garlic, thinly sliced
2 tbsp	Dijon mustard
1 tsp	red wine vinegar
1 tsp	dried thyme
¾ tsp	dried sage
¾ cup	reduced-sodium beef broth
¾ cup	unsweetened apple juice
¼ cup	apricot jam
1½ cups	peeled and chopped Granny Smith apples
2 tbsp	light (5%) sour cream
1 to 2 tbsp	cornstarch

MAKES 8 SERVINGS

PER SERVING

289 calories, 9.6 g total fat (3.2 g saturated fat), 10 g carbohydrate, 0.6 g fiber, 38 g protein, 95 mg cholesterol, 117 mg sodium

- Cut 8 deep slits in the top of roast using a very sharp knife. Insert garlic into slits.

- Mix mustard, vinegar, thyme and sage in a small bowl. Using a pastry brush, coat roast with all of the mustard mixture. Place roast in roasting pan.

- Warm the broth, apple juice and jam in a small pot over medium-high heat until jam melts. Pour over roast. Arrange chopped apples around roast. Cover and roast at 350ºF for 1¼ to 1½ hours, basting every 30 minutes or so.

- Remove roast from pan and keep warm. Reserve ½ cup pan juices. Pour remaining pan juices and apples into a medium pot. Skim off as much fat as possible. Into reserved ½ cup pan juices, add sour cream and cornstarch and whisk until lump-free.

- Bring pan juices and apples (in saucepan) to a boil. Add sour cream mixture and whisk over medium-high heat for 2 minutes, until gravy is bubbly and has thickened. Serve hot apple gravy over thin slices of pork roast.

He must be eating army food—everything goes to the front :)

Ham-Me-Down Dinner
Baked ham and pineapple with orange-mustard sauce

You'll pine over this simple ham and pineapple dinner that was handed down by our mother. It makes great leftovers, too, so you can play it again, ham.

You're such a ham!

1 can   (19 oz/540 mL) pineapple rings in juice, undrained
2 tbsp frozen orange juice concentrate, thawed
1 tbsp each yellow mustard and cornstarch
1   fully cooked lean ham (2 lbs/907 g—see tip)

- Drain juice from pineapple into a small pot. Set rings aside. You should have about 1 cup juice. Add orange juice concentrate, mustard and cornstarch to juice in pot. Cook and stir over medium heat until mixture is bubbly and has thickened, about 2 minutes. Remove from heat.

- Slice ham into 8 pieces. Arrange pieces in a 9 x 13-inch baking dish, overlapping as necessary. Top each piece with a pineapple slice. Pour sauce evenly over ham and pineapple.

- Cover with foil and bake at 350°F for 30 minutes, until ham is heated through and sauce is bubbly.

MAKES 8 SERVINGS

PER SERVING
181 calories, 4.1 g total fat (1.3 g saturated fat), 19 g protein, 18 g carbohydrate, 0.7 g fiber, 53 mg cholesterol, 854 mg sodium

Recipe Tip: When shopping for ham, choose a brand that contains the least amount of sodium. Even "reduced-sodium" ham can be high in salt.

Rumbles and Grumbles and Growls, Oh My!

Ever wonder what makes our stomachs growl? Some people find the rumbling embarrassing, but it's actually a normal part of digestion. There's a lot of pretty amazing stuff going on in that belly of yours, you know! Stomach growls happen when muscles in the stomach or upper intestine contract to "clean house," moving food and digestive juices down the digestive tract (a chew-chew train, of sorts). Rumbles are more common after you've gone several hours without eating, which is why many people associate a growling stomach with hunger. But growls also occur when there's incomplete digestion of food, which can lead to excess gas in the intestine. (This is called borborygmus, just in case you were looking for a new Scrabble word.) In rare cases, excessive abdominal noise may be a sign of other digestive conditions or diseases. Since a good chunk of your immune system resides in your gut, it's wise to listen to what it's telling you and it'll reward you by keeping you feeling and looking your best.

Trivial Tidbit

Where do pineapples grow?
(a) on the ground;
(b) in trees;
(c) inside volcanoes; or
(d) beside Tom Selleck's pool.
And the answer is...
(a) on the ground!
So why aren't they called "earth apples"? Because that's a nickname taken by potatoes!

Nutrition Nugget
Have supper for breakfast! Who says breakfast has to be cereal, toast or a muffin? Leftovers from dinner, especially if they involve veggies and lean protein like chicken and salmon, are a filling, satisfying, nutritious way to start your day.

The Blah-Shank Redemption

Baked bone-in ham with a maple-mustard glaze

We've turned a plain ol' boring ham into something sensational! Why confine yourself to the same mundane recipe every Easter dinner? Break out of the rut and escape the ordinary with our delectable, yet simple, maple-mustard glazed ham. We've kept the recipe under lock and key until now.

Pig Out!

1	fully cooked smoked bone-in ham (about 8 lbs/3.6 kg)
15	whole cloves
¼ cup	pure maple syrup
3 tbsp	grainy Dijon mustard
1 tbsp	cider vinegar
1 tsp	ground ginger

- Preheat oven to 325°F. Move oven rack to bottom third of oven.

- Using a sharp knife, score surface of ham crosswise and lengthwise, forming a crosshatch pattern about ¼ inch deep and 2 inches apart. Push a clove into the center of each square.

- Place ham on a rack in a shallow roasting pan. Cover loosely with foil. Roast for 1 hour and 40 minutes.

- While ham is cooking, prepare glaze. Combine maple syrup, mustard, vinegar and ginger in a small bowl.

- Remove ham from oven and brush with glaze. Use all of it and cover every square inch of ham. Return to oven and roast, uncovered, for 20 to 30 more minutes, until a meat thermometer inserted in deepest part of ham registers 140°F.

- Let ham rest for about 10 minutes before slicing. Slice thinly and serve hot.

MAKES 16 TO 20 SERVINGS

PER SERVING (BASED ON 20 SERVINGS)
169 calories, 5.6 g total fat (1.8 g saturated fat),
25 g protein, 3 g carbohydrate, 0 g fiber, 55 mg cholesterol,
1329 mg sodium

Viva Vinegar!

If you have diabetes or are at high risk for the disease, you might find help in the most unlikely of places—your kitchen cabinet! According to *Science News*, vinegar can help fight diabetes. Two tablespoons of vinegar taken before eating has been shown to reduce spikes of insulin and glucose that usually occur after meals. These jumps can cause complications in people with Type 2 diabetes and they can also cause heart disease. In one study, researchers found that blood-sugar levels of diabetics were cut by 25 percent with the vinegar regimen, and those who were prediabetic found their blood glucose was cut by almost half. In a longer diabetes study at Arizona State University, subjects were encouraged to consume two teaspoons of vinegar twice a day for a month. To the researchers' surprise, the subjects lost weight! It seems the acetic acid in vinegar likely interferes with the enzymes that digest carbohydrates. And if carbohydrates don't digest properly, they pass through the body much like fiber. So if you were thinking of cutting carbs, maybe you should try adding vinegar instead!

Nutrition Nugget

Chai it! You'll like it! Cloves are most commonly used in sweet and spicy Indian dishes, but they're also one of the main flavor boosters in chai tea. If you want to prevent aging, clove is a little longevity secret you should definitely add to your arsenal. Heck, its super-potent volatile oils may prevent your *arse*nal from expanding, since they've been proven to stabilize blood sugar, helping you to stay slim. They also battle free radicals that can make you old before your time. Clove's oils even kill bacteria, viruses, parasites and fungi that can plague your body and rob you of nutrients. Gotta clove it!

CLOVES

Flank 'n' Stein
Beer-and-spice-marinated grilled flank steak

This juicy, grilled steak will fill you up when you're Igor to tame a monstrous appetite. Tastes delicious with grilled or roasted vegetables or in fajitas. And let's be flank, the lager you marinate it, the better!

Marinade

⅓ cup   light beer
⅓ cup   hickory-flavored barbecue sauce
1 tbsp   freshly squeezed lemon juice
2 tsp   Montreal steak spice
1 tsp   grated lemon zest
1 tsp   balsamic vinegar
¼ tsp   dried rosemary, crushed

1½ lbs (680 g) flank steak, trimmed of fat

MAKES 4 SERVINGS

PER SERVING
279 calories,
12.2 g total fat
(5.2 g saturated fat),
33 g protein,
6 g carbohydrate,
0.1 g fiber,
80 mg cholesterol,
493 mg sodium

- Whisk together all marinade ingredients in a medium bowl. Place flank steak in a large, heavy-duty, resealable plastic bag. Add marinade and seal bag. Turn bag several times to coat steak with marinade. Marinate in refrigerator for at least 2 hours or as long as 24 hours.

- Preheat grill to high setting. Remove steak from bag and place on a grill rack that has been lightly brushed with oil. Grill for about 6 minutes per side, or to desired degree of doneness.

- Let steak rest for 5 minutes before slicing. To serve, slice steak thinly across the grain using a very sharp knife.

> It is not the quantity of the meat, but the cheerfulness of the guests, which makes the feast.
>
> *Edward Hyde*

A Wok in the Pork

Stir-fried pork tenderloin, vegetables and pineapple chunks in a sweet-and-sour sauce

You'll squeal with delight when you discover that this sweet-and-sour pork dish won't make you porky.

2 tsp	peanut oil
1¼ lbs	(568 g) pork tenderloin, cut into cubes or strips
2 tsp	grated gingerroot
1 tsp	minced garlic
1½ cups	each chopped green bell pepper and sliced carrots
1 cup	chopped onions
1 can	(14 oz/398 mL) pineapple chunks, undrained
¼ cup	each ketchup and white or rice vinegar
3 tbsp	brown sugar
2 tbsp	reduced-sodium soy sauce
1 tbsp	cornstarch
½ tsp	chili powder
4 cups	hot cooked brown rice or quinoa

- Heat oil in a large wok or skillet over medium-high heat. Add pork, gingerroot and garlic. Cook and stir for 6 to 7 minutes, until pork is cooked through and begins to brown. Remove pork from wok and keep warm. Add green pepper, carrots and onions to wok. Cook and stir for about 5 minutes, or until vegetables are tender.

- Meanwhile, prepare sauce. Drain pineapple, reserving ½ cup juice. In a small bowl, combine reserved pineapple juice, ketchup, vinegar, brown sugar, soy sauce, cornstarch and chili powder. Add sauce to vegetables in wok, along with cooked pork and pineapple chunks. Cook until sauce is bubbly and has thickened, and pork and pineapple are heated through. Serve over hot rice or quinoa.

MAKES 4 SERVINGS

PER SERVING (WITH RICE)
570 calories,
9.7 g total fat (2.1 g saturated fat),
37 g protein, 83 carbohydrate,
7.8 g fiber, 92 mg cholesterol,
571 mg sodium

Nutrition Nugget

You've probably heard that MSG can cause all sorts of reactions, from headaches to dizziness to seizures—the so-called Chinese Food Syndrome. But you may not realize that MSG can also cause weight gain! In animal studies, rats fed MSG became obese. In fact, scientists induce obesity in laboratory animals by feeding them MSG. Better not chow down on the chow mein unless you're certain it's MSG-free.

The Big Chili

Spicy beef chili with two kinds of beans

You and your pals can chill out and pig out on this filling chili. Just don't fight for seconds, or you may end up with a chili concussion.

1 tbsp	olive oil
1½ lbs	(680 g) stewing beef, cut into 1-inch cubes
1 cup	each chopped red and green bell peppers
1 cup	chopped red onions
2 tsp	minced garlic
3 cups	reduced-sodium beef broth
1½ cups	salsa (see tip)
1 can	(19 oz/540 mL) no-salt-added diced tomatoes, undrained
1½ tbsp	chili powder
1½ tsp	each ground cumin and dried oregano
1 tsp	ground coriander
½ tsp	freshly ground black pepper
1 can	(19 oz/540 mL) no-salt-added black beans, drained and rinsed
1 can	(19 oz/540 mL) no-salt-added red kidney beans, drained and rinsed
¼ cup	minced fresh cilantro
2 tbsp	freshly squeezed lime juice
1 tbsp	liquid honey

MAKES 8 SERVINGS

PER SERVING
312 calories, 7.1 g total fat
(2.2 g saturated fat), 27 g protein,
33 g carbohydrate, 11 g fiber,
52 mg cholesterol, 250 g sodium

- Heat olive oil in a large pot over medium-high heat. Add beef. Cook and stir until beef is lightly browned. Add peppers, onions and garlic. Reduce heat to medium. Cook and stir for 4 to 5 minutes, until vegetables begin to soften.

- Add broth, salsa, tomatoes and their juice, chili powder, cumin, oregano, coriander and black pepper. Bring to a boil. Reduce heat to low and simmer, covered, for 1½ hours, stirring occasionally.

- Add beans and simmer for 15 more minutes. Remove from heat. Stir in cilantro, lime juice and honey. Serve hot.

Recipe Tips You can control the heat of this beef chili by choosing mild, medium or hot salsa. The long, slow simmering is necessary to make the beef tender. If you're in a hurry, you can replace the stewing beef with extra-lean ground beef or cubed, boneless chicken breast, and simmer for 30 minutes instead of 1½ hours. By the way, The Big Chili tastes great served with a batch of our delicious corn muffins (see recipe on p. 296).

Heart-Warming News

Want to keep your heart happy? Eat black beans! They're a good source of magnesium. When your body has enough magnesium, the veins and arteries relax and breathe a sigh of relief, which improves blood flow, increasing oxygen and nutrient delivery to the body. But that's not all these little nuggets of nutrition can do for you. Black beans have levels of disease-fighting antioxidants that are equal to those found in oranges, grapes and cranberries! Interestingly, in Brazil, a country that, along with India, grows more black beans than any country in the world, beans have even been given an exclusive place on the Brazilian Food Pyramid. In other words, beans are recommended as their own unique food group! Here on this continent, we say eat 'em to your heart's content!

Deja Moo:
The feeling that you've heard this bull before :)

The Great Pretenderloin

Roasted whole beef tenderloin with rosemary and thyme

Actually, there's no use pretending—this is truly the most succulent, mouthwatering beef you'll ever taste. A real showstopper! You might want to save it for special occasions or holidays, though. It costs a lotta moo-la, but it's worth every penny.

Only you... can make this roast just right

Seasoning Rub

1 tbsp   softened butter or olive oil
1 tbsp   Dijon mustard
1 tbsp   brown sugar
1 tbsp   steak sauce (such as A1)
1 tbsp   minced fresh rosemary
1 tbsp   minced fresh thyme
2 tsp   minced garlic
1½ tsp   salt (we like sea salt)
1 tsp   freshly ground black pepper
1 tsp   grated lemon zest

1   whole beef tenderloin (3 lbs/1.4 kg), trimmed of visible fat

MAKES 8 SERVINGS

PER SERVING
225 calories, 11.3 g total fat (4.6 g saturated fat), 26 g protein, 3 g carbohydrate, 0.2 g fiber, 82 mg cholesterol, 533 mg sodium

- Preheat oven to 450°F. Move oven rack to bottom third of oven.

- Mix together rub ingredients in a small bowl. Rub all over beef. Let stand at room temperature for 30 minutes. Place beef on a rack in a shallow roasting pan. Place pan in oven and reduce temperature to 400°F.

- Roast meat, uncovered, for 45 to 55 minutes, or until meat thermometer inserted in the center registers 140°F for medium-rare. Remove roast from oven and let stand, uncovered, for 10 minutes before slicing. (Note: Exact cooking time will depend on thickness of roast. Temperature will continue to rise as meat rests. Don't overcook beef tenderloin!)

Nutrition Nugget

Blood pressure going up? Get some olive oil down! All you need is a few teaspoons of olive oil a day to help reduce blood pressure and also to prevent blood clots. Pair that with some garlic and you'll have one healthy heart: Garlic also helps normalize blood pressure and can thin the blood, much like the effects of aspirin.

Barbiechop Quartet
Spicy, marinated pork chops grilled on the barbie

This spicy number hits a high note where flavor's concerned. On the pork chop taste-o-meter, it rates a perfect ten-or!

4	boneless pork loin chops (about 5 oz/142 g each), trimmed of fat
⅓ cup	orange juice
3 tbsp	each liquid honey and ketchup
3 tbsp	mango chutney
1 tbsp	freshly squeezed lemon juice
2 tsp	chili powder
¾ tsp	ground cumin

MAKES 4 SERVINGS

PER SERVING
297 calories, 8.7 g total fat (2.9 g saturated fat), 24 g protein, 31 g carbohydrate, 0.9 g fiber, 66 mg cholesterol, 354 mg sodium

• Arrange pork chops in a single layer in a glass baking dish. Whisk together remaining ingredients in a small bowl. Pour over pork chops. Turn pieces to coat both sides with marinade. Cover with plastic wrap and refrigerate for at least 4 hours, or overnight if possible.

• Preheat grill to medium-high setting. Brush grill rack lightly with oil. Cook pork chops over hot coals for 6 to 7 minutes per side, basting with leftover marinade. Serve immediately.

FOOD BITE
The word barbecue comes from the Spanish *barbacoa*, meaning "frame of sticks." When early Spanish explorers landed on Haiti in the mid-17th century, they used this word to describe the Haitian Indians' method of grilling and smoking their meat outdoors on wooden racks over open fires.

Say It Ain't Soda!
No doubt you've heard that soft drinks have about 10 cubes of sugar per can. And you've probably glanced at those scary posters in the dentist's office showing how soda decays, corrodes and discolors our teeth. If the prospect of rotting teeth doesn't stop you (or more importantly, your kids) from guzzling gallons of the carbonated, sweet stuff, maybe rotting bones will: Did you know that something called phosphoric acid in soft drinks causes calcium to be leached from our bones? Can you say osteoporosis? Remember: Soft drinks = soft bones.

> A smiling face is half the meal.
> *Latvian proverb*

A Full Plate at Home Plate

Take me out to the ball game, take away my restraint,
Buy me some hot dogs and fattening snacks, I don't care if I fit in my slacks,
It's just eat, eat, eat, for the whole game, I'm feeling sick—what a shame,
I've gained one, two, three extra pounds, at the old ball game.

You'll have to admit, the snacks at stadium concession stands don't exactly qualify as health foods. But what's a ball game without a hot dog and a beer? It's not like they're going to blow your dietary record in the long run, especially if you keep the following tips in mind: (1) Sometimes a single is better than a triple. Do you really need that second or third slice of pizza? Why not opt for some unbuttered popcorn when hunger strikes? (2) You don't have to get loaded just because the bases are. When your friend declares, "We sure could use a new pitcher," do you head straight for the draft taps? Downing three jugs of beer might increase your chugging percentage, but it'll also make your Buttwider. A wiser move would be drinking one bottled water for each beer you chug. (Oh, and always buy seats near the restrooms!)

Lick Your Chops

Juicy pork loin chops in a zesty lemon-rosemary barbecue sauce

The lemon and molasses give 'em zest and zing. It's a "lick your lips, lick your fork, lick your plate" kinda thing.
You'll make them lickety-split, too!

Sauce

½ cup	ketchup
2 tbsp	freshly squeezed lemon juice
2 tbsp	molasses
2 tbsp	minced shallots or onions
1¼ tsp	chili powder
1 tsp	minced garlic
1 tsp	grated lemon zest
½ tsp	dried rosemary
¼ tsp	freshly ground black pepper

4	boneless pork loin chops (about 5 oz/142 g each)

Recipe Tip: If you have the time, you can marinate the pork chops in the sauce overnight. You don't have to cook the sauce first. Then, just throw the chops on the grill and wait for the standing ovation you're sure to receive!

MAKES 4 SERVINGS

PER SERVING
282 calories, 9 g total fat (3.1 g saturated fat),
36 g protein, 13 g carbohydrate, 0.6 g fiber,
91 mg cholesterol, 403 mg sodium

- To make sauce, combine all sauce ingredients in a small pot. Bring to a boil over medium-high heat. Reduce heat to low and simmer for 2 minutes, stirring occasionally.

- Preheat grill to medium-high setting. Place pork chops on a grill rack that has been lightly brushed with oil. Grill pork chops for about 6 minutes per side, depending on thickness of chops. Pork should be just slightly pink in the center. Be careful not to overcook them or they will be dry. Brush pork generously with sauce during last 5 minutes of cooking time.

- Brush any remaining sauce on pork chops just before serving.

Nutrition Nugget

Happily marinated: When you marinate meat in citrus or vinegar, or a rub containing rosemary, you reduce carcinogenic compounds formed during grilling.

Jellystone Pork

Grilled pork tenderloin with a tangy apple jelly and Dijon mustard sauce

When you bearly have the energy to prepare dinner, and you can't see the forest for the trees, try this scrumptious pork tenderloin recipe with an amazing (and simple!) apple-mustard sauce. It's approved for all taste buds by both the Pork Ranger and the Loin Ranger!

2	pork tenderloins (12 oz/340 g each)
½ tsp	each salt and freshly ground black pepper

Sauce

1 tbsp	butter
⅓ cup	finely minced shallots
2 tbsp	grated gingerroot
1 tsp	minced garlic
⅓ cup	apple jelly (see tip)
3 tbsp	Dijon mustard
2 tbsp	cider vinegar
¼ tsp	salt and freshly ground black pepper
¼ cup	light (5%) sour cream

Recipe Tip: Look for apple jelly near other jams and spreads at your grocery store.

MAKES 6 SERVINGS

PER SERVING
226 calories,
6.5 g total fat (2.6 g saturated fat),
25 g protein, 16 g carbohydrate,
0.2 g fiber, 80 mg cholesterol,
241 mg sodium

- Before grilling pork, get all of the sauce ingredients ready so you can whip up the sauce quickly while the cooked pork is resting.

- Preheat grill to medium-high heat. Sprinkle pork with salt and pepper. Place pork on a grill rack that has been lightly brushed with oil. Grill pork for about 15 minutes, turning occasionally. The outside should be nicely browned and the center should have just a trace of pink. Transfer pork to a plate, cover with foil and let rest while you make the sauce. (You could also roast pork in the oven: brush pork lightly with olive oil, then sprinkle with salt and pepper. Roast at 350°F for about 40 minutes.)

- To make sauce, melt butter in a small, non-stick skillet over medium heat. Add shallots, gingerroot and garlic. Cook and stir until shallots begin to soften, about 2 minutes. Be careful not to burn them.

- Add apple jelly, Dijon mustard, vinegar, salt and pepper. Mix well. Cook and stir for 3 minutes, until jelly completely melts and sauce begins to thicken. Reduce heat to low if it's bubbling too much. Remove from heat and stir in sour cream.

- To serve pork, slice it thinly and arrange on a small platter. Drizzle sauce over pork.

Trivial Tidbit

What part of the pig is regular bacon made from? (a) pork bellies; (b) pork livers; (c) pork rump; (d) Pork Rangers. The answer is...(a)! Kinda takes the sizzle out of your bacon addiction, doesn't it?

Butter Versus Margarine

Which is butter: Better or margarine? Ooops! Having trouble with our vowel movements again. Simply put, butter is a natural fat with many health-promoting qualities. In fact, 30 percent of butter's fat is monounsaturated—the kind that gives olive oil its good name! Margarine, on the other hand, is a man-made, manufactured fat. Even the new "designer" spreads aren't all they're cracked up to be. They may claim to have "no trans fats," but take a closer look at the ingredients list and you might see "partially hydrogenated soybean oil," which cannot be manufactured without creating trans fatty acids. How can they get away with that? Well, the claim takes advantage of health-industry regulations that allow rounding to zero a trans-fat value below 0.5 grams per serving. Sneaky! Plus, many of these spreads are made with highly processed, often-rancid vegetable or soybean oils to begin with, along with a host of additives. How do they make those oils spreadable, anyway? By what process? By what chemical means? Butter, on the other hand, is yellow because of the natural pigment carotene, which is also why butter is a source of vitamin A. Enough said. We trust cows over scientists any old day!

Life in the Fast Loin

Skillet pork loin chops drizzled with apricot-mustard sauce

Suppertime rush hour got you frazzled? Here's the ticket: A speedy and simple stovetop pork chop recipe that'll shift your family's appetite into high gear.

Sauce

⅓ cup	water
½ cup	no-sugar-added apricot preserves
2 tbsp	each balsamic vinegar and Dijon mustard
¾ tsp	ground ginger
¼ tsp	each salt and freshly ground black pepper

4	boneless pork loin chops (about 5 oz/142 g each)
¼ tsp	salt and freshly ground black pepper
1 tbsp	olive oil

- Whisk together all sauce ingredients in a medium bowl and set aside.

- Sprinkle both sides of pork chops with salt and pepper and let stand for a few minutes. Heat olive oil in a 10-inch, non-stick skillet over medium heat. Add pork chops and cook for about 6 minutes per side, until nicely browned on the outside and just slightly pink in the center. Cover skillet with lid if they're splattering.

- Remove pork chops from skillet, cover with foil and keep warm. Pour sauce ingredients into same skillet. Using a whisk, cook and stir sauce for about 5 minutes, or until it thickens. Make sure you scrape up any brown bits on the bottom of the skillet for added flavor. Serve pork chops drizzled with hot apricot-mustard sauce.

MAKES 4 SERVINGS

PER SERVING
267 calories, 9.9 g total fat (2.7 g saturated fat), 30 g protein, 13 g carbohydrate, 0.3 g fiber, 89 mg cholesterol, 260 mg sodium

Waste/Waist Management, Inc.

Got high cholesterol? How 'bout constipation? Both? Actually, that's not surprising. High cholesterol and constipation often go hand in hand. Think of your body as a magnificently engineered waste-management facility. Normally, nasty LDL cholesterol, harmful fats and other debris are swooshed quickly out of your body via the colon. But if you become constipated as a result of eating too much junk food, the sludge just kind of sits there. And sits there. After a while, some of the toxic guck (including bad cholesterol) gets reabsorbed through the lining of your intestine and ends up back in the bloodstream where it started. Yikes! Avoiding a backlog is as easy as one, two, three: First, get yourself the best "Colon Hoover" money can buy—otherwise known as soluble fiber. That's the kind found in oat bran, beans, flaxseed, fruit (especially apples and pears) and veggies. Second, get your bowels moving by getting your butt moving. Literally! Exercise is like a kick in the pants to your intestinal tract and can be your bowel's best buddy. The more regularly you exercise, the more regular you'll become. Finally, don't treat your body like a dump. For successful waste (and waist) management, stop eating so much garbage!

My friend got some vinegar in his ear and now he suffers from pickled hearing :)

FOOD BITE

Who needs Viagra? In the West African country of Senegal, women weave belts of gingerroot to restore their mates' sexual potency.

STEWpendous Beef

Slow-simmered, scrumptious beef stew with chunks of colorful vegetables and French herbs

*Quit stewing and get stewing! From our TV show, **Eat, Shrink & Be Merry!**, comes this delectable beef stew that'll have your family racing to the dinner table.*

2 lbs	(907 g) stewing beef (cut into 1- to 1½-inch cubes)
½ tsp	seasoned salt
2 tbsp	olive oil
1½ cups	coarsely chopped onions
1 cup	chopped celery
2 tsp	minced garlic
2 tsp	Herbes de Provence (see tip, p. 142)
2½ cups	reduced-sodium beef broth
2 tbsp	tomato paste
2 tbsp	balsamic vinegar
2	bay leaves
1 tsp	granulated sugar
½ tsp	each salt and freshly ground black pepper
1	large thin-skinned potato (such as Yukon Gold), unpeeled, cut into ¾-inch pieces
1	large carrot, chopped
1	small sweet potato, peeled, cut into ¾-inch pieces
2 tbsp	cornstarch
¾ cup	frozen green peas
2 tbsp	minced fresh parsley

- Pat beef dry with paper towels. Sprinkle beef lightly all over with seasoned salt. Heat 1 tbsp olive oil in a large pot (preferably non-stick) over medium-high heat. Add half the beef cubes and cook, turning occasionally, until all sides are lightly browned. Remove from pot and keep warm. Repeat with remaining 1 tbsp olive oil and beef cubes. Set browned beef aside.

- Add onions, celery and garlic to same pot (you may add a bit more olive oil or ¼ cup beef broth to pot if necessary to prevent sticking). Reduce heat to medium. Cook and stir until vegetables begin to soften, about 5 minutes. Return beef cubes to pot and stir in Herbes de Provence. Add beef broth, tomato paste, vinegar, bay leaves, sugar, salt and pepper. Bring to a boil. Reduce heat to low, cover and simmer for 1 hour and 15 minutes. (Make sure it's a low simmer and that mixture is not boiling or it will burn.)

- Stir in white potatoes and carrots. Cover and simmer for 25 more minutes. Stir in sweet potatoes and simmer for 20 to 25 more minutes, until vegetables are tender. Mix cornstarch with 2 tbsp water until smooth. Add to stew. Mix well and continue to cook until stew is bubbly and has thickened. Stir in peas and parsley and cook just until peas are heated through, about 2 minutes.

MAKES 6 SERVINGS

PER SERVING
399 calories,
12.6 g total fat
(3.9 g saturated fat),
39 g protein,
31 g carbohydrate,
4.4 g fiber,
91 mg cholesterol,
699 mg sodium

> When love and skill work together, expect a masterpiece.
> *John Ruskin*

Stick to Your Ribs

Pork tenderloin "ribs" with zesty, lemon-rosemary barbecue sauce

Avoiding fatty ribs since they go directly from your lips to your hips? Our boneless version, made with lean pork tenderloin, will satisfy your rib-meat craving without weighing you down!

Spice Rub

1 tbsp	brown sugar
1½ tsp	paprika
1 tsp	chili powder
½ tsp	ground cumin
½ tsp	seasoned salt
¼ tsp	freshly ground black pepper
¼ tsp	garlic powder
¼ tsp	onion powder
⅛ tsp	cayenne pepper
2	large pork tenderloins (about 1¼ lbs/568 g each)

Barbecue Sauce

1 tbsp	butter
2 tbsp	finely minced onions
1 tsp	minced garlic
½ cup	ketchup
⅓ cup	hickory-flavored barbecue sauce
2 tbsp	freshly squeezed lemon juice
2 tbsp	molasses
1¼ tsp	chili powder
1 tsp	grated lemon zest
½ tsp	each ground cumin and paprika
½ tsp	dried rosemary
¼ tsp	freshly ground black pepper

- Mix all spice rub ingredients together in a small bowl. Set aside.

- Using a meat mallet, pound the pork uniformly into about ¾-inch thickness. Using a sharp knife, score the pork in 1-inch intervals so that it looks like ribs. Cut about halfway into the meat, not all the way through. Use about 1½ tbsp spice rub per slab of "ribs" and rub into both sides of meat and into score marks. Cover with plastic wrap and refrigerate overnight for best flavor.

- To make sauce, melt butter in a small pot over medium heat. Add onions and garlic. Cook and stir until onions have softened, about 1 minute. Add all remaining sauce ingredients. Mix well. Simmer, uncovered, over low heat for about 5 minutes, stirring occasionally. Remove from heat and let cool. Sauce will thicken slightly as it cools.

- Preheat grill to high setting. Place pork on a grill rack that has been lightly brushed with oil. Grill pork for about 10 minutes, turning occasionally and basting often with barbecue sauce. Grill marks are mandatory! Be sure not to overcook the pork, as it will be dry. It's OK for pork to be a little pink in the middle. Remove pork from grill and let rest for 1 minute, then cut along score marks into individual "ribs." Serve hot.

MAKES 5 SERVINGS

PER SERVING

393 calories, 10.5 g total fat (4.2 g saturated fat), 49 g protein, 24 g carbohydrate, 1.2 g fiber, 154 mg cholesterol, 708 mg sodium

Dressed to Grill Pork Chops

Chili-and-garlic-marinated grilled pork loin chops

And grill you will! When you fire up the barbecue for savory pork chops with a drop-dead delicious marinade, all the neighbors will be talkin'. Prepare for the grill of a lifetime!

6	pork loin chops, trimmed of fat (about 5 oz/142 g each)
1 cup	reduced-sodium V8 juice
2 tbsp	brown sugar
1½ tbsp	Worcestershire sauce
1 tbsp	minced garlic
1½ tsp	each chili powder and ground cumin
¾ tsp	dried oregano
½ tsp	freshly ground black pepper

- Arrange pork chops in single layer in shallow pan. Combine remaining ingredients and pour over pork chops. Turn pork chops to coat both sides with marinade. Cover and marinate in refrigerator for at least 8 hours or overnight.

- Preheat grill to medium-high setting. Lightly brush grill rack with oil. Grill pork chops for about 6 to 7 minutes per side, basting with any leftover marinade.

MAKES 6 SERVINGS

PER SERVING
219 calories, 6.9 g total fat (2.2 g saturated fat), 31 g protein, 8 g carbohydrate, 0.9 g fiber, 89 mg cholesterol, 146 mg sodium

Nutrition Nugget

Cumin get it! Historically, cumin has been used to aid digestion and, more recently, it's emerged as a powerful anticarcinogen. By boosting the liver's ability to detoxify enzymes, cumin helps decrease the incidence of colon, stomach and liver cancers. Just half a teaspoon of these tiny seeds carries more than double the antioxidants found in half a cup of chopped tomatoes!

The Shape of Our Future

An apple a day keeps the doctor away, but if you've got an apple-shaped core, you might want a cardiologist on speed dial. Tons of studies show that abdominal fat isn't just a cosmetic issue—it's far more dangerous than lower-body fat, putting you at risk for heart disease and other health complications. In fact, a groundbreaking 12-year study (Iowa Women's Health Study) found that women with the thickest waist circumferences were more likely to die early. And a Harvard study showed that allowing your belt size to increase by just five inches during adulthood can double your risk of diabetes. Yikes! How 'bout them apples! Belly fat is dangerous because it sits close to critical organs like the heart and liver, and that abdominal fat may also be metabolized differently than other types of fat, contributing to higher cholesterol, blood fats and blood pressure. Those conditions, in combination with an apple shape, are often a sign of insulin resistance, a precursor to diabetes also referred to as Syndrome X or Metabolic Syndrome. Basically, when you're insulin resistant, your pancreas is fed up with your poor eating. To figure out if your figure is putting your health in jeopardy, get out a tape measure (and don't suck in your gut!). A waist size of more than 35 inches for women or 40 inches for men is a serious signal to tighten your belt by shaping up and slimming down. Given all the health risks surrounding belly fat, don't diddle when trimming your middle!

Once Upon a Thai

Roasted pork tenderloin in a sizzling-hot, Thai-inspired marinade

Our spicy Thai pork tenderloin is a must-try recipe for those who enjoy fiery tales.
Your taste buds will live happily ever after!

Marinade

⅓ cup	molasses
¼ cup	reduced-sodium soy sauce
1 tbsp	freshly squeezed lemon juice
1 tbsp	grated gingerroot
2 tsp	minced garlic
2 tsp	Thai red curry paste (see tip)
1 tsp	grated lemon zest
1 tsp	sesame oil
¼ tsp	ground coriander

2 lbs	(907 g) pork tenderloin (2 large pieces)

MAKES 6 SERVINGS

PER SERVING
219 calories,
5.6 g total fat (1.8 g saturated fat), 32 g protein, 8 g carbohydrate,
0 g fiber, 98 mg cholesterol, 322 mg sodium

- Whisk together all marinade ingredients in a medium bowl. Place pork in a large, heavy-duty, resealable plastic bag. Add marinade and seal bag. Turn bag several times to coat pork with marinade. Marinate in refrigerator for at least 2 hours.

- Remove pork from marinade (discard marinade). Place pork on a baking sheet that has been lined with foil. Roast at 400°F for about 25 minutes. Pork should still be slightly pink in the middle. Let pork rest for 5 minutes before slicing. Slice into ½-inch-thick medallions. Tastes great served with jasmine rice (see recipe on p. 252) and steamed broccoli.

Recipe Tip Thai red curry paste is an aromatic, concentrated blend of hot red chilies and Thai seasonings. Look for it in a small jar in the Asian food aisle of your grocery store. Two brands we like are "A Taste of Thai" and "Thai Kitchen."

Nutrition Nugget

Unlike refined white sugar and corn syrup, which are stripped of virtually all nutrients except simple carbohydrates, blackstrap molasses is a sweetener that's actually good for you! It has a variety of minerals, but it's most famous as a storehouse of iron. In comparison to red meat, another well-known source of iron, blackstrap molasses gives you more iron for fewer calories and it's totally fat-free! Oh, and for those who think a milk mustache is all the rage, a blackstrap molasses mustache may soon be a trend that really sticks. Two tablespoons of the gooey stuff contains as much calcium as a glass of milk! Got molasses?

C'mon Baby, do the Locomotion!

If you love to boogie, you're making great strides toward a longer, healthier life. That's because dancing is a far-out fat burner, a magnificent muscle toner and a hip-hop heart helper. Vigorous dancing burns upwards of 400 calories an hour and elevates your heart rate as much as running or cross-country skiing. Even moderate ballroom dancing burns about 250 calories an hour. Maybe that's why folks all over the map are dancing to their heart's content. There's the waltz in Tennessee, the polka in Pennsylvania, the last tango in Paris and the cha-cha in Chattanooga. Um, excuse the jive talking...that's choo-choo! Even square dancing qualifies as a top-notch aerobic activity. In fact, it's been estimated that square dancers often travel as far as three miles a night. (You'd think they could find a closer hall.) Swing yer partner round and round, get your heart rate up and your fat way down!

Stir Crazy

Orange-ginger pork stir-fry with broccoli and peppers

Our insanely delicious pork and ginger stir-fry will make your taste buds go gaga! The flavor's so irresistible, it's sure to cause a stir.

½ cup	reduced-sodium chicken broth
¼ cup	hoisin sauce
¼ cup	orange marmalade
1 tbsp	seasoned rice vinegar (see tip)
1 tbsp	cornstarch
1 tsp	each sesame oil and grated gingerroot
1 tsp	minced garlic
¼ tsp	Chinese five-spice powder or garam masala
1 lb	(454 g) pork tenderloin
2 tsp	olive oil
3 cups	broccoli florets
1 cup	each sliced red and yellow bell peppers
4 cups	hot cooked brown rice or quinoa

MAKES 4 SERVINGS

PER SERVING (WITH RICE)
513 calories, 10 g total fat (2.5 g saturated fat),
32 g protein, 75 g carbohydrate, 6 g fiber,
74 mg cholesterol, 411 mg sodium

- In a medium bowl, whisk together chicken broth, hoisin sauce, marmalade, vinegar, cornstarch, sesame oil, gingerroot, garlic and five-spice powder. Set aside.

- Trim any visible fat from pork. Cut pork into cubes or strips.

- Heat oil in a large, non-stick wok or skillet. Add pork. Cook and stir over high heat until no longer pink. Add broccoli and peppers. Reduce heat to medium-high. Cook for 3 more minutes. Add sauce and cook until sauce is bubbly and has thickened. Serve pork and vegetables over hot rice or quinoa.

Recipe Tip: Rice vinegar is a mild and slightly sweet vinegar made from fermented rice. Used widely in Japanese and Chinese cooking, you can buy it in both seasoned and unseasoned varieties. Seasoned rice vinegar has added salt and sugar. With the popularity of Asian cooking, you should have no trouble finding rice vinegar next to the regular vinegars at your grocery store.

If they like it, it serves four; otherwise, six.

Elsie Zussman

The Roast of Christmas Past

Classic pot roast with vegetables cooked in a savory cranberry sauce

If it's a scrumptious pot roast you want to be goblin, here's a down-home dinner that'll leave you in good spirits.

2 tsp	olive oil
1	boneless top sirloin roast (4 lbs/1.8 kg)
½ tsp	salt
1 can	(10 oz/284 mL) reduced-sodium beef broth, undiluted
½ cup	cranberry sauce with whole cranberries
½ cup	ketchup
1 pkg	(1 oz/28 g) dry onion soup mix
2 tsp	minced garlic
1 tsp	dry mustard
½ tsp	each dried marjoram and dried thyme
¼ tsp	freshly ground black pepper
8	medium potatoes, unpeeled, halved
4	large carrots, cut into quarters

- Heat oil in a large, non-stick skillet over medium-high heat. Sprinkle roast all over with salt. Add to skillet and brown roast on all sides. Transfer meat to a large roasting pan.

- In a medium bowl, whisk together broth, cranberry sauce, ketchup, onion soup mix, garlic, dry mustard, marjoram, thyme and black pepper. Pour sauce over roast. Cover and roast at 350°F for 2 hours, basting occasionally with sauce.

- Add potatoes and carrots to roasting pan. Spoon sauce over vegetables. Cover and roast for 1 more hour.

- Slice roast thinly and serve it on a platter surrounded by the vegetables. Skim off as much fat as possible from sauce in pan. Serve sauce on the side.

FOOD BITE Why are cranberries called bounceberries? Though the origin of this term is lost to legend, here's the part of the story most agree upon: John Webb, a 19th-century New Jersey farmer who had lost one of his legs, was unable to lug all of his berries down the hayloft where he stored them. Instead, he decided to pour them down the stairs, and discovered that the mushy, overripe berries would stick to the stairs, but the perfectly ripe, plump berries would bounce down to the floor below. To this day, leading cranberry producers like Ocean Spray separate their berries by bouncing them over a four-inch barrier.

MAKES
8 SERVINGS

PER SERVING
512 calories,
12.5 g total fat
(4.2 g saturated fat),
60 g protein,
38 g carbohydrate,
3.9 g fiber,
172 mg cholesterol,
674 mg sodium

Mad Over Cow Products

"I'm on a high-protein diet. Can I eat red meat 'til the cows come home?" Only if you want to mooove a kidney stone and have udderly bad breath! While animal protein is fine in moderation, science has proven that excess saturated fat can spell disaster for your overall health. Beef it up morning, noon and night, and there's not much room left for fiber and nutrient-packed plant foods. That paves the way for chronic constipation, headaches, bad breath and hair loss, some of the common side effects experienced by high-protein dieters. Eating too much meat can make your body very acidic, too. That can lead to fatigue, bone loss, kidney and liver damage, and it's also the environment in which disease—especially cancer—thrives. Our bodies operate best when we eat alkaline foods, such as fruits and veggies, more often. Sure, including some protein with each meal is a good idea since it keeps our blood sugar in check and helps us build muscle and lose weight, but that doesn't mean we should pile our plates sky-high with slabs of ribs and mountains of steak. We run into trouble when we take things too far, a common occurrence with high-protein dieters. If you eat red meat often, be doubly sure to pair it with proven cancer-fighting vegetables. Forget meat and potatoes—go for meat and garlic, meat and onions, meat and broccoli. Meat and just about anything green will do the trick. Most importantly, think smaller portions. Don't have a *whole* cow, man!

Beijing Beauty
Asian-glazed, grilled pork tenderloin

This sensational, grilled pork tenderloin is a beauty and a feast, not difficult in the least. Just baste and repeat 'til it's ready to eat!

MAKES 6 SERVINGS

PER SERVING
267 calories,
8.7 g total fat
(2.4 g saturated fat),
37 g protein,
9 g carbohydrate,
0.5 g fiber,
111 mg cholesterol,
362 mg sodium

Glaze

¼ cup   hoisin sauce
2 tbsp   freshly squeezed lemon juice
1 tbsp   each Dijon mustard and liquid honey
1 tbsp   each sesame oil and reduced-sodium soy sauce
1 tbsp   grated gingerroot
2 tsp   minced garlic
2 tsp   grated lemon zest

3   pork tenderloins (12 oz/340 g each)

- To make glaze, combine all glaze ingredients in a small bowl and mix well. Set aside.

- Preheat grill to medium-high setting. Brush grill rack lightly with oil. Grill pork for about 15 minutes, turning occasionally. Pork should be just slightly pink in the center. Do not overcook pork or it will be dry.

- Brush pork generously with glaze during last 5 minutes of cooking time. Baste, baste, baste! The more you baste, the better the taste!

- Place pork on a cutting board, cover loosely with foil and let rest for 5 minutes. Cut pork into thin slices and serve.

Trivial Tidbit

A little hot under the collar? Better hold your temper or you might end up holding a temperature! Research at The Institute of HeartMath showed that one five-minute episode of anger is so stressful it impairs the body's immune system for more than six hours, making it susceptible to colds, flu and other ailments.

I get distracted by all the meats in the deli section because of my short attention SPAM :)

In this chapter...

Ground Keepers

These scrumptious, family-pleasing, ground meat recipes are real keepers!

Glad Thai Dings, p. 249

Hawowii Meatballs

Grilled meatball and pineapple kebobs with sesame-ginger barbecue sauce

Zowie! When you taste these meatballs, you'll scream "Wowie!"
If you liked our Wowie Maui Chicken recipe in **Looneyspoons***,*
you'll love the similar flavor of these grilled meatball and
pineapple kebobs.

⅓ cup	your favorite barbecue sauce
5 tsp	reduced-sodium soy sauce
1 tbsp	grated gingerroot
2 tsp	liquid honey
1 tsp	sesame oil
32	precooked lean meatballs (see tip)
32	1-inch chunks fresh pineapple
16	1-inch chunks red bell pepper
16	1-inch chunks green bell pepper
8	12-inch metal skewers

MAKES 8 SERVINGS

PER SERVING (1 SKEWER)
178 calories, 6.3 g total fat (3.1 g saturated fat), 11 g protein,
20 g carbohydrate, 2.6 g fiber, 27 mg cholesterol, 556 mg sodium

Recipe Tip: If you're not a fan of bell peppers, just omit them. Increase the number of meatballs and pineapple chunks to 40 each, so you'll be threading 5 meatballs and 5 pieces pineapple on each skewer. Red onions would make a colorful addition to these skewers!

- To make sauce, whisk together barbecue sauce, soy sauce, gingerroot, honey and sesame oil in a small bowl. Set aside.

- Preheat grill to medium-high setting. For each skewer, thread meatballs, pineapple, red pepper and green pepper in this order: 1 meatball, 1 piece pineapple, 1 piece red pepper, 1 meatball, 1 piece pineapple, 1 piece green pepper, then repeat, so that each skewer contains 4 meatballs, 4 pieces pineapple, 2 pieces red pepper and 2 pieces green pepper.

- Brush grill rack lightly with oil. Grill skewers for 12 to 15 minutes, turning and basting generously with sauce every 2 minutes. Serve hot!

Recipe Tips If you have the time, prepare the meatballs on p. 249 up to Step 3. Let them cool before using them for this recipe. Or, make them a day in advance and keep them covered in the refrigerator until you're ready to assemble the kebobs. Alternatively, buy frozen, precooked, lean meatballs (beef, chicken or turkey)—preferably *not* Italian meatballs, since their flavor would be an odd match for our yummy sesame-ginger sauce. Make sure you thaw the frozen meatballs before threading them onto the skewers.

Crock-a-Doodle-Do Beef and Sausage Chili

Slow-cooked, hearty chili with beef, sausage and two types of beans

Wake up your taste buds with this super-satisfying, hungry-man chili. It makes great leftovers, too!

MAKES 8 SERVINGS

PER SERVING
297 calories,
8.8 g total fat
(3.3 g saturated fat),
30 g protein,
23 g carbohydrate,
7.5 g fiber,
77 mg cholesterol,
514 mg sodium

8 oz	(227 g) light Italian sausage
1½ lbs	(680 g) extra-lean ground beef
1 cup	chopped onions
2 tsp	minced garlic
1 can	(19 oz/540 mL) no-salt-added diced tomatoes, undrained
1 can	(19 oz/540 mL) no-salt-added red kidney beans, drained and rinsed
1 can	(19 oz/540 mL) no-salt-added navy beans or black beans, drained and rinsed
1 can	(10 oz/284 mL) reduced-sodium beef broth, undiluted
1 can	(5.5 oz/156 mL) tomato paste
1½ cups	chopped celery
1 cup	medium salsa
1½ tbsp	chili powder
2 tsp	dried Italian seasoning
1½ tsp	ground cumin
2 tbsp	minced fresh cilantro or parsley (optional)

- Remove casing from sausage and break into small pieces in a large, non-stick skillet. Add ground beef, onions and garlic. Cook and stir over medium-high heat until meat is no longer pink, about 5 minutes. Drain liquid/fat from skillet and transfer meat mixture to a slow cooker.

- Add all remaining ingredients, except cilantro, to slow cooker. Mix well. Cover and cook on low heat setting for about 5 hours. Stir in cilantro just before serving, if desired. (Note: Exact cooking time depends on the size of your slow cooker. The larger the slow cooker, the less time it takes to cook the chili.)

Recipe Tip: Freeze your leftovers in individual serving containers so you'll always have a convenient, healthy lunch or supper on days when you don't feel like cooking!

With everything you read about spray cans and the ozone layer, it's enough to scareosol to death :)

Crying Over Spilt Milk

Think milk is the only food that gives your bones a boost? Well moooove over, Elsie! Though onions may bring a tear to your eye, it seems they might also bring you stronger, healthier bones. The super-brainy folks over at the *Journal of Agricultural and Food Chemistry* have apparently identified a compound in onions that inhibits the activity of osteoclasts. That's science speak for "cells that break down bone." When animals in the study were given this onion compound, bone breakdown was inhibited. For crying out loud! This is great news for women who are at risk for osteoporosis as they go through menopause! Fosamax, the drug typically prescribed to prevent excessive bone loss, works in a similar manner (by destroying the osteoclasts so they don't break down bone). Potential negative side effects of Fosamax include irritation of the stomach lining, acid regurgitation, esophageal ulcers and erosions. Potential negative side effects of eating onions: onion breath! By the way, bone-building isn't the only reason onions have ap*peel*. Their sulfur compounds are potent liver detoxifiers and they contain loads of age-defying antioxidants, too. Plenty of reasons to cry for joy!

Nutrition Nugget

For such a humble vegetable, celery is surprisingly nutritious! Because of its antioxidant content, including vitamin C, it's a great protector against free radicals that can cause us to look older than our years. Truth is, celery is excellent "skin food" since it contains compounds that strengthen our connective tissue. Sure seems like reason to *celerb*rate!

Taco of the Town

Warm, spicy ground chicken, peppers and onions wrapped in a soft flour tortilla

We heard it through the grapevine: These tacos are di-vine. Rumor has it they're a real family-pleasing treat.

1½ lbs	(680 g) ground chicken
1 cup	diced onions
¾ cup	diced green bell pepper
1 tsp	minced garlic
2 cups	seeded and diced tomatoes, divided
½ cup	grated carrots
¼ cup	ketchup
1 tbsp	each chili powder and red wine vinegar
2 tsp	brown sugar
1 tsp	ground cumin
⅛ tsp	freshly ground black pepper
8	7-inch whole-grain flour tortillas
8	lettuce leaves
1 cup	packed shredded light old (sharp) cheddar cheese (4 oz/113 g)
½ cup	light (5%) sour cream

MAKES 8 TACOS

PER TACO
288 calories, 6.3 g total fat
(2.3 g saturated fat),
30 g protein,
29 g carbohydrate, 2.8 g fiber,
52 mg cholesterol, 390 mg sodium

Recipe Tip: Forgo the salt-laden, store-bought pouches of taco seasoning and make your own! Combine 4 tsp chili powder, 1½ tsp ground cumin, 1 tsp paprika, 1 tsp granulated sugar, ½ tsp seasoned salt, ½ tsp black pepper, ½ tsp garlic powder, ½ tsp ground coriander and ¼ tsp onion powder in a small bowl. You can double or triple this recipe and store it in an airtight container for months.

FOOD BITE Before starring on *Bonanza* and *Little House on the Prairie*, Michael Landon was a machine operator, sealing hot cans of Campbell's Tomato Soup for a living. He traded tin for Tinseltown in a mmm mmm good career move!

- Add chicken, onions, green pepper and garlic to a large, non-stick skillet. Cook and stir over medium-high heat until chicken is no longer pink, about 7 to 8 minutes. Drain off any liquid.

- Add 1 cup tomatoes, carrots, ketchup, chili powder, vinegar, brown sugar, cumin and pepper to chicken. Reduce heat to medium-low. Cover and simmer for 10 minutes, stirring occasionally. If mixture is too saucy, simmer uncovered for a few more minutes, until most of the liquid has evaporated. Remove from heat.

- To assemble tacos, place one lettuce leaf in center of a tortilla. Spoon ⅛ chicken mixture over top. Sprinkle some of the cheese and some of the remaining tomatoes over chicken, followed by a dollop of sour cream. Roll up bottom of tortilla to cover filling, then fold in sides. Serve immediately. A little messy, but worth it!

Hang Your Whites Out to Dry

If you're trying to lose fat, then plan for a whiteout! Despite their saintly color, sugar and flour can be dietary devils that encourage overeating and weight gain. These highly processed foods cause a quick rise in blood sugar, followed by a rise in blood insulin levels. Insulin is a hormone that can lead to weight gain, either by making the body store fat or by lowering blood-sugar levels so much that it causes intense hunger later on. The result: "I want a Hostess Ding Dong and I want it NOW!" Plus, sugar and white flour provide only "empty" calories, and usually lots of them. Now, we're not looney enough to suggest you never eat cake again. Heaven knows, we love our desserts! Moderation is the key. But if you're really serious about losing flab, you can jump-start your fat loss by avoiding ALL sweets and white flour for two weeks. Instead, choose whole, unprocessed, nutritious foods, including veggies, beans, quinoa, nuts, seeds and lean sources of protein like fish, chicken, turkey and eggs. You should see quick results, especially around your midsection. You know what they say: We all have a washboard stomach. Some of us just have a little extra laundry on top!

All You Need is Loaf

Easy weekday meat loaf with barbecue sauce

Loaf, loaf, loaf. Tired of the same ol' song and dance for dinner Eight Days a Week? Don't worry, We Can Work it Out. Here's some Help!: A recipe you just can't Beatle— especially after A Hard Day's Night. Sure to Please Please everyone.

1½ lbs	(680 g) extra-lean ground beef or ground sirloin
½ cup	dry unseasoned bread crumbs
½ cup	your favorite barbecue sauce, divided
¼ cup	minced fresh parsley
⅓ cup	minced onions
2 tbsp	freshly grated Parmesan cheese
1	egg
1 tsp	minced garlic
½ tsp	dried basil, thyme or oregano
½ tsp	each salt and freshly ground black pepper

MAKES 8 SERVINGS

PER SERVING
187 calories,
8.3 g total fat
(4.3 g saturated fat),
18 g protein,
10 g carbohydrate,
0.6 g fiber,
80 mg cholesterol,
503 mg sodium

- Preheat oven to 350°F. Spray a broiler pan with cooking spray and set aside.

- Combine beef, bread crumbs, ¼ cup barbecue sauce, parsley, onion, Parmesan cheese, egg, garlic, basil, salt and pepper in a large bowl. Mix well using your hands. Shape mixture into an oblong loaf, about 8 x 5 inches in size, and place directly on rack of broiler pan. Spread remaining barbecue sauce all over meat loaf.

- Bake for 50 minutes to 1 hour, or until meat loaf is nicely browned and meat is cooked through. Let stand 5 minutes before slicing.

Recipe Tips: To make individual, mini loaves, divide meat mixture among 6 mini loaf pans and bake for 30 minutes. Try sneaking some vegetables into the loaf—your kids will never notice! Add ½ cup each grated carrots and grated zucchini. By the way, cooking the meat loaf on a broiler pan instead of in a loaf pan is a smart idea because the fatty juices will drip away as the meat cooks.

> Tell me what you eat,
> I'll tell you who you are.
> *Jean Anthelme Brillat-Savarin*

Burger, She Wrote

Teriyaki-seasoned beef or chicken burgers for the barbecue

It's an unsolved mystery: How could burgers that taste this great also be low in fat?
All clues point to the same suspect: Teri Yaki. Throw the cookbook at her!

1½ lbs	(680 g) extra-lean ground beef, chicken or turkey
⅓ cup	dry unseasoned bread crumbs
⅓ cup	minced green onions
1	egg
¼ cup	ketchup
2 tbsp	reduced-sodium soy sauce
1 tbsp	brown sugar
1½ tsp	grated gingerroot
1 tsp	minced garlic
½ tsp	sesame oil
6	whole-grain hamburger buns

Lettuce, sliced tomatoes and your favorite
burger toppings (optional)

MAKES 6 BURGERS

PER BURGER
353 calories, 12 g total fat (4.4 g saturated fat), 34 g protein,
27 g carbohydrate, 1.9 g fiber, 108 mg cholesterol, 521 mg sodium

*Practice safe eating—
always use condiments :)*

- In a large bowl, combine beef, bread crumbs, onions and egg. Mix well (using your hands works best).

- In a small bowl, combine ketchup, soy sauce, brown sugar, gingerroot, garlic and sesame oil. Add 3 tbsp of this mixture to ground meat and mix well. Reserve remaining sauce to brush on burgers while grilling.

- Shape meat mixture into 6 patties. Preheat grill to medium-high setting. Brush grill rack lightly with oil. Grill burgers for about 5 to 6 minutes per side, or until center is no longer pink. Baste with reserved sauce during last 2 minutes of cooking time.

- Serve on hamburger buns with your favorite toppings.

The Better Burger Bureau

Let's be frank about burgers. We all love them! But there's a way to enjoy burgers—great taste and all—without becoming fatty like the patty. Try homemade more often, so you can use extra-lean ground beef and avoid the evil trans fats lurking in some fried fast-food burgers. Many burger joints add insult to injury by nuking their patties, making their junk food even junkier. Microwaving protein denatures or corrupts the protein molecules, making them difficult for your body to handle. Why bother when it's so easy to create a juicy, scrumptious, healthy masterpiece of your own? Now, if you do order out, at least pile on lots of fresh veggie fixin's and skip the fatty mayo, bacon, cheese and "special" sauces. You won't think they're so special when they end up on your rump later! Salsa is a flavorful burger topper. Give it a try. And yes, Annie, get your bun, but choose the whole-grain variety instead of the plain, gluey, white kind. (Many restaurants are now offering whole wheat buns.) Not only do they taste better, but they're also a good source of fiber (your weight-loss ally) and you'll get more magnesium, zinc and B vitamins than if you choose the lowly, nutrient-poor, albino kind. Follow these suggestions and you won't set off a *burger* alarm!

Pie Caramba!

Mexican pizza with seasoned ground beef, black beans, tomatoes and corn

Ai, ai, ai! It's a zesty pizza pie! If you want to experience the joy of Mex, say "si" to this uniquely topped pizza that's bursting with fabulous southwestern flavor. It's hot, hot, hot!

Taco 'bout delicious!

8 oz	(227 g) extra-lean ground beef
⅓ cup	minced red onions
1 tsp	minced garlic
½ cup	diced grape tomatoes
¼ cup	each grated carrots and diced green bell pepper
¼ cup	frozen or canned corn
¼ cup	canned no-salt-added black beans, drained and rinsed
1 tbsp	minced fresh cilantro
1 tsp	chili powder
½ tsp	ground cumin
¼ tsp	each salt and freshly ground black pepper
½ cup	pizza sauce
1	12-inch prebaked whole-grain thin-crust pizza shell
1 cup	packed shredded light old (sharp) cheddar cheese (4 oz/113 g)
2 tbsp	minced green onions

Garnishes: Light sour cream, salsa and guacamole (optional)

MAKES 1 PIZZA, 8 SLICES

PER SLICE
186 calories, 6.8 g total fat (3.4 g saturated fat),
12 g protein, 18 g carbohydrate, 1.9 g fiber,
28 mg cholesterol, 455 mg sodium

- Preheat oven to 425°F.

- Cook beef, onions and garlic in a large, non-stick skillet until beef is no longer pink. Add tomatoes, carrots, green pepper, corn and beans. Cook and stir for 2 more minutes. Add cilantro, chili powder, cumin, salt and pepper. Cook 1 more minute. Remove from heat.

- Spread pizza sauce evenly over crust. Top with half the cheese. Spoon beef mixture evenly over pizza. Top with remaining cheese, followed by green onions.

- Place pizza directly on middle oven rack and bake for 8 to 10 minutes, or until cheese is completely melted and crust is lightly browned.

- Tastes great with fajita-like accompaniments, such as sour cream, salsa and guacamole.

FOOD BITE The world's largest circular pizza was built on Dec. 8, 1990, at Norwood Hypermarket, just outside of Johannesburg, South Africa. It measured more than 122 feet in diameter (12,159 square feet) and weighed in at 26,883 pounds. The gigantic pizza contained 9,920 pounds of flour, 3,968 pounds of cheese and 1,984 pounds of sauce. Mamma Mia!

Unrolled Cabbage Rolls
Layered cabbage-roll casserole

This recipe was transported across the Atlantic in the late 1940s by our mother, Alfreda, who felt North America deserved a taste of authentic Polish cuisine. Finally, a recipe that unravels the mystery behind creating ultra-flavorful cabbage rolls without a lot of fuss. (Actually, we've unrolled them to make it even easier!)

2 tsp	olive oil
1 cup	chopped onions
1 tsp	minced garlic
1½ cups	reduced-sodium beef or chicken broth
¾ cup	uncooked brown rice (see tip)
1	medium head cabbage (about 3 to 4 lbs/1.4 to 1.8 kg)
1½ lbs	(680 g) extra-lean ground beef, chicken or turkey
1	egg
¼ cup	minced fresh parsley
1 tsp	dried marjoram
½ tsp	each salt and freshly ground black pepper
2 cans	(10 oz/284 mL each) reduced-sodium condensed tomato soup, undiluted

MAKES 8 SERVINGS
PER SERVING
314 calories, 9.4 g total fat (3.1 g saturated fat), 24 g protein, 35 g carbohydrate, 5.8 g fiber, 78 mg cholesterol, 469 mg sodium

- Heat olive oil in a medium pot over medium heat. Add onions and garlic. Cook and stir for about 3 minutes, until onions begin to soften. Add broth and rice. Bring to a boil. Reduce heat to medium-low. Cover and cook for 20 to 25 minutes, until rice is tender and liquid has been absorbed. Remove from heat.

- Meanwhile, bring a large pot of water to a boil. Cut cabbage into 8 wedges. Boil cabbage wedges for 5 minutes. Drain. Remove tough inner pieces. Separate individual leaves and set aside.

- In a large bowl, combine cooked rice with beef, egg, parsley, marjoram, salt and pepper. Mix well.

- Spray a 9 x 13-inch baking pan with cooking spray. Line bottom with ½ the cabbage leaves. Spread beef-rice mixture evenly over cabbage. Top with remaining cabbage leaves.

- Empty both cans of soup into a medium bowl. Add 1 can water and mix well. Pour soup evenly over cabbage. Cover and bake for 1 hour at 350°F. Reduce heat to 325°F and cook for another 45 minutes. Let cool for 5 minutes before serving.

Recipe Tips
Make sure your brown rice is the quicker-cooking variety (cooks in 20 minutes), but not instant rice. For a flavor variation, use 1 lb (454 g) extra-lean ground beef mixed with 8 oz (227 g) light Italian sausage.

Nutrition Nugget
Getting more of the antioxidant lycopene (from tomatoes, papaya and watermelon, for instance) may help older people stay active longer. In an *unconventional* study of 88 nuns ages 77 to 98, researchers found that those who got the most lycopene were the ones least likely to need help with daily activities, such as getting dressed and walking. A good reason to cultivate healthier *habits*!

> Wit is the salt of conversation, not the food.
> *William Hazlitt*

Someone Pasta Meatballs!

Italian sausage and beef meatballs

If you're looking for the tastiest, juiciest Italian meatballs to serve with spaghetti, our simple and succulent recipe will pasta test!

1½ cups	fresh whole-grain bread crumbs (see tip)
½ cup	1% milk
1 lb	(454 g) extra-lean ground sirloin
8 oz	(227 g) light mild Italian sausage, casing removed
⅓ cup	packed freshly grated Parmesan cheese
1	egg
1 tbsp	minced fresh flat-leaf parsley
1 tsp	minced garlic
¼ tsp	each salt and freshly ground black pepper
2 tbsp	olive oil

MAKES 24 MEATBALLS

PER MEATBALL
80 calories, 3.8 g total fat (1.4 g saturated fat),
8 g protein, 3 g carbohydrate, 0.3 g fiber,
27 mg cholesterol, 136 mg sodium

- Place fresh bread crumbs in a small bowl and pour milk over crumbs. Let stand for 5 minutes or until crumbs have absorbed milk.

- In a large bowl, combine crumbs with all remaining ingredients, except olive oil. Mix well (using your hands works best). Shape meat mixture into uniform-sized meatballs. (Tip: Pack meat mixture into ⅓-cup measuring cup. Use this amount to make 2 meatballs.)

- Heat olive oil in a deep, non-stick, 14-inch skillet. Add meatballs and cook over medium-high heat until lightly browned on all sides. Be careful not to break them.

- To finish cooking meatballs, either (1) Add two jars (about 6 cups/1.5 L) of your favorite tomato pasta sauce to the skillet. Reduce heat, cover and simmer until meatballs are cooked through, about 25 minutes; or (2) Remove meatballs from skillet and transfer to a large baking pan. Bake meatballs at 400°F for about 20 minutes, or until cooked through.

Recipe Tip: To make fresh bread crumbs for this recipe, tear 3 slices of whole-grain bread into chunks and place in a food processor or mini chopper. Pulse on and off until soft crumbs are formed.

Trivial Tidbit

Unlike Betty Crocker, Chef Boyardee was *not* a fictional advertising icon. There really was a Chef Boyardee and, believe it or not, he was a pretty good chef! Hector Boiardi was born in Italy in 1898 and began working in kitchens at 11 years of age. In 1914, he immigrated to New York and began working in hotel kitchens. He later moved to Cleveland and opened his own restaurant, Il Giardino d'Italia, which became quite popular, with patrons requesting portions of his meals to take home. Hector packaged up uncooked pasta and cheese along with milk bottles filled with his popular sauce. Demand grew and he eventually built a small processing plant in 1928. He marketed the pasta as Chef Boy-ar-dee, spelled phonetically so Americans could properly pronounce it. Ten years later, his pasta was enjoyed nationwide.

Cowabunga Beef Burgers

Smokin'!

Thick, juicy, smoky beef burgers with "kick"

Hickory dickory, dude
Don't eat your burger nude
When the clock strikes one
Grab a whole-grain bun
Cowabunga! That's kickin' food!

1¼ lbs	(568 g) extra-lean ground beef
¾ cup	fresh whole-grain bread crumbs or ⅓ cup dry unseasoned bread crumbs
3 tbsp	hickory-flavored barbecue sauce
2 tbsp	minced fresh parsley
2 tsp	prepared horseradish
1	egg
1 tsp	minced garlic
½ tsp	each salt and freshly ground black pepper

Extra barbecue sauce for basting burgers (optional)

MAKES 4 BURGERS

PER BURGER (PATTY ONLY)
271 calories, 12.9 g total fat (6.6 g saturated fat),
29 g protein, 12 g carbohydrate, 1.4 g fiber,
141 mg cholesterol, 531 mg sodium

- Combine all ingredients in a large bowl and mix gently using your hands. For juicier burgers, try to handle the meat as little as possible. Shape meat into 4 large patties, about 1 inch thick.

- Preheat grill to high setting. Brush grill rack lightly with oil. Grill burgers for about 5 to 6 minutes per side, or until center is no longer pink. Baste with extra barbecue sauce during last 2 minutes of cooking time, if desired. Resist the temptation to press down on burgers with a spatula. Every drop of juice and fat that you squeeze out makes the burgers that much drier.

- Serve burgers on whole-grain hamburger buns with your favorite burger toppings.

Nutrition Nugget

Add a tablespoon of oregano to your burgers or meatloaf and you'll do your body a flavor and a favor! When researchers at Kansas State University tested the bacteria-fighting abilities of various spices by adding them to ground beef, they discovered dried oregano was one of the best at wiping out E. coli bacteria!

Tidy Joes

Ground chicken sloppy Joes with "hidden" beans for added fiber

Meet Sloppy Joe's wholesome and healthy cousin, Tidy, from down south. Underneath a shipshape exterior lurks a wilder, spicier alter ego. Smmmmokin'!

1 lb	(454 g) ground chicken or turkey
½ cup	diced onions
2 tsp	minced garlic
½ cup	minced celery
¼ cup	grated carrots
1 cup	cooked Romano or pinto beans, mashed
1 cup	cooked brown rice or quinoa
1 cup	diced tomatoes
⅔ cup	ketchup
½ cup	chopped green onions
2	jalapeño peppers, seeded and minced (see tip)
2 tbsp	white vinegar
1 tbsp	each Worcestershire sauce and brown sugar
1½ tsp	chili powder
1 tsp	each ground cumin and yellow mustard
½ tsp	crushed red pepper flakes
¼ tsp	freshly ground black pepper
8	whole-grain hamburger buns

MAKES 8 SERVINGS

PER SERVING
304 calories, 8.2 g total fat
(2 g saturated fat), 18 g protein,
42 g carbohydrate, 4.8 g fiber,
45 mg cholesterol,
485 mg sodium

- Spray a large pot or skillet with cooking spray. Add ground chicken, onions, garlic, celery and carrots. Cook over medium-high heat until chicken is cooked through, about 8 minutes. Stir often. Break up any large chunks of chicken with a fork. Drain off any fat.

- Stir in remaining ingredients. Reduce heat to medium-low. Cover and simmer for 10 minutes, stirring occasionally. Spoon chicken mixture over bottom half of hamburger bun, cover with top half and enjoy!

Recipe Tip Since jalapeño peppers contain capsaicin, the source of their fiery flavor, they should be handled with care. Let's just say it doesn't tickle if this compound gets in your eye! After chopping a hot pepper, make sure you immediately wash your hands, as well as all surfaces that came in contact with the pepper. If you're not a lover of spicier fare, you can eliminate the jalapeños altogether from this recipe.

A man named Charles fell into a meat grinder. Now he's ground Chuck :)

Your Nonstop, Fat-Burning Shop

Think exercise can't possibly burn off enough calories to nix the six Oreos you just ate? Think again! One of the great secrets behind vigorous exercise is its "residual effect"—the calorie burning doesn't stop when your legs do! How's that happen? Well, when you run or lift weights, you break down a large number of muscle fibers. These broken fibers have to be repaired (that's how you build and grow muscle) and all this rebuilding takes energy (calories!). You also have to replace the glycogen (muscle fuel) that was used up during exercise—again, more energy required! So, when all is said and done, you haven't burned just 160 calories, you've burned 250, 300, maybe even 375 calories! Muscle is like the 24-hour supermarket of fat burning—it never shuts down. In fact, one study showed that more than two-thirds of fat-burning activity takes place after the actual exercise session. That phenomenon is technically known as PECBO (post-exercise calorie burn-off). Actually, Greta just made that up!

Shepherd's Pie with Squashed Potatoes

Seasoned beef and vegetables topped with cheesy mashed potatoes and squash

A fan favorite from our TV show
Eat, Shrink & Be Merry!

Meat and Vegetables

1½ lbs	(680 g)	extra-lean ground beef
1 cup		chopped onions
2 tsp		minced garlic
1 tsp		paprika
½ tsp		dried thyme
1 cup		frozen mixed peas and carrots
1 cup		frozen or canned corn (drain if using canned)
⅓ cup		reduced-sodium beef broth
2 tbsp		chili sauce (such as Heinz)
1½ tbsp		all-purpose flour
1 tbsp		Worcestershire sauce
¼ tsp		each salt and freshly ground black pepper

Potato Topping

2 lbs	(907 g)	Yukon Gold potatoes, peeled and cut into large chunks
2 cups	(about 8 oz/227 g)	peeled and chopped butternut squash
½ cup + 2 tbsp		freshly grated Parmesan cheese
½ cup		light (5%) sour cream
¼ tsp		salt
Dash		nutmeg
Minced fresh parsley for garnish (optional)		

Recipe Tip: Cut potatoes and squash into equal-sized pieces for even cooking.

MAKES 6 SERVINGS

PER SERVING
462 calories,
14 g total fat
(7.5 g saturated fat),
32 g protein,
58 g carbohydrate,
5.8 g fiber,
82 mg cholesterol,
538 mg sodium

- To make filling, cook beef, onions and garlic in a large pot or skillet over medium-high heat until meat is no longer pink and onions are tender. Stir in paprika and thyme. Cook 1 more minute. Add peas and carrots and corn. Mix well.

- In a medium bowl or measuring cup, whisk together broth, chili sauce, flour and Worcestershire sauce. Add to meat mixture in pot, along with salt and pepper. Reduce heat to medium-low. Let simmer, uncovered, for 5 minutes. Mixture will thicken slightly. Remove from heat, cover and keep warm while you prepare potato topping.

- To make topping, place potatoes in a large pot and cover with water by 2 inches (salt water if desired). Bring to a boil. Add squash. Cook until both potatoes and squash are tender, about 12 to 14 minutes. Drain potatoes and squash in a colander. Return to pot. Sprinkle ½ cup Parmesan over vegetables. Cover with lid and let stand 1 minute for cheese to melt. Add sour cream, salt and (tiny!) dash nutmeg. Mash well using a potato masher. Try to get out as many lumps as possible.

- To assemble casserole, spread meat mixture evenly over the bottom of a 2-quart casserole dish. Top with potato-squash mixture. Fluff with fork so small peaks are formed. Sprinkle remaining 2 tbsp Parmesan over potatoes. Bake at 375°F for 25 minutes, until completely heated through. Remove from oven. Sprinkle top with parsley, if desired. Let stand for 5 minutes before serving (it's hot!).

Loafstyles of the Rich and Famous

Deliciously different ground turkey loaf with apples, onions and herbs

Enquiring minds want to know: What's the secret behind this low-fat loaf that "everyone who's someone" is raving about? Well, according to the Psychic to the Stars, the secret ingredient is ground turkey, of all things, and apparently it has a very bright future ahead of it. First, loaves. Then, the world! You'll just fall in loaf with it!

2 tsp	butter
2 cups	chopped Granny Smith apples (unpeeled)
¾ cup	chopped onions
1½ lbs	(680 g) ground turkey
½ cup	quick-cooking rolled oats
⅓ cup	1% milk
¼ cup	minced fresh parsley
1	egg
1 tsp	Dijon mustard
1 tsp	minced garlic
¾ tsp	dried marjoram
½ tsp	each dried sage, salt and freshly ground black pepper

- Preheat oven to 350°F.

- Melt butter in a medium, non-stick skillet over medium heat. Add apples and onions. Cook and stir for about 5 minutes, until onions are tender. Let cool.

- In a large bowl, mix together apples, onions and all remaining ingredients.

- Spray a 9 x 5-inch loaf pan with cooking spray. Pat turkey mixture into pan. Bake for 1 hour, or until no longer pink in center. Pour off any liquid from pan. Invert onto a platter, slice and serve.

MAKES 6 SERVINGS

PER SERVING
270 calories, 11.7 g total fat (3.5 g saturated fat), 24 g protein, 18 g carbohydrate, 3.1 g fiber, 130 mg cholesterol, 326 mg sodium

Trivial Tidbit

It's the accidental apple! The city of Ryde, New South Wales, Australia, holds an annual Granny Smith festival celebrating the life and legacy of one of the district's most famous citizens, Maria Ann Smith—aka Granny Smith— who, back in 1868, "accidentally" grew the first batch of tart green apples that bear her name. As the story goes, Smith, who was a gardener, found an unusual seedling growing from a pile of bad apples she had thrown out. It's thought the seedling had sprouted from the remains of a French crab apple. She began using the distinctive, light green fruit for cooking, folks eventually began cultivating her new seedling tree and Granny Smith apples went on to achieve worldwide fame and glory.
How 'bout them apples?

Nutrition Nugget
Turkey is a lean, mean, fat-fighting machine! Not only does it give you muscle-building, metabolism-boosting protein, but it also supplies conjugated linoleic acid (CLA), which helps your body gobble up fat rather than store it.

Your body hears everything your mind says.
    Naomi Judd

Ooh-la-la-sagna!

Italian sausage and beef lasagna with whole wheat noodles

Va-va-voom! This meat-filled lasagna's got attitude, without a whole lotta fattitude! It's all dressed up but won't make you grow.

8 oz	(227 g) light mild Italian sausage
8 oz	(227 g) extra-lean ground beef
1 cup	chopped onions
2 tsp	minced garlic
1 tsp	dried oregano
¼ tsp	crushed red pepper flakes
1 jar	(22 oz/700 mL) your favorite tomato pasta sauce
1 can	(19 oz/540 mL) diced tomatoes with Italian herbs, undrained
⅓ cup	chopped fresh basil leaves
1 tbsp	balsamic vinegar
½ tsp	freshly ground black pepper
12	uncooked whole wheat lasagna noodles
2 cups	part-skim ricotta cheese
1 pkg	(10 oz/300 g) frozen spinach, thawed, squeezed dry and chopped
⅓ cup	freshly grated Parmesan, Romano or Asiago cheese
1	egg
1½ cups	packed shredded light mozzarella cheese (6 oz/170 g)

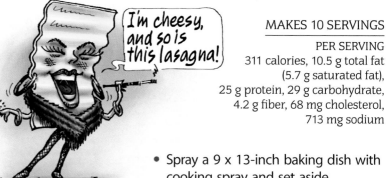

I'm cheesy, and so is this lasagna!

MAKES 10 SERVINGS

PER SERVING
311 calories, 10.5 g total fat
(5.7 g saturated fat),
25 g protein, 29 g carbohydrate,
4.2 g fiber, 68 mg cholesterol,
713 mg sodium

- Spray a 9 x 13-inch baking dish with cooking spray and set aside.

- To make sauce, spray a large, non-stick pot or deep, non-stick skillet with cooking spray. Remove casing from sausage and break into small pieces in skillet. Add ground beef, onions and garlic. Cook and stir over medium-high heat until meat is no longer pink. Stir in oregano and crushed red pepper flakes. Cook 1 more minute. Add pasta sauce, tomatoes, basil, vinegar and black pepper. Bring mixture to a boil. Reduce heat to low. Cover and simmer for 20 minutes.

- While sauce is simmering, cook lasagna noodles according to package directions. Drain. Rinse with cold water and drain again.

- In a medium bowl, mix together ricotta, spinach, Parmesan cheese and egg. Refrigerate until ready to use.

- To assemble lasagna, spread 1 cup meat sauce over bottom of baking dish. Top with 4 noodles, cutting pieces to fit, if necessary. Spread ⅓ remaining sauce over noodles, followed by ⅓ mozzarella. Top with 4 more noodles, ⅓ sauce, all of the ricotta mixture and ⅓ mozzarella. For top layer: 4 noodles, ⅓ sauce, ⅓ mozzarella.

- Cover lasagna with foil and bake at 375°F for 35 minutes. Uncover and bake for an additional 15 minutes. Let lasagna stand, uncovered, for 15 minutes before serving.

Taking the "Lack" Out of Lactose Intolerance

Cow's milk contains a special sugar called lactose, and many people around the world don't produce enough of the enzyme called lactase needed to digest this special sugar. The result is lactose intolerance, and symptoms can range from cramps and digestive problems to sinus congestion to asthma to more serious health issues. Not fun stuff at all, and staying away from dairy products usually makes most folks feel 100 percent better. "But what about cheese?" you ask. "If I can't digest the lactose in milk do I have to cut the cheese, too?" Maybe not. While a cup of cow's milk contains about 10 to 12 grams of lactose, the bacteria used to produce cheese and the time required for cheese to ferment both help to lower lactose levels. Soft cheeses typically contain only half the lactose as the milk from which they were made. But here's the really gouda news: Aged cheeses, including most hard cheeses like cheddar, Swiss and Parmigiano-Reggiano, have very little lactose left, making them pretty safe in small quantities for people who are lactose intolerant. Say cheese!

The dentist told me I grind my teeth at night. So now before I go to sleep, I fill my mouth with hot water and coffee beans and set my alarm for 7:30 :)

Mighty Meaty Pasta Sauce

Thick, rich, meaty and flavorful Bolognese sauce

If you make this super-meaty pasta sauce for your meat-loving family members, they'll think you're a culinary superhero!

1 tbsp	olive oil
1½ cups	chopped red onions
½ cup	each diced celery and diced carrots
1 tbsp	minced garlic
1¼ lbs	(568 g) extra-lean ground beef
8 oz	(227 g) light spicy Italian sausage, casing removed
2 tsp	dried Italian seasoning
½ tsp	dried fennel seeds
1 can	(28 oz/796 mL) no-salt-added diced tomatoes, undrained
1 can	(14 oz/398 mL) no-salt-added tomato sauce
1 can	(5.5 oz/156 mL) tomato paste
1 tbsp	balsamic vinegar
1 tbsp	brown sugar
½ tsp	each salt and freshly ground black pepper
¼ cup	minced fresh basil leaves

MAKES 8 SERVINGS

PER SERVING
240 calories, 9 g total fat (3 g saturated fat),
23 g protein, 15 g carbohydrate, 3.2 g fiber,
69 mg cholesterol, 459 mg sodium

- Heat olive oil in a large pot over medium heat. Add onions, celery, carrots and garlic. Cook and stir until vegetables begin to soften, about 5 minutes. Add beef and sausage. Cook and stir until meat is no longer pink. Break up any large pieces of meat as it's cooking. Add Italian seasoning and fennel seeds and cook 1 more minute.

- Add tomatoes, tomato sauce, tomato paste, vinegar, sugar, salt and pepper. Bring mixture to a boil. Reduce heat to low, cover and simmer for 30 minutes, stirring occasionally. Stir in basil and remove from heat. Serve sauce over hot, cooked pasta.

Trivial Tidbit

A clove of garlic is also called a: (a) toe; (b) nob; (c) petal; or (d) vampire's tooth. And the answer? (a) toe! We prefer an entire foot in our spaghetti sauce!

Turk du Soleil

Flavorful Thai-inspired turkey burgers with zesty peanut sauce

In a daring feat of culinary acrobatics, we've teamed extra-lean ground turkey with a Thairific circus of bold flavors to create a showstopping burger that'll make everyone flip!

⅓ cup	bottled light peanut sauce
1 tsp	sesame oil
1 tsp	reduced-sodium soy sauce
1 tsp	grated lemon zest
1 tsp	grated gingerroot
1½ lbs	(680 g) ground turkey or chicken
1 cup	fresh whole-grain bread crumbs or
	½ cup dry unseasoned bread crumbs
¼ cup	finely minced green onions
2 tbsp	minced fresh cilantro
1	egg
½ tsp	salt
¼ tsp	freshly ground black pepper
6	whole-grain hamburger buns

Lettuce and sliced tomatoes

MAKES 6 BURGERS

PER BURGER (PATTY ONLY)
229 calories,
11.2 g total fat
(2.6 g saturated fat),
26 g protein,
8 g carbohydrate,
1.2 g fiber,
105 mg cholesterol,
485 mg sodium

Note: The label on the package of hamburger buns will give you the nutritional information per roll. Just add these numbers to our analysis above to get the most accurate nutritional count.

- To make sauce, combine peanut sauce, sesame oil, soy sauce, lemon zest and gingerroot in a small bowl. Mix well and set aside.

- In a large bowl, combine ground turkey, bread crumbs, green onions, cilantro, egg, salt, pepper and 3 tbsp of the peanut sauce mixture (you will use the rest of the sauce to baste the burgers). Mix gently using your hands. Form mixture into 6 patties, about ½ inch thick. Cover and refrigerate until ready to grill.

- Preheat grill to high setting. Brush grill rack lightly with oil. Grill burgers for about 5 minutes per side, or until cooked through and no longer pink in the center. Brush burgers with reserved sauce during last 2 minutes of cooking time.

- Serve burgers on lightly toasted buns with sliced tomatoes and lettuce or any of your favorite burger toppings.

> Most turkeys taste better the day after; my mother's tasted better the day before.
>
> *Rita Rudner*

The Ladle in Red

Everyone's favorite classic beef chili. A staple recipe!

Never seen you cookin' so healthy as you did tonight. Never seen you dine so right.
You were amazing. I hardly know…this chili by my side. Never forget…
the way you cooked, tonight.

1½ lbs	(680 g) extra-lean ground beef
2 tsp	minced garlic
1 cup	each diced celery, diced green bell pepper and diced red onions
1½ tbsp	chili powder
1½ tsp	each ground cumin and dried oregano
1 tsp	ground coriander
¼ tsp	freshly ground black pepper
1 can	(19 oz/540 mL) no-salt-added diced tomatoes, undrained
1 can	(14 oz/398 mL) no-salt-added tomato sauce
1 cup	reduced-sodium beef broth
¼ cup	chopped celery leaves
1 tbsp	hickory-flavored barbecue sauce
1 can	(19 oz/540 mL) no-salt-added red kidney beans, drained and rinsed
1 can	(14 oz/398 mL) beans in tomato sauce (see tip)
3 tbsp	minced fresh cilantro
1 tbsp	freshly squeezed lime juice
2 tsp	liquid honey

MAKES 8 SERVINGS

PER SERVING
283 calories,
8 g total fat
(3.9 g saturated fat),
25 g protein,
30 g carbohydrate,
10 g fiber,
53 mg cholesterol,
346 mg sodium

Recipe Tips If you can, make this chili one day before you want to serve it. It thickens as it sits overnight and tastes even better the next day! Heinz Beans in Tomato Sauce are a good choice for this recipe and are usually available in every grocery store.

- Cook beef and garlic in a large, deep, non-stick skillet or pot over medium-high heat until beef is no longer pink. Stir in celery, green pepper and red onions. Cook and stir for 3 minutes, or until vegetables begin to soften.

- Stir in chili powder, cumin, oregano, coriander and black pepper. Cook for 1 more minute. Add tomatoes, tomato sauce, beef broth, celery leaves and barbecue sauce. Bring mixture to a boil. Reduce heat to low. Cover and simmer for 20 minutes, stirring occasionally.

- Add beans and simmer, covered, for 10 more minutes. Remove from heat. Stir in cilantro, lime juice and honey. Serve hot.

Nutrition Nugget

The spice is right! If you want to turn back the clock, use fresh and dried spices and herbs more often. These pungent powerhouses truly are the fountain of youth— from cinnamon to turmeric, oregano to ginger, dill to rosemary, cloves to cayenne. By weight, they're the most densely packed anti-aging foods you can find. Not only do they make your food look, smell and taste great, but they're also loaded with antioxidants that'll keep you looking and feeling hot, hot, hot!!

Tooth or Consequences

Your good ol' toothbrush may be one of the best tools for protecting your heart and your brain. Recent studies suggest that regularly flossing and brushing your teeth could cut your risk of stroke in half. In a 12-year study of 14,000 men, researchers found that those with the healthiest teeth and gums were also the least likely to have a stroke. That's because the bacteria that causes periodontal disease can sometimes sneak into the bloodstream, damaging blood vessels and increasing the risk of stroke. Our *flossify*? To maintain healthy arteries, avoid plaque like the plague.

No Weigh, José! Mexican Lasagna

Layered Mexican casserole with ground chicken, beans, vegetables, tortillas and cheese

José, can you see…that your meal's really light? It's hard to believe that a scrumptious Mexican lasagna like this one won't produce a paunch under your poncho, but with tons of veggies, beans and other lean good stuff, there's no weigh!

Eats unbelievable!

1½ lbs	(680 g) ground chicken
1 cup	each diced red onions and diced green bell pepper
2 tsp	minced garlic
1 cup	canned no-salt-added black beans, drained and rinsed
1 cup	diced tomatoes
½ cup	frozen or canned corn
1½ tsp	chili powder
1 tsp	ground cumin
2 cups	your favorite tomato pasta sauce
1 cup	medium salsa
¼ tsp	freshly ground black pepper
2 tbsp	minced fresh cilantro
4	large or 8 small whole-grain flour tortillas
1½ cups	packed shredded light old (sharp) cheddar cheese (6 oz/170 g)
1 cup	light (5%) sour cream
¼ cup	chopped green onions

MAKES 8 SERVINGS

PER SERVING
323 calories, 8 g total fat (3.7 g saturated fat),
30 g protein, 30 g carbohydrate, 6.2 g fiber,
73 mg cholesterol, 643 mg sodium

- Preheat oven to 375°F. Spray a 9 x 13-inch baking pan with cooking spray and set aside.

- In a large, non-stick pot or skillet, cook ground chicken, onions, green pepper and garlic over medium-high heat until meat is no longer pink. Break up any large pieces of chicken as it's cooking.

- Add black beans, tomatoes, corn, chili powder and cumin. Cook and stir for 2 more minutes. Add pasta sauce, salsa and black pepper. Bring to a boil. Reduce heat to low. Cover and simmer for 5 minutes, stirring occasionally. Stir in cilantro and remove from heat.

- To assemble lasagna, spread ⅓ sauce mixture over bottom of prepared pan. Top with ½ the tortillas, overlapping and cutting them as necessary to fit. Top with ⅓ sauce mixture, followed by ½ the cheese. Cover cheese with the remaining tortillas, followed by remaining sauce. Sprinkle remaining cheese over sauce.

- Cover with foil and bake for 35 minutes. Uncover and bake for 10 more minutes. Let lasagna stand at least 10 minutes before slicing for easier serving. Top each piece with a dollop of sour cream and some chopped green onions.

Recipe Tip: If you prefer, you can replace the ground chicken with extra-lean ground beef and the cheddar cheese with Monterey Jack.

*Why did the cooks play poker?
Because they wanted to win some pots :)*

Trivial Tidbit

It's no wonder television became known as the "boob tube." Researchers at Kansas State University found that people who had just watched television for a mere 15 minutes had diminished brain-wave activity. In fact, your brain is more active while you're sleeping than it is while you're watching TV! Switch off the telly or your brain turns to jelly!

FOOD BITE

In the Middle Ages, it was customary for peasants to toss their daily food scraps and leftovers into iron pots simmering over open fires. They often had no idea what was actually cooking, so when an unexpected visitor was asked "to take pot luck," he was invited to dine on whatever was available in the pot. It was a matter of luck—what meal was actually in the pot and whether there would be enough of it to go around. Today, the expression refers to a gathering where each of the guests brings food to be shared by all.

Glad Thai Dings

Asian meatballs in a zesty, Thai-inspired sauce

Rejoice! Whether you serve these succulent meatballs with stir-fried vegetables, rice noodles or alone as an appetizer, they're sure to bring your taste buds great comfort and joy.

Meatballs

1½ lbs	(680 g) extra-lean ground beef
¼ cup	hoisin sauce
¼ cup	dry unseasoned bread crumbs
3 tbsp	finely minced green onions
1 tbsp	minced fresh cilantro
1	egg
2 tsp	minced garlic
1 tsp	grated gingerroot
1 tsp	sesame oil
¼ tsp	each salt and freshly ground black pepper

Sauce

1 cup	light coconut milk
⅓ cup	hoisin sauce
2 tbsp	reduced-sodium soy sauce
2 tbsp	light peanut butter
2 tbsp	minced fresh basil leaves or fresh cilantro
1 tbsp	grated gingerroot
1 tsp	grated lemon zest
⅛ tsp	crushed red pepper flakes

MAKES 40 MEATBALLS

PER MEATBALL
46 calories, 2.4 g total fat (1.2 g saturated fat), 4 g protein, 3 g carbohydrate, 0.2 g fiber, 16 mg cholesterol, 125 mg sodium

- Preheat oven to 400°F. Spray a rimmed cookie sheet or large baking pan with cooking spray and set aside.

- To make meatballs, combine all meatball ingredients in a large bowl (using your hands works best). Form meat mixture into 1- to 1½-inch meatballs, about 40 in total. Place on prepared pan.

- Bake for 15 to 18 minutes, until meatballs are cooked through and nicely browned on the outside.

- While meatballs are cooking, prepare sauce. In a deep, non-stick skillet, whisk together all sauce ingredients. Heat over medium-high heat, stirring constantly, until sauce boils. Reduce heat to medium and cook sauce, uncovered, for 3 minutes, stirring often. Sauce will thicken a bit. Add cooked meatballs to sauce and mix well. Serve hot.

Nutrition Nugget

In the 1940s, farmers attempted to use cheap coconut oil to fatten up their animals, since larger cows yielded more meat and therefore more money. But, to their surprise, they discovered the oil made their cattle leaner and more active! Try adding a little coconut oil to your diet and see if it makes *your* loin a little leaner.

In this chapter...

The Rice is Right,
p. 266

The Bright Sides

When you're forced to choose sides,
pick these!

All That Jasmine

Sticky cinnamon-and-coconut-scented Thai jasmine rice

You can jazz up your dinner when you pair jasmine rice with fragrant spice. They make beautiful music together!

1 cup	light coconut milk
1 cup	reduced-sodium chicken or vegetable broth
¼ tsp	salt
1¼ cups	uncooked jasmine rice, rinsed and drained (see tip)
¼ cup	dried currants
2 tsp	olive oil
1 cup	diced onions
2 tsp	grated gingerroot
¾ tsp	ground cinnamon
¼ tsp	each ground coriander and ground ginger
2 tbsp	minced fresh cilantro

MAKES 6 SERVINGS

PER SERVING
207 calories, 3.7 g total fat (2.2 g saturated fat), 4 g protein, 40 g carbohydrate, 1.8 g fiber, 1 mg cholesterol, 174 mg sodium

- Combine coconut milk, broth and salt in a medium pot. Bring to a boil over high heat. Stir in rice. Reduce heat to low. Cover and simmer until liquid is absorbed and rice is tender, about 12 minutes. Remove from heat and stir in currants. Cover and let stand for 10 minutes.

- Meanwhile, heat olive oil in a large, non-stick skillet over medium heat. Add onions. Cook and stir until onions are tender, about 3 to 4 minutes. Add gingerroot, cinnamon, coriander and ginger. Mix well. Add cooked rice. Cook and stir for 2 more minutes, until mixture is well blended and spices are evenly distributed. Stir in cilantro and serve hot.

Recipe Tip Similar to Indian basmati rice, jasmine rice is a fragrant rice from Thailand and it should be rinsed before cooking to remove starchiness. Place the uncooked rice in a sieve and rinse under cold running water for a minute or so. Drain well. You can substitute basmati rice for the jasmine rice if you prefer.

Bursting at the Seams

Physical activity shouldn't be a shortcut to losing weight; it should become part of the fabric of your life, as natural a part of your day as your morning shower. And making it a habit is a lot easier if you aim for frequency, not duration. Instead of exercising for one hour, three times a week, try to incorporate simple, small bouts of activity into your everyday life. Fifteen minutes here and 10 minutes there seems like a cinch compared to cramming your entire week's worth of exercise into one marathon torture session. You wouldn't brush your teeth 21 times in one day and say "There. That'll do 'til next week!" If you want physical activity to become routine, learn to do it in short, frequent bursts. 'Cause it's better to exercise in short bursts than burst shorts!

Nutrition Nugget

Scentsational news: Cinnamon has one of the highest antioxidant levels of any spice—second only to cloves. A mere half teaspoon has as many antioxidants as a half cup of raspberries or strawberries! And researchers in Pakistan found that a half teaspoon of cinnamon a day can lower blood-sugar levels in Type 2 diabetics by 20 percent! This super spice is also known to boost metabolism, so it can help us shed fat. Because cinnamon is naturally sweet, it makes a great sugar substitute. Sprinkle it on your favorite dishes, use it in coffee or tea, on breakfast cereals or oatmeal or on a baked sweet potato.

Pea Diddy

Sautéed green peas with green onions and mint. Simple but delicious!

Why do peas get such a bad rap? Dress 'em up with some bling (a.k.a. green onions and mint) and they're the tastiest thing! Hip hop to it!

1 tbsp	butter
½ cup	chopped green onions (with white parts)
3 cups	frozen green peas, thawed
2 tbsp	minced fresh mint leaves (see tip)
¼ tsp	each salt and freshly ground black pepper

• Melt butter in a medium, non-stick skillet over medium heat. Add onions. Cook and stir until onions are softened, about 3 minutes. Add peas. Cook and stir until peas are heated through, about 3 more minutes. Add mint, salt and pepper. Mix well and remove from heat. Serve immediately.

MAKES 6 SERVINGS

PER SERVING
72 calories, 2.3 g total fat
(1.2 g saturated fat),
4 g protein, 10 g carbohydrate,
3.3 g fiber, 5 mg cholesterol,
200 mg sodium

Recipe Tip: Please don't use dried mint for this recipe. It's just not the same as fresh mint and your peas won't be very tasty.

FOOD BITE At weddings in the Czech Republic, it's customary to throw peas at the bride and groom instead of rice. Hence the origin of the expression, "Speak now, or forever hold your peas!"

The best six doctors anywhere
And no one can deny it
Are sunshine, water, rest and air
Exercise and diet.
These six will gladly you attend
If only you are willing
Your mind they'll ease
Your will they'll mend
And charge you not a shilling.

Nursery rhyme quoted by Wayne Fields
What the River Knows, 1990

Mr. Bean

Steamed green beans tossed with lemon, honey mustard and bacon

We realize preparing dinner is no laughing matter, so we've concocted a tasty bean side dish that's unspeakably simple. It mutters not whether you can cook. You really can't goof up this one.

1 lb	(454 g) fresh green beans, trimmed
2 slices	reduced-sodium bacon, finely chopped
½ cup	minced red onions or shallots
1 tsp	minced garlic
1 tbsp	each honey mustard and freshly squeezed lemon juice
¼ tsp	each salt and freshly ground black pepper

- Place beans in a steamer basket over boiling water. Steam for about 6 minutes, until beans are tender-crisp.

- While beans are steaming, cook bacon, onions and garlic over medium heat in a 10-inch, non-stick skillet until bacon is crisp and onions are tender, about 5 minutes. Be careful not to burn them.

- Remove skillet from heat. Add honey mustard and lemon juice. Mix well. Add beans and stir to coat beans with onion-bacon mixture. Sprinkle with salt and pepper and serve immediately.

MAKES 5 SERVINGS

PER SERVING
62 calories,
2.4 g total fat
(1 g saturated fat),
2 g protein,
8 g carbohydrate,
1.9 g fiber,
3 mg cholesterol,
106 mg sodium

Recipe Tip: If you prefer, you can substitute frozen cut green beans for fresh beans.

If you think you have someone eating out of your hands, it's a good idea to count your fingers :)

Trivial Tidbit
Chew on this: In 1915, to promote his chewing gum, William Wrigley sent four sticks of gum to 1.5 million U.S. homes listed in telephone directories, figuring that anyone who could afford a phone could also afford his product. The marketing ploy worked! The popularity of chewing gum spawned another development—vending machines. The first vending machines were used to sell chewing gum in New York subways.

The Edge of Nitrate

You can bring home the bacon and fry it up in the pan—just don't pig out on the stuff. Sodium nitrate, a common preservative used in bacon, packaged deli meats, cold cuts, hot dogs and sausages, changes into something evil called nitrosamines when it mixes in the stomach with other compounds found in protein-containing foods. Trouble is, even small amounts of nitrosamines have been shown to cause cancer in animals. Fortunately, there are more and more butchers who make their own preservative-free meats and sausages, and now health-conscious manufacturers are nixing the nitrates in favor of natural preservatives like vinegar. Always check ingredients lists and just don't overdo it. Most of us enjoy eating bacon every now and then, but you really shouldn't go hog wild. On a positive note, if you slice up plenty of veggies or fruit on the side, their potent, cancer-fighting phytonutrients can help counteract the negative effects of nitrates. For example, vitamin C is known to prevent the conversion to nitrosamines in your stomach, so slice up an orange as a side dish and you'll be makin' bacon a lot healthier!

Britney's Spears

Roasted asparagus with balsamic vinegar and feta cheese

Oops! We did it again! We've created a sensational side dish that'll have everyone in your family singing and dancing with delight.

1½ lbs	(680 g) asparagus spears
1 tbsp	olive oil
1 tsp	minced garlic
2 tsp	balsamic vinegar
¼ tsp	each salt and freshly ground black pepper
¼ cup	crumbled light feta cheese (1 oz/28 g) or freshly grated Parmesan cheese

MAKES 6 SERVINGS

PER SERVING
55 calories, 3.5 g total fat
(1.1 g saturated fat), 3 g protein,
5 g carbohydrate, 2 g fiber,
4 mg cholesterol,
152 mg sodium

Recipe Tip: You can substitute fresh, whole green beans for the asparagus.

- Preheat oven to 450°F. Trim tough ends off asparagus.

- Spray a small baking pan with cooking spray. Arrange asparagus in a single layer. Drizzle with olive oil and sprinkle with garlic. Mix asparagus around a bit to make sure they're well coated with oil and garlic (use your hands for this…it's the easiest way).

- Roast for about 8 to 10 minutes, depending on thickness of asparagus. Be careful not to overcook them. Soggy asparagus is no fun and no yum!

- Arrange cooked asparagus on a serving plate. Sprinkle with vinegar, salt and pepper. Top with crumbled feta and serve immediately.

Really Swell News

If you have "issues with your tissues," then stalk up on asparagus! Asparagus is a good source of potassium and quite low in sodium. This, combined with an active amino acid in asparagus called asparagine, makes it an effective diuretic. That's why, historically, asparagus has been used to treat problems involving swelling, such as arthritis and rheumatism. And it may also be useful for the dreaded PMS-related water retention that makes putting on a pair of jeans the equivalent to squeezing 10 pounds of potatoes into a five-pound sack! More good news: Asparagus can prevent a hangover! When researchers in South Korea exposed human liver cells to asparagus extract, it suppressed free radicals and almost doubled the liver's ability to metabolize alcohol. Hic, hic, hurray!

All in the Yamily

Roasted sweet potatoes with a hint of apple and ginger

You'd be no meathead for filling up on creamy-tasting, nutrient-rich gingered yams or sweet potatoes. They're loaded with potassium, beta-carotene, vitamins A and C and calcium. Eatith as much as you like!

4	medium yams or sweet potatoes, peeled and sliced crosswise into ¼-inch-thick rounds
¾ cup	unsweetened apple juice
1 tbsp	brown sugar
2 tsp	grated gingerroot

Salt and freshly ground black pepper to taste

MAKES 4 SERVINGS
***
PER SERVING
171 calories, 0.4 g total fat
(0 g saturated fat), 2 g protein,
40 g carbohydrate, 3.9 g fiber,
0 mg cholesterol,
23 mg sodium

- Preheat oven to 425°F.

- Combine all ingredients in a large bowl and mix well. Spread mixture evenly in a medium casserole dish. Bake, uncovered, for 30 minutes. Yams will be golden brown and most of the liquid will have evaporated. Add salt and freshly ground black pepper to taste, if desired. Serve hot.

Metabolic Meltdown

Experts tell us that as we age, we're going to suffer some memory loss, grow bigger ears and put on weight. It's so depressing—no wonder we're also expected to slouch! They predict that by age 55, we'll need about 150 to 200 fewer calories a day than younger folks, and that if we don't cut back on our food intake, we'll be walking around with a couple of bowling balls worth of blubber around our waistlines. Ah, the dreaded metabolic meltdown. A sluggish resting metabolism—the energy our bodies expend to sustain basic functions like breathing and heart beating—is due primarily to loss of muscle mass. It's not an "inevitable" metabolic decline as we age. The more muscle we have, the more calories we'll continue to burn, even when we're resting comfortably in our rocking chairs. Proposed solution to the meltdown crisis: Exercise! By conditioning our bodies, we can turn these so-called experts into false prophets (at least on the weight gain issue). Walk, swim, bike or dance—and don't just do aerobic exercises either. Lift something—anything! Weights, phone books, grandkids, whatever! Oh, by the way, exercise won't stop your ears from growing. But look at the bright side—you'll forget about them eventually.

Nutrition Nugget

Gram for gram (and yam for yam), sweet potatoes have fewer calories, more calcium and more vitamin C than white potatoes. But where the sweet potato really shines is in its beta-carotene content. White potatoes have a smidgen, but sweet potatoes are loaded with the stuff! As a result, eating sweet potatoes can help improve vision, prevent some kinds of cancer and boost immunity. Well, I'll be yammed!

> Artificial substances have created within you artificial appetites.
>
> *Marianne Williamson*

These Beets Were Made for Walkin'

Roasted beets and whole shallots with fresh thyme

There's no way these beets will get the boot! They're so darn tasty, they'll walk off the dinner table in no time.

6	medium whole fresh beets (about 1½ lbs/680 g)
12	small to medium shallots, peeled
1 tbsp	olive oil
2 tsp	minced fresh thyme
1 tsp	balsamic vinegar
¼ tsp	each salt and freshly ground black pepper

MAKES 6 SERVINGS

PER SERVING
87 calories, 2.5 g total fat
(0.3 g saturated fat), 2 g protein,
15 g carbohydrate, 3.2 g fiber,
0 mg cholesterol, 91 mg sodium

- Preheat oven to 425°F. Wrap beets individually in foil. Place on middle oven rack and roast for about 1 hour, until beets are tender (you can pierce them with a fork), but not soft. Exact roasting time will depend on size of beets.

- While beets are roasting, prepare shallots. Place peeled shallots in an 8 x 8-inch baking pan. Add olive oil and thyme and toss to coat. Set aside.

- When beets are finished roasting, remove from oven and place pan of shallots in oven. Unwrap beets and let cool while shallots are roasting. Roast shallots for 15 minutes, stirring once, halfway through cooking time.

- When beets are cool enough to handle, peel them. If you cut off the stem end, the skin should come off very easily. (We like to wear latex gloves while handling cooked beets since their juice will stain your hands.) Slice each beet into six wedges. Place in serving bowl. Add hot shallots and any olive oil and thyme you can scrape from the pan (using a rubber spatula helps). Sprinkle with balsamic vinegar, salt and pepper and toss lightly. Serve hot.

The Beet Goes On

We love beets. They're the beet-all and the end-all of vegetables, in our opinion. We could eat them every day and never get sick of them. In fact, if we ate beets every day, we'd probably never get sick! Beets are a super-good-for-you root vegetable, full of powerful nutrients that help fight heart disease and certain cancers, especially colon cancer. Your liver loves beets as much as we do, too. Beets are great for detoxifying! But forget all the health mumbo jumbo. We just love the way beets taste: fattening and buttery. We probably love beets because we started eating them when we were quite young. Our Polish mom prepared fried beets (cooked in bacon fat, if we remember correctly!), pickled her homegrown beets and, of course, whipped up batch after batch of her famous borscht soup. Can't beet that!

Posh Squash

Roasted butternut squash with rosemary and sage

This high-class, high-flavor roasted squash recipe makes an elegant addition to your Thanksgiving dinner menu.

6 cups	cubed butternut squash (about 2.2 lbs/1 kg)
1 tbsp	olive oil
1 tsp	balsamic vinegar
1 tsp	dried sage leaves
½ tsp	dried rosemary
¼ tsp	each salt and freshly ground black pepper or to taste
1 tbsp	pure maple syrup

MAKES 6 SERVINGS

PER SERVING
84 calories, 2.4 g total fat
(0.3 g saturated fat), 1 g protein,
17 g carbohydrate, 2.9 g fiber,
0 mg cholesterol, 103 mg sodium

Recipe Tip: You can use 1 tbsp minced fresh sage leaves and 1½ tsp minced fresh rosemary if you prefer.

- Combine all ingredients except maple syrup in a 9 x 13-inch, non-stick baking pan and toss until squash is well coated with seasonings.

- Roast, uncovered, at 400°F for 30 minutes. Remove from oven and drizzle with maple syrup. Mix well. Return to oven and roast for another 5 to 10 minutes, or until squash is tender when pierced with a fork. Serve hot.

FOOD BITE

Native Americans referred to winter squash as "the apple of God" and planted its seeds near their homes, believing they would promote fertility. They also held squash in such high regard that they buried it along with their dead to provide them with nourishment on their final journey.

The Grain from Spain

Quick and easy Spanish rice—a perfect accompaniment to tacos, enchiladas or fajitas

La Chihuahua esta sombrero cerveza. Por favor no padre si Ponce de Leon. Speedy Gonzales bienvenido siesta. Al right, all right—so maybe we don't know how to speak Spanish, but we sure know how to make a wickedly delicious Spanish rice!

2 tsp	olive oil
1 cup	chopped onions
½ cup	diced green bell pepper
1 tsp	minced garlic
2⅓ cups	reduced-sodium chicken broth
1 cup	uncooked brown rice (the quicker-cooking variety, but not instant)
1 cup	chunky-style salsa (mild, medium or hot)
½ tsp	each chili powder and ground cumin
¼ tsp	each salt and freshly ground black pepper
2 tbsp	minced fresh cilantro

MAKES 6 SERVINGS

PER SERVING
163 calories, 2.8 g total fat
(0.5 g saturated fat),
3 g protein, 31 g carbohydrate,
3.3 g fiber, 2 mg cholesterol,
269 mg sodium

- Heat olive oil in a medium pot over medium heat. Add onions, green pepper and garlic. Cook and stir until vegetables are tender, about 5 minutes.

- Add remaining ingredients, except cilantro, and mix well. Bring to a boil. Reduce heat to medium-low, cover and cook for another 15 to 20 minutes, or until liquid has been absorbed and rice is tender. (Cooking time depends on brand of rice. Check package instructions.)

- Remove from heat, stir in cilantro and serve hot.

A Matter of Fat

Muscle is a terrible thing to waste. But when you diet without exercising, that's exactly what you're doing. When you lose more than two pounds a week, typically half of the weight lost comes from muscle. That's bad news. Muscle is your calorie-burning, fat-incinerating furnace, using energy even when you're sleeping. Fat pretty much just sits there. Sure, if you starve yourself on a super-low-calorie diet, you'll lose weight. But it'll be an unfavorable type of weight loss. Though the scale says you're five pounds lighter, you've really just changed your body composition. You're simply a lighter fat person! That's not what you had in mind when you were subsisting on celery sticks, was it? To make matters worse, when you go off the diet (and you will), you'll gain back the weight you lost and then some. By sacrificing muscle on the restrictive diet, you've turned your body into a less efficient fat burner, so you'll gain weight even though you're eating less. What a great plan! To transform your body for the better, don't lose muscle—use muscle!

Nutrition Nugget

We hate to sound like a broken record, a broken record, a broken record, but we're not big fans of white foods. Just like white flour, white rice has been refined and stripped of most things good—the fiber, the vitamins and the minerals, plus it's high on the Glycemic Index. That means white rice basically acts like sugar in your body, causing you to pack on the pounds around your belly and, over time, that could lead to problems like diabetes. North Americans tend to pile their rice sky high, whereas Asians wisely eat small portions of rice as a complement to their vegetables and protein. Follow their lead by keeping your portions small to prevent your belly from becoming large!

Sellers of dried grapes are always raisin awareness :)

Rice 'n' Easy Casserole

Cheesy broccoli, cauliflower and rice casserole

Traditional broccoli and rice casserole has taken an abrupt "lite" turn. Our version is so creamy and satisfying, you won't believe it's lower in fat. Cauliflower lends a little excitement to this classic, uncomplicated favorite.

1 pkg	(6.3 oz/180 g) Uncle Ben's Long Grain & Wild Rice original recipe
2 cans	(10 oz/284 mL each) reduced-fat cream of mushroom soup, undiluted
¾ cup	packed shredded light old (sharp) cheddar cheese (3 oz/85 g)
2 tsp	Dijon mustard
1½ cups	each small broccoli and cauliflower florets

- Prepare rice according to package directions, omitting butter. Set aside.

- Preheat oven to 350°F. In a medium bowl, stir together soup, cheese and Dijon mustard. Mix well.

- Spray a medium casserole dish with cooking spray. Layer ½ soup mixture over bottom. Top with ½ the broccoli and cauliflower, followed by ½ the rice. Repeat layers. Cover and bake for 1 hour. Let cool for 5 minutes before serving.

MAKES 6 SERVINGS

PER SERVING
213 calories, 7.3 g total fat
(2.7 g saturated fat),
8 g protein, 27 g carbohydrate,
2.4 g fiber, 12 mg cholesterol,
586 mg sodium

Nutrition Nugget

Turn back the clock with brocc and bok! Researchers in Sweden, Australia and Indonesia studied the diets of 400 elderly men and women and found that those who ate the most leafy or dark green vegetables had the fewest wrinkles. Seems that those leaves are packed with compounds that help prevent and repair wear and tear on your skin cells as you get older. *Lettuce* leave wrinkles behind!

> As a child, my family's menu consisted of two choices: take it or leave it.
>
> *Buddy Hackett*

Small Changes, Big Payoff

When you're trying to lose fat, little things make a big difference. The simple, smart choices you make each day really do matter—like choosing purified water over soda, fruit instead of ice cream for dessert, quinoa in place of white rice or a small nonfat latte over a large one made with full-fat cream. Rather than attempting a radical, sweeping overhaul of bad habits you've developed over a lifetime, try incorporating one new, healthy habit into your life each week. A little here, a little there. It all adds up. Honest! If you're still not convinced that small, gradual changes pay huge health dividends, take note: scaling back a measly 100 calories a day can translate into 10 pounds of weight loss over the course of one year!

My Yammy Spice

Seasoned sweet potato wedges:
A nutritious twist on regular, oven-baked fries

Police! Put your yams up! You're under arrest for tasting so good! You have the right to remain spicy! Any fries you bake can, and will, be used to lure your kids to the dinner table.

4	medium yams or sweet potatoes
1 tbsp	olive oil
½ tsp	each ground cumin, paprika and dried oregano
¼ tsp	each salt and freshly ground black pepper

MAKES 4 SERVINGS

PER SERVING
170 calories, 3.9 g total fat
(0.5 g saturated fat), 2 g protein,
32 g carbohydrate, 4.1 g fiber,
0 mg cholesterol, 157 mg sodium

- Spray a baking sheet with cooking spray and set aside.

- Wash potatoes and pat dry using paper towels. Leave skins on. Slice potatoes into French-fry-like wedges, about ½ inch thick. Toss wedges with olive oil and remaining seasonings in a large bowl, until they're evenly coated with spices.

- Arrange potatoes in a single layer on baking sheet. Bake at 450°F for 15 to 20 minutes, turning wedges over halfway through cooking time. (Baking time will depend on thickness of wedges.) Serve hot.

Trivial Tidbit

Here's to your health! It is said that the Romans used to toast a woman's health by drinking a glass of wine for every letter in her name. Oh, what merry times were had when Cornelia Theodora Agrippina attended a party!

Glazed and Confused Carrots

Baby carrots with a peachy, orange-Dijon glaze

Pardon the confusion, but you can't really blame the carrots. After all, they're about to undergo a rather dramatic transformation—from humdrum, run-of-the-mill carrots to zesty, zingy carrots extraordinaire! Quick and easy.

1 lb	(454 g) baby carrots
3 tbsp	peach or apricot jam
1 tsp	each grated orange zest and Dijon mustard
¼ tsp	each dried thyme and salt

- Steam or boil carrots until tender, about 15 minutes.

- While carrots are cooking, prepare glaze. Combine jam, orange zest, mustard and thyme in a very small pot or skillet. Cook and stir over medium heat until jam has melted, about 2 minutes.

- Toss hot, cooked carrots with glaze and salt. Serve immediately.

MAKES 4 SERVINGS

PER SERVING

61 calories, 0.7 g total fat (0.1 g saturated fat), 1 g protein, 14 g carbohydrate, 2.1 g fiber, 0 mg cholesterol, 192 mg sodium

FOOD BITE

Baby carrots aren't a different breed or a shorter, stunted version of regular carrots. Farmers simply plant these carrots closer together to keep them slim and trim and easier to cut. Once picked, they're peeled, cut to a cute snack size and then packaged. By the way, cooked carrots are actually better for you than raw ones. Carrots get their crisp texture from cell walls stiffened with the indigestible food fibers cellulose, hemicellulose and lignin. Cooking dissolves some of the cellulose-stiffened walls, making the nutrients inside more readily available.

Trivial Tidbit Did you know that if you take the word "kitchen" and you shape-shift it (meaning, you rearrange the letters to come up with another word), you get the word "thicken"? And that's fitting, because it's in the kitchen where soups and sauces and stews and gravies are thickened, but it's also where relationships are thickened. Family gatherings, holidays, celebrations, conversations, togetherness—a lot of them revolve around the kitchen. Fortunately, if you follow the advice in this book, the kitchen will not be the place where your waistline thickens!

Merry-Go-Brown

Brown rice pilaf with cranberries and pistachios

Round and round it goes…your wooden spoon, that is, as you cook up a batch of this berry nutty, berry wholesome brown rice pilaf. It's the fairest of the fare!

2 tsp	olive oil or butter
2 cups	finely chopped mushrooms (try shiitake)
1 cup	minced red onions
1 tsp	minced garlic
1 cup	uncooked brown rice (see tip)
2 cups	reduced-sodium chicken or vegetable broth
½ tsp	salt
¼ cup	each chopped dried cranberries and chopped pistachios
2 tbsp	minced fresh parsley
2 tsp	grated lemon zest

MAKES 6 SERVINGS

PER SERVING
202 calories, 5 g total fat (0.7 g saturated fat),
6 g protein, 34 g carbohydrate, 3 g fiber,
2 mg cholesterol, 268 mg sodium

- Heat olive oil in a medium pot over medium-high heat. Add mushrooms, onions and garlic. Cook and stir until vegetables begin to soften, about 3 minutes.

- Stir in rice. Cook 1 more minute. Add broth and salt. Bring to a boil. Reduce heat to low and simmer, covered, for about 20 minutes (check suggested cooking time on rice package since brands vary).

- Remove from heat. Stir in cranberries, pistachios, parsley and lemon zest. Let stand, covered, for 10 minutes before serving.

> She's in such bad shape, she breathes hard when her stockings run :)

Recipe Tip You can use just about any type of rice or grain for this recipe, as long as you cook the grain for the recommended time on the package and adjust the amount of broth needed. There are some fabulous varieties of brown rice in the health food section of your grocery store. Don't be afraid to try some of them! Look for rice grown by Lundberg Family Farms in California. That brand of rice is amazing (and organic!) and many grocery stores now stock it. Or try quinoa, bulgur or wheat berries to expand your grain horizons.

Nutrition Nugget

More than just an awesome ice-cream flavor, pistachio is a nut worth noting! Interestingly, it gets its emerald hue from chlorophyll, the same super-healthy compound that gives green leaves their vibrant color. Rich in protein, fiber and antioxidants, pistachios are an ally in the battle of the bulge. In fact, researchers have reported greater weight loss and blood-lipid reductions when dieters ate pistachios instead of salted pretzels. The nuts are high in potassium, too, so they can help normalize blood pressure, maintain water balance and strengthen muscles. Stick with unsalted pistachios, otherwise the added sodium counteracts the potassium present in the nuts.

Bok in a Wok

Stir-fried bok choy and mushrooms with hoisin sauce

Does your family bok at the idea of eating leafy greens? Our quick and delicious Chinese side dish will have them coming bok for seconds.

1	large head bok choy
2 tsp	peanut oil
1 tsp	sesame oil
1 tsp	minced garlic
1 tsp	grated gingerroot
3 cups	sliced mixed mushrooms
1 can	(8 oz/227 mL) sliced water chestnuts, drained (optional)
1 bunch	green onions, coarsely chopped (white and green parts)
3 tbsp	hoisin sauce

- Before you begin, separate the bok choy into stalks, wash and dry thoroughly. Trim ¼ inch from the bottom of each stalk. Chop the stalks and leaves into ½-inch-thick slices. Separate the stalks from the leaves, since you'll be cooking them at different times.

- Heat both oils in a large, non-stick wok over medium-high heat. Add garlic and gingerroot and cook for 30 seconds. Add bok choy stems and mushrooms. Cook and stir until vegetables are tender, about 5 minutes. Add bok choy leaves, water chestnuts (if desired), green onions and hoisin sauce. Cook and stir for 2 more minutes, until leaves are wilted and mixture is hot. Remove from heat and serve immediately.

MAKES 4 SERVINGS

PER SERVING
99 calories,
4.4 g total fat
(0.6 g saturated fat),
5 g protein,
13 g carbohydrate,
2.9 g fiber,
0 mg cholesterol,
314 mg sodium

Nutrition Nugget

Few vegetables pack more of a nutritional punch than bok choy, a.k.a. Chinese white cabbage. For fewer calories than a stick of gum, bok choy delivers a potent vitamin cocktail, including a big dose of rare cancer-fighting nitrogen compounds called indoles. But what bok choy is most famous for is its unique calcium availability. Compared to other leafy greens, bok choy is lower in oxalate, a substance that binds with calcium and prevents it from being absorbed. The human body can absorb 54 percent of the calcium in bok choy. Compare this to five percent in spinach, a high-oxalate vegetable, and 32 percent in milk. So, as far as calcium goes, you get the most bang from your bok!

The Bulgur, The Better

Bulgur pilaf with five-spice powder and cranberries

We know what you're thinkin': Bulgur? You gotta be kidding! Is that something that comes from Bulgaria? Just calm down. There's no need to report us to the Better Bulgur Bureau. We just felt it was time for you to try something new, that's all.

2 tsp	olive oil
1 cup	diced celery
¾ cup	minced onions
2 tsp	minced garlic
1 cup	coarse bulgur (see tip)
¼ cup	dried cranberries
1 tsp	grated orange zest
½ tsp	Chinese five-spice powder
2 cups	reduced-sodium chicken broth
¼ tsp	salt

MAKES 6 SERVINGS
PER SERVING
128 calories, 2 g total fat,
(0.1 g saturated fat),
4 g protein, 25 g carbohydrate,
5.3 g fiber, 0 mg cholesterol,
214 mg sodium

- Heat oil in a medium pot over medium heat. Add celery, onions and garlic. Cook and stir until vegetables begin to soften, about 3 minutes. Add bulgur, cranberries, orange zest and five-spice powder. Cook and stir for 1 more minute.

- Add broth and salt. Bring to a boil. Reduce heat to low. Cover and simmer for 10 to 15 minutes, until liquid has been absorbed and bulgur is tender. Remove from heat and let stand, covered, for 5 minutes before serving.

Recipe Tip
Bulgur is a nutritious, quick-cooking form of whole wheat. It's often confused with, but is not exactly the same as, cracked wheat. Bulgur is created when wheat kernels are steamed, dried and crushed, whereas cracked wheat skips the cooking and drying steps. When cooked, bulgur has a nutty flavor and chewy texture. Look for it in well-stocked supermarkets or natural food stores.

Americans are just beginning to regard food the way the French always have. Dinner is not what you do in the evening before something else. Dinner is the evening.

Art Buchwald

Model Behaviour

If you're working on changing your body shape, don't model it after supermodels or celebrities. It's tough to measure up (or more likely, down) to the figures of Hollywood stars who have 24-hour private chefs, personal trainers, yoga gurus, tai chi instructors and massage therapists (not to mention plastic surgeons to fix whatever problems are left). Then there's airbrushing, good lighting and other photographic wizardry. Let's face it, Hollywood isn't reality—it's a very small and distorted part of the world. If you're trying to whip your body into shape, be realistic to avoid disappointment and do it for the right reasons: to develop a sense of well-being, improve self-esteem and boost energy so you can enjoy life fully. Anyone, of any body type, of any age, can become fit through regular exercise and a healthy diet. It's smarter to make fitness—not thinness—your No. 1 priority. Besides, who wants to deal with the paparazzi anyway?

The Rice is Right

Scentsational vegetable fried rice without all the fat!

Come on down! Vegetable fried rice is the next concoction on The Rice is Right! When it comes to savory side dishes, this colorful rice and veggie medley is Showcase No. 1!

WE HAVE A WINNER!

"DOG" BARKER

PREMIUM RICE

2	eggs
1½ tsp	sesame oil, divided
1 tsp	peanut oil
1 cup	finely chopped onions
1 cup	finely chopped mushrooms
¾ cup	finely chopped red bell pepper
½ cup	finely chopped celery
1 tbsp	grated gingerroot
2 tsp	minced garlic
1 cup	frozen mixed peas and carrots, thawed
4 cups	cooked basmati rice
½ cup	chopped green onions
2 tbsp	reduced-sodium soy sauce
2 tbsp	hoisin sauce

• Whisk together eggs and ½ tsp sesame oil in a small bowl. Spray an 8-inch, non-stick skillet lightly with cooking spray (or add a bit of oil or butter) and heat over medium-high heat. Add eggs and cook without stirring (as you would an omelette), until underside is cooked. Flip and cook other side. Remove cooked egg from skillet and chop into bite-sized pieces. Set aside.

• Heat remaining 1 tsp sesame oil and peanut oil in a wok or large skillet. Add onions, mushrooms, red pepper, celery, gingerroot and garlic. Cook and stir over medium-high heat until vegetables are tender, about 5 minutes. Add peas and carrots and cook just until heated through, about 2 more minutes. Stir in cooked rice, green onions, chopped egg, soy sauce and hoisin sauce. Mix well and continue to cook just until rice is heated through. Serve hot.

MAKES 8 SERVINGS

PER SERVING
172 calories, 3.3 g total fat
(0.7 g saturated fat), 6 g protein,
31 g carbohydrate, 2 g fiber,
54 mg cholesterol, 243 mg sodium

Nutrition Nugget

Bet you didn't know that the fried rice you eat in Chinese restaurants can have up to two tablespoons of oil per cup. That's 28 grams of fat just in your rice! Holy chow! Remember what Confucius said: He who eats too much Chinese food may not fit into his *Beijing* suit!

The Greater Scalloped Potater

Cheesy layered potato casserole with Canadian bacon and mushrooms

These slimmed-down scalloped potatoes get a flavor punch from lean Canadian bacon, shiitake mushrooms and a blend of tasty cheeses. A real knockout!

I AM THE GREATEST!

1 tbsp	butter or olive oil
1	medium onion, thinly sliced
2 tsp	minced garlic
2 cups	thinly sliced shiitake mushrooms
1 cup	finely diced Canadian bacon
¼ tsp	dried thyme
1 can	(14 oz/370 mL) 2% evaporated milk
1½ cups	reduced-sodium chicken broth
3 tbsp	all-purpose flour
½ tsp	dry mustard
¼ tsp	each salt and freshly ground black pepper
¾ cup	packed shredded light old (sharp) cheddar cheese (3 oz/85 g)
¼ cup	freshly grated Parmesan cheese
4	large thin-skinned potatoes, unpeeled, very thinly sliced (about 2½ lbs/1.1 kg)

MAKES 8 SERVINGS

PER SERVING
289 calories, 6.4 g total fat
(3.2 g saturated fat), 16 g protein,
42 g carbohydrate, 3.7 g fiber,
31 mg cholesterol, 552 mg sodium

- Melt butter over medium heat in a large pot. Add onion and garlic. Cook and stir until onion begins to soften, about 3 minutes. Add mushrooms and cook until mushrooms are tender, about 4 minutes. Add bacon and thyme. Cook and stir for 1 more minute.

- Whisk together milk, broth, flour, dry mustard, salt and pepper. Add to pot with onion-mushroom mixture. Cook and stir until sauce is bubbly and has thickened, about 5 minutes. Remove from heat. Add cheddar and Parmesan and stir until cheeses are melted.

- Spray a medium casserole dish with cooking spray. Layer ⅓ potatoes over bottom, overlapping as necessary. Spoon ⅓ sauce over potatoes. Repeat layering two more times, ending with sauce. Cover with foil and bake at 375°F for 1 hour, 20 minutes. Uncover and bake for 20 more minutes, or until top is golden brown and potatoes are tender. Let stand 15 minutes to cool before serving. It's hot!

Not a Dud Spud

Contrary to popular belief, potatoes are not the evil archenemy of a slim waistline. Like bread and rice, some people have turned a blind eye to the potato based on its high score on the Glycemic Index. But it's important to remember that potatoes do contain valuable nutrients like vitamin C and fiber—people have been subsisting on them for generations, for gosh sakes! In fact, a large baked potato has nearly four times the potassium of a banana, so it's good for the heart. And with lots of vitamin B6, it's good for the brain, too, even helping you produce more of the feel-good neurotransmitter serotonin. If you dig potatoes, you simply need a strategy that allows you to eat them every once in a while. First, keep your eyes on their size! Potatoes are a food we tend to overeat and in unhealthy forms: deep-fried, hash-browned or chipped 'n' dipped. Have a small portion (about half a cup) as an accompaniment to veggies and lean protein. And when you're hankerin' for a spud, make it a spud light. Choose new potatoes (a lower-glycemic option) and stick to healthier preparation methods like baked, steamed or roasted. Finally, by pairing potatoes with protein, fiber and good fat (like olive oil), you'll transform the high-glycemic food into a moderate-glycemic meal. As long as you think portion size, balance and moderation, potatoes won't go to waist.

Everybody Salsa

Fresh-tasting, colorful corn and black bean salsa

Whether spooned over chicken, fish or baked potatoes, stuffed in a pita pocket with tuna and chopped lettuce or eaten all by itself, this delicious salsa is sure to get your taste buds dancing!

2 tsp	avocado oil or olive oil
1 cup	whole-kernel corn (thaw first if using frozen)
1 cup	diced tomatoes
1 cup	canned no-salt-added black beans, drained and rinsed
½ cup	each diced onions and diced red bell pepper
¼ cup	grated carrots
1	jalapeño pepper, seeded and minced
1 tsp	minced garlic
1 tsp	ground cumin
½ tsp	chili powder
¼ tsp	each salt and freshly ground black pepper
2 tbsp	minced fresh cilantro

MAKES 4 CUPS

PER SERVING (½ CUP)
72 calories, 1.6 g total fat (0.2 g saturated fat), 3 g protein, 13 g carbohydrate, 3.3 g fiber, 0 mg cholesterol, 132 mg sodium

- Heat oil in a medium pot over medium heat. Add all ingredients except cilantro. Cook and stir for 5 to 7 minutes, until onions are tender and vegetables are heated through.

- Remove from heat and stir in cilantro. Serve warm or cold.

14-Carrotenoid Gold

You may have heard that yellow-orange veggies—squash, carrots, sweet potatoes, pumpkin—are chock-full of carotenoids. Why care about carotenoids? Well, these good-for-you plant compounds fight the DNA damage that can make your body old or sick. Yes, carrots and squash can help keep you young and healthy! How can they do that? Well, whether you spend your life loafing along the French Riviera or struggling to climb the corporate ladder, your DNA accumulates damage naturally. Another way your DNA gets damaged is when it gets copied to create a new cell. It's like when you use a photocopier to make a copy of a copy of a copy. Eventually, little flaws and imperfections start to show up. Same thing can happen with your DNA, and that can lead to the ultimate cell-replication error— cancer! Researchers suspect that carotenoids might protect against this kind of DNA damage that occurs with aging. So eat enough carrots and you'll never have to say, "What's up, doc?"

Nutrition Nugget

Want to slow down the aging process and prevent wrinkles? Duh! Who doesn't? Our best advice for saving face is to yank your sweet tooth. Elevated insulin levels (as a result of eating too much sugar and processed white foods) are one of the key contributors to rapid aging. It's true! Ask any dermatologist and they'll tell you that sugar weakens the elasticity of skin, causing wrinkles and sagging. Translation: The more sugar you eat, the faster you age!

Trivial Tidbit

*Weak*end willpower? According to the *Obesity Journal*, we eat an average of 236 more calories on Saturday.

Viva Las Veggies

Roasted vegetable gratin with tomatoes, zucchini, mushrooms and onions

When the stakes are high and you feel like adding some glitz and glamour to ordinary veggies, bake this sinsational side dish and get your dinner party swingin'! It makes slots, so there's enough to feed everyone. Just remember: What happens in the oven, stays in the oven.

4	medium tomatoes, cut into chunks
2	medium zucchini, chopped
2	large portobello mushrooms (about 5-inch diameter), chopped (see tip)
1	medium red onion, coarsely chopped
1 tsp	minced garlic
1 tbsp	each olive oil and balsamic vinegar
1 tbsp	chopped mixed fresh herbs, such as rosemary, basil, oregano or thyme
¼ tsp	each salt and freshly ground black pepper
1 cup	fresh whole-grain bread crumbs (see tip, p. 239)
½ cup	freshly grated Parmesan cheese
½ tsp	dried thyme

MAKES 6 SERVINGS

PER SERVING
139 calories, 5.7 g total fat (2 g saturated fat), 8 g protein, 18 g carbohydrate, 4.1 g fiber, 7 mg cholesterol, 323 mg sodium

Recipe Tips Using a small spoon, scrape off (and discard) the gills from the underside of the portobello mushrooms before using them in this recipe. Please, please buy fresh Parmesan cheese and grate it yourself. The cheap stuff you buy in the pasta aisle is fine on spaghetti, but it doesn't really melt, so you need to buy a small chunk of the good stuff to make this gratin.

- Spray a 9 x 13-inch baking dish with cooking spray. Add tomatoes, zucchini, mushrooms, onion and garlic. Mix well (using your hands works best). Add olive oil, vinegar, fresh herbs, salt and pepper. Mix again to coat vegetables with dressing.

- Roast, uncovered, at 425°F for 25 minutes. While vegetables are roasting, prepare topping. Combine bread crumbs, Parmesan cheese and dried thyme in a small bowl and mix well.

- Remove vegetables from oven. Sprinkle crumb mixture evenly over vegetables. Return to oven for 5 minutes, until cheese is melted and crumbs turn a light golden brown. Serve hot.

> The more you eat, the less flavor; the less you eat, the more flavor.
> *Chinese proverb*

Doctored 'Bellos

Grilled portobello mushrooms with basil and Parmesan cheese

I dream of in-Jeannie-ous side dishes! If you do, too, these flavor-packed, grilled portobellos are just what the dinner doctor ordered!

⅓ cup	bottled light Italian dressing
1 tbsp	minced fresh basil leaves
2 tsp	balsamic vinegar
⅛ tsp	freshly ground black pepper
8	medium portobello mushrooms (about 4-inch diameter), stems removed
¼ cup	freshly grated Parmesan cheese or crumbled light feta cheese (1 oz/28 g)

- Combine dressing, basil, vinegar and black pepper in a small bowl. Set aside.

- Wipe mushrooms clean. Using a pastry brush, generously brush both sides of mushrooms with prepared dressing. Let mushrooms stand at room temperature while you preheat the grill to high setting.

- Brush grill rack lightly with oil. Grill mushrooms for 2 to 3 minutes per side, until tender with nice grill marks. Remove from heat. Slice mushrooms and place in a serving bowl. Sprinkle with Parmesan cheese. Serve immediately.

Cashew: The sound a nut makes when it sneezes :)

Magically delicious mushrooms? It's sheer jeannie-ous!

MAKES
4 SERVINGS

PER SERVING

92 calories, 4.5 g total fat (1.1 g saturated fat), 5 g protein, 11 g carbohydrate, 2.6 g fiber, 6 mg cholesterol, 396 mg sodium

Trivial Tidbit

In 1969, when Neil Armstrong and Buzz Aldrin sat down to their first meal on the moon, what was the main course? Was it (a) roast turkey; (b) meatloaf; (c) a Quarter Pounder with Cheese or (d) Kraft Dinner? The answer? (a) roast turkey. But what they really craved was a Milky Way or Mars bar!

Pain, Pain, Go Away

If you think nagging arthritis pain or that old rotator-cuff tear gives you license to retire to the sofa with a remote control, a bottle of soda and a bag of chips, think again! Twenty years ago, doctors said arthritis and other age-related aches and pains were reason enough to donate your sneakers to The Salvation Army. These days, they recommend some form of exercise for almost everyone. Orthopedic specialist Dr. William Raasch put it best: "My older patients who exercise complain they have arthritis pain in their knees for a few hours after exercising. But my patients who don't exercise have arthritis pain 24 hours a day." As you grow older, it's important to find a fitness routine that suits your age. After all, you wouldn't drive a vintage car the same way you would a modern sports car. Your body might need kinder, gentler handling. Trade high-impact sports for lower-impact ones like walking, swimming and biking. If you want a good "quality-of-life" insurance policy, focus on flexibility and strength. Yoga, Pilates, stretching and weight training should keep your moving parts lubricated, prevent your chassis from expanding and give you unlimited mileage. C'mon! Shift out of park and take your body for a spin!

Darth Tater

Cheesy, gooey, roasted-potato casserole for a special occasion

If you think all potatoes are evil, think again! It's time to restore justice to the beloved spud with our lightened-up roasted-potato casserole. It's the best in the galaxy! A real lifesaber when you need a special side dish.

May the forks be with you!

MAKES
10 SERVINGS

PER SERVING
190 calories,
5.9 g total fat
(2.4 g saturated fat),
6 g protein,
28 g carbohydrate,
3.2 g fiber,
10 mg cholesterol,
454 mg sodium

4	large, unpeeled, thin-skinned potatoes (about 2½ lbs/1.1 kg)
1 cup	chopped onions
1 tbsp	olive oil
1 tsp	minced garlic
½ tsp	each salt and dried thyme
¼ tsp	each freshly ground black pepper and paprika
1 can	(10 oz/284 mL) condensed cheddar cheese soup, undiluted
⅓ cup	freshly grated Parmesan cheese
2 tbsp	minced fresh dill or fresh parsley
½ cup	packed shredded light old (sharp) cheddar cheese (2 oz/57 g)
1	green onion, chopped

- Preheat oven to 425°F. Cut potatoes into 1-inch chunks and place in a 9 x 13-inch baking dish that has been sprayed with cooking spray. Add onions, olive oil, garlic, salt, thyme, pepper and paprika and mix well. Roast potatoes for 30 minutes, stirring once, halfway through cooking time. Remove from oven. Reduce oven temperature to 375°F.

- In a medium bowl, mix together soup, Parmesan cheese and dill. Pour over potatoes. Mix well. Sprinkle shredded cheddar on top, followed by green onion. Return potatoes to oven and bake, uncovered, for 25 minutes, until cheese is bubbly and potatoes are golden brown around edges. Let stand 5 minutes before serving.

Nutrition Nugget

Keep your eyes on the size of your fries! If your cravings take over and you just can't resist an order of French fries, then at least opt for the small size. By replacing a large serving of fries with a small serving just once a week, you'll save 9,360 calories and 520 grams of fat in a year. That's more than seven days' worth of fat! So if you don't want French fries to form a merger with your waistline, downsizing is the way to go.

271

Twice as Nice Coconut Rice

A fragrant rice dish to pair with stir-fried vegetables

If you're tired of serving plain, ol' white rice with a meal, but don't have time to prepare anything too fancy, this doubly delicious recipe will rice to the occasion.

1 tsp	coconut oil or olive oil
2 tsp	grated gingerroot
1 tsp	minced garlic
1½ cups	uncooked brown or basmati rice
¾ cup	light coconut milk
1 tsp	each liquid honey and grated lemon zest
½ tsp	salt

- Heat oil in a medium pot over medium heat. Add gingerroot and garlic. Cook and stir for 1 minute. Add rice and cook for 1 more minute.

- Stir in coconut milk, 2¼ cups water, honey, lemon zest and salt. Bring to a boil. Reduce heat to low. Cover and simmer for 20 minutes, or until liquid is absorbed and rice is tender. (Exact cooking time depends on brand of rice. Check instructions on package.)

- Fluff rice with a fork and serve immediately.

MAKES 6 SERVINGS

PER SERVING
208 calories, 4.6 g total fat (3.1 g saturated fat), 4 g protein, 38 g carbohydrate, 1.7 g fiber, 0 mg cholesterol, 203 mg sodium

Special K Diet

We have a bone to pick with you! Seems that calcium's been hogging all the attention when it comes to bone health. Too bad. There's a bona fide bone-builder working silently in the background that deserves some time in the spotlight. Let's hear it for vitamin K! You'll get it from kale, cucumber, spinach, Swiss chard, bok choy, asparagus, parsley and most dark, leafy greens. Vitamin K-rich foods help maintain bone mass, protecting us from osteoporosis. And it's vitamin K that's required for blood to clot, so if you don't want to bleed to death from that paper cut, better eat your greens! (Yowch! How can something so small be so excruciating, anyway?) One of the best food sources of vitamin K is kale. One cup contains 10 times your daily requirement! Often relegated as a salad bar garnish, most people don't know what the heck to do with kale. Try adding finely chopped kale to a salad with other leafy greens or lightly sautéing it with olive oil, black pepper, garlic and sea salt, much like you would sauté spinach. Slice it up with a bunch of other veggies for a dee-lish stir-fry or toss it into soups and stews. You can even buy dehydrated kale chips—a salty, crunchy substitute for potato chips that won't go from your lips to your hips. Give 'em a try, K?

The golden rule when reading the menu is, if you cannot pronounce it, you cannot afford it.

Frank Muir

Sammy Salsa

Mango salsa that makes an excellent topping for grilled fish or chicken

It's going, going, gone! Our mango salsa is a big hit—a real dinger! We think it's the best salsa you'll ever have cross your plate.

1	large mango, peeled and diced
⅔ cup	minced red bell pepper
½ cup	minced red onions
1	jalapeño pepper, seeded and minced
2 tbsp	each freshly squeezed lime juice and minced fresh cilantro
2 tsp	granulated sugar
1 tsp	olive oil
¼ tsp	ground cumin
⅛ tsp	salt

MAKES 3 CUPS

PER SERVING (¼ CUP)
36 calories, 0.5 g total fat
(0 g saturated fat),
0 g protein,
9 g carbohydrate,
1 g fiber,
0 mg cholesterol,
26 mg sodium

- Combine all ingredients in a medium bowl. Mix well. Let salsa stand at room temperature for 30 minutes before serving. Cover and refrigerate any leftovers.

FOOD BITE The mango tree is considered sacred in India, where the fruit first appeared. This exceedingly juicy fruit is not only delicious, but also rich in vitamins A, C and D. You need to be careful when eating mango, though—the juice can stain your clothing!

Pine 'n' Dandy Salsa

I just love doing the salsa

Our grilled pineapple salsa is a flavorful accompaniment to grilled meats

Don't cha-cha just love the taste of juicy, fresh pineapple? Grilling this fabulous fruit intensifies its dandy flavor by caramelizing its natural sugars… and that's not just a bunch of mambo jumbo!

1	whole fresh pineapple (see tip)
1	medium red bell pepper
⅓ cup	minced red onions
1	jalapeño pepper, seeded and minced
2 tbsp	freshly squeezed lime juice
1½ tbsp	minced fresh cilantro
⅛ tsp	salt

MAKES 3½ CUPS

PER SERVING (¼ CUP)
23 calories, 0.2 g fat
(0 g saturated fat),
0 g protein,
6 g carbohydrate, 0.8 g fiber,
0 mg cholesterol, 22 mg sodium

- Preheat grill to high heat.

- If your pineapple needs peeling and coring, go ahead and do that now. Slice the pineapple into 6 rings, each about ¾ inch thick. Cut the bell pepper in half and remove the stem and seeds.

- Brush grill rack lightly with oil. Place pineapple rings and bell pepper halves on grill. Close lid. Cook for about 4 minutes per side, until heated through with nice grill marks on the surface. Remove from heat.

- When cool enough to handle, dice pineapple and bell pepper and place in a medium bowl. Add remaining ingredients and mix well. Serve immediately or cover and refrigerate until ready to serve. Tastes best when eaten within 1 day.

Recipe Tip: Make sure the pineapple is ripe or your salsa won't be very tasty. We suggest the precored pineapples that are sold refrigerated in plastic containers in the produce section. They're the same price, so why bother with the extra work?

The Spice of Rice

Brown rice with dried apricots and lots of spice

There's variety in the spice of rice! Four fragrant spices add jazz and pizzazz to this savory, flavory rice dish.

1 tsp	olive oil
½ cup	each diced carrots, diced green bell pepper and minced onions
1 cup	uncooked brown rice
1 tsp	ground coriander
½ tsp	ground cumin
¼ tsp	each ground ginger and ground cinnamon
2¼ cups	reduced-sodium chicken or vegetable broth
¼ tsp	salt
½ cup	chopped dried apricots (see tip)
2 tbsp	minced fresh cilantro or parsley

MAKES 6 SERVINGS

PER SERVING
157 calories, 1.2 g total fat (0.1 g saturated fat), 4 g protein, 33 g carbohydrate, 2 g fiber, 0 mg cholesterol, 281 mg sodium

- Heat olive oil in a medium pot over medium heat. Add carrots, green pepper and onions. Cook and stir until vegetables begin to soften, about 3 minutes.

- Add rice, coriander, cumin, ginger and cinnamon. Cook and stir for 1 more minute. Add broth, salt and apricots. Bring to a boil. Reduce heat to low. Cover and simmer for 15 to 20 minutes, until liquid has been absorbed and rice is tender. (Exact cooking time will depend on brand of rice. Check package for instructions.) Stir in cilantro. Remove from heat and let stand, covered, for 5 minutes before serving.

Recipe Tip Use kitchen shears or a very sharp knife to chop dried apricots. To prevent the fruit from sticking, spray the scissors or knife with cooking spray or dip them in hot water every once in a while. You can soften dried fruit that has hardened by covering it with boiling water and letting it soak for 15 minutes. Blot the fruit dry with paper towels before using.

What do you call a parrot in a raincoat?
Polly Unsaturated :)

Spud Light

Very simple, very delicious roasted mini red potatoes and onions

Even if you're watching your weight, there's no need to be a tater hater. As long as you keep your eyes on portion sizes, you can still be buds with spuds.

2 lbs	(907 g) mini red potatoes, unpeeled
1	medium red onion, cut into 8 wedges (see tip)
2 tbsp	olive oil
1 tbsp	minced fresh rosemary or fresh thyme, or a bit of both
2 tsp	balsamic vinegar
1 tsp	minced garlic
¼ tsp	each salt and freshly ground black pepper or to taste

- Preheat oven to 425°F. Spray a 9 x 13-inch baking pan with cooking spray. Cut potatoes in half or in quarters if they're larger, and place in baking pan. Add onion, olive oil, herbs, vinegar and garlic. Toss vegetables until well coated.

- Roast, uncovered, for about 30 minutes. Check for doneness of potatoes. Can you stick a fork in them? If not, stir the vegetables around a bit, return to oven and continue to roast until potatoes are tender. (It's a bit tricky to predict how long to cook the potatoes, since it depends entirely on their size.)

- Remove vegetables from oven and transfer to a serving dish. Sprinkle with salt and pepper and serve immediately.

Recipe Tip: You can substitute 8 large, peeled shallots for the red onion wedges.

MAKES 8 SERVINGS

PER SERVING
148 calories, 3.5 g total fat (0.5 g saturated fat), 3 g protein, 27 g carbohydrate, 2.8 g fiber, 0 mg cholesterol, 81 mg sodium

The Hydrogenated Bomb

Time to tune in to trans fats—the evil, dietary bogeymen lurking below the surface of many popular foods. These man-made fats are created by bubbling hydrogen through vegetable oil. That gives packaged foods like potato chips, crackers and cookies the taste and texture we love, and embalms them so they can sit on store shelves forever. Problem is, your body struggles to deal with trans fats. How bad are they? Bad! They block your arteries, tinker with your heart, weaken your liver, interfere with your immune system, inhibit fertility and basically wreak hormonal havoc. Did we mention they make you fat? No doubt you've heard that trans fats are hiding in fast foods, donuts, some margarines, peanut butter and shortening, but you might be shocked to find that these health corrupters have crept into many common convenience foods: frozen pizzas, toaster waffles, pastries, microwave entrées, frozen fries, chicken nuggets, microwave popcorn, chocolate bars, candy, granola bars...even some breakfast cereals! Fruity O-no! Thankfully, manufacturers have been pressured to trash the trans and now have to spell it out on labels. But buyer beware: Nutrition labeling regulations allow manufacturers to round to zero any trans-fat value below 0.5 grams per serving, so even if a package screams "0 Trans Fat!" the product might still have some. And even a little of this nasty stuff is a lot for your body to handle. Look for the words "partially hydrogenated vegetable or soybean oil" on ingredients lists. That spells T.R.O.U.B.L.E.

Trivial Tidbit

Placing this in your shoes at night will keep the leather soft and the shoes smelling fresh and clean: (a) a raw potato; (b) a bar of soap; (c) a pine cone; or (d) a foot. The answer is...(a) a raw potato! If you have stinky feet, this spud's for you!

The Fennel Frontier

Simple roasted fennel topped with Parmesan cheese

If you love fennel, this simple-yet-Enterprising creation will Shatner all expectations. Uhura in for a treat! This is the real McCoy, a recipe you'll wanna Klingon to, no Bones about it!

2	large fennel bulbs
2 tbsp	olive oil
½ tsp	each dried thyme, salt and freshly ground black pepper
⅓ cup	freshly grated or shaved Parmesan cheese

- Trim off and discard stalks and ½ inch off bottom of fennel bulbs. Cut bulbs in half. Place flat side down on cutting board. Cut each fennel half into generous ½-inch-thick slices and place in a 9 x 13-inch baking dish.

- Add oil, thyme, salt and pepper. Mix well. (Using your hands works best.) Roast at 400°F for 20 minutes. Remove from oven, stir and sprinkle with Parmesan. Bake for 15 to 20 more minutes, until fennel is very tender and begins to caramelize around edges. Serve hot.

> EAT WELL AND PROSPER

MAKES 6 SERVINGS

PER SERVING
95 calories, 6.2 g total fat
(1.7 g saturated fat), 3 g protein,
8 g carbohydrate, 3.2 g fiber,
4 mg cholesterol, 285 mg sodium

Nutrition Nugget

Eating fennel is like downing a huge vitamin C pill—it helps prevent disease and keeps you looking young. Plus, it contains compounds that block inflammation, which scientists are discovering is at the root of many diseases, including cancer and heart disease. We love it because it tastes like one of our favorite childhood treats—licorice!

Chew the Right Thing

Did you know that it takes 50 hours for a snake to digest one frog? If you did, you must have way too much time on your hands! Actually the snake is not alone in battling digestion challenges. Today, millions of folks are suffering from digestive difficulties, largely due to our "standard" diet of processed, refined junk foods. Unfortunately, foul play in the gut is often a major contributor to serious, chronic illness. Here's a simple tip to get your body on the right digestive track: Chew your food! Thoroughly chewing each bite at least 20 to 30 times is very important because the process of digestion actually begins in the mouth. There's an enzyme in saliva that starts breaking down starches as you chew. When you scarf down an order of fries like Janet does a box of Turtles at Christmas, your stomach's left to deal with your mouth's hasty, incomplete work. That would be fine if we had an extra set of teeth in our stomach, but since we don't, your stomach can't do its job properly. That puts a huge burden on your pancreas, which is responsible for supplying the remaining digestive enzymes. After years of dealing with poor chewing and poor *chewsing*, your pancreas can become exhausted and wave the white flag. A whole chain reaction occurs right through your digestive tract, with organs straining and suffering from overexertion. By the time those fries end up in your large intestine, they're an incompletely digested mass of spuds just sitting there and fermenting—perfect feed for the disease-causing bacterial critters that live in that organ. Gross! If you want to get on the right health track, then train yourself to chew. Chew, chew, train!

Hail a Cabbage

Braised red cabbage with apples and onions

You won't find better fare anywhere in town! Simple to prepare, this tremendously tasty cabbage will have the flavor-meter in a ticking tizzy.

2 tsp	olive oil
1	small onion, thinly sliced into rings
1 tsp	minced garlic
½ cup	apple juice
1 cup	peeled and finely chopped or grated apples
2 tbsp	red wine vinegar
1½ tbsp	brown sugar
1	bay leaf
½ tsp	salt
¼ tsp	freshly ground black pepper
4 cups	shredded red cabbage
2 tbsp	minced fresh parsley

- Heat olive oil in a large pot over medium heat. Add onions and garlic. Cook and stir until onions are tender, about 5 minutes.

- Dilute apple juice with ½ cup water to make 1 cup total. Add to onions and garlic, along with apples, vinegar, brown sugar, bay leaf, salt and pepper. Mix well and bring mixture to a boil. Stir in cabbage. Cover and simmer over medium heat until cabbage is tender-crisp, about 12 to 15 minutes. Remove from heat, discard bay leaf and stir in parsley.

MAKES 4 SERVINGS

PER SERVING
96 calories, 2.6 g total fat (0.4 g saturated fat), 2 g protein, 18 g carbohydrate, 2.8 g fiber, 0 mg cholesterol, 310 mg sodium

> Things turn out best for the people who make the best out of the way things turn out.
>
> *Art Linkletter*

Trivial Tidbit

Caution: Mass mail-outs could be hazardous to your waistline! Licking a postage stamp will set you back anywhere from two to eight calories, depending on how well you lick it.

In this chapter...

Bring Home the Bakin'

Put some lovin' in your oven with these mouthwatering muffins, loaves and cookies

Rolls Royce,
p. 292

The Rolling Scones

These delectable, cranberry-orange scones are perfect for tea time

Taste buds can't get no satisfaction? This old-time favorite treat will get them rockin'.

1½ cups	all-purpose flour
½ cup	oat bran
½ cup	sweetened dried cranberries, chopped
⅓ cup	packed brown sugar
2 tsp	baking powder
1 tsp	baking soda
½ tsp	salt
1 cup	buttermilk
2 tbsp	butter, melted
2 tsp	grated orange zest
½ tsp	vanilla
1	egg

MAKES 12 SCONES

PER SCONE
125 calories, 3 g total fat (1.5 g saturated fat), 3 g protein, 22 g carbohydrate, 1.2 g fiber, 24 mg cholesterol, 311 mg sodium

- Preheat oven to 400°F. Spray a large baking sheet with cooking spray and set aside.

- In a large bowl, combine flour, oat bran, cranberries, brown sugar, baking powder, baking soda and salt. Set aside.

- In a medium bowl, whisk together buttermilk, butter, orange zest and vanilla. Add wet ingredients to dry ingredients. Stir until a soft dough is formed. Add a bit more flour if dough is too sticky. Turn dough out onto a lightly floured surface. Divide into 2 pieces. Shape each piece into a ball. Place balls on baking sheet. Roll out or pat dough to ¾-inch-thick circles, about 6 inches in diameter. Using a sharp knife, cut each circle into 6 wedges, but do not separate them.

- To make glaze, lightly beat egg and 1 tbsp water in a small bowl. Brush glaze lightly over top of dough (you will use less than half of it). Bake for 15 to 17 minutes, until scones are puffed up and golden. Cool slightly. Pull scones apart and serve warm.

Nutrition Nugget

Drinking coffee might help perk up a drunk person, but it does nothing to sober him or her up. In fact, it may actually increase the adverse effects of alcohol because it worsens dehydration and gives the liver one more thing to detoxify. Your best bet to sober up? H_2O on the rocks or a drink containing electrolytes (trace minerals), like coconut water. So, when your friend offers you a cappuccino after a night of drinking vino, just say, "Nay, Bob!"

Did you hear about the man who used counterfeit money to pay his lunch bill? He had been served decaffeinated coffee with non-dairy creamer and artificial sweetener :)

Sweet Home Alabanana

Banana bread with oat bran, pecans and chocolate chips

Does your conscience bother you when all your banana Skynyrds are turnin' brown? Tell the truth! Here's a tasty solution: Whip up this guilt-free banana bread with crunchy pecans and mini chocolate chips—and make sure you save room for a Second Helping!

1¾ cups	all-purpose flour
½ cup	oat bran
2 tsp	baking powder
1 tsp	baking soda
1 tsp	ground cinnamon
½ tsp	salt
1½ cups	mashed ripe bananas (about 4 medium or 3 large)
¾ cup	buttermilk or plain yogurt
2	eggs
½ cup	packed brown sugar
2 tbsp	butter, melted
2 tsp	vanilla
½ cup	chopped pecans
⅓ cup	mini semi-sweet chocolate chips

Note: You absolutely must use ripe bananas (with brown spots!) for this recipe. Most banana bread recipes use a lot more sugar than we use in ours, so the sweetness from the ripe bananas is really important.

MAKES 2 SMALL LOAVES, 8 SLICES EACH

PER SLICE
171 calories, 6.2 g total fat (2 g saturated fat), 3.9 g protein, 28 g carbohydrate, 1.9 g fiber, 31 mg cholesterol, 236 mg sodium

- Preheat oven to 350ºF. Spray two 8 x 4-inch loaf pans with cooking spray and set aside.
- In a large bowl, combine flour, oat bran, baking powder, baking soda, cinnamon and salt. Mix well and set aside.
- In a medium bowl, whisk together bananas, buttermilk, eggs, brown sugar, butter and vanilla until well blended.
- Add wet ingredients to dry ingredients and mix just until dry ingredients are moistened. Fold in nuts and chocolate chips. Do not overmix batter.
- Divide batter evenly among loaf pans. Bake for 30 to 35 minutes, or until a wooden pick inserted in center of loaves comes out clean. Cool loaves in pans on a wire rack for 10 minutes. Remove loaves from pans and (1) slice and eat warm, or (2) cool completely on rack, then store covered in plastic wrap (they won't last long!).

Banana Banter

Please help us settle an argument/bet. We were having this really deep discussion recently about the proper way to eat a banana. Things got quite heated as we both presented our opposing banana-eating strategies. Greta peels the entire banana first, throws away the peel and holds the banana in her hand to eat it. Janet eats her banana like a monkey, peeling it halfway down, then holding the unpeeled bottom portion while eating the top portion. Greta thinks Janet looks like one of the characters from *Planet of the Apes* when she eats bananas this way, but what does she know? Maybe that's how everyone eats bananas. Janet's other preferred banana-eating method is to MASH the banana and eat it like baby food! (Veins in Greta's neck bulging.) If you're reading this, please, please take a minute to let us know how you eat a banana. This is not about taking sides or feeling sorry for Janet because Greta called her a monkey. Just send a note to janetandgreta@janetandgreta.com and tell us your preferred banana-eating method. We'll see which one of us wins the 20 bucks!

Note from Greta: Don't be influenced by this photo, which depicts Janet's ridiculous method of eating a banana.

The Grateful Bread

Super-moist and cake-like, this sweet apple and oat bread can be served for dessert

Grated apples, grated carrots, grated coconut—grate Scott! This bread has grate flavor!

You'll thank me for this!

1½ cups	all-purpose flour
1 cup	quick-cooking rolled oats (not instant)
1 cup	granulated sugar
2 tsp	each baking powder and ground cinnamon
½ tsp	salt
¼ tsp	ground nutmeg
⅓ cup	each sweetened shredded coconut and chopped walnuts
½ cup	2% evaporated milk
⅓ cup	unsweetened applesauce
2	eggs
2 tbsp	high-quality vegetable oil (see tip, p. 286)
2 tsp	vanilla
2 cups	peeled, grated apples
½ cup	grated carrots

- Preheat oven to 350°F. Spray a 9 x 5-inch loaf pan with cooking spray and set aside.

- In a large bowl, combine flour, oats, sugar, baking powder, cinnamon, salt and nutmeg. Add coconut and walnuts. Mix well.

- In a medium bowl, whisk together evaporated milk, applesauce, eggs, oil and vanilla. Stir in apples and carrots.

- Add wet ingredients to dry ingredients. Mix just until dry ingredients are moistened. Pour batter into pan. Spread evenly. Bake for 55 to 60 minutes, or until a wooden pick inserted in center of loaf comes out clean. Cool for 10 minutes in pan. Remove bread from pan and let cool completely on a wire rack. Cover with plastic wrap and store in the refrigerator.

MAKES 1 LARGE LOAF, 12 SLICES

PER SLICE
241 calories, 7.4 g total fat (2.1 g saturated fat), 5 g protein, 40 g carbohydrate, 2.3 g fiber, 37 mg cholesterol, 203 mg sodium

> **Losing weight is a triumph of mind over platter.**
> *Author unknown*

Donut Try This at Home!

Did you know that a bagel has more calories and sodium than a glazed donut? Not that we're encouraging you to choose the donut! The point is that healthy breakfast choices outside your own home are few and far between compared with lunch and dinner options. In fact, studies show that eating breakfast "out" doubles your odds of becoming obese! Double cream, double sugar, double-chocolate muffin...double chin! The best way to start your day, and your engine, is with a high-protein, high-fiber, high-octane breakfast that you prepare yourself, like a scrumptious whey protein shake with frozen berries, or poached eggs and whole-grain toast with almond butter, for example. Protein and fiber are your fat-loss friends, keeping you full and satisfied and fueled for action. Who knew that breakfast in bed could help prevent love handles?

FOOD BITE The earliest known advocate of a high-fiber diet was Hippocrates. He urged his fellow countrymen to bake their bread with bran for its "salutary effect upon the bowels." His being a big fan of bran surely has something to do with the Hippocratic *Oat*.

Everybody Loves Raysins

Soft and chewy oatmeal raisin cookies

Getting your family to sitcalm while these scrumptious cookies are baking is no laughing matter!

2 cups	quick-cooking rolled oats (not instant)	⅓ cup	butter, at room temperature
1 cup + 2 tbsp	all-purpose flour	⅓ cup	unsweetened applesauce
1 tsp	ground cinnamon	1	egg
½ tsp	baking powder	1 tsp	vanilla
½ tsp	salt	¾ cup	raisins
1 cup	lightly packed brown sugar		

- Preheat oven to 350°F. Spray a large cookie sheet with cooking spray and set aside.

- Combine oats, flour, cinnamon, baking powder and salt in a medium bowl. Mix well.

- In a large bowl, beat brown sugar and butter on low speed of electric mixer until mixture resembles wet sand. Add applesauce, egg and vanilla and beat again until well blended. Add oat mixture to sugar mixture. Using a wooden spoon, stir until dry ingredients are moistened. Stir in raisins.

- Drop dough by spoonfuls onto prepared cookie sheet. (Use about 2 tbsp dough per cookie and space 2 inches apart.) Flatten cookies to ¼-inch thickness using a fork. Dip the fork in water to prevent it from sticking to cookies. Bake for 12 to 14 minutes, until tops of cookies are dry to touch. Cookies may seem underbaked but that's OK. Do not overbake! Let cool on cookie sheet for 5 minutes, then carefully remove to cooling rack.

MAKES 20 COOKIES

PER COOKIE
130 calories, 4 g total fat
(2 g saturated fat),
2 g protein,
22 g carbohydrate,
1.3 g fiber,
19 mg cholesterol,
78 mg sodium

Nutrition Nugget
Why are oats so oatstanding? Well, besides the headline-making, cholesterol-lowering super fiber beta-glucan they contain, oats also harbor unique plant chemicals called avenanthramides, which prevent bad cholesterol from oxidizing and causing arterial plaque. Plus, oats can help stabilize blood sugar, so they're a helpful food for diabetics and for weight watchers. Throw in muscle-building protein, free-radical scavenging selenium, energy-producing vitamin B1 and feel-good, sleep-promoting tryptophan, and you can see why we're "doughing" our oats in this cookie recipe!

Sinnamon Apple Muffins

Aromatic cinnamon is paired with soft apple bits and nutritious oats in these highly addictive muffins

These sinfully delicious cinnamon-filled apple muffins are so mouthwatering and moist, they're certain to lead you into temptation.

THEY'RE SIN FREE

1½ cups	quick-cooking rolled oats (not instant)
1½ cups	boiling water
1 cup	all-purpose flour
½ cup	whole wheat flour
¾ cup	brown sugar (not packed)
2 tsp	baking powder
1 tsp	baking soda
1 tsp	ground cinnamon
½ tsp	salt
¼ cup	each liquid honey and unsweetened applesauce
1	egg
3 tbsp	butter, melted
1 tsp	vanilla
1½ cups	peeled, cored and finely chopped apples

Cinnamon sugar to sprinkle on top (optional)

- Preheat oven to 350°F. Spray a 12-cup muffin tin with cooking spray and set aside. Pour boiling water over oats in a medium bowl. Stir and let stand for 20 minutes.

- Combine both flours, sugar, baking powder, baking soda, cinnamon and salt in a large bowl. Set aside.

- In a small bowl, whisk together honey, applesauce, egg, butter and vanilla. Add applesauce mixture to oats and stir until smooth. Add oat mixture to flour mixture and stir until dry ingredients are moistened. Fold in chopped apples.

- Divide batter among 12 muffin cups. Sprinkle each muffin lightly with cinnamon sugar, if desired. Bake for 20 minutes, or until a wooden pick inserted in center of muffin comes out clean. Remove from pan and let cool.

MAKES 12 MUFFINS

PER MUFFIN
189 calories, 4.3 g total fat
(2 g saturated fat),
4 g protein,
35 g carbohydrate,
2.3 g fiber,
25 mg cholesterol,
252 mg sodium

Recipe Tip Wouldn't it be nice to have freshly baked muffins available first thing in the morning? Well, there's "muffin to it!" Separately mix the wet and dry ingredients the night before. Cover the dry ingredients and keep them at room temperature overnight. Cover the wet ingredients and refrigerate. Before hopping in the shower in the morning, simply preheat the oven, spray the muffin tin with cooking spray, combine the wet and dry ingredients, fill the muffin cups and pop them in the oven. The muffins can bake while you shower and get dressed!

Hay fever is much achoo about nothing :)

Barking Up the Right Tree

One of the oldest spices used by man, cinnamon is the inner bark of a tropical evergreen tree. After it's harvested, the bark curls up and it dries, then it's cut into sticks or ground into powder. Sprinkling cinnamon on your oatmeal or whole-grain toast may give you more than just a flavor boost: Research shows that cinnamon not only stimulates digestion, but it also boosts the activity of insulin, helping the body process sugars much more efficiently. That's sweet news for diabetics and for those at risk for Type 2 diabetes. By adding half a teaspoon to their daily diets, people with diabetes may help stave off complications related to impaired glucose metabolism, including fatigue, blurred vision and increased risk of kidney failure. And if your taste buds crave adventure, consider the following little-known cinnamon factoid: In the fourth century AD, a Chinese Taoist alchemist wrote that if one ingested cinnamon along with toad brains for seven years, that person could walk on water and avoid aging, and even death! Interestingly, this hypothesis has not yet been tested by modern science. Wanna sign up for the clinical trials?

Bananaberry Bombs

Moist banana-blueberry muffins with oats and flaxseed

You'll be blown away by the great taste and moist texture of these banana-blueberry muffins! Flavor explosion! Ka-pow!

1 cup	quick-cooking rolled oats (not instant)
½ cup	each all-purpose flour and whole wheat flour
½ cup	granulated sugar
¼ cup	ground flaxseed or wheat germ
1½ tsp	baking powder
1 tsp	baking soda
½ tsp	salt
1½ cups	mashed ripe bananas (about 3 large or 4 small)
¼ cup	butter, melted
1	egg
1 cup	fresh or frozen blueberries

- Preheat oven to 375°F. Spray a 12-cup muffin tin with cooking spray and set aside.

- Combine oats, both flours, sugar, ground flaxseed, baking powder, baking soda and salt in a large bowl. Mix well and set aside.

- In a medium bowl, whisk together bananas, butter and egg. Add banana mixture to dry ingredients and stir just until dry ingredients are moistened. Gently fold in blueberries.

- Divide batter among 12 muffin cups. Bake for 20 minutes, or until a wooden pick inserted in center of muffin comes out clean. Cool on a wire rack.

MAKES 12 MUFFINS

PER MUFFIN
183 calories, 5.7 g total fat (3 g saturated fat), 3.7 g protein, 30 g carbohydrate, 3.1 g fiber, 26 mg cholesterol, 209 mg sodium

The Facts on Flax

With a list of health benefits as long as Wayne Gretzky's scoring records, it's no wonder scientists have gone nuts over flaxseed. It's one of the richest sources of omega-3 fatty acids, a type of fat that your body can't manufacture. You can only get omega-3s from food and, sadly, due to our poor eating habits and (even poorer) food manufacturing processes, North Americans' diets are dreadfully deficient in them. But omega-3s are vitally important to our health. In short, they keep our brains healthy (even preventing depression), they fire up our immune systems, ease inflammation and arthritis and help control diabetes. They're also heart-healthy and cholesterol-lowering, they protect against some cancers, make our skin glow and relieve constipation. Heck, they even help us shed pounds. Imagine! A fat that helps fight fat! Seeding your body with omega-3s is a no-brainer. Flaxseed oil is very sensitive to heat, oxygen and light, so keep it refrigerated, don't ever cook with it (that corrupts the oil) and throw it out after six to eight weeks. Add a tablespoon of flaxseed oil to juice, smoothies and sauces, or use it to make salad dressings. You can also grind whole flaxseed in a coffee grinder and sprinkle it on oatmeal or cereal, or use it in baking for a mega-dose of fiber and cancer-fighting lignans.

Isn't She Loafly?

Chocolaty, chocolate-chip zucchini loaf

Isn't she wonderful? Isn't she special? She's a delectable, chocolate-chip zucchini loaf that's moist and delicious without a ton of fat. A real beauty!

2 cups	all-purpose flour
½ cup	whole wheat flour
½ cup	unsweetened cocoa powder
1½ tsp	baking powder
1 tsp	each baking soda and ground cinnamon
½ tsp	salt
1½ cups	granulated sugar
3	eggs
½ cup	unsweetened applesauce
⅓ cup	high-quality vegetable oil (see tip)
2 tsp	vanilla
2 cups	packed, grated zucchini
½ cup	mini semi-sweet chocolate chips

MAKES 2 LOAVES, 10 SLICES EACH

- Preheat oven to 350°F. Spray two 8 x 4-inch loaf pans with cooking spray and set aside.

- In a large bowl, combine both flours, cocoa, baking powder, baking soda, cinnamon and salt. Set aside.

- In a medium bowl, whisk together sugar, eggs, applesauce, vegetable oil and vanilla. Stir in zucchini. Add wet ingredients to dry ingredients and mix just until dry ingredients are moistened. Fold in chocolate chips.

- Spread batter evenly in prepared pans. Bake for 50 minutes, or until a wooden pick inserted in center of loaves comes out clean. Cool for 5 minutes in pans. Remove from pans and let cool on a wire rack before serving.

PER SLICE
181 calories, 5.4 g total fat (1 g saturated fat), 4 g protein, 31 g carbohydrate, 1.8 g fiber, 32 mg cholesterol, 169 mg sodium

FOOD BITE

In 1890, women baking at home produced more than 80 percent of the bread eaten in the United States. In 1910, 70 percent of the bread in the U.S. was baked at home by women. By the late 1920s, 94 percent of the bread eaten was baked by men in commercial bakeries. Apparently, there's no business like dough business!

Recipe Tip It pays to pay attention to your oils! For baking and other high-temperature cooking, look for "high-oleic" safflower or sunflower oil (preferably organic) at well-stocked grocery stores or health food stores. Oleic acid is a monounsaturated fatty acid and it's much less susceptible to heat damage than the polyunsaturated fatty acids normally found in regular safflower or sunflower oil. The high heat of cooking damages the oil's molecules and also destroys a lot of its precious antioxidants and nutrients. Protect your oil and you protect yourself!

> A crust eaten in peace is better than a banquet partaken in anxiety.
>
> *Aesop*

Pumpkin and Spice and Everything Nice

Pumpkin spice muffins with chocolate chips and walnuts

If you feed these tasty pumpkin muffins to your family, they sure won't be plump kin! That's because we've carved out the fatty ingredients and left in the yummy ones. No tricks. Just treats!

1¼ cups	all-purpose flour	½ cup	plain low-fat yogurt
½ cup	wheat bran or whole wheat flour	½ cup	pure maple syrup or liquid honey
2 tsp	pumpkin pie spice (see tip)	¼ cup	butter, melted
1½ tsp	baking powder	1	egg
1 tsp	baking soda	1 tsp	vanilla
½ tsp	salt	1 cup	finely grated carrots
1 cup	canned pure pumpkin (not pumpkin pie filling)	½ cup	mini semi-sweet chocolate chips
		½ cup	chopped walnuts or pecans

- Preheat oven to 375°F. Spray a 12-cup muffin pan with cooking spray and set aside.

- In a large bowl, combine flour, wheat bran, pumpkin pie spice, baking powder, baking soda and salt. Set aside.

- In a medium bowl, whisk together pumpkin, yogurt, maple syrup, butter, egg and vanilla. Stir in carrots. Add wet ingredients to dry ingredients and stir using a wooden spoon just until moistened. Fold in chocolate chips and walnuts. Batter will be thick.

- Divide batter evenly among 12 muffin cups. Bake for 20 to 22 minutes, or until a wooden pick inserted in center of muffin comes out clean. Cool on a wire rack.

MAKES 12 MUFFINS

PER MUFFIN
199 calories, 8.7 g total fat
(3.5 g saturated fat),
5 g protein, 28 g carbohydrate,
2.7 g fiber, 30 mg cholesterol,
291 mg sodium

Recipe Tips: Look for wheat bran in boxes or bags in the cereal aisle or in the bulk foods section of your grocery store. If you don't have pumpkin pie spice, use 1½ tsp ground cinnamon plus ¼ tsp each ground ginger and ground nutmeg.

Trivial Tidbit

Butter was one of the two gifts Little Red Riding Hood was delivering to her sick grandmother when she met the Big Bad Wolf.

Peanut-BETTER Gingersnaps

A thin and chewy cross between a peanut butter cookie and a gingersnap

These scrumptious cookies can be made in a snap!

MAKES 20 COOKIES

PER COOKIE
108 calories, 3.4 g total fat
(1.6 g saturated fat), 2 g protein,
17 g carbohydrate, 0.8 g fiber,
15 mg cholesterol, 100 mg sodium

¾ cup   all-purpose flour
⅓ cup   whole wheat flour
1 tsp   baking soda
2 tsp   ground cinnamon, divided
½ tsp   ground ginger
¼ tsp   each salt and ground allspice
2 tbsp   granulated sugar
1 cup   lightly packed brown sugar
⅓ cup   light peanut butter
3 tbsp   butter, at room temperature
1   egg
2 tbsp   molasses
1 tsp   vanilla

Recipe Tips

It's really important that your oven is properly preheated before you put these cookies in to bake. An oven thermometer is a good investment—ovens are notoriously inaccurate! Don't overbake the cookies or they'll be very dry. You want them chewy in the middle, not crispy. Seven minutes goes by very quickly, so don't start sorting socks or coloring your hair while the cookies are baking (promise?).

• Preheat oven to 350°F. Spray a large cookie sheet with cooking spray and set aside.

• In a medium bowl, stir together both flours, baking soda, 1 tsp cinnamon, ginger, salt and allspice. Set aside. Combine granulated sugar and remaining 1 tsp cinnamon in a small bowl. Set aside.

• In another medium bowl, beat together brown sugar, peanut butter and butter on medium speed of electric mixer for about 1 minute. Add egg, molasses and vanilla. Beat again until smooth.

• Using a wooden spoon, stir flour mixture into peanut butter mixture. You will be making a stiff dough. Using your hands, shape dough into 1½-inch balls. Roll balls in reserved cinnamon-sugar mixture. Place on cookie sheet at least 2 inches apart (they spread a lot while baking). Flatten cookies slightly using a fork.

• Bake cookies for 7 minutes. They may appear undercooked, but that's OK. Remove cookies from oven and cool on pan for 1 minute, then transfer from pan to a wire rack to cool completely.

Who keeps track of the cookies you eat? The kitchen counter :)

Oatstanding Choco-Chip Muffins

Oatmeal-chocolate-chip muffins with a hint of peach

Muffins sent directly from chocolaty, chewy heaven! Oatbursts of flavor make these a surefire, oat-of-this-world hit!

1¼ cups	quick-cooking rolled oats (not instant)
1 cup	1% milk
½ cup	puréed canned peaches (see tip)
1	egg
¼ cup	butter, melted
1 tsp	vanilla
1½ cups	Nutri Flour Blend (see tip)
½ cup	firmly packed brown sugar
2 tsp	baking powder
1 tsp	each baking soda and ground cinnamon
½ tsp	salt
½ cup	mini semi-sweet chocolate chips

- Preheat oven to 375°F. Spray a 12-cup muffin tin with cooking spray and set aside.

- Pour milk over oats in medium bowl. Stir and let stand for 20 minutes. Stir in puréed peaches, egg, butter and vanilla. Set aside.

- Combine flour, brown sugar, baking powder, baking soda, cinnamon and salt in a large bowl. Add oat mixture to flour mixture and stir just until dry ingredients are moistened. Fold in chocolate chips. Batter will be thick.

- Divide batter among 12 muffin cups. Bake for 20 minutes, or until a wooden pick inserted in center of muffin comes out clean. Remove muffins from pan and let cool on a wire rack.

Recipe Tips: Robin Hood makes an excellent baking flour called Nutri Flour Blend. It's a combination of all-purpose flour and wheat bran. If you can't find it, use 1 cup all-purpose flour plus ½ cup whole wheat flour in this recipe. Drain the canned peaches well and purée them in a blender or food processor before adding to the oats.

MAKES 12 MUFFINS

PER MUFFIN
187 calories, 6.2 g total fat
(3.2 g saturated fat), 5 g protein,
30 g carbohydrate, 2.8 g fiber,
29 mg cholesterol, 304 mg sodium

Nutrition Nugget

Are uncontrollable chocolate cravings playing Twix on you? A lack of magnesium in your diet could be causing your urge to splurge. Yes, chocolate contains magnesium, which explains your illicit lust affair with Oh Henry!, but how 'bout we throw some waist-friendlier options into the mix? If it's a nut, a bean or a seed, odds are it's a good source of magnesium. Other magnesium-rich foods are spinach and dark, leafy greens, broccoli, salmon, halibut, quinoa, chia seeds, pumpkin seeds and flaxseed.

Shrink Your Muffin Top

Tired of wearing baggy sweatshirts to cover the bulge hanging over the top of your jeans? Zoinks! The dreaded muffin top! If you're serious about whittling your waistline, you've got to kick the habit. Nothing to fear, Sister Mary Theresa—we're talkin' sugar habit here! Sugar is not only the evil archenemy of a healthy body, but it's also as addictive as cocaine, say experts, so it's not an easy habit to break. Rather than quitting sugar cold turkey, which might be a bit harsh for the serious addict, here's a simple and effective strategy to painlessly jump-start your way to a lean belly: Have half! If you want a sweet treat, just cut the usual amount in half. Instead of eating two Girl Guide cookies, have one. Hankering for a muffin? Break it in two and give the other half to your co-worker. Can't resist dessert? *Halve* your cake and eat it, too! When you share that cheesecake with your dinner companion, remember that the banquet is in the first bite. No bite will taste as good as the first, anyway. If you keep eating, you'll be getting more calories but not necessarily more pleasure. The less sugar you eat overall, the more fat will melt from your middle. We guarantee it! Have half and you'll halve your muffin top!

Naughty Biscotti

Lemon, cranberry and pistachio biscotti

If you were to make a list of the tastiest low-calorie snacks ever, and you checked that list twice, you'd discover this biscotti's not naughty—it's nice!

1¾ cups	all-purpose flour	2	eggs
½ cup	oat bran	1	egg white
1½ tsp	baking powder	1½ tbsp	grated lemon zest
¼ tsp	salt	1 tbsp	freshly squeezed
⅓ cup	granulated sugar		lemon juice
⅓ cup	lightly packed	1 tsp	vanilla
	brown sugar	½ cup	chopped dried
2 tbsp	butter, at room		cranberries
	temperature	½ cup	chopped pistachios

MAKES 18 BISCOTTI

PER BISCOTTI
119 calories, 3.4 g total fat
(1.1 g saturated fat), 3 g protein,
20 g carbohydrate, 1.2 g fiber,
24 mg cholesterol, 77 mg sodium

- Preheat oven to 350°F. Spray a cookie sheet with cooking spray and set aside.

- Combine flour, oat bran, baking powder and salt in a medium bowl. Set aside.

- In a large bowl, beat together both sugars and butter on medium speed of electric mixer for 1 minute. Add eggs, egg white, lemon zest, lemon juice and vanilla. Beat again until well blended. Using a wooden spoon, add flour mixture to sugar mixture and stir just until blended. Dough will be thick. Add cranberries and pistachios and mix well.

Divide dough in half. Using lightly floured or greased hands, shape each half into an 8 x 3 x ¾-inch loaf and place on prepared cookie sheet, about 3 inches apart. Add a bit more flour if dough is too sticky.

Bake on middle oven rack for 20 minutes. Remove loaves from cookie sheet and cool on a wire rack for 15 minutes. Reduce oven temperature to 275°F. Transfer loaves to a cutting board. Using a very sharp knife, cut each loaf crosswise on a diagonal into 9 slices. (You'll have some scraps from the end pieces, so go ahead and eat them. Everyone knows that scraps have zero calories.) Place slices, cut-side down, on same cookie sheet. Return to oven and bake for 8 minutes. Turn biscotti over and bake for 8 more minutes. Cool completely on wire rack. Biscotti will harden as they cool.

Recipe Tips: You can store these cookies for a month in a resealable plastic bag in the freezer. If you prefer super-hard biscotti, increase baking time from 8 minutes to 10 minutes per side.

FOOD BITE Biscotti, twice-baked Italian biscuits served in hip coffeehouses, were part of Christopher Columbus' food supply on his long voyages because of their mold-resistant properties. In fact, biscotti have a shelf life of fourteen hundred and ninety-two years (give or take)!

Morning Gloryous Muffins

Moist and marvelous everything-but-the-kitchen-sink muffins

Rise and dine on these glorious, fully loaded muffins with carrots, pineapple, coconut, raisins, walnuts and lots of spice. Nice!

1½ cups	all-purpose flour
¾ cup	whole wheat flour
2 tsp	baking soda
2 tsp	ground cinnamon
½ tsp	each ground nutmeg and salt
1 cup	well-drained crushed pineapple
1 cup	finely grated carrots
½ cup	unsweetened applesauce
½ cup	packed brown sugar
¼ cup	high-quality vegetable oil
1	egg
1 tsp	vanilla
½ cup	sweetened shredded coconut
½ cup	raisins
⅓ cup	chopped walnuts or pecans

- Preheat oven to 375°F. Spray a 12-cup muffin tin with cooking spray and set aside.

- In a large bowl, combine both flours, baking soda, cinnamon, nutmeg and salt. Mix well and set aside.

- In a medium bowl, whisk together pineapple, carrots, applesauce, sugar, oil, egg and vanilla. Add wet ingredients to dry ingredients and stir just until dry ingredients are moistened. Fold in coconut, raisins and nuts.

- Divide batter among 12 muffin cups. Bake for 20 minutes, or until a wooden pick inserted in center of muffin comes out clean. Cool on a wire rack.

IT'S A GLORYOUS DAY!

MAKES 12 MUFFINS

PER MUFFIN
238 calories,
9.7 g total fat
(2.7 g saturated fat),
5 g protein,
36 g carbohydrate,
2.9 g fiber,
17 mg cholesterol,
322 mg sodium

FOOD BITE

It is believed that the name muffin comes either from the German word *muffen* (plural of *muffe*, a small cake) or from the French word *moufflet*, meaning soft bread. Our theory is that the word muffin was created so people wouldn't feel guilty about eating cake for breakfast!

Gluten for Punishment

Over the last few years, we've been getting more and more requests for gluten-free recipes, not only from folks with Celiac disease who must avoid gluten, the protein in wheat, barley and rye, but also from others who suspect that wheat might be at the root of their digestive or other health problems. Wheat happens to be one of the most common food allergies, perhaps because it has been so genetically altered over the years, making it tough for the body to recognize. The wheat we eat is not the wheat our grandparents used to eat! And, in fact, more people than you think are sensitive to or even allergic to gluten, but they just don't know it yet. We humans don't digest wheat very well because we have only one stomach—and one may not be enough to digest wheat. Cows have four chambers within one stomach, so Betsy the Bovine can tolerate wheat, no problemo. It goes from one stomach to another to another and, by the time it reaches gut number four, it's fully digested and Betsy's feelin' groovy. Symptoms of gluten intolerance stretch beyond digestive discomfort (gas, bloating, constipation, heartburn, acid reflux) to include fatigue, headaches, brain fog, weight gain, joint and bone pain, depression, respiratory problems such as asthma and even autism and ADHD. So if you suffer from some of these symptoms, don't be a *gluten* for punishment! Go easy on the wheat for a couple of weeks and see if your symptoms improve.

Rolls Royce

Ooey, gooey cinnamon rolls with a hint of whole wheat and flax, drizzled with cream-cheese glaze

They're the Cadillac of cinnamon rolls! The Mercedes of bunz! The limousine of baked cuisine! OK, you get the point. These luxurious cinnamon rolls will drive you wild!

MAKES 12 ROLLS

PER ROLL
269 calories,
7.1 g total fat
(3.7 g saturated fat),
6 g protein,
47 g carbohydrate,
3 g fiber,
33 mg cholesterol,
227 mg sodium

Dough

2 cups	all-purpose flour
1 cup	whole wheat flour
¼ cup	ground flaxseed
1 pkg	(8 g) or 2¼ tsp quick-rising yeast
1 tsp	salt
1 cup	1% milk
¼ cup	brown sugar
2 tbsp	butter
1 tsp	vanilla
1	egg, lightly beaten

Filling

⅔ cup	brown sugar
1 tbsp	ground cinnamon
2 tbsp	butter, at room temperature

Glaze

2 tbsp	light cream cheese, at room temperature
1 tbsp	butter, at room temperature
½ cup	icing (confectioner's) sugar
½ tsp	vanilla

- To make dough, combine both flours, flaxseed, yeast and salt in a medium bowl. Mix well and set aside.

- Add milk, sugar, butter and vanilla to a small pot. Heat over medium heat, stirring often, just until milk is warmed, butter is melted and sugar is dissolved. Do not simmer or boil. Remove from heat and carefully pour into a large mixing bowl. Add half the flour mixture and egg. Stir using a wooden spoon until well blended. Add remaining flour mixture and stir until a soft ball forms. Turn dough out onto a lightly floured surface. Add a bit more flour if dough is too sticky. Knead dough until smooth and elastic, about 1 minute. Place dough in a clean bowl that has been lightly oiled. Cover with a tea towel and let rise in a warm place for 30 minutes or until double in size.

- Meanwhile, make filling. Mix brown sugar and cinnamon in a small bowl and set aside.

- Line a 9 x 13-inch baking pan with parchment paper and set aside.

- When dough has risen, turn out onto a lightly floured surface. Roll out dough to a 12 x 14-inch rectangle. Using a butter knife, spread 2 tbsp butter evenly over dough. Sprinkle with brown sugar-cinnamon mixture and spread evenly to edges. Roll up dough jelly-roll style. You should end up with a 12-inch long roll. Using a very sharp knife, slice roll into 12 equal pieces. Arrange rolls in a single layer in prepared pan. Cover with a tea towel and let rise in a warm place for 30 minutes.

- Preheat oven to 350°F. Bake rolls for 25 minutes. They should be puffed up and light golden brown. Remove from oven and let cool slightly while you prepare glaze. Using an electric mixer, beat together all glaze ingredients in a small bowl until smooth. Spread evenly over warm rolls. (Note: Add 1 tbsp milk to drizzle glaze as pictured in photo.)

> You know, I really don't need buns of steel. I'd be happy with buns of cinnamon.
>
> *Ellen DeGeneres*

Little Miss Muffin Tops

Oatmeal, blueberry and banana muffin tops

Elaine from "Seinfeld" made muffin tops famous. Your kids will love them! Look for muffin-top pans (sometimes called muffin-cap pans) in specialty bakeware stores or online. You may never make muffins in regular pans again!

You've never tried muffin like it!

1 cup	quick-cooking rolled oats (not instant)
1 cup	all-purpose flour
½ cup	oat bran
½ cup	granulated sugar
⅓ cup	sweetened shredded coconut (optional)
1 tsp	each baking powder and ground cinnamon
½ tsp	each baking soda and salt
1 cup	mashed ripe bananas
½ cup	plain low-fat yogurt
3 tbsp	butter, melted
1	egg
1 tsp	vanilla
1 cup	fresh blueberries

MAKES 12 MUFFIN TOPS

PER MUFFIN TOP
169 calories,
4.4 g total fat
(2.2 g saturated fat),
4 g protein,
31 g carbohydrate,
2.5 g fiber,
26 mg cholesterol,
108 mg sodium

- Preheat oven to 375°F. Spray two 6-cup muffin-top pans with cooking spray and set aside.

- In a large bowl, combine oats, flour, oat bran, sugar, coconut (if desired), baking powder, cinnamon, baking soda and salt. Mix well.

- In a medium bowl, whisk together bananas, yogurt, butter, egg and vanilla. Add wet ingredients to dry ingredients and mix just until dry ingredients are moistened. Batter will be thick. Gently fold in blueberries.

- Divide batter evenly among muffin-top cups. Bake for 12 to 14 minutes, or until muffin tops are puffed up and a wooden pick inserted in center comes out clean. Remove muffin tops from pans and cool on a wire rack.

Trivial Tidbit

Who'da thunk? Some people actually polish their leather shoes with banana peels! Apparently, the slippery skin shines and conditions shoes quite nicely. But what if shoes were actually *made* from banana peels? Would we call them slippers? Maybe someone should use banana peels to create a nifty briefcase for attorneys. It could be used exclusively by lawyers who want to *appeel* their cases!

Cracking the Protein Code

Eggs are the perfect protein. You might even call eggs the mother of all protein because they're the standard against which all proteins are compared. Not only that, they're packed with some of nature's most synergistic nutrients: For a mere 75 calories and five grams of fat, you get six grams of protein, vitamins A and D, B12, folate and just about every other important vitamin and mineral there is. Nowadays, you can even buy omega-3 eggs, laid by sorority-pledging chickens. Truthfully, they come from chickens that are fed flaxseed. The best-laid plan when it comes to buying eggs? Shell out a few eggstra cents and get them from a local farmer. Chances are, the chickens doing the laying will be allowed to roam freely in a pasture and forage for their own, natural choice of food (as opposed to being fed grains). And they'll be antibiotic-free, too. Remember: We are what we eat, but we're also what our food eats. Healthy, happy chickens produce healthier eggs with deep-orange, nutrient-filled yolks and plenty of perfect protein. And that should make a healthy, happy you!

Loaf Potion #9

Cranberry-orange loaf with zucchini, carrots and walnuts

Meet the loaf of your life! A spellbinding combination of ingredients ensures love at first bite.

1½ cups	all-purpose flour
⅔ cup	oat bran
½ cup	lightly packed brown sugar
1 tbsp	baking powder
1 tsp	baking soda
1 tsp	ground cinnamon
½ tsp	salt
⅔ cup	chopped dried cranberries
⅓ cup	chopped walnuts or chopped pecans
1 cup	plain low-fat yogurt
3 tbsp	high-quality vegetable oil
2	eggs
2 tbsp	frozen orange juice concentrate, thawed
2 tsp	grated orange zest
1 cup	each grated carrots and grated, unpeeled zucchini

MAKES 1 LARGE LOAF, 16 SLICES

PER SLICE
157 calories, 5.3 g total fat (0.8 g saturated fat), 4 g protein,
25 g carbohydrate, 1.7 g fiber, 28 mg cholesterol, 268 mg sodium

- Preheat oven to 350°F. Spray a 9 x 5-inch loaf pan with cooking spray and set aside.

- In a large bowl, combine flour, oat bran, brown sugar, baking powder, baking soda, cinnamon and salt. Make sure you get all of the lumps out of the brown sugar. Stir in cranberries and nuts.

- In a medium bowl, whisk together yogurt, oil, eggs, orange juice concentrate and orange zest. Stir in carrots and zucchini. Add wet ingredients to dry ingredients and mix just until dry ingredients are moistened.

- Spoon batter into prepared pan and smooth top. Bake for 45 to 50 minutes, or until loaf is lightly browned and a wooden pick inserted in center of loaf comes out clean.

- Cool loaf in pan on a wire rack for 10 minutes. Remove loaf from pan and cool completely on rack. Cover with plastic wrap and store at room temperature or in the refrigerator. To serve, cut loaf into 8 thick slices, then cut each slice in half. (This is easier than trying to cut 16 thin slices!)

Sometimes You Feel Like a Nut

We're nuts about nuts, and for good reason! Almonds, pistachios, cashews, walnuts and their nutty relatives are good sources of protein, calcium, magnesium and potassium, not to mention healthy fats. Got high blood pressure? Nuts to you! Diabetes got your blood sugar swingin'? More nuts to you! Got a few pounds to lose? Go nuts. Yes...really! They're like potent appetite suppressants, even in small quantities, making them an ideal weight-loss aid. But listen up, waist watchers. That doesn't mean you should squirrel away bowlfuls like you're eating popcorn. Remember that nuts are packed with calories—shelling out roughly 800 calories a cup! To keep their high-calorie content from going straight to your butt, use nuts sparingly as a condiment, garnish or as a light snack. For instance, add some slivered almonds to cereal, oatmeal, salads or steamed veggies, or throw a few peanuts or cashews into a stir-fry. Choose raw, unsalted nuts over the roasted (overly processed and overly salted) variety. And always store nuts in the fridge or freezer to prevent their oils from oxidizing and becoming rancid. An ounce a day is a good target and, since nuts are a satisfying snack, you'll still get your fil, Bert.

Nutrition Nugget

Probiotics, the healthy bacteria in fermented foods like yogurt, kefir and sauerkraut can help you lose weight! What does the bacteria in your gut have to do with your waistline? A lot! Multiple studies have shown that obese people have different intestinal bacteria than slim people and, regardless of weight, most people don't have the optimal balance of good and bad bacteria in their intestines. This imbalance can wreak havoc on your health in many ways and, yes, it may even contribute to being overweight or having difficulty shedding excess weight. In one study, obese people were able to reduce their belly fat by nearly five percent and their visceral fat (near organs) by more than three percent, simply by drinking a probiotic-rich fermented milk beverage (kefir) for 12 weeks. Pass the sauerkraut, please!

Cookies for Rookies

Peanut-butter, oatmeal and chocolate-chip cookies

*If you're kookie over cookies, these easy-to-make treats
are no sweat and no threat, even for the confirmed kitchen klutz.*

1¼ cups	all-purpose flour
1 cup	quick-cooking rolled oats (not instant)
½ tsp	each baking soda and salt
¾ cup	packed brown sugar
⅓ cup	butter, at room temperature
⅓ cup	light peanut butter
1	egg
⅓ cup	mini semi-sweet chocolate chips

- Preheat oven to 350°F. Spray a large cookie sheet with cooking spray and set aside.

- In a medium bowl, combine flour, oats, baking soda and salt. Set aside.

- In another medium bowl, beat together brown sugar, butter, peanut butter and egg on low speed of electric mixer until well blended. Add dry ingredients and chocolate chips and mix well using a wooden spoon. Dough will be stiff.

- Roll dough into 1½-inch balls and place 2 inches apart on prepared cookie sheet. Using a fork dipped in flour, flatten cookies to ¼-inch thickness. Bake for 10 minutes. Be careful not to overbake, as cookies will dry out.

- Remove cookies from tray immediately and cool on a wire rack. Store covered with plastic wrap or in an airtight container.

MAKES 24 COOKIES

PER COOKIE
91 calories, 2.4 g total fat
(0.7 g saturated fat),
2 g protein,
16 g carbohydrate,
0.6 g fiber,
9 mg cholesterol,
98 mg sodium

*He's so argumentative,
he won't even eat food
that agrees with him :)*

FOOD BITE Though most Europeans, starting with the ancient Romans, fed oats to their horses, the savvy Scots took advantage of oats' nutritious nature and made them a national breakfast dish. In fact, up until a few generations ago, most working-class households in Scotland had a kitchen cabinet with a "porridge drawer." On the weekend, they would make a large batch of oatmeal and pour it into the drawer. That way, during the week, chunks of porridge could be sliced off for meals.

Corn in the U.S.A.

Comforting corn muffins for dunking in chili or stew

If Utaht corn muffins were O-high-o in fat, think again! In our revamped version, oil's no longer the Maine ingredient, so you Kentucky an extra one in your lunch bag and still fit into that New Jersey.

1 cup	all-purpose flour
1 cup	yellow cornmeal
2 tbsp	granulated sugar
1½ tsp	baking powder
½ tsp	baking soda
¼ tsp	salt
1 can	(14 oz/398 mL) cream-style corn
½ cup	buttermilk
1	egg
2 tbsp	butter, melted
1 can	(4.5 oz/128 mL) diced green chilies

MAKES 12 MUFFINS

PER MUFFIN
147 calories, 3 g total fat
(1.4 g saturated fat),
4 g protein,
27 carbohydrate,
1.3 g fiber,
24 mg cholesterol,
341 mg sodium

- Preheat oven to 375°F. Spray a 12-cup muffin tin with cooking spray and set aside.

- In a large bowl, combine flour, cornmeal, sugar, baking powder, baking soda and salt. Set aside.

- In a medium bowl, whisk together corn, buttermilk, egg, butter and chilies. Add wet ingredients to dry ingredients. Stir just until dry ingredients are moistened.

- Divide batter among 12 muffin cups. Bake for 20 minutes, or until a wooden pick inserted in center of muffin comes out clean. Be careful not to overbake. Remove muffins from tin and cool slightly on a wire rack. Best served warm.

Nutrition Nugget

Seems that North America has a drinking problem on its hands, thanks to diet soda. Studies have shown that those who drink one can of diet soda a day have a 34 percent increase in their risk of developing metabolic syndrome (a pre-diabetic condition) and a 41 percent increase in their risk of becoming overweight or obese. Gulp! That's because fake sweeteners interfere with the body's hormonal response to foods. Basically, they confuse the brain, tricking it into thinking we ate something sweet. But when the calories aren't there to match up, it causes us to crave more and more sweets to satisfy the deficit. We keep eating and eating and eating. The end result? A fatter end!

Shake It Up, Baby!

If you want to get ahead in the healthy living game, you've gotta become a mover and a shaker! Continuous physical movement that elevates your heart rate is the best way to fight flab and build a leaner, healthier, fabulous you. The human body was designed for movement (not for sitting at a computer or in front of a TV), so any kind of movement will do: walk, bike, hike, jog, ski, golf, Rollerblade, play tennis, plant a garden, rake some leaves or do what Greta does and dance naked in your front window to really loud music. (She's the most popular resident on her street!) And it doesn't have to be a torturous marathon session, either. Ten minutes of doing something you love is better for your body and your spirit than doing half an hour of an activity that you absolutely detest. Pick the physical activity that best suits your lifestyle and personality and then "shake your wiggly things 'til they don't shake no more!"

> It is a scientific fact that your body will not absorb cholesterol if you take it from another person's plate.
>
> *Dave Barry*

Greta's Gluten-Free Miracle Brownies

Chewy, fudgy, gluten-free double-chocolate brownies

These super-chocolaty brownies have miraculous taste and deliver mouthfuls of chewy moistness, thanks to the addition of a "secret," non-detectable ingredient: pumpkin!

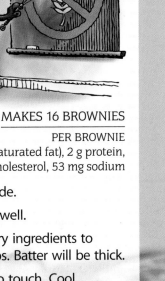

½ cup Greta's Gluten-Free Flour Blend (see tip)
⅓ cup unsweetened cocoa powder
¼ tsp each baking powder and salt
¾ cup lightly packed brown sugar
½ cup canned pure pumpkin (not pumpkin pie filling)
¼ cup butter, melted
1 egg
1 tsp vanilla
⅓ cup chopped walnuts or pecans
⅓ cup mini semi-sweet chocolate chips

MAKES 16 BROWNIES

PER BROWNIE

110 calories, 5.6 g total fat (2.5 g saturated fat), 2 g protein, 14 g carbohydrate, 1.4 g fiber, 21 mg cholesterol, 53 mg sodium

- Preheat oven to 350°F. Spray an 8 x 8-inch baking pan with cooking spray and set aside.

- In a medium bowl, combine flour blend, cocoa powder, baking powder and salt. Mix well.

- In a large bowl, whisk together brown sugar, pumpkin, butter, egg and vanilla. Add dry ingredients to wet ingredients and stir vigorously until well blended. Fold in nuts and chocolate chips. Batter will be thick.

- Spread batter evenly in prepared pan. Bake for about 25 minutes, until top feels dry to touch. Cool completely on a wire rack. Cover and refrigerate overnight for best flavor. Cut into 16 2-inch squares. These brownies taste great cold!

Recipe Tip After days of tinkering and lots of research, we're certain that the best gluten-free baking results are achieved by creating your own gluten-free flour blend. Our blend works very well in most muffin, cookie and brownie recipes. You can buy these ingredients at a health food store or bulk food store. **Combine 2 cups sorghum flour, 2 cups potato starch (not potato flour), ½ cup coconut flour, ½ cup brown rice flour and 1 tbsp xanthan gum.** Mix well and store in an airtight container in the fridge for up to one month.

GRAINola Bars

Chewy homemade granola bars with oats, flax, pumpkin, cranberries, nuts and mini chocolate chips

Why bother buying expensive boxes of granola bars full of questionable ingredients when it's easy and fun to make your own? You can individually wrap and refrigerate the bars to make portable, grab-and-go snacks.

- Preheat oven to 350°F. Line a 9 x 13-inch baking pan with parchment paper, letting the paper overhang on two opposite sides (so you can use it as a sling to pick up the granola bars after baking).

- Combine first 9 ingredients in a large bowl. Mix well. In a medium bowl, whisk together pumpkin, honey, butter and vanilla. Pour wet ingredients over dry ingredients. Mix using a wooden spoon until dry ingredients are coated with pumpkin mixture. Make sure there aren't any dry oats in the bottom of the bowl! Stir, stir, stir!

- Pour the wet granola mixture into the prepared pan and spread it evenly to the edges. Using your hand, press down firmly on the granola so that it's tightly packed in the pan.

- Bake on middle oven rack for about 25 minutes, until top turns a light golden brown and feels dry to touch. Remove pan from oven and cool completely on a wire rack. Lift cooled slab of granola from pan by holding on to parchment paper and transfer to a cutting board. Using a large, sharp knife, cut the granola into 16 bars, about 1½ x 4 inches each. (Tip: Press down with the knife to cut the bars and avoid a sawing motion.) Wrap bars tightly in plastic wrap and store in an airtight container, either at room temperature or in the fridge.

2½ cups	quick-cooking rolled oats (not instant)
1 cup	unsweetened shredded coconut
½ cup	chopped raw almonds, pecans or pistachios
½ cup	chopped dried cranberries
½ cup	mini semi-sweet chocolate chips
⅓ cup	whole wheat flour (see tip)
¼ cup	ground flaxseed
1 tsp	ground cinnamon
½ tsp	salt
¾ cup	canned pure pumpkin (not pumpkin pie filling)
½ cup	liquid honey
¼ cup	butter, melted
1 tsp	vanilla

MAKES 16 BARS

PER BAR
214 calories, 9.7 g total fat
(5 g saturated fat), 4 g protein,
30 g carbohydrate, 3.4 g fiber,
9 mg cholesterol,
83 mg sodium

Variation: For banana-nut granola bars, use mashed ripe bananas instead of pure pumpkin and replace the dried cranberries with chopped walnuts.

Recipe Tips The smaller you chop your dried cranberries and nuts, the better the bars will hold together. You can use just about any dried fruit and nuts you like, but please keep the quantities the same, or the bars may not hold together properly. For a gluten-free version, make sure your oats are certified gluten-free. Replace the whole wheat flour with oat flour. To make it, simply measure an additional cup of oats and place them in a food processor, then pulse on and off until the oats are ground to a super-fine consistency, like flour. Measure ⅓ cup oat flour and use it instead of the wheat flour.

Bisquito Bites

Mouthwatering buttermilk and mashed potato biscuits for dunking in chili, soup or stew

These scrumptious biscuits are definitely worth making from scratch, especially if you're itching for melt-in-your-mouth texture and a taste guaranteed to cause a real buzz at dinner parties.

1¼ cups	all-purpose flour
½ cup	whole wheat flour
1 tbsp	granulated sugar
1½ tsp	baking powder
1 tsp	baking soda
¼ tsp	salt
1 cup	cooked mashed potatoes
1 cup	buttermilk
3 tbsp	butter, melted

TRY ONE, I MADE THEM FROM SCRATCH

- Preheat oven to 425°F. Spray a large baking sheet with cooking spray and set aside.

- Combine both flours, sugar, baking powder, baking soda and salt in a large bowl. Mix well and set aside.

- In a medium bowl, whisk together potatoes, buttermilk and butter. Add buttermilk mixture to flour mixture and stir until a soft ball forms. Knead for 1 minute on a lightly floured surface (add a bit more flour if dough is too sticky). Roll out dough to ¾-inch thickness. Cut into 2½-inch rounds using a cookie cutter. Transfer biscuits to prepared baking sheet. Bake for 13 to 15 minutes, until biscuits have puffed up and are golden brown.

MAKES 14 BISCUITS

PER BISCUIT
99 calories, 2.8 g total fat
(1.7 g saturated fat),
3 g protein,
16 g carbohydrate, 1 g fiber,
7 mg cholesterol,
203 mg sodium

Did you hear about the employee who fell into a huge vat of gum? His boss chewed him out :)

Recipe Tip The worst part about making your own dough is trying to clean up the little bits that stick to your countertop. If you don't have a slab of marble to work on (like the professionals use), here's a tip that will help save on clean-up time: When rolling out dough for pizza crusts or biscuits, work on a large piece of parchment paper or wax paper that has been "anchored" to the countertop. Simply moisten the back of the paper with water before laying it down. This will hold it in place while you work. Just toss it out when you're done and voilà—no sticky mess!

The Whole-Grain Truth

We've got an APB on a fiber impostor! We repeat. A fiber impostor! Be on the lookout for "enriched" whole wheat bread pretending to be as nutritious as whole-grain bread. Don't be fooled! The only way to play it safe is to read labels first, ask questions later. To get the benefit of the dough, here's what you need to know: Plain ol' whole wheat bread is like white bread in disguise. All the good stuff has been stripped from it during the milling process. No bran. No germ. You know what that spells: no fiber, no B vitamins, no minerals, no antioxidants! That's why food scientists routinely add back synthetic nutrients to replace what they've stripped out, and even use caramelized sugar to get that faux-tanned, brown bread look. Beware the word "enriched"—a sure indication this is NOT a true whole-grain product. Also, labels might woo you with "made with whole-grain wheat" but, in reality, as long as "some" of the bread is made from whole grain—even 10 percent of it—the bread can legally be sold as "whole wheat." Keep on your toes! For the healthiest breads (and cereal products), always make sure the words "whole grain" or "100% whole wheat" appear as the first ingredient on labels. That means all the good stuff is still there, whole and intact and close to its original, natural form. There's no fake 'n' bake, no faux dough. And that's all your body is really asking for: the whole-grain truth and nothin' but the truth!

Goody Two Chews

Cranberry and peanut-butter granola clusters

It actually takes more than two chews to get these tasty granola clusters down, but we just couldn't swallow the fact that our title didn't make sense, so we went with it anyway! A perfect treat for your perfect kids!

So good, you'll swear they're bad for you!

⅓ cup	light peanut butter
⅓ cup	pure maple syrup
2	egg whites
1 tsp	pumpkin pie spice
2½ cups	low-fat granola (see tip)
¾ cup	chopped dried cranberries

- Preheat oven to 250°F. Spray a 12-cup muffin tin with cooking spray and set aside.

- In a medium bowl, beat together peanut butter and maple syrup on medium speed of electric mixer. Add egg whites and pumpkin pie spice and beat again until smooth.

- Stir in granola and cranberries. Divide mixture evenly among muffin cups. Bake for 45 minutes. Remove from oven and cool completely on a wire rack before removing clusters from pan. Store in an airtight container.

MAKES 12 CLUSTERS

PER CLUSTER
124 calories, 3.2 g total fat (0.5 g saturated fat), 4 g protein, 22 g carbohydrate, 1.2 g fiber, 0 mg cholesterol, 65 mg sodium

Recipe Tip When shopping for granola for these yummy clusters, look for a brand that *doesn't* contain fruit or raisins, otherwise these treats might be too sweet. Our very favorite brand of granola is made by Nature's Path, a Canadian company. Its Pumpkin Flax Plus Granola is absolutely perfect for this recipe and also tastes great mixed with fruit and yogurt.

Trivial Tidbit

Pumpkins were once recommended for: (a) cleaning ovens; (b) warding off ghosts and spirits; (c) shrinking hemorrhoids; or (d) removing freckles. The answer is...(d) removing freckles! It was believed that eating pumpkins (not rubbing them on your skin!) could help fade the little brown spots.

A Bran New World

Scrumptious bran muffins with sweet potato and currants

Who says bran has to be bland? By keeping up with currant events, we've discovered a bran new way to load up on flavor and nutrition. Muffin compares!

At last! The discovery we've been waiting for!

1 cup	cooked, mashed sweet potato (see tip)
¾ cup	buttermilk
½ cup	packed brown sugar
3 tbsp	high-quality vegetable oil
2	eggs
2 tsp	grated orange zest
4 cups	bran flakes cereal
1¼ cups	all-purpose flour
½ cup	dried currants
½ cup	chopped pecans or walnuts (optional but recommended)
2 tsp	baking powder
1 tsp	baking soda
1 tsp	ground cinnamon
½ tsp	salt
¼ tsp	each ground nutmeg and ground allspice

- Preheat oven to 375°F. Spray a 12-cup muffin tin with cooking spray and set aside.

- In a large bowl, whisk together sweet potato, buttermilk, brown sugar, oil, eggs and orange zest. Add bran flakes and mix well. Set aside.

- In another large bowl, combine flour, currants, nuts (if using), baking powder, baking soda, cinnamon, salt, nutmeg and allspice. Add wet ingredients to dry ingredients and mix just until dry ingredients are moistened. Batter will be thick.

- Divide batter evenly among muffin cups. There's lots of batter, so fill the cups right up! Bake for 17 to 18 minutes, or until muffins are golden brown and a wooden pick inserted in center of muffin comes out clean. Remove muffins from pan and cool on a wire rack.

Recipe Tips: Steam or boil the peeled, cubed sweet potatoes until tender, then mash with a fork. Cool before using. If you prefer, you can substitute ½ cup chopped, dried cranberries for the currants.

MAKES 12 MUFFINS

PER SERVING
191 calories, 4.8 g total fat (0.9 g saturated fat), 4 g protein, 35 g carbohydrate, 3.2 g fiber, 36 mg cholesterol, 363 mg sodium

> The biggest seller is cookbooks and the second is diet books—how not to eat what you just learned how to cook.
>
> *Andy Rooney*

Arterial Motive

Wanna lower your cholesterol and blood pressure and protect against heart disease? Well, there's nuttin' to it! Walnuts, unlike most other nuts, not only contain heart-healthy monounsaturated fat, but they also carry a hefty dose of omega-3 fats—more omega-3s than wild salmon, in fact! In one study, scientists gave test subjects an ounce and a half of walnuts after they ate a high-fat meal and, lo and beyold, the walnuts reduced arterial stiffening within four hours, even outperforming the heart-health mega-superstar, olive oil. We knew they were good for us, but that's kinda nutty. A measly ounce and a half a day helps keep plaque away!

Berry Maniloaf

This easy lemon loaf with raspberries makes a great afternoon snack

Our raspberry loaf will come along, just like a song, and brighten your day. You'll be singing its praises when you discover how simple it is to make.

1¼ cups	all-purpose flour
½ cup	whole wheat flour
½ cup	granulated sugar
2 tsp	baking powder
1 tsp	baking soda
½ tsp	salt
1 cup	lemon-flavored yogurt (see tip)
¼ cup	high-quality vegetable oil
2	eggs
1 tsp	grated lemon zest
1 cup	fresh or frozen raspberries (see tip)

MAKES 1 LOAF, 12 SLICES

PER SLICE
169 calories,
6 g total fat (0.7 g saturated fat),
4 g protein, 26 g carbohydrate,
1.7 g fiber, 36 mg cholesterol,
307 mg sodium

- Preheat oven to 350ºF. Spray a 9 x 5-inch loaf pan with cooking spray and set aside.

- In a large bowl, combine both flours, sugar, baking powder, baking soda and salt. Set aside.

- In a medium bowl, whisk together yogurt, oil, eggs and lemon zest. Add wet ingredients to dry ingredients and stir just until dry ingredients are moistened. Gently fold in raspberries.

- Pour batter into prepared pan and bake for 50 minutes, or until a wooden pick inserted in center of loaf comes out clean. Cool loaf in pan for 10 minutes. Remove from pan and let cool completely on a wire rack before slicing.

Recipe Tips: If using frozen raspberries in baked goods, make sure they're whole berries without syrup. Don't bother thawing them before adding to the batter. You may need to add a few minutes to the baking time, however, since frozen berries make the batter cold. If you can't find lemon yogurt, use vanilla yogurt then add 2 tbsp freshly squeezed lemon juice to the wet ingredients and increase lemon zest from 1 tsp to 2 tsp.

FOOD BITE

If you boil an egg while singing all five verses and choruses of the hymn "Onward, Christian Soldiers," it'll be a perfectly soft-cooked egg when you come to amen.

Dig the Berried Treasure

Yo, ho, ho and a lot of yum! Berries not only satisfy our cravings, but are also a treasure trove of amazing, health-promoting compounds. For instance, a cup of strawberries offers nearly double your daily dose of vitamin C and also contains a potent anticancer agent called ellagic acid. Raspberries contain anthocyanins, which boost insulin production and lower blood-sugar levels, making them a strong defender against diabetes. And blueberries contain more antioxidants (compounds that ward off cancer, heart disease and other age-related ills) than nearly any other fruit. In fact, feeding blueberry extracts to aging lab rats markedly improved their memory and balance. Imagine what blueberries could do for you? You'll remember where you left your keys and you won't topple over trying to pick them up! All berries are nuggets of fiber, your best fat-loss buddy, and fresh berries contain live enzymes that improve digestion and act like spark plugs for your cells. Plus, they're low on the Glycemic Index, so they won't spike your blood sugar. You're making a huge mistake if you cut these carbs out of your diet. They're as good as gold!

People who eat yogurt are well-cultured :)

Risky Biscuits

Mouthwatering sour cream and sweet potato biscuits

Cruisin' for a tasty, innovative biscuit recipe? We risked adding wholesome sweet potatoes and a hint of cinnamon to the mix, since ordinary biscuits are sooo '80s!

1¼ cups	all-purpose flour		¼ tsp	ground cinnamon
½ cup	whole wheat flour		¾ cup	light (5%) sour cream
2 tbsp	brown sugar		¾ cup	mashed or puréed sweet potato
2 tsp	baking powder			(see tip)
1 tsp	baking soda		3 tbsp	butter, melted
¼ tsp	salt			

Preheat oven to 425°F. Spray a large baking sheet with cooking spray and set aside.

In a large bowl, combine both flours, brown sugar, baking powder, baking soda, salt and cinnamon. Set aside.

In a medium bowl, whisk together sour cream, sweet potato and melted butter. Add wet ingredients to dry ingredients and stir using a wooden spoon until mixture forms a ball. The dough may seem dry at first but keep stirring!

- Turn dough out onto a lightly floured surface. Roll out or pat dough to ¾-inch thickness. Cut into 2½-inch rounds using a biscuit or cookie cutter. Re-roll scraps of dough to make 12 biscuits total. Transfer biscuits to prepared baking sheet. Bake for about 10 minutes, until biscuits have puffed up and are light golden brown. Serve warm.

Recipe Tip: Peel, chop and boil the sweet potatoes until tender, then mash well with a fork or purée until smooth in a food processor. Cool before using.

MAKES 12 BISCUITS

PER BISCUIT
123 calories, 3.6 g total fat (2.1 g saturated fat), 3 g protein, 20 g carbohydrate, 1.3 g fiber, 20 mg cholesterol, 255 mg sodium

Nutrition Nugget

The Tipsy Chicks? Females are more likely to mix alcohol with artificial sweeteners in an effort to save calories, but here's a word of caution to save you from drunk dialing your ex-boyfriend at 3 a.m.: Researchers say that booze mixed with artificial sweeteners gets you almost twice as drunk as booze mixed with sugar!

Berried Treasure

Moist and luscious blueberry-bran muffins

You'll gladly walk the plank for these mouthwatering muffins that hide blueberry nuggets inside a treasure chest of bran and peaches!

I'll be hooked on these!

1¼ cups	all-purpose flour
1½ tsp	baking soda
1 tsp	ground cinnamon
½ tsp	salt
1 can	(14 oz/385 mL) peaches in light syrup, undrained
⅔ cup	packed brown sugar
2	eggs
3 tbsp	high-quality vegetable oil
4 cups	bran flakes cereal
¾ cup	blueberries (fresh or frozen)

MAKES 12 MUFFINS

PER MUFFIN
195 calories, 4.7 g total fat
(0.8 g saturated fat), 3 g protein,
37 g carbohydrate, 3.4 g fiber,
35 mg cholesterol, 369 mg sodium

Recipe Tip: Try adding 2 or 3 tbsp ground chia seeds to these muffins for a healthy dose of omega-3 fats!

- Preheat oven to 375°F. Spray a 12-cup muffin tin with cooking spray and set aside.

- In a medium bowl, combine flour, baking soda, cinnamon and salt. Set aside.

- Drain peaches but reserve ⅓ cup syrup. Pour peaches and reserved syrup into a blender and purée until smooth. In a large bowl, whisk together puréed peaches, brown sugar, eggs and oil. Add bran flakes and mix well. Add flour mixture and stir just until dry ingredients are moistened. Do not overmix. Gently fold in blueberries.

- Divide batter among 12 muffins cups. Bake for 20 minutes, or until a wooden pick inserted in center of muffin comes out clean. Serve warm.

Mamma Mia! Hurray for Chia!

Look out flax! There's a new seed in town. It's chia! If the name sounds familiar, that's because it's the very same seed used in the retro '80s Chia Pet, those novelty gifts that allowed you to sprout "hair" on pottery figures. This ancient plant is an "almost-too-good-to-be-true" superfood. Chia is one of the richest whole food sources of omega-3 fatty acids and fiber found in nature, making it an amazing fat-loss aid and blood-sugar stabilizer. It has four times the fiber of flaxseed! And that's not all: chia contains calcium, magnesium, iron, vitamin C—even antioxidants. What's more, chia seeds are rich in protein, which delays hunger and helps you build muscle and burn fat. There's a whole lotta nutrition crammed into these tiny packages! Remember, your body craves nutrients, not calories. Because chia seeds are so nutritionally dense, you won't be a craving lunatic for a long time after eating them. It's best to add whole chia seeds to something moist, like oatmeal, yogurt or a smoothie, as the tiny seed can hold up to 20 times its weight in water. The outer shells are easily digested, unlike flaxseed, which need to be ground up, and they're also mild-tasting compared to flaxseed, making chia a great addition to baked goods and sauces. If you're a parent, adding this superfood to your kids' cereal is a no-brainer. You'll be sowing the seeds of optimum health for your family!

Poppy Love

Light and lemony poppy seed bread

Once you've had a taste of our pupular lemon bread, you'll dog-ear this page for sure! It's a doggone simple recipe that everyone will fall in loaf with.

1¼ cups	all-purpose flour		1 cup	2% milk
¾ cup	granulated sugar		¼ cup	butter, melted
½ cup	oat bran		1	egg
1 tbsp	poppy seeds		2 tbsp	freshly squeezed
2 tsp	baking powder			lemon juice
½ tsp	salt		2 tsp	grated lemon zest

- Preheat oven to 350°F. Spray an 8 x 4-inch loaf pan with cooking spray and set aside.

- In a large bowl, mix together flour, sugar, oat bran, poppy seeds, baking powder and salt.

- In a medium bowl, whisk together milk, butter, egg, lemon juice and lemon zest. Add wet ingredients to dry ingredients and mix just until dry ingredients are moistened. Spread batter in prepared pan. Bake for 40 to 45 minutes, or until loaf is light golden brown and a wooden pick inserted in center of loaf comes out clean.

- Cool loaf in pan on a wire rack for 10 minutes. Remove loaf from pan and cool completely on rack. Cover with plastic wrap and store at room temperature or in the fridge.

Trivial Tidbit

The tiny poppy seed comes from the same plant that produces opium. In fact, if you go nuts eating poppy seeds, you just might fail a drug test! The botanical name for the poppy flower actually means "sleep bearing," which is why it's long been used as a folk remedy for aiding sleep. In *The Wizard of Oz*, it was poppies that were used to put Dorothy to sleep! Today, we know poppy seeds are a source of calcium and magnesium, so they can help prevent high blood pressure and osteoporosis. Talk about specks appeal!

MAKES 1 LOAF, 12 SLICES

PER SLICE
158 calories, 5.1 g total fat (2.7 g saturated fat), 3 g protein, 27 g carbohydrate, 1.1 g fiber, 29 mg cholesterol, 195 mg sodium

In this chapter...

House of Carbs

The home sweet home of cakes, puddings and pies

Tir-riffic Tiramisu Trifle,
p. 319

Bonbon Jovi

Chewy, chocolaty, oatmeal and coconut clusters

Hunky treats that will make your heartthrob for more! Not technically bonbons, but we loved the name and figured these were pretty close.

2 cups	granulated sugar
6 tbsp	unsweetened cocoa powder
½ cup	2% evaporated milk
⅓ cup	butter
½ tsp	vanilla
3 cups	quick-cooking rolled oats (not instant)
1 cup	sweetened shredded coconut

- In a medium pot, combine sugar, cocoa powder, evaporated milk and butter. Cook and stir over medium-high heat until mixture comes to a boil. Boil for 1 minute, stirring constantly.

- Remove from heat. Stir in vanilla. Add rolled oats and coconut and mix well. Drop by tablespoonfuls onto a cookie sheet lined with parchment paper. Refrigerate until firm, about 30 minutes to 1 hour. Store in an airtight container in the refrigerator or at room temperature.

MAKES 35 BONBONS

PER BONBON
102 calories, 3.1 g total fat (1.7 g saturated fat), 1 g protein, 18 g carbohydrate, 1 g fiber, 5 mg cholesterol, 11 mg sodium

Did you hear about the hockey player who was kicked out of cake-decorating class? He was always called for icing :)

Nutrition Nugget

Let's hear it for cocoa—raw! raw! raw! Antioxidants are nutritional superheroes, fighting free radicals, those unstable molecules in the body that can cause DNA damage. There's actually a method of measuring the antioxidant capacities of different foods called Oxygen Radical Absorbance Capacity (ORAC). The higher the ORAC score, the more antioxidant superpowers contained in the food. Pure, raw, unprocessed cocoa scores a whopping 55,653 on the ORAC scale—far ahead of elderberries at 14,697, blueberries at 9,621 and black beans at 8,494. Chocoholics, rejoice!

Make it Splurge-Worthy

When you get the urge to splurge (and we all do!), don't waste valuable calories and stomach space on tasteless, mediocre treats. As a rule of *tongue*, before any high-fat, high-calorie, belt-busting food crosses your lips, make sure it's "splurge-worthy." Rate the indulgent food from 1 to 10. If it isn't a 9 or a 10, don't bother—it's not worthy! Who really wants to gorge on 600 sugar-loaded, headed-straight-to-your-hips calories in the form of Gram and Gramps' 70th anniversary sheet cake? Be polite, enthusiastically taste a small forkful, then slip the rest to Aunt Gertrude's Pomeranian. Same goes for your mother-in-law's fruitcake, chock-full of those scrumptious artificial fruit globules and the ever-so-tasty FD&C red No.3. It's not worthy! Repeat: Not worthy! Every single high-calorie indulgence should have a high "worth it" factor and should be a food that you absolutely love, love, love. For Greta, it would be pizza or gooey chicken wings. For Janet, just about anything chocolate will do. There's nothing worse than having to loosen your belt after eating a meal or food that you didn't really enjoy. Talk about *waisting* calories!

La Crème de la Cream Pie

Chocolate-banana cream pie with peanut-butter graham crust

It's the cream of the crop, la crème de la crumb, the best of the best banana cream pies!

Crust
1½ cups	graham crumbs
⅓ cup	light peanut butter
1	egg white (save yolk)

Filling
1 can	(14 oz/370 mL) 2% evaporated milk
1 pkg	(¼ oz/7 g) unflavored gelatine
½ cup	packed brown sugar
⅓ cup	unsweetened cocoa powder
3 tbsp	cornstarch
1½ cups	light (5%) cream
1	egg
1 tsp	vanilla
1 oz	(28 g) dark or semi-sweet chocolate

3	medium bananas, sliced
1 oz	(28 g) dark or semi-sweet chocolate, melted, for drizzling on top

Light whipped topping and more banana slices for garnish (optional)

MAKES 8 SERVINGS

PER SERVING
382 calories,
14 g total fat (5 g saturated fat),
14 g protein, 53 g carbohydrate,
3.2 g fiber, 75 mg cholesterol,
397 mg sodium

- To make crust, place crumbs, peanut butter and egg white in the bowl of a mini food processor and pulse on and off until well blended. Spray a 9-inch, deep-dish pie plate with cooking spray. Press crumb mixture evenly over bottom and part way up sides of pie plate. Bake at 350°F for 10 to 12 minutes, until edges turn golden and crust feels dry to touch. Let cool.

- Pour ¼ cup evaporated milk into a small, shallow bowl and sprinkle gelatine over top to soften. Set bowl aside.

- Combine brown sugar, cocoa powder and cornstarch in a medium, non-stick pot. Whisk in remaining evaporated milk and cream. Cook and continue to whisk over medium heat until mixture is bubbly and has thickened. Don't rush it by cranking up the heat. You will burn the pudding. Remove from heat but leave burner on. Reduce heat to low.

- In a medium bowl, whisk egg and reserved egg yolk (from crust) until lightly beaten. Add 1 cup of hot pudding mixture to beaten eggs and whisk quickly until well blended. Pour egg mixture into pot with remaining pudding and return to heat. Add reserved gelatine mixture and chocolate. Cook and stir for 1 more minute, whisking constantly, until chocolate is completely melted.

- Remove pudding from heat. Stir in vanilla. Let cool to room temperature (press plastic wrap over surface of pudding to prevent a skin from forming). Transferring the pudding to a metal bowl and refrigerating it will speed up the process.

- To assemble pie, layer sliced bananas over cooled pie crust. Spoon pudding evenly over bananas and spread to edges. Dish should be full. Cover with plastic wrap and refrigerate for 8 hours (or overnight) so filling can set. Yes, this is a long time to wait!

- To serve pie, slice into 8 wedges and garnish individual pieces with a dollop of light whipped topping, if desired. Place one banana slice on whipped topping. Drizzle with melted chocolate.

Fantasy Island Cake

Coconut, pineapple and banana snack cake with chocolate chips

Taking a bite of this luscious, moist cake is like being whisked away to a tropical paradise. Dream-come-true delicious!

1 cup	all-purpose flour	
1 cup	whole wheat flour	
½ cup	mini semi-sweet chocolate chips	
½ cup	sweetened shredded coconut	
1 tsp	baking powder	
1 tsp	baking soda	
1 cup	crushed pineapple with juice	
⅔ cup	mashed ripe bananas	
½ cup	packed brown sugar	
2	eggs	
2 tbsp	high-quality vegetable oil (see tip, p. 286)	
1 tsp	vanilla	

MAKES 12 PIECES

PER PIECE
198 calories,
5.7 g total fat
(2 g saturated fat),
4 g protein,
35 g carbohydrate,
2.4 g fiber,
35 mg cholesterol,
170 mg sodium

- Preheat oven to 350°F. Spray an 8 x 8-inch baking pan with cooking spray and set aside.

- Combine both flours, chocolate chips, coconut, baking powder and baking soda in a large bowl.

- In a smaller bowl, whisk together pineapple, bananas, brown sugar, eggs, oil and vanilla. Add wet ingredients to dry ingredients and stir just until dry ingredients are moistened.

- Spread batter evenly in prepared pan. Bake for 40 to 45 minutes, or until a wooden pick inserted in center of cake comes out clean. Cool cake in pan on a wire rack. Cut into 12 pieces and store in an airtight container or cover tightly with plastic wrap.

Nutrition Nugget

Stranded on a dessert island?
When faced with a humongous slab of
Double-Fudge-Brownie-Mocha-Coca-Kahlua
Cheesecake, try this experiment: Have three bites,
then stop and put the rest aside for a few minutes.
Most of the time, a little nibble is just as satisfying as eating
the whole slice. The banquet is in the first bite! Really!

The Carbs are on the Table

Think low-carb, high-protein products are the ticket to weight loss and better health? Just like the fat-free craze of yesterday, today's obsession with low-carb this and high-protein that has people overindulging—and bulging! Low carb, high protein doesn't necessarily mean healthy. Often, these packaged, heavily processed products (like energy bars and other snacks) are loaded with additives and preservatives, artificial sweeteners and cheap, "junky" protein concoctions like soy protein isolate—all created by men in white lab coats, most containing ingredients we can't pronounce in a list the size of The Yellow Pages. If you can't understand an ingredient, you can bet your body can't either. Indulge in these weirdo, chemical cocktails with reckless abandon (like we used to when we ate fat-free cookies!), and that's when health problems and often weight gain start creeping up. When given a choice, you're almost always better off choosing a natural food (like nuts, seeds, fruits and veggies) as a snack than you are opting for trendy, packaged food, no matter what health claims are emblazoned on the label. Make smarter choices and your healthy lifestyle efforts won't collapse like a house of *carbs*!

> We don't see things as they are...
> we see things as *we* are.
>
> *Anaïs Nin*

A Bundt in the Oven

Blueberry streusel coffee cake

Oh, baby! Whaaaaa smells so yummy? It's the tastiest treat from here to maternity—the mother of all coffee cakes! This easy-to-bake, scrumptious cake is guaranteed to ward off hunger and pacify a growling tummy.

This baby's ready to come out!

Streusel Topping

¼ cup	chopped pecans
3 tbsp	all-purpose flour
2 tbsp	brown sugar
1 tbsp	butter, melted

Cake

2 cups	Bisquick baking mix
1 cup	whole wheat flour
1 cup	granulated sugar
1 tsp	ground cinnamon
¾ cup	lemon-flavored yogurt (see tip)
2	eggs
⅓ cup	1% milk
¼ cup	high-quality vegetable oil
2 tsp	grated lemon zest
1 tsp	vanilla
2 cups	fresh blueberries

- Preheat oven to 350°F. Spray a bundt cake pan with cooking spray and dust lightly with flour. Set aside.

- To prepare streusel topping, combine all streusel ingredients in a small bowl and mix well using a fork. Set aside.

- Combine baking mix, flour, sugar and cinnamon in a large bowl. In a medium bowl, whisk together yogurt, eggs, milk, oil, lemon zest and vanilla. Add wet ingredients to dry ingredients and mix just until dry ingredients are moistened. Batter will be thick. Gently fold in blueberries.

- Spoon batter evenly into prepared cake pan. Sprinkle streusel topping evenly over batter. Bake for 40 to 45 minutes, or until a wooden pick inserted in center of cake comes out clean. Cool cake in pan on a wire rack. Loosen edges using a knife or small spatula and carefully transfer cake to a serving plate. Can be covered with plastic wrap and stored at room temperature for a couple of days.

Recipe Tip: If you can't find lemon-flavored yogurt, use plain yogurt and add 2 tbsp freshly squeezed lemon juice plus 1 tbsp sugar to wet ingredients.

MAKES 16 SERVINGS

PER SERVING
225 calories,
8.6 g total fat (1.8 g saturated fat),
4 g protein, 35 g carbohydrate,
2.2 g fiber, 29 mg cholesterol,
176 mg sodium

FOOD BITE

Let them eat kaka! The word cake was derived from the Old Norse *kaka*. Not exactly the type of word you'd expect the Vikings to contribute to the English language!

Marsha Marsha Marshmallow Squares

Our toasted-oat cereal squares are sure to be a hit with children

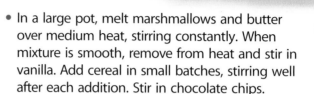

Why do our chewy cereal squares get all the attention? 'Cause they're packed with a delicious combination of crispy oat flakes, almonds, marshmallows and chocolate chips! Makes a big batch for a big bunch.

1 bag	(14 oz/400 g) marshmallows
⅓ cup	butter
1 tsp	vanilla
1 box	(17 oz/475 g) Oatmeal Crisp Crunchy Almond cereal
½ cup	semi-sweet chocolate chips

• In a large pot, melt marshmallows and butter over medium heat, stirring constantly. When mixture is smooth, remove from heat and stir in vanilla. Add cereal in small batches, stirring well after each addition. Stir in chocolate chips.

• Spray a 9 x 13-inch baking pan with cooking spray. Press cereal mixture evenly into pan. Cover with plastic wrap and refrigerate until firm, about 1 hour. For crunchy squares, store in an airtight container in the refrigerator. For chewy squares, store at room temperature.

MAKES 24 SQUARES

PER SQUARE
173 calories,
5.2 g total fat
(2.3 g saturated fat),
3 g protein,
31 g carbohydrate,
1.6 g fiber,
7 mg cholesterol,
51 mg sodium

He who eat too much sweet, have too much seat :)

The Weight-Loss Aid That Ain't

Artificial sweeteners have been controversial throughout history. A quick search on the Internet for some "artificial intelligence" will reveal thousands of conflicting opinions about the safety of sugar substitutes. If aspartame doesn't cause migraines, reading about it sure will! Personally, we decided not to use artificial sweeteners in our desserts chapter, or in any of our recipes. There are so many dark clouds swirling around the subject, we'd rather not be human guinea pigs while science (or the government) tries to figure out what's safe and what isn't. Side effects aside, another problem with sugar substitutes is that they encourage people to make junky sweets and processed "diet" foods part of their everyday life. Daily doses of sweet nothin's sure can add up and may leave a sour taste in your mouth: NutraSweet in your morning coffee, Splenda in your yogurt, aspartame in your diet soft drink, xylitol in your chewing gum, sucralose in your energy bar. Eeek! That much fake is hard for your liver to take! Also, just because those foods are sugar-free or low-calorie certainly doesn't mean they're healthy. Most are nutrient-free, too! More red flags: Recent studies show that artificial sweeteners boost insulin, just like real sugar does, and that can make you fat. Plus, regular use of sugar substitutes can change your perception of what's sweet, making you crave more and more sugar in order to be satisfied. Some diet plan, huh? The best thing that you can do for your health is develop less of a taste for sweets in general and view them as occasional, special treats. Treat treats as treats! And if you're craving something sweet, have a small portion of the REAL deal and savor every magnificent morsel.

Trivial Tidbit

In a popular 1970s TV commercial, what product "fooled" Mother Nature? (a) Parkay Margarine; (b) Chiffon Margarine; (c) Imperial Margarine; (d) I Can't Believe It's Not Butter! Answer: (b) Chiffon Margarine! Dena Dietrich starred as the forest matron with her trademark catchphrase, "It's not nice to fool Mother Nature!" Gotta love the melodic jingle: "If you think it's butter but it's not, it's Chiffon."

Must Bake Carrot Cake

Two-tiered spiced carrot cake with orange-cream-cheese frosting

This jazzed-up, TV-show version of our popular carrot cake recipe (from 1999!) includes a dreamy, creamy frosting and a luscious, layered presentation that's perfect for special occasions.

Frosting

1½ pkgs	(12 oz/375 g total) light cream cheese, at room temperature
¼ cup	butter, at room temperature
1½ cups	icing (confectioner's) sugar
1 tbsp	frozen orange juice concentrate
1 tsp	grated orange zest

Cake

1¾ cups	all-purpose flour
¼ cup	ground flaxseed or ground chia seeds
1 tbsp	ground cinnamon
2 tsp	baking soda
1 tsp	baking powder
½ tsp	each ground nutmeg and ground ginger
½ tsp	salt
1 cup	canned pure pumpkin (not pumpkin pie filling)
1 cup	brown sugar (not packed)
¾ cup	buttermilk
¼ cup	high-quality vegetable oil (see tip, p. 286)
3	eggs
1 tsp	vanilla
2 cups	finely grated carrots
½ cup	each chopped walnuts and sweetened shredded coconut

- Prepare frosting. In a medium bowl, beat together cream cheese and butter until well blended. Gradually add icing sugar and beat until smooth. Add orange juice concentrate and orange zest and mix well. Cover and refrigerate until ready to use.

- To make cake, preheat oven to 350°F. Spray two 9-inch round cake pans with cooking spray. Cut circles of parchment paper to fit bottoms. Lightly spray paper. Set pans aside.

- In a medium bowl, combine flour, ground flaxseed, cinnamon, baking soda, baking powder, nutmeg, ginger and salt. Set aside.

- Using low speed of electric mixer, beat together pumpkin, brown sugar, buttermilk, oil, eggs and vanilla until well blended. Add dry ingredients to wet ingredients and mix using a wooden spoon just until dry ingredients are moistened. Do not use a mixer for this step. Gently fold in carrots, walnuts and coconut.

- Divide batter evenly among baking pans. Bake on middle oven rack for about 30 minutes, or until a wooden pick inserted in center of cakes comes out clean. Cool cakes in pans on a wire rack for 10 minutes. Remove cakes from pans and cool completely before frosting.

- To frost cake, place one cake layer on a pretty plate. Spread 1 cup frosting over top. Top with second cake layer. Frost top and sides of cake with remaining frosting. If desired, press finely chopped walnuts into sides of cake. Store cake in refrigerator.

Don't Be Afraid of the Dark Fudge

Creamy, foolproof chocolate and peanut-butter fudge

This spooktacular, melt-in-your-mouth, dark-chocolate fudge recipe will vanish before your eyes!

2 cups	dark chocolate chips (such as Hershey's Special Dark)
1 cup	milk chocolate chips
½ cup	light peanut butter
½ cup	light cream cheese (in a brick, not in a tub)
2 tbsp	butter, at room temperature
¼ cup	1% milk
1 tsp	vanilla
2 cups	icing (confectioner's) sugar
1 cup	finely chopped walnuts

MAKES 36 PIECES

PER PIECE
132 calories,
7.5 g total fat
(3.1 g saturated fat),
3 g protein, 14 g carbohydrate,
0.7 g fiber, 4 mg cholesterol,
36 mg sodium

YOU'LL BE GOBLIN THESE UP IN NO TIME!

- Melt chocolate chips (on defrost setting of microwave or over double boiler). In a medium bowl, beat together peanut butter, cream cheese and butter on medium speed of electric mixer until well blended. Add melted chocolate and beat again. Add milk and vanilla and beat until smooth. Gradually add icing sugar and beat after each addition, scraping down sides of bowl as necessary. Stir in walnuts using a wooden spoon.

- Line an 8 x 8-inch baking pan with parchment paper and spoon fudge into pan. Spread to edges. Cover with plastic wrap and refrigerate until firm, about 3 hours. Remove fudge from pan and cut into 36 squares. Cover and store in refrigerator. Fudge will soften if left at room temperature.

> Fudge is a noun, a verb, an interjection...and delicious!
>
> *Jessi Lane Adams*

Wake Up and Smell the Coffee Cheesecake

Deceptively delicious coffee-flavored cheesecake with a graham crust

"I love the taste of coffee," Joe said perkily (and it's especially good in this sumptuous, creamy cheesecake).

Crust

1½ cups	graham crumbs
3 tbsp	butter, melted
1 tbsp	granulated sugar

Filling

⅔ cup	granulated sugar
⅓ cup	all-purpose flour
1 tbsp	cornstarch
1½ cups	1% cottage cheese
1 pkg	(8 oz/250 g) light cream cheese
2	eggs
1 tsp	vanilla
2 tbsp	instant coffee granules
½ cup	1% milk
⅓ cup	light (5%) sour cream
3	egg whites, at room temperature
4 tbsp	granulated sugar

MAKES 12 SERVINGS

PER SERVING
251 calories, 9.7 g total fat
(5.4 g saturated fat), 10 g protein,
30 g carbohydrate, 0.8 g fiber,
59 mg cholesterol, 333 mg sodium

Recipe Tip: Be sure to use a 9-inch pan and NOT a 10-inch pan for this recipe. A 10-inch pan will result in a flat, overcooked cheesecake.

- Preheat oven to 375°F.

- Combine graham crumbs, butter and sugar in a small bowl. Mix well. Press onto bottom (not sides) of a 9-inch springform pan that has been sprayed with cooking spray. Bake just until edges feel firm and dry, about 8 minutes. Let cool.

- Reduce oven temperature to 300°F. Combine ⅔ cup sugar, flour and cornstarch in a small bowl. Set aside.

- Process cottage cheese in a food processor or blender until completely smooth. Transfer to a large bowl. Add cream cheese. Beat with an electric mixer on high speed until smooth, about 3 minutes. Add eggs and reserved flour mixture and beat until well blended. Add vanilla and beat again.

- Mix coffee granules with milk until dissolved. Add to cheese mixture along with sour cream. Beat until smooth.

- In a separate, clean bowl, beat egg whites on high speed of electric mixer until soft peaks form. Add sugar, 1 tbsp at a time, beating at high speed until stiff peaks form. Gently fold egg white mixture into cheese mixture.

- Pour batter into prepared crust. Bake for 1 hour and 10 minutes, or until almost set. Turn oven off.

- Leave cake in oven for 1 hour. Remove from oven and cool completely. Cover and refrigerate for 8 hours or overnight. Run knife along edges of cake before removing sides of pan.

FOOD BITE Here's a sampling of world coffee trivia to perk you up: Coffee was first known in Europe as Arabian wine. As a world commodity, it's second only to oil. In Greece and Turkey, the oldest person is almost always served their coffee first. If travelling abroad, it's helpful to know that "latte" is the Italian word for milk. So if you order a latte in Italy, you'll be served a glass of milk. And, finally, coffee is so important in Turkey that bridegrooms were once required to make a promise during their wedding ceremonies to always provide their new wives with coffee. If they failed to do so, it was *grounds* for divorce.

Copabanana Cake

Super-easy banana snack cake with mini chocolate chips

Her name was Lola. She was a showgirl. But that was 30 years ago, when she used to have a show. Today she prefers to stay home and bake scrumptious cakes like this one.

1½ cups	all-purpose flour
½ cup	whole wheat flour
1 tsp	each baking powder and baking soda
½ tsp	salt
1 cup	granulated sugar
2	eggs
¼ cup	butter, at room temperature
1 cup	mashed ripe bananas
½ cup	light (5%) sour cream
1 tsp	vanilla
½ cup	mini semi-sweet chocolate chips

MAKES 16 SERVINGS

PER SERVING
173 calories, 4.9 g total fat
(2.7 g saturated fat), 3 g protein,
31 g carbohydrate, 1.4 g fiber,
36 mg cholesterol, 199 mg sodium

- Preheat oven to 350°F. Spray a 9 x 13-inch baking pan with cooking spray and set aside.

- In a medium bowl, combine both flours, baking powder, baking soda and salt. Set aside.

- In a large bowl, beat together sugar, eggs and butter on medium speed of electric mixer. Add bananas, sour cream and vanilla. Beat again until smooth.

- Gradually add flour mixture to banana mixture, beating after each addition. Batter will be thick. Fold in chocolate chips.

- Spoon batter into prepared pan and spread evenly using a spatula. Bake for 25 to 28 minutes, or until a wooden pick inserted in center of cake comes out clean. Cool completely on a wire rack. Cut into 16 pieces and store in an airtight container.

Nutrition Nugget
Bananas could actually help you lose weight: The kind of starch found in bananas (especially those on the greenish-yellowish side) is called resistant starch. It passes through your digestive tract largely undigested and helps feed the good bacteria in your gut, promoting overall health. Plus, it keeps you feeling full longer, so you eat less. And banana's potassium helps balance fluid levels in your cells, preventing bloating. It's always better to eat a naturally sweetened food when you have a sugar craving rather than turning to processed junk food. Incidentally, our good friend, Leanne, eats four bananas a day—sometimes five. We're serious! Not only is she slim and fit, but you should see her climb trees!

How Sweet It Isn't

The sweeter your diet, the more nutrient deficient it is. If you just can't yank your sweet tooth, at least choose "sweet somethin's" over "sweet nothin's." Try cutting back on refined white sugar and artificial sweeteners that serve up nothing but empty calories. Instead, choose natural sweeteners that offer some health benefits. Raw honey, for instance, contains vitamins (the Bee vitamins?), minerals and enzymes, plus antioxidants that protect against illness. Pure maple syrup—especially grade B maple syrup—is loaded with nutrients, too. Then there's blue agave nectar, which has a minimal impact on blood sugar. Another good choice is stevia, derived from an herb native to South America. It's calorie-free and actually helps balance blood-sugar levels, making it a great alternative for diabetics or those watching their weight. It's much sweeter than sugar and can have a little bit of an aftertaste, but a little goes a long way. Oh, and keep your eyes peeled for two rising sugar stars: coconut sugar (dee-lish and low-glycemic) and yacon syrup (a natural sweetener that balances blood sugar and also acts as a prebiotic, helping the digestive system to better absorb calcium and other nutrients). Whether sweets contain natural or refined sugars, please remember to consider ALL desserts, including the sugary cake on this page, as occasional indulgences and not daily delights!

Rhapsody in Blueberry

Old-fashioned blueberry crisp with oatmeal crumb topping

This classical dessert gets jazzed up with a symphony of flavors and textures that'll make your mouth water and your heart sing!

Filling

6 cups	(3 pints) fresh blueberries
⅓ cup	granulated sugar
2 tbsp	cornstarch
2 tbsp	freshly squeezed lemon juice
2 tsp	grated lemon zest

Topping

1 cup	quick-cooking rolled oats (not instant)
½ cup	all-purpose flour
⅓ cup	lightly packed brown sugar
½ tsp	ground cinnamon
¼ cup	butter, melted
2 tbsp	apple juice or orange juice
1 cup	thick lemon-flavored yogurt or light whipped topping (optional)

MAKES 8 SERVINGS

PER SERVING
256 calories, 6.9 g total fat
(3.7 g saturated fat),
3 g protein,
48 g carbohydrate,
4.4 g fiber, 16 mg cholesterol,
12 mg sodium

Recipe Tip: Make this recipe when fresh blueberries are in season. It just isn't the same when you make it with frozen blueberries.

- Preheat oven to 375°F. Spray a 9 x 13-inch baking dish with cooking spray. Add blueberries. Sprinkle blueberries with sugar, cornstarch, lemon juice and lemon zest. Mix well and set aside.

- To make topping, combine oats, flour, brown sugar and cinnamon in a medium bowl. Add melted butter and juice. Using a fork, stir until mixture resembles coarse crumbs. Sprinkle crumb mixture evenly over coated blueberries.

- Bake for 30 minutes, until blueberries are bubbling around edges of pan and crumb topping is golden brown. Cool for 10 minutes before serving (it's hot!). Serve with a dollop of lemon yogurt or light whipped topping, if desired. Also tastes great with a small scoop of vanilla ice cream.

FOOD BITE

If all the blueberries grown in North America in one year were spread out in a single layer, they would cover a four-lane highway that stretched from New York to Chicago.

*Sign in bakery window:
Cakes $ .66.
Upside-Down Cakes $ .99 :)*

Hot Fudge Monday

A heavenly fudgy cake smothered in a hot, chocolaty sauce

You read it right—it's not "sundae" and there's no ice cream, either. Tasty any day of the week, this unusual and unusually simple dessert is a chocolate-lover's dream!

I LOVE MONDAYS!

COCOA

Cake

½ cup	each all-purpose flour and whole wheat flour
¾ cup	brown sugar (not packed)
2 tbsp	unsweetened cocoa powder
2 tsp	baking powder
¼ tsp	salt
½ cup	1% milk
2 tbsp	high-quality vegetable oil

Sauce

¾ cup	brown sugar (not packed)
¼ cup	unsweetened cocoa powder
1¾ cups	boiling water

MAKES 6 SERVINGS

PER SERVING
278 calories,
5.7 g total fat
(0.8 g saturated fat),
4 g protein,
55 g carbohydrate,
3 g fiber,
1 mg cholesterol,
87 mg sodium

- Preheat oven to 350°F.

- To prepare batter, combine both flours, brown sugar, cocoa powder, baking powder and salt in a medium bowl. Mix well and set aside.

- Pour milk into measuring cup, add oil and whisk until blended. Add milk mixture to flour mixture. Using a wooden spoon, stir vigorously until well blended (you may also use an electric mixer on low speed). Pour batter over the bottom of an ungreased 8 x 8-inch baking pan. Spread evenly.

- To make sauce, mix together brown sugar and cocoa powder in a small bowl. Sprinkle mixture evenly over batter. Pour boiling water over top. DO NOT STIR! At this point you may think we're nuts, but stick with us. Bake for 40 to 45 minutes, until top of cake feels dry to touch. Remove from oven and let stand 5 minutes before serving. Cut into 6 pieces. Spoon sauce from bottom of pan over individual servings of cake.

Trivial Tidbit
In the early 1920s, the Washburn Crosby Company (later merged into General Mills) created the fictional character Betty Crocker to answer letters from consumers with a more personal touch. They combined the last name of a retired company executive, William Crocker, with the first name "Betty," which was thought of as "warm and friendly."

A Dark Secret
Looks like what's good for your sweetheart may be good for your heart, too. Chocolate is rich in flavonoids, the natural antioxidants that are also credited with making red wine heart-healthy. Researchers say an ounce a day can lower blood pressure, reduce bad cholesterol and even increase the flow of blood to the brain. Perhaps best of all, dark chocolate is full of anandamide and phenylethylamine, compounds that boost the same feel-good endorphins triggered by sex, drugs (like heroin and marijuana) and rockin'/rollin' physical exertion. Does that mean you should run to the supermarket and load your cart with Kit Kats and Milky Ways for "medicinal purposes"? Whoa, Henry! It's only the high-quality dark stuff that's good for you—at least 60 percent cocoa or higher. Sorry to burst your Aero bubble, but research published in *Nature* found that adding milk to chocolate seems to cancel out its antioxidant properties. Plus, the cheaper milk chocolate bars usually contain partially hydrogenated oils (trans fats) and a lot more sugar than their darker cousins. Pssst! Some high-quality, dark chocolate bars actually have four times the flavonoids of an apple! Could an ounce a day keep the doctor away?

Aerobics: A series of strenuous exercises which help convert fats, sugars and starches into aches, pains and cramps.

Author unknown

Tir-riffic Tiramisu Trifle
Lightened-up and lavishly layered tiramisu

It's a trifle that isn't trifle, if you know what we mean!
Simple to make yet looks very impressive!

Filling

½ cup	pure maple syrup
1 pkg	(¼ oz/7 g) unflavored gelatine
2 cups	part-skim ricotta cheese
2 pkgs	(8 oz/250 g each) light cream cheese
1½ cups	extra rich and thick vanilla-flavored yogurt (see tip)
4 tbsp	(2 oz) coffee-flavored liqueur (such as Kahlúa), divided
1 tsp	vanilla
¼ tsp	ground cinnamon
36 to 40	ladyfinger cookies
1 cup	extra-strong brewed coffee, cooled or
	1 cup boiling water mixed with
	1 tbsp instant espresso powder
1 oz	(28 g) semi-sweet chocolate (chunk)

Fresh raspberries and mint leaves for garnish (optional)

MAKES 10 SERVINGS

PER SERVING
386 calories, 12.6 g total fat (7.1 g saturated fat),
14 g protein, 49 g carbohydrate, 1.2 g fiber,
75 mg cholesterol, 228 mg sodium

Recipe Tip: Make sure the yogurt you buy for this recipe is vanilla-flavored (not plain) and that it's very thick. We like Liberté Méditerranée brand. While we're huge fans of Greek yogurt, it's a bit too tart for this recipe.

- To make filling, warm the maple syrup in a very small saucepan (or in microwave) and sprinkle gelatine over top to soften. Set aside.

- Add ricotta, cream cheese and yogurt to the bowl of a food processor and whirl until completely smooth. Stir warm syrup-gelatine mixture and add to cheese mixture along with 2 tbsp coffee liqueur, vanilla and cinnamon. Whirl until smooth.

- Combine cooled coffee and remaining 2 tbsp liqueur in a shallow bowl. Working one at a time, quickly dip ladyfingers in coffee mixture and shake off excess. You don't want to soak them, just a very quick dunk. Line sides of trifle dish with ladyfingers (stand them up). Cover bottom of trifle dish with more dunked ladyfingers, cutting or breaking them as necessary to fit bottom. Spoon ¼ cheese filling over ladyfingers. Grate ¼ chocolate directly over filling (use finest holes of grater). Repeat layering: dunked ladyfingers, ¼ filling, ¼ grated chocolate, dunked ladyfingers, ¼ filling, ¼ grated chocolate, dunked ladyfingers, ¼ filling, finishing with ¼ grated chocolate. Cover with plastic wrap and refrigerate at least 8 hours or overnight. To serve, spoon into dessert dishes. Top with fresh raspberries and garnish with mint leaves, if desired.

Nutrition Nugget

OK, let's be realistic: Tiramisu is not a health food! It's a once-or-twice-a-year indulgence. A special treat for a special occasion. There are no whole grains to be added, no flax or other sources of fiber, no omega-3s and no sneaking in grated vegetables. Nope, let's call this treat a treat. Enjoy it, smile while you're eating it, love every morsel, then get right back on the healthy eating track the next day.

Lovin' My No-Oven Cheesecake

Light and velvety no-bake pumpkin cheesecake

Our famous no-bake pumpkin cheesecake is the perfect finish to Thanksgiving dinner. And you can make it no sweat, since you don't use an oven! Plus, we've carved out the heavy stuff and left in the light stuff, so even though you're feeling stuffed, you can still eat some sweet stuff.

Smile Gourdious!

Crust

1½ cups	graham crumbs
2 tbsp	brown sugar
½ tsp	ground cinnamon
3 tbsp	butter, melted

Filling

1 cup	2% evaporated milk
¼ cup	frozen orange juice concentrate, thawed
2 pkgs	(¼ oz/7 g each) unflavored gelatine
1½ pkgs	(12 oz/375 g total) light cream cheese, at room temperature
1¼ cups	packed brown sugar
1 tbsp	vanilla
2 cups	light (5%) sour cream
2 cups	canned pure pumpkin (not pumpkin pie filling)
2 tsp	ground cinnamon
½ tsp	each ground nutmeg, ground ginger and ground allspice

Light whipped topping (optional)

MAKES 16 SERVINGS

PER SERVING
227 calories, 7.8 g total fat (4.6 g saturated fat), 6 g protein, 33 g carbohydrate, 1.5 g fiber, 24 mg cholesterol, 184 mg sodium

- To make crust, combine graham crumbs, brown sugar and cinnamon in a medium bowl. Add melted butter and stir using a fork until crumbs are moistened. Spray a 9-inch springform pan with cooking spray. Press crumb mixture firmly and evenly over bottom of pan (not sides). Refrigerate for 1 hour.
- Meanwhile, combine evaporated milk and orange juice concentrate in a small saucepan. Sprinkle gelatine over top and let stand for 5 minutes. Whisk gelatine into milk mixture and cook over medium-high heat, stirring constantly, until mixture just starts to boil. Remove from heat immediately and let cool while crust is setting.
- To make filling, beat together cream cheese, brown sugar and vanilla on high speed of electric mixer until smooth. Add sour cream, pumpkin and spices. Beat again on medium speed until well blended. Add milk mixture and beat again until well mixed.
- Pour batter over crust and smooth top. Cover with plastic wrap and refrigerate for at least 8 hours (overnight is best). To serve, run a sharp, thin knife around edge of pan to loosen cake. Remove sides of pan. Serve individual slices with light whipped topping, if desired.

What do you get when you divide the area of a pumpkin by its radius? Pumpkin pi :)

The Hallowed Pumpkin

Too bad pumpkins are destined to spend their lives in patches or on porches rather than on dinner tables where they belong! A pumpkin is just really a huge squash, and it's the beta-carotene king, too. Like carrots and sweet potatoes, pumpkins are chock-full of carotenoids. These good-for-you plant chemicals fight nasty cellular damage that can make you feel sick or make you look old. Yes, eating pumpkin can help keep you young and healthy! And you don't have to sharpen your carving knife, either. Canned pumpkin will do the trick (and it's a treat!). A half a cup has about 200 percent of the daily amount of beta-carotene recommended by experts. Plus, pumpkins have lots of fiber and a ton of iron, which is really important for women because we need to replenish the iron we lose during monthly cycles. Pssst! Hey, guys! Don't forget about the seeds. They're brilliant at preventing prostate issues.

You're Pudding Me On

Warm banana bread pudding with chocolate chips and pecans

You'll be a super duper when you fool your friends with this lightened-up banana bread pudding. No one will believe it's lower in fat and contains multigrain bread! Better hide the recipe, jest in case!

It's foolproof!

10 to 12	large slices multigrain bread (about 1 lb/454 g)
2 cups	2% milk
2 cups	mashed ripe bananas
1 cup	vanilla-flavored yogurt
4	eggs, lightly beaten
¾ cup	packed brown sugar
1 tsp	each vanilla and ground cinnamon
¾ cup	semi-sweet chocolate chips
⅔ cup	chopped pecans

MAKES 12 SERVINGS

PER SERVING
276 calories, 8.7 g total fat
(2.2 g saturated fat), 9 g protein,
45 g carbohydrate, 4 g fiber,
3 mg cholesterol, 221 mg sodium

- Break bread into 1-inch pieces and place in a 9 x 13-inch glass baking dish that has been sprayed with cooking spray. Dish should be full.

- In a large bowl, whisk together milk, bananas, yogurt, eggs, brown sugar, vanilla and cinnamon. Pour mixture over bread. Using your hands (yeah, it's a little messy), mix bread cubes with milk mixture so that all pieces are coated. Let stand for 15 minutes while you preheat the oven to 350°F.

- Just before popping dish into oven, mix in most of the chocolate chips and pecans, saving a little of each to sprinkle on top. Now, go ahead and sprinkle them on top!

- Bake for 50 to 55 minutes, until pudding is puffed up and golden brown and center is set. Remove from oven and let stand for 10 minutes before serving. You can cut the dessert into squares and serve it on a plate or spoon it into dessert bowls. If you feel like splurging, serve the sliced version with a small scoop of vanilla ice cream or frozen yogurt, and the spooned version with a drizzle of real whipping cream.

Merry Cherry Cheesecake

Simple and scrumptious cherry cheesecake squares with a hint of lemon

Your dinner guests will be very merry when they taste this light-and-lemony cherry cheesecake. A crowd favorite!

Crust

1½ cups	graham crumbs
½ tsp	ground cinnamon
3 tbsp	butter, melted

Filling

¼ cup	freshly squeezed lemon juice
1 pkg	(¼ oz/7 g) unflavored gelatine
2 pkgs	(8 oz/250 g each) light cream cheese
2 cups	light (5%) sour cream
1 can	(10 oz/284 mL) low-fat sweetened condensed milk (such as Eagle Brand)
2 tsp	grated lemon zest
2 cans	(19 oz/540 mL each) reduced-sugar cherry pie filling

- To make crust, combine graham crumbs and cinnamon in a medium bowl. Add melted butter and stir using a fork until crumbs are moistened. Spray a 9 x 13-inch baking dish with cooking spray. Press crumb mixture firmly and evenly over bottom of dish. Refrigerate while you prepare the filling.

- Measure lemon juice in a measuring cup. Sprinkle gelatine over lemon juice and let stand for 1 minute. Add ¼ cup boiling water. Mix well, until gelatine is dissolved. Set aside.

- To make filling, beat together cream cheese and lemon-juice mixture on high speed of electric mixer until smooth. Add sour cream, sweetened condensed milk and lemon zest. Beat again until well blended. Pour filling over prepared crust and spread to edges of pan. Cover and refrigerate for at least 3 hours until set. Spread cherry pie filling over cream-cheese mixture. Cover and refrigerate until ready to serve.

MAKES 18 SQUARES

PER SQUARE
248 calories, 8.9 g total fat
(5.5 g saturated fat),
7 g protein,
37 g carbohydrate,
0.3 g fiber,
28 mg cholesterol,
212 mg sodium

Recipe Tips: Take the cream cheese out of the fridge about 30 minutes before you make this cake. It's easier to beat cream cheese if it isn't cold. Don't omit the lemon juice from this recipe— it, along with the gelatine, helps the filling set. (If you leave it out, the filling will be runny.) Don't forget to grate the zest from the lemon before cutting it in half to squeeze out its juice.

Nutrition Nugget
Three cheers for cherries! Cherries contain "natural aspirin" that helps detoxify inflammation-related substances in the body's tissues and joints. That makes cherries helpful in relieving arthritis pain and gout. Tired of counting sheep to get some quality zzz's? Reach for tart cherries! Montmorency sour cherries—the same kind found in cherry pie—contain readily absorbable dietary melatonin, the precious hormone responsible for sleep. (No, this is not permission to polish off a can of cherry pie filling!) A study at the University of Rochester Medical Center showed that the consumption of tart cherry juice significantly reduced the severity of insomnia and lessened "wake periods" after sleep onset. Cherr-io!

Oops! There it is! Chocolate Cake
Chocolate snack cake with mini chips and a hint of cinnamon

The accidental dessert—that's what this is! We still don't know how or why this combination of ingredients ended up in the pan, but what a tasty result! Super moist and chocolaty, you won't believe this cake isn't loaded with fat. Kids love it!

OOPS! LOOKS LIKE I'VE DONE IT AGAIN

1 cup	all-purpose flour
⅓ cup	unsweetened cocoa powder
1½ tsp	baking powder
1 tsp	baking soda
½ tsp	ground cinnamon
¼ tsp	salt
1¼ cups	packed brown sugar
2	eggs
3 tbsp	high-quality vegetable oil
1 cup	light (5%) sour cream
1 tsp	vanilla
¼ tsp	almond extract
½ cup	mini semi-sweet chocolate chips

MAKES 12 SERVINGS

PER SERVING
214 calories, 6.5 g total fat (1.6 g saturated fat), 4 g protein, 37 g carbohydrate, 1.4 g fiber, 39 mg cholesterol, 257 mg sodium

- Preheat oven to 350°F. Spray an 8 x 8-inch baking pan with cooking spray and set aside.

- In a small bowl, mix together flour, cocoa powder, baking powder, baking soda, cinnamon and salt. Set aside.

- In a medium bowl, beat together brown sugar, eggs and oil using an electric mixer on medium speed. Add sour cream, vanilla and almond extract. Beat on low speed until well blended.

- Gradually add flour mixture to sour cream mixture, beating on medium speed. Fold in chocolate chips.

- Spread batter evenly in prepared pan. Bake for 40 to 45 minutes, or until a wooden pick inserted in center of cake comes out clean. Be sure to check cake after 40 minutes, since you don't want to over-bake it. Remove from oven and let cool in pan for 15 minutes. Cut into 12 squares. For maximum moistness, store at room temperature in an airtight container.

Nutrition Nugget

We'll bet dollars to peanuts that once you've tried almond butter, you'll never want plain ol' Jiffy again. Almond butter is a great source of protein and good fats like monounsaturated and omega-3. Its only ingredients are almonds and a wee bit of oil. That's it. That's all! Almond butter is pricey (around $10 a jar), but you get what you pay for. We guarantee your kids will gobble it up and, since it's much healthier than peanut butter, that should soften the blow about the extra dough. And while you're at it, give smooth and creamy almond milk a try. It's a great source of calcium and good fats, plus, unlike regular milk, it's a low-carbohydrate choice that's lactose free. Time for a new flavor of milk mustache!

Playing the Percentages

Don't eat this. Avoid that. This'll make you fat. That raises cholesterol. Ugh! What's a guy or gal to do? Like real estate's mantra for success, "location, location, location," the sane way to navigate the murky waters of today's nutritional landscape is to think "moderation, moderation, moderation." Most foods in moderation are OK. Most foods in excess—even some healthy foods—are not OK. It's our excesses (dietary and otherwise) that can lead to problems. (Just ask Charlie Sheen!) Obesity, cancer, diabetes and heart disease are not the result of eating "unhealthy" or "taboo" foods every once in a while. They're usually the result of regular consumption of unhealthy foods—day in and day out, year after year. A helpful and realistic healthy-eating guideline is the 80/20 rule: 80 percent of the time, try choosing foods that are whole, natural and nutritious. Twenty percent of the time, let yourself have an indulgence. Craving chocolate ice cream? Scoop up a small serving and savor every spoonful. Then, get back on the healthy-eating track for the rest of the day. It's not every morsel of food you eat that's important—it's what you do consistently, over the long haul, that matters most.

Puddin' on the Ritz

Warmly spiced cinnamon-raisin bread pudding with apples

Traditional bread pudding gets all jazzed up with cinnamon-raisin bread in place of the ordinary stuff, and chopped apples tossed in for a pleasing texture and tasty goodness. A treat for breakfast with a light drizzle of maple syrup!

4 cups	cubed cinnamon-raisin bread (slightly stale)
1 cup	peeled and chopped Granny Smith apples
½ cup	packed brown sugar
2	eggs
1 cup	2% evaporated milk
½ cup	skim or 1% milk
1½ tsp	vanilla
¼ tsp	ground cinnamon
⅛ tsp	ground nutmeg

MAKES 6 SERVINGS

PER SERVING
243 calories, 4.1 g total fat
(1 g saturated fat), 8 g protein,
44 g carbohydrate, 2 g fiber,
78 mg cholesterol, 218 mg sodium

- Preheat oven to 350°F. Spray an 8 x 8-inch baking pan with cooking spray and set aside.

- Toss bread cubes and apples together in a large bowl. In a separate bowl, whisk together brown sugar and eggs. Add evaporated milk, skim milk, vanilla, cinnamon and nutmeg. Whisk again.

- Pour milk mixture over bread cubes and apples. Mix well. Let stand for 15 minutes for bread to absorb liquid.

- Transfer mixture to baking pan. Make sure apples are evenly distributed throughout pan. Bake for 50 minutes, until bread is a deep golden brown and puffed up. A knife inserted in the center should come out clean. Slice into 6 squares and serve warm.

FOOD BITE

Call the Spice Squad! You're busted! Though most commonly used to flavor eggnog, pies and cakes, nutmeg can also be a hallucinogenic drug. It's true! Nutmeg contains the chemical myristicin, which has properties similar to the drug mescaline and, if taken in large quantities, nutmeg can actually produce hallucinations and a feeling of euphoria. No need to trash your stash, though. You'd have to down an absurd amount to reach Fantasy Island— and you'd probably get sick to your stomach before you got there. In culinary proportions, you can rest assured that nutmeg is a safe spice, not a Scary Spice.

Thieves Escape Death!

What do you get when you combine the oils of cinnamon, cloves, lemon, rosemary and eucalyptus? A delicious-smelling, powerful protector against infectious disease, that's what! Bye-bye flu and cold bugs! See ya later mold and fungi! This versatile, potent blend of essential oils is available in a product called Thieves Essential Oil from Young Living Essential Oils (www.youngliving.com). The blend is based on a historical tale of 15th-century thieves who rubbed oils on themselves to avoid contracting the plague while they robbed the dead and dying. When apprehended, the thieves disclosed their secret formula of herbs, spices and oils used to protect themselves in exchange for a more lenient punishment. Much scientific research has proven this blend to be highly antimicrobial— germs don't stand a chance! You can put a drop in a glass of water or under your tongue (it's strong!) or apply it directly to the bottom of your feet or your chest. And as an added bonus, you'll smell like a cinnamon bun, so don't be surprised if throngs of people are suddenly drawn to you like bees to honey!

A farmer brought a bucket of milk to church so it could get pastorized :)

Shockolate Cheesecake

Rich-tasting, double-chocolate cheesecake with a chocolate brownie crust

Electrify your guests with this shockingly good cheesecake! It's chock-full of chocolate and its rich, decadent taste will send chills up your spine!

1 box	(15.5 oz/440 g) low-fat brownie mix (such as Betty Crocker Fudge Brownies)
2 cups	1% cottage cheese
1 cup	light (5%) sour cream
1 pkg	(8 oz/250 g) light cream cheese, at room temperature
1 cup	granulated sugar
⅓ cup	unsweetened cocoa powder
¼ cup	all-purpose flour
6 oz	(170 g) semi-sweet chocolate squares, melted and cooled slightly (see tip)
4	eggs
1 tsp	vanilla

Melted chocolate for drizzling (optional)

MAKES 16 SERVINGS

PER SERVING
317 calories, 10 g total fat (5.9 g saturated fat),
11 g protein, 47 g carbohydrate, 2.2 g fiber,
65 mg cholesterol, 299 mg sodium

- Spray a 10-inch springform pan with cooking spray. Prepare brownies according to package directions, baking in springform pan instead of regular cake pan. Brownies should bake in about 20 minutes. Remove pan from oven and reset oven temperature to 325°F. Set brownie crust aside to cool slightly while you prepare filling.

- To make filling, whirl cottage cheese, sour cream and cream cheese in the bowl of a food processor or blender until perfectly smooth. Scrape out mixture into a large mixing bowl. In a small bowl, sift together sugar, cocoa powder and flour. Gradually add sugar mixture to cream-cheese mixture and beat on medium speed of electric mixer until well blended. Add melted chocolate and beat again, scraping down sides of bowl as necessary. Add eggs and vanilla. Beat just until eggs are incorporated into batter.

- Before pouring batter over crust, lightly grease sides of pan. This will help prevent cheesecake from cracking as it cools. Pour batter over brownie crust and smooth top. Place on middle oven rack and bake for 60 to 70 minutes. Cake will be puffed up and center will jiggle slightly when pan is shaken. Turn off oven, open oven door halfway and leave cake in oven to cool for 1 hour. Remove from oven, run knife around edge of pan to loosen cake from sides and cool completely. Cover with plastic wrap and refrigerate overnight.

- To serve, remove sides of pan, slice thinly (it's rich!) and drizzle melted chocolate over individual pieces, if desired.

Recipe Tip To melt chocolate, place chocolate squares in a microwave-safe bowl and microwave on medium-low power (or defrost setting) until chocolate is melted. For 6 squares, it should take about 3 minutes, depending on the strength of your microwave. Be careful not to burn chocolate! Remove bowl from microwave and stir chocolate until smooth. Cool slightly before using in recipe.

In this chapter...

Miscellooneyous

A mishmash of marvelous, mismatched recipes (you know, stuff that doesn't fit anywhere else!)

Acropolis Sandwich,
p. 345

The LEANing Tower of Pizza

Thin-crust chicken pizza with sun-dried tomatoes, zucchini, olives and feta cheese

A sight to behold! This pizza's stacked so high to the sky with tasty toppings, it's hard to believe it's not towering with fat! We're a little mixed up with our geography, though. This leaning tower has Greek-style toppings, not Italian. Oh well.

2 tsp	olive oil
1 cup	each thinly sliced zucchini and red onions
½ cup	pizza sauce
1	12-inch prebaked whole-grain thin-crust pizza shell
1 cup	chopped cooked chicken breast
5	sun-dried tomatoes, soaked and chopped
3	extra-large pitted black olives, thinly sliced
2	plum tomatoes, thinly sliced
¼ cup	crumbled light feta cheese (1 oz/28 g)
½ cup	packed shredded light mozzarella cheese (2 oz/57 g)

MAKES ONE 12-INCH PIZZA, 8 SLICES

PER SLICE
163 calories, 5.3 g total fat (1.7 g saturated fat), 10 g protein, 18 g carbohydrate, 2.6 g fiber, 20 mg cholesterol, 302 mg sodium

- Heat olive oil in a medium skillet over medium heat. Add zucchini and onions. Cook and stir until vegetables are tender, about 5 minutes. Remove from heat.

- Spread sauce evenly over crust. Layer toppings in the following order: chicken, onions and zucchini, sun-dried tomatoes, olives, tomato slices, feta, mozzarella. Bake at 425°F for about 10 minutes, or until cheese is melted and crust is golden brown.

Recipe Tip: Feel like making the crust from scratch?
Use the recipe on p. 343 and increase baking time to 15 minutes.

I worked at a diet food company, but the chances for promotion were slim :)

Nutrition Nugget

"Take two teaspoons and call me in the morning!" Did you know there's a compound in olive oil that has the same pain-relieving effect as ibuprofen (Motrin, Advil)? Or that olive oil can help protect against breast cancer? Studies show that women who consume at least two teaspoons of olive oil a day have a 73 percent reduced risk of breast cancer compared with women who take in little or no olive oil.

FOOD BITE

Pizza-delivery drivers report the following peculiar customer habits: Those who have pierced noses, lips or eyebrows ask for vegetarian toppings 23 percent more often than meat toppings. Not surprisingly, women are twice as likely as men to order vegetables on their pizza. People who have wind chimes on the porch are four times more likely than the average to request olives. And men who wear muscle shirts order pepperoni three times more often than any other topping. You wanna *pizza* me?

Erik Eggstrata

Layered breakfast strata with Italian sausage and veggies

When the CHiPs are down, you can call on this satisfying breakfast strata to tame a hungry crowd. Colorful veggies and super-light ingredients mean you won't develop a Ponch.

3 cups	whole-grain herb-seasoned croutons
8 oz	(227 g) light mild Italian sausage
1 cup	diced zucchini
½ cup	minced onions
½ cup	diced red bell pepper
1 cup	packed shredded light old (sharp) cheddar cheese (4 oz/113 g)
8	eggs
1 cup	2% evaporated milk or light (5%) cream
¼ tsp	each salt and freshly ground black pepper

MAKES 8 SERVINGS

PER SERVING
245 calories, 11.4 g total fat (4.4 g saturated fat), 19 g protein, 17 g carbohydrate, 2 g fiber, 241 mg cholesterol, 607 mg sodium

- Spray an 11 x 7-inch casserole dish with cooking spray. Spread croutons evenly in bottom of dish. Set aside.

- Spray a medium, non-stick skillet with cooking spray or add a bit of olive oil. Remove and discard casing from sausage. Break or cut sausage into small pieces and add to skillet. Cook over medium-high heat until no longer pink, breaking up any large pieces. Add zucchini, onions and red pepper. Reduce heat to medium. Cook and stir for about 3 more minutes, until vegetables begin to soften.

- To assemble strata, spoon sausage mixture evenly over croutons. Top with shredded cheese. Whisk together eggs, milk, salt and pepper in a medium bowl. Pour egg mixture evenly over sausage and vegetables. Let strata stand for 15 minutes while you preheat oven to 350°F.

- Bake, uncovered, for 40 minutes, until eggs are completely set. Let stand 5 minutes before serving.

Recipe Tips You can use just about any flavor of croutons for this recipe: sun-dried tomato and basil, Caesar, onion and garlic, but please look for whole-grain croutons. Turkey kielbasa is a good substitute if you can't find light Italian sausage. It's already cooked, however, so just cut it up and heat it with the vegetables in the skillet. (The spiciness of the kielbasa will lend some flavor to the vegetables as they cook.)

Pizzazzy Pizza Sauce

Traditional tomato-and-herb pizza sauce with pizzazz

Can the canned stuff and get cooking! This zesty and zingy pizza sauce with punch and panache will perk up any pizza, pronto!

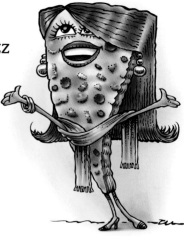

2 tsp	olive oil	
½ cup	minced red onions	
2 tsp	minced garlic	
2 cups	no-salt-added tomato sauce	
1 can	(5.5 oz/156 mL) tomato paste	
2 tsp	dried oregano	
2 tsp	balsamic vinegar	
2 tsp	brown sugar	
½ tsp	dried basil	
½ tsp	dried rosemary	
¼ tsp	freshly ground black pepper	
Salt to taste		

MAKES ABOUT
2 ½ CUPS

PER SERVING (½ CUP)
116 calories,
3.8 g total fat
(0.3 g saturated fat),
4 g protein, 18 g carbohydrate,
3.5 g fiber, 0 mg cholesterol,
180 mg sodium

- Heat olive oil over medium heat in a medium pot. Add onions and garlic. Cook and stir until onions are softened, about 3 minutes. Be careful not to burn them.

- Add all remaining ingredients and mix well. Bring sauce to a boil. Reduce heat to low and simmer, covered, for 15 minutes. Taste and add salt, if needed. Cool before using. Keeps for 1 week in an airtight container in the refrigerator and may be frozen for up to 2 months.

Recipe Tip: If you like your pizza sauce hot 'n' spicy, add ½ tsp crushed red pepper flakes or ¼ tsp cayenne pepper.

Trivial Tidbit

If you were a "sage" warden, what herb would you ban from jailhouse cooking? Is it (a) rosemary; (b) thyme; (c) dill; or (d) oregano? The answer? (d) oregano! It's been said that some inmates will roll an oregano joint while doing *thyme*.

> **The remedies for every human illness are concealed within nature.**
>
> *Paracelsus, 16th century physician*

Eat, Drink & Be Flabby

Think beverage calories don't count? Better think before you drink! North Americans are guzzling more fruity, juicy concoctions, designer coffees and sugary sports or energy drinks than ever before. But have you ever stopped to consider how many empty calories you're sucking up through that straw? Two hundred? Three hundred? Maybe even four hundred? And those calories are just "add-ons"—meaning you don't consume them in place of food calories, you have them in *addition* to food. If you don't cut back on what you eat to make up for what you drink, you could end up pouring on the pounds. Another problem is that fluids don't help our brains register that same "full" feeling we get when we eat solids, so we consume more. When you swig back that frothy mocha latte before lunch or suck back that margarita after work, they don't feel like a rich, creamy slab of cheesecake but, to your fat cells, there's no difference. Chug it or chew it, a calorie is a calorie. And sugar is sugar. When a drink contains 10 teaspoons of sugar, like most soft drinks and fruity beverages do, you can pretty much guarantee your blood sugar's going to Mars and back. That'll send your hormones into a fat-storing frenzy! The final straw: Experts believe that high-fructose corn syrup, the inexpensive sweetener found in many beverages, ranks right up there with trans fats as one of the most health-defeating substances you could ever put in your body.

Thai Kwon Dough

Thai chicken pizza with zesty peanut sauce

Martial in the troops for this Thai-inspired work of art! It's a kickin' pizza topped with peanut sauce instead of tomato sauce, packing a real flavor punch!

Peanut Sauce

¼ cup	light peanut butter
¼ cup	hoisin sauce
1 tbsp	freshly squeezed lemon juice
2 tsp	sesame oil
2 tsp	grated gingerroot
1 tsp	each liquid honey, reduced-sodium soy sauce and red wine vinegar
1 tsp	minced garlic
Pinch	crushed red pepper flakes
1 cup	chopped cooked chicken breast (see tip)
1	12-inch prebaked whole-grain thin-crust pizza shell
1 cup	packed shredded light Monterey Jack cheese (4 oz/113 g), divided
⅓ cup	bean sprouts
¼ cup	each grated carrots and chopped green onions
2 tbsp	chopped roasted peanuts
1 tbsp	minced fresh cilantro

- Preheat oven to 425°F.

- To make sauce, combine all sauce ingredients in a small pot and heat over medium-high heat until bubbly, stirring constantly. Remove from heat and let cool slightly.

- Mix 1 heaping tbsp of peanut sauce with chicken pieces and set aside. To assemble pizza, spread remaining peanut sauce evenly over crust. Top with half the shredded cheese. Distribute chicken cubes evenly over cheese. Top with bean sprouts (break them into smaller pieces if you prefer), carrots, green onions and peanuts, in that order. Sprinkle remaining shredded cheese over toppings.

- Place pizza directly on middle oven rack and bake for about 8 to 10 minutes, until cheese is completely melted and edges are lightly browned. Sprinkle with cilantro before serving.

Recipe Tip: We like using the breast meat from a rotisserie chicken because it's so moist. However, grilled chicken would work in this recipe, too, as long as it's not overcooked.

MAKES 1 PIZZA, 8 SLICES

PER SLICE
220 calories, 9.6 g total fat (2.7 g saturated fat), 12 g protein, 22 g carbohydrate, 1.7 g fiber, 18 mg cholesterol, 398 mg sodium

Nutrition Nugget

Monterey Jack cheese is low in tyramine, a compound found in many cheeses and other foods that can trigger headaches or migraines in some people. So if you're prone to a throbbin' noggin', this variety might be your best cheese choice.

Welcome Back, 'Cotta

Lemon-ricotta pancakes with fresh blueberry sauce

Ricotta cheese is a welcome addition to these light and lemony pancakes. They're no sweat to make and so tasty, you'll want to hog them all for yourself. (P.S. Our pal Vinnie from Washington Gabe us the recipe!)

UP YOUR NOSE WITH A RUBBER HOSE

Blueberry Sauce

2 cups	fresh blueberries
¼ cup	water
¼ cup	granulated sugar
2 tbsp	freshly squeezed lemon juice
1½ tsp	cornstarch

Pancakes

1¼ cups	all-purpose flour
⅓ cup	oat bran
¼ cup	granulated sugar
2 tsp	baking powder
½ tsp	baking soda
¼ tsp	salt
1 cup	part-skim or extra-smooth ricotta cheese
⅓ cup	1% milk
¼ cup	freshly squeezed lemon juice
2	eggs
2 tbsp	butter, melted
2 tsp	grated lemon zest
1 tsp	vanilla

MAKES 8 LARGE PANCAKES

PER PANCAKE
197 calories,
6.7 g total fat
(4 g saturated fat),
8 g protein,
27 g carbohydrate,
2 g fiber,
74 mg cholesterol,
255 mg sodium

SAUCE (PER ¼ CUP)
76 calories,
0 g total fat
(0 g saturated fat),
0 g protein,
20 g carbohydrate,
1.5 g fiber,
0 mg cholesterol,
3 mg sodium

- To make sauce, combine blueberries, water and sugar in a small pot. Heat over medium-high heat until mixture comes to a boil. Reduce heat to medium-low and simmer, uncovered, for about 2 minutes, until some of the blueberries begin to burst.

- Combine lemon juice and cornstarch in a small bowl and mix well. Add to blueberry mixture. Cook and stir until sauce thickens, about 1 more minute. Remove from heat, cover and keep warm.

- Preheat griddle to medium-high heat. To make pancakes, combine flour, oat bran, sugar, baking powder, baking soda and salt in a large bowl. Mix well. In a medium bowl, whisk together ricotta, milk, lemon juice, eggs, butter, lemon zest and vanilla.

- Add wet ingredients to dry ingredients and stir just until dry ingredients are moistened. Batter will be thick. (You'll notice an almost instant chemical reaction and the batter will begin to fluff up…that's the baking powder and baking soda in action! Don't dillydally, get these babies on the griddle!)

- Spoon batter by ½-cupfuls onto preheated griddle that has been lightly coated with cooking spray. Gently spread batter to about a 5-inch diameter. Cook for about 1½ minutes per side, until pancakes are light golden brown and cooked through. Be careful not to burn them. Serve hot, topped with blueberry sauce.

If Aunt Jemima wrote a cookbook, would it sell like hotcakes? :)

332

Bohemian Wrapsody

Stir-fried chicken and vegetables with brown rice, wrapped in warm flour tortillas

I see a little silhouette-o of a wrap. Add the rice!
Add the sauce! Can you fill the tortilla?

MAKES 4 WRAPS

PER WRAP
273 calories,
6.5 g total fat
(0.7 g saturated fat),
21 g protein,
37 g carbohydrate,
5.2 g fiber,
37 mg cholesterol,
365 mg sodium

1 tbsp	each reduced-sodium soy sauce and ketchup
2 tsp	each liquid honey and freshly squeezed lime juice
1½ tsp	grated gingerroot
1 tsp	each sesame oil and cornstarch
¼ tsp	ground coriander
4	7-inch whole-grain flour tortillas
1 tsp	olive oil
2	boneless skinless chicken breasts, cut into thin strips (about 12 oz/340 g)
1 cup	each bean sprouts, halved snow peas and sliced red bell pepper
1 cup	hot cooked brown rice
½ cup	grated carrots

- In a small bowl, combine soy sauce, ketchup, honey, lime juice, gingerroot, sesame oil, cornstarch and coriander. Set aside.

- Wrap tortillas in a clean, damp kitchen towel and place in 250°F oven for 10 minutes to warm.

- Meanwhile, heat olive oil in a large wok or skillet over medium-high heat. Add chicken. Cook and stir until chicken is no longer pink. Continue to cook until chicken is lightly browned. Add bean sprouts, snow peas and red pepper. Cook for 2 more minutes. Add reserved sauce. Cook until sauce is bubbly and has thickened. Remove from heat.

- To assemble wraps, place a warm tortilla on a serving plate. Spoon ¼ rice in center, followed by ¼ grated carrots. Spoon ¼ hot chicken-vegetable mixture over top. Fold bottom of tortilla up to cover part of filling, then fold in sides. Serve immediately.

Nutrition Nugget

As silly and obvious as this may sound, make sure you eat off plates or out of bowls. (What? This isn't the kind of insightful advice you expected for $35?) Nibbling from packages of crackers or bags of chips, taking forkfuls of cake from a platter or eating ice cream straight from the container can add up to plenty o' calories leading to plenty o' pounds! Put the packages, boxes and bags away. Out of sight, out of mouth!

> **I like rice. Rice is good if you're hungry and want 2,000 of something.** *Mitch Hedberg*

Boozing and Bulging

If you're wondering where those love handles came from, ever consider the possibility that more weight could be accumulating from booze than from burgers? Here's proof: Research has shown that meals consumed with alcohol often contain 350 to 500 more calories than those consumed without it. Plus, alcohol has almost twice as many calories per gram as carbohydrates and protein. In addition to the calorie wallop, drinking also whittles away at your self-control. And it's been shown that diners spend nearly three times longer at the table when they're drinking. Here's the last call on alcohol: Two or more drinks at one sitting can dramatically increase insulin levels, shifting your body's fat-forming processes into overdrive and reducing its ability to burn fat by about one-third. One-third! You booze, you *don't* lose!

Spring Chickens

Warm chicken tortilla spring rolls with peanut sauce

Bounce for bounce, our nutritious, oven-baked chicken spring rolls with whole-grain tortillas are lower in fat and calories than traditional fried spring rolls. Your taste buds will flip when spring has sprung from the oven!

6	7-inch whole-grain flour tortillas (see tip)
1 tbsp	sesame oil
¾ cup	packed shredded light Monterey Jack cheese (3 oz/85 g)
1	large chicken breast, cooked and thinly sliced (see tip)
2 tbsp	minced fresh cilantro
¼ cup	chopped green onions
6	thin strips red bell pepper
⅓ cup	grated carrots
½ cup	bean sprouts
¾ cup	bottled light peanut sauce for dunking (see tip)

MAKES 6 SERVINGS

PER SERVING
244 calories, 9.6 g total fat
(3.2 g saturated fat),
13 g protein,
24 g carbohydrate,
3 g fiber,
24 mg cholesterol,
503 mg sodium

- Preheat oven to 450°F. Working one tortilla at a time, coat one side of tortilla with sesame oil using a pastry brush. Lay coated side down on your work surface. Evenly distribute about ⅙ of each ingredient (except peanut sauce) on lower half of uncoated side. Starting at edge closest to you, roll up tortilla into a tight cigar shape, tucking in sides as you roll, so filling is completely enclosed. Place tortilla seam-side down on a baking sheet. Repeat with remaining tortillas and filling. Make sure you space tortillas at least 1 inch apart on baking sheet.

- Bake tortillas on middle oven rack for about 8 minutes, until lightly browned and heated through. Slice warm tortillas in half diagonally (on an angle) and arrange them on a platter with a bowl of warmed peanut dipping sauce in the center.

Recipe Tips When buying tortillas, make sure they're very soft and fresh. If they're a little old, they'll crack when you roll them (frustrating!). To revive slightly stale tortillas, just wrap them in a lightly dampened, clean kitchen towel and microwave them for 15 to 20 seconds (adjust time according to the strength of your microwave and the number of tortillas you're heating). Roasted chicken breast tastes great in this recipe, as does grilled teriyaki chicken (see recipe, p. 159). Look for bottled peanut sauce in the Asian food aisle of your grocery store or in the section where stir-fry sauces are sold.

Nutrition Nugget

Edible sunblock? If you're heading south for a winter getaway, be sure to stash some dark chocolate, tomatoes, pomegranate or green tea in your suitcase (or, better yet, score some from your resort's buffet table so the friendly folks at Customs and Immigration don't confiscate your suitcase!). These superfoods contain a type of antioxidant that can migrate to the upper layers of your skin and boost your resistance to damaging ultraviolet rays. And they sure taste a lot better than sunscreen!

Trivial Tidbit

Which of the following kitchen helpers is considered to be the worst food contaminant?
(a) blender;
(b) can opener;
(c) cutting board; or
(d) husbands who drink straight from the milk carton.
The answer?
(b) can opener!
(Though four out of five wives would argue otherwise!)

Phony Pepperoni Pizzas

Turkey pepperoni, mushrooms and green peppers on whole-grain pita crusts

We know what you're thinking: "Turkey on pizza? What a bunch of phony baloney!" But here's the truth: Turkey pepperoni is an ideal kitchen counterfeit. After one slice you'll shout, "Impostorble taste!"

I've got 'em all fooled!

1½ cups	thinly sliced mushrooms
½ cup	thinly sliced turkey pepperoni or turkey pepperettes (see tip)
½ cup	diced green bell pepper
½ tsp	dried oregano
1 cup	pizza sauce (see recipe, p. 330)
4	7-inch whole-grain pitas
¼ cup	freshly grated Parmesan, Romano or Asiago cheese
1 cup	packed shredded light Monterey Jack or mozzarella cheese (4 oz/113 g)

Recipe Tip: Look for turkey pepperoni or turkey pepperettes where packaged cold cuts are sold at your grocery store.

MAKES 4 SERVINGS

PER SERVING
309 calories, 9 g total fat (5.3 g saturated fat), 20 g protein, 35 g carbohydrate, 5.2 g fiber, 27 mg cholesterol, 638 mg sodium

- Preheat oven to 425°F.

- Spray a medium, non-stick skillet with cooking spray or add a bit of olive oil. Add mushrooms, pepperoni and green pepper. Cook and stir over medium heat until mushrooms are tender, about 5 to 6 minutes. Stir in oregano and cook 30 more seconds. Remove from heat.

- For each pizza, spread about ¼ cup sauce over pita, leaving a ½-inch border. Sprinkle 1 tbsp Parmesan cheese over sauce. Top with ¼ pepperoni mixture, followed by ¼ shredded cheese.

- Place pizzas directly on middle oven rack and bake for about 10 minutes, until cheese is completely melted and edges are beginning to brown. Transfer from oven to cutting board and let stand 1 minute before slicing.

FOOD BITE

Although we consider the beloved pizza to be Italian, it actually originated in Greece. The Greeks came up with the concept of the edible plate, which is really what a pizza is—a big, delicious plate with many types of food served on it.

Gaining weight is something that just kinda snacks up on you :)

A Lotta Enchilada

Flavor-packed chicken, black bean and corn enchiladas

These authentic-tasting chicken enchiladas have a lotta flavor and, yes, a lotta ingredients. But they're pretty simple to make, so you just gotta try them!

Sauce

2 tsp	olive oil
1½ cups	diced onions
2 tsp	minced garlic
1 tbsp	chili powder
2 tsp	ground cumin
1 tsp	dried oregano
1 can	(28 oz/796 mL) no-salt-added crushed tomatoes
1 cup	reduced-sodium chicken broth
1 tbsp	brown sugar
½ tsp	each salt and freshly ground black pepper
3 tbsp	minced fresh cilantro

Filling

2 cups	chopped cooked chicken breast
1 cup	canned no-salt-added black beans, drained and rinsed
½ cup	each grated carrots, minced red bell pepper, chopped green onions and whole-kernel corn
1 tbsp	freshly squeezed lime juice
½ tsp	each ground cumin and chili powder
2 tbsp	minced fresh cilantro
10	7-inch whole-grain flour tortillas
2 cups	packed shredded light old (sharp) cheddar cheese, divided (8 oz/227 g)

Light (5%) sour cream and chopped green onions for garnish (optional)

MAKES 10 ENCHILADAS

PER ENCHILADA
332 calories, 9.5 g total fat (3.7 g saturated fat), 22 g protein, 42 g carbohydrate, 6.4 g fiber, 40 mg cholesterol, 532 mg sodium

- You will need two 9 x 13-inch baking dishes or one very large baking pan for this recipe.

- To make sauce, heat olive oil over medium heat in a large pot. Add onions and garlic. Cook slowly and stir until onions begin to soften, about 3 minutes. Stir in chili powder, cumin and oregano. Mix well. Add all remaining sauce ingredients, except cilantro. Bring sauce to a boil. Reduce heat to low. Cover and simmer for 15 minutes. Remove from heat and stir in cilantro.

- While sauce is simmering, prepare filling. Combine all filling ingredients in a large bowl and mix well. Set aside.

- Preheat oven to 375°F. Spray two 9 x 13-inch baking dishes with cooking spray. Add ½ cup sauce to filling and mix well. Set aside 1 cup cheese for sprinkling over rolled enchiladas.

- Working one at a time, spread a heaping ⅓ cup filling in center of tortilla. Top with 1 heaping tbsp cheese. Roll up tightly and place seam-side down in baking dish. Each dish will hold 5 enchiladas. Repeat with remaining tortillas, filling and cheese. Spoon sauce evenly over enchiladas, making sure each enchilada is covered with sauce. Top with reserved cheese. Cover loosely with foil and bake for 30 minutes. Uncover and bake an additional 5 to 10 minutes, until cheese is bubbly. Serve enchiladas hot with a dollop of sour cream and a sprinkle of green onions on top, if desired.

Fitness Protection Program

Did you know your body comes with a lifetime warranty? Keep your muscles—your body's fat-burning engine—tuned and toned, and they'll remain strong, flexible and well-balanced throughout your life. By creating a bigger, stronger engine through strength-training, you can postpone age-related weakness by a decade or longer. Both men and women lose about a third of a pound of muscle each year after age 40, and they gain as much fat, if not more. But it doesn't have to be that way. In a study at Tufts University, a group of out-of-shape volunteers followed a high-intensity, strength-training regimen for eight weeks, and the results were quite impressive. Some achieved three- and fourfold increases in strength. Not bad, considering they were all in their 90s! A true story!

Tongue Thai'd
Pad Thai: Stir-fried rice noodles with shrimp and tofu

Cat got your tongue? Too bad. You won't be able to savor the flavor of this zesty, zingy Pad Thai recipe with shrimp and tofu. Never tried Thailand's most famous noodle dish? It's about Thai!

I'm speechless!

23rd ANNUAL Yummy AWARDS

3 tbsp	each freshly squeezed lime juice and Asian fish sauce (see tip)
2 tbsp	each ketchup and brown sugar
1 tbsp	each grated gingerroot and reduced-sodium soy sauce
1 tsp	sesame oil
¼ tsp	crushed red pepper flakes or hot pepper sauce
8 oz	(227 g) rice stick noodles, about ⅛ inch wide
2 tsp	peanut oil
½ cup	very thinly sliced red onions or shallots
2 tsp	minced garlic
1	medium red bell pepper, diced or thinly sliced
8 oz	(227 g) uncooked medium shrimp, peeled and deveined
1 cup	diced extra-firm tofu (see tip)
2 cups	bean sprouts
½ cup	chopped green onions
¼ cup	chopped fresh cilantro
¼ cup	chopped dry-roasted peanuts

- First, gather all the ingredients you'll need for this recipe and get them ready (chop the red pepper, peel the shrimp, etc.). Once you're ready to go, the meal comes together very quickly. You don't want to be hunting for the bean sprouts while the shrimp burns!

- To prepare sauce, whisk together lime juice, fish sauce, ketchup, brown sugar, gingerroot, soy sauce, sesame oil and crushed red pepper flakes in a medium bowl. Set aside.

- Place rice noodles in a large bowl and pour boiling water over top. Let soak 7 minutes. Drain.

- While noodles are soaking, heat peanut oil in a large, non-stick wok. Add onions and garlic. Cook and stir over medium-high heat until onions are tender, about 2 minutes. Add red pepper and cook for 2 more minutes, stirring often. Add shrimp and tofu. Cook and stir until shrimp turn pink, about 3 minutes. Add reserved sauce, noodles, bean sprouts, green onions and cilantro. Toss and cook until mixture is hot, about 1 minute. Serve immediately, topped with chopped peanuts.

MAKES 6 SERVINGS

PER SERVING
306 calories, 7.1 g total fat
(0.9 g saturated fat),
16 g protein,
46 g carbohydrate,
3.6 g fiber,
57 mg cholesterol,
766 mg sodium

Recipe Tips Fish sauce makes Pad Thai taste authentic—please don't leave it out! Once you buy it, you can keep it for months. Look for it in the Asian food aisle of your grocery store. Fish sauce smells awful, but tastes very good when mixed with other ingredients. Just hold your breath when adding it to the sauce (we're not joking!). Oh, and don't taste the raw sauce…you'll think we've "lost it" completely! Trust us, the finished product will be wonderful. Buy extra-firm tofu for this recipe or any stir-fry recipe that includes tofu. Soft or silken tofu will turn to mush when you try to stir-fry it.

Yumola Granola

Scrumptious homemade granola with oats, nuts, seeds, dried cranberries, peanut butter and honey

When heart-healthy oats are blended with almonds, coconut, pumpkin seeds, cinnamon, peanut butter and a touch of honey, then baked to perfection and tossed with dried cranberries, there's only one word to describe the result: YUMOLA!

3 cups	old-fashioned oats (see tip)
½ cup	unsweetened shredded coconut
½ cup	sliced or chopped raw almonds
½ cup	raw pumpkin seeds
⅓ cup	raw sunflower seeds
2 tbsp	whole flaxseed
½ cup	liquid honey
⅓ cup	natural peanut butter
2 tsp	ground cinnamon
½ cup	chopped dried cranberries or other dried fruit

MAKES ABOUT 6 CUPS

PER SERVING (½ CUP)
311 calories, 14 g total fat (3.9 g saturated fat), 10 g protein, 40 g carbohydrate, 5.4 g fiber, 0 mg cholesterol, 8 mg sodium

Recipe Tip: Old-fashioned oats are sometimes called large flake oats. They're bigger and thicker than quick-cooking oats and are better suited to making granola.

- Preheat oven to 350°F. Line a large, shallow baking pan with parchment paper and set aside.

- In a large bowl, combine oats, coconut, almonds, pumpkin seeds, sunflower seeds and flaxseed. Mix well. In a medium bowl, whisk together honey, peanut butter and cinnamon until well blended.

- Add peanut-butter mixture to oat mixture and stir using a wooden spoon until oat mixture is completely coated. Spread oat mixture evenly in prepared pan. Bake for 10 minutes. Remove pan from oven, give granola a stir, then bake another 10 to 12 minutes, until granola is golden brown and feels dry to touch. Be careful not to burn it. Let cool. Stir in dried cranberries. Store in an airtight container for up to 5 days.

Nutrition Nugget

With so many tasty, packaged granolas out there, why bother making it from scratch? Well, in theory, granola's a healthy choice since it's loaded with good-for-you nuts and oats. Unfortunately, the store-bought varieties contain oil to make them crisp and they also cram in tons of sugar for more yum factor. The result: One serving can pack around 500 calories. *Groanola!*

We have just received news that Betty Crocker has passed away. Funeral services are being held tomorrow at 3:50 for 25 to 30 minutes :)

Pimped-Out Pumpkin Pie Pancakes

Fluffy and flavorful pancakes made with classic pumpkin pie ingredients

Bling it on! Topped with creamy vanilla yogurt and a drizzle of pure maple syrup, these warmly spiced pumpkin pie pancakes will get your taste buds hip-hoppin'.

THESE CAKES ARE KICKIN'!

1 cup	whole wheat flour
1 cup	all-purpose flour
1½ tsp	baking powder
1½ tsp	pumpkin pie spice (see tip)
½ tsp	each baking soda and salt
1 can	(14 oz/370 mL) 2% evaporated milk
1 cup	canned pure pumpkin
¼ cup	brown sugar (not packed)
2	eggs
2 tbsp	butter, melted
1 tsp	vanilla
¾ cup	each vanilla-flavored yogurt and pure maple syrup

- Preheat griddle to medium-high heat. Combine both flours, baking powder, pumpkin pie spice, baking soda and salt in a large bowl. Mix well. In a medium bowl, whisk together milk, pumpkin, sugar, eggs, butter and vanilla.

- Add wet ingredients to dry ingredients and stir just until dry ingredients are moistened.

- Spoon batter by ⅓-cupfuls onto preheated griddle that has been lightly coated with cooking spray. Gently spread batter to about a 4-inch diameter. Cook for about 1½ minutes per side, or until pancakes are golden brown and cooked through. Be careful not to burn them. Serve immediately topped with vanilla yogurt and maple syrup.

MAKES 12 MEDIUM PANCAKES

PER PANCAKE (WITH YOGURT AND SYRUP)
217 calories, 3.9 g total fat (1.7 g saturated fat),
6 g protein, 40 g carbohydrate, 2.1 g fiber,
47 mg cholesterol, 270 mg sodium

Recipe Tip: Look for Club House brand pumpkin pie spice in a small tin beside the regular spices at your grocery store. If you can't find it, use 1 tsp ground cinnamon + ¼ tsp ground ginger + ¼ tsp allspice in this recipe.

FOOD BITE

In the early 1800s, hotcakes cooked in bear grease or pork lard were the most popular fast-food item at carnivals and country fairs. Anyone who kept a hotcake stand was sure to make a killing. In fact, they were so popular that by the beginning of the 19th century, the expression "sell like hotcakes" came to mean anything that sold quickly and effortlessly in huge quantities. But bear grease and pork lard? A more accurate expression would be "selling like fatcakes!"

Nutrition Nugget

You know those jack-o'-lantern innards you mindlessly toss into the trash each Halloween? You're throwing out the baby with the bathwater! Pumpkin seeds, also called pepitas, are a nutrient-charged super-snack. For men, they help support prostate health due to their high magnesium and zinc content. Magnificent magnesium plays a role in more than 300 bodily processes and, according to French researchers, men with the highest levels have a 40 percent lower risk of early death than those with the lowest levels. And gals, you oughtta know that magnesium can curb cravings for sweets, protect your heart, calm you down, help you sleep deeply and even lessen PMS symptoms. Add raw (not roasted) seeds to a salad, oatmeal, cereal or even to soup for added texture and crunch.

Wise Guy Pizza Pie

Italian sausage pizza with mushrooms and red onions

You wanna pizza me? Who can blame you! All da boys will wanna pizza the action, too. You'd be wise to double this recipe so you don't get mobbed when everyone wants more.

It's really good, fellas.

8 oz	(227 g) light mild Italian sausage
¾ cup	thinly sliced red onions
2 cups	thinly sliced mushrooms
1 tbsp	minced fresh oregano or basil leaves, or 1 tsp dried
½ cup	pizza sauce (see recipe, p. 330)
1	12-inch prebaked whole-grain thin-crust pizza shell
¼ cup	freshly grated Parmesan cheese
1 cup	packed shredded light provolone cheese (4 oz/113 g—see tip)

MAKES 1 PIZZA, 8 SLICES

PER SLICE
182 calories, 7.5 g total fat (3.3 g saturated fat), 13 g protein, 16 g carbohydrate, 1.8 g fiber, 24 mg cholesterol, 487 mg sodium

Recipe Tip: If you can't find light provolone cheese, use light Monterey Jack instead.

- Preheat oven to 425°F.
- Spray a 10-inch, non-stick skillet with cooking spray or add a bit of olive oil. Remove and discard casing from sausage. Break or cut sausage into small pieces and add to skillet along with onions. Cook and stir over medium-high heat until sausage is cooked through and onions begin to soften, about 3 minutes. Break up any large pieces of sausage as it's cooking.
- Stir in mushrooms and cook until mushrooms are tender, about 5 more minutes. Add oregano, mix well and remove from heat.
- Spread pizza sauce evenly over crust. Top with Parmesan cheese. Spoon sausage mixture evenly over cheese. Sprinkle shredded cheese evenly over sausage mixture.
- Place pizza directly on middle oven rack and bake for about 10 minutes, until cheese is completely melted and edges are lightly browned.

Nutrition Nugget

Another reason to lick your salt habit: Salt is a bone robber! Sodium decreases the amount of calcium your body's able to absorb, and it also increases the amount of calcium that it excretes. So the more salt in your diet, the more calcium ends up flushed down the toilet!

Steeping Beauty

Looking for a way to burn fat, protect against cancer and delay the aging process? Well, the answer may lie in the tea leaves. No need to visit your local clairvoyant, though. We're talking white tea here! White tea comes from the young leaves of the tea plant, before the buds have fully opened. The young leaves are covered in fine, silvery hair, which gives the slightly sweet-tasting tea its name. White tea's created a big brew-ha-ha because it's thermogenic. That's a fancy-schmancy way of saying that it boosts your metabolism, helping you to burn more calories. (And you thought "thermogenic" meant "looks good in a thermos." Ha!) Plus, white tea has more disease-preventing antioxidants than any other type of tea, including green. That's because it's minimally processed, so it retains the highest level of powerful polyphenols, natural compounds also found in grapes, kidney beans, prunes, raisins and red wine. White tea is also lower in caffeine than both black and green teas, so if you like to savor a nice, hot cup of tea in the evening, no worries about white keeping you awake. And, tooth be told, white tea is far less likely to stain your teeth than drinking coffee or other tea varieties. With white tea, good health is in the bag!

The Sound of Muesli

A high-fiber breakfast blend of oats, yogurt and fresh fruit

The thrills are alive with the sound of muesli! And our healthy, satisfying breakfast just might Alp you lose weight, too!

We can make beautiful muesli together!

3 cups	quick-cooking rolled oats (not instant)
1½ cups	strawberry-flavored yogurt
1 cup	orange juice
⅓ cup	light (5%) cream
2 tbsp	liquid honey
1½ cups	each fresh raspberries and diced strawberries
1 cup	fresh blueberries
1	medium apple, peeled, cored and coarsely grated

- In a large bowl, combine oats, yogurt, orange juice, cream and honey. Let stand 5 minutes.

- Gently fold in fresh fruit. Cover and refrigerate overnight. Serve cold.

Recipe Tip:
Refrigerating the muesli overnight makes it thicker and creamier. Sprinkle individual servings with a tablespoon of granola if you want to add some crunch. Keeps for 3 days in the fridge.

MAKES 6 SERVINGS

PER SERVING
270 calories, 4.6 g total fat
(1.1 g saturated fat), 10 g protein,
8.2 g fiber, 53 g carbohydrate,
5 g cholesterol, 33 mg sodium

> He that eats till he is sick must fast till he is well.
>
> *English proverb*

An OATstanding Way to Start Your Day

There's nothing like a hearty bowl of oatmeal to warm you up on a chilly morning. Famous as a comfort food, its main claim to fame is its soluble fiber that helps keep cholesterol in check. But oats are not a one-trick pony. They also contain a generous helping of protein—more than most other cereal grains. And the slower your oatmeal cooks, the better it is for you. Instant, flavored oatmeal might be quick and easy, but you pay a price for that convenience. In order for your oats to be ready in a flash, they're cut thinly and some of the good stuff (fiber and nutrients) are stripped out. Plus, those instant varieties contain tons of sugar. Fortunately, you can beef up instant oatmeal's nutritional resumé by adding your own sources of fiber, which act like a "sugar stopper." Some good stir-ins include berries, raisins or chopped apples. Ground flaxseed or chia seeds and slivered nuts will add fiber and healthy fats. If you have time, choose slow-cooking oats (ready in 15 minutes)—they haven't been processed to death. Even better is old-fashioned, steel-cut oatmeal (sometimes called Irish oatmeal). Nothing's been stripped from it—the nutrients and fiber are still intact. Stir in some Greek yogurt for a hit of calcium and protein. Now your oats are oatta this world!

Batter-Be-Good-To-Me Pancakes

Scrumptious blueberry and banana pancakes with strawberry sauce

Grab your pancake Turner, Tina! These flapjacks are flippin' fabulous, so come and get 'em while they're hotcakes!

Strawberry Sauce

2 cups	diced fresh strawberries
3 tbsp	pure maple syrup
¼ cup	orange juice
1 tbsp	cornstarch

Pancakes

1⅓ cups	all-purpose flour
⅔ cup	oat bran
2 tsp	baking powder
1 tsp	baking soda
1¾ cups	buttermilk
½ cup	mashed ripe bananas
2 tbsp	butter, melted
1	egg
1 tbsp	pure maple syrup
½ tsp	vanilla
1 cup	fresh blueberries
1 cup	vanilla-flavored yogurt

- To make sauce, mix together strawberries and maple syrup in a medium pot. Whisk together orange juice and cornstarch in a small bowl. Add to strawberries. Cook over medium-high heat, stirring constantly, until mixture is bubbly and has thickened, about 2 minutes. Remove from heat.

- Preheat electric griddle to medium-high heat. Combine flour, oat bran, baking powder and baking soda in a large bowl. Set aside.

- Whisk together buttermilk, bananas, butter, egg, maple syrup and vanilla in a medium bowl. Add wet ingredients to dry ingredients and mix just until dry ingredients are moistened. Do not overmix! Fold in blueberries.

- Spray griddle lightly with cooking spray. For each pancake, spoon about ½ cup batter onto hot griddle and spread to make 5-inch circles. Cook until undersides are lightly browned. Flip pancakes and cook until other sides are lightly browned, 2 to 3 more minutes. Top pancakes with generous dollops of vanilla yogurt and strawberry sauce.

MAKES 10 PANCAKES

PER PANCAKE (WITH SAUCE AND YOGURT)
181 calories, 4 g total fat (2 g saturated fat),
6 g protein, 33 g carbohydrate, 2.8 g fiber,
29 mg cholesterol, 292 mg sodium

I don't like hanging out at the pancake house. That place gives me the crepes :)

The Benefit of the Dough

Quick-rising, whole wheat and ground flax pizza dough

No doubt about this dough! It's the best-tasting healthy pizza crust you've ever tried. And it's a pizza cake to make—simple and quick enough for a weeknight supper.

1 cup	all-purpose flour
½ cup	whole wheat flour
2 tbsp	flax meal or ground flaxseed
1 pkg	(8 g) or 2¼ tsp quick-rising yeast
½ tsp	salt
⅔ cup	very warm water
2 tsp	olive oil
2 tsp	liquid honey
1 tbsp	cornmeal
Olive oil cooking spray	

MAKES 1 12-INCH PIZZA CRUST

PER SERVING (⅛ CRUST)
122 calories, 2.8 g total fat
(0.3 g saturated fat), 4 g protein,
21 g carbohydrate, 2.6 g fiber,
0 mg cholesterol, 148 mg sodium

- In a medium bowl, combine both flours, flax meal, yeast and salt. Mix well.

- Measure warm water in measuring cup, then stir in olive oil and honey. Pour this mixture over dry ingredients and mix using a wooden spoon to form a ball. Turn dough out onto a lightly floured surface. Knead for 2 minutes. Spray another medium bowl with olive oil spray (or coat lightly with olive oil) and place dough inside. Cover with plastic wrap. Let rise in a warm place until double in size, about 20 minutes. Meanwhile, spray a 12-inch pizza pan with olive oil spray and dust with cornmeal.

- When dough has risen, turn out onto a lightly floured surface and, using a rolling pin, roll dough into a 12-inch circle. Transfer dough to prepared pizza pan. You can top it with your favorite toppings at this point and bake in a 425°F oven for about 15 minutes. Or, prick crust in several places with a fork and bake untopped for 6 minutes. Remove crust from oven, add your favorite sauce and toppings, then slide pizza directly onto middle oven rack and bake for an additional 8 to 10 minutes.

FOOD BITE

Flaxseed comes from the same blue-flowered plant, *Linum usitatissimum* (wouldn't want to tackle that word in a spelling bee!), that brings us linen fabric and the linseed oil used in woodworking.

Healthy Eating is a Pizza Cake

We must! We must! We must decrease our crust! Just because you're watching your weight doesn't mean you can't have a pizza the action. To lessen the blow from the dough, ask for whole wheat, thin-crust pizza instead of the regular kind that's fluffed up with refined, white flour. You'll add fiber and subtract calories, so your pizza slices won't multiply all over your thighs. What about deep dish? Picture deep cellulite dimples. Stuffed crust? Only if you want stuffed fat cells. Choose thin to stay thin. Then pile your pizza with veggies, top it with lean protein, such as chicken or Canadian bacon, and ask for reduced-fat cheeses. And here's a simple trick to cut more grease: When your pizza arrives, blot it lightly with a paper towel (half a Bounty will do!) to soak up about a tablespoon (120 calories worth) of saturated fat.

Pump Up the Jambalaya
Spicy jambalaya with turkey sausage and scallops

With traditional jambalaya, you'd be hammin', but with our healthier version, you'll be jammin'—all kinds of tasty ingredients into one big pot. Get ready for ragin' Cajun flavor!

1 tbsp	olive oil
1 cup	each chopped onions, chopped green bell pepper and chopped celery
1 tsp	minced garlic
8 oz	(227 g) turkey kielbasa, casing removed, cut into bite-sized pieces
2½ cups	reduced-sodium chicken broth
1⅓ cups	salsa (see tip)
1¼ cups	uncooked brown rice (see tip)
1	bay leaf
1 tsp	Cajun seasoning
½ tsp	each dried thyme and dried oregano
12 oz	(340 g) uncooked bay scallops
¼ cup	minced fresh parsley

- Heat oil in a large pot over medium-high heat. Add onions, green pepper, celery and garlic. Cook and stir until vegetables begin to soften, about 4 minutes.

- Add kielbasa and cook for 2 more minutes. Add all remaining ingredients, except scallops and parsley. Bring to a boil. Reduce heat and simmer, covered, for 15 minutes, or until rice is tender. Exact cooking time will depend on brand of rice. Stir occasionally to prevent rice from sticking to bottom of pot.

- Stir in scallops and parsley. Cook for 5 more minutes, until scallops are cooked through. Let stand, covered, for 5 minutes before serving.

MAKES 6 SERVINGS

PER SERVING
292 calories, 6.4 g total fat (1.2 g saturated fat), 23 g protein, 41 g carbohydrate, 2 g fiber, 45 mg cholesterol, 691 mg sodium

Recipe Tip Jambalaya (pronounced juhm-buh-LI-yah) is a hallmark of Creole cooking. The name comes from the French word jambon, meaning "ham," the star ingredient in many of the first jambalayas. This spicy dish is typically a concoction of rice, tomatoes, onions, green peppers and just about any kind of shellfish, poultry or meat. You can substitute shrimp for the scallops in this recipe, and use cubed chicken breasts instead of the kielbasa. If you like your food spicy, use hot salsa. Make sure your brown rice is the quicker-cooking variety (cooks in 15 to 20 minutes), but not instant rice.

Time for the Bar Exam

Though energy bars might give off an aura of health, don't go nuts eating them. Once in a while, they're just fine. But remember, in scientific terms, "energy" means calories. And that's exactly what you're getting—up to 350 calories, in some cases. Many energy bars are really just glorified chocolate bars. Scour the fine print on the label and you'll likely uncover some not-so-great ingredients right near the top of the list. The usual suspects? High-fructose corn syrup and hydrogenated vegetable oil! Plus, the cheap, synthetic vitamins and soy protein isolate (a junky by-product of the soybean industry) might be more of a burden than a blessing to your body's cells if you eat them every day. When you need a snack and you're called to the bar, choose those with natural (preferably organic!) high-fiber main ingredients, such as oats, seeds, nuts and dried fruit. The final verdict: Eating an energy bar is healthier than eating a bag of potato chips, but there's a lot more nutrition packed into a handful of almonds and an apple—bar none!

Acropolis Sandwich

Lemon-oregano chicken in a whole-grain pita with veggies and tzatziki sauce

Finding a better-tasting Greek-style sandwich would be a Herculean task, for sure.

1½ tbsp	freshly squeezed lemon juice
1 tsp	dried oregano
1 tsp	minced garlic
4	boneless skinless chicken breasts, cut into strips (about 1½ lbs/680 g)
2 tsp	olive oil
4	7-inch Greek-style pitas (see tip)
4	lettuce leaves
1 cup	chopped tomatoes
1	small red onion, thinly sliced
¾ cup	tzatziki sauce (see recipe, p. 16)

MAKES 4 SERVINGS

PER SERVING

433 calories, 8.6 g total fat (2.7 g saturated fat), 48 g protein, 38 g carbohydrate, 5.1 g fiber, 106 mg cholesterol, 444 mg sodium

- Combine lemon juice, oregano and garlic in a medium bowl. Add chicken strips and toss until well coated. Let stand 10 minutes.

- Heat olive oil in a large wok or skillet over medium-high heat. Add chicken and cook, stirring often, until no longer pink. Continue to cook until chicken is lightly browned.

- Meanwhile, wrap pitas in foil and warm in a 350°F oven for 8 minutes.

- To assemble, place lettuce leaf and ¼ chicken on one pita bread. Top with chopped tomatoes, onions and 3 tbsp tzatziki. Fold pita over filling and serve immediately. (Wrap bottom half of sandwich in aluminum foil to secure).

Recipe Tip: Greek-style pitas are similar to Italian flatbread, only they're slightly thinner and a bit softer. When warmed, you can easily fold them over without breaking them in half (ideal for sandwiches). A distinguishing feature of Greek-style pitas is the absence of a hollow "pocket" inside. Also called "East Indian-style pitas," they're sold in most well-stocked supermarkets. These pocketless pitas make fantastic pizza crusts!

Nutrition Nugget

Mood ring turning black? Gotta get some green! Green leafy vegetables like romaine lettuce, kale, Swiss chard and spinach are chock-full of important B vitamins, which are part of the assembly line that manufactures feel-good hormones like serotonin, dopamine and norepinephrine. They're good mood food!

I'm Dreaming of a White Chili

Creamy and delicious tomato-less chicken chili

Unlike the ones you used to know, this dramatically different chili is an enticing blend of mostly white ingredients. Bing would sing of its zest and zing!

2 tsp	olive oil
4	boneless skinless chicken breasts, cut into 1-inch cubes (about 1½ lbs/680 g)
1½ cups	chopped onions
1 cup	diced celery
2 tsp	minced garlic
1 tbsp	chili powder
2 tsp	each ground cumin and dried oregano
½ tsp	ground coriander
¼ cup	all-purpose flour
3 cups	reduced-sodium chicken broth
1 can	(14 oz/370 mL) 2% evaporated milk
2 cans	(19 oz/540 mL each) no-salt-added navy beans, drained and rinsed
1 can	(4.5 oz/128 mL) diced green chilies (look near taco kits)
½ tsp	each salt and freshly ground black pepper
¼ tsp	cayenne pepper
1 cup	light (5%) sour cream
2 tbsp	minced fresh cilantro

Shredded light Monterey Jack cheese and chopped green onions for garnish (optional)

MAKES 8 SERVINGS

PER SERVING
329 calories, 4.4 g total fat
(2.2 g saturated fat),
34 g protein, 38 g carbohydrate,
9.5 g fiber, 63 mg cholesterol, 353 mg sodium

- Heat oil in a large pot over medium-high heat. Add chicken and cook for 3 to 4 minutes, stirring constantly, until no longer pink. Add onions, celery and garlic. Cook and stir for 4 to 5 more minutes, until vegetables begin to soften.

- Add chili powder, cumin, oregano and coriander to chicken. Mix well and cook for 1 more minute. Add flour and stir until chicken is well coated. Stir in broth and evaporated milk. Bring mixture to a boil. Reduce heat to medium and simmer, uncovered, for 5 minutes.

- Add navy beans, green chilies, salt, pepper and cayenne pepper to chicken mixture. Reduce heat to medium-low. Cover and simmer for 15 minutes, stirring occasionally.

- Remove chili from heat. Stir in sour cream and cilantro. Ladle chili into serving bowls and top with shredded cheese and a few chopped green onions, if desired.

When Bad is Good

If you remember only one thing from this book, let it be this: Food that goes bad is good for you. Food that doesn't go bad is bad for you! Say what? The more processed a food, the longer its shelf life and the less nutritious it typically is. Real food, on the other hand, is alive, so it will eventually rot and die. That's a good thing! So get real and choose whole, natural, fresh foods more often and limit foods that are concocted in factories. There are now more than 3,000 ingredients on the government's list of "safe" food additives—and any of these preservatives, artificial sweeteners, colorings and flavor enhancers could end up on your plate. Do we really know what these chemicals do to our waistlines and, more importantly, our health? It's anyone's guess. Food immortality is not a virtue! When buying processed, packaged foods, always choose products with the fewest ingredients on the label. (Incidentally, an exception to the "bad is good" rule is honey, a healthy, natural food that never spoils!)

Trivial Tidbit

Did you know that Americans eat more on Super Bowl Sunday than on any other day of the year except Thanksgiving? After 3,000 calories, your tight end might look more like a fullback!

Funny Bones Dog Treats

Homemade peanut butter and banana dog cookies with spelt flour and ground flax

Why bake for your barking companions? 'Cause dogs are people, too! Our canine children love these healthy, wholesome dog treats with peanut butter and banana flavor.

2 cups	spelt flour (see tip)
3 tbsp	ground flaxseed
1 tsp	ground cinnamon
½ cup	natural peanut butter
⅓ cup	mashed ripe banana
2	eggs
¼ cup	pure maple syrup

Recipe Tip: Look for bags of spelt flour in the health food aisle of your grocery store. We buy Bob's Red Mill brand.

MAKES ABOUT 24 DOG COOKIES

PER COOKIE
94 calories, 3.7 g total fat (0.6 g saturated fat), 3.5 g protein, 12 g carbohydrate, 1.4 g fiber, 18 mg cholesterol, 7 mg sodium

- Preheat oven to 300°F. Combine flour, flaxseed and cinnamon in a medium bowl. Set aside.

- In a large bowl, whisk together peanut butter, banana, eggs and maple syrup until smooth. Add dry ingredients to wet ingredients and mix well. Roll out dough on a lightly floured surface to about ¼-inch thickness. Add a bit more flour if dough is too sticky. Cut cookies with a 3-inch, bone-shaped cookie cutter and place on large cookie sheet. Bake for 30 minutes. Cool completely on a wire rack. Store cookies in the fridge in an airtight container or large, resealable plastic bag. May be frozen.

When baking dog biscuits, be sure to use Collie flour :)

Trivial Tidbit

Please don't overfeed the animals! A recent survey found that as people get fatter, so do their pets. In fact, a full 25 percent of dogs and cats in North America and Europe are now overweight. Only you can stop the bingeing and purring!

In this chapter...

Italian cream cake with coconut, pecans and a rich cream-cheese frosting

Slow-cooked pork back ribs with a smoky rub and gooey barbecue sauce

Triple-decker, triple-decadent chocolate layer cake

WARNING

Highly addictive. Do not exceed recommended dosage. Regular consumption may cause large deposits of fat on abdomen, back, thighs, buttocks, face and arms leading to saddle bags, love handles, spare tires, muffin tops, potbellies, cellulite dimples and double chins.

Other common side effects include increased salivation, gastrointestinal difficulties, severe blood-sugar fluctuations, rapid heartbeat, drowsiness or alertness, nausea and possibly hallucinations.

In extreme cases where excessive belching becomes unbearable or lasts for more than 4 hours, consult a physician immediately. Not recommended for those with non-existent willpower, lack of self-discipline or CPS (Couch-Potato Syndrome).

The authors and the publisher expressly disclaim any responsibility for any split seams, popped buttons or stretch marks resulting as a consequence, directly or indirectly, of the over-consumption of the food contents of this chapter.

Side effects can be minimized by following authors' orders and keeping to the lowest dosage possible.

Splurge-Worthy

Totally "worth it," over-the-top,
once-a-year indulgences

Italian Dream Cream Cake,
p. 350

Italian Dream Cream Cake

Incredibly moist and delicious Italian cream cake with coconut, pecans and a rich cream-cheese frosting

If you're looking for a special-occasion dessert with serious wow factor, "questa torta prende la torta!" (This cake takes the cake!)

Frosting & Filling

1½ pkgs	(12 oz/375 g total) cream cheese, at room temperature
½ cup	butter, at room temperature
1 tsp	vanilla
1 tsp	grated orange zest (optional)
4 cups	icing (confectioner's) sugar
¾ cup	each sweetened shredded coconut and finely chopped pecans

Cake

2 cups	all-purpose flour
1½ tsp	baking powder
½ tsp	baking soda
1 cup	butter, at room temperature
1¾ cups	granulated sugar
4	eggs, separated
1 tsp	vanilla
1 cup	buttermilk
¾ cup	sweetened shredded coconut

Toasted coconut and chopped pecans for decorating cake (optional)

Recipe Tip: To toast coconut, place coconut in a dry, non-stick skillet over medium heat. Stir continuously and heat until coconut turns golden brown. Remove from heat and let cool before using.

MAKES 12 SERVINGS

PER SERVING
We're not telling!

- To make frosting, beat together cream cheese, butter, vanilla and orange zest (if desired) in a large bowl using high speed of electric mixer. Gradually add icing sugar and beat until smooth. Divide frosting in half. Stir coconut and pecans into one half and mix well. This will be used as filling. Other half will be used to frost outside of cake. Cover and refrigerate both until ready to use.

- Preheat oven to 350°F. Lightly grease bottom and sides of three 8-inch round cake pans. Do not use 9-inch pans for this cake—they are too big. Cut circles of wax paper or parchment paper to fit bottom of pans and place in pans. Lightly grease paper. Set pans aside.

- In a medium bowl, combine flour, baking powder and baking soda. Set aside. In a large bowl, beat butter and sugar on high speed of electric mixer until fluffy, about 2 minutes. Add egg yolks and vanilla. Beat again until well blended. Gradually add flour mixture and buttermilk in batches, beginning and ending with flour mixture. Stir in coconut.

- Clean and dry beaters thoroughly. Beat egg whites in a deep stainless steel or glass mixing bowl until stiff peaks form. Fold beaten whites into batter. Divide batter evenly among prepared pans. Bake for about 25 minutes, or until a wooden pick inserted in the center of cakes comes out clean. Cool cakes in pans on wire rack for 10 minutes. Run a knife around edges of cakes to loosen from sides. Invert cakes onto cooling rack, remove paper and cool completely before frosting.

- To frost cake, place one layer on a pretty cake plate. Spoon ½ the coconut-pecan filling over top and spread to edges. Repeat with next layer. Place final layer on top. Ice top and sides of cake with reserved frosting. If desired, sprinkle toasted coconut evenly over top of cake and press chopped pecans into sides. Refrigerate for at least 2 hours before serving. Keep cake stored in the refrigerator.

Nutrition Nugget Can't curb crazy cravings for carbs? Then at the very least, follow this simple but effective rule of tongue to curtail packing on serious poundage: No sweet carbs after 7 p.m.! We repeat: NO SWEET CARBS AFTER 7 P.M.! If you just have to indulge in a sweet treat, have it earlier in the day. That way, you're at least giving yourself a fighting chance to burn off those sugar-laden calories with activity over the course of the day. Eat sweets at night and your hormones will slam the brakes on fat-burning and shift into fat-making mode. Don't let your sweet dreams turn into a nightmare!

SPLURGE-WORTHY

Ribs Van Winkle

Slow-cooked, succulent pork back ribs with a smoky rub and gooey barbecue sauce

A meat-lover's dream, these super-tender, finger-lickin' pork ribs will awaken your taste buds at the first mouthwatering bite! (Thanks to our friends at CTV's "Dan for Mayor" for this seriously punny recipe title.)

Rib Rub

2 tbsp	brown sugar
1 tbsp	chili powder
1 tbsp	ground cumin
2 tsp	ground coriander
1 tsp	each smoked paprika, dried oregano, salt and freshly ground black pepper
¼ tsp	cayenne pepper
2	large racks pork back ribs (about 5 lbs/2.3 kg total)
1 cup	smoky barbecue sauce (bottled or homemade— see tip)

MAKES ABOUT 5 SERVINGS

PER SERVING
Never mind!

- Combine all rub ingredients in a small bowl. Mix well.

- Place each slab of ribs on a large piece of aluminum foil. Remove thin membrane from back of ribs, if desired. Rub rib rub all over ribs while repeating tongue-twisting instructions. Wrap ribs tightly in foil and place side by side on a large, rimmed baking sheet or pan. Bake at 275°F for 2½ hours.

- Remove ribs from oven and let stand, covered, while you preheat grill to medium-high setting. Carefully remove ribs from foil and place on grill rack that has been lightly brushed with oil. Slather ribs with barbecue sauce on both sides and allow sauce to caramelize a bit, turning ribs a few times so both sides get lightly browned and yummy. Be careful not to burn them! Serve hot with extra warmed sauce for dipping, if desired.

> I always wanted to be somebody, but now I realize I should have been more specific.
>
> *Lily Tomlin*

Recipe Tip When buying a bottled sauce for this recipe, look for the words "smokehouse," "chipotle," or "hickory" on the label. Smoky sauces are darker in color than regular barbecue sauces and are well matched to ribs. Or, make your own sauce: Heat 2 tbsp butter in a small pot over medium heat, add ½ cup finely minced onions and 1 tsp minced garlic. Cook until onions are tender, about 5 minutes. Add 1 cup ketchup, 3 tbsp freshly squeezed lemon juice, 3 tbsp molasses, 1 tbsp Worcestershire sauce, 1 tsp grated lemon zest, 1 tsp chipotle chili powder, 1 tsp paprika, 1 tsp ground cumin and ¼ tsp freshly ground black pepper. Cover and simmer on low heat for 15 minutes. Store for up to 1 week in fridge.

Died-and-Gone-to-Heaven Chocolate Layer Cake

Triple-decker, triple-decadent chocolate layer cake

If you've been a dietary saint all year, go ahead and treat yourself to a little piece of heaven: A slice of divine chocolate cake that's packed with decadent, splurge-worthy ingredients. C'mon! It's not like you're going to burn in hell or anything! Just make sure you burn off the calories later.

Cake

3 cups	granulated sugar
2½ cups	all-purpose flour
1 cup	unsweetened cocoa powder
2 tsp	baking soda
1 tsp	baking powder
1 tsp	salt
3	eggs
1½ cups	buttermilk
1 cup	strong brewed coffee, cooled
¾ cup	high-quality vegetable oil
1 tsp	vanilla
4 oz	(113 g) unsweetened chocolate squares, melted and cooled slightly

Frosting

1¼ cups	granulated sugar
⅓ cup	unsweetened cocoa powder
1 cup	whipping (35%) cream
6 oz	(170 g) semi-sweet chocolate squares
2 tsp	vanilla
1 pkg	(8 oz/250 g) light cream cheese, at room temperature
1 cup	butter, at room temperature

MAKES 16 SERVINGS

PER SERVING
Trust us, you don't want to know!

- Preheat oven to 350°F. Lightly grease bottom and sides of three 9-inch round cake pans. Cut circles of wax paper or parchment paper to fit bottom of pans and place in pans. Lightly grease paper. Set pans aside.

- Combine sugar, flour, cocoa powder, baking soda, baking powder and salt in a large bowl. Set aside.

- In another large bowl, beat eggs on high speed of electric mixer for about 3 minutes, until they have thickened slightly and are lemon colored. Add buttermilk, coffee, oil, vanilla and melted chocolate. Mix on low speed until well blended.

- Gradually add dry ingredients to wet ingredients and mix on medium speed until batter is smooth. Divide batter evenly among pans. Bake for 25 to 30 minutes, until a wooden pick inserted in center of cakes comes out clean. Cool in pans on a wire rack for 10 minutes. Remove cakes from pans, peel off paper and cool completely before frosting.

- To make frosting, whisk together sugar, cocoa powder and whipping cream in a medium pot. Cook slowly over medium heat, whisking constantly, until mixture comes to a gentle boil. Cook 1 minute. Remove from heat and stir in chocolate until melted. Stir in vanilla. Let cool to room temperature.

- In a large bowl, beat cream cheese and butter on high speed of electric mixer until smooth. Add cooled chocolate mixture and beat on medium speed until well blended. Refrigerate frosting until desired spreading consistency is reached, about 1 hour. Don't let it get too firm, or you won't be able to spread it.

- To frost cake, place one cake layer on a pretty plate. Spread 1 cup frosting over top. Repeat with second layer. Place final layer on top. Ice top and sides of cake with remaining frosting. Decorate cake with chocolate curls and/or chocolate-covered strawberries, if desired. Cover and refrigerate. Let cake stand at room temperature for 30 minutes before serving.

Splurge on This!

Don't eat this! Cut back on that! So much of the weight-loss process involves limiting or cutting out. But exercise is the exception—the more you get up and move, the more you're doing your body some good. Being active not only produces tremendous physical gains, but it can also lead to dramatic psychological benefits. And we're not just talking about a runner's high or an endorphin buzz, either. Exercise can relieve depression, anxiety and stress, improve self-esteem and better your outlook on life in general. Think about how great you feel when someone compliments the way you look, or when you can zip the zipper that hasn't zipped in years. When it comes to exercise, it's OK to have the urge to splurge!

It was an emotional wedding. Even the cake was in tiers :)

Metric Conversion

Use these charts to convert the recipes in this book to metric measurements.

VOLUME		
Conventional Measure	Exact Metric Conversion (mL)	Standard Metric Conversion (mL)
¼ teaspoon	1.2 mL	1 mL
½ teaspoon	2.4 mL	2 mL
1 teaspoon	4.7 mL	5 mL
2 teaspoons	9.4 mL	10 mL
1 tablespoon	14.2 mL	15 mL
2 tablespoons	28.4 mL	30 mL
3 tablespoons	42.6 mL	45 mL
¼ cup (4 tablespoons)	56.8 mL	60 mL
⅓ cup (5⅓ tablespoons)	75.6 mL	75 mL
½ cup (8 tablespoons)	113.7 mL	125 mL
⅔ cup (10⅔ tablespoons)	151.2 mL	150 mL
¾ cup (12 tablespoons)	170.5 mL	175 mL
1 cup (16 tablespoons)	227.3 mL	250 mL
4 cups	909.2 mL	1000 mL (1 L)

WEIGHT		
Ounces (oz)	Exact Metric Conversion (g)	Standard Metric Conversion (g)
1 oz	28.3 g	30 g
2 oz	56.7 g	55 g
3 oz	85.0 g	85 g
4 oz	113.4 g	125 g
5 oz	141.7 g	140 g
6 oz	170.1 g	170 g
7 oz	198.4 g	200 g
8 oz	226.8 g	250 g
16 oz (1 lb)	453.6 g	500 g
32 oz	907.2 g	1000 g (1 kg)

OVEN TEMPERATURES	
Fahrenheit (°F)	Celsius (°C)
175°	80°
200°	95°
225°	110°
250°	120°
275°	140°
300°	150°
325°	160°
350°	175°
375°	190°
400°	205°
425°	220°
450°	230°
475°	240°
500°	260°

The J & G Diaries

A random sampling of our favorite blog entries from the past few years—some silly, some serious, some seriously hilarious! More blog postings can be found on our website www.janetandgreta.com. See you there!

Taste Not, Want Not

Posted by Greta (May 2006)

I can't breathe. Honestly…I am so stuffed up right now with the worst cold possible that when I inhale through my nose, nothing happens. Not a sound, not a bit of air, zilch. It's like someone stuffed wine corks up both my nostrils. If only I had listened to Don Cherry on TV and started taking Cold-Fx, I might be better by now. But this is day number seven and things are getting worse!

We all know that our sense of smell is connected to our sense of taste, so my taste buds are totally euchred. Good thing I don't have to develop any recipes today cuz they wouldn't taste very good! However, my inability to taste has led me to dream up an ingenious weight-loss idea, a product that would revolutionize the dieting world and make me super-rich and famous. Here's the gist of it: If Quarter Pounders, french fries, pizza, chicken wings, cheesecake and fettuccine Alfredo didn't taste good, would we eat them? Of course not! We love these foods and all the other rich, fatty ones because of the way they taste. So, what if we *couldn't* taste them?

Introducing, the *No Taste/No Waist Taste-Bud Zapper*™! Yes, intentionally zap your taste buds so you won't eat junky, fattening foods! I can see the reviews already in *Time* and *Newsweek*: "A Matter of Taste: Revolutionary Taste-Bud Zapper™ Helps Millions Shed Unwanted Pounds!" or "This Bud's For You! When Taste Buds Become Taste Bads, Everyone Loses (Weight)!" etc., etc. Every magazine and scientific journal will be writing about my invention and even Oprah will want to talk to me!

My *Taste-Bud Zappers*™ would come in the form of those little Listerine breath strips. You'd just place the patented *Taste-Bud Zapper*™ strip on your tongue, wait 'til it dissolves, and voilà! Can't taste a thing! The strips will come in three nifty flavors: Beef Tenderloin, Chocolate Layer Cake and Mamma's Lasagna, since that'll be the last thing you taste for a while! This is so exciting! Excuse me for a second—I'm going to perform a clinical trial right now just to make sure I'm really as smart as I think I am. Tick tock. Tick tock. I'm back. Wow! It really works! Not having taste buds

means I have no interest in chocolate! I just ate an Oreo cookie and it tasted like…well…NOTHING! Didn't enjoy it at all! What a waste of calories! Might as well have eaten a bland rice cake cuz it would taste identical! Get the idea?

Now, you wouldn't go zapping your taste buds every day. That's not the idea. After all, Janet and I are the queens of "everything in moderation." Plus, I love eating and I love food and I love the way food tastes and food is meant to be enjoyed. However, I can see many occasions when *Taste-Bud Zappers*™ would come in handy…times when we're sure to be led into pig-out temptation and just need a little help with our willpower, such as:

• A bridal shower, which is just an excuse for women to get together, drink wine and enjoy an all-you-can-eat dessert buffet.

• When you have PMS and would kill your husband and/or children for a piece of chocolate; also, any other time a mad craving hits you.

• When you attend a sporting event and the choice of snacks consists of hot dogs, sausage, burgers, pizza and beer.

• If you belong to Weight Watchers, the day before weigh-in day would be a good taste-bud zapping day!

• When you're feeling down in the dumps and don't want to turn to food for comfort.

• When you're invited over to your mother-in-law's house for her famous stroganoff, which you despise, or any other occasion where you're forced to eat a meal you can't stand.

Taste-Bud Zappers™ are discreet and can fit in your pocket or purse. Imagine this scenario: You're at the dinner table and your husband's boss presents you with a goat-cheese-caper-and-sardine frittata. You conveniently drop your napkin under the table, bend over to retrieve it, insert *Taste-Bud Zapper*™, dig in and enjoy! The possibilities are endless! It all makes perfect sense! Why would you eat a slice of pepperoni pizza if a banana tasted exactly the same? Why would you binge on potato chips when celery tastes identical? You wouldn't! Oh, this is going to be HUGE! I wouldn't be surprised if Proctor & Gamble contacts me about this. Fame and fortune are near. I can just taste it! ■

Get the Gunk Out!

Posted by Janet (August 2006)

We live in a much different world today than the one our grandparents or even our parents lived in. Unfortunately, we're faced with toxins and pollutants at every corner. The typical North American diet is laden with preservatives, additives, MSG, aspartame, pesticides, caffeine, sugar and trans fats. On top of that, we have to deal with environmental pollutants, with chlorine in our drinking water (not good!) and with a witch's brew of chemicals in cosmetics, hair products and household cleaning products. These toxins can accumulate in your body's tissues (especially in fat tissue) and prevent it from operating on all cylinders. Plus, if your body's overloaded with toxins, it's almost impossible to lose weight because your organs are so busy dealing with the immediate danger of poisons, they can't focus on their "to-do list," which includes fat metabolism. Geez, this is depressing! I need a stiff drink!

But fret not, my friend. Seriously! The human body is extraordinarily resilient and there are ways to protect yourself from the toxic onslaught. Nowadays, you just need to give your body a helping hand in ridding itself of the gunk, and you need to do it on a regular basis— kinda like brushing your teeth to prevent plaque buildup. Love your liver and it'll love ya back!

One of the easiest and most effective "gunk-prevention" strategies going is adding a "greens supplement" to your daily regimen. Green food supplements are whole-food supplements. They're not synthetic, manufactured, isolated vitamins and minerals, but concentrated "real food," derived from real food. And that's good, because everyone knows that Mother Nature is the best manufacturer! Most contain wheat grass, barley grass, chlorella, blue-green algae, spirulina, and other concentrated whole herbs, plants, dehydrated vegetable and fruit juices and sprouts. You're getting a whole whack of vitamins, minerals, enzymes and amino acids. But you're also getting a mega-detox potion and enough "wonderfuel" to keep your cells alkaline and charged like the Energizer Bunny! Incidentally, I've talked to several people who said that after taking their greens in the a.m., they eventually gave up coffee because the supplement gave them the energy boost they needed in the morning.

There are lots of high-quality greens supplements on the market today. Greens+, Green Magma, Nu-Greens,

Simmon's Super Food and Perfect Food are good examples. My absolute favorite by a million is called BioSuperfood, technically a whole-food product, but more like nature's vitamin chest in a bottle. They call it "the culmination in cellular nutrition" and I don't doubt it. Because it literally contains more than 5,000 individual nutrients in a highly usable form, I've kissed most other supplements goodbye, and don't miss them one bit. I've never loved a greens product more (and my wallet seems happier, too!). You can read about BioSuperfood at www.bioage.com.

10 More Ways to Get the Gunk Out

1. Get sloshed regularly! Drink like a fish! That's right, you need to drink plenty of pure, filtered water in order to flush out toxins. Eight to 10 glasses is good. If you drink bottled water, shove a lemon slice into the bottle. Lemon is an excellent liver detoxifier and blood cleanser. Lemon also helps balance your body's pH, making it more alkaline, an environment in which your body thrives. A gentle, effective way to keep your body squeaky clean is to drink lemon water each morning. Simply squeeze the juice of half a lemon into a mug of

Janet demonstrates tip No. 5

warm, filtered water and drink. If you want a livelier liver, pledge to eat lemons more often!

2. Get rubbed the right way! Deep tissue massage is great for mobilizing toxins stored in tissue.

3. Tea it up! Go for herbal teas that have gentle detoxifying action. Milk thistle and dandelion are excellent choices. You can also buy milk thistle and dandelion supplements or tinctures at your local health food store. Worth it! These are gentle enough that you could take them on a regular basis to give your liver a boost.

4. Do sweat it! Skin is the largest organ in the body and is responsible for one-fourth of the body's detoxification each day. Skin's also known as the "3rd kidney." That's why exercise is so important to our health—we need to sweat! If you have access to a sauna, take advantage of its amazing detoxifying effects. "Far infrared saunas" are very popular nowadays. They're great for your health and when you're in one you don't get that suffocatingly hot feeling you get in a regular sauna. Some health clubs offer them now, but if you have extra cash stashed away, you can invest in one for your home.

5. Make like a kangaroo! That is, buy a rebounder. Bouncing up and down on a mini-trampoline for only seven to 10 minutes a day is one of the best ways to stimulate your lymphatic system (your body's sewer) to release wastes. It also tones and trims your legs and butt like you wouldn't believe. You'll find rebounders at most fitness stores.

6. Eat detoxifying foods. Onions, garlic, artichoke, avocado, cabbage, celery, beets, kale, spinach and other leafy greens are just a few of the potent foods that help your body purge the garbage. Actually, just about any fruit or veggie will do the trick! (Organic is even better, if you can afford it.) Herbs like cilantro and dill draw heavy metals like mercury and lead out of your system, and watermelon contains a compound that's a good liver detoxifier.

7. Do a seven- to 10-day cleanse. It's worth contacting a nutritionist or naturopathic doctor who can give you guidance about doing a good liver, colon and kidney cleanse. You'll be taking cleansing herbs or homeopathic remedies while you're following a strict diet free of junk like sugar, white flour, alcohol and caffeine. Cleanses are very beneficial for long-term health and I'd recommend doing one in the spring and one in the fall.

8. Rub-a-dub-dub. Detox in a tub! Add one to two cups of Epsom salts (magnesium sulfate) to a nice hot bath, and its sulfur compounds will draw toxins from your body through the skin. Epsom salts also relax the nervous system and muscles and help reduce swelling and soreness. It's no wonder massage therapists routinely suggest clients soak in Epsom salts after treatments. Epsom salt is inexpensive. Look for it at your local pharmacy or well-stocked supermarket.

9. Eat your beans, bran and broccoli! What I'm talking about is fiber, fiber and more fiber. You don't want toxic wastes sitting around, lingering in your nether regions for long periods of time. That can lead to auto-intoxication (toxic sludge gets re-absorbed through your intestinal lining and goes back into the bloodstream). Eeeewww! In fact, they say that "death begins in the colon." (I'm not sure who "they" are but what "they" said certainly got my attention!) If you find you don't eat enough foods with fiber, try adding ground or powdered flaxseed or chia seeds to smoothies, oatmeal, cereal or yogurt.

10. Try dry skin brushing. What the heck is that? Well, remember what I said earlier about the skin being a huge detoxifying organ? Brushing your skin all over with a special bristle brush while your skin is dry is an excellent way to help rid your body of toxins that can gather beneath the skin's surface. When you brush your skin, you help your lymph system cleanse itself of waste that accumulates in the lymph glands. You use a simple technique to improve the surface circulation on the skin and keep the pores of the skin open, encouraging your body to purge metabolic wastes. Your skin looks healthier, plus it's supposed to help get rid of cellulite! Yeehaaa! Just Google dry skin brushing and you'll find detailed instructions.

Here's to a cleaner, leaner, much healthier you! ■

Recipe Titles That Didn't Quite Make the Cut

Posted by Janet and Greta (March 2006)

You can probably imagine how difficult it is to write and self-publish a cookbook, never mind having to dream up 150 punny, absolutely silly recipe titles for each book! We still can't believe we've managed to name 450 recipes so far between our three books. We are truly warped. What happened to us as children that we now regularly think, speak and probably dream in puns?

We dug up a list of some funny, mostly ridiculous, recipe titles that never made it into any of our cookbooks so you can have a good laugh at our expense. Oh well, at least we were trying!

Drumroll…

Celery Clinton
Gnocchi Night in Canada
Hallowed Weenies (Sounds a little scary!)
Bread Pitt (Date loaf)
Basil Passages (Heaven *nose* what we were thinking!)
Days of Our Chives
Snacquille O'Neal (Stuff for dunking?)
Ricotta Montálban
Edgar Allan Poultry (For when you're *raven*-ous)
Metric Cookies (Made with "gram" crackers)
Tori Spelling's Alphabet Soup
Pamela Anderson's Melon Balls
Chili Bean's Not My Lover (Michael Jackson's chili recipe)
Kate Moss's Ribs
Anti-Separatist Breakfast (French toast made with English muffins)

Silence of the Yams
Much Fondue About Nothing
The Best of the Breast (Chicken breasts, that is!)
Whose Loin is it, Anyway? (Loin chops? Tenderloin? Striploin?)
Tinker Bell Peppers
Hippocratic Oat Cookies
Davey Crockpot
Franky Scallop, I Don't Give a Ham (Ham and scalloped potatoes)
Master Peas
Olivey Twists (Braided bread sticks with olives)
Chili's Angels
Ham I Am
The Steaks are High (on what?)
Central Pork (Pork chops with Big Apple sauce)
Veggie Jackson

Hey Y'all! We Met Paula Deen!

Posted by Greta (June 2008)

Yesterday, Janet and I were lucky enough to meet Paula Deen, U.S. Food Network mega-star, while visiting QVC (the huge U.S. shopping network) in West Chester, Pennsylvania. She was as nice and cheerful and delightful as we expected her to be, and not pretentious at all, considering her phenomenal success: appearances on *Oprah*, TV shows, cookbook empire, restaurants and food products (and the list goes on).

In fact, when we met Paula, she was standing in the kitchen, ironing her pink linen shirt before going on the air. She called me "hon" and "darlin'" and I was instantly drawn to her warm demeanor. We chatted briefly, I showed her our *Eat, Shrink & Be Merry!* cookbook and told her about our Food Network Canada TV show, and she said something like "Well, I'll be! Gosh darn that's somethun' else, ain't it?" (At least that's what I think she said. Because, just in case you haven't seen or heard

Paula Deen, her Southern accent's pretty thick. And so charming!)

Janet and I chatted with her about the importance of having fun in the kitchen and having a good sense of humor, not taking cooking too seriously, etc., and she told us she wanted to have a look through our book, so we signed it for her and left it in her dressing room. All y'all never know, we could end up having an Iron Chef cook-off someday: The Pod Squad vs. Paula. (She'd probably kick our butts.)

I've also decided that I'm going to start speaking like her. Since I'm from the South, too (Southern Ontario), I just fell in love with her accent and I want one for myself. After micro-analyzing the way she speaks, I know I've mastered her style and lingo. For example, I would normally say something very boring and typical like this: "I really hate my hair." Now, with my charismatic, Paula Deen Southern accent, I'll sound like this: "Uh rilly hate ma hay-er." Totally different, isn't it? This is so exciting! Oh, the people I'll meet and places I'll go now that I'm charming! Thanks Paula! Luv yuh, hon! ■

Duck, Duck, Goose!

Posted by Janet (April 2010)

I just had to write to tell you about yesterday's harrowing experience while walking at High Park in Toronto. I've been there a million times with my Jack Russell terrier, Lacey Lou. We always enjoy hiking along the lovely, tree-lined path beside the lake. (Well, it's actually called Grenadier *Pond*, but it sure doesn't seem like a pond to me at all. Ponds are small, scummy and have pollywogs that turn into frogs sitting on lily pads eating gross insects. Unless it's a "see-ment" pond, like on *The Beverly Hillbillies*.)

Anyway, I was nonchalantly walking along the lake and on this day, the cherry trees were in full, pink bloom, crowds of tourists were snapping photos of swans and diving ducks, children were frolicking, the sun was shining—everyone was happy-go-lucky and all was good in the world. Until "they" arrived….

Lacey and I were on a particularly narrow part of the path when, all of a sudden, I could see in the distance two crazed, wildly cackling geese, flying low and very fast along the path like airplanes coming in for a landing. Only they seemed more like fighter jets coming in for an attack!

They headed straight for us, beaks open, pink tongues flapping, intent on…well…beaking us! These were huge, honkin' geese! My first instinct was to duck, but since it was a goose, I dove sideways off the path and into a mucky, icky bog (wrecking my brand-new Merrell hiking shoes that I just bought on sale at Mountain Equipment Co-op). Then I screamed at Lacey Lou, "Run, Lacey! Run!" And she did. Only the dive-bombing "head goose" flew even faster and bit her right on the bum! Thinking the nutso, 20-pound goose was going to pick my tiny, nine-pound Jack Russell up by the collar and drop her into the lake (I mean pond), I made a wild, screeching fuss, arms flailing, legs kicking, muck flying everywhere, until the goose got the message that I was NOT to be messed around with now that my new hiking shoes were ruined and my dog's derriere was dented. And the bird flew. Boy did it fly! Phew!

I must have looked like a truly crazy person but, thankfully, no one was there to witness us getting goosed. Perhaps the geese were protecting their babies or something, but gosh, why all the fuss and drama? Such trauma over flying geese. Now I know how Captain Chesley Sullenberger must have felt! ■

Take the Dessert Personality Test!

Posted by *Greta* (January 2008)

My sister, Margie, sent me this fun personality test today so I thought I'd pass it along. If all of the desserts listed below were sitting in front of you, which one would you choose? Do not cheat—go with the first dessert you pick! (Sorry, you can only pick one.) Choose your dessert, then read what psychiatrists have to say about you.

Here are your choices:

1. **Angel Food Cake**
2. **Brownies**
3. **Lemon Meringue**
4. **Vanilla Cake with Chocolate Icing**
5. **Strawberry Shortcake**
6. **Chocolate on Chocolate**
7. **Ice Cream**
8. **Carrot Cake**

You can't change your mind after you've read the descriptions, so think carefully about what your choice will be! OK, now that you've made your choice, this is what the research says about you:

1. ANGEL FOOD CAKE — Sweet, loving, cuddly. You love all warm and fuzzy items. A little nutty at times. Sometimes you need an ice-cream cone at the end of the day. Others perceive you as being childlike and immature at times.

2. BROWNIES — You are adventurous, love new ideas and are a champion of underdogs and a slayer of dragons. When tempers flare up, you whip out your saber. You are always the oddball with a unique sense of humor and direction. You tend to be very loyal.

3. LEMON MERINGUE — Smooth, sexy and articulate with your hands, you are an excellent after-dinner speaker and a good teacher. But don't try to walk and chew gum at the same time. A bit of a diva, but you have many friends.

4. VANILLA CAKE WITH CHOCOLATE ICING — Fun-loving, sassy, humorous, not very grounded in life; very indecisive and lack motivation. Everyone enjoys being around you, but you are a practical joker. Others should be cautious in making you mad. However, you are a friend for life.

5. STRAWBERRY SHORTCAKE — Romantic, warm, loving. You care about other people, can be counted on in a pinch and expect the same in return. You can be assertive. Intuitively keen. You are intelligent, but can be very emotional at times.

6. CHOCOLATE ON CHOCOLATE — Sexy; always ready to give and receive. Very creative, adventurous, ambitious and passionate. You can appear to have a cold exterior but are warm on the inside. Not afraid to take chances. Will not settle for anything average in life. Love to laugh.

7. ICE CREAM — You like sports, whether it be baseball, football, basketball or soccer. If you could, you would like to participate, but you enjoy watching sports. You don't like to give up the remote control. You tend to be self-centered and high maintenance.

8. CARROT CAKE — You are a very fun-loving person who likes to laugh. You are fun to be with. People like to hang out with you. You are a very warm-hearted person and a little quirky at times. You have many loyal friends.

I'd love to tell you which dessert I picked, but I suffer from *selectophobia*, a paralyzing mental disorder that prevents me from choosing my favorite ANYTHING! *Favorite song*. I dunno. *Favorite food?* That's a ridiculous question. *If I was stranded on a desert island and could only bring one book to read for the rest of my life?* That's so stupid I'm not even justifying it with an answer. (It would be *Looneyspoons*.) Plus, I absolutely hate hypothetical questions. *Best friend*? It's really not nice to rank people. *Favorite color*? To wear? To paint my kitchen? For a car? For toenail polish? Please clarify!

Naturally, when my sister sent me this email "test" (I despise tests, too), I was in complete protest. Mostly because cheesecake isn't on the list, but also because my paralysis by analysis kicked in and threw off my body's equilibrium and stressed me out for the whole day. How am I supposed to pick a dessert without answers to the following questions?: Does the carrot cake have cream-cheese icing? Because if it doesn't, then I don't want carrot cake at all. What does "lemon meringue" mean? Lemon meringue pie or just lemon-flavored meringue? There's a difference, you know. Are the strawberries for the shortcake in season, or am I eating flavorless winter strawberries or (gasp!) soggy frozen berries? Are the brownies homemade or from a hydrogenated mix? With icing? Do they contain nuts? Are we talking about plain ice cream here or a Dairy Queen large vanilla cone dipped in that amazing hot melted chocolate? Answers! I need answers!

Come on…fess up. You had all kinds of questions, too, and probably thought about which answer would turn out to be "the best" answer, didn't you? *Didn't you*? What do you think a psychiatrist would say about *that*? ■

Time for an Oil Change!

Posted by Janet (November 2007)

According to Penn State chemical engineers, cooking oils and salad oils could lubricate machinery like cars and boats. Tests found that when blended with an additive developed at Penn State, some vegetable oils performed as well or better than commercial motor oils (though very few motor oils tasted good on a garden salad!). These polyunsaturated oils might be beneficial for your car's valves, but as far as your heart's valves are concerned, it's a slippery situation.

Unfortunately, most commercial cooking oils found in grocery stores today (such as vegetable, corn, soybean, sunflower, canola and safflower) are not as healthy as they could be, thanks to the tinkering and tampering of manufacturers. In order to extend shelf life, cooking oils are usually overly refined and processed, subjected to intense heat, then bleached and deodorized during the manufacturing process. In short, they've been run through the ringer! That changes the oil's chemical structure, making it really tough for your body to handle. Plus, these chemically treated and super-heated oils have lost most of their antioxidants and beneficial plant chemicals. Manufacturers are simply doing what's best for their bottom lines, not what's best for the human body.

Another problem with regular cooking oils (the cheap ones you find in clear bottles on grocery store shelves) is oxidation. Here's the deal: Oils are very sensitive to heat, light and oxygen, and overexposure to any of these can cause the oil to spoil and go rancid. Ick! Not only will it taste bitter, but the oil's molecules also become corrupt or damaged. Your body doesn't know what the heck to do with the stuff. That interferes with how your cells function, and that's when health problems start creeping up—heart disease, cancer, arthritis, autoimmune disease, infertility, liver damage and other not-so-fun things. Cheap, rancid oils are so bad for your body, I don't even want to talk about them! But I just did. Rancid=very bad. Trust me. Damaged oils cause free-radical damage in our bodies, helping us to "rust from the inside out." JEEPers!

No worries, though! A basic oil change is all that's required to keep your pipes clear and your engine running smoothly:

1. Ditch the huge jug of 10W40 (also known as vegetable oil) that's been sitting in your pantry just waiting for a French fry-up. Trash it now!

2. At the store, check your oil and make sure the label says "expeller-pressed" or "cold-pressed"—that means minimal heat was used in manufacturing. Organic is even better since it (usually) has fewer pesticides and doesn't involve genetic modification. In general, olive oil is not subjected to these harsher manufacturing processes, so even if the label on a bottle of olive oil doesn't say "expeller-pressed," it's usually OK.

3. Poor-quality cooking oils come in clear containers. Buy only the kind in dark-tinted bottles. That protects the oil from the harsh grocery store lighting and other sources of light exposure. Reach to get the bottle farthest back on the shelf (away from the light).

4. Buy the smallest bottle you can and use it within three months. Once opened, air will degrade the oil slowly. The longer it's stored, the fewer the polyphenols and other healthy stuff. If your olive oil has witnessed both the delivery of your firstborn and her high-school prom, NOW is the time to go shopping for a new bottle! (Interestingly, researchers have found that adding rosemary to olive oil might help prevent this drop in its health qualities.)

5. Store oils in a cool, dry place. Avoid leaving them out on your kitchen counter where they'll be exposed to more light and heat. No matter how decorative a bottle looks, definitely don't keep it next to the stove or right by the kitchen window. Protect your oil and you'll protect yourself!

Given what I've said about how high heat changes the molecular structure of oils, hopefully you'll understand why overindulging in deep-fried foods is such a health no-no. You really don't want to be a frequent fryer! Seductive as they may be to your taste buds, the fact is, fries, donuts, potato chips and that finger-lickin' chicken are all leading you toward an inevitable heartbreak (literally!). Even if you take a healthy oil like olive oil or canola, and you subject it to the very high heat involved with deep frying, you end up altering the oil's molecular structure in a bad way (you change a good fat into a bad fat), and that ends up altering YOUR molecular structure over time.

The Best Oils to Use for Cooking

Avocado Oil: An oil that's naturally 12 percent saturated and 72 percent monounsaturated, avocado oil is all the rage (and my fave!) because it has one of the highest smoke points of all vegetable oils at 520°F. Plus, its super-antioxidants and beneficial plant chemicals can keep you looking young and feeling healthy! What's not to love? With a mild taste, it's great for most of your stovetop needs.

Coconut Oil: Loaded with health benefits (see p. 80), coconut oil is also very stable in high heat, making it great for sautéing vegetables, making stir-fries and popping corn. Use it in recipes where the mild flavor of coconut is acceptable.

High-Oleic Safflower or Sunflower Oil: For baking (where you need a mild-flavored oil) and other high-temperature cooking, look for "high-oleic" oils. Oleic acid is a monounsaturated fatty acid, which is much less susceptible to heat damage than the polyunsaturated fatty acids normally found in regular safflower or sunflower oil. Worth it!

Grapeseed Oil: With the same powerful antioxidants as green tea, berries and red wine, grapeseed oil can do wonders for your skin and overall health. It withstands heat well, so you can use the oil for stir-fries, marinades, salad dressings, baking and most of your stovetop needs.

Extra-Virgin Olive Oil: You can't say enough about the health benefits of olive oil. Its mega-nutrients and antioxidants are easily destroyed by heat and light, though, so you don't want to crank the heat when using olive oil. In fact, it's best to use it only for light sautéing, making sauces and, of course, for salad dressings. (See p. 73 for a tip about combining olive oil with butter—wonderful for sautéing!)

Look for these oils at health food stores and well-stocked grocery stores. Sure, you'll pay a bit more for organic, expeller-pressed oils, but for the price of a bottle of wine, it's one of the smartest investments you could ever make for your health and *well*fare. Your heart's valves are worth the extra expense!

And that's oil she wrote!

How to Procrastinate

Posted by Greta (May 2007)

Some days I just don't feel like working and today is one of those days. I've been procrastinating since 8 a.m. It's now 3:19 p.m. and I've basically accomplished nothing. However, I DID manage to have a very deep discussion with Janet via email exchanges that went something like this:

G: I have three types of beets growing in my organic garden. Perhaps I will set up a booth at the St. Jacobs market to sell them.

J: What makes your garden "organic" anyway? "Beets Me" would be a good name for your booth, BTW.

G: I am training my dog Lexi to go to the bathroom in the garden so I don't have to use pesticides or fertilizers. That's why it's organic.

J: FYI, If Donna (our sister and part-time gardener) uses those bags of "3-in-1 mix," then your garden is not "technically" organic, cuz that stuff is not all-natural and actually deposits more chemicals into the water table. Hate to burst your organic bubble. (But I'll still eat and enjoy every mouthful of your roasted beets!)

Signed,
Janetski Suzuki

G: She isn't using ANYTHING. It's all-natural, so no bubbles are bursting. I am charging 50 cents per beet. You can choose from Detroit Dark Red, Golden Beets or the hard-to-find Italian Chioggia with red-and-white striped flesh (looks like a bull's-eye). So there.

J: With that many beets to offer, you should call your booth, "The Beet Goes On." Fifty cents a beet? Rip-off! You better throw in some organic basil leaves as a gift with purchase or you'll be one lonely booth-tender.

G: People will drive for miles and miles to buy my beets, like they did in the movie *Field of Dreams*. Not that they bought beets in *Field of Dreams*, but cars lined up for miles and miles. You know what I mean. Plus, I will offer free recipe cards for my delicious beet recipes, printed on recycled paper with soy inks.

J: No response.

G: All this talk of organic gardening makes me want to buy a pair of Birkenstocks. Do they sell those at Winners?

J: No response.

G: Did you know that the average chocolate bar contains four to eight insect legs?

J: Beet it!

OK, fine. It's time to get back to work anyway. But not before I read the flyers that arrived in my mailbox this morning. *What?* There could be an amazing sale on at LensCrafters or something! Yes, yes, I did have laser eye surgery (twice!) and don't need glasses anymore. Good point. But, I know people who wear glasses. Perhaps I'll organize my rubber bands and colored paper clips next, since it drives me crazy when things are intertwined and all tangled like that. That should take up 30 minutes or so. Then I'll Google my name and the names of friends to see what comes up. That'll occupy at least 20 minutes. Plus, I really should check the weather forecast to see if rain is on the way or if I need to water my beets tonight. I just stared at my hair, searching for split ends for 10 whole minutes! How time flies! Hmm. How many words can I create using only the middle row of letters on a keyboard? Fad, gas, has, lash, lad, lag, gaga, lala, kaka…oh, I give up. Guess what? Writing this blog as slowly as possible has now taken up 56 minutes. See ya later…it's quittin' time!

A Brilliant Disguise

Posted by Janet (May 2008)

With our TV show airing four times a week on Food Network Canada, a Dempster's Ancient Grains bread commercial that we filmed earlier in the year playing a gazillion times and with our monthly *Reader's Digest* column having been in circulation for two years, I'm noticing that it's harder and harder to go anywhere without being recognized. It's not like I'm being stalked by nasty, pushy, prying, ruthless paparazzi or anything. No, no, most people who approach me are superpolite and very enthusiastic. I actually love chatting with our book and show fans.

Just the other day, a woman tapped me on the back while I was waiting in line at Shoppers Drug Mart.

"Oh…my…gawd!! Are you one of the Looney cooking sisters? Those crazy spoons with that *Eat, Drink & Be Merry* TV show?"

"Why, yes. Yes, I am. Uh… *Eat, SHRINK & Be Merry*, that is," I said, smiling politely and enthusiastically.

"I just love yous guyses show. You and yer sister are SO funny! And my husband Durk just loves your books! He makes Jurassic Pork and Chicken Teriwacky faithfully almost every week!"

"Gee, thanks!" I'm turning a bit red now, not from all of this fan's gushing, but because I'm standing in line juggling the biggest possible, jumbo, super-duper, family-sized package of double-roll two-ply toilet paper imaginable. (Note: I live alone and this was enough paper for a small village, but, first of all, it was on sale and, second, I HAVE been trying to add more fiber to my diet lately.) Oh well. I could've been standing there clutching a tube of Preparation H.

Because more and more people are recognizing me (and sometimes I haven't put much effort into my appearance and don't want fans to think I look like a hag), I've decided to go out incognito. I now wear my ball cap and big sunglasses everywhere, just like those mysterious, aloof Hollywood stars you see in trashy celeb mags. OK, I'm busted! Ball caps and sunglasses ARE my usual attire. It's my "look" and has been for years now, I admit it. In fact, it's what I live in when we're not filming or touring, and it's great for bad hair days, too (which occur frequently).

So last week I went for a walk with my dog, Lacey Lou, at the Arboretum in Ottawa. We were there no more than 10 minutes when out of the forest emerged a 20-something-ish girl with her rather sheepish-looking sheep dog.

"Excuse me, aren't you from *Eat, Shrink & Be Married?*"

"Yes, yes I am," I laughed. I mentioned that she wasn't the first person to mistakenly call our show by that name. A five-year-old boy calls it that (his mom wrote to say he sings the theme song to our show with the improvised words). Plus, our mother, Alfreda, adds an even funnier twist with her Polish mispronunciation of the same incorrect title. Guess it's her subliminal messaging to her two youngest daughters, both single.

So my disguise didn't work, not surprisingly, but I decided to keep it up. On the weekend, I ran into my favorite takeout food joint, The Wild Oat in Ottawa, to grab some of their super-yummy vegetarian chili. Ball cap and sunglasses shielding my identity, I stood in the long lineup at the cash for what seemed like an eternity, paid for the chili and then turned to exit. As I was leaving, a young couple walked confidently toward me, obviously recognizing me.

"Excuse me…," they began. Anticipating their next line, I said, "Yes, yes I am."

The man looked at me quizzically and responded, "Just wanted to tell you that the price tag on your sweatshirt is hanging out the back. You got it on sale! Way to go!"

Eeeek! The tag was HUMONGOUS and it was dangling off the hood of my new purple hoodie and down my spine. On it was a neon red sale sticker (the same color as my face) screaming $19.99!! Gasp! I must have been standing in line for a good 10 minutes before these kind people had the decency to intervene. My only saving grace was that they had no clue who I was. Phew!

"By the way, we love your show!" they waved as they left the building.

Yes, yes, I am the host of *Eat, Shriek & Be Mortified!*

Life's a Gas

Posted by Greta (April 2008)

It's finally grilling season, which means just about everything I cook for dinner will be prepared over burning-hot coals if possible. Fish, vegetables, steak, pork tenderloin and even pizza just somehow taste better when cooked on the barbecue, don't they? I've already lugged my two huge propane tanks to the gas station for their annual fill-up. (Can you believe the price of gas? That's it. I'm buying a scooter.) What I WON'T ever do again is *run out of propane* while in the middle of cooking expensive steaks, as I did last winter while entertaining eight hungry, out-of-town guests.

The story goes something like this: It was mid-January and about 20 degrees below zero, but that didn't stop me from hauling out my well-worn Weber barbecue so I could impress my guests with perfectly seasoned, medium-rare beef tenderloin steaks. Problem was, I forgot to check my fuel level and just as I put the zillion-dollar steaks on the grill, the fire went out. Kaput. No heat. No sizzle, just fizzle. Oh no! Now what? I'm the ultimate perfectionist, and admitting that I goofed and that my steaks would have to be cooked in a pan on the stovetop (gasp!) would be the kiss of culinary death for me. I'd rather have a branding iron sear my rear than deliver bland slabs of beef to the dinner table. People have high expectations when they come to my house for supper and I must not disappoint! What to do? Think, Greta! Think!

Then I remembered my spare tank. Phew! I'm saved! But, there was a small problem: The spare tank was stored in my garden shed, out in the backyard, about 150 snowbank-covered feet from the garage where I stood panicking in my high heels, sheer control-top pantyhose and short black party skirt. Still, I didn't hesitate for a second. I fumbled and stumbled my way through drift after drift in the pitch-black darkness (remember, it was January!) on a mission to find my spare propane tank. Never mind that the sharp, ice-covered snowbanks were cutting into my legs and shredding my nylons to pieces! Never mind that I fell twice and sliced my hand on the snow fence! Never mind that I was developing frostbite as I took step after icy step in my brand-new Isaac Mizrahi pumps that I just bought off the clearance rack at the Designer Shoe Warehouse in Florida! These were beef tenderloin steaks, after all, and they needed saving!

The spare tank was full, thank goodness, so I dragged all 30 pounds of it back through the snow drifts and into the garage, my bare legs now completely exposed as the snow had literally "eaten" my pantyhose right off my body, my hair tangled in ratty knots from the gusting, freezing winds combined with copious amounts of firm-hold hairspray (unscented) and my skirt now on totally backward, with the sexy, 12-inch slit positioned straight up the front. But, never mind! There's meat to cook! Hungry mouths to feed! I attached my spare tank to the barbecue nozzle with trembling, frozen hands and ta-da! I had fire! Halleluialuja! (Or however you spell it!)

About 10 minutes later, as if nothing unusual had transpired, I calmly delivered, in Martha Stewart-like fashion, eight perfectly cooked, medium-rare beef tenderloin steaks and their accompanying grilled vegetables with balsamic reduction to my ravenous guests at the dining-room table. They were either too polite or too shocked to comment on my appearance. The steaks, on the other hand, drew rave reviews, and for that I'm *tankful*. ■

Soy Story

Posted by Janet (March 2008)

Even though I must confess to having more than my fair share of chai tea lattes made with soy milk over the last couple of years, I've never been a big fan of soy. It's not the taste of soy products that bothers me, although I can't say I crave watery soy milk on my Multigrain Flakey-O's in the morning. (Incidentally, I'm an almond milk girl!) It's just that the whole subject of soy is fraught with more controversy than an episode of *The Real Housewives of New Jersey*. Fifty percent say soy's soooo great for your health. Fifty percent say it's not. For that reason, I've tried to stay fairly neutral and drink in as many of the facts as I can. But after doing lots of reading on the subject, and being a registered holistic nutritionist to boot, I realize I share the perspective of natural practitioners who give processed soy products (especially soy protein isolate and soybean oil, which are in just about everything nowadays) the big thumbs-down. That's in contrast to the multi-billion-dollar soy industry and its lobbyists who tout it as being the answer to all our dietary prayers.

The soy that has acclaimed health benefits is the fermented kind: miso, tempeh, soy sauce, fermented tofu and natto, for example. Even so, we weren't meant to eat mountains of the stuff. When the soy industry, and then the government, announced that soy was "soy good for you," they pointed to the Asian diet, which they claim contains a lot of soy. In fact, soy consumption is relatively low in Asia, ranging from two tablespoons a day in Japan to two teaspoons a day in China. And the kind of soy they eat is not the processed-to-death kind but the fermented kind mentioned above.

One problem with soy is that it's a goitrogen. Huh? That's souped-up, science mumbo jumbo that really means "you're gonna get fat!" Goitrogens slow your thyroid gland function. When your thyroid gland is sluggish, your metabolism slows (among other not-so-pleasant things), putting the brakes on fat loss, helping you gain weight even when you eat very little. Dang! Interestingly, even with the small amounts of soy eaten in Asia, thyroid problems are widespread there, particularly in China.

Another problem with soy is that it's one of the most genetically modified crops going, and the jury's still out on what that can mean for your overall health. Animal studies carried out in 1974 showed that soy protein isolate, the major ingredient in modern soy foods, increases the requirement for vitamins D, E, K and B12 and causes deficiencies in many important minerals. What's more, overconsumption of processed, unfermented soy products can interfere with protein digestion over time. Some health food, huh? Most holistic practitioners agree that soy is just downright difficult to digest and, for that reason, many, many folks are intolerant or allergic to soy products—most of them without even knowing it!

Soy's claim to health fame comes from its estrogen-like substances called isoflavones. Isoflavones mimic estrogen in the body and can increase the amount of estrogen that can bind onto estrogen receptors. Soy isoflavones are a kinder, gentler version of the body's regular estrogen (kinda like a cheap knockoff) so they might cause less harm binding onto estrogen receptors than the more potent "bad" estrogens kicking around in your body. That's why phytoestrogens, in moderate quantities, can be very helpful to menopausal and pre-menopausal women who have declining levels of estrogen. But what about people who don't need the extra estrogen jolt? Young girls, for instance. Or adult women nowhere near menopause. Two glasses of soy milk a day is enough to throw off menstrual patterns. Say it ain't soy! And what about men? What happens when they have too much processed soy? Can you say "man boobs"? And don't even get me started on soy infant formula. Ohhh, baby! Tinkering with hormones is serious stuff.

While small portions of soy would probably do no harm, the truth is, we're gobbling up massive quantities. And it's not surprising. People listen to media hype proclaiming something to be "the next greatest thing" and they just go soy nuts! They take it too far. Much too far. Today, processed soy is found in more than 60 percent of packaged foods, from protein bars and shakes, meal replacements, cereal, ice cream, cheese, sausages, burgers, soy milk and tofu-based "mock meats." Heck, Ford Motor Company even uses by-products of soybeans to make plastic window frames, steering wheels and upholstery! Soy's ubiquitous, and that's drivin' me around the bend.

Obviously, moderation is key. Rather than me babbling on and on (I'm prone to that), I think it's best to do your own research and form your own opinion. Hopefully you'll find this a good starting point. I should tell you I'm officially on the wagon. "My name is Janet and it's been 14 weeks since my last soy chai tea latte." (That's my soy story and I'm sticking to it.) ■

Burnin' Ring of Desire

Posted by Janet (April 2006)

It's all fun and games 'til someone loses a gallbladder. Let me explain what happened: The evening started with the best of intentions. My friend Leanne and I decided to meet after work for a high-energy power walk along the Ottawa River. (We were trying to whip ourselves into shape for a fast-approaching spa vacation.) Anyway, about 15 minutes into it, she gasped, "I'm so hungry, I could chew my new shoes!" Her leather sneakers sure looked yummy to me, too, and I couldn't muffle the sound of my stomach's urgent SOS calls. "Who needs exercise? Let's eat!"

When your body's running on fumes, it drives you to make some pretty desperate, impulsive, evil-yet-oh-so-deeply-satisfying food choices. What would it be? Pizza? Pasta? Boston cream donuts with a large, hot-chocolate chaser? Nope. Feeling proud of ourselves, we resisted and settled on a new, trendy restaurant that serves organic, home-style burgers. We'd just say no to fries and choose salad on the side, like good girls do. There we were, in total control, everything fine and dandy, until I caught a glimpse of a little card on our table nestled beside the condiments. "Tower of Rings! Voted Best Onion Rings in Town!" Well, I couldn't, for the life of me, tell you the last time I had onion rings. Had to be back in high school (so that would be around 1995—wink!). Leanne confessed that earlier in the day she'd experienced an intense craving for…none other than… onion rings! A co-inky-dink? I think not. Needless to say, we caved to the crave.

The Tower was delivered to our table by a waif of a waitress who struggled under the sheer weight of the dish. "Here ya go, ladies! These are my favorite! I eat 'em every day at work," she smiled.

"Uh, yeah, right," I thought. The Tower glistened before us. Twelve crispy, near-donut-sized rings neatly stacked one on top of another. Spicy barbecue dipping sauce on the right. Zesty ranch dressing on the left. This should be good! We sat in silence, eagerly devouring our first ring. Then another. Then another. At that point I noticed Leanne daintily and discreetly blotting her fourth ring in a napkin.

With only half a Bounty, she absorbed enough Crisco to coat the bottom of an industrial-sized wok. Ick!

"Grease is the word, is the word, is the word," I sang, doing my best Frankie Valli imitation.

"Where exactly is the gallbladder located?" Leanne was holding her belly. "Is it to the right or left in the abdomen? Under the rib cage?" I told her it was closer to the center.

"Yep, that's where I'm feelin' the pain," she admitted. By then, our bun-less, five-herb, organic burgers had arrived, along with our garden salads. We picked at them, our appetites dampened and spirits sunken by the weight of the Exxon Valdez onion rings. When our bill came, Leanne clumsily dropped a $20 bill on the floor by the leg of my chair. I couldn't bend over to retrieve it, and neither could she. We were in the midst of a serious oil crisis.

"That's it! I'm NEVER doing this again! I was skinny when I came in here! That wasn't even splurge-worthy!" Leanne ranted, making reference to the universal code for rating indulgences.

And you know, if I had to rate those rings for splurge-worthiness, with 10 being "totally worth it," and anything below 9 being "not worthy," I'd score the first ring at 9, the second ring at 5 and all the rings that followed at 1. It just goes to show, savoring a few little bites of a treat or an indulgence is usually all that's needed to satisfy a craving…and save a gallbladder. ■

A one-week stay at a fat farm/detox spa was needed to recover from the oil spill.

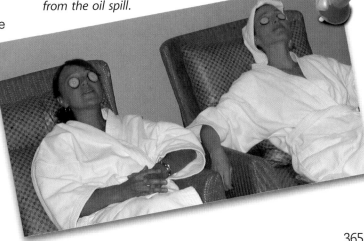

Life in the Country's Not *Bat* at All

Posted by Greta (April 2006)

There's never a dull moment when you live in a 150-year-old farmhouse in the middle of a cornfield. One day the police drove right through my backyard and straight into the field searching for a stash of marijuana (not mine!). The next day my dog was lured into a boxing match with a big, fat raccoon, resulting in a $250 vet bill. And the day after that I discovered yet another mouse under my kitchen sink, happily munching away on a box of S.O.S pads. I've lived in this house for six years now and, thankfully, have never seen a bat...until yesterday.

While checking emails on my computer, I noticed a faint chirping/clicking/cooing noise coming from a corner of my living room. I knew I wasn't hearing things because my dog gave me one of those quizzical head tilts that, in doggy language, means, "What the heck was that?" The noise grew louder and louder, crisper and clearer. It didn't sound like a bird. I've had many birds in my house before and once ended up with a dead bird in my bed, under the covers, a "gift" from my proud, sparrow-loving dog. After scanning the room for potential invaders, I spotted a tiny bat dangling from my built-in bookshelf. Eeeek!!! I totally freaked out and ran from the room, grabbed a blanket and a staple gun (I'm very resourceful) and "sealed off" the doorway like it was the entrance to a bloody crime scene. Panic-stricken, I phoned my brother-in-law and left him an anxious, "you're-not-going-to-believe-what-I-found, please-come-fast-and-save-me-before-I-die" type of voice-mail message. He knows that I hate critters.

Two long hours of nerve-wracking chirping/clicking/cooing later, my brother-in-law Don arrived (he lives out of town), wearing rubber work gloves and a Montreal Canadiens ball hat for protection. Feeling a bit like MacGyver, I armed Don with my long-handled mesh sieve and a glass saucepan lid and told him to "catch" the bat using the sieve, like it's a butterfly net. "Good idea," said batman-in-law. Interestingly, I noticed that the bat was suddenly silent...not making a single peep. Strange, since it had been driving me insane for two hours straight.

Don made his way around my makeshift iron curtain and into the living room.

"Where's the bat?" he asked. "I can't see it."

"On the bookshelf, second shelf from the top, left-hand side," I responded, my voice quivering.

"I can't find it!" Don yelled through the red-and-white, French-toile barricade.

I pulled out a couple staples and reluctantly stuck my head into the living room, pointed to the bat dangling

bat!

from the second shelf of the bookcase and screamed, "Right there! Right in front of you!"

"That thing right there?" asked Don, pointing straight at the bat.

"Yes! Yes! That's what small bats look like! They look like big moths!" I screamed through the blanket, covering my head with a dish towel, just in case. "Get it before it takes off!"

"Got it," Don calmly announced. "And you've *gotta* see this."

"No! Don't bring it in here! Please! Just get rid of it!" I pleaded.

"No, I really think you should see this," Don declared as he appeared from behind the fabric doorway. "Here's your bat."

I shrieked as he pushed the sieve toward me, then I fell silent, absolutely dumbfounded. Inside the sieve was an antique, leather-bound book (Robinson Crusoe!) with a dark, thick, silk bookmark dangling out the bottom. Despite the fact that I've had laser eye surgery, I actually believed that a blue silk bookmark was a nasty, rabid, baby bat. Just so you don't think I'm totally nuts, I've attached a photo of the phantom bat above. You have to understand, I was a good 15 feet away and it was kinda dark in the room, plus my eyes were fuzzy from staring at the computer monitor for so long. Honest!

Still, there's no explanation for the weird chirping/clicking/cooing noise that I heard. In fact, after my brother-in-law departed in his batmobile (I sent him home with a pot of chili to ease my guilt), the "bat" started up again and yakked for a good 15 minutes, probably laughing at me. I still haven't found the mysterious creature, but my dog and I know for sure that it's hiding in the house. Somewhere. ■

All the Juicy Details

Posted by Janet (July 2007)

I have a good friend named Gaye whom everyone is always complimenting for her youthful, glowing, gorgeous skin and striking, clear, sky-blue eyes. If it wasn't for her full head of equally gorgeous, equally striking, shoulder-length gray hair, you'd swear that she was 49 instead of her real age: 63. I've begged her many times for her secret "fountain of youth" formula, but she won't fess up. Is it an overall healthy lifestyle? Attitude? Lack of stress? A special wrinkle-obliterating night cream? Maybe it's a combination of the above. What the heck is her secret? Enquiring minds want to know! I want to know!

Well, I think I'm finally on to her. What I've noticed is that every time I'm at her house, Gaye's juicing fresh, organic vegetables like kale, beets, carrots, cilantro, parsley and cucumbers. In fact, she often talks about her juicer—not a regular, run-of-the-mill blender or basic citrus juicer that you'd use to squeeze fresh oranges. No siree, it's a "juice extractor." Hers is an ancient beast, a "Green Power" contraption/thing-a-majiggy that she's had for 15 to 20 years and I reckon it's about the same size as a compact car, taking up most of her kitchen counter space and even encroaching on her dining room when she uses it. But man, it works miracles, as Gaye's beautiful skin demonstrates!

Envious of my friend's vitality, I decided to do some detective work into juice extractors and the benefits of this type of juicing for health in general. I was really impressed by what I found. Here are the juicy details:

When it comes to juicing, there are really two types of juicers: centrifugal and masticating. A centrifugal juicer is the most common type you see in stores and on groovy TV infomercials. (Remember Jack LaLanne? Or The Juice Lady? Act now! Don't delay! Operators are standing by!) This type of juicer spins at high speeds and, during the spinning process, the vegetables that you've shoved down the chute are ground to a pulp. The spinning motion then forces the juice away from the pulp.

The definition of "mastication" (not to be confused with a similar-sounding, non-food-related word!) is "to chew, grind or knead into a pulp." Your teeth are an excellent example of mastication in action. Thing is, most people skip the chewing thing and scarf back their food so fast (you reading this, Greta?) they hoover large chunks that are then difficult to digest and absorb. That's nastification! (Cows are masters at mastication, by the way. Go Elsie!) A masticating juicer grinds vegetables and literally squishes out the juice, leaving behind pulp that's almost powdery. Since they spin at low speeds, they tend to juice many vegetables more efficiently, especially the most important ones for our health: the leafy greens, such as kale, cilantro, parsley, spinach

and the like. You get more juice out of your vegetables with a masticating juicer, so you get more nutritional bang for your buck. Plus, a masticating juicer is so good at getting the juice out, you need fewer vegetables to create more juice.

But here's the real reason a masticating juice extractor is all the rage for improving your health. We all know that colorful and dark green veggies are loaded with vitamins, minerals and, most importantly, antioxidants that are critical to good health and anti-aging. Well, when a juicer's blades spin at very fast speeds, like they do with centrifugal juicers or even in a blender that you'd typically make a smoothie in, that produces too much heat, which then damages a portion of the vitamins and destroys almost all of the live enzymes in the vegetable. That's not good. You're wasting all those nutrients. And remember, they say that the moment a vegetable is plucked from the vine or from the ground, it quickly loses up to 50 percent of its vitamin/mineral content. So you're already working with an inferior product. You need to get the most out of what you have!

Masticating juicers, however, spin at a low speed and that prevents oxidation and damage to those precious, health-promoting nutrients and enzymes. You're getting the very, very best part of the vegetable—the part that will infuse your body's cells with life and vitality and health.

"But what about the pulp? Don't I want all that fiber, too?" you ask. Sure, you definitely want fiber, but not necessarily in your juice. Let's deal with this pulp fiction: A lot of the beneficial stuff that's stored in fruits and veggies are stored in the (pulp) fiber, but the problem is that the body doesn't break fiber down well. It acts as bulk and is whooshed out via your colon, and along with it goes some of the nutrients that are bound up in there. However, when fruit and vegetables are juiced, all the good stuff is released from the fibers, the nutrients are made available to your body and they're readily absorbed. There's probably not a healthier thing you could put into your body! That's why so many people juice for health reasons—the phytochemicals in plants help remove carcinogens, detoxify the liver, protect our cells' DNA, help repair and regenerate cells, give us energy and make us feel and look great. So treat your juice as a supplement or an addition to your diet, and get your all-important fiber elsewhere through smart food choices.

I personally ended up buying an Omega 8005 Juicer (stainless steel to match my kitchen) and experimented by making juice every day for 40 days straight to see if I would end up looking all radiant and glowy like my friend. My favorite concoction consisted of carrot, beet, celery (one of the best vegetables to *Continued...*

juice to promote healthy skin), kale and parsley along with one apple. Gingerroot is yummy, too. (I used only organic vegetables.) Beets are one of the best liver detoxifiers, and those leafy greens, well, they're just loaded with so much goodness, it's radicchio!

Anyway, to make this long story longer, all I can say is I LOVE, LOVE, LOVE my Omega juice extractor! Did I mention that I LOVE it? Within five days or so, I noticed a huge improvement in my energy level. My sleep improved dramatically and I looked very well rested. After a week or so, I noticed that the skin on my hands, feet and legs, which had been dry and a little scaly, was looking and feeling moist and nourished. People have commented on how good my skin looks lately. Heck, I've even had a couple guys in their 20s tell me I'm hot! And I don't mean they were *born* in the '20s

either! (Still, I checked my armpits for sweat stains in case I was misinterpreting their use of the word "hot." I wasn't. Yay!) I also noticed that my cravings for sugar were dramatically reduced, probably because I was giving my body the nutrients that it really needed and wanted. In fact, my appetite was substantially reduced and, as a result, I've dropped unnecessary weight, mostly in the form of bloating. Bloat be gone! Goodbye, wrinkles and cellulite! Hello, healthy glow and boundless energy!

In general, I think purchasing this juicer and using it regularly is one of the best things I've ever done for my health. EVER! I'm planning on having a glass of fresh juice every single day. It seems to me that the Fountain of Youth may very well spew forth freshly extracted, masticated vegetable juice! (Don't worry, Gaye. Your secret's safe with me! Well…sorta.) ■

Hairspray! (Not the Musical...)

Posted by Greta (August 2008)

We're having another argument, only this time I know I'm right (for a previous argument on the proper way to eat a banana, visit p. 281 and read article "Banana Banter").

I can't stand pump hairspray. I'm an aerosol girl! Yes, I'm conscious of the environment and all that mumbo jumbo, but most aerosols no longer have those nasty PCBs or NBCs or XYZs or whatever they're called. Pumps are meant for shoes, not for hair. Whenever I borrow Janet's pump hairspray, I end up with half of it on my body, all over my neck and arms, because the drops of hairspray are so big and heavy, which means I actually have to WASH MY ARMS if I'm wearing a tank top or take my silk shirt to the dry cleaner because it's splattered in goopy-sticky hairspray gunk.

On the other hand, my wonderful aerosol can delivers an even, gentle, fine mist of tacky hair adhesive exactly where I want it: on my hair, not on my body! Janet says

aerosol hairspray's "so stupid…it doesn't even hold anything, so what's the point?" Um. I'm pretty sure I wouldn't be using it if it didn't "hold anything." I'm the queen of hairspray, after all, and, like my American Express card (which I don't actually own, but I'm trying to make a point here), never leave home without it (on my head).

A little aside: I've always thought that if I was chosen as a contestant on *Survivor*, my one "luxury" item that I would bring along would be a can of hairspray. And why not? I figure it's a smart choice because it could serve several purposes: (1) hold my hair; (2) help start a fire; (3) could be sprayed in the eyes of other contestants who annoy me; and (4) if I brought along the ultra stinky 1970s Final Net hairspray, could act as bug repellent.

Anyway, please send me an email at janetandgreta@ janetandgreta.com and tell me that I'm right and Janet's wrong, that aerosol is the only way to go and that pump hairspray sucks. ■

Freaky-Finger Friday

Posted by Janet (April 2006)

(Warning: This blog entry is not for the faint of heart!) Let me start by saying that this is the first time I've been physically able to blog since last Friday, April 21st, which I'll heretofore refer to as "Freaky-Finger Friday." (If you discover any typos in this text, you'll soon find out why, and hopefully forgive me.)

For me, Freaky-Finger Friday started out like most other days—rushed. That's a familiar state for me. Must be an Aries trait. I'm actually quite well-known for getting too many speeding tickets and also for never giving myself enough time to get to appointments, to catch planes or to even make golf tee times. For example, on the day before Freaky-Finger Friday—which happened to be my birthday—I thought I was going to be late for a dentist appointment. In typical fashion, I flew out the door, high-jumped into my SUV and drove like Dale Earnhardt, Jr., skillfully weaving in and out of rush-hour traffic to get there. Sighing in relief that I did, indeed, make it on time, I was escorted into the dentist's chair. As the chair reclined, I gasped. Looking down at my feet, I could see that I had two different shoes on! One brown. One black. A high heel and a flat. And I didn't even notice! I must've literally jumped into my shoes as I raced out the door!

On Freaky-Finger Friday, as I was similarly racing out for a breakfast meeting, somehow (and I'm still not exactly sure how) the heavy, steel front door of my house slammed violently shut onto my right index finger. Yeeee-oooowch! That's not exactly what I said—more like Bleep! Bleepin'! Bleepety Bleep!! (Censored for our young readers.) I lapsed into semi-shock when I noticed the door had ripped through the tip of my finger. It was literally hangin' by a thread. Almost off. Ugghh!

You see, I don't have a fingernail on that particular finger, so there was nothing to protect it from the blow. Why no nail? Well, that's a story in itself:

The year was 1965, and Alfreda Podleski was about seven months pregnant with little fetus, Janet. Alfreda was cleaning the floor using an electric floor polisher when out of nowhere she received a huge shock—a jolt so strong that she couldn't free her hands from the polisher for several seconds. My father, nearby, rushed into the room and pulled the plug from the wall. When my mom delivered me a couple of months later, she said to the doctor (in her adorable Polish accent), "Look at the baby's hands! Look at the baby's hands!" Apparently, being intuitive, she suspected the shock would translate into some kinda weirdo deformity—and it did...sorta. I was born without fingernails on both of my index fingers. When they grew in, they were really, really crooked. The right one was so badly ingrown and crooked and painful that I had to have it pulled out by a doctor when I was in the sixth grade. (In biology class, I used to entertain everyone by putting the

deformed digit under a microscope. Gross!) Needless to say, I'll never star in Palmolive Dishwashing Liquid commercials.

Back to Freaky-Finger Friday. My next-door neighbor, Felicity, frantically drove me to the emergency ward, my throbbing finger packed in ice. The hospital was bustling. A four-hour wait, I was told. "Oh, I hope my poor finger can hang on that long," I thought. I waited patiently and very stoically, as Felicity later told me. I was even cracking jokes with the other patients. (Pretending to be a PA announcer: "Dr. Pepper. Dr. Pepper to emergency.") Then something really freaky happened. You know, I've never been one who enjoys people fussing over me for being an author or recognizing me as "a celebrity," as they say. I especially feel uncomfortable receiving any preferential treatment or privileges. But, in this case, I welcomed it with open arms and nine and three-quarter fingers. Turns out the reception nurse recognized my name from our cookbooks. "Oh my gosh! I have *Looneyspoons* and *Eat, Shrink & Be Merry!* My teenage boys and I loooovvvve them!" she exclaimed. I was blushing. My finger was dripping blood. She examined it. "Wow, you really have a big boo-boo there! Ick! Let's get you in to see a doctor right away."

From there, it seemed there was a parade of nurses and emergency workers who were familiar with our books and who were fans. It was really nice to hear their compliments. I was still in the reception area when I felt a tap on the shoulder. "Hi, I'm Becky. I'm you're biggest fan! Wow, it's really you. I'm gonna get you in and out of here really quick. This is so exciting!" While I wouldn't classify my traumatic, excruciatingly painful pointer problem as "exciting," I soon discovered why she said what she did.

Nurse Becky, who was young, very pretty and very engaging, told me her story. She'd been overweight her entire life. "Obese," she said. It was tough growing up like that, with the teasing from other kids. Her four other sisters were blessed with fast metabolisms and had always been thin. She was the oddball. Her teenage years were very difficult. She weighed more than 200 pounds, which I found hard to believe as I observed this sleek, healthy-looking woman applying Polysporin to my injury. Then, in her late teens, she ended up buying a copy of *Looneyspoons*. She loved the food. She followed the nutrition advice. She laughed at the jokes. It worked. Her weight now hovers around 135 and she looks gorgeous. She's recently moved in with her boyfriend and says they'll be getting married soon. She looked me in the eye and told me that our book changed her life. Wow!

As I listened intently to every word Becky said, it's funny how I completely forgot about my almost-severed finger and the intense, throbbing pain I'd been experiencing. As she tended my wound, I realized that I had helped tend her wound, too. Nothing is more satisfying than the knowledge that you've positively impacted someone's life. And that made me feel really, really good—a lot better than the Tylenol 3 with codeine that the doctor sent me home with. ▪

The Big 4-0? Big Deal!

Posted by Greta (April 2006)

I wish everyone would stop bugging me about turning 40, like it's some kinda huge, important milestone that comes around only once in a lifetime or something. I don't understand all the fuss and I'm getting tired of it. And don't think I'm posting this rant exactly one week before my birthday so you'll send me presents, either. I'm not like that, plus I don't even like presents. Or birthdays—especially my upcoming 40th (one week from today, in case you missed that part).

I'm not worried about getting older. Not one bit. Just last summer I was asked to show ID at a Detroit Tigers baseball game when I ordered a beer. Flattered, I smiled, flipped my blonde hair Farrah-Fawcett style and smugly slid my driver's license over to the elderly gentleman behind the bar. (I think I may have winked at him, too, but my memory's fading.) "New rules," he explained as he pointed to the small sign over his left shoulder, which read, "We ID anyone under 40." Hmm. Guess it could've been worse, like if he didn't ask me for ID.

I don't know what my boyfriend's going to do for entertainment when "the big day," as he annoyingly calls it, comes and goes. He's been razzing me about turning 40 since I turned 35. "How's it feel to be in your late thirties?" he sarcastically inquired at one minute past midnight on April 12, 2001. "Pretty soon I'll be dating a forty-year-old!" I fully expected this statement to be followed by "How gross!" or "Yuck!" judging by the tone of his voice, but he's a pretty sharp guy and probably realized mid-sentence that Mr. Gray Temples himself was turning 40 later that same year. It was his not-so-subtle, wildly embellished reaction to my low-rise jeans just a few months ago that got me thinking about turning 40 for the first time ever. I honestly hadn't given my upcoming birthday a

moment's thought, 'til the following scenario transpired:

Me: "Just let me get these bags out of the backseat, honey." I bend over to reach for some shopping bags, wearing my favorite 7 For All Mankind low-rise jeans.

He: (Sounding utterly mortified) "My gawd, Greta! Honestly! Pull up your pants! Do you really think I need to see your plumber butt and your thong underwear? That's absolutely ridiculous! For Pete's sake, you're almost 40!"

Me: (Trying not to sound hurt, immature or like a complete idiot) "So…um…like…what EXACTLY is that supposed to mean? That when you're 40, you have to wear granny underpants and elastic-waist jeans up to your boobs? That if I was just 25 or 30, you'd be glad to see my plumber butt and thong underwear but, since I'm "pushing 40," you don't? Is it my age that's the problem here or do you not want to see my "ridiculous" butt ever?" (Bottom lip starts quivering right about now.) "Are you saying that a 40-year-old woman can't have sex appeal? Can't wear "cool" clothes? Has to dress like a nun? Fine then. "Sister Greta" it is from now on. I'll even cover my ugly, old face if you want me too!"

"It's my (40th birthday) party and I'll cry if I want to! Wearing my low-rise jeans, of course."

And away I went, wailing and sulking and turning a little nothing statement into a huge ordeal, the way I have since I was "sweet sixteen." (Another birthday "milestone" that annoyed me!)

The truth is, April 12, 2006 (one week from today!) is just another Wednesday on the calendar. Whoop-dee-doo. But if it makes the people around me happier, heck, I'll go out, eat too much cake and celebrate this grand achievement. After all, someone very smart and famous once said, "Turning forty is just turning twenty for the second time, and it is far better to reach this milestone than to not." Actually, I just made that up, but you can go ahead and quote me if you want. ■

Royal Meeting!!

Posted by Janet (September 2008)

We're still pinching ourselves! Yowch! A little while ago, Greta and I were fortunate enough to have had a lunch meeting with Sarah Ferguson, the Duchess of York. (Not tea—lunch!) And yes, you read that right… with Fergie herself! How royally cool!

This is how it shook down: We found out that Fergie was coming to Waterloo to do a speaking engagement, and since a friend of ours knows her quite well, we begged him to get us a meeting with her. You know, so we could chat about Weight Watchers, what really happened to Princess Di, if Hugh Grant really is that charming in person, what the Queen serves for Thanksgiving dinner, etc. Well, lo and behold, our friend Rob managed to get us a meeting…for real! (What does one wear to lunch with a Royal? Why, a stylish hat, obviously. Dang! My Nike ball cap just wouldn't cut it.)

We met at a fantastic restaurant in Waterloo called Wildcraft. It was 2:30 in the afternoon, so the restaurant was quiet and we were tucked away into a far corner. It was so great to meet her. At first, she didn't say much. She had just flown in from Halifax and her schedule had been exhausting, so she seemed very tired. I'm sure the last thing she felt like doing was having lunch with a couple of perky, wide-eyed, cookbook-writing strangers. We were grateful this was happening at all!

Our friend Rob asked us to tell Sarah "our story." So we did. At first she just observed us, took it all in as we rambled on and on. She ate her lunch (a scrumptious salmon salad), listening intently. Then we gave her a copy of *Eat, Shrink & Be Merry!* She really seemed to like it! She flipped through it, giggling at some of the cartoons and recipe titles. Told Rob it was "her" sense of humor. Told us it was "very modern." Told us that David Beckham is coming out with a line of food products and is using cute cartoons on his packaging. Told us she's never cooked a meal in her entire life! Pity!

Next we shared with her our latest "secret project" we've been working on. (Just so you know, it was our grEATing cards we were developing for Hallmark.) Well, she really went gaga over it. (A good sign!) We also told her our saga about how we've been trying to break into the American market this fall with our book and our TV show, and how difficult it is. The U.S. market is so celebrity-centric, much more so than Canada. It takes a mini-miracle to get anyone to return a phone call or email or to open a courier package. It's very humbling. It's like we're back to our 1996 *Looneyspoons* days, with rejection after rejection after rejection. Everyone keeps telling us we're perfect for both *Oprah* and *Ellen*, yet getting their producers to listen is next to impossible. We have to find a creative way to rise above the noise. We told her that despite the rejections, we refused to give up. We wouldn't give up because we truly believe that we can impact the lives of millions of Americans. We know we can get Americans on the healthy-eating bandwagon. We just know it!

Well, after our impassioned sister-soliloquy, she generously offered to help us (even though we didn't ask her for help). She put her hands on our cookbook and said, "I'm a facilitator. I know a lot of people. I believe that you should be given a chance in the U.S. How can I help? What can I do? Is there someone you'd like me to call?" Greta and I were looking at each other, stunned and in disbelief. How amazing can she possibly be?

What we discovered is that she really IS amazing. She was full of interesting, innovative ideas in our meeting. One after another after another. She is tireless and dedicated and passionate in her charity work involving disadvantaged children. She is a fantastic storyteller. She is a fighter who's had to bounce back from being pushed to the ground many times, and she's always come out on top. And after listening to her speech the following day in front of 700 adoring women, what was most obvious to us is that she has a heart the size of Great Britain (and that's pretty darn big!).

I have to admit that at one point in the meeting, I was sitting there listening to Sarah, The Duchess of York, and I sorta tuned out, my eyes glazing over. My thought bubble was thinking, "A BILLION people tuned in to watch your wedding on TV! You were pals with Lady Di!" It was bizarre and surreal. Was this really happening? Greta admitted later that the same thing happened to her. Sarah's mouth was moving as she was talking, but my sister could only hear her own thought, "So, your daughters would say things like, 'Mummy, can we go to Grandma's castle this weekend?'" This lunch meeting was a lot for two commoners to digest!

After two hours, we hugged, smiled and said our goodbyes. She said it was lovely to meet us and gave us her business card. (It was very regal looking. Her email address is on it, but I haven't had the guts to "drop the Duchess a line," you know, to see if she wants to grab a latte or catch a movie or somethin'.) Sarah even asked for our contact information, because she suggested that "perhaps we should work together some time." Imagine.

You know, even if nothing else ever comes of our royal meeting, it's an experience that made my sister and me feel like queens for a day. ▪

Recipe for Disaster

Posted by Greta (March 2008)

Woe is me. I get very sad when someone tells me that they tried one of "my" recipes and that it didn't "work." It's only happened a few times, but it still really bothers me. After chatting with the disgruntled cookbook fan and asking a series of questions, I always discover that they "sorta, kinda, not really" followed the recipe and used a million substitutions, then decided to blame me for their wasted time and money! Sigh.

Some recipes are easy to adapt or modify and others aren't. Making one substitution probably isn't going to hurt, unless you're using cinnamon in place of chili powder or something radical like that. I like it when people write to us to say, "I prefer chicken breasts to thighs so I used breasts in your Sticky Chicky recipe and it was fantastic!" I'm not saying never alter a recipe (that would be silly), plus giving recipes your own special twist (if you know what you're doing!) can be fun, but please realize that if you decide to change this and substitute that, then it really isn't "my" recipe anymore, it's yours! If it's good, go ahead and take all the credit for it! If it's bad, don't get mad at me!

In case you can't tell, I'm a little down in the recipe dumps today (haven't slept for days because I can't breathe due to my ridiculous head cold), but instead of throwing a pity party, I've decided to dig deep and write a poem to cheer myself up! I hope you enjoy it. I feel better already!

Recipe for Disaster

You didn't have the pasta so you substituted rice
You didn't have the curry so you used another spice
You didn't add the onions plus you used a different pan
Forgot to buy tomatoes so you used them from a can
You simmered it too long because your mom called on the phone
The chicken that you bought was not the kind without a bone
"There must be something wrong with it, I couldn't even eat it!"
Well what do you expect when all the good stuff's been deleted?
Oh tell me, upset cookbook fan, whatever can I do
To make you follow recipes so that they'll "work" for you?

The end.

Index

Z

W

Y

Acknowledgments

Risking wife and limb, **Ted Martin**, our cartoonist superhero, has now drawn more than 700 brilliant, one-of-a-kind cartoons for our four cookbooks. Phew! We challenge anyone to draw with Ted's incredible attention to detail and imagination. A chunk of blue cheese that looks like Neil Diamond? A "Risky Biscuit" that looks just like Tom Cruise? A dancing Tina Turner tuna fish? No problem, since Ted is crazy talented! We also appreciate his "right-hand gal," wife **Dawn Martin**, who smoothly coordinated this huge cartooning project.

What do you get when you pair Ted's amazing cartoons with **Pierre Loranger**'s artistic flair and digital colorization talents? A masterpiece! Thanks, Pierre, for your beyond-beautiful work and the speed at which you delivered it!

"Unflappable" is her middle name! Gorgeous page design and layout is her game! **Mary Lou Core** went WAY above and beyond the call of duty, working days, nights, weekends, holidays and every day in between to help us put this book together in record time. We think her middle name should be "Lifesaver."

Fina Scroppo, author of the soon-to-be-published reference manual, *Hyphens-R-Us* (kidding!), was our dream-come-true, keen-eye-for-detail, proper-punctuation editor-in-chief. Thanks, Fina, for working all summer long (even while on vacation!) to meet our crazy deadlines and for allowing us to use words like "zoinks," "eeek," "a lotta," and "zowie" even though we are grown women.

Our sisters, **Donna**, **Theresa** and **Margie** deserve Medals of Valor for bravely volunteering to be Greta's "Kitchen Aids" when knee surgery landed her on crutches, unable to cook. All summer long, our sisters shopped, chopped, sliced, diced, minced, whisked, whirled and whipped their way to carpal tunnel syndrome, dishpan hands and aching feet, just so our book could be completed on schedule. We owe you big time! (Your Workers' Compensation checks are in the mail.)

Thank you to **our sister**, **Helen**, and **our Aunt Grethe** for enduring three long, mentally exhausting days of painstaking proofreading. These Polish gals polished their eyeglasses to help polish our pages.

Our 24-hour, on-call, moral-support hotline, **Leanne Cusack** also acted as Greta's sous-chef and photo-studio lighting manager. (Translation: She held up a cookie sheet to reflect the sun's light, since Greta doesn't actually have a photo studio). Luv ya, Leanne!

Who needs a composter when you have **Peter McMenemy**, **Doug Ridge**, **Sourov De** and **Ryan Burgio** eagerly waiting to "dispose of" Greta's recipe creations? The boys at the office were enthusiastic supporters and constant cheerleaders (male cheerleaders—gotta love that!).

Finally, we have to say how truly grateful and honored we are to have such a widespread, loyal and incredibly enthusiastic fan base from coast to coast. From Linda Ratcliffe and The Bench Babes to "The Empress" (Seaneen Wasch) to our *Looneyspoons* Fan Club in Edmonton. From Suzie the Foodie to Detective Constable Jim Brady to young fans Ola and Hleb to Facebook fans Celine Girard, Dave Leclair and Helen Street Jennings. Thanks to Weight Watchers members who held up our books in meetings, bought copies for all their friends and talked our recipes up on their message boards. (We owe you commission! We'll start deducting it from Greta's pay immediately.) There's no way we'd be where we are today without your ongoing support over the last 15 years. This book is for you! Thank you so much from the very bottom of our hearts.

Hungry for more? See what's cooking at www.janetandgreta.com